The *Charles W. Morgan*, Yankee whaleship of 1841 at Mystic Seaport Museum, Connecticut, is a recipient of the World Ship Trust Award for 2000. The award is given to vessels of outstanding historical importance. See more on the *Morgan* on pages 281-2.

Previous World Ship Trust Awards

1980 film "Ghosts of Cape Horn"   **1982** *Vasa*, Sweden   **1983** *Mary Rose*, UK
1985 *Jylland*, Denmark   **1987** USS *Constitution*, USA   **1988** HMS *Warrior*, UK   **1988**
Polly Woodside, Australia   **1992** *Subanahongsa*, Thailand   **1992** *Mikasa*, Japan   **1995** *Huascar*,
Chile   **1995** *Buffel*, Netherlands   **1996** *Great Britain*, UK   **1997** *Bergantim Real*, Portugal
1998 *Argonaute*, France   **1999** *Dom Fernando II e Gloria*, Portugal   **1999** *Star of India*, USA

HISTORIC SHIPS

THE
INTERNATIONAL
REGISTER OF

HISTORIC
SHIPS

THIRD EDITION
Completely Revised and Updated

· · · · ·

Norman J Brouwer

SEA HISTORY PRESS
NATIONAL MARITIME HISTORICAL SOCIETY
PEEKSKILL, NEW YORK

Historic vessels often survive because they have a continuing commercial use, a common function being that of floating restaurant. Few have as picturesque a setting as the Russian barquentine KRONVERK at St Petersburg. (see page 243)

THE INTERNATIONAL REGISTER OF HISTORIC SHIPS

PATRONS

Starboard Watch

PETER A. ARON

ALAN BURROUGH, CBE

GUY E. C. MAITLAND, ESQ.

OPERATION SAIL, INC.

HOWARD SLOTNICK

EDWARD G. ZELINSKY

Port Watch

JOHN C. COUCH

KRISTINA BARBARA JOHNSON, ESQ.

MARINE SOCIETY OF NEW YORK

RALPH M. PACKER, JR.

EDMUND A. STANLEY, JR.

ALIX T. THORNE

DAVID B. VIETOR

———— 🐚 ————

The National Maritime Historical Society acknowledges an important grant from Furthermore, the publication program of The J. M. Kaplan Fund, to help us reach a broader public with this work to educate Americans in their heritage in historic ships.

Copyright © Norman Brouwer 1999

First published in North America in 1999 by Sea History Press, National Maritime Historical Society, 5 John Walsh Blvd., PO Box 68, Peekskill NY 10566-0068

First published in Great Britain in 1999 by Chatham Publishing, 61 Frith Street, London W1V 5TA

ISBN 0-930248-11-2

A Library of Congress Catalog Card No. is available on request.

Printed and bound in Great Britain

Restoration is an ongoing process for many vessels. The Australian barque JAMES CRAIG is being returned to sailing condition in time for the 2001 centenary of the Federation of Australia. (see page 26)

Contents

Preface

RECOGNIZED today as the authoritative field guide to the world's historic ships, this *International Register* is often known by the name of its author, simply as 'Brouwer's Register'. It comes to you from the hand of a quiet person, but one whose mind and spirit have ranged to the far corners of the world in quest of our heritage in ships, garnering the truth of the lives of these ships - a heritage which in sum has done so much to affect our lives and development of human purpose on this watery planet.

Norman Brouwer, the author of this work, has sought out these ships where they live, from the choppy, windswept waters of San Francisco Bay on the US west coast, to the still tidal pool of hilly Bristol in England, the shallows of Russia's oft-embattled city St Petersburg, the golden creeks of the Parana above Buenos Aires, or the muddy, busy purlieus of the Irrawaddy in Myanmar. Wherever he goes, he finds the ships and talks to their people. He has hunted out glass plate negatives of the South Street Seaport Museum's ship *Wavertree* in Port Stanley, Falkland Islands, where the big full-rigger put in after being dismasted off Cape Horn in 1910. More than that - he has interviewed

the men who danced on the ship's foredeck, using stringed shovels as banjos, in the long years she lay as a coal hulk in the Straits of Magellan sheltered behind the islands of Tierra del Fuego. And he walked through the ship with James Roberts, who sailed aboard the *Wavertree* in 1896 when Roberts was fifteen.

Ask Norman Brouwer about a ship - as people have done for years now - and he will quite likely say that he doesn't really know the whole story of that particular ship. But if you persist in your question, you'll find the ship's story taking shape before your eyes, seemingly drawn from thin air. He doesn't know the whole story - he just knows it better than anyone else.

Brouwer has sailed Cape Horn waters himself. After graduating from the Maine Maritime Academy, he served as mate in the National Science Foundation ship *Hero* - a stout vessel most appropriately named for the little sloop sailing out of Stonington, Connecticut, USA, in which Captain Nathaniel B. Palmer first raised the desolate shores of Antarctica.

After the seafaring chapter of Brouwer's life ended, he apprenticed himself to museum studies at historic Cooperstown in upstate New York. From there, in 1972 he came to South Street Seaport Museum on the historic sailing ship waterfront of New York City, where he serves today as the senior ship historian. From his arrival in his mid-twenties he brought needed depth of knowledge and sea experience to the then-new museum, as one of a worldwide network of historic ship people - a wonderful group we had already made contact with through the Cape Horn

These days few genuine maritime museums are without floating exhibits, and the willingness to devote scarce resources to the expensive restoration of ships has done much for the preservation movement. This is the Aegean Maritime Museum's Thalis O Milissios at Piraeus. (see page 189)

The end of the Cold War not only revealed some hitherto unknown preserved vessels behind the old Iron Curtain, but also released a number of older vessels for exhibition in the West. This 'WHISKY' class conventional boat at Stockholm is one of a number of ex-Soviet submarines now on show around the world. (see page 265)

veteran Karl Kortum of San Francisco, founder of the National Maritime Historical Society. The Australian deepwater sailorman and historian Alan Villiers was a mainstay of this group, with the superb Australian marine artist Os Brett, the US West Coast historian Captain Harold Huycke, a leading authority on the German Cape Horners, the naval architect Howard Chapelle at the Smithsonian Institution, and Britain's extraordinary ship historian Frank G G Carr, yachtsman, deckhand on sailing barges and former director of Britain's National Maritime Museum. Brouwer was the youngest in that salty company, which he served as a kind of secretary in pursuit of historic ships.

It was Kortum - who did not suffer fools gladly - who called Norman in Cooperstown and told him to get down to New York City and join the South Street Seaport crew. Kortum had come to know of Brouwer's work while Brouwer was a student at George Washington University. He had spent his spare time, as you might by now expect, doing volunteer work for the National Maritime Historical Society, then headquartered in Washington DC. And the two had met at the San Francisco Maritime Museum (as it was called then) when the steamship *Calmar*, aboard which Brouwer was serving as mate, put into port there in 1965. Karl Kortum appreciated people who had salt spray in their faces as well as visions of tall ships in their heads!

In 1974 Frank G Carr came to the United States at the invitation of the National Maritime Historical Society to advocate the cause of the yet-to-be-founded World Ship Trust. He knew that Brouwer had started publishing lists of historic ships in the NMHS journal *Sea History*. At first Frank resisted becoming chairman of the nascent World Ship Trust, but ultimately he agreed that as a worldwide organization the Trust would be most effectively based in Britain, home of Greenwich Mean Time and 0 degrees longitude, and that he was the choice of all of us as chairman. So we founded the American Ship Trust in 1978 with Carr as International Chairman and then met in London the following year to found the World Ship Trust in December 1979. Frank decreed that the first order of business should be the publication of a definitive version of Brouwer's ship lists.

So the World Ship Trust, dedicated to the preservation of historic ships from every trade or mission, and from every quarter of our water-girded planet, became the publisher of the *International Register*. In the process England's Maldwin Drummond of the Sail Training Association, James Forsythe of the Norfolk Wherry Trust, Captain Peter Elphick, and other dedicated ship people lent their time and talents to the work, recognizing its importance to a priceless heritage of mankind.

This third edition is enriched by the new-on-the-scene ships that have come to light since the first edition was published in 1985. That edition had some 700 ships, this one nearly three times that number, thanks to ship keepers and aficionados around the world pooling their knowledge in Brouwer's Register.

The book before you makes an absorbing field to browse through, for greenhorns and old hands alike. But its best use is surely as a field guide - first to get to know the ships that brought us so far, and then to visit the actual ships. A remarkably complete bibliography opens the door to the ships' stories, and the ship-keeping institutions (listed with each ship entry) are usually glad to send you more about their ships - and to welcome you aboard.

This then is the genesis of the work you have before you - a work that may be said to have concerns as old as King Solomon's wonder at the way of a ship in the sea, and as young as the wonder of today's city youngster thinking the long, long thoughts of youth and feeling the pull of the far horizons the ships of our voyaging past have ever steered for.

PETER STANFORD
President
National Maritime Historical Society

9

The end of the Cold War has seen a flow of information to the West about many aspects of the old Soviet Union, including preserved ships. One common feature of Soviet war memorials was the mounting of whole vessels on concrete plinths. Like this armoured river launch BKA-181, they are mostly small craft, but they survive in larger numbers than this Register has been able to record.

Introduction

THE first edition of this *Register* appeared in 1985, containing information on over 700 vessels located in forty-three countries. This third edition provides data on over 1800 ships in seventy-two countries. Each year sees further efforts to preserve historic vessels, either undertaken by maritime museums or by groups of enthusiasts. Some of the increase is also attributable to better communications with areas that were semi-inaccessible during the years of the recent 'Cold War'. Still more ships have come to light through the internet. Web sites, for ships or organizations, or simply created by knowledgeable enthusiasts of various vessel types, many with useful further 'links', seem to have proliferated almost overnight.

As in previous editions, all vessels currently being preserved by museums or other non-profit groups for their historic or educational value have been included regardless of age. Vessels substantially intact and of particular significance, in private hands, are included if built prior to 1950. A few additional significant ships in this category, dating from the 1950s or 1960s, have also been included in this edition.

In general, the minimum size for inclusion in the *Register* is 40 feet overall length of hull, anything smaller falling into the category of small craft. One exception to this rule is the Isle of Man schooner *Peggy*, due to her remarkable age, and because the concept of size of vessels was so different when she was built in 1791. Ships included in the main body of the Register should at least be complete hulls, the only exception being the British warship *Mary Rose* of 1510, one side of which is largely complete from keel to rail. An appendix was added to the second edition of the *Register* published in 1993 which lists many significant remnants of ships, ranging from exposed wreckage on remote beaches to portions of vessels installed as museum exhibits.

Other appendices include lists of vessels by type, a list of ships that have changed nationality or name or have been dropped since the last edition, a list of addresses for many of the owners of vessels, and a bibliography that has been greatly expanded since the previous edition.

Once again, I would like to thank the many people who helped make this edition of the Register possible. Particularly helpful were: Graeme Andrews and Lindsay Rex in Australia; Herbert Klein in Austria; James Delgado in Canada; Gert Uwe Detlefsen in Germany; Alistair Deayton and Peter Elphick in Great Britain; Ron van den Bos and Dick Schouten in the Netherlands; Olaf Engvig in Norway; Vladimir Chepelev in Russia; Lars Bruzelius in Sweden; and Kevin Foster, Ted Miles and William Worden in the United States. Finally, I would like to express my appreciation to Robert Gardiner of Chatham Publishing for his labours in seeing this edition through to completion, and to my dear friend and invaluable travelling companion Marilyn Alexander for all her patience and moral support.

NORMAN BROUWER

Updating the Register

In producing this Register, the Trustees of the World Ship Trust, with both Author and Publisher, are fully aware that its publication will be followed by numerous letters calling attention to errors needing correction, to incomplete information where full details are lacking, and to the omission of historic craft which should be included. Such letters will be warmly welcomed; for this printing of the Register should be regarded as only a start to open up new lines of research, which it is hoped will add materially to the existing state of knowledge, and enable the records to be kept up to date.

All such reports will be gratefully acknowledged, and should be addressed to: The World Ship Trust, 202 Lambeth Road, London SE1 7JW, United Kingdom.

Terms used in the Register

Dimensions

For purposes of measurement the ships in the Register fall into two groups. Where a ship was employed in a commercial enterprise such as carrying cargo, carrying passengers or fishing, the system of measurement relates to income-producing capacity. In this case the tonnage listed is 'gross register tonnage', the total internal volume of the hull and superstructure computed in tons equal to 100 cubic feet. Length in this case is 'registered length', measured at the main deck from the fore side of the stem to the after side of the sternpost.

Where a ship was designed for a non-income-producing function, as in the case of warships, yachts and various service craft, the actual weight of the vessel is given in tons equal to 2240 lbs. This is termed 'displacement', as it also represents the weight of water displaced by the vessel's hull when afloat. In this case 'overall' length is given, which is the total length of the structure of the hull excluding any projecting spars.

Bibliography

Works which provide useful histories or descriptions of ships in the Register are listed in a Bibliography at the back of the book. Entries in this Bibliography are indicated by letter and number designations accompanying the listing for the ship in the main body of the Register.

Current owners of ships

An appendix at the back of the book lists full mailing addresses for the owners of most of the ships listed.

The Register

Argentina

Argentina occupies over one thousand miles of the Atlantic coast of South America. Its major rivers, the Parana and the Uruguay, which are navigable well into the interior of the continent, both flow into the broad estuary known as the Rio de la Plata, on which is located the capital, Buenos Aires, an important seaport. Argentina maintains a merchant fleet engaged in overseas, coastal, and inland trades, and one of the larger navies in Latin America. A major peacetime activity of the Argentine Navy is the support of research bases in the Antarctic where, prior to the current Antarctic Treaty moratorium, the country claimed territory extending to the Pole that included the Antarctic Peninsula. Argentina's two museum ships are both naval vessels, one a former training ship of the country's naval academy, and the other a cruising gunboat that is a veteran of the early activities in the Antarctic on which the country bases its territorial claims. An Argentine candidate for preservation is the former presidential yacht Tequara, built in 1922 and once used by Juan and Eva Peron, which for years has been stored indoors in poor condition in an active shipyard.

Marjory Glen
steel barque

Built 1892 by Grangemouth Dockyard Co, Grangemouth, Scotland
Original owners W Blair & Co, Glasgow
Propulsion Sail, barque rig
Tonnage 1087 gross
Length 213.0ft/64.92m
Breadth 34.1ft/10.39m
Depth 19.4ft/5.91m
Materials Steel hull, deckhouse, masts
Original use Cargo
Condition Intact burned-out hull, remains of lowermasts
Location Near Rio Gallegos, Argentina
History Beached in 1911 with cargo of coal on fire through internal combustion. Now lies well ashore, near Rio Gallegos, with hull largely intact though deformed by the fire and missing wood decks.

Presidente Sarmiento
sail training ship

Built 1897 by Laird Brothers, Birkenhead, England
Original owners Argentine Navy
Propulsion Steam, 3-cylinder compound, 1000hp, ship rig
Tonnage 2750 displacement
Length 265ft/80.77m
Breadth 43.0ft/13.11m
Draught 18.5ft/5.64m
Materials Steel hull, deckhouses, masts
Original use Training ship
Condition Rigged, fully restored
Present owners Argentine Navy
Location Buenos Aires, Argentina
History The last intact cruising training ship of the generation of the 1890s. Built for the Argentine naval academy, she made thirty-seven annual training cruises, including six circumnavigations of the globe. Retired as a seagoing vessel in 1938, she continued to serve as a stationary training ship until 1961. She is now maintained in her original 1898 appearance as a floating exhibit near the centre of Buenos Aires.
Bibliography A14, C21, C96

Uruguay
steam gunboat

Built 1874 by Laird Brothers, Birkenhead, England

Presidente Sarmiento

Uruguay

Original owners Argentine Navy
Propulsion Steam, compound,
barque rig
Tonnage 550 displacement
Length 142.75ft/43.51m
Breadth 25.0ft/7.62m
Draught 11.75ft/3.58m
Materials Iron hull; wood
deckhouses, masts
Original use Cruising gunboat
Condition Rigged, fully restored
Present owners Argentine Navy
Location Buenos Aires or Tigre,

Argentina
History Originally built as a cruising
gunboat for the Argentine Navy. She is
now preserved as a memorial to
Argentina's past activities in the
Antarctic. In 1903 this vessel rescued
the Nordenskjold expedition from an
island off the Antarctic Peninsula. She
served as a hulk for many years, before
being completely restored to her 1903
appearance in the 1960s.
Bibliography A15, C21

Australia

The only country that occupies
an entire continent, Australia still
has large areas, including some
stretches of coastline, that are
sparsely populated. Europeans
first came in 1788, finding a native
aboriginal population with little
involvement in seafaring. Because
of its long distance from Europe,
Australia was one of the last
regions served by deepwater
sailing ships. Immigration under
sail ended in the late-1800s, but
Australian grain was being
transported to Europe under sail
through the 1930s and, to a
limited extent, for a few years
after the Second World War. The
last such cargoes were brought
east around Cape Horn in 1949.
Two British-built deepwater
sailing vessels later owned in
Australia and New Zealand,
POLLY WOODSIDE, and JAMES
CRAIG are now preserved in
Melbourne and Sydney. Survivors
of the Australian grain trade
preserved elsewhere include
PASSAT in Germany, VIKING in
Sweden, POMMERN in Finland, and
MOSHULU in the United States.
Smaller sailing craft built locally
were employed in the Australian
coastal trade and fisheries, and in
a unique pearl fishery in the
northwest. Australia has few
navigable internal waterways, with
the exception of one extensive
river system composed of the
Murray and its two tributaries,
the Darling and Murrumbidgee,
which pass across much of the
southeast. Maritime historic
preservation is a very active field
in Australia, involving a wide
range of vessel types. In addition
to many vessels preserved by
museums as static exhibits, there
are a number of traditional sailing
craft maintained in sailing
condition, and a steadily growing
fleet of distinctly Australian
shallow-water paddlewheel
steamers restored to operating
condition on the Murray River.

A1

outrigger barge

Built 1911 probably by C Felshaw,
Echuca, Victoria, Australia
Original owners Murray River Sawmills
Propulsion Towed
Length 92.0ft/30.2m
Breadth 16.0ft/5.25m
Materials Wood throughout
Original use Log barge
Condition Intact
Present owners River and Riverboat
Historical and Preservation
Location Mildura, Victoria, Australia
History Typical Murray River outrigger
barge for transporting red gum logs.
Built for operation with (now
restored) paddle steamer ADELAIDE.
Currently on river bank at Mildura,
Victoria. Acquired by present owner in
1992 for restoration and eventually
operation at Mildura, Victoria with
paddle steamer SUCCESS which is also
planned to be restored. Name (A)
indicates the first such barge built for
Murray River Sawmills in 1911.

Ada

towed barge

Built 1898 at Echuca, Victoria, Australia
Original owners Permewan, Wright
and Co Ltd
Propulsion Towed
Tonnage 172 gross
Length 108.0ft/32.92m
Breadth 23.0ft/7.01m
Draught 1.5ft/0.46m
Materials Iron frames and topsides,
wood planking
Original use Cargo
Condition Intact
Present owners Echuca City Council
Location Echuca, Victoria, Australia
History Large inland river cargo barge
often towed by restored steamer
PEVENSEY during river trade. Acquired
by present owners in 1974, restored in
1980 and exhibited afloat at Echuca,
Victoria.

Adelaide

paddle tug

Built 1866 by G Link, Echuca, Victoria,
Australia
Original owners J G Grassie
Propulsion Steam, sidewheel,
2-cylinder, 36hp, wood fired; engine
built by Fulton and Shaw, Melbourne
Tonnage 58 gross
Length 76.4ft/23.29m
Breadth 17.0ft/5.18m
Draught 2.3ft/0.71m

Materials Hull wood over iron frames; wood superstructure
Original use Towing
Condition Fully restored
Present owners Echuca City Council
Location Echuca, Victoria, Australia
History Believed to be the oldest wooden-hulled steamer operating in the world, and one of the oldest of any construction. Built mainly for towing barges on the Murray River around Echuca, wool being the main cargo until 1872. For the next 85 years until 1957 ADELAIDE was a logging boat, towing up to three barges loaded with red gum logs from forests along the Murray to sawmills at Echuca. In 1963 she was moved to shore and exhibited close to the river in the town of Echuca. Interest in the history of the Port of Echuca, Australia's busiest inland port of the past, increased over the following years. This resulted in wharf restoration, purchase and restoration of the paddle steamer PEVENSEY, acquisition of barges and other port-related facilities and eventually to the decision to refloat and restore ADELAIDE to steaming condition. As a result ADELAIDE was refloated in 1984 and recommissioned after extensive restoration at the Port complex in 1985. Since that time ADELAIDE has been regularly steamed for demonstration purposes or for special occasions. To celebrate her 125th birthday in 1991, ADELAIDE towed restored outrigger barge D26 loaded with red gum logs from the Barmah forest to Echuca, thus simulating her 85 years of such work on the Murray River in the past.

ADELAIDE still has her original engine which was built by Fulton and Shaw in Melbourne. The two 14-inch

diameter by 36-inch stroke double-acting cylinders are arranged one each side of the marine type boiler, directly connected by the main shaft to the 14ft diameter paddles. Operating boiler pressure remains at 120psi. A new boiler was fitted around 1936. The engine has Stephenson's reversing gear. Like almost all paddle steamers which operated on the Murray and tributary inland rivers, ADELAIDE is wood-fired. This is due to the abundance of suitable wood along most of the river banks and the lack of other fuel such as coal in the areas around the rivers.

ADELAIDE is the most significant vessel located at the historic Port of Echuca complex. The site includes two other operating historic paddle steamers, PEVENSEY and ETONA, and two barges together comprising the most significant such collection at one location in Australia. At least three other historic steamers are under restoration for operation at the Port.
Bibliography B66, C71, D101, D393

Advance
fast patrol boat

Former name HMAS ADVANCE
Built 1968 by Walkers Ltd, Maryborough, Queensland, Australia
Original owners Royal Australian Navy
Propulsion Two diesel engines, 1725hp each, twin screw
Tonnage 146 displacement
Length 107.5ft/32.8m
Breadth 20.0ft/6.1m
Draught 7.3ft/2.2m
Materials Steel throughout
Original use Coastal patrol
Condition Intact, in operating condition

Adelaide

Advance

Present owners Australian National Maritime Museum
Location Sydney, Australia
History Australian fast patrol boat of the 1960s transferred to the National Maritime Museum in 1988 to serve as a floating exhibit.

Akarana
sailing yacht

Built 1888 by R Logan, Auckland, New Zealand
Original owners R Logan
Propulsion Sail, cutter rig
Tonnage 8.35 displacement
Length 39.0ft/11.89m
Breadth 6.7ft/2.04m
Draught 5.75ft/1.73m
Materials Wood throughout
Original use Racing yacht
Condition Intact, in sailing condition
Present owners Australian National Maritime Museum
Location Sydney, Australia
History Built for and competed in the 1888 Centennial Regatta in Melbourne. Purchased by the New Zealand government in poor condition in 1987 and fully restored that year in Auckland. Presented to the Australian Government as New Zealand's bicentennial gift to Australia in 1988. On exhibit at Darling Harbour, Sydney.
Bibliography D176, D177

Alexander Arbuthnot
sidewheel river steamer

Built 1923 by Charles Felshaw, Koondrook, Australia
Original owners Estate of A Arbuthnot
Propulsion Steam, sidewheel, 2-cylinder, 4hp, wood burning

Tonnage 46 gross
Length 76.0ft/23.16m
Breadth 15.3ft/4.66m
Draught 2.0ft/0.61m
Materials Hull wood over steel frames; wood deckhouse
Original use Towing
Condition Fully restored to operating condition
Present owners Echuca City Council
Location Echuca, Victoria, Australia
History Last cargo carrying steamer completed for the Murray River. Built on a barge hull dating from 1916. Brought to Echuca in 1989 and restored there to operating condition. Now makes regular river excursions alternating with the restored steamers ADELAIDE and PEVENSEY.
Bibliography B2, C71

Alison
outrigger barge

Built 1907 at Koondrook, Victoria, Australia
Original owners A Arbuthnot
Propulsion Towed
Tonnage 60 gross
Length 82.0ft/24.99m
Breadth 15.3ft/4.66m
Draught 1.5ft/0.46m
Materials Wood throughout
Original use Cargo
Condition Intact
Present owners Echuca City Council
Location Echuca, Victoria, Australia
History Outrigger barge built to transport logs on the Murray River, towed by sidewheel steamers. Acquired by the Echuca City Council for exhibition on shore near that city's historic riverfront.
Bibliography C71

Alma Doepel
topsail schooner

Built 1903 by Frederick Doepel,
Bellinger River, New South Wales,
Australia
Original owners Frederick Doepel
Propulsion Sail, 3-masted topsail
schooner rig; engines added
Tonnage 151 gross
Length 116.1ft/35.4m
Breadth 26.6ft/8.1m
Draught 7.5ft/2.29m
Materials Wood throughout
Original use Cargo
Condition Fully restored, operational
Present owners Sail and Adventure Ltd
Location Melbourne, Australia
History ALMA DOEPEL is the only
Australian built commercial square
rigged sailing vessel to have survived.
She was also the last such vessel when
her yards were removed in 1937. She
was built by Frederick Doepel in 1903
at the isolated town of Bellinger on the
Bellinger River in northern New South
Wales for the trade between there and
Sydney. After 13 years in this service,
except for some initial voyages to New
Zealand, ALMA DOEPEL was sold to
Henry Jones IXL of Hobart to become
one of his well known 'jam' fleet of
wooden sailing vessels. Her first
(small) engine was installed in 1916
and her first real auxiliary in c1936.
Over the period from 1916 until 1959
when the decision was made to cease
interstate trading, ALMA DOEPEL made
578 Bass Strait crossings, the most of
any sailing vessel. The most common
cargoes were explosives and general
southbound, with bottles and wheat
especially before the Second World
War and timber northbound.

In 1943 the Australian government
requisitioned ALMA DOEPEL for army
service. As a result she was modified in
Sydney emerging as AK (Army Ketch)
82 with the lower foremast only and
diesel engines. Subsequently she served
in northern Australian and New
Guinea waters. ALMA DOEPEL survived
the war and in 1946 returned to Hobart
where she was refitted as a 3-mast
'bald-headed' (no topmasts) to re-
enter the Hobart-Melbourne trade in
1947. After lay up in 1959 ALMA
DOEPEL again had her main and
mizzen masts removed and was
employed as a motorized barge
carrying limestone from Southport to
Electrona in southern Tasmania from
1961 until 1975.

In 1976 the badly knocked-about
hull was purchased by a Melbourne

Alma Doepel

organization for restoration as a sail
training vessel and motored to
Melbourne. The subsequent 12-year
restoration, carried out substantially
by volunteers, required immense effort
due to the initial condition of the
vessel and the changes necessary to fit
the ship for her new role on Port
Phillip Bay. The hull required new
decks, bulwarks, bulkheads, rudder
and centreboards. Deckbeams, knees
and planks were replaced. New
deckhouses and galley were arranged
together with accommodation,
showers, heads etc for 18 boys, 18 girls
and a crew of up to 15. The ship was
completely rerigged with a sailplan
similar to the original. A new diesel
engine was obtained, overhauled and
installed to provide reliable twin-
engine twin-screw reliability. A
hydraulically-driven bow thruster was
installed to assist in handling the
vessel. The cost of all work exceeded $3
million. This was provided by
substantial corporate sponsorship
particularly from the company which
had previously taken control of the old
Henry Jones company supplemented
by ongoing fund raising.

After final fitting out in Adelaide in
1987 ALMA DOEPEL sailed to Sydney to
join the Australian Bicentennial

celebrations on 26 January 1988. She
fittingly took second place in the Tall
Ships Parade-of-Sail that day on
Sydney harbour. On return to
Melbourne youth training voyages
commenced. These typically involve 10
days within Port Phillip Bay. In
addition weekend and other cruises
and special charters are operated, with
management training being offered in
more recent times. ALMA DOEPEL is
now a familiar sight under sail on Port
Phillip and is the most significant
historic sailing vessel in service in
Australia today.
Bibliography A15, B2, D353

Ancel
pearling lugger

Built 1952 by A S Male, Broome,
Western Australia
Original owners A S Male
Official number B46
Propulsion Sail, ketch rig; diesel engine
(removed c1972)
Tonnage 33 gross
Length 52.3ft/15.94m
Breadth 14.2ft/4.33m
Draught 5.7ft/1.74m
Materials Wood throughout
Original use Pearl fishing
Condition Intact

Present owners Western Australian
Museum
Location Fremantle, Western Australia
History Representative of later type of
traditional northern Australian
wooden pearl fishing vessels known as
'pearling luggers'. Built to withstand
regular tidal strandings. Acquired and
brought to Fremantle in early 1970s.
Later restored and now displayed
ashore at the Western Australian
Maritime Museum, Fremantle, WA.

Annie Watt
trading ketch

Built 1870 by J Wilson, Port Esperance,
Tasmania
Original owners G Watt
Propulsion Sail, ketch rig; auxiliary
engine installed in 1925
Tonnage 44 gross
Length 63.7ft/19.42m
Breadth 18.0ft/5.49m
Draught 5.6ft/1.71m
Materials Wood throughout
Original use Cargo
Condition Unrigged, needs extensive
restoration
Present owners South Australian
Maritime Museum
Location Port Adelaide, South Australia
History Representative earlier

Tasmanian and South Australian trading ketch and the second oldest to survive. Trading in South Australian waters from 1874 until approximately 1970. Acquired for restoration around 1980, but project was not successful. Hull has now deteriorated beyond the point of restoration, but is preserved as an exhibit.
Bibliography B3, C44, C69a

Ardent
patrol boat

Former name HMAS ARDENT
Built 1968 by Evans Deakin Ltd
Original owners Royal Australian Navy
Official number P 87
Propulsion Diesel engines, twin screw, 3500hp. Engine built by Paxman
Tonnage 146 displacement
Length 107.5ft/32.8m
Breadth 20.0ft/6.1m
Draught 7.3ft/2.2m
Materials Steel throughout
Original use Patrol boat
Condition Intact
Present owners Museum of Defence
Location Darwin, Northern Territories, Australia
History A sistership of the ADVANCE on exhibit in Sydney. Recently retired and preserved as an exhibit.

Australia II
racing yacht

Built 1982 by S W Ward & Co, Perth, Western Australia
Original owners A Bond
Propulsion Sail, cutter rig
Tonnage 32 gross
Length 63.0ft/19.2m
Breadth 12.3ft/3.74m
Draught 8.5ft/2.59m
Materials Aluminium throughout except lead keel
Original use Racing yacht (America's Cup)
Condition Intact
Present owners National Museum of Australia, Canberra
Location Sydney, Australia
History Australian challenger for the 25th challenge for the America's Cup held at Newport, Rhode Island, USA in 1983. Finally won that trophy from the New York Yacht Club in the seventh and deciding race after a 113-year history of successful Cup defence, the longest in international sporting history. The design by Ben Lexcen incorporated a controversial winged keel. On loan to the Australian National Maritime Museum, Sydney,

Baragoola

where yacht is exhibited inside museum building and fully rigged.
Bibliography D19, D490

Australien
sidewheel river steamer

Built 1897 by R Wilson, Echuca, Victoria, Australia
Original owners W Wilson
Propulsion Steam, sidewheel, 16hp, wood fired; later diesel
Tonnage 58 gross
Length 80.0ft/24.38m
Breadth 16.0ft/4.88m
Draught 1.7ft/0.51m
Materials Iron frames and topside

Australia II

plating, wood planking and deck
Original use Cargo and towing
Condition Restoration in progress
Present owners Australien Syndicate
Location Echuca, Australia
History Traded mainly on Murray and Murrumbidgee Rivers. Holds record for voyage Echuca to Hay and return of 11 days. Later used in the logging trade until c1958 with a diesel engine. Subsequently became derelict and sank in Lake Mulwala. Purchased and raised in 1989 by present owners (Echuca residents) and taken by road to a property at Echuca. Restoration to full steaming condition on the Murray River at Echuca is planned, including the installation of a recently acquired engine similar to the original.

B22
log barge

Built 1922 probably by C Felshaw, Echuca, Victoria, Australia
Original owners Murray River Sawmills
Propulsion Towed
Length 82.0ft/25.0m
Breadth 17.0ft/5.18m
Draught 1.3ft/0.41m
Materials Wood throughout
Original use Log barge
Condition Intact but deteriorated
Present owners Echuca City Council
Location Echuca, Australia
History Typical Murray River log barge built for use with the now restored paddle steamer ADELAIDE. Name (B)indicates the second such barge built for Murray River Sawmills (in 1922). Currently lying grounded at Echuca awaiting restoration as an exhibit.

Baragoola
harbour ferry

Built 1922 by Mort's Dock and Engineering Co, Balmain, New South Wales, Australia
Original owners Port Jackson and Manley Steamship Co
Propulsion Steam, screw, triple expansion; diesel electric since 1960
Tonnage 498 gross
Length 199.5ft/60.8m
Breadth 34.1ft/10.4m
Draught 12.2ft/3.71m
Materials Steel hull, steel and wood superstructure
Original use Ferry
Condition Intact, showing neglect
Present owners Waterview Wharf Pty Ltd
Location Sydney, Australia
History Last of six similar BINNGARRA class single funnel double-ended Manly ferries built from 1905. Diesel electric engines fitted 1959/60. Retired 1981. Currently laid up at Sydney, future uncertain.

Boomerang
schooner yacht

Former name BONA
Built 1903 by W Homes, Sydney, Australia. Designed by Walter Reeks
Original owners C D Wallace
Propulsion Sail, schooner rig; auxiliary engine
Tonnage 42 gross
Length 73.2ft/22.31m
Breadth 16.9ft/5.15m
Draught 7.74ft/2.36m
Materials Wood throughout
Original use Yacht

Condition Operating condition
Present owners Sydney Maritime
Museum
Location Sydney, Australia
History Designed by the noted
Australian naval architect Walter
Reeks. Has not been operated as a
sailing yacht since the 1930s. After 1929
was owned by the Albert family, who
donated BOOMERANG to the Sydney
Maritime Museum, now Sydney
Historic Fleet, in 1987. Maintained in
operating condition as a motor yacht
making cruises in Sydney Harbour.
Bibliography D223

C L S (Commonwealth Light Ship) No 2
lightship

Former name CARPENTARIA
Built 1918 in Sydney, Australia
Original owners Australian
Government lighthouse service
Materials Steel throughout
Original use Lightship
Condition Intact
Present owners Queensland Maritime
Museum
Location Brisbane, Queensland,
Australia
History Unmanned lightship used to
mark the route for shipping around
the north of Australia. Maintained as a
floating exhibit at the maritime
museum in Brisbane.

C L S (Commonwealth Light Ship) No 4
lightship

Former name CARPENTARIA No 2
Built 1918 by Cockatoo Island
Dockyard, Sydney, New South Wales,
Australia
Original owners Australian
Department of Transport
Propulsion Towed to station
Tonnage 146 displacement
Length 76.0ft/23.16m
Breadth 25.7ft/7.83m
Draught 9.0ft/2.74m
Materials Steel throughout
Original use Lightship
Condition Intact
Present owners Australian National
Maritime Museum
Location Sydney, Australia
History Veteran Australian unmanned
lightship which served in northern
Australia and later in the Bass Strait.
Retired in 1985 and currently a floating
exhibit at the National Maritime
Museum in Sydney.

Castlemaine

Castlemaine
minesweeper

Former name HMAS CASTLEMAINE
Built 1942 by Melbourne Harbour
Trust, Williamstown Dockyard,
Williamstown, Victoria, Australia
Original owners Royal Australian Navy
Propulsion Steam, triple expansion,
twin screw, 2000hp
Tonnage 815 displacement
Length 186.0ft/56.69m
Breadth 31.0ft/9.45m
Draught 8.5ft/2.59m
Materials Steel throughout
Original use Minesweeper
Condition Intact
Present owners Maritime Trust of
Australia
Location Williamstown, Victoria,
Australia
History One of sixty BATHURST Class
minesweepers built in Australia during
the Second World War. Served in the
Pacific during the war. Later a
stationary training vessel until
transferred to present owners in 1974.
Restored to original appearance as a
floating museum berthed near
Melbourne.
Bibliography B2, B3, B24

Cerberus
coast defence monitor

Former name HMAS PLATYPUS,
HMVS CERBERUS
Built 1868 by Palmer Shipbuilding and
Iron Co, Jarrow-on-Tyne, England
Original owners Royal Victorian Navy
Propulsion Steam, twin screw
Tonnage 3340 displacement
Length 225.0ft/68.58m
Breadth 45.0ft/13.72m
Draught 15.3ft/4.66m
Materials Iron hull; wood over iron
beam decks
Original use Coast defence monitor
Condition Largely intact but beginning
to collapse
Present owners Black Rock Yacht Club
Location Black Rock, Melbourne,
Australia
History Construction of the
USS MONITOR during the American
Civil War revolutionized warship
design by introducing a major
armament mounted in a revolving
turret. The next significant step in the
evolution of the modern warship came
with the completion of the British-
built breastwork monitor CERBERUS in
1870. The original MONITOR was
eventually lost at sea in heavy weather
due to her low freeboard and
vulnerable openings on her main deck.
CERBERUS eliminated this weakness by
having her turrets mounted on a 7ft
high breastwork. She as also the first
British warship to have a raised
superstructure, low freeboard, fore and
aft turrets and the first major warship
to totally dispense with sails. This latter
feature was facilitated by having twin
screws which greatly reduced the
danger of loss of propulsion due to
propeller shaft failure and by the
vessel's role of providing defence near
sources of coal.

CERBERUS's entire active career was
spent protecting Melbourne and Port
Phillip Bay in the Australian colony of
Victoria. From 1901 she was port
guardship and during the First World

War (as a unit of the new Royal Australian Navy) a stores ship at Williamstown. From 1921 as HMAS PLATYPUS II she was a submarine depot ship. In 1924 CERBERUS was largely stripped and paid off. She was later sold for use as a breakwater at Black Rock, Victoria and was sunk in 15ft of water in 1926 for this purpose. Though she has now functioned solely as a breakwater for 65 years, her armour and armament are remarkably intact. Her four 10-inch, muzzle-loading, rifled guns are still mounted in the turrets. Unfortunately, the hull plating is badly deteriorated, and the structure cannot be expected to support the heavy loadings much longer.

Several attempts have been made to preserve CERBERUS since the early 1970s, but to date the necessary funds have not been forthcoming. The vessel lies on a sandy bottom a short distance offshore at Black Rock in Port Phillip Bay, 18 kilometres from the city of Melbourne, forming a breakwater for a yacht harbour.
Bibliography B3, B24, D229

Cheynes II
steam whale catcher

Former name LOOMA II, THORBRYN
Built 1947 by Smith's Dock Co, Middlesborough, England
Original owners Bryde & Dahls Hvalfangerselskab A/S
Propulsion Steam, screw, triple expansion, 45hp; later diesel. Engine built by Smith's
Tonnage 440 gross
Length 157.1ft/47.88m
Breadth 27.6ft/8.41m
Draught 16.1ft/4.91m
Materials Steel throughout
Original use Whale catcher
Condition Intact, in poor condition
Present owners D Seray
Location Albany, Western Australia
History Steam whale catcher last operated from Cheynes Beach Whaling Co shore station at Albany, WA, which was closed in 1978. Subsequently sailed to Hobart, Tasmania in 1984 as a proposed museum ship but insufficient support forced the ship's sale. Brought back to Albany for possible use as a floating restaurant. Laid up.

Cheynes IV
steam whale catcher

Former name WILFRED FEARNHEAD
Built 1948 by A/S Framnaes,

Sandefjord, Norway
Original owners Union Whaling Co, South Africa
Propulsion Steam, screw, 4-cylinder compound
Tonnage 534 gross
Length 149.1ft/45.45m
Breadth 29.7ft/9.0m
Draught 17.0ft/5.2m
Materials Steel throughout
Original use Whale catcher
Condition Intact
Present owners Jaycees Community Foundation
Location Albany, Western Australia
History Steam whale catcher formerly operating out of the Cheynes Beach Whaling Co station near Albany which closed in 1978. Since 1983 has been an exhibit on shore at the side of the station.

City Of Adelaide
rescue lifeboat

Former name PRESIDENT VAN HEEL
Built 1894 by R & H Green, Blackwall, England
Original owners South Australian Lifeboat Service
Propulsion Steam, compound, waterjet turbine; screw after 1911
Tonnage 30 displacement
Length 52.0ft/15.8m
Breadth 15.0ft/4.6m
Draught 3.3ft/1.0m
Materials Steel throughout
Original use Rescue lifeboat
Condition Deteriorated
Present owners City of Port Lincoln
Location Port Lincoln, South Australia
History Rare surviving jet-propelled lifeboat. Intended for service in South Holland but delivery refused. Purchased for lifeboat service in South Australia in 1895 and operated in this capacity at Beachport from 1896 until 1930. Currently exhibited on shore at Port Lincoln in very poor condition.
Bibliography B2, B3, D491

Colonel
sidewheel river steamer

Built 1895 by A J Inches, Echuca, Victoria, Australia
Original owners Permewan, Wright and Co
Propulsion Steam, sidewheel, 12hp, wood fired
Tonnage 57 gross
Length 80.5ft/24.12m
Breadth 13.9ft/4.24m
Draught 1.5ft/0.46m
Materials Iron frames and topsides,

D26 logging barge showing outriggers

wood planking
Original use Towing and cargo
Condition Restoration in progress
Present owners S A Moritz
Location Murray Bridge, Australia
History Inland river steamer employed mainly on Murrumbidgee, Edwards and Wakool river trades. Vessel stripped and engine removed *c*.1941 in Mildura. Sank at Renmark in 1952. Present owner raised hull in 1986, towed it to Murray Bridge in 1987 and in 1988 slipped vessel. Restoration is planned at Murray Bridge including installation of a 16nhp steam engine similar to previous unit.

D26
outrigger barge

Built 1926 by C Felshaw, Echuca, Victoria, Australia
Original owners Murray River Sawmills
Propulsion Towed
Length 81.5ft/24.84m

Breadth 17.0ft/5.18m
Draught 1.3ft/0.41m
Materials Iron keel, otherwise wood
Original use Log barge
Condition Fully restored
Present owners Echuca City Council
Location Echuca, Victoria, Australia
History Typical Murray River outrigger barge for transporting red gum logs. Built for operation with (now restored) paddle steamer ADELAIDE. Bought by present owners in 1987 after part restoration and subsequently fully restored at Echuca by 1990. Displayed afloat at Echuca and occasionally demonstrated with ADELAIDE as an outrigger barge carrying red gum logs.

Dart
river barge

Built 1912 by E A Milne, Goolwa, South Australia
Original owners Engineering and Water Supply Department, South

Australia
Propulsion Towed
Length 75.6ft/23.05m
Breadth 17.4ft/5.3m
Draught 1.0ft/0.3m
Materials Iron frames and topsides, wood planking
Original use Lock maintenance barge
Condition Restored
Present owners Signal Point Murray River Interpretive Centre
Location Goolwa, South Australia
History Believed built to operate with (now restored) paddle steamer INDUSTRY. Used for lock servicing including pile driving and for transporting fresh water and oil fuel. Purchased by present owners in 1986 and after repairs displayed afloat at Goolwa, SA.

Defender
trading ketch

Built 1895 by G Frost, Kincumber, New South Wales, Australia
Original owners G Fraine
Propulsion Sail, ketch rig; auxiliary engine added
Tonnage 67 gross
Length 92.0ft/28.04m
Breadth 22.0ft/6.7m
Draught 7.5ft/2.29m

Materials Wood throughout
Original use Cargo
Condition Fully restored, operational
Present owners L W Dick
Location Launceston, Tasmania
History Only surviving sailing vessel from the Bass Strait 'mosquito fleet' of ketches and auxiliaries. Set a sailing record of 18 ½ hours from Smithton, Tasmania to Port Phillip Heads in 1923. Operated in southeastern Australian waters, particularly in South Australia. From c1921 operated in Bass Strait services under many owners until laid up in the mid-1950s. Purchased for use as a houseboat and taken to Hobart in 1958. Lay there until after a succession of owners and one sinking in the early 1980s, was purchased by present owner and towed to Launceston in 1982 as a derelict hull for restoration. Restoration involved replanking below waterline, new stern, deck, bulwarks and deckhouses. On completion DEFENDER sailed to Hobart in January 1988 and competed in the Australian Bicentennial Tall Ships race to Sydney. DEFENDER now operates both for community activities and as a private vessel from her home port of Launceston, Tasmania.
Bibliography D372

Diamantina

Diamantina
frigate

Former name HMAS DIAMANTINA
Built 1945 by Walkers Ltd, Maryborough, Queensland, Australia
Original owners Royal Australian Navy
Official number 266
Propulsion Steam, two triple-expansion, twin screw, 5500hp
Tonnage 1420 displacement
Length 301.5ft/91.96m

Breadth 36.5ft/11.13m
Draught 12.0ft/3.66m
Materials Steel throughout
Original use Anti-submarine warship
Condition Intact
Present owners Queensland Maritime Museum
Location Brisbane, Queensland, Australia
History Australian 'River' class frigate built in time for brief service in the Second World War. Has been preserved as an exhibit, in a former graving dock in South Brisbane, since 1981.
Bibliography B2

Ena
steam yacht

Former name AURORE, HMAS SLEUTH
Built 1901 by W Ford, Sydney, Australia
Original owners T A Dibbs
Propulsion Steam, screw, 2-cylinder compound, 25hp
Tonnage 65 gross
Length 100.0ft/30.48m
Breadth 16.2ft/4.88m
Draught 7.5ft/2.29m
Materials Wood throughout
Original use Yacht
Condition Operating condition
Present owners Privately owned
Location Sydney, Australia
History Only surviving steam yacht of her type in Australia. Expensively built for entertaining on Sydney Harbour. Sold to Royal Australian Navy in 1916, gun mounted forward and served in Torres Strait until return to Sydney in 1917. Sold by the Navy in 1920 and c.1933 taken to Hobart for carrying fruit in southern Tasmania. This was unsuccessful and ENA was subsequently sold and for a time

Defender

operated as a steam trawler on the east coast of Tasmania. In *c*1950 she was converted to diesel and as Aurore operated as a fishing boat under several owners until she sank in 100ft of water in 1981. After several months the vessel was raised and in 1982 towed to Sydney where later restoration was begun. Recommissioned in Sydney in 1988 as Ena at a reported cost of $4.5 million. The restoration was carried out in painstaking detail, using the best and most authentic materials, fittings and finishes available consistent with current safety and operational standards. A new engine was assembled based on a unit almost identical to the original, obtained from the derelict steamer Excella. It is considered that Ena is now perhaps the finest vessel of her type in the world, her condition being described as immaculate and without flaw. In 1986/7 Ena steamed around the continent of Australia. She was sold in 1991 but remains in Sydney and is currently located at Berrys Bay. Used for charter.
Bibliography B2, D492, D505

Enterprise
sidewheel river steamer

Built 1878 by W L Keir, Echuca, Victoria, Australia
Original owners W L Keir
Propulsion Steam, sidewheel, 2-cylinder, 12hp
Tonnage 55 gross
Length 56.8ft/17.31m
Breadth 15.6ft/4.75m
Draught 2.0ft/0.61m
Materials Wood throughout, iron frames added in the 1920s
Original use Cargo
Condition Operating condition
Present owners National Museum of Australia
Location Lake Burley Griffin, Canberra, Australia
History Operated on the inland rivers mainly towing barges with a period as a 'hawking' vessel (mobile floating store) on the Darling River. In 1919 became a fishing and house boat. Purchased for present owners in 1984 and restored at Echuca with new boiler but original engine. Restoration completed in 1988 and vessel transported to Lake Burley Griffin in Canberra by road. Now regularly steamed there. Second oldest operating steamer in Australia.
Bibliography C71, D164

Enterprise
trading ketch

Built 1902 by Charles Lucas, Hobart, Tasmania
Original owners Harry Purdon
Propulsion Sail, ketch rig; oil engine added in 1913
Tonnage 37 gross
Length 69.0ft/21.03m
Breadth 18.0ft/5.49m
Depth 5.0ft/1.52m
Materials Wood throughout
Original use Cargo
Condition Intact
Present owners Sea Life Centre
Location Bicheno, Tasmania
History First scow type (flat bottom, hard chine, centreboard) Tasmanian trading ketch or 'barge'. Employed in southern Tasmanian trades. Open to the public fully rigged on shore at Bicheno.
Bibliography B2, C44

Etona
sidewheel river steamer

Built 1899 by Ross, Milang, Australia
Original owners Church of England Missions
Propulsion Steam, sidewheel, 2-cylinder, 9hp
Length 62.4ft/19.02m
Breadth 20.0ft/6.1m
Draught 2.0ft/0.61m
Materials Wood throughout
Original use Mobile mission chapel; later used as a yacht
Condition Fully restored, operational
Present owners Phil Symons and Ian Stewart
Location Echuca, Victoria, Australia
History Built as a floating mission vessel for use on the Murray River. Became fishing boat in 1912 and occasionally carried cargo until 1956. Acquired for restoration in 1961 and subsequently restored and maintained in operating condition at Echuca, Victoria. Believed to be the only vessel of her type in existence. Name believed to be derived from Eton College in England.
Bibliography B2, B66, C71, D168

Falie
sailing fishing vessel

Former name Hollands Trouw
Built 1919 by W Richter, Maassluis, Netherlands
Original owners W Richter
Propulsion Sail, ketch rig; diesel auxiliary 64hp, now 290hp
Tonnage 182 gross
Length 118.2ft/36.03m
Breadth 21.67ft/6.61m
Depth 9.83ft/3.0m
Draught 9.5ft/2.9m
Materials Steel hull
Original use Cargo
Condition Fully restored
Present owners Government of South Australia
Location Port Adelaide, South Australia
History Built as a gaff Schooner ('logger') Hollands Trouw on 'spec' and owned by builder until 1922 when purchased at Maassluis by Spencer's Gulf Transport Co. Then completed including fitting of oil engine by JS Figee, who had purchased builder's yard, renamed Falie and sailed to Australia. Operated as auxiliary mainly in south eastern Australian waters until 1982 except for period 1940–45 when as HMAS Falie operated by Royal Australian Navy in Sydney and New Guinea waters. Purchased by Government of South Australia from Spencer's Gulf Transport Co in 1982. Fully restored between 1983 and 1986 with ketch rig. Maintained at and used as a museum and operating vessel by Falie Project Ltd, Port Adelaide.
Bibliography B2, D461, D518

Fearless
steam tug

Former name Rockwing, Tapline, Abqaiq
Built 1945 by Midland Shipyards Ltd, Midland, Ontario, Canada
Original owners British Ministry of Transport
Propulsion Steam, triple expansion, 1000hp
Tonnage 249 gross
Length 113.5ft/34.59m
Breadth 30.2ft/9.2m
Draught 12.5ft/3.81m
Materials Steel throughout
Original use Tug
Condition Intact
Present owners South Australian Maritime Museum
Location Port Adelaide, South Australia
History Steam harbour tug serving early with the Royal Navy in Pacific waters. Subsequently owned in the Middle East until sale to Brisbane, Queensland owners in 1954. Served in Brisbane until sold in 1972 and steamed to Adelaide for preservation. Moved to dry berth in Birkenhead, SA in 1983. Transferred to present owners in 1989. Not currently open to the public.

Florrie
river steamer

Built 1880 by R Davis, Blackwall, New South Wales, Australia
Original owners F G Crouch
Propulsion Steam, screw, 2-cylinder, 15hp; later diesel
Tonnage 36 gross
Length 67.7ft/20.63m
Breadth 13.2ft/4.01m
Draught 3.5ft/1.07m
Materials Wood throughout
Original use Cargo and passengers
Condition Hull and superstructure intact
Present owners Ballina Shire Council
Location Ballina, New South Wales, Australia
History Built for service between Casino on the Richmond River and Ballina. Wrecked in 1882 and rebuilt. Later used for towing sugar cane barges, as a dredger and a workboat. Upon retirement donated to present owners and moved ashore for display in 1975. Located near the Ballina Maritime Museum, NSW.
Bibliography B2

Forceful
steam tug

Built 1925 by A Stephen & Sons Ltd, Glasgow, Scotland
Original owners Macdonald Hamilton & Co
Propulsion Steam, triple expansion, 1050hp, coal fired
Tonnage 288 gross
Length 121.0ft/36.88m
Breadth 27.0ft/8.23m
Draught 13.4ft/4.08m
Materials Steel throughout
Original use Tug
Condition Fully restored, in operating condition
Present owners Queensland Maritime Museum
Location Brisbane, Australia
History Steam tug based in Brisbane during commercial life. Operated by Royal Australian Navy 1942–43 in Australian and New Guinea waters. Retired in 1970 and handed over to present owners in 1971. Preserved in steaming condition as a floating museum at Brisbane.
Bibliography B3, D344

Gem
sidewheel river steamer

Built 1876 by Air & Westergaard, Moama, New South Wales, Australia

Original owners E C Randell
Propulsion Steam, sidewheel
Tonnage 228 gross
Length 133.5ft/40.69m
Breadth 20.5ft/6.25m
Draught 4.5ft/1.37m
Materials Hull wood over metal frames; house wood
Original use Cargo and passengers
Condition Intact
Present owners Swan Hill Folk Museum
Location Swan Hill, Australia
History Largest steam passenger and cargo vessel to operate on Australia's inland rivers. Built as 82 tons gross, 93.4ft registered length, cargo boat but converted to 143 tons gross steamer in 1877. Lengthened by 40ft in 1883 and passenger accommodation increased. Ceased regular passenger services in 1952 and made last trip under own power in 1954. Engine removed in early 1960s. GEM was sold to present owners in 1962 and soon after towed from Mildura to Swan Hill. Subsequently placed in a small lake at Swan Hill Pioneer Settlement Museum, Victoria where GEM serves as museum entrance etc. The Swan Hill Folk Museum is a museum village which also exhibits the cargo barge VEGA.
Bibliography A17, B2, B66, C71, D38, D443

Gretel II
racing yacht

Built 1970 by W Barnett, Sydney, Australia
Original owners Sir Frank Packer
Propulsion Sail, sloop rig
Tonnage 31.5 displacement
Length 63.0ft/19.2m
Breadth 12.2ft/3.72m
Draught 9.3ft/2.83m
Materials Wood hull, aluminium mast
Original use Racing yacht (America's Cup)
Condition Intact
Present owners Sydney Maritime Museum
Location Sydney, Australia
History Unsuccessful 1970 challenger for the America's Cup. Won one race in the challenge series. Campaigned unsuccessfully as a challenger in 1977. One of the last wooden hulled 12m yachts built. Donated to Museum in 1987. Displayed afloat and in sailing condition at Australian National Maritime Museum, Darling Harbour, Sydney.

Hecla
trading ketch

Built 1903 by Thomas Beauchamp, Birkenhead, South Australia

Original owner Captain C C Dale, Birkenhead
Official number 117421
Propulsion Sail, ketch rig; auxiliary engine in 1915
Tonnage 14.96 gross
Length 60.0ft/18.2m
Breadth 13.5ft/4.1m
Depth 4.5ft/1.3m
Materials Wood throughout
Original use Cargo
Condition Intact
Present owners Axel Stenross Maritime Museum
Location Port Lincoln, South Australia
History South Australian trading ketch that in the 1930s was part of a fleet of similar vessels bringing grain to Port Lincoln for shipment to Europe in large sailing ships. Later an onshore exhibit.
Bibliography C69a

Hero
sidewheel river steamer

Built 1874 by G Linklater, Echuca, Victoria, Australia
Original owners J Maultby
Propulsion Steam, sidewheel, 2-cylinder. Engine built by Atlas Engine Works, Melbourne
Tonnage 137 gross
Length 92.2ft/28.0m

Breadth 17.0ft/5.1m
Draught 6.3ft/1.9m
Original use Cargo and towing
Condition Recently salvaged after being sunk since 1957. Proposed active steamer.
Present owners Gary Byford
Location Strathmerton, Australia

Hong Hai
motor fishing boat

Built 1970 by Truong Van Soi, An-Hoa, Vietnam
Original owners Tran Thi Nga
Propulsion Petrol outboard motor
Tonnage 24 gross
Length 61.4ft/18.7m
Breadth 11.2ft/3.4m
Materials Wood throughout
Original use Fishing
Condition Intact
Present owners National Museum of Australia
Location Sydney, Australia
History Former Vietnamese fishing boat used by `boat people' leaving that country. Arrived in Darwin, Northern Territory in November 1978 with 38 people. Acquired by present owners in 1983 and subsequently fully restored for use as an exhibit on shore.

Industry
sidewheel river steamer

Built 1911 by A J Inches, Goolwa, Australia
Original owners Engineering and Water Supply Dept of South Australia
Propulsion Steam, sidewheel, 2-cylinder, 30hp, wood fired
Tonnage 91 gross
Length 112.0ft/34.14m
Breadth 18.6ft/5.67m
Draught 3.1ft/0.94m
Materials Hull wood over iron frames, iron topsides, wood house
Original use Snag boat and general work boat
Condition Operating condition
Present owners Corporation of the Town of Renmark
Location Renmark, South Australia
History Sidewheel steamer employed in keeping the channels of the Murray River clear for navigation. Could be fitted out for snag removal, lock repair and maintenance, or dredging. Retired in 1969, and exhibited afloat at Renmark after 1975. Overhauled in 1990 and returned to steaming condition.
Bibliography B2, B66, C71

Industry

James Craig
trading barque

Former name CLAN MACLEOD
Built 1874 by Bartram, Haswell & Co, Sunderland, England
Original owners Thomas Dunlop
Propulsion Sail, barque rig
Tonnage 671 gross
Length 179.5ft/54.71m
Breadth 31.3ft/9.54m
Depth 17.5ft/5.33m
Materials Iron hull, lowermasts; planked deck
Original use Cargo
Condition Final stages of restoration
Present owners Sydney Maritime Museum
Location Sydney, Australia
History JAMES CRAIG was built as CLAN MACLEOD for Thomas Dunlop of Glasgow, Scotland for worldwide trading. From 1883 she was engaged in the New York to New Zealand trade. CLAN MACLEOD rounded Cape Horn 23 times before sale to J J Craig of Auckland in 1900. She then served in the intercolonial trade between Australia and New Zealand and was renamed JAMES CRAIG in 1905. From 1911 until 1918 JAMES CRAIG served as a storage hulk at Port Moresby. In 1918, due to a shortage of ships, she was bought by H Jones and Co Ltd of Hobart and refitted in Sydney to re-enter the intercolonial trade. After some eventful voyages JAMES CRAIG was sold in 1925 for service as a coal hulk near the Catamaran coal mines in Recherche Bay in southern Tasmania. After the mines closed in the early 1930s JAMES CRAIG broke her moorings and grounded in a sheltered part of Recherche Bay where she lay for around 40 years.

In 1972 enthusiastic members of the organization which was to become the Sydney Maritime Museum began attempts to refloat and recover JAMES CRAIG for restoration. The ship was finally refloated in October and towed to Hobart in 1973. Repairs were progressed over subsequent years culminating in towing the repaired hull to Sydney in 1981. In 1985 the hull was placed on a specially constructed floating pontoon which is now located in Darling Harbour. Work has included stripping the hull back to bare metal, the fitting of new frames, plating and other metal work, timber deck and lower masts and bowsprit. The project is open to the public for inspection as part of the Museum's Sydney Seaport. Plans call for full restoration to sailing condition by the year 2001, the centenary of Federation in Australia, and currently in final stages of restoration to sailing condition.
Bibliography B37, C9, D13, 80, 109, 403, 521

John Louis
pearling lugger

Built 1957 by Male and Co, Broome, Western Australia
Original owners L Placanico
Propulsion Sail, ketch rig; diesel engine
Tonnage 34.45 gross
Length 60.02ft/18.3m
Breadth 14.4ft/4.4m
Draught 5.7ft/1.73m
Materials Wood throughout
Original use Fishing for pearls
Condition In sailing condition
Present owners Australian National Maritime Museum
Location Sydney, Australia
History Preserved in late 1980s as an example of the later type of traditional wooden 'pearling' lugged used around the northern coast of Australia. Built to withstand regular tidal strandings.

Maintained in sailing condition as a floating exhibit at the National Maritime Museum in Sydney.

John Oxley
steam pilot vessel/lighthouse tender

Built 1927 by Bow, McLachlan & Co, Paisley, Scotland
Original owners Government of Queensland
Propulsion Steam, triple expansion, 1270hp, coal fired
Tonnage 544 gross
Length 168.0ft/51.21m
Breadth 32.0ft/9.75m
Draught 13.9ft/4.23m
Materials Steel throughout
Original use Pilot vessel
Condition Intact, needs some restoration
Present owners Sydney Maritime Museum
Location Sydney, Australia
History Example of small steam coaster. Based at Brisbane during her active career. JOHN OXLEY was employed both as a pilot vessel and in the maintenance of aids to navigation along the Queensland coast.

Accommodation is provided for around 38 personnel. After retirement in 1968 the vessel was made available to the present owners and steamed to Sydney in 1970. Since last steaming in 1973 JOHN OXLEY has been retained afloat awaiting restoration. She is currently moored at the Museum's Rozelle Bay restoration site partly dismantled.
Bibliography B37, D519

Julie Burgess
sailing fishing vessel

Built 1936 by E E Jack, Launceston, Tasmania
Original owners H R Burgess
Propulsion Sail, ketch rig; auxiliary engine
Tonnage 38 gross
Length 64.0ft/19.5m
Breadth 17.0ft/5.18m
Draught 8.0ft/2.44m
Materials Wood throughout
Original use Fishing
Condition In operation
Present owners Captain R J Burgess
Location Devonport, Tasmania
History Only remaining Tasmanian

Julie Burgess

fishing ketch in the period in original condition and the last to operate commercially with a full suite of sails. Fished in Tasmanian and Victorian waters with some cargo and livestock voyages to and from Bass Strait islands until 1987. Participated in Australian Bicentennial Tall Ships race from Hobart to Sydney in January 1988. Regularly sailed since, mainly for sail training from her home port of Devonport, Tasmania.
Bibliography C44

Kanangra
harbour ferry

Built 1912 by Mort's Dock & Engineering Co, Balmain, New South Wales, Australia
Original owners Sydney Ferries
Propulsion Steam, screw, triple expansion; later diesel
Tonnage 295 gross
Length 149.2ft/45.48m
Breadth 32.0ft/9.75m
Draught 10.9ft/3.32m
Materials Steel hull, wood decks and superstructure
Original use Ferry
Condition Largely intact, some restoration in progress
Present owners Sydney Maritime Museum
Location Sydney, Australia
History Only survivor of the once-popular 'K' series double-ended Sydney Harbour ferries. Retired in 1985 and donated to present owners by the New South Wales Government. Restored to serve as a floating exhibit at Sydney.

Bibliography B2, C1, D173

Karya Sama
sailing fishing vessel

Built c1970 at Papela, Roti, Indonesia
Propulsion Sail, sloop rig
Length 42.1ft/12.84m
Breadth 13.0ft/3.95m
Draught 4.0ft/1.23m
Materials Wood throughout
Original use Fishing
Condition Intact
Present owners Northern Territory Museum of Arts and Science
Location Darwin, Northern Territory, Australia
History Indonesian 'perahu lambo' type sailing fishing boat, confiscated for illegal fishing in Australian waters and now exhibited indoors with sails rigged at Darwin.

Kathleen Gillett
sailing yacht

Built 1939 by C Larson, Sydney, Australia; designed by Colin Archer
Original owners J Earl
Propulsion Sail, ketch rig
Tonnage 20.9 displacement
Length 43.2ft/13.18m
Breadth 14.9ft/4.54m
Draught 6.9ft/2.1m
Materials Wood throughout
Original use Yacht
Condition Intact
Present owners Australian National Maritime Museum
Location Sydney, Australia
History Designed by Norwegian naval architect Colin Archer. Participated in

Krait

first Sydney-Hobart yacht race in 1945. Second Australian yacht to circumnavigate the world in 1947-48. Purchased by Norwegian government and fully restored to original condition in Sydney as Norway's bicentennial gift to Australia. Work completed in 1991 with assistance of original owner. Floating exhibit at the National Maritime Museum in Sydney.
Bibliography D489

Krait
motor fishing boat

Former name PEDANG, HMAS KRAIT, SUEY SIN FAH
Built 1934 by Hamaguni Shipyard, Nagahama, Shikoku, Japan
Original owners Fugisawa family
Propulsion Diesel engine
Tonnage 68 gross

Length 70.0ft/21.33m
Breadth 11.0ft/3.35m
Draught 4.9ft/1.5m
Materials Wood throughout
Original use Fishing
Condition Intact
Present owners Australian War Memorial, Canberra
Location Sydney, Australia
History Impounded at Singapore in December 1941 and initially used for rescue and supply work in that area before being sailed to India in 1942. Subsequently shipped to Australia and over time prepared as KRAIT for Operation Jaywick, a successful commando raid on Japanese shipping in the Singapore area, in 1943, which sank or damaged 37,000 tons of shipping. Purchased and returned to Australia from Borneo in 1964; was a war memorial. On loan as a floating exhibit at the National Maritime Museum in Sydney.
Bibliography B2, B3, D211, D467

KS8-1192
motor fishing boat

Built pre-1991 in Cambodia
Propulsion Diesel engine
Length 46.6ft/14.2m
Breadth 12.1ft/3.7m
Materials Wood throughout
Original use Fishing
Condition Intact
Present owners Northern Territory Museum of Arts and Sciences
Location Darwin, Northern Territory, Australia
History Cambodian motor fishing boat used by refugees from that country to travel to Australia. Preserved as an exhibit on shore at Darwin.

Kanangra when in service, 1980

Lady Denman
harbour ferry

Built 1912 by J Dent, Huskisson, Australia
Original owners Balmain Ferry Co
Propulsion Diesel engine; formerly steam screw
Tonnage 95 gross
Length 110.0ft/33.53m
Breadth 25.0ft/7.62m
Draught 8.0ft/2.44m
Materials Wood throughout
Original use Ferryboat
Condition Intact
Present owners Lady Denman Heritage Complex
Location Huskisson, New South Wales, Australia
History One of the oldest surviving Sydney Harbour ferries. Retired in 1979 and two years later towed to Huskisson, where she was originally built, to serve as an onshore maritime museum.
Bibliography B2, C1

Lady Forrest
steam rescue lifeboat

Built 1902 by J Samuel White, East Cowes, Isle of Wight, England
Original owners Fremantle Harbour Trust
Propulsion Steam, screw; later diesel
Tonnage 31 displacement
Length 56.5ft/17.23m
Breadth 15.0ft/4.6m
Materials Steel throughout
Original use Pilot vessel
Condition Intact
Present owners Western Australian Museum
Location Fremantle, Western Australia
History Built to a Royal National Lifeboat Institution rescue lifeboat design and employed as a pilot boat at Fremantle until 1967. Restored and exhibited under cover together with original steam engine in B Shed, Historic Boats Museum, Western Australian Maritime Museum, Fremantle, WA.
Bibliography B3

Lady Hopetoun
steam launch

Built 1902 by Watty Ford, Sydney, Australia
Original owners Maritime Services Board
Propulsion Steam, triple expansion
Tonnage 38 gross, 30 displacement
Length 77.0ft/23.47m

Lady Hopetoun

Breadth 13.8ft/4.21m
Draught 6.75ft/2.06m
Materials Wood throughout
Original use VIP and inspection launch
Condition Operational
Present owners Sydney Maritime Museum
Location Sydney, Australia
History Edwardian steam launch formerly employed carrying VIPs and as an inspection vessel in Sydney Harbour. Acquired for preservation in 1966 and extensively restored and refitted in 1990-91. Currently maintained as a floating exhibit and operating steam vessel.
Bibliography A17, B3, B37

Maid Of Sker
paddle steamer

Former name THE MAID OF SKER
Built 1884 by J W Sutton, Brisbane, Queensland, Australia
Original owners C H Philpott
Propulsion Steam, sidewheel
Tonnage 52 gross
Length 74.8ft/22.8m
Breadth 17.0ft/5.18m
Materials Iron throughout
Original use Passengers and cargo
Condition Restored
Present owners Town of Nerang
Location Nerang, Queensland, Australia
History Paddlewheel steamer built to operate between Brisbane and

Southport. Later reduced to a gravel barge. Moved ashore and restored as an exhibit in a park at Nerang.
Bibliography B2

Marion
sidewheel steamer

Built 1897 by A H Landseer, Milang, Australia
Original owners W Bowring
Propulsion Steam, sidewheel, 2-cylinder, 20hp
Tonnage 157 gross
Length 107.9ft/32.89m
Breadth 22.6ft/6.89m
Draught 3.3ft/1.0m
Materials Iron hull, wood decks and superstructure
Original use Cargo
Condition Intact, restored
Present owners National Trust of South Australia
Location Mannum, South Australia
History Intended as steamer by G S Fowler but after his death completed as barge and laid up. Sold to W Bowring 1900 and completed as hawking steamer for operation on Darling River. Converted for cargo and passengers in 1908. Third passenger deck added 1915 and operated on Murray River as passenger vessel until 1953. Purchased by present owners in 1963 and exhibited afloat. Recently restored to steaming.
Bibliography A17, B2, B66, C71, D197

Matilda
sailing fishing vessel

Built c1889 by T Chandler, Hobart, Tasmania
Original owners Moody Brothers
Propulsion Sail, cutter rig; engine added
Length 37.5ft/11.43m
Breadth 10.5ft/3.2m
Draught 3.5ft/1.06m
Materials Wood throughout
Original use Fishing
Condition Restored
Present owners Port Arthur Historic Site Management
Location Port Arthur, Tasmania
History Representative Tasmanian 'double ender' fishing and 'passage' (farm produce) boat of the period. Won last sailing fishing boat race at Royal Hobart Regatta in 1955. Acquired by present owner in 1985. Maintained in sailing condition as a floating exhibit at Port Arthur.

May Queen
trading ketch

Built 1867 by A Lawson, Franklin, Tasmania
Original owners W Thorpe
Propulsion Sail, ketch rig; engine added in 1924
Tonnage 30 gross
Length 70.0ft/21.3m
Breadth 17.5ft/5.33m

Draught 5.0ft/1.52m
Materials Wood throughout
Original use Cargo
Condition Intact, afloat and rigged, some restoration needed
Present owners Marine Board of Hobart
Location Hobart, Tasmania
History MAY QUEEN is the oldest surviving sailing cargo vessel in Australia. Her design represents a type of wooden sailing vessel developed in Tasmania. The design incorporated shallow draught, centreboard, ketch rig, lofty jackyard topsails to extend the topsail capability. These vessels, known locally as 'barges', were constructed basically unchanged up until the 1930s. A feature of many earlier vessels, including MAY QUEEN, was the use of wood fastenings, known as 'trennels' (treenails). These contributed to the long working lives of vessels so constructed. Hundreds of these craft were built, mostly in southern Tasmania for local trades but many operated in Bass Strait, South Australia and other south eastern Australian waters.

MAY QUEEN was built by shipwright Alexander Lawson at Franklin on the Huon River in 1867 and registered in the ownership of William Thorpe. Henry Chesterman had interests in the vessel from the outset and MAY QUEEN's ownership was association with the Chesterman family for all her working life, except for the period 1924 until 1940 when she was owned by C Boxall. She was employed most of her life transporting timber, particularly from Raminea in southern Tasmania, to Hobart.

'Barge' races were a feature of the annual Royal Hobart Regatta until the last race in 1954. MAY QUEEN maintained a consistent record in these races, despite the more yacht-like and larger ketches with special racing sails competing in later years. MAY QUEEN won four years in succession from 1882 to 1885, in 1927, 1946 (2 races), 1949 and 1951. Following her participation in the last race in 1954, MAY QUEEN had her topmasts removed and bowsprit shortened. She continued to transport timber largely under power until finally in 1973, after 106 years of trading and as the sole survivor of her type trading commercially she was laid up. The following year she was presented by her owners to the Tasmanian Government and as a result the Marine Board of Hobart acquired MAY QUEEN. By 1979 she had been rerigged and restored by the Marine Board as a floating exhibit in Waterman's Dock near the centre of Hobart where she remains. Cannot be boarded and is not in sailing condition.
Bibliography B2, B3, C44

Melbourne
sidewheel river steamer

Built 1912 by Government Dockyard (assembled at Koondrook, Victoria), Williamstown, Victoria, Australia
Original owners Government of Victoria
Propulsion Steam, sidewheel, compound, 25hp, wood fired
Tonnage 78 gross
Length 106.0ft/32.31m
Breadth 21.0ft/6.4m
Draught 3.0ft/0.91m

Materials Iron frames and topsides, wood planking and deckhouse
Original use Snag removal and workboat
Condition In operation
Present owners A E and F O Pointon
Location Mildura, Victoria, Australia
History Formerly employed keeping the upper River Murray open for navigation and in general construction. Later used for logging at Echuca and retired c1942. Purchased by present owner in 1965, restored, converted for passenger service and recommissioned in 1966 at Mildura, Victoria. Currently maintained in steaming condition making excursions out of Mildura.
Bibliography B2, B66, C71

Nelcebee
iron-hulled cargo steamer

Built 1883 by T B Seath & Co, Rutherglen, Scotland. Prefabricated at Port Adelaide, Australia
Original owners Adelaide Milling & Mercantile Co
Propulsion Steam, screw, compound, 30hp; later diesel. Present engine built by Fairbanks Morse
Tonnage 168 gross
Length 120.0ft/36.6m
Breadth 18.8ft/5.73m
Draught 8.2ft/2.5m
Materials Iron hull, wood superstructure and masts
Original use Cargo
Condition Intact
Present owners South Australian Maritime Museum
Location Port Adelaide, South Australia
History Former iron steamer built for

cargo and towing lighters etc in Spencer Gulf ports in South Australia. Converted to an auxiliary ketch in 1927 for the gulf trades. From 1965 operated to Kangaroo Island. Laid up in 1982 after 99 years of continuous service and at the time the oldest ocean-going vessel in service in Australia. Handed over to the present owners in 1985 and exhibited afloat at the Museum at Port Adelaide.
Bibliography B2

North Head
harbour ferry

Former name BARRENJOEY
Built 1913 by Mort's Dock and Engineering Co, Woolwich, New South Wales, Australia
Original owners Port Jackson and Manley SS Co, Sydney
Propulsion Steam, screw, triple expansion; later diesel electric
Tonnage 466 gross
Length 210.0ft/64.0m
Breadth 32.2ft/9.81m
Draught 12.2ft/3.71m
Materials Steel hull, wood and steel superstructure
Original use Ferry
Condition Intact
Present owners North Head Pty Ltd
Location Hobart, Tasmania
History Fifth of six similar BINNGARRA class single funnel double-ended Manly ferries built from 1905. Diesel-electric propulsion and twin funnels fitted 1948-51. Sailed to Melbourne and operated excursions on Port Philip Bay in 1964 and again in 1966 and 1967. Retired in 1985 after almost 72 continuous years' service on the Manly run. Sold to present owners in 1987 and sailed to Hobart in March 1987, where she serves as a floating restaurant.
Bibliography D358

Onslow
submarine

Former name HMAS ONSLOW
Built 1968 by Scott's Shipbuilding and Engineering Co, Greenock, Scotland
Original owners Royal Australian Navy
Propulsion Diesel and electric motors, 6000hp
Tonnage 2030 displacement
Length 295.2ft/90.0m
Breadth 26.5ft/8.1m
Draught 18.0ft/5.5m
Materials Steel throughout
Original use Submarine
Condition Intact
Present owners Australian National

Melbourne

Maritime Museum
Location Sydney, New South Wales,
Australia
History Fleet submarine of the 1960s
British OBERON class turned over to
the Australian National Maritime
Museum upon retirement in 1999, for
use as a floating exhibit at Sydney.

Oscar W
sidewheel river steamer

Built 1908 by F O Wallin, Echuca,
Victoria, Australia
Original owners F O Wallin
Propulsion Steam, sidewheel,
2-cylinder, 7hp
Tonnage 83 gross
Length 104.1ft/31.72m
Breadth 20.7ft/6.31m
Draught 5.1ft/1.55m
Materials Composite hull, wood
superstructure
Original use Cargo and towing
Condition Restored to operating
condition
Present owners Tourism South
Australia (Government of South
Australia)
Location Goolwa, South Australia
History River steamer that spent most
of her early career towing wool barges.
Spent much of the time to 1942 towing
wool barges on the inland rivers. From
1943 to 1959 was used by the South
Australian Government as a service
craft on the lower Murray River.
Restored for the Australian
Bicentenary in 1988. Now based at the
Signal Point River Murray Interpretive
Centre at Goolwa, SA and regularly
steamed. In 1991 made a historic
voyage on the Murray River to Echuca
where she was built, a distance of 1168
river miles in each direction.
Bibliography B2, B66, C71, D535

Our Svanen
trading schooner

Former name SVANEN, H C ANDERSEN,
PACIFIC, MATHILTE
Built 1922 by K Andersen,
Frederikssund, Denmark
Original owners L Hedaa
Propulsion Sail, 3-masted schooner rig;
auxiliary engine since 1955
Tonnage 119 gross
Length 130.0ft/39.6m
Breadth 21.8ft/6.7m
Draught 10.0ft/3.05m
Materials Wood throughout
Original use Cargo
Condition In operation
Present owners Svanen Charters Pty Ltd

Location Sydney, Australia
History Former 3-masted schooner,
now rigged as a barquentine, built to
carry cargo in the Danish Baltic and
coastal trades. Later rebuilt for sail
training and charter work based in
Canada. Sailed to Australia for the
bicentenniel of the 1988 First Fleet Re-
enactment and subsequently bought
there by the present owners for
excursion and charter work.
Bibliography A11, A15, D85

Ovens
submarine

Former name HMAS OVENS
Built 1967 by Scott's Shipbuilding and
Engineering Co, Greenock, Scotland
Original owners Royal Australian Navy
Official number S70
Propulsion Diesel and electric motors,
6000hp
Tonnage 2030 displacement
Length 295.2ft/90.0m
Breadth 26.5ft/8.1m
Draught 18.0ft/5.5m
Materials Steel throughout
Original use Submarine
Condition Intact
Present owners Western Australian
Maritime Museum

Location Fremantle, Western Australia
History Fleet submarine of the 1960s
turned over to the museum in
Fremantle in 1999. Sistership ONSLOW
is a museum in Sydney, and others of
this class are preserved in England and
Brazil. Recently retired and preserved
as a floating exhibit.

Parry Endeavour
racing yacht

Former name CHALLENGER
Built 1978 by P Curran, Perth, Western
Australia
Original owners Dr J Chute
Propulsion Sail, sloop rig; auxiliary
engine
Tonnage 12.2 displacement
Length 46.0ft/14.02m
Breadth 13.1ft/4.0m
Draught 7.2ft/2.19m
Materials Fibreglass hull, aluminium
mast
Original use Yacht, ocean racing
Condition Intact
Present owners Western Australian
Maritime Museum
Location Fremantle, Western Australia
History After modification by D Piesse
and R Tasker, sailed by Australian
single-handed sailor Jon Sanders in his

record-breaking non-stop triple
circumnavigation of the world which
was completed in March 1988. The
voyage involved sailing 71,023 nautical
miles (131,535 kilometres) in 658 days.
PARRY ENDEAVOUR is exhibited under
cover in B Shed, Historic Boats
Museum, Western Australian Maritime
Museum, Fremantle, QA together with
the 34ft long yacht PERI BANOU in
which Sanders had set the previous
record non-stop double
circumnavigation of the world.

Penguin
sailing fishing vessel

Former name MERCIA
Built 1908 at Thursday Island, Australia
Propulsion Sail, ketch rig; auxiliary
engine
Materials Wood throughout
Original use Pearl fishing
Condition Intact
Present owners Queensland Maritime
Museum
Contact address PO Box 3098, South
Brisbane, Queensland 4101
Location Onshore exhibit, Brisbane,
Queensland, Australia
History Auxiliary sailing vessel used in
pearl fishery in northern Australia.

Our Svanen

Pevensey
sidewheel river steamer

Former name MASCOTTE
Built 1910 at Moana, Victoria, Australia
Original owners Permewan, Wright and Co
Propulsion Steam, sidewheel, 2-cylinder, 20hp, wood fired
Tonnage 130 gross
Length 111.5ft/34.0m
Breadth 23.0ft/7.01m
Draught 2.3ft/0.7m
Materials Iron frames and topsides, wood planking
Original use Cargo and towing
Condition In operating condition
Present owners Echuca City Council
Location Echuca, Victoria, Australia
History Large inland river cargo and towing vessel originally employed on the Murrumbidgee River. Recorded as having carried a record 1950 bales of wool down the Murrumbidgee, with one barge in tow. Rebuilt 1933-35 following a fire in 1932. In the 1930s operated a regular cargo service between Morgan, South Australia and Mildura, recorded as the last such service in the inland rivers. Served as a museum at Mildura in the 1960s but became derelict and was sold to the present owners for restoration in 1973. Recommissioned in 1979. Now maintained in fully restored condition at Echuca, Victoria and regularly steamed on the Murray River with passengers as part of the Port complex.
Bibliography B2, B66, C71

Polly Woodside
iron trading barque

Former name RONA
Built 1885 by Workman, Clark & Co, Belfast, Northern Ireland
Original owners William J Woodside & Co
Propulsion Sail, barque rig
Tonnage 678 gross
Length 186.5ft/56.85m
Breadth 30.15ft/9.19m
Draught 14.0ft/4.27m
Materials Iron hull and deckhouse, iron and wood masts
Original use Cargo
Condition Restored, except officers' accommodations
Present owners National Trust of Australia
Contact address Tasma Terrace, Parliament Place, Melbourne, Victoria 3002
Location Melbourne, Victoria, Australia
History Employed by original owners

Polly Woodside

in worldwide trading until sold to New Zealand owners and renamed RONA in 1904. From then until 1922 had four New Zealand owners. RONA was employed in the intercolonial trade (Australia to New Zealand) and on the New Zealand coastal trade from 1904 until 1916. This was followed by trade mainly between New Zealand and San Francisco until mid 1920 following which RONA carried coal from Newcastle, NSW to New Zealand. Her last such sailing ended at Wellington on 30 September 1921 after which the ship was laid up.

In 1922 RONA was sold for service as a coal lighter, was stripped in Sydney and in 1925 towed to Melbourne for this service. From 1943 until return to Melbourne in 1946 RONA was requisitioned for service as a dumb lighter in New Guinea waters in connection with the war effort. In 1962 the National Trust of Australia

(Victoria) decided to save RONA. In 1968 the Trust was presented with the ship by the owners following the end of her coaling days. The subsequent extensive and painstaking restoration involving some 60,000 hours of voluntary labour led to the ship being renamed POLLY WOODSIDE and berthed afloat in the old Duke's and Orr's timber dry dock which had been closed down in 1975. The ship is now the centrepiece of the Melbourne Maritime Museum located on the Yarra River near the city centre.

In 1988 the World Ship Trust awarded their seventh maritime heritage award to POLLY WOODSIDE for supreme achievement in the preservation of Maritime Heritage. POLLY WOODSIDE is recognized as one of the most authentically rigged restored sailing vessels of her type in the world.
Bibliography A15, B3, D119, D377, D435

Port Fairy Lifeboat

Built 1858 by Government Dockyard, Williamstown, Victoria, Australia
Original owners Government of Victoria
Propulsion Rowed, also dipping lug sail
Tonnage 4 displacement
Length 30.0ft/9.14m
Breadth 7.5ft/2.29m
Draught 1.4ft/0.43m
Materials Iron keel, otherwise wood, diagonal planked
Original use Rescue lifeboat
Condition Intact
Present owners Borough of Port Fairy
Location Port Fairy, Victoria, Australia
History With the Portland Lifeboat, believed to be the oldest lifeboat in the world. In service at Port Fairy 1858-1941 as lifeboat, then used (with Warrnambool Lifeboat) as a catamaran vessel for a dredging pump until c1975. No significant rescues. Exhibited on shore in a lifeboat house built for it in 1861.

Portland Lifeboat

Built 1858 by Government Dockyard, Williamstown, Victoria, Australia
Original owners Government of Victoria
Propulsion Rowed, also dipping lug sail
Tonnage 4 displacement
Length 30.0ft/9.14m
Breadth 7.5ft/2.29m
Draught 1.4ft/0.43m
Materials Iron keel, otherwise wood, diagonal planked
Original use Rescue lifeboat
Condition Intact
Present owners City of Portland
Location Portland, Victoria, Australia
History With the Port Fairy Lifeboat, believed to be the oldest lifeboat in the world. In service at Portland until 1915. Involved in rescue of 19 survivors of ss ADMELLA in 1859 on Carpenter's Rocks, SA. Currently stored indoors there awaiting restoration for exhibition.

Pyap
river barge/steamer

Built 1896 by W Westergaard & Sons, Mannum, South Australia
Original owners C Oliver
Propulsion Steam, sidewheel, 10hp, wood fired
Tonnage 117 gross
Length 94.0ft/28.6m
Breadth 16.8ft/5.12m
Draught 2.0ft/0.61m

Materials Iron frames and topsides, wood planking
Original use Cargo
Condition In operation
Present owners Swan Hill Pioneer Settlement
Location Swan Hill, Victoria, Australia
History Built as a cargo barge for use on the Murray River, but converted to a steamer in 1898. Served as a hawking steamer (travelling general store) and for carrying cargo and passengers. Restored to operating condition in the 1970s with a diesel engine for excursions out of Swan Hill. Acquired by present owners around 1986.
Bibliography B2, B66, C71

Queenscliffe Lifeboat

Built 1926 by A MacFarlane & Sons, Port Adelaide, South Australia
Original owners Government of Victoria
Propulsion Petrol engine; later diesel engine
Tonnage 27 displacement
Length 45.0ft/13.7m
Breadth 12.5ft/3.8m
Draught 4.0ft/1.22m
Materials Steel throughout
Original use Rescue lifeboat
Condition Intact
Present owners Queenscliffe Lifeboat Preservation Society
Location Queenscliffe, Victoria, Australia
History Motor rescue lifeboat built on British design, formerly stationed at Queenscliffe at the entrance to Port Phillip, the approaches to the Port of Melbourne. Restored and exhibited in a specially-built building at Queenscliffe since 1985.
Bibliography D313

Ranger
sidewheel fishing vessel

Former name BARHAM
Built by C W Felshaw, Echuca, Victoria, Australia (date not known)
Original owners A H Conner
Propulsion Steam, sidewheel, 4hp, wood fired
Tonnage 11 gross
Length 50.0ft/15.24m
Breadth 10.1ft/3.08m
Draught 1.3ft/0.38m
Materials Wood throughout
Original use Fishing
Condition Fully restored, operational
Present owners D and S Fitton
Location Echuca, Victoria, Australia
History Originally used for fishing on

Pyap

Murray River. Later employed as BARHAM, for towing and logging. Became derelict in 1960s and engine scrapped. Subsequently part rebuilt at Mildura. Acquired by present owner in 1990 and taken to Echuca, Victoria where restoration to original condition for excursion work is progressing. A 6nhp engine similar to second original has been installed. Moored on the Murray River beside the Historic Port complex.

Reemere
river steamer

Built 1909 by Purdon and Featherstone, Battery Point, Tasmania, Australia
Original owners R and C Calvert
Propulsion Steam, screw, compound, 14hp; later diesel
Tonnage 50 gross
Length 81.1ft/24.7m
Breadth 17.5ft/5.33m
Draught 6.1ft/1.85m
Materials Wood throughout
Original use Cargo and passengers
Condition Afloat, largely restored
Present owners The Reemere Steamship Co Ltd
Location Melbourne, Australia
History Typical ex-Tasmanian river steamer now owned by a preservation

group intending to fully restore vessel as an excursion steamer in Hobart. As a steamer traded mainly in southeast Tasmanian waters until 1963. Subsequently had several owners until in 1966 the steam plant was placed in a working steam museum in southern Tasmania and REEMERE was stripped and converted into a diesel fishing boat. In 1989 she was laid up and acquired by Hobart group in 1991. Recently moved to Melbourne by new owners.
Bibliography D65, D557a

Reginald M
trading ketch

Built 1921 by John Henry Murch, Birkenhead, South Australia
Original owners John Henry Murch
Propulsion Sail, ketch rig; auxiliary engine installed in 1925
Tonnage 68 gross
Length 87.1ft/26.55m
Breadth 21.6ft/6.58m
Draught 5.6ft/1.71m
Materials Wood throughout
Original use Cargo
Condition Fully restored
Present owners Flagstaff Hill Maritime Museum
Location Warrnambool, Australia
History South Australian trading ketch

built with flat bottom and centreboard in style of inland river vessels. Used for carrying explosives in Tasmania from 1960 and later as a training vessel. Acquired by present owners in 1975 and in 1977 transported overland to present position afloat in man-made harbour at Warrnambool, Victoria, adjacent to a historical museum and a created museum village.

Rowitta
river steamer

Former name TARKARRI, SORRENTO
Built 1909 by Purdon and Featherstone Ltd, Hobart, Tasmania, Australia
Original owners The River Tamar Trading Co
Propulsion Steam, screw, triple expansion, 45hp; later diesel
Tonnage 121 gross
Length 111.0ft/33.8m
Breadth 20.5ft/6.25m
Draught 6.8ft/2.07m
Materials Wood throughout
Original use Passengers and cargo
Condition Restored to original appearance; no engine
Present owners Flagstaff Hill Maritime Museum
Location Warrnambool, Victoria, Australia
History The only Tasmanian river

steamer restored to original appearance. Operated on Tamar River until 1941. Subsequently operated in Hobart, then after modification as SORRENTO in Melbourne, Sydney and again in Hobart. In 1967 sold for fishing, gutted, diesel engine installed and renamed TARKARRI. Purchased by present owners and moved to present site in man-made harbour at Warrnambool in 1975. Subsequently restored to original appearance without engine. Open to public.

Ruby
sidewheel river steamer

Built 1907 by David Milne, Morgan, South Australia
Original owners Hugh King
Propulsion Steam, sidewheel, wood fired
Tonnage 205 gross
Length 130.9ft/39.9m
Breadth 18.75ft/5.72m
Draught 2.5ft/0.76m
Materials Composite hull, iron topsides, wood superstructure
Original use Passengers
Condition Intact, engines missing, poor condition
Present owners Town of Wentworth
Location Wentworth, Australia
History Originally employed as a passenger steamer on the Murray River. Withdrawn from regular service in 1928 and later became a houseboat. Engine and boiler removed. Acquired by present owners in 1969 and towed to Wentworth. Restored and now exhibited ashore in a park beside the Darling River at Wentworth, NSW.
Bibliography B66, C71, D444

Sam Male
pearling lugger

Former name KIMBERLEY MALE
Built 1957 by Streeter and Male, Broome, Western Australia
Original owners Streeter and Male
Propulsion Sail, ketch rig; diesel engine
Tonnage 30 gross
Length 56.4ft/17.2m
Breadth 13.5ft/4.1m
Draught 6.0ft/1.83m
Materials Wood throughout
Original use Pearl fishing
Condition Intact
Present owners Broome Shire Council
Location Broome, Western Australia
History An example of the later type of wooden 'pearling lugger' employed around the north coast of Australia. Built to withstand regular tidal

Rowitta

strandings. Displayed on foreshore at Broome since 1974 but hull subsequently deteriorated badly. Major hull restoration work was begun in Broome in 1990 and completed in 1992. Plans are for SAM MALE to be moved into a new shopping arcade for permanent undercover display complete with masts and rigging.
Bibliography B2

Santiago
iron-hulled trading barque

Built 1856 by Balfour, Methill, Scotland
Original owners Balfour, Williamson & Co
Propulsion Sail, barque rig
Tonnage 484 gross
Length 160.6ft/48.95m
Breadth 25.9ft/7.89m
Depth 17.4ft/5.3m
Materials Iron hull and lowermasts, otherwise wood
Original use Cargo
Condition Intact hull sunk in shallow water
Location Near Port Adelaide, South Australia
History Probably the oldest intact iron-hulled sailing ship still in existence. Employed by British, and later Norwegian, owners in world trade. Hulked at Port Adelaide, Australia and

now lying abandoned in mangrove swamps near there.

Sekar Aman
Indonesian 'lete lete'

Built 1950s by Haji Maturi, Raas Island, Indonesia
Original owners Haji Maturi
Propulsion Sail, single mast, proto-lateen (2 booms) rig
Length 41.63ft/12.69m
Breadth 15.8ft/4.81m
Draught 2.6ft/0.8m
Materials Wood throughout
Original use Cargo
Condition Intact
Present owners Australian National Maritime Museum
Location Sydney, New South Wales, Australia
History Traditional Indonesian sailing trading vessel known as a 'lete lete' exhibited afloat at the National Maritime Museum in Sydney.
Bibliography D359

Shin Hsun Yuan
fishing vessel

Built Taiwan
Materials Wood throughout
Original use Fishing
Condition Intact

Present owners Town of Mackay
Location Mackay, North Queensland, Australia
History Taiwanese fishing boat confiscated in Australian waters, displayed on shore near the Mackay visitor centre.

South Steyne
harbour ferry

Built 1938 by Henry Robb Ltd, Leith, Scotland
Original owners Port Jackson & Manley Steamship Co
Propulsion Steam, 4-cylinder, triple expansion, 3250hp
Tonnage 1203 gross
Length 222.5ft/67.82m
Breadth 38.2ft/11.64m
Draught 12.3ft/3.81m
Materials Steel throughout
Original use Passenger ferry
Condition Intact, apparently well maintained
Location Sydney, New South Wales, Australia
History Best known and largest ferry ever on Sydney harbour and the last operating steam ferry. Engine believed to be the most powerful marine steam reciprocating engine now in service in the world. The double-ended SOUTH STEYNE was the last of the 'push-pull'

steam ferries built for the Sydney harbour service from Circular Quay to Manly. The vessel served the Port Jackson & Manly Steamship Co Ltd from 1938 to 1974. Built by Henry Robb Ltd of Leith in Scotland, SOUTH STEYNE has a riveted steel hull, steel superstructure and bulwarks and teak decks and wheelhouses. The engine, manufactured by Harland & Wolff Ltd in Belfast, is directly connected to both fore and aft propellers. Speed was over 17 knots.

SOUTH STEYNE made the delivery voyage to Sydney under her own power in nine weeks, an amazing feat for a vessel designed to operate a 7-mile harbour ferry service. A maximum of 1781 passengers could be carried in harbour service. From 1953 to 1973 SOUTH STEYNE operated weekend ocean cruises, usually to Broken Bay north of Sydney. On 25 August 1974, shortly after being withdrawn from service the vessel was bought and sold by a variety of syndicates, all hoping to restore the vessel, but unable to generate sufficient funds. In 1983, SOUTH STEYNE was towed to Balina, NSW, where major restoration work began. The interior was lavishly and extensively refurbished to provide restaurants, lounges, accommodation and other facilities at a reported cost of 8-10 million Aus$.

In March 1988 SOUTH STEYNE left Ballina for Melbourne, where she entered service as a floating restaurant and excursion vessel on Port Phillip Bay, including a luncheon for Queen Elizabeth II and Prince Phillip during an Australian tour. Unfortunately this venture soon encountered financial difficulties and SOUTH STEYNE was laid up at the end of 1988. Two years later, the vessel was purchased by a consortium of businessmen from Newcastle, NSW, and arrived there in January 1991. Since then, SOUTH STEYNE has operated as a function and excursion vessel at Newcastle, with occasional trips to Sydney.
Bibliography B2, C1, D415

South Steyne in service, 1974

Success
sidewheel river steamer

Built 1877 by G B Air, Moama, New South Wales, Australia
Original owners J P Westward and G B Air
Propulsion Steam, sidewheel, wood fired
Tonnage 129 gross
Length 82.7ft/25.2m
Breadth 16.5ft/5.4m
Draught 2.3ft/0.70m
Materials Iron frames, otherwise wood
Original use Cargo and towing
Condition Vessel and engine undergoing restoration
Present owners River and Riverboat Historical and Preservation
Location Mildura, Victoria, Australia
History Last active cargo steamer on the Darling River when retired and abandoned in 1957. Rescued from the riverbank in 1991 for full restoration to steaming condition.
Bibliography C71

Terima Kasih
Indonesian 'perahu konteng'

Built c1965 at Brondong-Blimbing, East Java, Indonesia
Propulsion Sail, single mast, proto-lateen (two boom) rig
Length 41.5ft/12.66m
Breadth 12.0ft/3.66m
Draught 3.5ft/1.05m
Materials Wood throughout
Original use Fishing
Condition Intact
Present owners Northern Territory Museum of Arts and Sciences
Location Darwin, Australia
History Indonesian 'perahu konteng' used for net fishing on the north coast of Java. Hull covered with elaborate painted decoration. Exhibited indoors, rigged, at Darwin.

Thinh Vuong
motor fishing vessel

Built c1970s probably in Vietnam
Propulsion Diesel engine
Length 55.8ft/17.0m
Materials Wood throughout
Original use Fishing
Condition Intact
Present owners Northern Territory Museum of Arts and Sciences
Location Darwin, Northern Territory, Australia
History Vietnamese fishing boat that arrived in Darwin in June 1978 carrying refugees from the Communist takeover of South Vietnam. Restored for exhibition in a museum building at Darwin.

Ti Tu
private launch

Built 1901 by A E Brown, Fremantle, Western Australia
Original owners S Burt
Propulsion Steam, screw; later petrol engine
Tonnage 10 gross
Length 42.8ft/13.04m
Breadth 8.7ft/2.66m
Materials Wood throughout
Original use Yacht
Condition Intact, engine removed
Present owners Western Australian Museum
Location Fremantle, Western Australia
History Private launch used for entertaining VIPs at Fremantle. Restored in 1977 and now an exhibit in a shed at the maritime museum there.

Titipan
Indonesian fishing vessel

Built Indonesia
Materials Wood throughout
Original use Fishing
Condition Undergoing restoration
Present owners Broome Historical Society
Location Broome, Australia
History Example of a traditional Indonesian fishing boat undergoing restoration indoors for use as an exhibit.

Tp
cargo barge

Former name WANERA
Built 1900 by Permewan, Wright and Co, Echuca, Victoria, Australia
Original owners Permewan, Wright

and Co
Propulsion Towed
Length 112.0ft/34.1m
Breadth 20.9ft/6.37m
Draught 2.0ft/0.61m
Materials Iron frames, steel topsides, wood planking
Original use Cargo
Condition Fully restored
Present owners I, R and K Mansell, Colignan, Victoria
Location Mildura, Victoria, Australia
History Converted to a paddle steamer by original owners in 1911 and renamed WANERA. After the Second World War used for carting wood and increasingly for passengers and in stages modified for 5-day river cruises in the Mildura-Wentworth area. Converted from steam to diesel power in 1955, thus becoming the first diesel paddle boat on the inland rivers. In January 1985 was burnt to the waterline at Wentworth, NSW. The hull was subsequently acquired by the present owners and has since been rebuilt in her original configuration as a cargo barge.
Bibliography C71

Trixen
fishing schooner

Built 1904 by H Miller, Broome, Western Australia
Original owners E Miller
Propulsion Sail, schooner rig; later diesel auxiliary
Tonnage 30 gross

Length 56.0ft/17.07m
Breadth 14.4ft/4.4m
Draught 4.9ft/1.5m
Materials Wood throughout
Original use Pearl fishing
Condition Basic hull in poor condition
Present owners Western Australian Museum
Location Broome, Western Australia
History Early 'pearling lugger' off northern Australia built to withstand regular tidal strandings. Ceased pearling in early 1960s and then used as a trawler and for lobster fishing. Later, after cargo and passenger service off Fremantle, became derelict. Donated to present owners in 1981 and partly restored in 1986, for eventual exhibit as part of the boat collection of the maritime museum in Fremantle.

Tu Do
motor fishing boat

Built c1968 at Phu Quoc Island, Vietnam
Propulsion Diesel engine
Length 63.6ft/19.4m
Breadth 17.1ft/5.2m
Draught 5.9ft/1.8m
Materials Wood throughout
Original use Fishing
Condition Intact
Present owners Australian National Maritime Museum
Location Sydney, New South Wales, Australia
History South Vietnamese motor fishing boat that arrived in Darwin,

Australia, in November 1977 carrying refugees from the Communist takeover of that country. Restored for exhibition afloat at the National Maritime Museum in Sydney.
Bibliography D527

Vampire
destroyer

Former name HMAS VAMPIRE
Built 1959 by Cockatoo Docks and Engineering Co, Sydney, New South Wales, Australia
Original owners Royal Australian Navy
Official number D 11
Propulsion Steam turbines, 54,000hp, twin screw
Tonnage 3600 displacement
Length 388.5ft/118.4m
Breadth 43.0ft/13.1m
Draught 14.4ft/4.4m
Materials Steel throughout
Original use Destroyer
Condition Intact
Present owners Commonwealth of Australia
Location Sydney, New South Wales, Australia
History Largest preserved vessel in Australia. Australian built destroyer of the British DARING class design. Decommissioned in 1986 and loaned to the Australian National Maritime Museum in 1991. Exhibited afloat and open to the public at Darling Harbour, Sydney, NSW.
Bibliography C28

Vega
river barge

Built 1911 by Franz O Wallin, Moama, New south Wales, Australia
Original owners Franz O Wallin
Propulsion Towed
Tonnage 96 gross
Length 104.0ft/31.7m
Breadth 20.7ft/6.31m
Draught 1.8ft/0.96m
Materials Iron frames and topsides, otherwise wood
Original use Cargo
Condition Intact
Present owners Swan Hill Pioneer Settlement
Location Swan Hill, Victoria, Australia
History Typical inland river wool barge. Towed from Mildura to Swan Hill in 1972, restored and fitted out with the appearance of a loaded wool barge; the wool bales actually house a theatre for historic presentations. Sits on frame in artificial pond at Pioneer Settlement at Swan Hill, Victoria.

Victoria
steam tug

Former name LYTTELTON II
Built 1939 by Lobnitz & Co, Renfrew, Scotland
Original owners Lyttelton Harbour Board, Lyttelton, New Zealand
Propulsion Steam, 6-cylinder, triple expansion, 1250hp
Tonnage 303 gross
Length 123.0ft/37.5m

Vampire during her naval service

Breadth 31.3ft/9.54m
Draught 12.3ft/3.75m
Materials Wood wheelhouse and decks, otherwise steel
Original use Tug
Condition Intact, needing some restoration
Present owners Bay Steamers Ltd
Location Melbourne, Victoria, Australia
History Last working steam tug in commercial service in New Zealand and last coal-fired steamship to cross the Tasman Sea. Sailed to Sydney in 1981 for preservation. Later sold and sailed to Melbourne in 1985 but laid up. Purchased by present Melbourne owners in 1992 for restoration to steaming condition and conversion to excursion vessel.
Bibliography D470

Vivienne
pearling lugger

Former name WHITE STAR
Built c1945 at Broome, Western Australia
Original owners W R Scott
Propulsion Sail, ketch rig; auxiliary diesel engine
Length 50.5ft/15.4m
Breadth 14.4ft/4.38m
Draught 5.4ft/1.65m
Materials Wood throughout
Original use Pearl fishing
Condition Intact
Present owners Northern Territory Museum of Arts and Sciences
Location Darwin, Northern Territory, Australia
History Example of a later pearl fishing vessel from northern Australia of the type known as a pearling lugger. Last such vessel to operate out of Darwin in 1982. Donated to present owners in 1983, and restored to serve as an exhibit, with masts and sails, in a museum building at Darwin.

Waitangi
racing yacht

Built 1894 by Robert Logan, Devonport, New Zealand
Original owners J Jamieson
Propulsion Cutter rig
Length 74.0ft/22.56m
Breadth 11.0ft/3.35m
Draught 9.0ft/2.74m
Materials Wood throughout
Original use Racing yacht
Condition Fully restored; in sailing condition
Location Melbourne, Australia
History Late Victorian racing yacht

Waratah

restored to original appearance and maintained in sailing condition by a private owner.
Bibliography D225

Waratah
steam tug

Former name BURUNDAH
Built 1902 by Cockatoo Dockyard, Cockatoo Island, Sydney, Australia
Original owners New South Wales Public Works
Propulsion Steam, 2-cylinder compound, 275hp, coal fired
Tonnage 132 gross
Length 108.5ft/33.07m
Breadth 20.25ft/6.17m
Depth 9.75ft/2.97m
Draught 10.3ft/3.15m
Materials Iron hull, wood decks and superstructure
Original use Tug
Condition Fully restored to operating condition
Present owners Sydney Maritime Museum
Location Sydney, New South Wales, Australia
History WARATAH is the oldest operational coastal steam tug in Australia. Her origins are obscure. She was shipped in sections from the UK and assembled in Sydney in 1902 for the State government and initially

named BURUNDA. Her service life involved work as a tug at the various river mouth bars in northern NSW, general port service and at times relief pilot vessel duty at Newcastle in particular. She was renamed WARATAH in 1918. During the Second World War WARATAH steamed as far as Nauru in the Pacific and Fremantle, WA. Her later life was spent increasingly at Newcastle until in 1968 she was presented by the NSW government to the forerunner of the Sydney Maritime Museum.

Extensive restoration was required to bring WARATAH to good condition and re-establish her original appearance. To achieve this over an extended period at minimum cost using Museum staff and volunteer labour, an abandoned graving dock formerly used by the local power authority to repair fuel barges was acquired. This was cleaned up and fitted with a new gate to accommodate WARATAH. Using the old deteriorated plates as templates, replacements were cut and rivetted to the hull. Most of the steel bulwarks also had to be replaced, as well as some deck beams and all of the timber decking. The superstructure was thoroughly restored and the engine completely overhauled. By the early 1980s WARATAH was steaming again, a

remarkable example of what can be accomplished by a team of dedicated amateurs.

Work on WARATAH set a standard that is now being followed in the Museum's restoration of the 1874 iron barque JAMES CRAIG. WARATAH is now regularly steamed and is exhibited at the Australian National Maritime Museum at Darling Harbour, Sydney.
Bibliography B3, B37, D172, D174

Wattle
steam tug

Former name CODECO
Built 1933 by Cockatoo Dockyard, Cockatoo Island, Sydney, Australia
Original owners Royal Australian Navy
Propulsion Steam, compound, 300ihp
Tonnage 99 gross
Length 81.25ft/24.76m
Breadth 18.5ft/5.64m
Depth 9.25ft/2.82m
Draught 9.25ft/2.82m
Materials Wood wheelhouse and foredeck, otherwise steel
Original use Tug
Condition Restored, in operating condition
Present owners Victorian Steamship Association Ltd
Location Melbourne, Victoria, Australia
History Operated as harbour tug at Sydney by Royal Australian Navy until

1969. Acquired by present owners in Sydney in 1978 and towed to Melbourne in 1979. Subsequently restored and re-entered commercial service in 1985. Operates regular cruises and charters on Port Phillip Bay. WATTLE is the only steamship operating regular public cruises on the Australian coast.
Bibliography B2, B3

Whyalla
minesweeper

Former name RIP, HMAS WHYALLA
Built 1942 by Broken Hill Proprietary Co, Whyalla, South Australia
Original owners British Admiralty
Official number J 153
Propulsion Steam, triple expansion, twin screw, 1750hp
Tonnage 815 displacement
Length 186.0ft/56.69m
Breadth 31.0ft/9.45m
Draught 8.5ft/2.59m
Materials Steel throughout
Original use Corvette/minesweeper
Condition Intact
Present owners City of Whyalla
Location Whyalla, South Australia
History One of 60 BATHURST class vessels built in Australia during the Second World War and the first ship built at The Broken Hill Proprietary Co Ltd shipyard at Whyalla. Served in Australian and Pacific waters during the Second World War and then laid up. Towed to Melbourne in 1974 and converted to a buoy and port service vessel by the Ports and Harbours Department. Sold to the City of Whyalla in 1984 and stored there for preservation. Hauled ashore in 1987 where originally built and transported 2 kilometres overland to the Whyalla Maritime Museum where she is now exhibited partly restored on cradles.
Bibliography B2, D498

Yambulla
motor workboat

Built 1945 by A T Brine and Sons, Perth, Western Australia
Original owners Australian Army Water Transport Division
Official number AM 409
Propulsion Diesel engine
Tonnage 33 gross
Length 40.0ft/12.2m
Breadth 12.1ft/3.68m
Draught 4.6ft/1.4m
Materials Wood throughout
Original use Launch, workboat
Condition In operation

Present owners Western Australian Museum
Location Fremantle, Western Australia
History Standard Australian services Second World War 40ft workboat. Donated to present owners in 1985 and used for educational/training purposes on the Swan River and Cockburn Sound. Operates from the Expedition Boat Shed in East Fremantle.

Yelta
steam tug

Built 1949 by Cockatoo Docks & Engineering Co, Sydney, Australia
Original owners Ritch & Smith, Port Adelaide
Propulsion Steam, triple expansion, 970hp, coal fired; later oil fired
Tonnage 233 gross
Length 103.3ft/31.5m
Breadth 26.7ft/8.14m
Draught 10.25ft/3.12m
Materials Wood wheelhouse, otherwise steel
Original use Tug
Condition Intact
Present owners South Australian Maritime Museum
Location Port Adelaide, South Australia
History The last steam tug in commercial service in Australia when retired. Employed as a harbour tug at Port Adelaide until 1976. Preserved by a private individual until acquired by the newly established South Australian Maritime Museum in 1985. Kept as an exhibit in steaming condition and operated occasionally.

Austria

Until the First World War the centre of the Austro-Hungarian Empire, with coastline on the Mediterranean and the Black Sea and one of Europe's larger navies, Austria is today a landlocked, largely mountainous, country. Its navigable waterways are the Danube River, and several scenic mountain lakes. The oldest paddlewheel vessels in active service on the Danube within Austria are two largely unaltered diesel-propelled boats of the 1930s. There are hopes that the last Austrian river steamer SCHÖNBRUNN may re-enter service one of these years, and reports that at least two steam-powered towing craft are currently being restored to operating condition by steam enthusiasts in the Vienna area. Two fine old sidewheel steamers operate out of Austrian lake ports during the summer months, the venerable GISELA on the Traunsee, and the somewhat younger HOHENTWIEL on the Bodensee, a lake shared with Germany.

Frédéric Mistral
river towboat

Former name COLUMBIA I
Built 1914 by Gertiundenburg Shipyard, Netherlands
Propulsion Steam, screw
Length 86.8ft/26.4m
Breadth 17.7ft/5.4m
Draught 5.9ft/1.8m
Materials Steel throughout
Original use River towboat
Condition Undergoing restoration
Location Vienna, Austria
History Danube River steam towboat. Awarded to France at the end of the First World War for further use on the river under that flag. Currently undergoing restoration back to steaming condition at Vienna.

Gisela
sidewheel steamer

Built 1872 by Schiffwerft Florisdorf, Lake Traunsee, Austria
Propulsion Steam, sidewheel, oscillating engine, 120hp. Engine built by Prager Maschinenfabrik, Prague

Tonnage 187 gross
Length 144.0ft/43.89m
Breadth 31.0ft/9.45m
Draught 7.0ft/2.13m
Materials Steel hull, wood superstructure
Original use Passengers
Condition In active service
Present owners Traunsee Schiffahrt Rud Ges
Location Lake Traunsee, Austria
History Last sidewheel steamer on the Traunsee and the oldest coal-fired steamer in Austria. Reconditioned and returned to service in 1984. Now converted to oil fuel.
Bibliography B16, B43, C98, D63

Hohentwiel
sidewheel steamer

Built 1913 by Escher-Wyss & Co, Zurich, Switzerland
Original owners Koniglich Wurttembergische Staatsbahnen
Propulsion Steam, sidewheel, 2-cylinder compound
Tonnage 378 displacement
Length 175.48ft/53.5m
Breadth 42.64ft/13.0m
Draught 4.69ft/1.43m
Materials Steel throughout
Original use Passengers
Condition Restored to operating condition
Present owners Verein Internationales Bodenseeschiffahrtsmuseum
Location Bodensee (lake), Austria
History Former German sidewheel steamer built for operation on the Bodensee (Lake Constance). Moved to the Austrian end of the lake following retirement in 1960 and used as floating headquarters for a boat club. Fully restored to operating condition in 1990, based at Hard, Austria.
Bibliography B16, B43, C98, D166, D278a

Kaiser Franz Josef I
sidewheel steamer

Built 1873 by Mayer Werft, Linz, Austria
Original owners Salzburger Lokalbahnen
Propulsion Steam, sidewheel; converted to diesel in 1954. Engine built by Klockner-Humboldt-Deutz (current)
Tonnage 81 gross, 46.4 displacement
Length 108.3ft/33.0m
Breadth 27.8ft/8.5m
Materials Steel hull, steel and wood superstructure
Original use Passengers
Condition In operation

Present owners Osterreichische Bundesbahn
Contact address Markt 35, 5360 St Wolfgang
Location St Wolfgang, Austria
History Built as a sidewheel steamer for operation on the Wolfgangsee. Converted to geared diesel propulsion in 1954, with alteration of stack. Otherwise little changed and still in regular service.
Bibliography B43

Pascal
river towboat

Former names LEINE, BERTHA ANNA, WEST HAVELLAND
Built 1907 by Weimann Brothers, Brandenburg, Germany
Propulsion Steam, screw
Length 71.5ft/21.8m
Breadth 14.4ft/4.4m
Draught 4.6ft/1.4m
Materials Steel throughout
Original use River towboat
Condition Undergoing restoration
Location Vienna, Austria
History Danube River steam towboat. Awarded to France at the end of the First World War for further use on the river under that flag. Currently undergoing restoration back to steaming condition at Vienna.

Schönbrunn
sidewheel steamer

Built 1912 by Obuda Werft, Budapest, Hungary
Original owners Donau-Dampfschiffahrts Gesellschaft
Propulsion Steam, sidewheel, 740hp
Tonnage 440 (net), 556 displacement

Kaiser Franz Josef I

Length 245.0ft/74.68m
Breadth 26.17ft/7.98m
Draught 5.67ft/1.73m
Materials Steel hull, wood superstructure
Original use Passengers
Condition Intact, afloat
Present owners Erste Donau-Dampfschiffahrts
Location Linz, Austria

History The last intact sidewheel river steamer in Austria. Has been out of service for a number of years, but plans were proposed for her to be refurbished and reactivated, possibly by the summer of 1999.
Bibliography B16, B43

St Josef
lake steamer

Built 1887 by Mayer, Linz, Austria
Propulsion Steam, converted to diesel
Tonnage 58 gross
Length 86.6ft/26.4m
Breadth 14.4ft/4.4m
Original use Lake passenger steamer
Condition In operation
Present owners Aachensee Schiffahrt
Location Aachensee (Lake), Austria
History Austrian lake steamer converted to diesel propulsion but otherwise little altered.

Stadt Innsbruck
lake steamer

Built 1911 by Stabilimento Technico Triestino Schiffwerk, Linz, Austria
Propulsion Diesel engine
Materials Steel hull

Original use Lake passenger vessel
Condition In operation
Present owners Aachensee Schiffahrt
Location Aachensee (Lake), Austria
History Austrian lake steamer built early in the century. Currently diesel-powered but otherwise unaltered.

Stadt Passau
sidewheel riverboat

Built 1940 by Werft Korneuburg, Vienna, Austria
Original owners DDSG
Propulsion Sidewheel, diesel electric, two 460hp engines. Engine built by Sulzer
Tonnage 650 displacement
Length 255.0ft/77.7m
Breadth 49.8ft/15.2m
Materials Steel hull
Original use Passengers
Condition In active service
Present owners DDSG
Location Vienna (home port), Austria
History Diesel-operated paddlewheel riverboat built for use on the Danube and still in service making excursions out of Vienna.
Bibliography B43

Schönbrunn lying at Vienna in 1962

Stadt Wien

Stadt Wien
sidewheel riverboat

Built 1939 by Werft Korneuburg,
Vienna, Austria
Original owners Erste Donau-
Dampfschiffahrts Gessellschaft
(DDSG)
Propulsion Sidewheel, diesel electric,
two 460hp engines. Engine built by
Sulzer
Tonnage 650 displacement
Length 255.0ft/77.7m
Breadth 49.8ft/15.2m
Materials Steel hull
Original use Passengers
Condition In active service
Present owners DDSG
Location Vienna (home port), Austria
History Diesel-operated paddlewheel
riverboat built for use on the Danube
River and still in service making
excursions out of Vienna.
Bibliography B43

Thalia
passenger steamer

Former name KLAGENFURT
Built 1909 by Dresdner
Maschinenfabrik & Schiffswerft
Ubigau, Dresden, Germany
Propulsion Steam, screw, compound,
150hp
Tonnage 132 gross
Length 126.3ft/38.5m
Breadth 18.0ft/5.5m
Materials Steel throughout
Original use Passengers
Condition Fully restored in the 1980s
Present owners Klagenfurter
Stadtwerke
Location Klagenfurt, Austria
History Veteran steamer employed on
the Worthersee for cruises. Retired in
1974 but fully restored after 1986
including removal of modernised
superstructure.

Bangladesh

Formerly an eastern region of
British India north of the Bay of
Bengal, Bangladesh became East
Pakistan in 1947 with the end of
colonial rule, and in 1971 an
independent nation when it
severed its link with West
Pakistan. Much of the country's
coastline is a labyrinth of river
estuaries, large and small, which
continue to be home to a
fascinating fleet of varied
traditional craft. Sailing, rowing,
poling, and hauling by humans or
animals are being increasingly
replaced by economical small
diesel engines, but the methods
used in constructing the wooden
hulls of these craft continue to be
quite foreign to westerners.
During the colonial period steam
navigation was introduced on the
larger rivers, and some of the
paddlewheel vessels of that
period reportedly survive, either
in use or in lay-up. News, aside
from random sightings by
travellers, is sparse, as those in
operation only serve the local
traffic, and are not promoted as
tourist transportation.

Kiwi
sidewheel river steamer

Built c1930
Propulsion Steam, sidewheel, inclined
triple expansion. Engine built by
Denny, Dumbarton, Scotland
Tonnage 630 gross
Length 235.0ft/71.6m
Materials Steel hull
Original use Passengers
Condition In operating condition
Location Pudda River, Bangladesh
History Large paddlewheel river
steamer, probably built in the British
Isles around 1930. Reportedly
maintained in operating condition and
employed for excursions on special
occasions.

Belgium

The surviving medieval cities of
Ghent and Bruges are testimonial
to Belgium's long history as a
centre of trade and commerce. In
recent centuries Antwerp, on the
Scheldt River which also forms
the country's boundary with the
Netherlands at the North Sea,
has served as one of Europe's
major seaports. Belgium has an
internal network of navigable
rivers and canals that both serve
its own needs, and also link it
with a large area of the interior
of the continent. Antwerp is the
location of the country's National
Maritime Museum, which deals
with oceangoing and inland
shipping, and preserves examples
of craft typical of the latter.

Cephee
canal barge

Built 1937 by Pruvost frères et Blond,
Merville, France
Original owners Marcel Ruyffelaere
Propulsion Towed by horses
Length 126.44ft/38.54m
Breadth 16.57ft/5.05m
Draught 6.56ft/2.0m
Materials Wood throughout
Original use Cargo; canal barge
Condition Intact, afloat
Present owners Rijn en
binnenvaartmuseum
Location Antwerp, Belgium
History Type of canal barge once used
to transport goods from northern
France to Antwerp. Usually towed by
horses. Currently a floating exhibit.

Delphine
steam yacht

Former name DAUNTLESS
Built 1921 by Great Lakes Engineering
Works, Detroit, Michigan, USA
Original owners Horace E Dodge
Propulsion Steam, screw, triple
expansion
Tonnage 1286 gross, 1950 displacement
Length 250.0ft/76.2m
Breadth 35.5ft/10.82m
Draught 14.6ft/4.45m
Materials Steel hull, steel and wood
superstructure
Original use Yacht
Condition Intact but poor
Location Bruges, Belgium

History Steam yacht built for automobile manufacturer Horace E Dodge. Converted to a patrol vessel during the Second World War and renamed USS DAUNTLESS. Later based at Washington DC as flagship of Chief of Naval Operations Admiral Ernest King. Returned to the Dodge family after the war. From 1968 to 1987 served as a training ship for a maritime union seamanship school at Piney Point, Maryland. Undergoing restoration to active steam at Bruges.
Bibliography D547

Lauranda
canal/river barge

Built 1928 by L van Praet-Dansaert, Baasrode, Belgium
Original owners Jan Verhayen
Propulsion Towed by horses
Length 126.21ft/38.47m
Breadth 15.64ft/5.04m
Depth 7.87ft/2.4m
Materials Iron hull, wood superstructure
Original use Cargo, barge
Condition Intact, on shore
Present owners Scheepvaartmuseum
Contact address Steenplein 1, 2000 Antwerpen, Belgium
Location Antwerp, Belgium
History Type of barge used to carry cargo on the canals and rivers of Belgium, France, Germany and the Netherlands. Towed on canals by horses and on rivers by steam towboats. Now an exhibit at Antwerp.

LS No 1
lightship

Former name WANDELAAR
Built 1950
Original use Lightship
Present owners NEMO
Location Ghent, Belgium
History Proposed use as restaurant/exhibit

LS No 2
lightship

Original use Lightship
Location Zeebrugge, Belgium
History Used as an exhibit

Mercator
sail training ship

Built 1932 by Ramage & Ferguson, Leith, Scotland
Propulsion Sail, barquentine rig (briefly topsail schooner); diesel auxiliary

Mercator

Tonnage 770 gross
Length 190.0ft/57.91m
Breadth 34.75ft/10.59m
Depth 16.75ft/5.11m
Materials Steel hull, deckhouses, and most spars
Original use Training ship
Condition Intact, rigged
Present owners Belgian Ministry of Transport
Location Ostend, Belgium
History Built as a training vessel for future officers in the Belgian merchant marine. Retired from seagoing use in 1961 and moored at Antwerp as a floating museum. Later moved to Ostend.
Bibliography A14, C96, D125, D193

Oudenaarde
minesweeper

Built 1958 by Mercantile Marine Yard, Kruibeke, Belgium
Original owners Royal Belgian Navy
Propulsion Diesel engines, 1260hp
Tonnage 190 displacement
Length 113.0ft/32.5m
Breadth 22.0ft/6.7m
Draught 7.0ft/2.1m
Materials Steel throughout

Original use Minesweeper
Condition Intact
Present owners National Scheepvaartmuseum
Location Antwerp, Belgium
History Belgian inshore minesweeper of the 1950s preserved as an onshore exhibit at Antwerp.

St Antonius
canal/river barge

Built 1914 at Merelbeke, Belgium
Original owners Desire van Reeth
Propulsion Sail, engine added
Length 88.94ft/27.11m
Breadth 15.62ft/4.76m
Draught 5.18ft/1.58m
Materials Iron hull
Original use Cargo, river barge
Condition Intact, restored
Present owners National Scheepvaartmuseum
Contact address Steenplein 1, 2000 Antwerpen, Belgium
Location Antwerp, Belgium
History Type of river and canal barge employed on the waterways of Belgium and the Netherlands. Exhibited on shore at Antwerp.

U-480
submarine

Built in Russia (date not known)
Original owners Soviet Navy
Materials Steel throughout
Original use Submarine
Condition Intact
Present owners Seafront
Contact address Oude Vismijn, Albertdok 1, Vismijnstraat 12, 8380 Zeebrugge
Location Zeebrugge, Belgium
History Russian conventionally-powered submarine of the Cold War era, now exhibited afloat in Belgium by a private firm.

West Hinder
lightship

Original owners Belgian Lighthouse service
Official number LS 3
Materials Steel throughout
Original use Lightship
Condition Intact, being refurbished
Present owners National Maritime Museum
Location Antwerp, Belgium
History Acquired for preservation.

Brazil

The largest country in South America, Brazil has many seaports along its long coastline. Much of its interior, particularly in the north and west was, until recent highway construction, an area of swamp or jungle only accessible by river transportation. The last stronghold of the paddlewheel steamer in Brazil is the Sao Francisco River, where one or more of the boats built to carry freight and inter-city passengers are believed to still be in use as excursion craft. Brazil has maintained one of the larger navies in Latin America, modernising its fleet in the post-Second World War period with warships originally built for the United States or Great Britain. Brazil ended naval training under sail in 1962, shortly before the international surge in interest in the 'tall ships'. The barque GUANABARA was sold to Portugal, where she still operates as the SAGRES. The four-masted topsail schooner ALMIRANTE SALDANHA, converted to a motor vessel in 1962, may now be rerigged, and there are reports that one or more new sailing vessels are to be built. Brazil has a Naval Museum on shore at Rio de Janeiro, and all the ships currently serving as exhibits in the country are retired naval craft.

Almirante Saldanha
sail training ship

Built 1933 by Vickers-Armstrong, Barrow in Furness, England
Original owners Brazilian Navy
Propulsion Sail, 4-masted topsail schooner rig; diesel auxiliary
Tonnage 3315 displacement
Length 262.4ft/79.9m
Breadth 52.0ft/15.8m
Draught 28.5ft/8.6m
Materials Steel throughout
Original use Training ship
Condition Rig removed, converted to motor vessel
Present owners Brazilian Navy
Location Rio de Janeiro, Brazil
History Built as a training ship for the Brazilian Navy. Converted to a research vessel in 1962 when the Navy gave up sail training. There have been recent proposals to rig her again.

Bahia
submarine

Former name USS PLAICE
Built 1943 by Portsmouth Naval Shipyard, Kittery, Maine, USA
Original owners United States Navy
Propulsion Diesel and electric motors
Tonnage 1525 displacement
Length 311.75ft/95.02m
Breadth 27.25ft/8.31m
Draught 15.25ft/4.65m
Materials Steel throughout
Original use Submarine
Condition Intact
Present owners Museum of Naval Technology
Location Santos, Brazil
History Fleet submarine of BALAO class that served in the United States Navy during the Second World War. Transferred to the Brazilian Navy in 1963, and now an onshore exhibit at Santos.
Bibliography C64

Bauru
destroyer escort

Former name USS REYBOLD
Built 1943 by Federal Shipbuilding Co, Newark, New Jersey, USA
Original owners United States Navy
Propulsion Diesel electric, 6000hp
Tonnage 1900 displacement
Length 306.0ft/93.27m
Breadth 36.7ft/11.19m
Draught 12.0ft/3.66m
Materials Steel throughout
Original use Destroyer escort
Condition Intact

Present owners Brazilian Navy
Location Rio de Janeiro, Brazil
History CANNON class destroyer escort built for the United States Navy during the Second World War. Transferred to the Brazilian Navy in 1944. Moored at Rio de Janeiro as a floating naval museum.
Bibliography C64

Benjamin Guimares
sternwheel river steamer

Built 1913 by James Rees Sons & Co, Pittsburgh, Pennsylvania, USA
Propulsion Steam, sternwheel, wood fuel
Tonnage 321 gross
Length 125.42ft/38.23m
Breadth 25.92ft/7.9m
Draught 2.39ft/0.73m
Materials Iron hull
Original use Passengers & cargo
Condition In active service
Present owners Companhia de Navegacao Sao Francisco, Pirapora, Minas, Brazil
Location Sao Francisco River, Brazil
History Built for Brazilian owners to carry cargo and passengers on one of the country's rivers. In recent years has been used for cruises on the Sao Francisco River between Juazeiro and Pirapora.

Laurindo Pitta
seagoing tug

Built 1910 by Vickers, Sons and Maxim, Barrow, England
Original owners Brazilian Government
Propulsion Steam, screw, 4-cylinder compound, twin screw
Tonnage 271 gross
Length 128.0ft/39.0m
Breadth 25.8ft/7.8m
Materials Steel hull
Original use Seagoing tug
Condition In operating condition
Present owners Brazilian Navy
Location Rio de Janeiro, Brazil
History Last surviving Brazilian Navy vessel that participated in the First World War. Was used between Dakar, Africa and the Cape Verde Islands. Later served as a Navy Yard tug at Rio de Janeiro. Being restored to carry historical exhibits on Brazilian participation in the First World War, and to serve as a ferry between the Navy Cultural Center and Fiscal Island at Rio. Operated by the League of Friends of the Naval Museum.

Riachuelo
submarine

Built 1975 by Vickers, Barrow, England
Original owners Brazilian Navy
Official number S 22
Propulsion Diesel and electric motors, 6000hp
Tonnage 1610 displacement
Length 295.0ft/89.9m
Breadth 26.4ft/8.07m
Draught 17.9ft/5.48m
Materials Steel throughout
Original use Submarine
Condition Intact
Present owners Brazilian Navy
Location Rio de Janeiro, Brazil
History One of three submarines built in England for the Brazilian Navy based on the Royal Navy's OBERON class. Decommissioned in November 1997. Preserved as a floating exhibit.

Saldanha Marinho
sidewheel steamer

Built in Brazil (date not known)
Propulsion Steam, sidewheel
Materials Steel hull, wood superstructure
Original use Passsengers and cargo
Condition Restored, with boiler but no engine
Location Juazeiro, Brazil
History Either restored example of a Rio Sao Francisco sidewheel steamer, or a convincing replica. Sits on shore with restaurant seating on open main and upper decks.

Wenceslau Braz
river steamer

Built 1913 by James Rees Sons & Co, Pittsburgh, Pennsylvania, USA
Propulsion Steam, sternwheel, wood fuel
Tonnage 321 gross
Length 125.42ft/38.23m
Breadth 25.92ft/7.9m
Draught 2.39ft/0.73m
Materials Iron hull
Original use Passengers and cargo
Condition Operative or laid up
Present owners Companhia de Navegacao Sao Francisco, Pirapora, Brazil
Location Pirapora, Brazil
History Sister vessel to the BENJAMIN GUIMARES. Last reported in active service in 1979. Currently either making excursions on the Sao Francisco River or laid up.

Bulgaria

This country achieved its independence, and virtually its current boundaries, in 1878. It borders on the Black Sea, and before the First World War also had coastline on the Aegean but this territory was lost to Greece because the country sided with Turkey in that conflict. Bulgaria's northern boundary with Romania is formed by the Danube River. After the Second World War, a sizeable fleet of sidewheel towboats was built in Hungary for service on the river, many of them for operation under the Bulgarian flag. One of these, the PLOVIOV of 1954, was converted in 1964 to an operating reproduction of the Austrian passenger steamer RADETSKY, scene of an incident in 1876 during the Bulgarian struggle for independence. She is no longer steaming, but is believed to survive as a museum and youth hostel at Kozloduj. The Bulgarian torpedo boat DERZKI, veteran of a war with Turkey in 1912, was one of the first steam-powered warships to be set aside for preservation.

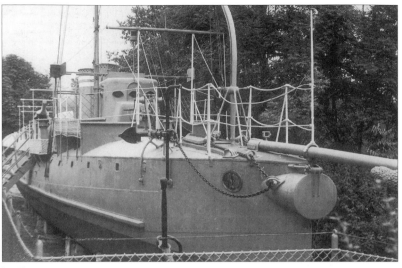
Derzki

Derzki
steam torpedo boat

Built 1904 by Schneider Creusot & Co, Toulon, France
Original owners Bulgarian Navy
Propulsion Steam, triple expansion
Tonnage 98 displacement
Length 124.67ft/38.0m
Breadth 14.42ft/4.4m
Draught 8.5ft/2.6m
Materials Steel throughout
Original use Torpedo boat
Condition Intact
Present owners Naval Museum
Location Varna, Bulgaria
History Prefabricated in France and assembled at Varna, Bulgaria. Veteran of the 1912 war with Turkey. Is an exhibit in a park in Varna.
Bibliography D469

Pioneer
trading cutter

Former name BOUZLOUDZHA, SHIPKA
Built 1945 by Neptune Shipyard, Varna, Bulgaria

Original owners Peroun Co Ltd
Propulsion Sail, cutter rig; semi-diesel, 90hp; later diesel, 150hp
Tonnage 80 gross
Length 61.66ft/18.8m
Breadth 21.32ft/6.5m
Draught 9.18ft/2.8m
Materials Wood throughout
Original use Cargo
Condition Intact, laid up, in need of restoration
Present owners Bourgas Town Council
Location Bourgas, Bulgaria
History Last surviving example of a type of double-ended sailing vessel once used to carry cargo under sail in the Black Sea. Laid up. Acquired for conversion to a sail training vessel.

Torpedo Cutter No 3
torpedo boat

Built 1942 by Varna Naval Arsenal, Varna, Bulgaria
Original owners Bulgarian Navy
Tonnage 25 displacement
Length 55.75ft/16.9m
Breadth 9.75ft/2.9m
Draught 5.0ft/1.5m
Materials Steel throughout
Original use Torpedo boat
Condition Intact
Present owners Varna Naval Museum
Location Varna, Bulgaria
History Bulgarian torpedo boat of the Second World War period preserved on shore as an exhibit and Naval memorial.

Veslets
auxiliary sailing vessel

Former name VOLA, MILKA
Built 1943 by Todor Szeliabov Shipyard, Kavalla, Greece

Original owners Todor Szeliabov
Propulsion Schooner rig; diesel auxiliary engine
Tonnage 120 gross
Length 81.04ft/24.7m
Breadth 20.83ft/6.35m
Draught 8.86ft/2.7m
Materials Wood hull, steel masts
Original use Cargo
Condition Intact
Present owners Autokombinat-Varna
Location Varna, Bulgaria
History Built as a cargo vessel, but converted to a sail training vessel by the Bulgarian Navy in 1949. Used for youth training from 1959 to 1972 and then moved on shore and converted to a youth club.

Pioneer lying at Bourgas in 1983

Canada

The United States' neighbour to the north has one of the longest coastlines in the world, bordering on the Atlantic Ocean, the Pacific Ocean, the Arctic Sea, and the Great Lakes. Much of the Arctic Sea waters are impassable the year around without icebreaker assistance, and the remainder of that coast, the Great Lakes, and the St Lawrence River ports of Montreal and Quebec are largely closed due to ice for many months of the year. In spite of this the country has had a rich and varied maritime history. The earliest French and British explorers learned how to use the lakes and rivers as highways from the native population. During the nineteenth century wooden sailing vessels built and owned in Canada were known around the world. When the plains of the Canadian west were settled, Great Lakes shipping became important to carry grain to the cities of the east. Discovery of gold in the late-1800s opened up areas of the far northwest to settlement when steamboats on winding, rapids-filled rivers were the only practical means of transportation. One of the largest preserved native-American craft, a Haida dugout canoe from the Pacific coast of Canada, is on exhibit at the American Museum of Natural History in New York. The most intact Canadian deepwater sailing vessel from the nineteenth century is the EGERIA of 1859, which continues to serve as a wharf and storeroom in the Falkland Islands. In Canada itself, a number of communities have taken on the preservation of vessels and others, like the riverboat KLONDIKE at Whitehorse, Yukon Territory, have been restored for exhibition by the national park system, Parks Canada. Specially formed groups have taken on the preservation of several Canadian warships of World War II or the 'Cold War' era, but a proposal to save the last 'Canadian Liberty' cargo ship surviving from World War II, the CAPE BRETON, has failed.

Acadia

Acadia
steam survey ship

Former name HMCS ACADIA
Built 1913 by Swan, Hunter & Wigham Richardson Ltd, Newcastle, England
Original owners Government of Canada
Propulsion Steam, triple expansion
Tonnage 846 gross
Length 170.0ft/51.82m
Breadth 33.6ft/10.24m
Draught 12.0ft/3.66m
Materials Steel throughout
Original use Hydrographic research
Condition Intact
Present owners Maritime Museum of the Atlantic
Location Halifax, Nova Scotia, Canada
History Veteran of many years' service as a Canadian surveying ship. Acquired for preservation unaltered externally or internally, and currently open to the public at Halifax as a floating museum.

Alexander Henry
icebreaker

Built 1959 by Port Arthur Shipbuilding, Thunder Bay, Ontario, Canada
Original owners Canadian Coast Guard
Propulsion Diesel engines, 3550hp
Tonnage 1674 gross
Length 210.0ft/64.01m
Breadth 44.0ft/13.41m
Draught 16.0ft/4.88m
Materials Steel throughout
Original use Icebreaker
Condition Intact
Present owners Marine Museum of the Great Lakes
Location Kingston, Ontario, Canada
History Retired Canadian icebreaker preserved as an exhibit and also serving as bed-and-breakfast accommodation. To be moved into the original shipyard graving dock next to the shipyard workshops now housing the museum's shoreside exhibits.

Annapolis
frigate

Former name HMCS ANNAPOLIS
Built 1963 by Halifax Shipyards Ltd at Halifax, Nova Scotia
Original owners Royal Canadian Navy
Official number DDE 265
Propulsion Gas turbines, twin screw, 30,000hp. Engine built by English-Electric.
Tonnage 3000 displacement
Length 371.0ft/113.1m
Breadth 42.0ft/12.8m
Draught 14.5ft/4.4m
Materials Steel throughout
Original use Frigate
Condition Intact, exhibit
Location North Vancouver, British Columbia, Canada

BCP-45
fishing vessel

Built 1927 at Vancouver, British Columbia
Original owners British Columbia Packers
Tonnage 28 gross
Length 47.0ft/14.8m
Materials Wood hull
Original use Seine fishing
Condition Intact
Present owners Vancouver Maritime Museum
Location Vancouver, British Columbia, Canada
History Typical fishing vessel employed on the Canadian Pacific Coast and preserved as a floating exhibit at Vancouver in conjunction with a land-based maritime museum.
Bibliography D228a

Black Duck
air sea rescue launch

Built 1954 at Dunville, Ontario, Canada
Original owners Canadian Armed forces
Propulsion Diesel engine
Materials Steel throughout

Original use Aviation rescue
Condition In operating condition
Present owners Vancouver Maritime
Museum
Location Vancouver, British Columbia,
Canada
History High speed motor boat
stationed at military air stations to
rescue aviators who have crashed in
the water. Preserved as a floating
exhibit and operational vessel at the
maritime museum in Vancouver.

Bradbury
lighthouse tender

Built 1915 by Dominion Shipyards,
Selkirk, Manitoba, Canada
Original owners Government of
Manitoba
Propulsion Steam, coal burning;
converted to diesel
Tonnage 379 gross
Length 151.0ft/46.02m
Breadth 27.0ft/8.23m
Draught 13.0ft/3.96m
Materials Iron hull, wood-sheathed;
steel superstructure
Original use Fish patrol, lighthouse
tender
Condition Intact
Present owners Marine Museum of
Manitoba
Location Selkirk, Manitoba, Canada
History Former Canadian lighthouse
tender and patrol vessel preserved as
an exhibit in a dry berth.

Bras D'Or
hydrofoil

Built 1967 by Marine Industries Ltd,
Sorel, Quebec, Canada
Original owners Canadian Navy
Propulsion Gas turbine and diesel
Length 150.8ft/45.96m
Breadth 21.5ft/6.55m
Draught 23.0/7.5ft / 7.01/2.29m
Materials Aluminium throughout
Original use Experimental hydrofoil
Condition Intact
Present owners Berniers Museum
Location L'Islet-sur-Mer, Quebec,
Canada
History Prototype anti-submarine
hydrofoil built for the Canadian Navy,
now exhibited on shore at a maritime
museum complex in L'Islet-sur-Mer on
the St Lawrence River below Quebec.
Bibliography D326

Canadian Princess
research vessel

Former name WILLIAM J. STEWART
Built 1932 by Collingwood Shipyards
Inc, Collingwood, Ontario, Canada
Original owners Government of
Canada
Propulsion Steam, triple expansion
Tonnage 1295 gross
Length 214.0ft/65.23m
Breadth 36.0ft/10.97m
Draught 13.5ft/4.11m
Materials Steel throughout

Original use Hydrographic research
Present owners Oak Bay Marina Ltd
Contact address 1327 Beach Drive,
Victoria, BC, V8S 2N4 Canada
Location Ucluelet, British Columbia,
Canada
History Retired from hydrographic
survey work in 1975. Was the subject of
a preservation effort under her original
name. Later sold for use as a floating
hotel and restaurant at Ucluelet,
British Columbia.

Cape Sable
trawler

Built 1962 at Leiden, Netherlands
Original owners National Sea Products,
Halifax
Propulsion Diesel engines
Tonnage 362 gross
Length 131.0ft/39.93m
Materials Steel throughout
Original use Fishing
Condition Intact
Present owners Nova Scotia
Department of Public Works
Location Lunenburg, Nova Scotia,
Canada
History Example of the type of trawler
used in the Canadian North Atlantic
fisheries before the introduction of the
stern ramp. Preserved as a floating
exhibit of the fisheries museum in
Lunenburg.

Chickama II
motor passenger vessel

Built 1942 at Selkirk, Manitoba, Canada
Original owners Selkirk Navigation Co
Propulsion Diesel engines
Tonnage 45 gross
Length 61.0ft/18.59m
Breadth 16.45ft/5.01m
Draught 5.5ft/1.68m
Materials Wood throughout
Original use Passengers
Present owners Marine Museum of
Manitoba
Location Selkirk, Manitoba, Canada
History Small 'feeder' passenger vessel
employed on a waterway connecting
with Lake Winnipeg. Currently an
exhibit at the marine museum in
Selkirk.

Daniel McAllister
steam tug

Former name HELEN M B, HELENA
Built 1907 by Collingwood
Shipbuilding Co, Collingwood,
Ontario
Propulsion Steam, screw, triple
expansion; converted to diesel
Tonnage 268 gross
Length 109.0ft/35.06m
Breadth 23.3ft/7.12m
Materials Steel throughout
Original use Tug
Condition Intact
Present owners Old Port of Montreal
Location Montreal, Quebec, Canada
History Former steam tug operated by
the Canadian Government. Was
stationed at Halifax, Nova Scotia, and
later St John, New Brunswick. Last
active service was as a diesel tug
operated by a private owner, based in
the port of Montreal. Used as an
exhibit.

Detector
coast guard survey vessel

Built 1915 by Canadian Government
Shipyard, Sorel, Quebec, Canada
Original owners Canadian Coast Guard
Propulsion Steam, compound, 532hp
Tonnage 584 gross
Length 147.0ft/44.81m
Breadth 35.0ft/10.67m
Draught 10.0ft/3.05m
Materials Steel hull
Original use Sounding vessel
Condition Intact
Location L'Islet-sur-Mer, Quebec,
Canada
History Canadian Government vessel
formerly used in charting the channels

Bras D'Or

Detector

of the St Lawrence River. After retirement was moved ashore at L'Islet-sur-Mer and converted to a restaurant.

Dredge No 4
mining dredger

Built 1941 by Yukon Consolidated Gold Corp, Bonanza Creek, Yukon Territory, Canada
Original owners Yukon Consolidated Gold Corp
Propulsion Winched into position
Length 139.76ft/42.6m
Breadth 65.62 ft/20.00m
Draught 3.04ft/0.93m
Materials Wood throughout

Dredge No 4

Original use Gold mining dredger
Condition Intact
Present owners Parks Canada, Klondike Historic Sites
Location Bonanza Creek, Yukon Territory, Canada
History Intact example of the type of dredger used for gold mining in the Yukon and Alaska. Winched itself from place to place by creating its own basin as it dug out gold-bearing gravel in front and deposited the processed gravel behind. Now preserved as a museum where it was last employed, by the Canadian national park system.
Bibliography D379

Ernest Lapointe
icebreaker

Built 1940 by Davie Shipbuilding & Repair, Lauzon, Quebec, Canada
Original owners Canadian Coast Guard
Propulsion Steam, compound, 2000hp
Tonnage 1179 gross
Length 172.0ft/52.43m
Breadth 36.0ft/10.97m
Draught 16.0ft/4.88m
Materials Steel throughout
Original use Icebreaker
Condition Intact
Present owners Bernier Museum
Location L'Islet-sur-Mer, Quebec, Canada
History Veteran of forty years service keeping channels clear in the winter and freeing frozen-in vessels. Now serving as an exhibit in permanent drydock.

Felicia
steam tug

Built 1923 at Sorel, Quebec
Propulsion Steam, screw, 54hp; replaced by diesel engine
Tonnage 183 gross
Length 85.0ft/25.8m
Breadth 24.0ft/7.3m
Materials Steel throughout
Original use Tug
Condition Intact
Present owners Exposition Maritime
Location Saint-Joseph-de-la-Rive,

Quebec, Canada
History Built as a steam tug and originally based in the Port of Montreal. Later converted to diesel propulsion and employed at Halifax. Now preserved by an outdoor museum in Saint-Joseph-de-la-Rive, Quebec.

Feu Follet
motor patrol boat

Built 1951 at St Laurent, Quebec
Propulsion Diesel engines
Tonnage 68 gross
Length 67.0ft/20.4m
Materials Wood throughout
Original use Patrol boat
Present owners Exposition Chantiers Maritimes
Location Saint-Joseph-de-la-Rive, Canada
History Preserved as an exhibit.

Fraser
destroyer escort

Former name HMCS FRASER
Built 1953 by Burrard Shipyard, Vancouver, British Columbia, Canada
Original owners Canadian Navy
Official number DDE-233
Propulsion Steam turbines, 30,000shp
Tonnage 2800 displacement
Length 366.0ft/111.6m
Breadth 42.0ft/12.8m
Draught 17.0ft/5.2m
Materials Steel throughout
Original use Destroyer escort
Condition Intact
Present owners Canadian Naval Heritage Foundation
Contact address 73 Davey Crescent, Kingston, Ontario K7N 1X7
Location Kingston, Ontario, Canada
History Canadian destroyer of the Korean War period preserved as a memorial and floating museum.

Grosse Ile
wooden coaster

Built 1951 at St Laurent, Quebec
Propulsion Diesel engine
Tonnage 48 gross
Length 57.0ft/17.3m
Materials Wood throughout
Original use Cargo
Condition Intact
Present owners Exposition Chantiers Maritime
Location Saint-Joseph-de-la-Rive, Quebec, Canada
History Small wooden cargo vessel built to operate on the Gulf of St Lawrence and the St Lawrence River,

known as a 'goelette'. Preserved as an exhibit at a museum devoted to this coastal trade.

Haida
destroyer

Former name HMCS HAIDA
Built 1941 by Vickers Armstrong, Newcastle, England
Original owners Royal Canadian Navy
Propulsion Steam turbines
Tonnage 1927 displacement
Length 355.6ft/108.39m
Breadth 36.6ft/11.16m
Draught 26.0ft/7.92m
Materials Steel throughout
Original use Destroyer
Condition Intact
Present owners Provincial Government of Ontario
Location Toronto, Ontario, Canada
History Last survivor of the British 'Tribal' class of destroyers that saw extensive service in the Second World War. Preserved as a floating exhibit and memorial on the waterfront of Toronto.
Bibliography A8, A16, B24, D448, D457, D459

Hydrofoil HD-4
experimental hydrofoil

Built 1914 by Bell-Baldwin, Baddeck, Nova Scotia, Canada. Designed by Alexander Graham Bell
Original owners Alexander Graham Bell
Propulsion Two aircraft engines, propellers. Engine built by Liberty Aviation
Length 59.97ft/18.28m
Materials Wood and canvas
Original use Experimental hydrofoil
Condition Intact
Present owners Parks Canada
Location Baddeck, Nova Scotia, Canada
History Built for early hydrofoil experiments by Alexander Graham Bell. Set a world speed record in 1919. Displayed indoors at the former Bell estate near Baddeck, Nova Scotia.

Ivanhoe
steam tug

Built 1907 by Wallace Shipyards Ltd, False Creek, Vancouver, British Columbia, Canada
Original owners George I Wilson

Propulsion Steam, triple expansion; diesel engine since 1937. Engine built by McKie & Baxter (steam); Union (diesel)
Tonnage 181 gross
Length 99.5ft/30.33m
Breadth 22.5ft/6.86m
Draught 14.5ft/4.42m
Materials Wood throughout
Original use Tug
Condition Intact
Present owners Ivanhoe Heritage Foundation
Location Vancouver, British Columbia, Canada
History Tug employed by a lumber company for coastal towing. Converted to diesel propulsion in 1937. Restored to operating condition by an enthusiast group in the early 1980s; floating exhibit.

Jean Yvan
motor cargo vessel

Built 1958 at La Petite Riviere St Francois, Quebec
Propulsion Diesel engine
Tonnage 113 gross
Length 84.0ft/25.6m

Materials Wood throughout
Original use Cargo
Condition Intact
Present owners Exposition Chantiers Maritime
Location Saint-Joseph-de-la-Rive, Canada
History Type of small wooden motor cargo vessel employed in the River and Gulf of St Lawrence known as a 'goelette'. One of the last to be built. Currently preserved as a museum exhibit as she appeared when in service.
Bibliography C20a

Joe Simpson
motor cargo vessel

Built 1963 by Selkirk Machine Works, Selkirk, Manitoba, Canada
Original owners Selkirk Navigation Co
Propulsion Diesel engines
Tonnage 168 gross
Length 94.5ft/28.7m
Breadth 20.0ft/6.1m
Draught 4.2ft/1.2m
Materials Steel throughout
Original use Cargo
Condition Intact
Present owners Marine Museum of Manitoba
Contact address Box 7, Selkirk, Manitoba R1A 2B1, Canada
Location Selkirk, Manitoba, Canada
History Small cargo vessel, formerly employed on Lake Winnipeg, preserved as an exhibit.

Keenora
cargo/passenger steamer

Built 1897 at Keenora, Ontario, Canada
Original owners Rainy River Navigation Co
Propulsion Steam screw, wood burning; converted to diesel
Tonnage 609 gross
Length 158.0ft/48.16m
Breadth 28.0ft/8.53m
Draught 8.9ft/2.71m
Materials Steel and wood hull; steel superstructure
Original use Passengers and cargo
Present owners Marine Museum of Manitoba
Contact address Box 7, Selkirk, Manitoba R1A 2B1, Canada
Location selkirk, Manitoba, Canada
History Steamer built to carry passengers and cargo on Lake Winnipeg and the Rainy River; later an excursion vessel. Converted from steam to diesel and lengthened 30ft in 1917. Now preserved as one of the

Haida

Keenora when operating as an excursion vessel

exhibits of the Marine Museum of Manitoba.

Keno
cargo/passenger steamer

Built 1922 by British Yukon Navigation Co, Whitehorse, Yukon Territory, Canada
Original owners British Yukon Navigation Co
Propulsion Steam sternwheel, wood burning
Length 140.6ft/42.85m
Breadth 30.4ft/9.27m
Materials Wood throughout
Original use Passengers and cargo
Condition Intact
Present owners Parks Canada, Klondike National Sites
Location Dawson City, Yukon Territory, Canada
History Built to carry passengers and cargo on the rivers of the Yukon Territory. Lengthened 11m in 1937. Now preserved as an onshore exhibit by the Canadian national park service. Was undergoing extensive restoration in 1998.
Bibliography B44, C24

Kipawo
ferry

Built 1925 at East Saint John, New Brunswick
Propulsion Diesel engine
Tonnage 200 gross
Length 113.0ft/34.44m
Breadth 26.0ft/7.92m
Materials Steel hull
Original use Ferry
Condition Intact, undergoing some restoration

Present owners Parrsboro Maritime Museum
Location Parrsboro, Nova Scotia, Canada
History Ferryboat used at Parrsboro, Nova Scotia, prior to the Second World War. Later owned in Newfoundland. Brought back to Parrsboro for use as a maritime museum.

Klondike
passenger/cargo steamer

Built 1937 by British Yukon Navigation Co, Whitehorse, Yukon Territory, Canada

Original owners British Yukon Navigation Co
Propulsion Steam sternwheel, wood burning
Tonnage 1362 gross
Length 235.0ft/71.63m
Breadth 41.75ft/12.73m
Draught 4.5ft/1.37m
Materials Wood throughout
Original use Passengers and cargo
Condition Fully restored
Present owners Parks Canada
Location Whitehorse, Yukon Territory, Canada
History Built to carry passengers and cargo on the rivers of the Yukon Territory. Preserved on shore, fully restored and fitted out, by the Canadian national park service.
Bibliography B44, C24

Kyle
coastal steamer

Former names ARCTIC EAGLE, KYLE
Built 1913 by Swan Hunter & Wigham Richardson, Newcastle, England
Propulsion Steam, triple expansion. Engine built by Swan Hunter & Wigham Richardson
Tonnage 1055 gross
Length 230.0ft/70.0m
Breadth 32.35ft/19.8m
Depth 20.5ft/6.2m
Draught 17.7ft/5.3m
Materials Steel throughout
Original use Passengers and cargo
Condition Largely intact
Location Harbour Grace, Newfoundland, Canada
History Canadian coastal steamship, abandoned intact on a mudbank in a small Newfoundland harbour. Currently being renovated for use as an onshore museum.

Lady Canadian
motor fishing vessel

Built 1944 at Selkirk, Manitoba
Original owners Canadian Fish Producers Ltd
Propulsion Diesel engine

Klondike

Tonnage 151 gross
Length 74.0ft/22.55m
Breadth 17.65ft/5.38m
Draught 9.33ft/2.84m
Materials Steel hull
Original use Fishing
Present owners Marine Museum of
Manitoba
Location Selkirk, Manitoba, Canada
History Former fishing vessel, later
used as an exhibit.

Lady Rose

passenger/cargo motor vessel

Former name LADY SYLVIA
Built 1937 by Inglis, Scotland
Original owners Union Steamship Co
Propulsion Diesel engines
Tonnage 199 gross
Length 104.8ft/31.9m
Breadth 21.2ft/6.4m
Materials Steel hull
Original use Passengers and cargo
Condition Largely unaltered; in
operation
Present owners Alberni Marine
Transportation Inc
Location Port Alberni, British
Columbia, Canada
History Small motor vessel built to
carry passengers and cargo on the
Pacific coast of Canada. Currently
making cruises in the Barkley Sound
area of British Columbia.
Bibliography D367a

Maple Leaf

sailing yacht

Former name MAPLE LEAF, PARMA,
CONSTANCE B
Built 1904 by Vancouver Shipyard Ltd,
Vancouver, British Columbia, Canada
Original owners Alexander MacLaren
Propulsion Sail, ketch rig; diesel
auxiliary engine. Engine built by
General Motors
Length 59.5ft/18.14m
Breadth 14.58ft/4.44m
Draught 8.42ft/2.57m
Materials Wood throughout
Original use Yacht
Condition Restored in 1980s
Present owners The Maple Leaf
Preservation Society
Location Duncan, British Columbia,
Canada
History First flagship of the Royal
Vancouver Yacht Club, and first
Canadian yacht to qualify for the
Trans-Pacific Yacht Race. Later
employed as a fishing vessel. Restored
by a group based in Richmond, British
Columbia, and employed in youth sail

Maple Leaf berthed near owner's lumber mill, Burrard Inlet

training. Now operating as a charter
vessel in the area of the Queen
Charlotte Islands of British Columbia.

Marion Elizabeth

fishing schooner

Built 1918 at Lunenburg, Nova Scotia
Propulsion Sail, schooner rig; diesel
auxiliary
Tonnage 146 gross
Length 117.2ft/35.72m
Breadth 26.3ft/8.02m
Materials Wood throughout
Original use Fishing
Condition Hull intact; in use
Present owners Schooner Museum
Location Margaree Harbour, Nova
Scotia, Canada
History Built for fishing out of Nova
Scotia. Later used to carry cargo.
Reportedly engaged in 'rumrunning'
during the American prohibition era.

Has served as a restaurant on shore at
Margaree Harbour, Nova Scotia since
the 1960s.

Master

steam tug

Built 1922 by Arthur Moscrop, False
Creek, British Columbia, Canada
Original owners Master Towing Co
Propulsion Steam, triple expansion
Length 70.0ft/21.34m
Breadth 19.7ft/6.0m
Depth 9.0ft/2.74m
Materials Wood throughout
Original use Tug
Condition Intact, in operating
condition
Present owners SS Master Society
Location Vancouver, British Columbia,
Canada
History Last surviving wooden steam
tug in British Columbia. Maintained in

operating condition as a museum and
active steam vessel by a group based in
Vancouver.
Bibliography A17, C87a

Missinaibi

log handling tug

Built 1952 at Owen Sound, Ontario,
Canada
Original owners Canadian
International Paper Co
Propulsion Diesel engine, 330hp
(removed), engine built by Cummins
Length 45.9ft/14.0m
Materials Steel throughout
Original use Log handling tug
Condition Intact, lacking engine
Present owners City of Hull
Location Hull, Quebec, Canada
History Ottawa River log handling tug
that appeared on Canadian $1 bill.
Now preserved as an onshore exhibit.

Moyie

sternwheel lake steamer

Built 1898 by James Bugler, Nelson,
British Columbia, Canada
Original owners Canadian Pacific
Railroad
Propulsion Steam sternwheel
Tonnage 835 gross
Length 162.0ft/49.38m
Breadth 33.0ft/10.06m
Draught 3.0ft/0.91m
Materials Hull steel and wood;
deckhouse wood
Original use Passengers and cargo
Condition Intact
Present owners Village of Kaslo
Location Kaslo, British Columbia,
Canada
History Last surviving Kootenay Lake
sternwheel steamboat. Preserved on
shore at Kaslo, British Columbia,
where she houses exhibits of the local
historical society.
Bibliography B44, C24, C87a, D540

Naramata

steam tug

Built 1914 by Western Dry Dock, Port
Arthur, Ontario (pre-fab); Okanagan
Landing, British Columbia
Original owners Canadian Pacific
Railroad
Propulsion Steam, compound
Tonnage 150 gross
Length 89.67ft/27.33m
Breadth 19.42ft/5.92m
Draught 8.0ft/2.44m
Materials Steel throughout
Original use Lake towboat

Condition Intact, restored in 1980s
Present owners Okanagan Landing
Community Association
Location Okanagan Landing, BC,
Canada
History Tug used to move freight
barges on Okanagan Lake. Pre-
fabricated at Port Arthur, Ontario.
Now maintained as a floating museum
at the former Canadian Pacific
Railroad Shipyard in Okanagan.
Bibliography C94, D541

Ned Hanlan
steam tug

Built 1932 by Toronto Drydock Co,
Toronto, Ontario, Canada
Original owners Corporation of the
City of Toronto
Propulsion Steam, 2-cylinder
Tonnage 105 gross
Length 74.8ft/22.8m
Breadth 19.1ft/5.82m

Naramata when working, about 1920

Draught 9.0ft/2.74m
Materials Steel throughout
Original use Tug
Condition Intact
Present owners City of Toronto
Historical Board
Contact address Exhibition Place,
Toronto, Ontario M6K 3C3, Canada
Location Toronto, Ontario, Canada
History Intact steam tug formerly
employed in Toronto Harbour. Has
been an exhibit on shore next to the
Toronto Maritime Museum for a
number of years. The museum is now
moving to a site on the waterfront, and
there are plans to refloat the tug and
restore her to operating condition.
Bibliography B44

Norgoma
passenger/cargo steamer

Built 1950 at Collingwood, Ontario,
Canada

Original owners Owen Sound
Transportation Co
Propulsion Steam, screw; converted to
diesel
Tonnage 1435 gross
Length 180.25ft/54.94m
Breadth 36.0ft/10.97m
Materials Steel throughout
Original use Passengers and cargo
Condition Intact
Present owners Sault Ste Marie
Maritime Museum
Location Sault Ste Marie, Ontario,
Canada
History Former overnight steamer
operated between ports on Lake
Huron. Maintained afloat as a
maritime museum at Sault Ste Marie,
Ontario.

Norisle
passenger/cargo steamer

Built 1946 at Collingwood, Ontario,
Canada
Original owners Owen Sound
Transportation Co
Propulsion Steam, screw, triple
expansion
Tonnage 1668 gross
Length 203.0ft/61.97m
Breadth 36.0ft/10.97m
Materials Steel throughout
Original use Passengers and cargo
Condition Intact
Present owners Town of Assignach,
Ontario
Location Manitowaning, Ontario,
Canada
History Former overnight passenger
steamer operating between ports on
Lake Huron. Maintained afloat at
Assignach housing a maritime
museum.
Bibliography B44

Nottingham Castle
steam launch

Former name CRESSET
Built 1943 by British Royal Navy
Original owners British Royal Navy
Propulsion Steam, screw, compound
Tonnage 40 displacement
Length 60.0ft/18.29m
Breadth 14.0ft/4.27m
Draught 5.25ft/1.6m
Materials Wood throughout
Original use Navy launch
Condition In operation
Present owners Upper Canada Steam
Navigation Co, Paignton House Hotel
Location Lake Rousseau, Ontario,
Canada
History British Royal Navy harbour

service steam launch brought to
Canada and restored as a private yacht.
Maintained in operating condition
based at a resort hotel on Lake
Rousseau.
Bibliography B26, B44

Our Lady of Lourdes
mission support ship

Built 1930 by George W Kneass, San
Francisco, California, USA
Original owners Oblate Fathers of
Mary Immaculate
Propulsion Diesel engine; sloop rig
Tonnage 30 gross
Length 55.0ft/16.76m
Materials Wood throughout
Original use Supply ship for missions
Condition Intact
Present owners Roman Catholic
Missions, Yellowknife
Location Tuktoyaktuk, Northern
Territory, Canada
History Employed from 1930 to 1957 as
a support ship for remote Inuit
settlements in the Arctic. Placed on
shore for preservation at the village of
Tuktoyaktuk in 1967.
Bibliography D139

Peguis II
motor tug

Built 1955 at Owen Sound, Ontario,
Canada
Original owners Ministry of Public
Works
Propulsion Diesel engines; 150hp
Tonnage 48 gross
Length 59.35ft/18.09m
Breadth 16.1ft/4.91m
Original use Tug
Condition Intact
Present owners Marine Museum of
Manitoba
Location Selkirk, Manitoba, Canada
History Tug used to move barges filled
with dredged mud and silt, now
exhibited afloat at the maritime
museum in Selkirk.

Phoebe
steam launch

Built 1914 by Davis Dry Dock Co,
Kingston, Ontario, Canada
Original owners Dr John Alfred
Brashear
Propulsion Steam, compound, 65hp
Length 48.0ft/14.63m
Breadth 9.15ft/2.79m
Draught 4.0ft/1.22m
Materials Wood throughout
Original use Yacht

Condition Intact
Present owners City of Kingston
Location Kingston, Ontario, Canada
History Intact covered steam launch built locally. Formerly an exhibit at the Pump House Steam Museum in Kingston, responsibility for her preservation has now been transferred to the Marine Museum of the Great Lakes in Kingston.

Radium King
motor tug

Built 1937 (prefabricated at Sorel, Quebec) at Fort Smith, Northwest

Territories, Canada
Original owners Eldorado Mine
Propulsion Diesel engines; 480hp
Tonnage 115 gross
Length 95.2ft/29.02m
Breadth 20.0ft/6.1m
Materials Steel hull
Original use Towing and cargo
Condition Intact
Present owners Northern Life Museum
Location Fort Smith, Northwest Territory, Canada
History Tug for use on a river in the Northwest Territories. Preserved as an onshore exhibit at Fort Smith.

Robertson II
sailing fishing vessel

Built 1940 at Shelburne, Nova Scotia, Canada
Original owners Robertson II Ltd
Propulsion Sail, schooner rig; auxiliary diesel engine
Tonnage 98 gross
Length 94.75ft/28.88m
Breadth 22.0ft/6.71m
Draught 12.0ft/3.66m
Materials Wood throughout
Original use Fishing
Condition Intact
Present owners Sail and Life Training

Robertson II

Society (SALT)
Location Victoria, British Columbia, Canada
History Built for fishing off the East Coast of Canada. Spent some years as a three-masted staysail schooner, but has now been restored to original two-masted rig. Later employed as a training vessel for young people based in Victoria, British Columbia. A new sail training vessel has been built to replace her. Her owners plan to preserve her in stationary use, primarily as an exhibit.
Bibliography D102

Royal Wave
motor fishing boat

Built 1962 at Parkers Cove, Nova Scotia, Canada
Original owners Floyd E Oliver
Propulsion Diesel engines, 170hp
Tonnage 41 gross
Length 57.33ft/17.47m
Breadth 16.25ft/5.0m
Materials Wood hull
Original use Fishing

Condition Intact
Present owners Fisheries Museum of the Atlantic
Location Lunenburg, Nova Scotia, Canada
History Small motor fishing boat formerly used in dragging for scallops off the coast of Nova Scotia. Preserved as a floating exhibit of the fisheries museum in Lunenburg.

Rudokop
steam tug

Built 1957 by the Naval Shipyard, Leningrad, Russia

Sackville

Original owners Russian Navy
Propulsion Steam, triple expansion, 600hp
Tonnage 208 gross
Length 107.6ft/32.8m
Breadth 25.0ft/7.62m
Draught 13.4ft/4.09m
Materials Steel throughout
Original use Tug
Condition Operating condition
Present owners Thordon Bearings, Burlington, Ontario, Canada
Location Burlington, Ontario, Canada
History Large Russian naval tug acquired after the breakup of the Soviet Union. Maintained as an operating steam vessel and travelling commercial exhibit. Apparently owned in Canada but registered in the Cayman Islands.

Sackville
corvette

Former name HMCS SACKVILLE
Built 1941 by St John Dry Dock Co, St John, New Brunswick, Canada
Original owners Royal Canadian Navy

Propulsion Steam, triple expansion
Tonnage 1085 displacement
Length 205.0ft/62.48m
Breadth 33.0ft/10.06m
Draught 14.5ft/4.42m
Materials Steel throughout
Original use Corvette
Condition Intact
Location Halifax, Nova Scotia, Canada
History Last surviving Canadian corvette to serve in the Second World War. Of the once numerous 'Flower' class, she was converted after the war to a research vessel. Now restored to her wartime appearance as a floating exhibit and memorial.

Saint Andre
motor cargo vessel

Built 1956 at La Malbaie, Quebec
Propulsion Diesel engine
Tonnage 222 gross
Length 98.3ft/29.9m
Breadth 29.9ft/9.2m
Materials Wood throughout
Original use Cargo
Condition Intact
Present owners Exposition Chantiers Maritime
Contact address 305 de l'Eglise, Saint-Joseph-de-la-Rive, Canada

Location Saint-Joseph-de-la-Rive, Canada
History Used as an exhibit.
Bibliography C20a

St Roch
Arctic patrol vessel

Built 1928 by Burrard Dry Dock, North Vancouver, British Columbia
Original owners Royal Canadian Mounted Police
Propulsion Diesel engines
Length 103.97ft/31.69m
Breadth 25.0ft/7.62m
Draught 12.99ft/3.96m
Materials Wood throughout
Original use Patrol vessel
Condition Intact, fully outfitted
Present owners Vancouver Maritime Museum
Location Vancouver, British Columbia, Canada
History Arctic patrol vessel of the Royal Canadian Mounted Police that became the first vessel to pass through the Northwest Passage from west to east, and the first to circumnavigate North America. Preserved as an indoor exhibit fitted out as she was for her historic voyage.
Bibliography A8, A14, D129, D150

San Mateo

Sam McBride
motor ferry

Built 1939 at Toronto, Ontario
Original owners Toronto Harbour Ferries
Propulsion Diesel engines
Tonnage 412 gross
Length 116.0ft/35.3m
Materials Steel throughout
Original use Ferry

Condition In operation
Present owners Toronto Harbour Ferries
Location Toronto, Ontario, Canada
History Double-ended diesel ferryboat built to operate to an island off the lakefront of the City of Toronto. Still in operation as a ferry on her original route, largely unaltered.

Samson V
sternwheel snag boat

Built 1937 by Star Shipyards, New Westminster, British Columbia, Canada
Propulsion Steam, sternwheel, 150hp
Length 112.8ft/34.38m
Breadth 31.0ft/9.45m
Draught 4.6ft/1.4m
Original use Snag removal
Condition Intact
Present owners New Westminster Hyack Festival Association
Location New Westminster, British Columbia, Canada
History Sternwheel steamer used to keep river channels clear of submerged dead trees. Open to the public as an exhibit at New Westminster.
Bibliography C87a

San Mateo
steam ferry

Built 1922 by Bethlehem Shipbuilding Corp, San Francisco, California
Propulsion Steam, screw, triple expansion
Tonnage 1782 gross
Length 216.7ft/66.05m
Breadth 42.1ft/12.83m
Materials Steel hull, wood superstructure

St Roch during her Arctic service

Original use Ferry
Condition Laid up; in need of restoration
Location Frazer River, British Columbia, Canada
History Steam ferryboat built to carry vehicles and passengers across San Francisco Bay. Was the subject of preservation efforts in the Seattle, Washington, area for a number of years, and was then taken to British Columbia where she now lies in the Frazer River.

Segwun

passenger steamer

Former name NIPISSING
Built 1887 at Gravenhurst, Ontario
Original owners Muskoka Steamship Lines
Propulsion Steam screw
Tonnage 272 gross
Length 123.5ft/37.64m
Breadth 21.0ft/6.4m
Depth 7.6ft/2.32m
Materials Iron hull, wood superstructure
Original use Passengers and cargo
Condition In operation
Present owners Segwun Steamboat Museum
Location Gravenhurst, Ontario, Canada
History By the turn of this century there were hundreds of lakes served by small passenger steamboats scattered across Canada and the United States. The steamboats first served as vital links in rail and water transportation networks when roads were few and poor in quality. Later they became a pleasant form of excursion, linking growing cities with weekend or summer resorts. SEGWUN is not only the last active steamboat on Ontario's

Segwun

Muskoka Lakes system, but a vessel whose career has spanned much of the history of steam navigation on those waters. She began life as the iron sidewheel steamboat NIPISSING, prefabricated in a shipyard on the River Clyde in Scotland and assembled at Gravenhurst, Ontario. Her engine was of the American walking beam type. It was trouble with this machinery, after thirty years of service, that caused her to be laid up in 1917. Her sturdy iron hull had held up well, and in 1924 she was rebuilt as a propeller-driven steamboat and renamed SEGWUN. The original steamboat company ceased operation in 1958 in the face of competition from the automobile. SEGWUN was sold to the town of Gravenhurst four years later to serve as a floating maritime museum. Many people fondly recalled the days of steamboating on the lakes, and wondered if they couldn't be brought back. In 1970 it was decided to undertake the extensive restoration needed to put SEGWUN back in operation. The maiden trip under steam following her second rebirth took place on 21 June 1981. Daily cruises are now made during the summer months, and the steamer can be chartered for special cruises in the evenings.
Bibliography B44, D514, D538

Sicamous

sternwheel steamer

Built 1914 by Western Dry Dock, Port Arthur, Ontario (prefab); Okanagan Landing, British Columbia
Original owners Canadian Pacific Railroad
Propulsion Steam sternwheel, tandem

Thomas F Bayard as a sealing vessel, 1913

compound
Tonnage 1787 gross
Length 200.5ft/61.11m
Breadth 40.0ft/12.19m
Draught 8.0ft/2.44m
Materials Wood throughout
Original use Passengers and cargo
Condition Intact
Present owners City of Penticton
Location Penticton, British Columbia, Canada
History Last surviving Okanagan Lake sternwheel steamboat. Designed to carry both passengers and cargo. Currently preserved as a museum on the shore of the lake.
Bibliography B27, C24, C94, D103, D541

Tarahne

motor passenger/cargo vessel

Built 1917 at Atlin, Yukon Territory, Canada
Propulsion Petrol engine
Tonnage 286 gross
Length 119.0ft/36.27m
Breadth 20.0ft/6.1m

Materials Wood throughout
Original use Passengers and cargo
Condition Intact
Present owners Town of Atlin
Location Atlin, Yukon Territory, Canada
History Vessel that formerly operated on Lake Atlin, Yukon Territory, carrying passengers and cargo. Lengthened from original 78ft in 1928. Preserved as an onshore exhibit in the town of Atlin.

Theresa E Connor

fishing schooner

Built 1938 by Smith & Rhuland Ltd, Lunenburg, Nova Scotia
Original owners Maritime National Fish Co
Propulsion Schooner rig, diesel engines, 300hp
Tonnage 185 gross
Length 130.5ft/39.78m
Breadth 27.25ft/8.31m
Draught 10.0ft/3.05m
Materials Wood throughout

Original use Fishing
Condition Intact
Present owners Fisheries Museum of the Atlantic
Contact address PO Box 1363, Lunenburg, Nova Scotia B0J 2C0
Location Lunenburg, Nova Scotia, Canada
History Fully restored and fitted out example of an auxiliary fishing schooner built by the same Lunenburg shipyard that launched the famous racing fisherman BLUENOSE. Exhibited afloat as part of the fleet of a large museum devoted to the fishing industry of eastern Canada.
Bibliography F10, F24

Thomas F Bayard
pilot schooner

Former name SANDHEADS NO 16, THOMAS F BAYARD
Built 1880 by C & R Poillon, Brooklyn, New York, USA
Original owners Captain Henry Virden, Lewes, Delaware
Propulsion Schooner rig
Tonnage 70 gross
Length 86.0ft/26.21m
Breadth 21.08ft/6.43m
Draught 8.5ft/2.59m
Materials Wood throughout
Original use Pilot vessel
Condition Hull intact; undergoing restoration
Present owners Thomas F Bayard Preservation Society
Location Vancouver, British Columbia, Canada
History Before the present unified organizations of pilots were formed, schooners raced to be first to meet an incoming vessel. The famous racing yacht AMERICA built at New York in 1851 was largely based on pilot schooner design. THOMAS F. BAYARD is the last surviving American pilot schooner built in the 19th century. She was the product of one of the most highly respected builders of these vessels, the Poillon shipyard in Brooklyn. The BAYARD was built for pilots stationed at the mouth of Delaware Bay who guided ships into the Port of Philadelphia. When the pilots began adopting steam pilot vessels in 1898 she was sold to a group called the Alaska Francisco to carry people and supplies in the Alaskan Gold Rush. After 1907 she was used as a sailing vessel in the northern Pacific by Canadian owners. Her sailing days ended when she was purchased by the Canadian Government to serve as the

first lightship on the Pacific coast. She operated in this capacity off the mouth of the Frazer River from 1913 to 1955. Replaced by a lighthouse, the BAYARD was then sold to a North Vancouver owner to who intended to restore her to sail again. The work was never completed. After laying afloat at North Vancouver for over two decades she was acquired by the Vancouver Maritime Museum. The Museum planned to restore the BAYARD to her appearance as a Pacific sealing schooner. This work is now being continued by a separate organization.

Trillium
steam ferry

Built 1910 at Toronto, Ontario
Original owners Corporation of the City of Toronto
Propulsion Steam sidewheel
Tonnage 673 gross
Length 150.0ft/45.72m
Breadth 30.0ft/9.14m
Materials Steel hull, wood superstructure
Original use Ferryboat
Condition In operating condition
Present owners Municipality of Toronto
Location Toronto, Ontario, Canada
History Steam ferryboat built to operate between the shorefront of the City of Toronto and a nearby island. Lay sunk and abandoned for several years, before being fully restored to operating condition in the 1980s.
Bibliography B44

U-521
submarine

Built 1974 by Sudomekh Shipyards, Russia

Original owners Russian Navy
Propulsion Diesel and electric motors
Tonnage 1950 displacement
Length 300.1ft/91.5m
Breadth 26.2ft/8.0m
Draught 21.0ft/7.1m
Materials Steel throughout
Original use Submarine
Condition Intact
Present owners Russian Submarine BC Ltd
Location New Westminster, BC, Canada
History Russian conventionally-powered submarine of the Cold War era. Exhibited afloat as a waterfront attraction at New Westminster by a private firm. She was reportedly moving to Seattle, around late 1998.

Wanda III
steam yacht

Built 1915 by Polson Iron Works, Toronto, Ontario, Canada
Propulsion Steam, triple expansion, 27nhp. Engine built by Polson Iron Works
Tonnage 60.0 gross
Length 94.0ft/28.6m
Breadth 12.0ft/3.6m
Materials Composite hull
Original use Yacht
Condition Intact
Present owners George A Thomson
Contact address 2052 Highwiew Avenue, Burlington, Ontario L7R 3X4
Location Lake of Bays, Ontario, Canada
History Eighty-year-old steam yacht with machinery intact, maintained by private owners.
Bibliography D96

William Inglis
motor ferry

Built 1935 at Toronto, Ontario
Original owners Toronto Harbour Ferries
Propulsion Diesel engines
Tonnage 238 gross
Length 91.0ft/27.7m
Materials Steel throughout
Original use Ferry
Condition In operation
Present owners Toronto Harbour Ferries
Location Toronto, Ontario, Canada
History Double-ended diesel ferryboat built to operate to an island off the lakefront of the city of Toronto. Still an active vessel on her original route, currently used only in the summer.

York Boat
sailing/rowing boat

Built c1920 by Hudson's Bay Co, Canada
Original owners Hudson's Bay Co
Propulsion Single square sail and oars
Tonnage 8 displacement
Length 43.66ft/13.3m
Breadth 10.5ft/3.1m
Draught 4.0ft/1.2m
Materials Wood throughout
Original use Cargo
Condition Intact
Present owners Lower Fort Garry National Historic Site
Location Lower Fort Garry, Manitoba, Canada
History Open double-ended sailing and rowing craft built to carry furs, trade goods, and supplies on the rivers of northern Manitoba. Boats of this type were last built in the 1920s. This last surviving example has been an indoor exhibit since 1935.
Bibliography D259a

Trillium

Chile

One of the world's more maritime-oriented nations, Chile occupies a strip of land between the Pacific Ocean and the Andes mountain range less than 200 kilometres in width, but more than 4300 kilometres in length in a north-south direction. Its long coastline ranges from desert in the north, with a scattering of poorly-sheltered harbours, to largely uninhabited fjords in the south towered over by spectacular snow-capped mountains. The southernmost populous region, the Territory of Magallanes, is only linked to the remainder of the country by air or by ships transiting over 800 miles of these gale-swept channels. Out of necessity, Chile has developed hardy seafarers capable of navigating its challenging coastal waters in tiny wooden sailing cutters or modern steamships. The country also administers the Juan Fernandez Islands and Easter Island well out in the Pacific, and maintains several research bases in the Antarctic. Chileans have long been proud of their nation's naval history. Their warships played an important role in the struggle for independence in the early 1800s, and in preventing a return by Spain in the 1860s. The War of the Pacific of 1879, in which Chile expanded northward at the expense of Bolivia and Peru, was largely won through a series of hard-fought encounters at sea. The captured Peruvian seagoing monitor HUASCAR, preserved by Chile as a museum and memorial, is today one of the world's more significant survivors from the early development of steam warships.

Amadeo
steam coaster

Built 1884 by Liverpool Forge Co, Liverpool, England
Propulsion Steam, compound
Tonnage 412 gross
Length 151.8ft/46.27m
Breadth 24.0ft/7.32m
Depth 11.9ft/3.63m
Materials Iron throughout, except wood wheelhouse
Original use Cargo
Condition Engines removed but otherwise intact, hull deteriorating
Present owners Soc Anon Ganadera y Comercial Menendez-Behety, Punta Arenas, Chile
Location Estancia San Gregorio, Chile
History First steamer based on the Straits of Magellan, owned in the Chilean city of Punta Arenas. After retirement she was beached on the shorefront of a large estancia (sheep ranch) belonging to her owners. Vessel is considered of historic importance and has plaque mounted on inshore side which receives some maintenance. Engines have been removed.

Ambassador
tea clipper

Built 1869 by William Walker, Rotherhithe, England
Original owners William Lund, London
Propulsion Ship rig
Tonnage 714 gross
Length 176.0ft/53.64m
Breadth 31.3ft/9.54m
Depth 19.1ft/5.82m
Materials Hull teak over iron frames
Original use Cargo
Condition Complete iron frame, most planking missing
Location Estancia San Gregorio, Chile
History The most nearly intact British tea clipper after the CUTTY SARK. Was condemned in the Falklands in 1895 while sailing under the Norwegian flag, as the result of damage sustained off Cape Horn. Served as a storage hulk in the Straits of Magellan after 1895. Now lies beached at a large sheep ranch on the eastern Straits.
Bibliography D60

Esmeralda
sail training schooner

Built 1952 by Echavarrieta y Larrinaga, Cadiz, Spain
Original owners Spanish Navy
Propulsion Sail, 4-masted topsail schooner rig; diesel engine, 1500hp
Tonnage 3500 displacement
Length 308.5ft/94.03m
Breadth 42.67ft/13.01m
Draught 19.67ft/5.99m
Materials Steel throughout
Original use Training ship
Condition In operation
Present owners Chilean Navy
Location Home port, Valparaiso, Chile
History Launched as a training vessel for the Spanish Navy but not placed in service. Sold to Chile for use by that country's naval academy in 1954 and still in operation.
Bibliography A10, A14, C25

Falstaff
iron sailing ship

Built 1875 by Barrow Shipbuilding Co, Barrow, England
Original owners J Beazley, Liverpool
Propulsion Ship rig
Tonnage 1465 gross
Length 238.0ft/72.54m
Breadth 38.0ft/11.58m
Depth 23.5ft/7.16m
Materials Iron hull, wood decks, iron & wood spars
Original use Cargo
Condition Intact hull
Present owners Chilean Navy
Location Punta Arenas, Magallanes, Chile
History Sailing vessel employed in world trade under the British flag. Later used as a storage hulk in the Straits of Magellan, and now beached at Punta Arenas where she serves as part of a breakwater of ships.

Esmeralda

Hipparchus
auxiliary steamship

Built 1867 by A Leslie & Co, Newcastle, England
Original owners Société de Navigation Royal Belge Sud Amérique
Propulsion Steam, compound, 170hp
Tonnage 1840 gross
Length 290.7ft/88.61m
Breadth 34.5ft/10.52m
Depth 28.2ft/8.6m
Materials Iron hull, deck wood over iron beams
Original use Cargo
Condition Hull intact
Present owners Chilean Navy
Location Punta Arenas, Magallanes, Chile
History The small harbour of Punta Arenas is one of the world's most interesting maritime graveyards. Late in the last century, when the Straits of Magellan were an important thoroughfare for coal-burning steamers, the roadstead there contained a sizeable fleet of anchored coaling hulks that had begun their careers as deepwater sailing vessels or early steamships. Three of these hulls were sunk in the 1930s to form a breakwater for the local ship repair yard. Two are iron sailing ships of the 1870s. The third belongs to a type even rarer today. She is a transitional, sail-carrying steamer of the 1860s, an example of the class of vessel first sought to compete with sail on the world's inter-oceanic trade routes. Hipparchus was among the first fleet of steam vessels to enter the China tea trade after the opening of the Suez Canal in 1869. In 1870 she went out to Shanghai by way of the Canal in 53 days, almost cutting in half the average time taken by sailing vessels. She also spent a number of years trading with South America under the Belgian flag before being hulked in the Straits early in this century. Her sturdy hull has withstood the severe weather conditions in those waters very well. A wooden catwalk passes through the ship, connecting her with the sailing ship Falstaff lying against her bow and the sailing ship Munoz Gamero, ex-County of Peebles, lying against her stern. Though the deck planking is gone, leaving her interior exposed to the elements, she is otherwise largely intact. Permission to board these ships can be obtained from the headquarters of the Naval District located near the central plaza of Punta Arenas.

Huascar

Huascar
coast defence turret ship

Built 1865 by Laird Brothers, Birkenhead, England
Original owners Peruvian Navy
Propulsion Steam crew, horizontal engine
Tonnage 1870 displacement
Length 190.0ft/57.91m
Breadth 35.5ft/10.82m
Draught 16.0ft/4.88m
Materials Iron hull and superstructure
Original use Seagoing monitor
Condition Intact
Present owners Chilean Navy
Location Talcahuano, Chile
History Seagoing monitor captured from Peru in the War of the Pacific after a fiercely fought battle. Had previously sunk the Chilean Esmeralda off Iquique. Preserved afloat as a museum and Naval memorial near the entrance to Chile's major Naval Base at Talcahuano.
Bibliography A15, D574

Micalvi
cargo steamer

Former name Boston Lincs, Bragi
Built 1925 by Ostsee Werft, Stettin, Germany
Propulsion Steam, triple expansion, 380hp
Tonnage 612 gross, 850 displacement
Length 181.5ft/55.32m
Breadth 28.75ft/8.76m
Draught 11.0ft/3.35m
Materials Steel throughout
Original use Cargo
Condition Intact
Present owners Chilean Navy
Location Near Puerto Williams, Chile
History Cargo steamer acquired by the Chilean Navy for use as a supply ship. Later anchored at Puerto Williams, Chile's southernmost Naval Base, as a storage hulk and living quarters.

Ministro Zenteno
destroyer

Former name USS Charles S Sperry
Built 1944 by Federal Shipbuilding Co, Newark, New Jersey
Original owners United States Navy
Propulsion Steam turbines, 60,000hp
Tonnage 3320 displacement
Length 376.5ft/114.8m
Breadth 40.9ft/12.4m
Draught 19.0ft/5.8m
Materials Steel throughout
Original use Destroyer
Condition Intact
Present owners Chilean Navy
Location Valparaiso, Chile
History Allen M Sumner class destroyer built for the US Navy during the Second World War and transferred to the Chilean Navy in 1974. Proposed as a public exhibit attached to the Chilean naval museum in Vina del Mar.
Bibliography C64

Micalvi

Munoz Gamero
iron four-masted ship

Former name COUNTY OF PEEBLES
Built 1875 by Barclay, Curle & Co,
Glasgow, Scotland
Original owners R & J Craig, Glasgow
Propulsion 4-masted ship rig
Tonnage 1691 gross
Length 266.6ft/81.26m
Breadth 38.7ft/11.8m
Depth 23.4ft/7.13m
Materials Iron hull, iron and wood
masts
Original use Cargo
Condition Intact hull with lowermasts
and deckhouses
Present owners Chilean Navy
Location Punta Arenas, Magallanes,
Chile
History First sailing vessel rigged as a
four-masted ship. Spent many years as
a coal storage hulk at a remote location
near the western end of the Straits of
Magellan. Later brought to Punta
Arenas and sunk as the outermost of a
breakwater of ships protecting the
local Naval shipyard.
Bibliography D58

Poderoso
steam tug

Built 1908 by Vickers Shipbuilders,
Liverpool, England
Original owners Luis Tronchel,
Valdivia, Chile
Propulsion Steam screw, coal burning
Tonnage 312 gross
Length 124.0ft/37.8m
Breadth 24.83ft/7.57m
Draught 13.75ft/4.19m
Materials Steel throughout
Original use Tug
Condition Intact, undergoing
conversion
Location Talcahuano, Chile
History Was the last active steam tug in
Chile. After retirement became the
subject of a preservation effort based
in Valparaiso. Was towed to
Talcahuano in 1994 for use as a
maritime museum.

China

With a long coastline, major
navigable rivers, and some of the
world's oldest man-made canals,
one would expect China to have
its share of interesting vessels.
Unfortunately, obtaining
information from official Chinese
sources remains very difficult.
And, little has turned up in
reports by visitors to the
country. The recent raising of the
gunboat ZHONGSHAN, sunk early
in the Second World War, appears
to be the first really serious
effort to preserve a vessel in
China as a floating museum. The
remarkable iron steamer YENG
HE lying on the grounds of the
Summer Palace in Beijing remains
largely a mystery. All letters sent
to likely government agencies
have gone unanswered. She
appears to date from the mid-
1800s, and to be the product of
British ship- and engine-building.

3139
high speed missile boat

Built c1966
Original owners People's Republic of
China Navy
Propulsion Diesel, 12,000hp
Tonnage 215 displacement
Length 126.66ft/38.6m
Breadth 25.0ft/7.6m
Draught 6.0ft/1.8m
Materials Steel throughout
Original use Guided missile fast
patrol boat
Condition Intact

Yeng He

Location Beijing, China
History Example of a high speed
missile boat of the 'Osa' class built in
large numbers in Russia and other
communist bloc nations during the
Cold War. Later used as an onshore
exhibit.

Yeng He
steam launch

Built Pre-1909 in Japan or Great
Britain
Original owners Emperor of Japan
Propulsion Steam, sidewheel
Length 65.6ft/20.0m
Breadth 11.81ft/3.6m
Materials Iron hull
Original use Yacht
Condition Intact, lacking any
deckhouse
Present owners The Summer Palace
Location Beijing, China
History Sidewheel steam launch with
original engine. Was Japan's gift to the
infant Emperor of China upon his
ascending the throne in 1909. May have
originally been presented to Japan by a
British nobleman in the late 1850s.
Displayed in the grounds of the
Summer Palace in Beijing.

Zhongshan
gunboat

Built 1913
Original owners Chinese Navy
Materials Steel throughout
Original use Gunboat
Location Hubei, China
History Chinese gunboat built early in
the century. Sunk during fighting with
Japanese forces in the late 1930s.
Recently raised and undergoing
restoration for use as a floating
museum.

Colombia

One of the nations created as a
result of Simon Bolivar's struggle
to free South America from Spain
in the early 1800s, Colombia has
coastline on both the Pacific
Ocean and the Caribbean, and
several important seaports. Until
recently, the old colonial city of
Cartagena on the Caribbean was
home to a large fleet of trading
schooners, and the long
Magdalena River could be
travelled on sternwheel
steamboats built in North
American shipyards. There have
been no recent reports of
surviving examples of these
vessels. Current ship preservation
in the country seems to be
limited to twentieth century
warships, maintained either by
the Colombian Navy or by
private individuals.

Boyaca
destroyer escort

Former name USS HARTLEY
Built 1957 by New York Shipbuilding
Corp, Camden, New Jersey
Original owners United States Navy
Tonnage 1877 displacement
Length 308.0ft/93.9m
Breadth 36.66ft/11.2m
Draught 11ft 10in/3.6m
Materials Steel throughout
Original use Destroyer escort
Location Colombia
History Destroyer escort of the 1950s
DEALEY class that served in the United
States and Colombian Navies.
Converted to a museum and tourist
attraction.

Cartagena
motor vessel

Built 1930 by Yarrow & Co, Scotstoun,
Scotland
Original owners Colombian Navy
Propulsion Diesel engines, 600hp
Tonnage 142 displacement
Length 137.25ft/41.83m
Breadth 23.5ft/7.16m
Draught 2.75ft/0.84m
Materials Steel hull
Original use Gunboat
Condition Intact
Present owners Colombian Navy
Location Puerto Laguizamo, Colombia

Gloria

History Veteran of the 1933 river war with Peru. Preserved on shore at the Colombian naval base in Puerto Laguizamo on the Putumayo River.

Cordoba
high-speed transport

Former name USS RUCHAMKIN
Built 1944 by Philadelphia Naval shipyard, Philadelphia, Pennsylvania, USA
Original owners United States Navy
Propulsion Steam turbines, 12,000hp
Tonnage 2114 displacement
Length 306.0ft/93.27m
Breadth 37.0ft/11.28m
Draught 12.65ft/3.86m
Materials Steel throughout
Original use Destroyer escort
Condition Intact
Present owners Duque family
Location 60 miles north of Bogota, Colombia
History High-speed transport version of BUCKLEY class destroyer escort built

for the United States Navy during the Second World War and transferred to the Colombian Navy in 1969. Cut into sections and transported overland for exhibition in a park *c*60 miles north of Bogota.
Bibliography C64

Gloria
sail training ship

Built 1968 by Celaya, Bilbao, Spain
Original owners Colombian Navy
Propulsion Barque rig, 1400m²; diesel 530bhp
Length 249.3ft/76.0m
Breadth 34.75ft/10.6m
Draught 21.66ft/6.6m
Materials Steel
Original use Sail training
Condition In service
Present owners Colombian Navy
Location Colombia
History First of a new generation of purpose-built sail training ships, she has facilities for 88 cadets.

Cuba

Once a popular 90-mile boat trip from Florida, the island nation of Cuba has since its adoption of communism in 1959, been the focus of United States travel restrictions and embargoes. This isolation has clearly held back any modernisation on the island and has had a detrimental effect on its prosperity. Cuba's economy continues to be largely dependent on one agricultural commodity, sugar. The country maintains a modest merchant fleet and a small navy, and apparently has little in the way of museums that deal with maritime history or technology. One full-size display in a memorial to the Revolution in Havana, representing the motor yacht GRANMA that played a role in the coming to power of the current government, is apparently a reproduction.

Pilar
cabin cruiser

Built 1934 by Wheeler Shipyard, Brooklyn, New York, USA
Original owners Ernest Hemingway
Propulsion Motor
Length 40.0ft/12.19m
Materials Wood throughout
Original use Yacht
Condition Intact
Present owners Cuban government
Location Havana, Cuba
History Cabin cruiser built in Brooklyn, New York, and used by the author Ernest Hemingway for sport fishing off Cuba and Florida. Preserved on shore at his former villa in Cuba.

Pilar

Czech Republic

Czechoslovakia was created in 1918, at the end of the Second World War, out of several ethnic regions in the northwestern portion of the defeated Austro-Hungarian Empire. In 1992, the two major ethnic groups, the Czechs in the west and the Slovaks in the east, agreed to peacefully form separate republics. The Czech Republic, which also borders on Germany, Poland, and Austria, has no seacoast and few lakes of any size. The major navigable river of this part of Europe, the Danube, passes south of the Republic through Austria. The major navigable river within the Czech Republic, and the waterway passing through the capital city of Prague, is the Vltava, actually the upper portion of the Elbe River that flows across Germany to enter the North Sea below the Port of Hamburg. A small group of sidewheel steamboats survives at Prague, one or two of which are used for excursions during the summer season. Off and on efforts to reactivate further boats for this service have led to some confusing name changes. Two boats, one inactive, at last report had the name VYSEHRAD.

Labe
river steamer

Built 1949 by Praga Yard, Prague, Czechoslovakia
Original owners Osobni Lodni Doprava
Propulsion Steam, sidewheel, compound diagonal, coal-fired, 150hp
Length 174.17ft/53.1m
Breadth 29.85ft/9.1m
Materials Steel throughout
Original use Passengers
Condition Out of service, in need of restoration
Present owners Osobni Lodni Doprava
Location Prague, Czechoslovakia
History River steamer under construction at Prague in 1940 but not completed until 1949 due to the Second World War. Withdrawn from service in 1987 and currently laid up at the company shipyard in Prague.
Bibliography B16, B43

Vltava
sidewheel passenger steamer

Former name MOLDAU
Built 1940 by Aussiger Schiffswerft (or
Ustecka Lod, Usti?), Prague,
Czechoslovakia
Propulsion Steam sidewheel,
compound diagonal, 150hp. Engine
built by CKD, Prague
Length 174.0ft/53.03m
Breadth 30.0ft/9.14m
Materials Steel throughout
Original use Passengers
Condition In active service
Present owners Osobni Lodni Doprava
Location Prague, Czechoslovakia
History Active sidewheel steamer based
at Prague. Converted from coal to oil
fuel in 1979. Currently making
passenger excursions between Prague
and Slapy Dam.
Bibliography B16, B43

Vysehrad
sidewheel river steamer

Former name DEVIN, T G MASARYK,
KARLSTEIN, ANTONIN SVEHLA
Built 1938 by Aussiger Schiffswerft (or
Ustecka Lod, Usti?), Prague,
Czechoslovakia
Propulsion Steam sidewheel,
compound diagonal, 220hp. Engine
built by CKD, Prague
Length 210.0ft/64.0m
Breadth 34.0ft/10.36m
Materials Steel throughout
Original use Passengers
Condition Out of service, undergoing
restoration
Present owners Osobni Lodni Doprava
Location Prague, Czechoslovakia
History Sidewheel river steamer based
at Prague which until 1993 operated
under the name DEVIN. (Since Devin is
a place in the now-separate Slovak
Republic, she was given the name of a
sistership that is currently laid up at
the company shipyard in Prague.)
Bibliography B16, B43

Vysehrad
sidewheel steamer

Former name DR EDVARD BENES,
WISCHERAD, LABE
Built 1938 by Aussiger Schiffswerft,
Prague, Czechoslovakia
Propulsion Steam, sidewheel,
compound diagonal, 220hp. Engine
built by CKD, Prague
Length 210.0ft/64.0m
Breadth 34.0ft/10.36m
Materials Steel throughout

Original use Passengers
Condition Laid up
Present owners Osobni Lodni Doprava
Location Prague, Czechoslovakia
History Czech sidewheel steamer
withdrawn from service around 1990
for re-boilering and alterations. Work
apparently stopped due to lack of
funds, and she remains laid up at the
company shipyard in Prague. Her
name has been given to her sister, the
ex-DEVIN, which is currently
operating.
Bibliography B16, B43

Denmark

Living on a peninsula and a large
number of islands of various sizes
in the Baltic and North Seas, the
Danes are seldom far from sight
of the water. Well into the
twentieth century, coastal
communities in Denmark built
and operated large fleets of
schooners and barkentines for
the Baltic and European coastal
trades, and the trades with
Greenland and North America. In
recent years a number of the
survivors have been returned to
sailing condition to serve as
youth training or charter vessels.
To this fleet of authentic sailing
craft have been added newly-built
vessels of similar appearance and
rig, with the result that traditional
sailing vessels are once again a
common sight sailing off the
Danish coast or berthed in the
country's ports large and small.
Denmark's wooden steam frigate
JYLLAND is the world's last
surviving warship of the type, and
the country can also claim the
world's only significant fleet of
surviving wooden lightships.

Ane Catherine
coastal ewer

Built 1887 at Nordby, Denmark
Propulsion Sail, sloop rig
Tonnage 15 gross
Length 45.59ft/13.87m
Breadth 12.59ft/3.84m
Draught 3.25ft/0.99m
Materials Wood throughout
Original use Cargo
Condition Intact
Present owners Fiskeri og
Sjofartsmuseet
Location Esbjerg, Denmark
History Example of a type of sailing
vessel used in the Danish coastal trades
known as a 'ewer'. Preserved on shore
as an exhibit at Esbjerg.
Bibliography A16

Anna Möller
sailing coaster

Former name ESTHER
Built 1906 by Peter Larsen, Randers,
Denmark
Propulsion Sloop rig, later ketch rig
Tonnage 49 gross
Length 65.0ft/19.81m
Breadth 18.0ft/5.49m
Draught 7.0ft/2.13m
Materials Wood throughout
Original use Cargo
Condition Fully restored
Present owners Nationalmuseet,
Vikingskibhallen, Roskilde
Location Copenhagen, Denmark
History Former sailing cargo vessel
employed in the coastal trade.
Exhibited afloat and used as a training
vessel for young people based in the
Nyhaven at Copenhagen.
Bibliography B33

Aron
coasting schooner

Built 1906 by L J Bager, Marstal,
Denmark
Propulsion Sail, schooner rig; auxiliary
engine
Tonnage 61.8 gross
Length 69.9ft/21.3m
Breadth 18.7ft/5.7m
Draught 6.8ft/2.1m
Materials Wood throughout
Original use Cargo
Condition In operation for charters
Present owners K Lund
Location Svendborg, Denmark
History Schooner built to carry cargo
in the Danish Baltic and coastal trades.
Maintained in sailing condition.
Bibliography B33, B38

Anna Moller

Bent II
motor fishing vessel

Built 1944 by P N Thomsen, near
Vorupor, Denmark
Official number LN 10
Propulsion Diesel engine, 36hp
Tonnage 7.87 gross
Length 34.7ft/10.6m
Breadth 13.4ft/4.1m
Draught 4.6ft/1.4m
Materials Wood throughout
Original use Fishing
Condition In operating condition
Present owners Kystfiskerimuseet
Contact address Det gamle
redningshus, Ndr. Strandvej, DK-9480
Lokken
Location Lokken, Denmark
History Example of a Danish fishing
boat of the 1940s preserved as an
exhibit.

Björn
steam harbour tug

Built 1908 by Seebeck A/G,
Geestemunde, Germany
Propulsion Steam, screw, 3-cylinder,
450hp
Tonnage 135 gross
Length 85.61ft/26.1m
Breadth 26.27ft/8.01m
Draught 9.84ft/3.0m

Materials Steel throughout
Original use Tug and icebreaker
Condition Intact, may not be
operational
Present owners Dansk Veteranskibsklub
Location Copenhagen, Denmark
History Veteran Danish steam harbour
tug maintained in operating condition
by steam enthusiasts based in
Copenhagen.

Bonavista
coasting schooner

Former name SYVEREN, THOMAS 3
Built 1914 by L Johansen, Marstal,
Denmark
Propulsion Sail, schooner rig; diesel
auxiliary, 230hp
Tonnage 97.2 gross
Length 85.28ft/25.7m
Breadth 22.96ft/6.8m
Draught 8.5ft/2.6m
Materials Wood throughout
Original use Cargo
Condition In operation
Present owners Per Thuesen
Location Home port Rungstedt,
Denmark
History Schooner built to carry cargo
in the Danish Baltic and coastal trades.
Maintained in sailing condition as a
charter vessel based at Rungstedt.
Bibliography B33, B38

Brita Leth
coasting schooner

Former name HILFRED, BRITA,
M A FLYVEBJERG
Built 1911 by J Ring Andersen,
Svendborg, Denmark
Propulsion Sail, schooner rig
Tonnage 87 gross
Length 75.44ft/23.0m
Breadth 19.68ft/6.0m
Draught 6.56ft/2.1m
Materials Wood throughout
Original use Cargo
Condition In operation
Present owners Brita Leth ApS
Location Home port Arhus, Denmark
History Schooner built to carry cargo
in the Danish Baltic and coastal trades.
Maintained in sailing condition as a
charter vessel based at Arhus.
Bibliography B33, B38

Broen
motor ferry

Former name KALUNDBORG
Built 1952 by Frederikshavn Vaerft &
Flydedok, Frederikshavn, Denmark
Propulsion Diesel engines, 5200hp
Tonnage 1582 gross
Length 263.0ft/80.16m
Breadth 43.3ft/13.2m
Draught 17.0ft/5.2m

Materials Steel throughout
Original use Ferry
Condition Intact, afloat
Location Arhus, Denmark
History Motor ferryboat employed
between Korsor and Nyborg, and
Kalundborg and Arhus. Currently
moored in the harbour of Arhus,
serving some stationary use
(restaurant?).

Carene Star
trading schooner

Former name CARENE, ARGUS, KARNA,
HANNE HANSEN, MONA, LARS
Built 1945 by J Ring Andersen,
Svendborg, Denmark
Propulsion Sail, schooner rig; auxiliary
motor, 169hp
Tonnage 99.3 gross
Length 89.3ft/27.2m
Breadth 23.0ft/7.0m
Draught 7.2ft/2.2m
Materials Wood throughout
Original use Cargo
Condition In operation
Location Home port Nyborg, Denmark
History Schooner built to carry cargo
in the Danish Baltic and coastal trades.
Maintained in sailing condition based
at Nyborg.

Claus Sörensen
motor fishing vessel

Built 1922
Official number E 1
Propulsion Motor
Tonnage 17 gross
Length 37.7ft/11.5m
Original use Fishing
Condition In operating condition
Present owners Fiskeri og
Sofartsmuseet
Contact address Tarphagevej, DK-6710
Esbjerg V, Denmark
Location Esbjerg, Denmark
History Example of a Danish motor
fishing vessel of the 1920s maintained
in operating condition by a maritime
and fisheries museum.

Daekspram No 19
lighter

Built 1907 by A Jensen, Svendborg,
Denmark
Propulsion None
Tonnage 63 gross
Length 86.0ft/26.2m
Breadth 26.0ft/7.9m
Draught 7.0ft/2.13m
Materials Wood throughout
Original use Cargo

Condition Intact
Present owners Nationalmuseet, Vikingskibhallen
Location Copenhagen, Denmark
History Type of wooden barge used in transporting goods within a port area. Preserved afloat as an exhibit in the Nyhaven at Copenhagen.

Dana
motor fishing vessel

Built 1922 at Skagen, Denmark
Official number S 49
Propulsion Motor, 45hp, sloop rig
Tonnage 16.63 gross
Length 44.3ft/13.51m
Breadth 14.0ft/4.25m
Draught 7.8ft/2.38m
Materials Wood throughout
Original use Fishing
Condition Intact
Present owners Fiskeri og Sofartsmuseet

Location Esbjerg, Denmark
History Small Danish motor fishing vessel preserved on shore as an exhibit of the museum in Esbjerg.

Danmark
sail training vessel

Built 1932 by Nakskov Skibs, Nakskov, Denmark
Original owners Danish Ministry of Shipping and Fisheries
Propulsion Ship rig; diesel engines, 486hp
Tonnage 790 gross
Length 178.83ft/54.51m
Breadth 32.83ft/10.01m
Draught 13.75ft/4.19m
Materials Steel, except decks and lighter spars
Original use Training ship
Condition In active service
Present owners Danish Ministry of Trade, Shipping and Industry

Location Home port Copenhagen, Denmark
History The countries of Northern Europe have not only continued to believe in the value of training under sail but also, until the Second World War, made it a prerequisite for any merchant marine licence. As the last cargo-carrying sailing vessels disappeared in the 1920s and 1930s, sailing ships designed purely for training were built to replace them. The full-rigged ship DANMARK is an excellent example of the training ships of that generation. Though her career has now spanned over half a century, she is still fully active, making an extended cruise each year usually to the West Indies and one or more ports in the United States. She visited that country in 1939 and was caught there by the outbreak of the Second World War. She lay in a Florida port until the United States entered the War and was then taken over to serve as the training ship of the Coast Guard Academy, located in New London, Connecticut. Because of the threat of German submarines, cruises were restricted to the sheltered waters of Long Island Sound. The Academy's experience with the DANMARK influenced their decision to acquire their present training ship, the barque EAGLE, in 1946. DANMARK has been a regular participant in the various gatherings of square-rigged training ships since the first one organized by the Sail Training Association in 1954. During the parade of sailing ships celebrating the American bicentennial in 1976 she was placed at the head of the procession behind the host ship EAGLE in honour of her service under the American flag. DANMARK's home port was recently shifted from Copenhagen to Frederikshavn, Denmark.
Bibliography C25, 75, 93, 96, D167, 220

Danmark

Dannebrog
royal yacht

Built 1931 by Royal Dockyard, Copenhagen, Denmark
Original owners Royal Family of Denmark
Propulsion Diesel engine. Engine built by Burmeister & Wain, Copenhagen
Tonnage 1070 gross
Length 207.17ft/63.15m
Breadth 34.08ft/10.39m
Draught 11.67ft/3.56m
Materials Steel, except wood decks
Original use Royal yacht
Condition In active service
Present owners Royal Family of Denmark
Location Home port Copenhagen, Denmark
History Designed and built as a yacht for the Royal Family of Denmark, and remains in active service after almost seventy years.
Bibliography C15

Elida
coasting schooner

Former name SUNDIA, FRITHIOF, MOLLE, MON
Built 1875 by Kockums Mekaniska Verkstad, Malmo, Sweden
Propulsion Sail, schooner rig; auxiliary motor, 135hp
Tonnage 120 gross
Length 81.4ft/24.8m
Breadth 20.0ft/6.1m
Draught 7.5ft/2.3m
Original use Cargo
Location Arhus, Denmark
History Schooner built to carry cargo in the Danish Baltic and coastal trades. Maintained in sailing condition based at Arhus.

Elinor
coasting schooner

Built 1906 by Otto Hansen, Stubbekobing, Denmark
Propulsion Sail, 3-masted schooner; diesel engine, 155hp
Tonnage 71.5 gross
Length 114.9ft/35.0m
Breadth 19.68ft/6.0m
Draught 6.56ft/2.1m
Materials Wood throughout
Original use Cargo
Condition In operation
Present owners Sejlskibskommanditselkabet Alta
Location Home port Copenhagen, Denmark
History 3-masted schooner built to

Dannebrog

carry cargo in the Danish Baltic and coastal trades. Maintained in sailing condition as a charter vessel based at Copenhagen.
Bibliography A15, B33

Ellen
motor fishing vessel

Built 1906 by Dolmers Vaerft, Vestero, Denmark
Official number FN 162
Propulsion Petrol motor
Tonnage 10.89 gross
Length 32.4ft/9.88m
Breadth 12.8ft/3.9m
Draught 5.5ft/1.68m
Materials Wood throughout
Original use Fishing
Condition Intact
Present owners Laeso Sofarts-og Fiskerimuseet
Contact address Versto Havnegade 5, DK-9940 Laeso, Denmark
Location Laeso, Denmark
History Small Danish motor fishing boat built early in the century maintained as a floating exhibit.

Else Dorothea Bager
coasting schooner

Former name JACQUELINE, MERCANTIC II, TALATA, KARIS
Built 1942 by J Ring Andersen, Svendborg, Denmark
Propulsion Sail, schooner rig; auxiliary motor, 135hp
Tonnage 95.1 gross
Length 88.9ft/27.1m
Breadth 23.0ft/7.0m
Draught 7.2ft/2.2m
Materials Wood throughout
Original use Cargo
Location Hals, Denmark
History Schooner built to carry cargo in the Danish Baltic and coastal trades. Maintained in sailing condition based at Hals.

Eron
motor fishing vessel

Built 1947 by K J C Bonde, Stenbjerg, Denmark
Official number T 117
Propulsion Motor, 30hp
Tonnage 9.1 gross

Materials Wood throughout
Original use Fishing
Condition Intact
Present owners Fiskeri og Sofartsmuseet
Location Esbjerg, Denmark
History Danish clinker-planked motor fishing boat preserved on shore as an exhibit of the museum in Esbjerg.

Freia
coasting schooner

Built 1896 by Bornholms Maskinfabrik, Ronne, Denmark
Propulsion Sail, schooner rig; auxiliary motor, 66hp
Tonnage 67.5 gross
Length 75.0ft/22.7m
Breadth 18.7ft/5.7m
Draught 6.2ft/1.9m
Materials Wood throughout
Original use Cargo
Condition In operation
Location Svendborg, Denmark
History Schooner built to carry cargo in the Danish Baltic and coastal trades. Maintained in sailing condition as a cruise vessel based at Svendborg.

Fulton

coasting schooner

Built 1915 by C L Johansen, Marstal,
Denmark
Original owners R B H Nielsen
Propulsion 3-masted schooner rig
Tonnage 102 gross
Length 116.0ft/35.36m
Breadth 23.0ft/7.01m
Draught 8.0ft/2.44m
Materials Wood throughout
Original use Cargo
Condition In active service
Present owners Nationalmuseet,
Vikingskibhallen, Roskilde
Location Home port Roskilde,
Denmark
History Fully restored Danish cargo
schooner employed in a programme
which gives sailing vessel experience to
young people of high school age.
Bibliography A15, B33, B38, C25, D110

Fylla

coasting schooner

Former name POLAR FREEZER,
ARCTIC FREEZER, FYN
Built 1922 by N P V Dreyer, Nyborg,
Denmark
Propulsion Sail, schooner rig; diesel
auxiliary, 175hp
Tonnage 122 gross
Length 94.14ft/28.7m
Breadth 24.11ft/7.35m
Draught 9.84ft/3.0m
Materials Wood throughout
Original use Cargo
Condition In operation
Present owners Fyns Amtskommune
Location Home port Odense, Denmark
History Schooner built to carry cargo
in the Danish Baltic and coastal trades.
Currently maintained in sailing
condition as a youth training vessel
based at Odense.
Bibliography B33

Fyrskib II

self-propelled lightship

Built 1916 at Faaborg, Denmark
Original owners Royal Danish
Lighthouse Authority
Propulsion Diesel engine, 130hp
Tonnage 179 gross
Length 115.9ft/35.33m
Breadth 23.0ft/7.01m
Draught 11.1ft/3.38m
Materials Wood throughout
Original use Lightship
Condition Afloat
Location Copenhagen, Denmark
History Early Danish self-propelled

lightship. Currently maintained as a
floating restaurant in Copenhagen.

Fyrskib X

lightship

Built 1877 by the Naval Dockyard at
Copenhagen, Denmark
Original owners Royal Danish
Lighthouse Authority
Propulsion Towed to station
Tonnage 139 gross
Length 103.4ft/31.52m
Breadth 19.0ft/5.79m
Draught 10.3ft/3.14m
Materials Wood throughout
Original use Lightship
Condition Afloat
Location Helsingor, Denmark
History Veteran Danish lightship
maintained afloat as a restaurant in
Helsingor (Elsinore). External
appearance unaltered.

Fyrskib XI

lightship

Built 1878 by Sparre, Nystad, Denmark
Original owners Royal Danish
Lighthouse Service
Propulsion Towed to station
Tonnage 138 gross
Length 103.4ft/31.52m
Breadth 19.0ft/5.79m
Draught 10.3ft/3.14m
Materials Wood throughout
Original use Lightship
Condition Afloat
Location Copenhagen, Denmark
History Veteran Danish lightship
maintained afloat as a private
residence, external appearance
unaltered.

Fyrskib X

Fyrskib XII

lightship

Built 1880 by the Naval Dockyard,
Copenhagen, Denmark
Original owners Royal Danish
Lighthouse Service
Propulsion Towed to station
Tonnage 137 gross
Length 103.4ft/31.52m
Breadth 19.0ft/5.79m
Draught 10.3ft/3.14m
Materials Wood throughout
Original use Lightship
Condition Afloat
Location Copenhagen, Denmark
History Veteran Danish lightship
maintained afloat as a private
residence at Copenhagen, external
appearance unaltered.

Fyrskib XIII

lightship

Built 1880 at Copenhagen, Denmark
Original owners Royal Danish
Lighthouse Authority
Propulsion Towed to station
Tonnage 136 gross
Length 103.6ft/31.58m
Breadth 19.4ft/5.91m
Draught 10.3ft/3.14m
Materials Wood throughout
Original use Lightship
Condition Afloat
Present owners Danish Ministry of
Justice
Location Copenhagen, Denmark
History Veteran Danish lightship
maintained afloat in Copenhagen,
external appearance unaltered.

Fyrskib XVII

lightship

Built 1895 by N F Hansen, Odense,
Denmark
Original owners Royal Danish
Lighthouse Authority
Propulsion Towed to station
Tonnage 170 gross
Length 116.0ft/35.36m
Breadth 21.0ft/6.4m
Draught 11.0ft/3.35m
Materials Wood hull, wood & steel
superstructure
Original use Lightship
Condition Intact
Present owners Nationalmuseet,
Vikingskibhallen, Roskilde
Location Copenhagen, Denmark
History Veteran Danish lightship
exhibited as a floating museum at

Fyrskib II

Copenhagen, external appearance unaltered since the last years of her active service.

Fyrskib XXI
lightship

Former name SKAGENS REV
Built 1911 by R Mollers Vaerft, Faaborg, Denmark
Original owners Royal Danish Lighthouse Authority
Tonnage 188 gross
Length 110.3ft/33.6m
Breadth 21.0ft/6.4m
Materials Wood throughout
Original use Lightship
Condition Intact
Location Ebeltoft, Denmark
History Former Danish lightship maintained as a floating museum in Ebeltoft near the preserved steam frigate JYLLAND.

Georg Stage
sail training ship

Built 1935 by Frederikshavn's Vaerft & Flydedok A/S, Frederikshavn, Denmark
Original owners Georg Stage Foundation
Propulsion Ship rig; diesel engine, 122hp
Tonnage 298 gross
Length 123.42ft/37.62m
Breadth 27.5ft/8.38m
Draught 12.5ft/8.38m
Materials Steel hull, steel & wood masts
Original use Training ship
Condition In active service
Present owners Georg Stage Foundation
Location Home port Copenhagen, Denmark
History Small full-rigged ship built as a replacement for the earlier Danish training vessel of the same name that is now preserved at Mystic, Connecticut, under the name JOSEPH CONRAD. Usually makes training cruises during the summer months in European waters.
Bibliography A14, C54, C75, C96

Hanne Lene
motor fishing vessel

Former name REX
Built 1938 by P N Thomsen, near Vorupor, Denmark
Official number A168
Propulsion Motor
Tonnage 7.53 gross

Georg Stage

Materials Wood throughout
Original use Fishing
Condition Intact
Present owners Fiskeri og Sofartsmuseet
Location Esbjerg, Denmark
History Small clinker-planked motor fishing boat preserved on shore as one of the outdoor exhibits of the museum in Esbjerg.

Helge
motor passenger vessel

Built 1924 by J Ring Andersen, Svendborg, Denmark
Propulsion Diesel engine, 180hp
Tonnage 27 gross
Length 61.1ft/18.62m
Breadth 17.5ft/5.33m

Draught 5.0ft/1.52m
Materials Wood throughout
Original use Passengers
Condition In operation
Present owners Sydfyenske Dampskibsselskab
Location Based at Svendborg, Denmark
History Small Danish motor passenger vessel preserved in operating condition and original appearance. In operation as an excursion vessel based at Svendborg.

Hellas
motor fishing vessel

Built 1943 by Bdr Lauersens, Esbjerg, Denmark
Official number E 718
Propulsion Motor, 140hp
Tonnage 40 gross
Materials Wood throughout
Original use Fishing
Condition Intact hull, roofed-over, with doors in sides
Present owners Fiskeri og Sofartsmuseet
Location Esbjerg, Denmark
History Hull of a wooden Danish fishing boat with corrugated metal roof protecting the deck and doors cut into the side for access, serving as an exhibit on shore at the museum in Esbjerg.

Hjalm
coasting ketch

Former name DYKKEREN, MAGDA, CHR JENSEN
Built 1901 at Assens, Denmark
Propulsion Sail, ketch rig; diesel auxiliary, 90hp
Tonnage 52 gross

Helge

Hjejlen

Length 67.0ft/20.42m
Breadth 18.0ft/5.49m
Materials Wood throughout
Original use Cargo
Condition In operation
Present owners Holbaek Kommune
Location Based at Holbaek, Denmark
History Ketch built to carry cargo in
the Danish Baltic and coastal trades,
later used for training. Maintained in
sailing condition based at Holbaek.
Bibliography C54

Hjejlen
excursion steamer

Built 1861 by Baumgarten &
Burmeister, Copenhagen, Denmark
Original owners A/S Hjejlen
Propulsion Steam sidewheel,
oscillating, coal-fired, 25hp
Tonnage 39 gross
Length 88.2ft/26.9m
Breadth 12.42ft/3.79m
Depth 5.5ft/1.68m
Materials Iron throughout
Original use Passengers
Condition In active service
Present owners A/S Hjejlen
Location Silkeborg-Seen, Denmark
History Steamboat that has operated
on the lakes near Silkeborg, Denmark,
for almost 140 years. The boiler has
been replaced more than once, but the
engine is original.
Bibliography A17, B16, B43, D304

Ingolf
fisheries patrol vessel

Built 1962 at Svendborg, Denmark
Original owners Danish Government
Official number F-350
Propulsion Diesel engines, 6400hp.
Engine built by General Motors
Tonnage 1650 displacement
Length 219.66ft/67.0m
Breadth 38.0ft/11.5m
Draught 16.0ft/5.0m
Materials Steel throughout
Original use Fisheries inspection vessel
Condition Intact
Present owners Aalborg
Marinemuseum
Contact address Vester Fjordvej 81, DK-
9000 Aalborg, Denmark
Location Aalborg, Denmark
History Danish fisheries patrol vessel to
be preserved as an exhibit.

Isefjord
coasting schooner

Former name MINNA, SKAGEN
Built 1874 by H V Buhl, Frederikshavn,
Denmark
Propulsion Sail, schooner rig; diesel
auxiliary added, 47hp
Tonnage 29.7 gross
Length 55.76ft/17.0m
Breadth 14.9ft/4.55m
Draught 5.3ft/1.6m
Materials Wood throughout
Original use Cargo
Condition In operation

Present owners H E B Gyldenkrone-
Rysensteen
Location Copenhagen, Denmark
History Schooner built to carry cargo
in the Danish Baltic and coastal trades.
Maintained in sailing condition as a
charter vessel based in Copenhagen.
Bibliography A15, B33

Jensine
sailing coaster

Built 1852 by J W Riis, Alborg,
Denmark
Propulsion Sail, cutter rig
Tonnage 31 gross
Materials Wood throughout
Original use Cargo
Condition In operating condition
Location Based at Haderslev, Denmark
History The oldest Danish sailing vessel
still afloat. Built to carry cargo in the
Baltic and coastal trades. Maintained
in sailing condition as a yacht based at
Haderslev.
Bibliography B33, B38

Jylland
wooden steam frigate

Built 1860 by Nyholm Naval Shipyard,
Copenhagen, Denmark
Original owners Danish Royal Navy
Propulsion Steam screw, horizontal
Tonnage 2450 displacement
Length 311.67ft/95.0m
Breadth 43.0ft/13.11m
Draught 19.67ft/6.0m

Materials Wood throughout
Original use Steam frigate
Condition Undergoing stabilisation
and restoration
Present owners Den Selvejende
Institution Fregatten Jylland
Location Ebeltoft, Denmark
History The earliest steam-propelled
warships were simply wooden sailing
warships with engines added. Since
paddlewheels were too vulnerable to
ramming and cannon fire, the screw
propeller was soon adopted, powered
by horizontal engines placed low in the
ship for protection from shots
penetrating the hull. JYLLAND is the
last major warship surviving from this
era. She currently lacks both her rig
and her original engines, but her
handsome figurehead and the fine
carved decoration that ornamented
her stern still exist. While a new vessel,
she saw action in a battle between a
Danish squadron and a combined
Austrian and Prussian squadron, off
Heligoland in the North Sea on 9 May
1864. JYLLAND sustained considerable
damage during the two-hour action,
which ended in a Danish victory when
the enemy was forced to withdraw
with their flagship SCHWARZENBERG on
fire. JYLLAND was eventually reduced
to stationary use at a Danish naval base
in 1890, and was on the verge of being
scrapped in 1908 when the decision
was made to preserve her. She was
brought to Ebeltoft in 1960 in the
hopes that she could be completely
restored there. Simply preserving the
ancient wooden hull afloat became a
major challenge. By the 1980s she was
badly hogged and much of her
structure was seriously deteriorated. A
few years ago her hull was placed in a
dry berth under cover. Major
restoration of the ship is now
underway. JYLLAND may never go back
into the water, but it is hoped she can
someday be restored where she now
lies to represent her appearance as an
active warship of the 1860s.
Bibliography A14, D289, D494

Kompas
motor fishing vessel

Former name CHR HUSTED, PER LOKKE
Built 1971 by Schiffswerft Hobro,
Hobro, Denmark
Propulsion Motor
Tonnage 97 gross
Materials Wood hull
Original use Fishing
Condition Intact, in use
Location Oddesund Bridge, Denmark

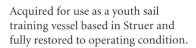

History Danish motor fishing boat, largely unaltered, serving as an exhibit and onshore tourist information bureau.

Kongechalup
royal barge

Built 1780 at Copenhagen, Denmark
Original owners King of Denmark
Propulsion Rowed
Length 36.1ft/11.0m
Breadth 8.2ft/2.5m
Draught 2.5ft/0.75m
Materials Wood throughout
Original use Royal barge
Condition Intact
Present owners Orlogsmusect
Location Copenhagen, Denmark
History Elegant rowing barge with small cabin at stern used to transport rulers of Denmark on ceremonial occasions. Now fully restored and displayed indoors at the Naval Museum in Copenhagen.

Lilla Dan
sail training vessel

Built 1951 by J Ring Andersen, Svendborg, Denmark
Original owners J Lauritzen & Co
Propulsion Sail, topsail schooner rig;

auxiliary diesel engine, 85hp
Tonnage 95 gross
Length 84.6ft/26.0m
Breadth 23.5ft/6.2m
Draught 9.4ft/2.5m
Materials Wood throughout
Original use Training vessel
Condition In operation
Location Home port Svendborg, Denmark
History Built as a training vessel for a maritime school operated by the J Lauritzen & Co shipping company. Continues to operate as a sail training vessel for young people based at Svendborg.

Lissy
motor fishing vessel

Built 1936 by Andersen & Ferdinandsen, Gilleleje, Denmark
Official number FN 164
Propulsion Diesel engine
Tonnage 19.86 gross
Length 44.3ft/13.5m
Breadth 13.7ft/4.17m
Draught 5.7ft/1.73m
Materials Wood throughout
Original use Fishing
Condition Intact
Present owners Nordsomuseet
Location Hirtsals, Denmark

History Danish motor fishing boat preserved on land as an outdoor exhibit of the museum in Hirtsals.

Marilyn Anne
trading schooner

Former name VEST, VESTVAG, FREM
Built 1919 by E Eriksen, Marstal, Denmark
Original owners Kromann of Marstal
Propulsion Sail, 3-masted schooner rig; diesel auxiliary, 256hp. Engine built by Scania
Tonnage 134.93 gross
Length 125.1ft/38.14m
Breadth 24.93ft/7.6m
Draught 8.9ft/2.7m
Materials Wood throughout
Original use Cargo
Condition In operation
Present owners Joint project; Struer, Herning, Holstebro Kommunes
Location Based at Struer, Denmark
History Sailing vessel built for the trade between Denmark, Iceland, Newfoundland, and Portugal. Sold to Swedish owners in 1939 for trading around Scandinavia and in the Baltic. Came under the Danish flag again in 1958. Bought by an American in 1968 who gave her her present name and attempted to restore her until 1977.

Acquired for use as a youth sail training vessel based in Struer and fully restored to operating condition.

Meta
coasting schooner

Built 1884
Propulsion Sail, schooner rig; auxiliary diesel engine, 120hp
Original use Cargo
Condition In operation
Location Home port Svendborg, Denmark
History Schooner built to carry cargo in the Danish Baltic and coastal trades. Maintained in sailing condition as a cruise vessel based at Svendborg.

MHV-67
motor patrol vessel

Former name VENDSYSSEL III
Built 1929 by C Nielsen, Frederikshavn, Denmark
Propulsion Diesel engine
Tonnage 35 gross
Length 60.4ft/18.4m
Breadth 17.1ft/5.2m
Draught 7.5ft/2.3m
Materials Wood throughout
Original use Government patrol vessel
Condition Intact
Location Ebeltoft, Denmark
History Patrol vessel built on the lines of a motor fishing boat, in active service based at Ebeltoft. Floating exhibit.

Mjölner
sailing coaster

Built 1922 by J Ring Andersen, Svendborg, Denmark
Propulsion Sail, cutter rig; auxiliary motor
Tonnage 19.83 gross
Length 51.9ft/15.81m
Breadth 16.4ft/5.0m
Materials Wood throughout
Original use Cargo
Condition In operating condition
Present owners Langelands Museum
Location Home port Rudkobing, Denmark
History Cutter-rigged vessel built to carry cargo in the Danish coastal trade. Maintained in sailing condition as a floating exhibit at the Langelands Museum. Currently an active sailing vessel.

Jylland at Ebeltoft before being moved to a dry berth

Mön

motor ferry

Built 1923 by Nakskov Skibsvaerft, Nakskov, Denmark
Propulsion Diesel engine, 136hp
Tonnage 79.46 gross
Length 72.0ft/21.94m
Breadth 20.0ft/6.12m
Draught 8.7ft/2.67m
Original use Ferry
Present owners Danmarks Faergemuseum
Location Nyborg, Denmark
History Danish motor ferryboat formerly employed on the Kalvehave-Lindholm route. Preserved as an exhibit of a museum devoted to ferries at Nyborg.

Motorfyrskib I

self-propelled lightship

Former name HORNS REV
Built 1913 by R Mollers Vaerft, Faaborg, Denmark
Original owners Royal Danish Lighthouse Authority
Propulsion Diesel engine, 125hp
Tonnage 181 gross
Length 110.2ft/33.58m
Breadth 22.4ft/6.82m
Draught 11.1ft/3.38m
Materials Wood throughout
Original use Lightship
Condition Intact
Present owners Fiskeri og sjofartsmuseet
Location Esbjerg, Denmark
History First Danish self-propelled lightship, and last Danish lightship in active service. Preserved as a floating exhibit at Esbjerg.

Nalle Puh

steam tug

Former name NALLE
Built 1923 by Oskarshamns Mekaniske Verksted, Oskarshamn, Sweden
Propulsion Steam, compound, 260hp
Tonnage 68.64 gross
Length 70.9ft/21.6m
Breadth 21.3ft/6.5m
Draught 10.5ft/3.2m
Materials Steel throughout
Original use Tug
Condition Afloat
Present owners Hans Heger
Location Copenhagen, Denmark
History Active until 1964 as a tug and harbour icebreaker. Currently moored at Copenhagen as a private residence, outwardly unaltered.

Nalle Puh

Palnatoke

galeass

Built 1894
Propulsion Sail, galeass rig; auxiliary diesel engine, 85hp
Length 54.13ft/16.5m
Breadth 17.06ft/5.2m
Draught 5.57ft/1.7m
Materials Wood throughout
Original use Cargo
Condition In operation
Location Home port Svendborg, Denmark
History Danish galeass built to carry cargo in the Danish Baltic and coastal trades. Maintained in sailing condition as a cruise or charter vessel based at Svendborg.

Ruth

sailing coaster

Built 1854 by P Willumsen, Svinor, Norge, Denmark
Propulsion Sloop rig
Tonnage 19 gross
Length 44.0ft/13.41m
Breadth 16.0ft/4.88m
Draught 5.0ft/1.52m
Materials Wood throughout
Original use Cargo
Present owners Nationalmuseet,
Vikingskibhallen, Roskilde
Location Roskilde, Denmark
History One of the oldest surviving coastal sailing vessels. Hull is intact and afloat, awaiting rerigging; floating exhibit.
Bibliography A16

Sjaelland

passenger motor ferry

Former name DRONNING INGRID
Built 1951 by Helsingor Skibsvaerft, Helsingor, Denmark
Propulsion Engines, 5450hp
Tonnage 3034 gross
Length 110.4m
Breadth 17.2m
Draught 4.1m
Materials Steel throughout
Original use Ferry
Condition Intact, in use
Location Copenhagen, Denmark
History Large ferryboat for vehicles and foot passengers preserved without external alterations as a floating restaurant and museum at Copenhagen.

Skjelskör

coastal passenger steamer

Built 1915 by J Ring Andersen,
Staalskibsvaerft, Svendborg, Denmark
Original owners Dampskibsselskabet Skjelskor
Propulsion Steam, compound, 75hp
Tonnage 49 gross
Length 67.6ft/20.6m
Breadth 14.1ft/4.3m
Depth 6.08ft/1.85m
Draught 6.2ft/1.9m
Materials Steel throughout
Original use Passengers
Condition In active service
Present owners Dansk Veteranskibsklub
Location Sakskobing, Denmark
History Veteran coastal passenger steamer kept in operation by steam enthusiasts. Operates between Sakskobing and Bandholm where it connects with an operating steam train.
Bibliography A17, B16, B38

Söbjörnen

torpedo boat

Built 1964 by Copenhagen Navy Yard, Copenhagen, Denmark
Original owners Danish Navy
Official number P512
Propulsion Gas turbine, 12,750hp. Proteus engine built by Bristol
Tonnage 120 displacement
Length 88.6ft/27.0m

Breadth 25.0ft/7.6m
Draught 6.2ft/1.9m
Materials Steel throughout
Original use Torpedo boat
Condition Intact
Present owners Aalborg
Marinemuseum
Contact address Vester Fjordvej 81, DK-9000 Aalborg, Denmark
Location Aalborg, Denmark
History Example of a Danish torpedo boat of the 1960s, based on a British design, maintained as an exhibit.

Springeren
submarine

Built 1963 by Copenhagen Navy Yard, Copenhagen, Denmark
Original owners Danish Navy
Propulsion Diesel and electric engines. Engines built by Burmeister & Wain
Tonnage 595 displacement
Length 178ft 10in/54.5m
Breadth 15ft 5in/4.7m
Draught 13ft/4.0m
Materials Steel throughout
Original use Submarine
Condition Intact
Present owners Aalborg Marine Museum
Contact address Vester Fjordvej 81, DK-9000 Aalborg, Denmark
Location Aalborg, Denmark
History Retired Danish submarine of the 1960s, exhibited on shore.

Sprogø
motor ferryboat

Built 1962 by Helsingor Skibsvaerft, Helsingor, Denmark
Original owners De Danske Statsbaner
Propulsion Engines, 8700hp. Engines built by Burmeister & Wain
Tonnage 6590 gross
Length 358.0ft/109.2m
Breadth 58.0ft/17.7m
Draught 15.0ft/4.6m
Materials Steel throughout
Original use Ferry
Condition Intact
Present owners Danmarks Faergemuseum
Location Nyborg, Denmark
History Large Danish motor ferryboat built to carry railway cars, now retired from service and preserved as a floating museum devoted to ferries at Nyborg.

U-359
submarine

Built c1955 in the USSR

Original owners Soviet Navy
Propulsion Diesel and electric motors
Tonnage 1350 displacement
Length 250.0ft/76.0m
Breadth 20.7ft/6.3m
Draught 15.8ft/4.8m
Materials Steel throughout
Original use Submarine
Condition Preserved
Present owners Kolding Submarine Center
Contact address Helligkorsdage 22, DK-6000 Kolding
Location Kolding, Denmark
History Russian non-nuclear submarine of the Cold War era preserved on shore as a tourist attraction since 1994.

U-461
submarine

Built 1964 by Krasnaya Sormovo Submarine Yard, Gorki, Russia
Original owners Soviet Navy
Propulsion Diesel and electric motors
Tonnage 3160 displacement
Length 285.5ft/87.0m
Breadth 32.8ft/10.0m
Draught 25.6ft/7.8m
Materials Steel throughout
Original use Submarine
Condition Intact
Present owners Ubads Museum
Contact address Kalvebod Brygge, Kajplads 110, DK-1560 Kobenhavn
Location Copenhagen, Denmark
History Russian non-nuclear submarine of the Cold War era open to the public at Copenhagen.

Viking
customs cutter

Built 1897 by N F Hansen, Odense, Denmark
Original owners Danish Customs Service
Propulsion Sail, cutter rig; auxiliary diesel engine, 135hp
Tonnage 19.57 gross
Length 45.0ft/13.72m
Breadth 14.0ft/4.27m
Draught 7.5ft/2.28m
Materials Wood throughout
Original use Customs cutter
Condition Afloat, in operating condition
Present owners Svendborg Museum
Location Svendborg, Denmark
History Former sailing customs patrol vessel fully restored to her original appearance as an exhibit afloat and active sailing vessel.
Bibliography B33, B38, D254

Dominican Republic

This Spanish-speaking West Indian nation shares the island of Hispaniola with the one-time French colony of Haiti. Hispaniola was the first large land mass discovered by Columbus, and Santo Domingo, the capital and largest port in the Dominican Republic, is the oldest continuous European settlement in the New World. The Dominican Republic is a primarily agricultural country. Its leading exports are sugar, rice and bananas. The native population died out early in the colonial period, and maritime trade and fishing have been carried out in craft based on European designs, in the earlier period using sail, and today motors. Dominican vessels are largely limited to the coastal and nearby inter-island trades. A small navy is maintained whose largest warships since the Second World War have tended to be veterans of the United States or Canadian Navies.

Mella
frigate

Former name PRESIDENTE TRUJILLO, CARLPACE
Built 1943 by Davie, Lauzon, Quebec, Canada
Original owners Canadian Navy
Materials Steel throughout
Location Dominican Republic
History An ex-Canadian 'River' class frigate, later converted to the presidential yacht. On exhibit.

Ecuador

Ecuador is located at the equator on the Pacific coast of South America, between Colombia to the north and Peru to the south. It has the major seaport of Guayaquil linked by rail with its inland capital of Quito, and administers the territory of the Galapagoes Islands well out in the Pacific. Ecuador has remained out of the naval wars of South America, apart from some brief conflicts with Peru over contested territory to the east in the upper Amazon Basin. Ecuador's only preserved ship is a relic of one of these wars fought in the twentieth century.

Calderon
steam coaster

Former name COTOPAXI, CHAIHUIN
Built 1884 at Glasgow, Scotland
Original owners Adam Greulich & Co, Valparaiso
Propulsion Steam, screw, 150hp
Length 131.0ft/39.93m
Breadth 16.0ft/4.88m
Draught 9.0ft/2.74m
Materials Iron hull
Original use Cargo
Condition Intact
Present owners Ecuadorian Navy
Location Guayaquil, Ecuador
History Former merchant vessel acquired by the Ecuadorian Navy in 1886 and converted into a gunboat. Took part in the Battle of Jambeli during war between Ecuador and Peru in 1941. Preserved grounded in a lagoon in a park in Guayaquil.
Bibliography D43

Calderon

Egypt

Egypt can claim the world's oldest ship, a vessel dating from the age of the Pharaohs that was found in a disassembled state in an underground stone chamber beside one of the pyramids, and later assembled for exhibition in a museum building. Egypt also has in the EL HORRIA one of the world's oldest steam yachts, though she has gone through many alterations in her 135 years. An even older sidewheel steam yacht was seen in Cairo in the 1970s, but it has been impossible to determine her subsequent fate. Tourist travel on the Nile by overnight steamer has been popular for over a century, and several older boats have been refurbished for this service in recent years. The steamers share the river with cargo-carrying feluccas, sailing craft that have changed little in general appearance over many centuries.

El Horria
state yacht

Former name MAHROUSSA
Built 1865 by Samuda Brothers, Poplar, England
Original owners Khedive of Egypt
Propulsion Steam sidewheel, oscillating; now steam turbine
Tonnage 3762 gross, 3140 displacement
Length 421.5ft/128.47m
Breadth 42.6ft/12.98m
Draught 17.5ft/5.33m
Materials Iron hull
Original use Royal yacht
Condition Intact
Present owners Egyptian Government
Location Home port Alexandria, Egypt
History Built as the Egyptian royal yacht. Originally a sidewheel steamer. Converted to screw propulsion in 1905 and lengthened twice. Converted to a naval training vessel after the last king of Egypt was deposed.
Bibliography C40

Indiana
sternwheel steamer

Built 1923
Original owners Egyptian Government
Propulsion Steam, sternwheel
Length 130.0ft/39.6m
Original use River survey steamer
Condition In operation
Present owners Egyptian Government
Location Cairo, Egypt
History Sternwheel steamer built for use as a survey vessel operating on the Nile River and still in service.

Karim
steam yacht

Built 1917 in Great Britain
Original owners Sultan Fuad of Egypt
Propulsion Steam, sternwheel
Length 151.0ft/46.0m
Breadth 32.8ft/10.0m
Draught 4.3ft/1.3m
Materials Steel hull
Original use Yacht
Condition In operation
Present owners Spring Tours, Cairo, Egypt
Location Aswan/Luxor, Egypt
History Built as a steam yacht for use on the Nile by the ruler of Egypt. After Fuad's death in 1936 she was inherited by King Farouk. Used after the Revolution of 1952 by President Nasser and later President Sadat. Fully converted to a passenger vessel and currently making one week excursions out of Luxor.
Bibliography D2

Mahabiss
steam fishing vessel

Built 1930 by Swan, Hunter & Wigham Richardson, Newcastle, England
Propulsion Steam, triple expansion. Engine built by Swan, Hunter & Wigham Richardson
Tonnage 317 gross
Length 138.2ft/42.12m
Breadth 28.7ft/8.75m
Materials Steel throughout
Original use Fishing
Condition In operating condition
Present owners Egyptian Government; Port & Lighthouse Administration
Location Home port Alexandria, Egypt
History Egyptian research vessel converted from a steam fishing vessel in 1960.

Memnon
passenger steamboat

Built 1910
Propulsion Steam, sidewheel

El Horria, 1976

Original use Passengers
Condition Needs renovation
Location Near Cairo, Egypt
History Veteran Nile River passenger
steamboat used in the film *Death on
the Nile*. Inactive since the late 1970s,
she is laid up and reportedly for sale.

Royal Ship of Cheops
wooden rowing vessel

Built 2500BC in Egypt
Original owners King Cheops
Propulsion Oars
Tonnage 45 displacement
Length 142.4ft/43.4m
Breadth 19.4ft/5.91m
Materials Wood throughout
Condition Intact
Present owners Egyptian Government
Location Cairo, Egypt
History The world's oldest existing ship
is also one of the best preserved. Every
timber from which it is constructed
was shaped by the original shipwrights
over 4000 years ago. Possibly a funeral
barge for King Cheops himself, its
existence was unknown in modern
times until 1954. In that year an
Egyptian archaeologist cut through
one of the 15-ton limestone blocks
forming the cover of its burial
chamber beside the Great Pyramid. He
saw inside over one thousand carefully
shaped pieces of wood, the
disassembled parts of a fairly large
vessel of the time of the Pharaohs.
Over ten years were spent assembling
the ship. The few clues available
beyond the pieces themselves were
limited to depictions of vessels of the
period in ancient murals, and present
day craft used on the Nile which retain
some of her characteristics. In 1970 the
completed vessel was installed in a
special building standing over the pit
in which she was found. The hull has a
very graceful shape, with elongated
bow and stern ending in the popular
Egyptian papyrus bud motif. This
shape is clearly a reflection of even
earlier reed boats used on the Nile. The
planks are stitched together with rope.
Half round wooden battens are used to
cover the seams on the inside. A
deckhouse of wooden panels stands on
the after half of the single deck, further
suggesting funerary or ceremonial use.
Oars were found with the disassembled
vessel, but no spars of sails. Recent
examination of a similar stone
chamber nearby confirmed the
existence of a second disassembled
wooden vessel of the same period.
Bibliography D258, D311

Royal Ship of Cheops

Sudan
sidewheel river steamer

Built 1921 by Bow McLachlan, Paisley,
Scotland
Original owners Cook's Tours
Propulsion Steam, sidewheel, 3-cylinder
inclined
Length 228.0ft
Materials Steel hull
Original use Passengers
Condition In operation
Present owners LTI Hotels
Location Aswan, Egypt
History Largest hotel boat operating on
the Nile River. Fully renovated and
returned to service, making overnight
cruises on the river in 1994.

Time Machine
sidewheel river steamer

Former name MAHASEN
Built 1930
Original owners King Farouk of Egypt
Propulsion Steam, sidewheel, 2-cylinder
compound (built 1908). Engine built in
Birmingham, England
Length 138.0ft/40.0m
Breadth 25.0ft/7.6m
Materials Steel throughout
Original use Steam yacht
Condition In operation
Location Luxor, Egypt
History Originally built for Nile River
cruises by ministers in the government
of King Farouk. Now employed in one
week cruises out of Luxor.

Eire (Ireland)

After centuries of English
colonisation, the majority of the
island of Ireland achieved self-rule
in 1923 as the Irish Free State,
and severed its last political
connections with the rest of
Great Britain in 1937, at which
time it adopted the name of Eire.
A primarily agricultural land, it
had been greatly de-populated in
the mid-1800s when many people
struggling to survive on an
uncertain potato crop left to
seek new lives across the sea,
mainly in the United States. Eire
has had its involvement in
shipbuilding and ship operation,
but never on the scale of the
more industrialised north that
remains a part of Great Britain.
On its rugged west coast hardy
villagers have long challenged the
sea to fish or trade in small craft
of local design, including the
cutter-rigged 'Galway hookers'
and open, tarred canvas over
frame beach boats known as
curraughs. The south coast
harbour of Queenstown, or
Cobh, with its sheltered bay
surrounded by green Irish hills,
was once the first and last port
of call for the great transatlantic
liners.

Asgard
ketch yacht

Built 1905 by Colin Archer, Larvik,
Norway
Original owners Erskine Childers
Propulsion Ketch rig
Tonnage 18 gross
Length 44.0ft/13.41m
Breadth 13.0ft/3.96m
Draught 7.5ft/2.29m
Materials Wood throughout
Original use Yacht
Condition Intact, in need of restoration
Present owners Kilmainham Museum
Location Kilmainham, Dublin, Ireland
History Former yacht of the author of
the popular sea novel *Riddle of the
Sands*. Later used to run guns to
Ireland for the Easter Uprising of 1916.
Used as an Irish sail training vessel
until replaced in 1980. Currently stored
under cover awaiting a decision either
to restore or exhibit as an artifact.
Bibliography C51, D242a

Guillemot
lightship

Built 1923 by Cran & Somerville, Leith, Scotland
Original owners Irish Lighthouse Service
Propulsion Towed to station
Length 102.0ft/31.09m
Breadth 24.0ft/7.32m
Depth 12.5ft/3.81m
Original use Lightship
Condition Intact
Present owners Wexford Maritime Museum
Location Wexford, Ireland
History Veteran Irish lightship, retired in 1968, later converted to a floating museum.

Naomh Eanna
passenger ferry

Former name NAOM EANNA
Built 1958 by Liffey Dockyard Co, Dublin, Ireland
Original owners Coras Iompair Eireann [Irish Railways], Galway
Propulsion Diesel engine
Tonnage 483 gross
Length 137.25ft/41.83m
Breadth 27.92ft/8.5m
Draught 8.42ft/2.57m
Materials Steel hull
Original use Ferry
Condition Intact
Present owners Irish National Trust
Location Dublin, Ireland
History Built to operate as a ferry between Galway and the Aran Islands off the west coast of Ireland. Currently a museum and headquarters of the Irish National Trust moored in the Grand Canal Basin in Dublin.

Saint Patrick
Galway hooker

Built 1911 by Padraig Casey, Mweenish, Ireland
Original owners Casey Brothers
Propulsion Sail, cutter rig
Length 40.15ft/12.24m
Breadth 11.75ft/3.58m
Draught 5.5ft/1.68m
Materials Wood throughout
Original use Cargo
Condition In sailing condition
Present owners Paddy Barry
Location Dublin, Ireland
History Small Irish working sailing vessel of the type known as a 'Galway hooker'. Fully restored to sailing condition as a yacht based in Dublin.
Bibliography C34, C87

Estonia

The nation of Estonia was established in 1920 in territory on the east shore of the Baltic Sea once controlled by Sweden, and more recently by Russia. Estonia was occupied by Germany during the Second World War, and absorbed into the Soviet Union after Germany's defeat. It became an independent nation again in 1991 after the break up of the Soviet Union. Russia promoted the industrialisation of Estonia and the expansion of its fishing industry, primarily with Russian management and re-located Russian labour. The capital city and major seaport of Talinn is the home of the country's national maritime museum, located in a large tower of the medieval city walls. The leading ship preservation projects, a submarine and an icebreaker, are relics of the country's first two decades of independence between the world wars.

Admiral
steam tug

Former name ADMIRALTEETS
Built 1956 at Leningrad, Soviet Union
Original owners Soviet Government
Propulsion Steam, screw
Length 98.4ft/30.0m
Breadth 24.4ft/7.5m
Materials Steel throughout

Suur Toll as Russian Volhynetz

Original use Tug, seagoing
Condition Intact
Location Talinn, Estonia
History Former Russian steam seagoing tug acquired for preservation as an operating vessel based in Talinn. Now reportedly a floating restaurant there.

Lembit
submarine

Built 1936 by Vickers-Armstrong, Barrow, England
Original owners Estonian Navy
Propulsion Diesel and electric motors
Tonnage 820 displacement
Length 190.0ft/57.91m

Lembit, 1988

Breadth 24.5ft/7.47m
Draught 11.5ft/3.5m
Materials Steel throughout
Original use Submarine
Condition Intact
Present owners Estonian State Maritime Museum
Location Talinn, Estonia
History Only surviving submarine of the Estonian Navy. Served with the Russian Navy during the Second World War. Now a floating exhibit at Talinn.
Bibliography A16, D499

Suur Toll
steam icebreaker

Former name VAINAMOINEN, VOLHYNETZ, TSAR MIKHAIL FEODOROVITCH
Built 1914
Original owners Government of Russia
Propulsion Steam, screw, 4500hp
Tonnage 3622 displacement
Length 236.5ft/72.08m
Breadth 57.0ft/17.37m
Materials Steel throughout
Original use Icebreaker
Condition Intact, undergoing restoration
Present owners Estonian State Maritime Museum
Location Talinn, Estonia
History Veteran steam icebreaker employed by Tsarist Russia, Estonia, and the Soviet Union. Undergoing restoration at Talinn to serve as a floating exhibit.
Bibliography D463

Falkland Islands

These sparsely-populated islands in the South Atlantic, settled by people from the British Isles, have played a unique role in the history of the deepwater sailing ship. During the period the 'Cape Horn trades' were at their height, from the 1840s to the early years of this century, the Falklands were the location of the only relatively convenient port downwind that vessels could head for after having been disabled in their battle with the Horn. Some were repaired and sent back to sea, but the Falklands lacked drydocks or cranes with which to effect major hull or rigging repairs. Many sailing vessels were condemned at Port Stanley, some to be sold for further use as storage hulks in South America. Others remained in the Falklands, where they were grounded to serve as warehouses or the substructure of jetties. By the 1970s the Falklands had become a sailing ship 'Valhalla,' able to boast among other relics the best-preserved surviving examples of mid-nineteenth century wooden sailing vessel construction in Great Britain, Canada, and the United States. Efforts have been made to document these ships, but as yet there has been no serious move to ensure their continued survival.

Golden Chance

Charles Cooper
packet ship

Built 1856 by William Hall, Black Rock, Connecticut, USA
Original owners Layton & Hurlbut, New York
Propulsion Ship rig
Tonnage 977 gross
Length 166.0ft/50.6m
Breadth 35.0ft/10.67m
Materials Wood throughout
Original use Cargo and passengers
Condition Dismasted, collapsing on starboard side, hull otherwise intact
Present owners Falkland Islands Government

Location Port Stanley, Falkland Islands
History In 1818 a group of New York sailing ship owners embarked on the experiment of providing scheduled transatlantic departures at regular intervals. Passengers, and the more valuable cargoes, were quickly drawn to these guaranteed sailings and the 'packet' trade was born. CHARLES COOPER, built over a century ago to operate between New York and Le Havre, is the last of the packet ships still in existence. She is also the most intact survivor of approximately 7000 square-rigged merchant vessels built in the United States. In 1866, while on a passage from Philadelphia to San Francisco when only ten years old, she put into Port Stanley in the Falkland Islands in need of repairs and was condemned. She was employed for a few years as an anchored storage hulk, and then grounded around 1870 at the end of the pier. Protected by a series of roofs, the hull served as a warehouse for almost a century. In 1968 it was bought for the South Street Seaport Museum in New York. Between 1976 and 1981 the Museum sent three expeditions to Port Stanley to record the ship and stabilize it. The interior of the hull was found to be remarkably well-preserved, including original decks supported by massive timber knees, and a large timber windlass. Until removed to the Port Stanley Museum in 1978 much of the carved stern decoration survived in place spanning the 30ft-wide transom. In early 1991 the South Street Seaport

Museum transferred responsibility for the preservation of the CHARLES COOPER to Falklands Conservation.
Bibliography B48, D61, D230

Egeria
wooden full rigged ship

Built 1859 at Millidgeville, St John, New Brunswick, Canada
Propulsion Ship rig
Tonnage 1066 gross
Length 176.5ft/53.8m
Breadth 36.3ft/11.06m
Depth 22.9ft/6.98m
Materials Wood throughout
Original use Cargo
Condition Dismasted, hull cut down in forward half, stern largely intact, lower bow survives under the wharf
Present owners Falkland Islands Co
Location Port Stanley, Falkland Islands
History Most intact remains of a Canadian-built nineteenth century sailing vessel employed in world-wide trade. Arrived in Port Stanley in a damaged condition in 1872 and was eventually grounded for use as a warehouse for stevedoring equipment.
Bibliography B48

Fleetwing
brig

Built 1874 by Jones, Porthmadog, Wales
Original owners W Prichard & Co, Caernarfon, Wales
Propulsion Brig rig
Tonnage 237 gross
Length 110.0ft/33.53m

Breadth 25.0ft/7.62m
Depth 14.6ft/4.45m
Materials Wood throughout
Original use Cargo
Condition Grounded, most of hull intact, without decks
Present owners Falkland Islands Co
Location Port Stanley, Falkland Islands
History Brig that traded out of North Wales until early this century. Arrived in Port Stanley in 1911 with a cargo of coal and was converted to a storage hulk. Now lies grounded and unused against the shore there.
Bibliography B48, C42

Garland
iron trading barque

Built 1865 by R & J Evans, Liverpool, England
Propulsion Barque rig
Tonnage 599 gross
Length 155.7ft/47.46m
Breadth 27.7ft/8.44m
Depth 17.8ft/5.43m
Materials Iron hull; iron & wood decks and masts
Original use Cargo
Condition Grounded, hull intact
Present owners British Crown Receiver of Wrecks
Location Darwin Harbour, Falkland Islands
History Intact iron hull of a small barque that traded under the British and Chilean flags. Arrived in the Falklands early this century with hull damaged by a corrosive cargo. Brought to Goose Green settlement to serve as a

storage hulk, but a gale drove her ashore across the harbour where she now lies.

Golden Chance
steam drifter

Built 1914 by John Chambers Ltd, Lowestoft, England
Propulsion Steam, screw, compound
Tonnage 90 gross
Length 84.0ft/25.6m
Breadth 19.0ft/5.79m
Materials Wood throughout
Original use Fishing
Condition Deteriorated but largely intact including engines
Present owners Crown Receiver of Wrecks, Port Stanley, Falkland Islands
Location Port Stanley, Falkland Islands
History Former British steam drifter brought to the Falklands in 1949 in an unsuccessful attempt to revive the sealing industry. Lies beached and abandoned in a cove near Stanley.
Bibliography B48

Jhelum
wooden trading vessel

Built 1849 by Steel, Liverpool, England
Propulsion Barque rig
Tonnage 428 gross
Length 123.1ft/37.52m
Breadth 27.1ft/8.26m
Depth 18.1ft/5.52m

Materials Wood throughout
Original use Cargo
Condition Grounded, intact hull
Present owners British Crown Receiver of Wrecks
Location Port Stanley, Falkland Islands
History Best-preserved example of a British wooden merchant sailing ship of the nineteenth century employed in world trade. Arrived in Port Stanley in damaged condition and later grounded to serve as a warehouse linked to shore by a jetty. Unused for many years and jetty now removed. Hull is being stabilized by the Merseyside Maritime Museum in Liverpool.
Bibliography B48, D47, D485

Lady Elizabeth
iron barque

Built 1879 by R Thompson Jr, Sunderland, England
Original owners J Wilson, London
Propulsion Barque rig
Tonnage 1208 gross
Length 223.0ft/67.97m
Breadth 35.0ft/10.67m
Depth 21.4ft/6.52m
Materials Iron hull; iron and wood decks & masts
Original use Cargo
Condition Intact, including deckhouse and lower masts
Present owners British Crown Receiver of Wrecks

Location Port Stanley, Falkland Islands
History Iron sailing ship employed in worldwide trade under the British and Norwegian flags. Arrived in Port Stanley in 1913 with hull damage and converted to a storage hulk. Grounded and abandoned there at the east end of the harbour since 1936.
Bibliography B48

Vicar of Bray
wooden barque

Built 1841 by Robert Hardy, Whitehaven, England
Propulsion Brig rig; later barque rig
Tonnage 282 gross
Length 97.0ft/29.57m
Breadth 24.25ft/7.39m
Depth 17.0ft/5.18m
Materials Wood throughout
Original use Cargo
Condition Intact hull
Present owners Falkland Islands Co
Location Goose Green, Falkland Islands
History Small sailing vessel employed in transporting copper ore between Chile and Wales in the mid-1800s. Took goldseekers from Chile to San Francisco in 1849, making her the last surviving vessel to take part in the California Gold Rush. Has served as support for a jetty at Goose Green for many years.

Faroe Islands

A group of eighteen islands located roughly midway between Scotland and Iceland, the Faroes are populated by around 50,000 people of Scandinavian descent. While largely self-governing, they maintain political ties with Denmark. Wool and fish are the leading exports.

Westward Ho
fishing ketch

Built 1884 by Leaver & Co, Grimsby, England
Propulsion Sail, ketch rig; diesel engine added
Tonnage 92.5 gross
Materials Wood throughout
Original use Fishing
Condition Intact, in sailing condition
Present owners Sluppen Foundation
Location Torshaven, Faroe Islands
History Former British North Sea sailing fishing vessel. Spent last sixty-five years of career based in the Faroe Islands. Fully restored externally, with interior converted to living accommodations.
Bibliography C54

Jhelum

Finland

The easternmost of the Scandinavian countries is probably best known for its extensive forests. A complex network of interconnected lakes provided the Finns with the means to exploit this resource. Forest products were transported on these inland waterways in cargo vessels and barges, and in rafts towed by steam tugboats. Specialised steam tugs were used in 'bundling' up logs for towing. Other European countries, such as the Netherlands, have been the scene of steam tug preservation by groups of private individuals, but Finland can claim to be the leader with over fifty operating steam tugboats maintained by members of its 'Tugboat Yachting Association'. In the nineteenth century the towns on the Finnish lakes were linked with the outside world by the construction of a canal to the Baltic. One of the steamers built to serve the lake and Baltic trade, the SALAMA of 1874, is a remarkable case of underwater survival, having been sunk in collision in 1898 and raised intact in 1971 for exhibition afloat. Finland was the last country to operate major deepwater sailing ships. The four-masted bark POMMERN preserved in the Åland Islands is an excellent example, and one of the few ships of this type to have never required significant restoration. Another noteworthy sailing vessel preserved in Finland is the bark SIGYN, the only intact wooden cargo vessel of her rig surviving in the world.

Ahkera
steam tug

Built 1871 by Paul Wahl & Co, Varkaus, Finland
Original owners Enzo-Gutzeit Co
Propulsion Steam, screw, 176hp
Tonnage 45.48 gross
Length 75.87ft/23.13m
Breadth 15.15ft/4.62m
Materials Iron throughout
Original use Tug

Condition Intact
Present owners Enzo-Gutzeit Co
Location Savonlinna, Finland
History Tug formerly used to move timber rafts on the Finnish lakes. Preserved on shore as an exhibit at the entrance to the Enzo-Gutzeit Shipyard near Savonlinna.

Ahti
steam tug

Former name LIITTO, SAITTA
Built 1892 by Hietalahti Workshop, Helsinki, Finland
Propulsion Steam, screw, 97hp
Length 69.0ft/21.03m
Breadth 14.3ft/4.37m
Draught 6.6ft/2.0m
Materials Steel throughout
Original use Tug
Condition In operating condition
Present owners Lauri Komulainen, Helsinki
Location Lake Saimaa, Finland
History Steam tug maintained in operating condition by a member of the Finnish Steamer Yachting Association.

Amanda
steam tug

Former name MAURI, TORNATOR II
Built 1905 by Paul Wahl & Co, Varkaus, Finland
Propulsion Steam, screw, 225hp
Length 43.9ft/22.5m
Breadth 16.0ft/4.9m
Draught 6.9ft/2.1m
Materials Steel throughout
Original use Tug
Condition In operating condition
Present owners Mikko Rytsola and Juhani Uusmaa
Location Helsinki, Finland
History Steam tug maintained in operating condition by members of the Finnish Steamship Yachting Association.

Ansio
steam tug

Former name KOTVIO, SALMI, CAROLUS, RUIJA
Built 1889 by Tampereen Pellava-ja Rautateollisuus Oy, Tampere, Finland
Propulsion Steam, screw, 80hp
Length 61.6ft/18.78m
Breadth 11.8ft/3.61m
Draught 7.9ft/2.4m
Materials Steel throughout
Original use Tug
Condition In operating condition

Ahkera

Present owners Pekka Kuronen and Heikki Riipinen, Helsinki
Location Paijanne, Finland
History Steam tug formerly operated on the Finnish lakes. Maintained in operating condition by members of the Finnish Steamer Yachting Association.

Antero
steam tug

Built 1924 by Lehtoniemi & Taipale, Joroinen, Finland
Propulsion Steam, screw, compound, 125hp
Tonnage 37.47 gross
Length 60.4ft/18.41m
Breadth 13.8ft/4.21m
Draught 6.9ft/2.1m
Materials Steel throughout
Original use Tug
Condition In operating condition
Present owners Ari and Arja Juva, Espoo
Location Lake Saimaa, Finland

History Steam tug formerly employed on the Finnish lakes. Maintained in operating condition by members of the Finnish Steamer Yachting Association.

Armas
steam tug

Former name TOINEN
Built 1908 by Paul Wahl & Co, Varkaus, Finland
Original owners Enso Trasliperi Ab
Propulsion Steam, screw, 257.5hp
Length 70.9ft/21.6m
Breadth 16.0ft/4.87m
Draught 6.9ft/2.1m
Materials Steel throughout
Original use Tug
Condition In operating condition
Present owners Ilkka Juva, Helsinki
Location Lake Saimaa, Finland
History Steam tug formerly employed on the Finnish lakes. Maintained in operating condition by a member of the Finnish Steamer Yachting Association.

Aure
steam tug

Built 1926 by A Ahlstrom Oy, Varkaus, Finland
Propulsion Steam, screw, 136hp
Tonnage 45 gross
Length 65.4ft/19.94m
Breadth 14.89ft/4.54m
Materials Steel throughout
Original use Tug
Condition In operation, shelter added to after deck
Present owners Hoyrylaivaosakeyhtio Aure
Location Tampere, Finland
History Steam tug built to operate on the Finnish lakes. Now operated as an excursion vessel on one of the lakes, based at Tampere.
Bibliography B16

Enso
steam tug

Built 1899 by Paul Wahl, Varkaus, Finland
Propulsion Steam, screw, 269hp
Length 75.1ft/22.89m
Breadth 16.3ft/4.98m
Draught 7.5ft/2.3m
Materials Steel throughout
Original use Tug
Condition In operating condition
Present owners Veikko Lindroos
Location Espoo, Finland
History Tug employed moving log rafts on Lake Saimaa. Now preserved by a member of the Finnish Steamer Yachting Association.

Figaro
lake steamer

Former name SAARISTO, NORRKULLA, NAGU
Built 1911 by Lehtoniemi & Taipale, Joroinen, Finland
Original owners Aktiebolaget Wulcan
Propulsion Steam, 2-cylinder, oil fired, 120hp
Tonnage 81 gross
Length 75.58ft/23.04m
Breadth 26.0ft/7.92m
Draught 6.92ft/2.11m
Materials Steel throughout
Original use Passengers
Condition In operation
Present owners Kyronsalmen Hoyrywenhe Oy
Location Savonlinna, Finland
History Veteran Finnish lake steamer maintained in active service as an excursion vessel.
Bibliography B16

Aure

Haapaniemi
steam tug

Former name RIIKKA
Built 1905 at Kokkola, Finland
Propulsion Steam, screw, 85hp
Length 59.2ft/18.04m
Breadth 13.3ft/4.06m
Materials Steel throughout
Original use Tug
Condition In operating condition
Present owners Heikki Saraste
Location Viitasaari, Finland
History Tug used to move log rafts on the Finnish lake system. Now maintained in operating condition by a member of the Finnish Steamer Yachting Association.

Halla IX
steam tug

Built 1896 by Stenberg & Soner, Helsinki, Finland
Propulsion Steam, screw, 100hp
Length 51.2ft/15.6m
Breadth 12.8ft/3.9m
Draught 4.0ft/1.2m
Materials Steel throughout
Original use Tug
Condition In operating condition
Present owners Pertti Hammar, Lahti
Location Lake Saimaa, Finland
History Steam tug maintained in operating condition by a member of the Finnish Steamer Yachting Association.

Halla XVII
steam tug

Built 1908 by Kotkan Rauta Oy, Kotka, Finland
Propulsion Steam, screw, 192hp
Length 71.9ft/21.9m
Breadth 15.8ft/4.83m
Draught 6.9ft/2.1m
Materials Steel throughout
Original use Tug
Condition In operating condition
Present owners Erkki Riimala, Helsinki
Location Lake Saimaa, Finland
History Steam tug maintained in operating condition by a member of

Heikki Peuranen

the Finnish Steamer Yachting Association.

Hame
passenger launch

Built 1903 by Sommers, Tampere, Finland
Propulsion Steam, screw, 39hp
Length 40.7ft/12.4m
Materials Steel throughout
Original use Passenger launch
Condition Restoration underway
Present owners L Elo
Location Tampere, Finland
History Passenger launch raised from the bottom of the lake near Tampere. Currently being restored by a private owner for return to steaming condition.

Heikki Peuranen
steam tug

Built 1897 by Gallen Workshop, Vyborg, Finland
Propulsion Steam, screw, 310hp
Length 75.67ft/23.07m
Breadth 17.15ft/5.23m
Materials Steel throughout
Original use Tug
Condition In operating condition
Present owners Seppo Ylasaari
Location Espoo, Finland
History Former steam tug employed on the Finnish lakes. Maintained in operating condition as a private yacht based in the Lake Saimaa region.

Heinävesi
passenger steamer

Former name HEINÄVESI I
Built 1906 by Paul Wahl & Co, Varkaus, Finland
Propulsion Steam, screw, 150hp
Tonnage 145 gross
Length 88.25ft/26.9m
Breadth 21.98ft/6.17m
Draught 6.89ft/2.1m
Materials Steel throughout
Original use Passengers
Condition In operation
Present owners Oy Savonlinnan Laivat
Location Kuopio, Finland
History Steamer built to carry passengers on the Finnish lakes. Still in active service making cruises out of Kuopio.
Bibliography B16

Helga
trading schooner

Built 1948 by Paul Gronqvist & Co, Valax, Finland
Propulsion Sail, 3-masted schooner rig; diesel engine, 365hp
Length 157.44ft/48.0m
Breadth 24.44ft/7.45m
Materials Wood throughout
Original use Cargo
Condition In operation

Location Finland
History Three-masted schooner built to carry cargo in the Finnish Baltic Sea trade. Restored to sailing condition for use as a charter vessel operating in Finnish waters.

Hovinsaari
steam tug

Built 1921 by Enso-Gutzeit Oy, Savonlinna, Finland
Propulsion Steam, screw, 50hp
Length 48.0ft/14.65m
Breadth 11.9ft/3.62m
Draught 5.0ft/1.5m
Materials Steel throughout
Original use Log bundling tug
Condition In operating condition
Present owners Reijo Pasanen and Lauri Multanen, Joensu
Location Lake Saimaa, Finland
History Steam tug employed in bundling up log rafts for towing on the Finnish lakes system. Maintained in operating condition by members of the Finnish Steamer Yachting Association.

Hurma
steam tug

Built 1901 by Vipurin Konepaja, Vyborg, Finland
Propulsion Steam, screw, 216hp

Tonnage 66 gross
Length 77.5ft/23.6m
Breadth 18.9ft/5.75m
Draught 7.2ft/2.2m
Materials Steel throughout
Original use Tug
Condition In operating condition
Present owners Tehdaspuu Oy, Kouvola
Location Lappeenranta, Finland
History Steam tug maintained in operating condition by members of the Finnish Steamer Yachting Association.

Hyöky
lightship

Former name HELSINKI, ARANDSGRUND, RELANDERSGRUND, LIBAUSKIJ
Built 1912 by Putilov Works, St Petersburg, Russia
Original owners Russian Lighthouse Service
Propulsion Steam, screw, coal-fired
Tonnage 275 displacement
Length 131.7ft/40.1m
Breadth 24.6ft/7.5m
Draught 7.2ft/3.0m
Materials Steel throughout
Original use Lightship
Condition Haminan Hoyrylaiva Oy
Location Hamina, Finland
History Built as a Russian lightship and later used by Finland as a survey vessel.

Currently maintained as an operating steamer.

Janne
steam tug

Former name NERKOO, PURUVESI
Built 1907 by Savonlinna Workshops, Savonlinna, Finland
Propulsion Steam, screw, 175hp
Length 69.0ft/21.0m
Breadth 16.6ft/5.05m
Draught 7.0ft/2.15m
Materials Steel throughout
Original use Tug
Condition In operating condition
Present owners Kari and Heikki Korpivaara, Espoo
Location Lake Saimaa, Finland
History Steam tug formerly employed on the Finnish Lakes. Maintained in operation condition by members of the Finnish Steamer Yachting Association.

Joh. Parviainen
steam tug

Built 1908 by Borga Mekaniska Verkstad, Porvoo, Finland
Propulsion Steam, screw, 175hp
Length 70.2ft/21.38m
Breadth 16.0ft/4.86m
Draught 7.2ft/2.2m
Materials Steel throughout
Original use Tug
Condition In operating condition
Present owners Jorma Manninen, Vaaksy
Location Paijanne, Finland
History Steam tug maintained in operating condition by a member of the Finnish Steamer Yachting Association.

Juno
steam tug

Former name TAUNOLA 2
Built 1907 by Borga Mekaniska Verkstad, Porvoo, Finland
Propulsion Steam, screw, compound, 77hp. Engine built by Borga Mekaniska Verkstad
Length 58.1ft/17.7m
Breadth 13.1ft/4.0m
Materials Steel hull
Original use Tug
Condition In operating condition
Present owners Esko Haro, Espoo
Location Paijanne, Finland
History Steam tug maintained in operating condition by a member of the Finnish Steamer Yachting Association.

Heinävesi

Kaima

passenger steamer

Built 1898 by Paul Wahl & Co, Varkaus, Finland
Propulsion Steam, screw, 87hp
Length 69.44ft/21.17m
Breadth 15.25ft/4.65m
Materials Steel throughout
Original use Passengers
Condition In operating condition
Present owners Olavi Ruutu, Helsinki
Location Paijanne region, Finland
History Small steamer formerly used to carry passengers on the Finnish lakes. Maintained in operating condition as a private yacht based in the Paijanne region.
Bibliography B16

Kajaani I

steam tug

Former name SALO II
Built 1911 at Kajaani, Finland

Karjalankoski

Propulsion Steam, screw, 112hp
Length 77.1ft/23.5m
Breadth 19.2ft/5.85m
Draught 5.9ft/1.8m
Materials Steel throughout
Original use Tug
Condition In operating condition
Present owners Jaakko Ebeling, Kauniainen
Location Oulujarvi, Finland
History Steam tug and 'wood warping vessel' formerly employed on the Finnish lakes. Maintained in operating condition by a member of the Finnish Steamer Yachting Association.

Kalle Tihveräinen

log bundling tug

Former name PURISTAJA IV, SAVO
Built 1916 by H Saastamoinen Oy, Kuopio, Finland
Propulsion Steam, screw, 60hp
Length 88.7ft/27.0m
Breadth 16.6ft/5.06m

Materials Steel throughout
Original use Log bundling vessel
Condition In operating condition
Present owners Tero Lehto and Pentti Roitto
Location Savonlinna, Finland
History Tug employed in bundling logs into rafts for towing. Maintained in operating condition by members of the Finnish Steamer Yachting Association.

Karjalankoski

passenger steamer

Former name APOLLO
Built 1905 by Lehtoniemi & Taipale, Joroinen, Finland
Propulsion Steam, screw, 134hp
Tonnage 107 gross
Length 79.47ft/24.23m
Breadth 21.48ft/6.55m
Draught 7.02ft/2.14m
Materials Steel throughout
Original use Passengers
Condition In operation
Present owners Imatran Hoyrylaivaosakeyhtio
Location Imatra, Finland
History Steamer built to carry passengers on the Finnish lakes. Still in service making excursions out of Imatra.
Bibliography B16

Keihäslahti

steam tug

Former name UNNUKKA
Built 1900 by Paul Wahl & Co, Varkaus, Finland
Propulsion Steam, screw, 37hp
Length 50.0ft/15.2m
Breadth 11.2ft/3.4m
Materials Steel throughout
Original use Tug
Condition In operating condition
Present owners Saastamoinen Oy
Location Kuopio, Finland
History Small steam tug formerly employed in the Finnish lakes. Maintained in operating condition by a group of members of the Finnish Steamer Yachting Association.

Keihassalmi

coastal minelayer

Built 1956 by Almel Ltd, Helsinki, Finland
Original owners Finnish Navy
Official number 05
Propulsion Two diesel engines, 1600hp. Engine built by Wartsila
Tonnage 290 displacement
Length 184.75ft/56.0m

Breadth 25.3ft/7.7m
Draught 6.5ft/2.0m
Materials Steel throughout
Original use Minelayer
Condition Intact
Location Turku, Finland
History Used as a floating exhibit.

Keitele

steam tug

Former name AANEKOSKI I
Built 1877 by Paul Wahl & Co, Varkaus, Finland
Propulsion Steam, screw, 95hp
Length 68.91ft/21.01m
Breadth 12.07ft/3.68m
Materials Iron hull
Original use Tug
Condition In operation
Present owners Imatran Hoyrylaivaosakeyhtio
Location Lake Keitele, Finland
History Built as a tug for use on the Finnish lakes. Later converted to a small passenger vessel. Maintained in operating condition as a private yacht based on Lake Keitele.

Kemi

lightship

Former name ARANSGRUND, RELANDERSGRUND, RAUMA
Built 1901 by Pori Machine Works, Pori, Finland
Original owners Finnish Board of Navigation
Propulsion Steam screw, 166hp
Length 101.38ft/30.9m
Breadth 22.74ft/6.93m
Draught 12.14ft/3.7m
Materials Steel hull; wood decks
Original use Lightship
Condition Fully restored
Present owners Hylkysaari Maritime Museum
Location Helsinki, Finland
History Veteran Finnish lightship fully restored and open to the public adjacent to a maritime museum located on an island off Helsinki.

Kouta

steam tug

Former name VUOKATTI II
Built 1921 by A Ahlstrom Oy, Varkaus, Finland
Propulsion Steam, screw, compound, 121hp
Length 73.96ft/22.55m
Breadth 17.51ft/5.34m
Materials Steel throughout
Original use Tug

Condition In operation
Present owners Matti Kuorikoski and
Allan Sointamo
Location Kajaani, Finland
History Built as a tug for use on the
Finnish lakes and rivers. Maintained in
operating condition as an excursion
vessel based at Kajaani on Lake
Oulujarvi.

Lahtis
sidewheel steamer

Former name Saari II, Lahti
Built 1865 by William Crichton, Turku,
Finland (assembled Lake Paijanne)
Original owners Johannes Parviainen
and Leopold Torpelius
Propulsion Steam, sidewheel; converted
to screw in 1904; later barge
Length 110.7ft/33.73m
Breadth 16.0ft/4.87m
Materials Iron hull
Original use Passengers
Condition Hull intact, restoration
unfinished
Location Jyvaskyla, Finland
History Paddlewheel steamer built for
operation on Lake Paijanne. Converted
to twin-screw propulsion in 1904, and
later reduced to a barge. Restored to
paddlewheel propulsion in 1979, but
lack of funds for further work led to
her being stored on shore near
Jyvaskyla.
Bibliography B43

Laitiala
passenger steamer

Former name Hopeasalmi, Mikkeli,
Orivesi II, Leppavirta I
Built 1903 by Paul Wahl & Co, Varkaus,
Finland

Propulsion Steam, screw, 138hp
Tonnage 168 gross
Length 87.9ft/26.8m
Breadth 21.32ft/6.5m
Draught 7.87ft/2.4m
Materials Steel throughout
Original use Passengers
Condition Intact
Present owners Pekka Kierikka
Location Lahti, Finland
History Steamer built to carry
passengers on the Finnish lakes. Until
recently was serving as a floating
restaurant at Savonlinna under the
name Hopeasalmi.
Bibliography B16

Läsäkoski
steam tug

Former name Vesilahti
Built 1904 at Tampere, Finland
Propulsion Steam, screw, 94hp
Length 62.0ft/18.9m
Breadth 12.5ft/3.8m
Draught 5.6ft/1.7m
Materials Steel throughout
Original use Tug
Condition In operating condition
Present owners Jukka Kaipomaki
Location Jamsa, Finland
History Tug employed in the Finnish
lakes. Maintained in operating
condition by a member of the Finnish
Steamer Yachting Association.

Lauri
steam tug

Built 1931 by A Ahlstrom, Varkaus,
Finland
Propulsion Steam, screw, 130hp
Length 65.27ft/19.9m
Breadth 15.58ft/4.75m

Lauri

Materials Steel throughout
Original use Tug
Condition In operating condition
Present owners Harri Lallukka and
associates
Location Lake Saimaa, Finland
History Tug built for use on the
Finnish lakes towing timber rafts.
Maintained in operating condition as a
private yacht based in the Lake Saimaa
region.

Leppävirta
lake steamer

Former name Leppävirta II
Built 1904 by Paul Wahl & Co, Varkaus,
Finland
Original owners Leppavirta Hoyrylaiva
Oy

Leppävirta

Kemi

Propulsion Steam, 2-cylinder compound, 129hp. Engine built by Warkauden konepaja
Tonnage 161 gross
Length 88.09ft/26.85m
Breadth 21.98ft/6.7m
Depth 7.22ft/2.2m
Draught 5.51ft/1.68m
Materials Steel throughout
Original use Passengers
Condition In operation
Present owners Municipality of Leppavirta
Location Leppavirta, Finland
History Finnish lake steamer maintained in operation as an excursion vessel.
Bibliography B16

Lokki
passenger steamer

Built 1913 by Paul Wahl & Co, Varkaus, Finland
Propulsion Steam, screw, compound, 129hp
Tonnage 124 gross
Length 81.77ft/24.93m
Breadth 20.17ft/6.15m
Draught 7.87ft/2.4m
Materials Steel throughout
Original use Passengers
Condition In operation
Present owners Roll-Laivat Oy
Location Kuopio, Finland
History Steamer built to carry passengers on the Finnish lakes. Still in service making cruises out of Kuopio.
Bibliography B16

Metsä
steam tug

Former name RAGNAR
Built 1896 at Rotterdam, Netherlands
Propulsion Steam, screw, compound, 104hp
Length 61.3ft/18.67m
Breadth 13.5ft/4.12m
Materials Steel hull, steel and wood superstructure
Original use Tug
Condition In operating condition
Present owners Esko Haro
Location Paijanne, Finland
History Steam tug maintained in operating condition by a member of the Finnish Steamer Yachting Association.

Mikko
cargo steamer

Former name ENSI
Built 1914 by Savonlinna Konepaja Oy,

Lokki

Savonlinna, Finland
Original owners Enso Gutzeit Oy
Propulsion Steam screw, 79hp
Tonnage 212 gross
Length 101.33ft/30.89m
Breadth 23.33ft/7.11m
Draught 8.0ft/2.43m
Materials Hull wood over steel frames
Original use Cargo
Condition Intact
Present owners City of Savonlinna
Location Savonlinna, Finland
History Steamer built to carry lumber on the Finnish lakes. Exhibited in fully restored condition with a fleet of historic vessels at Savonlinna.

Näsijärvi II
steam tug

Former name NEPTUN II
Built 1929 by A Ahlstrom Oy, Varkaus, Finland
Propulsion Steam, screw, 160hp
Length 68.98ft/21.03m
Breadth 16.83ft/5.13m
Materials Steel throughout
Original use Tug
Condition Intact
Present owners Town of Tampere
Location Tampere, Finland
History Steam tug formerly employed on the Finnish lakes. Preserved as a floating exhibit at Tampere.

Oberon III
steam tug

Built 1919 by A Ahlstrom Oy, Varkaus, Finland
Propulsion Steam, screw, 203hp
Length 85.87ft/26.18m
Breadth 16.47ft/5.02m
Materials Steel throughout
Original use Tug
Condition Intact, in operating condition
Present owners Harri Lallukka
Location Savonlinna, Finland
History Steam tug built for the timber industry on the Finnish lakes. Maintained in operating condition as a private yacht based in the Lake Saimaa region.

Olli
steam tug

Former name HALLA XV, OTSO
Built 1920 by Lehtoniemi & Taipale, Joroinen, Finland
Propulsion Steam, screw, 149hp
Length 63.2ft/19.25m
Breadth 14.9ft/4.55m
Draught 5.9ft/1.8m
Materials Steel throughout
Original use Tug
Condition In operating condition
Present owners Olavi Rasanen Oy, Mikkeli
Location Lake Saimaa, Finland
History Steam tug maintained in

Mikko

Oberon III

operating condition by members of the Finnish Steamer Yachting Association.

Osmo
cargo steamer

Built 1904 by Lehtoniemi & Taipale, Joroinen, Finland
Propulsion Steam, screw, 114hp
Length 100.9ft/30.75m
Breadth 20.9ft/6.38m
Draught 6.6ft/2.0m
Materials Steel throughout
Original use Cargo
Condition In operating condition
Present owners Allan Holopainen
Location Vehmersalmi, Finland
History Cargo steamer built for use in the forest products trade in the Finnish lakes. Maintained in operating condition by a member of the Finnish Steamer Yachting Association.

Otso
steam tug

Built 1919 by A Ahlstrom Oy, Varkaus, Finland
Propulsion Steam, screw, 90hp
Length 51.1ft/15.58m
Breadth 12.0ft/3.66m
Draught 4.5ft/1.37m
Materials Steel throughout
Original use Tug
Condition In operating condition
Present owners Jarmo Ruutu, Varkaus
Location Lake Saimaa, Finland
History Steam tug formerly employed on the Finnish lakes. Maintained in operating condition by a member of the Finnish Steamer Yachting Association.

Pallas
steam tug

Built 1923 by A Ahlstrom Oy, Varkaus, Finland
Propulsion Steam, screw, 124hp
Length 60.0ft/18.3m
Breadth 15.6ft/4.75m
Draught 5.9ft/1.8m
Materials Steel throughout
Original use Tug
Condition In operating condition
Present owners Allan Holopainen, Vehmersalmi
Location Lake Saimaa, Finland
History Steam tug formerly employed in the Finnish lakes. Maintained in operating condition by a member of the Finnish Steamer Yachting Association.

Papinniemi
steam tug

Former name KARTTULA
Built 1905 by Lehtoniemi & Taipale, Joroinen, Finland
Propulsion Steam, screw, 80hp
Length 65.0ft/19.8m
Breadth 15.0ft/4.57m
Draught 7.3ft/2.23m
Materials Steel throughout
Original use Tug
Condition In operating condition
Present owners Ari Reunanen, Mikkeli and Kaj Wickstrom, Helsinki
Location Lake Saimaa, Finland
History Steam tug formerly employed in the Finnish lakes. Maintained in operating condition by a member of the Finnish Steamer Yachting Association.

Parsifal
steam tug

Built 1915 by A Ahlstrom, Varkaus, Finland
Propulsion Steam, screw, 170hp
Length 70.2ft/21.4m
Breadth 16.1ft/4.9m
Draught 6.9ft/2.1m
Materials Steel throughout
Original use Tug
Condition In operating condition
Present owners Stig Tornqvist, Helsinki
Location Lake Saimaa, Finland
History Steam tug formerly employed on the Finnish lakes. Maintained in operating condition by a member of the Finnish Steamer Yachting Association.

Paul Wahl
passenger steamer

Former name PAASIVESI, JOENSUU, MIKKELI, VEHMERSALMI
Built 1919 by A Ahlstrom Oy, Varkaus, Finland
Propulsion Steam, screw, 150hp
Tonnage 125 gross
Length 88.56ft/27.0m
Breadth 19.68ft/6.0m
Materials Steel throughout
Original use Passengers
Condition Intact
Present owners Town of Varkaus
Location Varkhaus, Finland
History Steamer built to carry passengers on the Finnish lakes. Still in service making cruises out of Varkhaus during the summer months.
Bibliography B16

Peura III
steam tug

Former name VUOTJARVI
Built 1905 by Lehtoniemi & Taipale, Joroinen, Finland
Propulsion Steam, screw, 43hp
Length 40.0ft/12.16m
Breadth 10.0ft/3.04m
Draught 5.0ft/1.5m
Materials Steel throughout
Original use Tug
Condition In operating condition
Present owners Veikko Karjalainen, Kuopio
Location Lake Saimaa, Finland
History Steam tug formerly employed on the Finnish Lakes. Maintained in operating condition by a member of the Finnish Steamer Yachting Association.

Pohjola
passenger steamer

Built 1905 by Oy Sommers af Hallstrom & Waldens, Tampere, Finland
Propulsion Steam, screw, 185hp
Length 96.76ft/29.5m
Breadth 18.56ft/5.66m
Draught 7.38ft/2.25m
Materials Steel throughout
Original use Passengers
Condition Intact, laid up
Present owners Runoilijan Tir Oy
Location Tampere, Finland
History Steamer built to carry passengers on the Finnish lakes. Withdrawn from service in 1976 in need of engine repairs. There have been efforts to get her restored.
Bibliography B16

Pommern
trading barque

Former name MNEME
Built 1903 by J Reid & Co, Greenock, Scotland
Original owners B Wencke Sohne, Hamburg, Germany
Propulsion 4-masted barque rig
Tonnage 2376 gross
Length 310.5ft/94.64m
Breadth 43.33ft/13.21m
Draught 21.98ft/6.7m
Materials Steel hull; steel & wood decks & masts
Original use Cargo
Condition Intact
Present owners City of Mariehamn
Location Mariehamn, Aland Islands, Finland
History Sailing vessel built in a British shipyard for German owners, for use in worldwide trade. Spent her last active years in the Australian grain trade under the Finnish flag. Laid up as a result of the Second World War and later given by her owners to the Town of Mariehamn which maintains her as a floating exhibit.
Bibliography A14, C52, D511

Puhois
log bundling vessel

Former name PURISTAJA I, SAMPO
Built 1925 by Enzo-Gutzeit Oy, Tainionkoski, Finland
Original owners Enzo-Gutzeit Oy
Propulsion Steam, screw, 62hp
Length 77.8ft/23.7m
Breadth 16.7ft/5.1m
Draught 4.9ft/1.5m
Materials Wood hull
Original use Log bundling vessel
Condition In operating condition
Present owners N & E Rantapuu
Location Nummela, Finland
History Vessel used to bundle up log rafts for towing through the Finnish lake system. Maintained in operating condition by a member of the Finnish Steamer Yachting Association.

Rauha
steam tug

Former name HUMPPA
Built 1878 by Vyborg Workshop, Vyborg, Finland
Propulsion Steam, screw, 280hp
Length 85.2ft/25.95m
Breadth 17.7ft/5.4m
Draught 9.2ft/2.8m
Materials Iron hull
Original use Tug

Pommern

Condition In operating condition
Present owners Paavo Airas, Helsinki
Location Lake Saimaa, Finland
History Steam tug employed on the
Finnish lakes. Maintained in operating
condition by a member of the Finnish
Steamer Yachting Association.

Repola 5
steam tug

Former name MATTI, PIELAVESI
Built 1900
Propulsion Steam, screw, 142hp
Length 70.1ft/21.37m
Breadth 14.7ft/4.48m
Draught 6.9.0ft/2.1m
Materials Steel throughout
Original use Tug
Condition In operating condition
Present owners Rauma-Repola Oy,
Savonlinna
Location Lake Saimaa, Finland
History Steam tug formerly employed
on the Finnish lakes. Maintained in
operating condition by members of the
Finnish Steamer Yachting Association.

Riistavesi
passenger steamer

Former name VEHMERSALMI
Built 1927 by Lehtoniemi & Taipale,
Joroinen, Finland
Propulsion Steam, screw, compound,
148hp
Tonnage 99 gross
Length 80.36ft/24.5m
Breadth 19.35ft/5.9m
Materials Steel throughout
Original use Passengers
Condition In operating condition
Present owners O Eberling and R
Lunden, Helsinki
Location Kuopio, Finland
History Steamer built to carry
passengers on the Finnish lakes.
Currently preserved in operating
condition as a private yacht based at
Kuopio.
Bibliography B16

Saimaa
steam inspection vessel

Built 1893 by Crichton-Vulcan, Turku,
Finland
Original owners Board of Navigation
Propulsion Steam, screw, 180hp
Tonnage 71.23 gross
Length 81.02ft/24.7m
Breadth 17.71ft/5.4m
Draught 4.9ft/1.48m
Materials Steel throughout
Original use Inspection vessel

Salama

Condition In operation
Present owners Finnish Board of
Navigation
Location Savonlinna, Finland
History Built as a steam inspection
vessel for use on Finland's lakes and
inland waterways. Still in service based
at Savonlinna.

Salama
passenger/cargo steamer

Built 1874 by Vyborg Workshop,
Vyborg, Finland
Propulsion Steam, screw, 39hp
Length 101.68ft/31.0m
Breadth 22.96ft/7.0m
Materials Iron hull, wood deckhouse
Original use Passengers and cargo
Condition Intact
Present owners Navigational Society of
Savonlinna
Location Savonlinna, Finland
History Steamer built to operate
between the Finnish lakes and Lubeck,
Germany, through the Saimaa Canal.
Sunk in collision in the lakes in 1989 in
30m of water. Raised virtually intact in
1971, refurbished and placed on exhibit
afloat at Savonlinna.
Bibliography A16, B16, D433

Savonlinna
lake steamer

Former name SUUR-SAIMAA
Built 1904 by Paul Wahl & Co, Varkaus,
Finland
Original owners Saimaan Laivamaktat
Propulsion Steam, 2-cylinder, oil fired,
200hp
Tonnage 169 gross
Length 91.51ft/27.9m
Breadth 21.98ft/6.7m
Draught 8.0ft/2.44m
Materials Steel throughout
Original use Passengers
Condition Intact
Present owners City of Savonlinna
Location Savonlinna, Finland
History Retired Finnish lake steamer
preserved as a floating exhibit.

Sigyn
wooden trading barque

Built 1887 by Gamla Varvet,
Gothenburg, Sweden
Original owners A Landgrens,
Gothenburg
Propulsion Barque rig; later
barquentine rig
Tonnage 359 gross
Length 139.42ft/42.5m

Breadth 30.5ft/9.3m
Draught 13.0ft/3.96m
Materials Wood throughout
Original use Cargo
Condition Fully restored
Present owners Maritime Museum at
Abo Academy
Location Abo, Finland
History A century ago small wooden
barques were a common sight on every
ocean. Today SIGYN is the only
merchant vessel of this type surviving
in a restored state. She traded almost
entirely within the Atlantic Ocean
visiting such ports as Cape Town,
Buenos Aires and Galveston, Texas. She
visited Asia just once, rounding the
Cape of Good Hope and crossing the
Indian Ocean to Bangkok, Siam. In
1914 she was reduced in rig to a
barquentine. For the remainder of her
active career she remained in the Baltic
and North Sea trade. In 1927 SIGYN
became a Finnish vessel owned in the
Swedish-speaking Åland Islands. Soon
after its founding in 1936 the Maritime
Museum of the Åbo Akademi on the
mainland of Finland began to consider
acquiring a sailing vessel. Funds were
raised to purchase SIGYN and she was
towed to Abo in June 1939. During the
Second World War and for many years

Sigyn

afterwards the Museum was barely able to maintain the ship. In 1971 a full-scale restoration programme was finally initiated. By 1979 she had been returned to her original barque rig. Today SIGYN conveys much the appearance she would have had when in active service prior to 1914. Aside from being the only surviving merchant barque, she has a number of interesting features found on no other preserved sailing vessel, including large carved timber knees supporting the overhang of the deckhouse roof, and a windmill with furling canvas sails to operate the bilge pumps. In the early years of this century Scandinavian wooden sailing vessels were known as 'onkers', apparently because of the noise made by this type of windmill pump. Fully restored as a floating exhibit.
Bibliography A14, C52, D210, D405

Sunnan II
passenger steamer

Former name IMATRA II, LOUHEVESI, LAPPEENRANTA
Built 1906 Varkaus, Finland
Original owners Saimaan Hoyrylaiva Osakeyhho
Propulsion Steam, 2-cylinder, wood fired; converted to diesel

Tonnage 150 gross
Length 82.67ft/25.2m
Breadth 21.33ft/6.5m
Draught 7.83ft/2.39m
Materials Steel throughout
Original use Passengers
Condition In operation
Present owners Imatran Hoyrylaiva Osakehtio
Location Imatra, Finland
History Passenger steamer converted to diesel and still in operation.

Suomen Joutsen
steel full rigged ship

Former name LAENNEC, OLDENBURG
Built 1902 by Chantiers et Ateliers de St Nazaire, St Nazaire, France
Original owners Société des Armateurs Nantais
Propulsion Ship rig
Tonnage 2260 gross
Length 262.5ft/80.01m
Breadth 40.33ft/12.29m
Draught 17.0ft/5.18m
Materials Steel throughout
Original use Cargo
Condition Intact
Present owners Merchant Navy Seamen's School
Location Abo, Finland
History Last surviving French-built sailing vessel designed for worldwide trading. An example of the 'bounty ships' built under generous government subsidies. Later converted to a German cargo-carrying training ship, and sail training ship for the Finnish Navy, and finally a stationary training ship for the Finnish merchant marine. Now maintained as a floating restaurant and exhibit.
Bibliography A14, C52, C96, D300

Suomi
passenger steamer

Built 1905 by Lehtoniemi & Taipale, Joroinen, Finland
Propulsion Steam, screw, 200hp
Tonnage 239 gross
Length 104.07ft/31.73m
Breadth 21.98ft/6.7m
Draught 8.3ft/2.53m
Materials Steel throughout
Original use Passengers
Condition In operation
Present owners Paijanneristeilijat Hilden
Location Jyvaskyla, Finland
History Steamer built to carry passengers on the Finnish lakes, still in service making excursions out of Jyvaskyla during the summer months.

Suomen Joutsen

Tarjanne

Suur-Saimaa
passenger steamer

Former name KALLAVESI, PUIJO,
IMATRA, SINIKOLMIO, PUNKAJARJU
Built 1907 by Paul Wahl & Co,
Varkhaus, Finland
Propulsion Steam, screw, 135hp
Tonnage 148 gross
Length 90.53ft/27.6m
Breadth 21.32ft/6.5m
Draught 7.22ft/2.2m
Materials Steel throughout
Original use Passengers
Condition Intact, in operation
Present owners Kuopian-Roll-Risteilyt
Location Savonlinna, Finland
History Steamer built to carry
passengers on the Finnish lakes. Until
recently was making excursions out of
Kuopio under the name PUIJO. Now
serving as a floating restaurant at
Savonlinna.
Bibliography B16

Suvi-Saimaa
passenger steamer

Former name KALLAVESI, KUOPIO,
HEINAVESI II
Built 1907 by Paul Wahl & Co, Varkaus,
Finland
Propulsion Steam, screw, compound,
150hp
Tonnage 149 gross
Length 87.58ft/26.7m

Breadth 21.65ft/6.6m
Draught 6.9ft/2.1m
Materials Steel throughout
Original use Passengers
Condition In operation
Present owners Lapeenrannan Laivat
Oy
Location Lapeenranta, Finland
History Steamer built to carry
passengers on the Finnish lakes, still in
service making excursions out of
Lapeenranta during the summer
months.
Bibliography B16

Taimi III
passenger steamer

Former name PUNKAHARJU, KERTTU,
OSUUSKUNTA I
Built 1905 by Emil Kiiveri, Savonlinna,
Finland
Propulsion Steam, screw, 142hp
Tonnage 74 gross
Length 73.8ft/22.5m
Breadth 16.24ft/4.95m
Draught 6.56ft/2.0m
Materials Steel throughout
Original use Passengers
Condition In operation
Present owners Martti Sieranta,
Jarvenpaa
Location Joensu, Finland
History Small two-decked passenger
steamer built for operation on the
Finnish lakes. Still in service making

excursions out of Joensu during the
summer months.

Tapio
steam tug

Former name AKKAS
Built 1904 at Viiala, Finland
Propulsion Steam, screw, 87hp
Length 60.7ft/18.5m
Breadth 12.8ft/3.9m
Draught 4.9ft/1.5m
Materials Steel throughout
Original use Tug
Condition In operating condition
Present owners Lisveden Metsa Oy,

Suonenjoki
Location Keitele, Finland
History Steam tug formerly employed
on the Finnish lakes. Maintained in
operating condition by members of the
Finnish Steamer Yachting Association.

Tarjanne
passenger steamer

Built 1908 by Lehtoniemi & Taipale,
Joroinen, Finland
Propulsion Steam, screw, triple-
expansion, 300hp
Tonnage 133 gross
Length 96.76ft/29.5m
Breadth 20.34ft/6.2m
Draught 7.38ft/2.25m
Materials Steel throughout
Original use Passengers
Condition In operation
Present owners Runoilijan Tie Oy
Location Tampere, Finland
History Steamer built to carry
passengers on the Finnish lakes
between Tampere and Virrat. Still in
active service during the summer
months. Converted to oil fuel in 1954.
Bibliography B16

Tarmo
icebreaker

Former name APU
Built 1907 by Armstrong, Whitworth &
Co, Newcastle, England
Original owners Board of Navigation
Propulsion Steam, screw, 3850hp
Tonnage 1562.47 gross
Length 219.96ft/67.07m
Breadth 47.03ft/14.34m
Draught 17.88ft/5.45m
Materials Steel throughout
Original use Icebreaker
Condition Intact

Tarmo

Present owners Hylkysaari Maritime Museum
Location Helsinki, Finland
History Former Finnish icebreaker maintained as a floating exhibit at a maritime museum on an island off the City of Helsinki.

Tippa
steam tug

Former name REPOLA 3, STOR-KLAS
Built 1892 in Sweden
Propulsion Steam, screw, 70hp
Length 56.1ft/17.1m
Breadth 12.4ft/3.77m
Draught 6.9ft/2.1m
Materials Steel throughout
Original use Tug
Condition In operating condition
Present owners Arja and Kauko Ylasaari, Kuopio
Location Lake Saimaa, Finland
History Steam tug formerly employed on the Finnish Lakes. Maintained in operating condition by members of the Finnish Steamer Yachting Association.

Toimi
steam launch

Built 1898 by J D Stenberg & Co, Helsinki, Finland
Propulsion Steam, screw, compound, 57hp
Tonnage 26 gross
Length 51.0ft/15.55m
Breadth 10.82ft/3.3m
Materials Steel throughout
Original use Passengers
Condition In operating condition
Present owners Eero Puranen, Mikkeli, Finland
Location Lake Paijanne, Finland
History Small Finnish steam launch with enclosed cabin built to carry passengers. Currently maintained in operating condition as a private yacht based on Lake Paijanne.

Toimi II
steam tug

Built 1904 by Lehtoniemi & Taipale, Joroinen, Finland
Propulsion Steam, screw
Length 64.4ft/19.62m
Breadth 14.4ft/4.38m
Draught 5.9ft/1.8m
Materials Steel throughout
Original use Tug
Condition In operating condition
Location Lake Saimaa, Finland
History Steam tug formerly employed on the Finnish lakes. Maintained in

operating condition by members of the Finnish Steamer Yachting Association.

Tommi
steam tug

Former name TID 35
Built 1943 by Richard Dunston Ltd, Thorne, England
Original owners British Ministry of Transport
Propulsion Steam, screw, 205hp
Length 70.4ft/21.46m
Breadth 17.4ft/5.3m
Draught 6.9ft/2.1m
Materials Steel throughout
Original use Tug
Condition In operating condition
Present owners Jouko and Aila Kurppa
Location Vantaa, Finland
History One of a series of tugs built in Great Britain during the Second World War. Later employed in Finland. Maintained in operating condition by members of the Finnish Steamer Yachting Association.

Uitto 6
steam tug

Former name ALKU
Built 1899 Oulu, Finland
Propulsion Steam, screw
Length 49.2ft/15.0m
Breadth 11.81ft/3.6m
Materials Steel hull
Original use Tug
Condition Intact
Present owners Forestry Museum of Lapland
Location Rovaniemi, Finland
History Built for use as a timber warping tug on a lake in northern Finland. Preserved as an onshore exhibit in Rovaniemi.

Ukko-Pekka
lighthouse tender/inspection vessel

Former name HAMINA, TURKU
Built 1938 by Wartsila, Helsinki, Finland
Original owners Finnish Government
Propulsion Steam, screw, triple expansion
Tonnage 287 gross
Length 115.1ft/35.1m
Breadth 24.1ft/7.35m
Draught 11.8ft/3.6m
Materials Steel throughout
Original use Lighthouse tender, inspection
Condition In operation
Present owners Hoyrylaivaosakeyhtio SS Ukkopekka

Location Turku, Finland
History Former government lighthouse tender and inspection vessel. Converted to carry excursion passengers on daily cruises in the Turku archipelago in southwestern Finland.

Utra
steam tug

Former name LOYTO II
Built 1925 at Raahe, Finland
Propulsion Steam, screw, 108hp
Length 49.86ft/15.2m
Breadth 14.43ft/4.4m
Materials Steel hull
Original use Tug
Condition Intact
Present owners Northern Karelian Float Transport Association
Location Utra, Finland
History Small steam tug built for use on the Finnish lakes. Preserved as an exhibit on shore at Utra, near Joensuu.

Uurastaja
steam tug

Former name KARL BOSTROM
Built 1908 by Paul Wahl & Co, Varkaus, Finland
Propulsion Steam, screw, 60hp
Length 65.2ft/19.87m
Breadth 15.7ft/4.78m
Draught 5.9ft/1.8m
Materials Steel throughout
Original use Tug
Condition In operating condition
Present owners Kaisa and Pertti Virtanen, Tikkakoshi
Location Keitele, Finland
History Steam tug formerly employed on the Finnish lakes. Maintained in operating condition by members of the Finnish Steamer Yachting Association.

Vaajakoski
steam tug

Former name HELLNAS
Built 1920 by A Ahlstrom Oy, Varkaus, Finland
Propulsion Steam, screw, 80hp
Length 46.9ft/14.3m
Breadth 13.0ft/3.95m
Draught 6.1ft/1.85m
Materials Steel throughout
Original use Tug
Condition In operating condition
Present owners Pekka Salonen, Muurame and Timo Fredrikson, Jyvaskyla
Location Paijanne, Finland
History Steam tug formerly employed

on the Finnish lakes. Maintained in operating condition by members of the Finnish Steamer Yachting Association.

Vänni
steam tug

Former name SVEN
Built 1901 by Borga Mekaniska Verkstad, Porvoo, Finland
Propulsion Steam, screw, 83hp
Length 60.4ft/18.39m
Breadth 12.8ft/3.9m
Draught 6.6ft/2.0m
Materials Steel throughout
Original use Tug
Condition In operating condition
Present owners Arto Juva, Vaaksy
Location Paijanne, Finland
History Steam tug formerly employed on the Finnish lakes. Maintained in operating condition by a member of the Finnish Steamer Yachting Association.

Vega
trading barquentine

Built 1948 at Abo, Finland
Original owners Soviet Ministry of Mercantile Marine
Propulsion Sail, barquentine rig; diesel engine
Tonnage 322 gross
Length 129.0ft/39.32m
Breadth 29.0ft/8.84m
Draught 9.15ft/2.79m
Materials Wood throughout
Original use Cargo; later sail training
Condition Intact, in sailing condition
Present owners City of Jakobstad
Location Jakobstad, Finland
History One of a large series of wooden sailing vessels built in Finland in the late 1940s as Second World War reparations payments to Russia. Last based at Talinn, Estonia, where she was owned by the Estonian Maritime Museum. Has now been returned to Finland to be based at the City of Jakobstad.

Vesikko
submarine

Former name CV-707
Built 1933 by A/B Chrichton Vulkan, Abo, Finland
Original owners Finnish Navy
Propulsion Diesel engines, 700hp
Length 134.17ft/40.90m
Breadth 13.0ft/3.96m
Draught 13.5ft/4.11m
Materials Steel throughout
Original use Submarine

Wenno

Condition Intact
Present owners Solamuseo
Contact address 1 00170 Helsinki 17,
Finland
Location Suomenlinna, nr Helsinki,
Finland
History Last surviving Finnish
submarine of the Second World War
period. Preserved on shore at the
former fortress and Naval base of
Suomenlinna on an island off Helsinki.
Bibliography A6, A16, C88

Vetäjä V
steam tug

Former name ILMARI, WIENTI
Built 1891 by Lehtoniemi, Joroinen,
Finland
Propulsion Steam, screw, 143hp
Length 70.68ft/21.55m
Breadth 16.24ft/4.95m
Materials Steel throughout
Original use Tug
Condition Intact
Present owners Town of Turku
Location Turku, Finland
History Small steam tug built to
operate on the Finnish lakes. Preserved
in operating condition as a floating
exhibit based at Turku.

Visuvesi
steam tug

Built 1890 by Tampereen Pellava-ja
Rautateollisuus Oy, Tampere, Finland
Propulsion Steam, screw, 91hp
Length 68.1ft/20.75m
Breadth 14.2ft/4.33m
Draught 7.0ft/2.14m
Materials Steel throughout
Original use Tug
Condition In operating condition
Present owners Seppo Hakli, Rainer

Kokemaki, Sauli Korhonen, Tampere
Location Nasijarvi, Finland
History Steam tug formerly employed
on the Finnish lakes. Maintained in
operating condition by members of the
Finnish Steamer Yachting Association.

VMV II
patrol boat

Built 1935 at Turku, Finland
Original owners Finnish Navy
Propulsion Diesel engines, 1220hp
Tonnage 33 displacement
Length 86.0ft/26.21m
Breadth 13.5ft/4.11m
Draught 3.15ft/0.96m
Materials Wood hull
Original use Patrol vessel
Condition Intact
Present owners Rajavartiolaitos
Location Santahamina, Finland
History Finnish armed patrol boat that
saw service in the Second World War.
Preserved as an exhibit and memorial
at Santahamina.

Warkaus
steam tug

Built 1910 by A Ahlstrom Oy, Varkaus,
Finland
Propulsion Steam, screw, 149hp
Length 65.6ft/20.0m
Breadth 14.8ft/4.5m
Draught 6.6ft/2.0m
Materials Steel throughout
Original use Tug
Condition In operating condition
Present owners Pauli and Jaakko
Lopponen, Mekkeli
Location Lake Saimaa, Finland
History Steam tug formerly employed
on the Finnish lakes. Maintained in
operating condition by members of

the Finnish Steamer Yachting
Association.

Warkaus VII
steam tug

Built 1913 by A Ahlstrom Oy, Varkaus,
Finland
Propulsion Steam, screw, 180hp
Length 69.83ft/21.29m
Breadth 16.24ft/4.95m
Materials Steel throughout
Original use Tug
Condition In operating condition
Present owners A Ahlstrom Osakeyhtio
Location Varkaus, Finland
History Steam tug built for operation
on the Finnish lakes. Preserved in
operating condition at Varkaus by the
firm that originally built it.

Wellamo
steam tug

Built 1907 by Oy Sommers af
Hallstrom & Waldens, Tampere,
Finland
Propulsion Steam, screw, 170hp
Length 70.1ft/21.18m
Breadth 15.0ft/4.53m
Draught 4.6ft/1.4m
Materials Steel throughout
Original use Tug
Condition In operating condition
Present owners Osmo Norvasto,
Tampere
Location Vanajavesi, Finland
History Steam tug formerly employed
on the Finnish lakes. Maintained in
operating condition by a member of
the Finnish Steamer Yachting
Association.

Wenno
cargo steamer

Former name VETEHINEN
Built 1907 by Savonlinna Workshop,
Savonlinna, Finland
Original owners Enzo-Gutzeit Co
Propulsion Steam, screw, 96hp
Tonnage 167 gross
Length 101.02ft/30.8m
Breadth 21.98ft/6.7m
Materials Steel throughout
Original use Cargo
Condition Intact
Present owners Town of Puumula
Location Puumula, Finland
History Cargo steamer built to carry
timber on the Finnish lakes. Preserved
in operating condition, a floating
musuem, as the last steel-hulled vessel
of her type.
Bibliography B16

Wipunen
steam tug

Built 1908 by Paul Wahl & Co, Varkaus,
Finland
Propulsion Steam, screw, 93hp
Length 59.04ft/18.0m
Breadth 13.12ft/4.0m
Materials Steel throughout
Original use Tug
Condition In operating condition
Present owners Oy Gust Ranin
Location Kuopio, Finland
History Steam tug built to operate on
the Finnish lakes. Maintained in
operating condition as a private yacht
based at Kuopio.

Yhtiö
steam tug

Built 1878 by Paul Wahl & Co, Varkaus,
Finland
Propulsion Steam, screw, 41hp
Length 50.2ft/15.3m
Breadth 10.7ft/3.25m
Draught 4.8ft/1.45m
Materials Iron hull
Original use Tug
Condition In operating condition
Present owners Erkki Nieminen and
Juha Kytola, Jyvaskyla
Location Lake Saimaa, Finland
History Steam tug formerly employed
on the Finnish lakes. Maintained in
operating condition by members of the
Finnish Steamer Yachting Association.

Wipunen

France

Once one of the world's great maritime powers, with colonies scattered around the globe, France maintained a sizeable merchant marine and one of Europe's largest navies. Her deepwater sailing ship fleet prospered under a generous subsidy, or 'bounty,' into the early years of this century. The only surviving example of these ships is the ex-LAENNEC now located in Finland as the SUOMEN JOUTSEN. France herself has the bark BELEM, now restored to sailing condition, which was built for trading in the Atlantic. The once-numerous French codfishing fleet, built to work the Grand Banks off Newfoundland, is also represented by one survivor, the ex-COMMANDANT LOUIS RICHARD which is now the Italian training barkentine PALINURO. The French Atlantic coast is dotted with small harbours that once sent to sea fleets of sailing craft to fish and transport local cargoes. By the time interest in this heritage took hold in the 1980s the last survivals tended to be decaying wooden hulls in nearby marine graveyards. The majority have now been re-created in the form of carefully-researched and skillfully-built sailing reproductions, beyond the scope of this register.

Alose
submarine

Built 1904 by Arsenal de Toulon, Toulon, France
Original owners French Navy
Propulsion Petrol engines and electric motors, 95hp
Tonnage 73.6 displacement
Length 78.0ft/23.77m
Breadth 7.5ft/2.28m
Draught 8.5ft/2.59m
Materials Steel throughout
Original use Submarine
Condition Intact
Present owners Comex Co
Location Marseilles, France
History Early French submarine sunk as a target in 1918. Preserved as an exhibit on shore at the Comex plant.
Bibliography A6

Anna Rosa
trading sloop

Built 1892 in Norway
Propulsion Sloop rig; 'hardanger Jagt'
Length 71.5ft/21.8m
Materials Wood throughout
Original use Cargo
Condition Restored to sailing condition
Present owners Port-Musée, Douarnenez
Location Douarnenez, France
History One of last survivors of a type of Norwegian sloop once used to bring bait to Brittany. Now preserved in France as a restored sailing vessel and exhibit.

Ardeche
steam towboat

Built Date unknown
Propulsion Steam, screw
Original use Tug
Condition Largely intact, beached on the riverbank
Present owners L'Association des Amis de la Batellerie du Rhone
Location France
History Steam chain-hauled towboat formerly used on the river. Currently lying abandoned. Has for a number of years been the focus of preservation efforts, thus far unsuccessful.

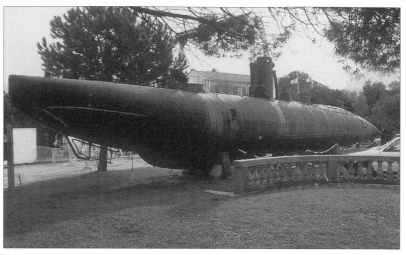

Alose

Argonaute
submarine

Built 1957 by Arsenal de Cherbourg, Cherbourg, France
Original owners French Navy
Propulsion Diesel and electric motors, 1300hp
Tonnage 543 displacement
Length 163.0ft/49.68m
Breadth 19.0ft/5.79m
Draught 13.0ft/3.96m
Materials Steel throughout
Original use Submarine
Condition Intact
Present owners Association des Amis du Musée de la Mer
Location La Villette, nr Paris, France
History French ARÈTHUSE class submarine of the 1950s preserved on shore in a suburb of Paris and open to the public.
Bibliography D128

Avel
sailing yacht

Built 1896 by Camper & Nicholson, Gosport, England. Designed by Charles Nicholson
Original owners René Calame, Nantes, France

Argonaute

Belem

Propulsion Sail, cutter rig
Length 60.0ft/18.17m
Breadth 11.4ft/3.46m
Draught 8.6ft/2.61m
Materials Wood throughout
Original use Yacht
Condition Fully restored to sailing
condition
Location Nantes, France
History Sailing yacht of the late-
Victorian era produced by leading
British designers and builders. Built for
a French owner and still sailing as a
yacht under the French flag after her
latest rebuilding.
Bibliography D89

bateau lavoir (floating public laundry)

Built at Nantes, France
Propulsion Stationary
Length 53.0ft/16.0m
Breadth 16.4ft/5.0m
Draught 1.3ft/0.4m
Materials Iron hull
Condition Intact
Location Nantes, France
History Barge moored in the centre of
a town to which residents could bring
their laundry and wash it using the
river water. Survives intact with
interior converted to a home.
Bibliography D402

bateau lavoir (floating public laundry)

Built c1909 at Laval, France
Propulsion Stationary
Length 72.2ft/22.0m
Breadth 16.7ft/5.1m
Original use Floating laundry
Condition Fully restored, open to
public
Present owners City of Laval
Location Laval, France
History Barge moored in the centre of
a town to which people could bring
their laundry and wash it using the
river water. Fully restored as a historic
exhibit in connection with the local
historical museum.
Bibliography D306

Belem
trading barque

Former name FANTOME II, GIORGIO CINI
Built 1896 by A Dubigeon, Nantes,
France
Original owners Denis Crouan & Co
Propulsion Barque rig; diesel engine
added
Tonnage 562 gross

La Belle Poule

Calypso
racing yacht

Built 1911 by Chantier Guedon, Lormont, France
Original owners Pictet de Rochemont
Propulsion Sail
Tonnage 3.0 displacement
Length 41.33ft/12.6m
Breadth 7.87ft/2.4m
Draught 5.0ft/1.53m
Materials Wood throughout
Original use Yacht
Present owners Amerami
Contact address Palais de Chaillot, 75116 Paris
Location Dives-sur-Mer, Normandy, France
History One of the famous Godinet racing yachts of Lake Leman, now exhibited at a maritime museum in Normandy.

canal tug

Built 1912 in France
Original owners Canal de la Marne |au Rhin
Propulsion Electric motors, hauled by chain
Materials Steel throughout

Original use Canal tug used in tunnel
Condition In operation
Present owners Canal de la Marne au Rhin
Location Mauvages, France
History Chain-hauled tug used to tow canal boats through a tunnel. Still in use near the village of Mauvages.

Canot Imperial
ceremonial barge

Built 1811 in France
Original owners Emperor Napoleon I
Propulsion Rowed
Length 56.45ft/17.21m
Breadth 10.99ft/3.35m
Materials Wood throughout
Original use Imperial barge
Condition On exhibit
Present owners Musée de la Marine
Location Paris, France
History Very ornate ceremonial barge built for Napoleon I. Later used by Napoleon III. Exhibited indoors as the centrepiece of the Musée de la Marine in Paris.
Bibliography C15

Calypso

Length 162.76ft/49.61m
Breadth 28.87ft/8.8m
Draught 11.48ft/3.5m
Materials Steel hull, steel & wood decks & spars
Original use Cargo
Condition Fully restored
Present owners Fondation Belem
Location France
History Built for the trade between France and Brazil. Later converted to a British yacht, and an Italian training vessel with barquentine rig. Eventually returned to France and restored to barque rig. Now serves as a sail training vessel.
Bibliography A15, C96, D200, 232, 365

Belle Etoile
fishing ketch

Built 1938 by Gourmelon Shipyard, Camaret, France
Propulsion Ketch rig
Length 60.0ft/18.3m
Materials Wood throughout
Original use Fishing (crayfish)
Condition Fully restored, in operation
Present owners Association Belle Etoile
Contact address Mairie, 29570 Camaret-Sur-Mer
Location Camaret-sur-Mer, France
History Former French ketch-rigged fishing vessel fully restored and currently making sailing excursions.

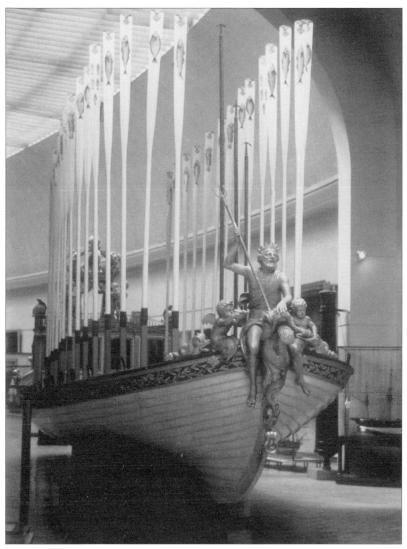

Canot Imperial

Cap Lizard
fishing sloop

Built 1924
Propulsion Sloop rig
Length 48.0ft/14.6m
Materials Wood throughout
Original use Crab fishing
Condition Undergoing restoration
Present owners Port-Musée,
Douarnenez
Location Douarnenez, France
History Last survivor of a fleet of
seventy crab fishing sloops once based
at Camaret. Undergoing restoration to
active sailing vessel and exhibit.

Clymene
racing yacht

Built 1924 by Camper & Nicholson,
Gosport, England
Original owners P de G Benson
Propulsion Sail, cutter rig; converted to
sloop
Tonnage 28 gross

Length 65.6ft/20.0m
Breadth 11.8ft/3.6m
Draught 8.86ft/2.7m
Materials Wood hull
Original use Yacht
Condition In sailing condition
Present owners Franck Pizzato
Location Bandol, France
History Classic 12-metre racing yacht
of the 1920s built by a leading British
yard. Maintained in sailing condition
by a private owner.

Colbert
cruiser

Built 1956 by Brest Navy Shipyard,
Brest, France
Original owners French Navy
Official number C 611
Propulsion Steam turbines 86,000shp
Tonnage 12,566 displacement
Length 593.0ft/180.8m
Breadth 65.0ft/20.2m
Draught 23.0ft/7.0m
Materials Steel throughout

Original use Cruiser
Condition Intact
Present owners French Navy
Contact address Face au 60, Quai des
Chartrons, 33000 Bordeaux, France
Location Bordeaux, France
History Cruiser built as an all-gun
vessel, but refitted with guided missiles
1970-72. After refit served as flagship of
the French Mediterranean fleet. Now a
museum.

D-6
steam-powered dredger

Built 1906 by Ateliers de Chantiers de
la Loire, Nantes, France
Propulsion Non-self-propelled, steam
dredging machinery
Tonnage 587 displacement
Length 140.38ft/42.3m
Breadth 32.54ft/9.92m

Draught 7.48ft/2.28m
Materials Steel throughout
Original use Dredger
Condition In operation
Present owners Port of La Rochelle
Location La Rochelle, France
History Last French steam-powered
'ladder' (or bucket) dredger. Converted
from coal to oil fuel in 1966. Recently
still in use in the port of La Rochelle,
but earmarked for preservation when
retired.
Bibliography B22

Déhel
pilot cutter

Built 1931 by Chantier Lacheray,
Honfleur, France
Propulsion Sail; auxiliary diesel engine,
13hp. Engine built by Bertliet
Tonnage 27 displacement

Clymene

Length 55.76ft/17.0m
Breadth 15.0ft/4.58m
Draught 6.26ft/1.91m
Materials Wood throughout
Original use Fishing
Present owners Amerami
Contact address Palais de Chaillot, Paris
Location Le Havre, France
History Typical Seine estuary pilot
cutter of the 1930s. Recently refitted at
Le Havre to serve as an exhibit afloat
and active sailing vessel.

Diadem
sailing yacht

Built 1907 by White Brothers, Itchen,
England. Designed by Fred Shepherd
Original owners M F B Wigfull
Propulsion Sail, yawl rig; later sloop rig
Length 79.0ft/21.0m
Breadth 13.8ft/4.2m
Materials Wood throughout
Original use Yacht
Condition Intact, in need of restoration
and rerigging
Present owners Yann Mauffret
Location Brest, France
History Yacht built in England early in
the century rigged as a yawl. Currently
stored indoors in France awaiting
restoration.
Bibliography D136

Dieu Protégé
sand barge

Built 1950
Length 72.2ft/22.0m
Original use Sand barge
Present owners Le Port Musée
Contact address Quai du Port-Rhu, BP
434, 29174 Douarnenez cedex
Location Douarnenez, France
History Example of a type of sand
barge employed in the coastal estuaries
of France. Preserved as an exhibit of
the maritime museum in Douarnenez.

Duchesse Anne
sail training vessel

Former name GROSSHERZOGIN
ELIZABETH
Built 1901 by J C Tecklenborg,
Geestemunde, Germany
Original owners Deutsche Schulschiff-
Verein
Propulsion Ship rig; auxiliary engine
Tonnage 1260 gross
Length 226.42ft/69.01m
Breadth 39.0ft/11.89m
Depth 20.67ft/6.3m
Materials Steel hull, steel & wood decks
& spars

Déhel

Original use Training ship
Condition Undergoing restoration to
sailing condition
Present owners Port of Dunquerque
Location Dunquerque, France
History Built as a training vessel for the
German merchant marine. Spent many
years as a hulk at the French Navy Yard
in Brest, but has now been restored
and rerigged at Dunkerque for an
eventual return to service as a sail
training vessel based at the Port.
Bibliography C26, C96, D298, D299,
D429

Dyck
lightship

Built 1935 by Forges et Chantiers de la

Méditeranée, Graville, France
Original owners French lighthouse
service
Propulsion Diesel-electric engines
Tonnage 500 displacement
Length 139.4ft/42.5m
Breadth 20.5ft/6.25m
Draught 15.74ft/4.8m
Materials Steel throughout
Original use Lightship
Condition Intact
Present owners City of Le Havre
Location Le Havre, France
History French lightship of the 1930s
maintained as a floating exhibit in the
Port of Le Havre.
Bibliography C78

Espadon
submarine

Built 1958 by A C Augustin-Normand,
France
Original owners French Navy
Propulsion Diesel and electric motors
Tonnage 1635 displacement
Length 257.0ft/78.33m
Breadth 26.0ft/7.9m
Draught 17.0ft/5.18m
Materials Steel throughout
Original use Submarine
Condition Intact
Present owners City of St Nazaire
Location St Nazaire, France
History French NARVAL class non-
nuclear submarine of the 1950s
maintained as a floating exhibit.

Etoile Molene
fishing ketch

Built 1954 by Auguste Tertu, Rostellec, France
Propulsion Ketch rig
Materials Wood throughout
Original use Fishing
Condition Fully restored, in operation
Present owners Etoile Marine SARL
Contact address 6 avenue Louis Martin, 35400 Saint-Malo
Location Saint-Malo, France
History French ketch-rigged fishing vessel fully restored and currently making sailing excursions.

France I
ocean weather ship

Built 1958 by Forges et Chantiers de la Méditeranée, Graville, France
Original owners French Government
Propulsion Diesel-electric engines, 932hp
Tonnage 1885.74 displacement
Length 249.61ft/76.1m
Breadth 41.16ft/12.55m
Draught 15.25ft/4.65m
Materials Steel throughout
Original use Weather ship
Condition Intact
Present owners Musée Maritime de La Rochelle
Location La Rochelle, France
History Weather ship and ocean station

France I

vessel employed by France for over thirty years. Serves as a floating exhibit at La Rochelle.
Bibliography D301

Havre II
lightship

Former name SANDETTIE II
Built 1912 at Graville, France
Original owners French lighthouse service
Propulsion Diesel engines
Tonnage 142 displacement
Length 131.2ft/40.0m
Breadth 21.91ft/6.68m
Materials Steel throughout
Original use Lightship
Condition Intact
Present owners City of Dunkirk
Location Dunkirk, France
History Lightship formerly stationed off the north coast of France. Preserved afloat as a headquarters for a small marina in an old basin of the Port of Dunkirk.
Bibliography C78

Hémérica
trawler

Built 1957 by Chantiers et Forges de l'Ouest, St Nazaire, France
Original owners Le Huede-Tonnerre, L'Orient
Official number CC4119
Propulsion Diesel engines
Tonnage 202 gross
Length 104.5ft/31.85m
Breadth 23.0ft/7.0m
Draught 11.5ft/3.51m
Materials Steel throughout
Original use Fishing
Condition Intact
Present owners Musée de la Peche, Concarneau

Hémérica

Location Concarneau, France
History Preserved as an example of a French trawler of the 1950s, prior to the use of stern ramps. Serves as a floating exhibit at the fisheries museum in Concarneau.
Bibliography B23, D297

Joble
Seine sailing barge

Former name ENFANT DE FRANCE
Built 1866 by Chantiers Pecquer, Petit-Quevilly
Original owners M Poncherot
Propulsion Sail, sloop rig; later converted to motor vessel
Length 65.6ft/20.0m
Breadth 21.32ft/6.5m
Materials Wood throughout
Original use Cargo
Present owners Parc Naturel Régional de Brotonne
Location Tancarville, France
History Oldest surviving sailing craft used to carry cargoes on the Seine River. Converted to a motor vessel in 1920. Currently preserved on shore at Tancarville.

La Belle Poule
sail training vessel

Built 1932 by Chantier Naval de Normandie, Fecamp, France
Original owners French Naval Academy
Propulsion Topsail schooner rig; diesel auxiliary engine
Tonnage 227 gross
Length 123.0ft/37.49m
Breadth 23.58ft/7.19m
Draught 11.83ft/3.61m
Materials Wood throughout
Original use Training ship
Condition In operation
Present owners French Naval Academy
Location Home port Brest, France
History Built as a sail training vessel for the French Navy, on the lines of a typical French coastal schooner. Still in active service.
Bibliography A10, A14, C25, C96, D165

La Leone
river sailing barge

Former name LA LORRAINE
Built 1903 by Prigent & Davais de Norkoise, Reze, near Nantes, France
Original owners Lajat & Henry de Nort-sur-Erdre
Propulsion Single square sail (river sailing barge)
Length 87.4ft/26.64m
Materials Steel throughout
Original use Cargo
Condition Fully restored, in sailing condition
Present owners Claude Rabet
Location Nantes, France
History Built as a barge that could be towed or sailed, for use on the rivers of

France. Has been restored to sailing condition based at Nantes.
Bibliography D307

LCA-1825
landing craft

Built 1944 in Great Britain
Original owners British Royal Navy
Official number LCA-1825
Propulsion Diesel engines
Tonnage 13 displacement
Length 41.25ft/12.65m
Materials Steel throughout
Original use Landing craft
Condition Intact
Present owners Military Museum, Arromanches
Location Arromanches, France
History Preserved on shore at Arromanches as an example of the type of landing craft used by British troops in the landings on the beaches of Normandy during the Second World War.

Lechalas
steam launch

Built 1913 by Blasse & Fils, Chantenay, France
Propulsion Steam, screw, compound
Length 55.1ft/16.78m
Breadth 12.7ft/3.88m
Draught 5.0ft/1.53m
Materials Steel hull, wood pilothouse

and cabin
Original use River steam launch
Condition In operating condition
Location Nantes, France
History Small steam launch with enclosed cabin formerly employed on the river at Nantes. Fully restored to serve as a floating exhibit and active steamer.
Bibliography D367

Les Deux Frères
Gironde sailing barge

Built 1892 on the Gironde River, France
Propulsion Sail, sloop rig
Tonnage 30 gross
Materials Wood throughout
Original use Cargo
Condition Fully restored to sailing condition in 1994
Location Bordeaux, France
History Built to carry cargo under sail on the Gironde River. Fully restored to sailing condition as a floating exhibit and active vessel.
Bibliography D338

L'Etoile
sail training vessel

Built 1932 by Chantier Naval de Normandie, Fecamp, France
Original owners French Naval Academy
Propulsion Topsail schooner rig; diesel auxiliary engine
Tonnage 227 gross
Length 123.0ft/37.49m
Breadth 23.58ft/7.19m
Draught 11.83ft/3.61m
Materials Wood throughout
Original use Training ship
Condition In operation
Present owners French Naval Academy
Location Home port Brest, France
History Built as a sailing training vessel for the French Navy on the lines of a typical Franch coastal schooner. Still in active service.
Bibliography A10, A14, C25, C96, D165

Lydia
passenger vessel

Former name MOONTA
Built 1931 by Burmeister & Wain, Copenhagen, Denmark
Original owners Adelaide Steamship Co
Propulsion Diesel engines, 2200hp
Tonnage 2696 gross
Length 298.33ft/90.93m
Breadth 43.67ft/13.31m
Draught 25.25ft/7.7m
Materials Steel throughout

Maillé-Brézé arriving at Nantes, June 1988

Marseillois

Original use Passsengers
Condition Intact
Present owners Société d'Economie
Mixte 'Semeta'
Location Barcares, France
History Small passenger vessel
originally based in Australia. Beached
at Barcares in 1967 to serve as a hotel
and amusement centre.

Maillé-Brézé
destroyer

Built 1954 by Arsenal de Lorient,
Lorient, France
Original owners French Navy
Official number D 627
Propulsion Steam turbines, 63,000hp
Tonnage 3900 displacement
Length 434.6ft/132.66m
Breadth 41.7ft/12.7m
Draught 21.4ft/5.8m
Materials Steel throughout
Original use Destroyer
Condition Intact
Present owners Nantes Marine
Tradition Association
Contact address Quai de la Fosse,
Nantes, BP 773, 44029 Cedex 04
Location Nantes, France
History One of a series of large *Surcouf*
class (T 47) destroyers built for the
French Navy in the 1950s. Preserved as

a floating museum and Naval
memorial.

Marie-Fernand
sailing pilot cutter

Built 1894 by Abel Lemarchand, Le
Havre, France
Original owners Eugene Prentout
Propulsion Sail, cutter rig
Tonnage 37.8 displacement
Length 52.2ft/15.9m
Breadth 14.0ft/4.25m
Draught 8.2ft/2.5m
Materials Wood throughout
Original use Pilot cutter
Condition Fully restored, in sailing
condition
Present owners Association Hirondelle
de la Manche
Contact address Hangar 22, Quai de
Norvege, 76600 Le Havre
Location Le Havre, France
History French sailing pilot vessel of
the late 19th century. Restored to
sailing condition by an organisation
based in Le Havre.
Bibliography D339

Marie-Therese
canal boat

Former name MARIA

Built 1855 at Toulouse, France
Propulsion Towed by horses; engine
installed in 1934
Tonnage 124 displacement
Length 84.0ft/25.6m
Breadth 17.4ft/5.3m
Materials Wood throughout
Original use Canal boat
Condition Hull was recently raised in
one piece
Location Sete, France
History Oldest surviving working
vessel in France. Was built for carrying
cargo on the Midi Canal. Later served
as a floating restaurant in Sete, where
she eventually sank. Recently raised for
restoration as an exhibit at a park or
museum to be created at a location on
the canal for which she was built.

Marseillois
trading schooner

Former name CALA VIRGILI, RAIDA DE
HUELVA, FARO BENICARLO
Built 1944 by Astilleros Atlantida,
Valencia, Spain
Propulsion Sail, schooner rig; diesel
engine; now barquentine rig
Tonnage 247 gross
Length 137.76ft/42.0m
Breadth 26.24ft/8.0m
Draught 13.12ft/4.0m

Materials Wood throughout
Original use Cargo
Condition Intact
Present owners ASCANFE 'Le
Marseillois'
Location Marseilles, France
History Schooner built to trade in the
Mediterranean under the Spanish flag.
Restored with barquentine rig as a
floating exhibit at Marseilles.

Merlandou
sailing river barge

Built 1904 by E Arnouil, Bergerac,
France
Original owners Pierre Berney, Mauzac
Propulsion Sail, single mast lug-rigged
Tonnage 9.5 displacement
Length 43.62ft/13.3m
Breadth 13.94ft/4.25m
Draught 4.26ft/1.3m
Materials Wood throughout
Original use Cargo
Condition In sailing condition
Present owners Société Nautique,
Mauzac
Location Mauzac, France
History Type of sailing craft formerly
used to carry sand and gravel on the
rivers of the Dordogne region. Petrol
engine installed in 1929. Recently
restored to original appearance and

sailing condition as a floating exhibit.
Bibliography D88

Mutin
sail training vessel

Built 1927 by Florimond-Guignardeau,
Sables d'Olonne, France
Original owners Pilotage School, Saint-
Servan, nr St Malo
Propulsion Sail, yawl rig; auxiliary
engine
Tonnage 57 displacement
Length 69.0ft/21.0m
Breadth 20.8ft/6.35m
Draught 11.2ft/3.4m
Materials Wood throughout
Original use Training
Condition In sailing condition
Present owners Group Écoles du
Poulmic
Location France
History Built on the lines of a typical
French sailing fishing vessel, but fitted
out as a training vessel for pilots. In
1968 was acquired by the French Navy,
who used her as a training vessel along
with the topsail schooners L'ÉTOILE
and LA BELLE POULE. Continues to
serve as a training vessel and a
travelling exhibit.

Nomadic
tender

Built 1911 by Harland & Wolff, Belfast,
Ireland
Original owners White Star Line
Propulsion Steam, screw, 4-cylinder
compound
Tonnage 1273 gross
Length 220.7ft/67.2m
Breadth 37.1ft/11.3m
Materials Steel throughout
Original use Tender for passenger liners
Condition Hull intact, superstructure
altered
Location Paris, France
History Currently inactive, used as a
floating restaurant.

Northdown
cargo sailing barge

Built 1924 by Anderson, Whitstable,
England
Original owners C Burley Ltd,
Sittingbourne
Propulsion Ketch rig; later spritsail yawl
Tonnage 86 gross
Materials Wood throughout
Original use Cargo
Condition Intact
Present owners Le Port Musée
Location Douarnenez, France

Ondee

History Built as a sailing barge to carry
cargoes on the rivers and estuaries of
eastern England. Currently a floating
exhibit in a French maritime museum.
Bibliography C74

Notre-Dame de Rumengol
coasting ketch

Built 1945 at Camaret, France
Propulsion Ketch rig
Length 94.0ft/28.5m
Materials Wood throughout
Original use Cargo
Condition Fully restored, in operation
Present owners Association an Test
Contact address Mairie, 29460
L'Hopital-Camfrout
Location L'Hopital-Camfrout, nr Brest,
France
History French ketch formerly
employed carrying cargo in the coastal
trades, now fully restored and
currently making sailing excursions.
Bibliography D309

Notre-Dame de Rocamadour
motor fishing vessel

Built 1959
Propulsion Motor vessel
Length 99.0ft/30.2m
Materials Wood hull
Original use Lobster fishing
Condition Intact
Present owners Le Port-Musée,
Douarnenez
Location Douarnenez, France
History Type of vessel once used in
lobster fishing off Mauretania,
preserved as a floating exhibit in a fleet
of former working craft at the museum
in Douarnenez.

Notre-Dame des Flots
fishing ketch

Built 1947 at Gravelines, France
Propulsion Sail, ketch rig; diesel engine
Length 67.0ft/20.4m
Materials Wood throughout

Original use Fishing
Condition In sailing condition
Present owners Jean-Pierre Despres and
associates
Location La Rochelle, France
History Currently used for charter.

Ondee
steam water-carrier

Built 1935 by Forges et Chantiers de la
Mediteranée, Le Havre, France
Original owners French Navy
Propulsion Steam, screw, triple
expansion, 300hp
Tonnage 437 gross
Length 123.66ft/37.7m
Materials Steel throughout
Original use Water boat
Condition Intact, in operating
condition
Present owners Francois Tremaud, Paris
Location France
History Steam vessel built to carry
fresh water at a French naval base. Last
steam-powered ship of the French
Navy when retired in the late 1980s.
Maintained in steaming condition as a
floating exhibit.
Bibliography D364

Pacifique
canal/river barge

Built 1931 in Belgium
Original owners Paul Penot
Propulsion Diesel engine
Materials Steel throughout
Original use Cargo, canal and river
barge
Condition In operating condition
Present owners Musée de la batellerie
de l'Ouest
Location France
History Exhibit and operating vessel.

Pasteur
steam river tug

Former name TURNU SEVERIN
Built 1913 at Linz, Austria-Hungary
Original owners Erste Donau-
Dampschiffahrts-Gesellschaft (DDSG)
Propulsion Steam, screw
Tonnage 279 gross
Length 125.0ft/38.07m
Breadth 21.4ft/6.52m
Draught 5.3ft/1.6m
Materials Steel throughout
Original use River towboat
Condition Intact
Present owners Amis du Musée régional
du Rhin
Contact address 11 rue de la Minoterie,
67000 Strasbourg

Pasteur

Location Strasbourg
History Steam river towboat built in Austria-Hungary. Maintained as a floating exhibit at the French river port of Strasbourg. Was operated by a French company after being awarded to that country as war reparations in 1919.
Bibliography D396

Pompon-Rouge
motorised cargo barge

Built 1949 at Tamise, Belgium
Propulsion Diesel engine
Length 126.4ft/38.5m
Breadth 16.7ft/5.1m
Materials Steel throughout
Original use Cargo; motor barge
Condition Intact
Present owners Musée Maritime de Rouen
Contact address Hangar 13, Quai Emile Duchemin, 76000 Rouen
Location Rouen, France
History Type of motorised cargo barge once common on the canals and inland waterways of France. Preserved as an exhibit at Rouen.
Bibliography D546

Princess Elizabeth
excursion steamer

Built 1927 by Day, Summers & Co, Southampton, England
Original owners Southampton, Isle of

Wight & South of England SP Co
Propulsion Steam, sidewheel, compound, 94hp
Tonnage 371 gross
Length 195.0ft/59.44m
Breadth 24.17ft/7.37m
Draught 8.0ft/2.44m
Materials Steel throughout
Original use Ferryboat
Condition Outwardly unaltered

Present owners Association de Défense des Arts Typographiques
Location Paris, France
History Built to operate as an excursion steamboat on the south coast of England, out of Bournemouth and Southampton. Took part in the rescue of British troops from the beaches of Dunkirk during the Second World War. Sold for scrap in 1967 but resold

for use as a floating restaurant in London, without engines. Sold to French owners in 1987 for use as a floating cultural centre and exhibit.
Bibliography B43

Principat de Catalunya
trading schooner

Former name LA LLEVANTINA, MIGUEL CALDENTAY
Built 1916 at Palma, Mallorca, Spain
Original owners Miguel Caldentay
Propulsion Sail, schooner rig
Length 80.85ft/24.65m
Materials Wood throughout
Original use Cargo
Condition Intact
Present owners Musée de la Voile Latine, Canet
Location Canet, France
History Schooner built to carry cargo in the Mediterranean under the Spanish flag. Served as a floating clubhouse in France, and is now part of a fleet of sailing craft exhibited afloat at Canet.
Bibliography B59

Racleur d'Ocean
motor fishing vessel

Built 1958 by Loussauarn a Treffiagat, France
Propulsion Diesel engine
Length 54.71ft/16.68m
Breadth 18.37ft/5.61m
Draught 9.5ft/2.9m

Racleur d'Ocean

Materials Wood throughout
Original use Fishing
Condition Intact
Present owners Musée de la Peche,
Concarneau
Location Concarneau, France
History Tunny fishing vessel retired in
1986. Exhibited as an example of the
type at the fisheries museum in
Concarneau.
Bibliography B23

S-622
midget submarine

Built c1945 in Germany
Original owners German Navy
Official number S 622
Propulsion Diesel engines
Tonnage 12.5 displacement
Length 39.69ft/12.1m
Breadth 4.26ft/1.3m
Draught 5.08ft/1.55m
Materials Steel throughout
Original use Midget submarine
Condition Intact
Present owners Musée de la Marine,
Brest
Location Brest, France
History German midget submarine
found in France at the end of the
Second World War. Used by the French
Navy for training after the war, and
now preserved as an onshore exhibit at
Brest.
Bibliography D544

Saint-Gilles
harbour tug

Built 1958 by Ateliers et Chantiers de La
Pallice, La Pallice, France
Original owners Union des
Remorquers de l'Ocean
Propulsion Diesel engines, 1000hp
Tonnage 188 gross
Length 88.6ft/27.01m
Breadth 24.66ft/7.52m
Draught 12.3ft/3.75m
Materials Steel throughout
Original use Tug
Condition Intact
Present owners Musée Maritime, La
Rochelle
Location La Rochelle, France
History French diesel harbour tug of
the 1950s preserved in operating
condition as a floating exhibit by the
maritime museum in La Rochelle.
Bibliography D543

Saint-Marc
hopper dredging vessel

Built 1931 by Forges et Ateliers de la

Méditeranée, Le Havre, France
Original owners Port of La Rochelle
Propulsion Diesel engine, 400hp
Tonnage 520 displacement
Length 140.38ft/42.8m
Breadth 30.18ft/9.2m
Draught 10.89ft/3.32m
Materials Steel throughout
Original use Hopper vessel for dredge
spoil
Condition In active service
Present owners La Rochelle Harbour
Authority
Location La Rochelle, France
History Hopper dredge used to dispose
of dredging spoil. Last used in
conjunction with the steam ladder
dredger *D6* (see above).
Bibliography B22

Sandettie
lightship

Former name DYCK
Built 1949 by Forges et Chantiers de la
Méditeranée, Graville, France
Original owners French lighthouse
service
Length 139.4ft/42.5m
Breadth 14.76ft/4.5m
Draught 8.69ft/2.65m
Materials Steel throughout
Original use Lightship
Condition Intact
Present owners City of Dunkirk
Location Dunkirk, France
History Last active French lightship,
retired around 1990. Preserved as a
floating museum in the harbour of
Dunkirk.
Bibliography C78

Scarweather
lightship

Built 1947 at Dartmouth, England
Original owners Trinity House
Propulsion None, towed to station
Materials Steel throughout
Original use Lightship
Condition Intact
Present owners Port Musée,
Douarnenez
Location Douarnenez, France
History British lightship formerly
stationed off Swansea on the south
coast of Wales. Acquired in 1991 for use
as a floating exhibit at Douarnenez.

ST-8
diesel tug

Former name USS ST-488
Built 1944 by J K Welding Co,
Brooklyn, New York, USA

Original owners United States Navy
Propulsion Diesel engine
Tonnage 190 displacement
Length 86.6ft/26.4m
Breadth 23.6ft/7.2m
Draught 8.7ft/2.64m
Materials Steel throughout
Original use Harbour tug
Condition Intact
Present owners Association
Remorqueur US ST-488
Contact address Musée Maritime et
Portuaire, hangar 22, 76600 Le Havre
Location Le Havre, France
History American harbour tug sent to
Europe to assist at the Normandy
landings. Exhibited afloat as a relic of
the Second World War.
Bibliography D340

St Denys
steam tug

Former name NORTHGATE SCOT
Built 1929 by William Beardmore & Co,
Glasgow, Scotland
Propulsion Steam, triple expansion
Tonnage 174 gross
Length 90.52ft/27.59m
Breadth 25.1ft/7.65m
Draught 14.0ft/4.27m
Materials Steel throughout
Original use Tug
Condition Intact
Present owners Le Port Musée
Location Douarnenez, France
History British steam harbour tug
retired in 1981. Originally acquired for
preservation afloat at Falmouth,
England. Now part of a fleet of
museum vessels at Douarnenez.

Zaca
sailing yacht

Built 1930 by Nunes Brothers,
Sausalito, California, USA
Original owners Templeton Crocker,
San Francisco
Propulsion Sail, schooner rig; diesel
auxiliary engine
Tonnage 122 gross
Length 118.0ft/35.97m
Breadth 23.75ft/7.24m
Draught 14.0ft/4.27m
Materials Wood throughout
Original use Yacht
Condition Undergoing restoration
Present owners Musée Naval et
Municipal de Balaquier, La Seyne
Location La Seyne, France
History Sailing yacht once owned by
the movie actor Errol Flynn. Recently
being restored to sailing condition.
Bibliography A1, D106

Germany

East and West Germany, products
of the Cold War, were finally
reunified in 1990 following the
collapse of the communist regime
in the former. Based on the
statistics, Germany has now
emerged as one of the most
active countries in the field of
maritime historic preservation.
Of the 400 plus vessels added to
this Register since the last
published edition, over 100 are
located in Germany. German
ports belonging to the 'Hanseatic
League' were very active in world
trade centuries before the first
unification of the country in
1871. In the decades before the
First World War, Germany
became the only country to
seriously challenge the then long-
standing maritime and naval
supremacy of Great Britain.
Germany was the last country to
build large sailing ships to carry
cargo. Surviving examples are the
PEKING in New York, the SEDOV
and KRUZENSHTERN sailing as
training ships under the Russian
flag, and the PASSAT preserved on
the Baltic coast of Germany.
German shipyards also launched
many of the surviving square-
rigged training vessels of the
world, with examples currently
under the flags of the United
States, Norway, Portugal,
Indonesia, R0mania, Yugoslavia,
and Germany herself. German
ship preservation not only
involves historic and traditional
seagoing and coastal craft, sail and
steam, but also many vessels of
the country's extensive network
of navigable internal waterways,
rivers, canals, and lakes. Dresden,
on the upper Elbe River, is home
to the world's largest fleet of
operating sidewheel excursion
steamers.

I Mai

dredger

Former name SWINEMUNDE
Built 1898 by Lubecker Maschinenbau-Gesellschaft, Lubeck, Germany
Tonnage 412 displacement
Length 154.3ft/47.0m
Breadth 29.8ft/9.08m
Materials Steel throughout
Original use Dredger
Condition Intact
Present owners Schiffahrtsmuseum der Hansestadt Rostock
Location Rostock, Germany
History Heavy lift salvage ship originally built as a dredger. Converted to a salvage vessel in 1946 to remove wrecks from The Second World War. Currently maintained as one of the floating exhibits of the maritime museum in Rostock.
Bibliography B13

925

torpedoboat

Built 1975 by VEB Peene-Werft, Wolgast, East Germany
Original owners East German Navy
Propulsion Diesel engines
Tonnage 28 displacement
Length 62.2ft/18.96m
Breadth 14.8ft/4.5m
Materials Light metal throughout
Original use Torpedoboat
Condition Intact
Present owners Wissenschaftliches Institut fur Schiffahrts
Contact address Elbchaussee 277, 22605 Hamburg
Location Hamburg, Germany
History Currently used as an onshore exhibit.

Absalon

sailing fishing boat

Built 1903 by I Poulsen, Frederiksund, Denmark
Propulsion Diesel engine, 80hp. Engine built by Volvo-Penta
Length 51.4ft/15.66m
Breadth 16.3ft/4.98m
Draught 5.4ft/1.65m
Original use Fishing
Condition Intact
Present owners Museumhafen Flensburg
Location Flensburg, Germany
History Danish sailing fishing boat with auxiliary engine preserved and exhibited in the German port of Flensburg near the Danish border.

Adolph Reichwein

motor fishing boat

Built 1949 by Boddenwerft, Damgarten, Germany
Original owners Fischerei Sassnitz
Official number SAS 95
Propulsion Diesel engines. Engine built by Buchau-Wolff
Tonnage 39 gross
Length 57.4ft/17.5m
Breadth 16.4ft/5.0m
Draught 7.54ft/2.3m
Original use Fishing
Condition Intact
Present owners Deutsche Museum fur Meereskunde und Fischerei
Location Stralsund, Germany
History Small German motor fishing boat of the 1940s preserved indoors as an exhibit on fishing technology.

Albatros

passenger/cargo steamer

Built 1912 by Jos L Meyer, Papenburg, Germany
Original owners Flensburg-Ekensunder DG
Propulsion Steam, compound, 260hp
Tonnage 214 gross
Length 119.87ft/36.54m
Breadth 20.3ft/6.19m
Draught 7.5ft/2.3m
Materials Steel hull, steel and wood superstructure
Original use Passengers, cargo
Condition Intact
Present owners Rettung uber See
Contact address 24531 Damp
Location Nr Ekenforde, Germany
History Passenger and cargo steamer that operated in the local coastal trade out of Flensburg for almost sixty years. Carried refugees out of East Prussia at the end of the Second World War. Served for a time as a floating restaurant and nightclub, and now preserved on shore at a holiday camp near Eckenforde.
Bibliography A17, B13, B16

Albatros

trading schooner

Former name ESTHER LOHSE, DAGMAR LARSEN, IRITHY
Built 1942 by K A Tommerup, Hobro, Denmark
Propulsion Sail, 3-masted topsail schooner; auxiliary diesel engine. Engine built by Alpha
Tonnage 109 gross
Length 117.2ft/35.7m
Breadth 22.6ft/6.9m

Alexandra

Draught 11.2ft/3.4m
Materials Wood throughout
Original use Cargo
Condition In operation
Present owners 'Clipper' Deutsches Jugendwerk zur See
Contact address Jurgensallee 54, 22609 Hamburg
Location Home port Bremerhaven, Germany
History Schooner built to carry cargo under the Danish flag. Currently operated as a youth training vessel by an organisation headquartered in Hamburg, Germany.
Bibliography B13

Alexandra

passenger/cargo steamer

Built 1908 by Janssen & Schmilsky, Hamburg, Germany
Original owners Flensburg-Ekensunder DG
Propulsion Steam, compound, 420hp
Tonnage 140.4 gross

Length 110.3ft/33.62m
Breadth 23.5ft/7.16m
Draught 8.53ft/2.3m
Materials Steel hull, steel and wood superstructure
Original use Passengers, cargo
Condition In operation
Present owners Forderverein Salondampfer Alexandra
Contact address Postfach 1616, 24944 Flensburg
Location Flensburg, Germany
History Last coastal passenger steamer active in Germany when retired in 1975. Ran between Flensburg, Germany, and Sonderburg, now in Denmark. Restored and returned to service as an excursion vessel in 1989.
Bibliography A17, B13, B16, B18

Amphitrite

schooner yacht

Former name DOLORES, JOY, HINEMOA
Built 1887 by Camper & Nicholson, Gosport, England

Original owners Colonel MacGregor
Propulsion Sail, 3-masted schooner rig;
diesel auxiliary. Engine built by
Mercedes
Tonnage 111 gross
Length 138.78ft/42.3m
Breadth 18.7ft/5.7m
Draught 12.14ft/3.7m
Materials Wood throughout
Original use Yacht
Condition In operation
Present owners Clipper-Deutsches
Jugendwerk zur See
Contact address Jurgensallee 54, 22609
Hamburg
Location Home port Bremerhaven,
Germany
History Large British sailing yacht of
the Victorian era. Acquired as a
training vessel in 1975 by a German
organisation patterned after the British
Outward Bound Trust. Maintained in
sailing condition based at Bremerhaven.
Bibliography A10, A15, B13, D285

Andreas
steam river tug

Built 1950 by Gebr Wiemann,
Brandenburg, Germany
Propulsion Steam, screw, triple
expansion, 224hp (1928 engine)
Tonnage 228 displacement
Length 115.5ft/35.18m
Breadth 22.7ft/6.93m
Draught 4.9ft/1.49m
Materials Steel throughout
Original use River towboat
Condition In operation
Present owners Berliner
Schiffahrtsgesellschaft
Location Berlin, Germany
History Steam towboat built for
operation on German rivers and
canals. Currently maintained in
operating condition as a floating
exhibit at Berlin.
Bibliography B13

Angela Von Barssel
Dutch tjalk

Former name ZELDENRUM, GEERTJE,
SANKT GEORG, KARL-HEINZ
Built 1896 by A Mulder, Stadskanaal,
Netherlands
Propulsion Sail, tjalk rig, diesel engine,
55hp
Tonnage 21 gross
Length 59.3ft/18.08m
Breadth 13.4ft/4.09m
Draught 2.6ft/0.8m
Original use Cargo
Present owners Verein 'Angela von
Barssel'

Contact address Hans Berkenbeger,
Marienstrasse 2, 26676 Barssel
Location Barssel, Germany
History Dutch sailing cargo vessel of
the 'tjalk' type formerly employed in
the coastal and inland trade. Preserved
as an exhibit in the harbour of Barssel.
Bibliography B13

Anna Von Amrum
coasting ketch

Built 1891 by D W Kremer Sohn,
Elmshorn, Germany
Propulsion Sail, ketch rig; diesel
auxiliary, 35hp
Tonnage 22 gross
Length 50.2ft/15.31m
Breadth 16.6ft/5.05m
Original use Cargo
Condition Intact
Present owners Pionierbataillon 1
Contact address Medem-Kaserne,
Bodenstrasse 9-11, 37603 Holzminden
Location Holzminden, Germany
History Ketch-rigged sailing vessel
designed to carry cargo in the
German coastal trades. Preserved
on shore as an exhibit at
Holzminden with complete rig
including sails.
Bibliography B13

Anna-Lisa Von Stade
coasting ketch

Former name MAHILDE
Built 1906 by J Junge, Wewelsfleth,
Germany
Propulsion Sail, ketch rig
Tonnage 41 gross
Materials Steel hull
Original use Cargo
Condition In operation
Present owners Municipality of Stade
Location Stade, Germany
History Ketch-rigged leeboard sailing
vessel built to carry cargo in the
German coastal trades. Maintained in
sailing condition based at Stade.
Bibliography B13

Astarte
sailing fishing vessel

Built 1903 by August Albers,
Finkenwerder, Germany
Official number HF 244
Propulsion Sail, ketch rig; diesel
auxiliary
Tonnage 34 gross
Length 94.5ft/28.8m
Breadth 19.9ft/6.05m
Draught 6.8ft/2.08m
Materials Wood throughout

Original use Fishing
Condition In operation
Present owners Schiffergilde
Bremerhaven
Contact address Van Ronzelen Str 2,
27568 Bremerhaven
Location Based at Bremerhaven,
Germany
History Sailing fishing vessel based at
Finkenwerder until 1919, and at
Schulau until retired in 1952. Used as a
research/training vessel until 1978.
Restored to original sailing rig at
Bremerhaven in 1979.
Bibliography B13

Atalanta
pilot schooner

Former name CUXHAVEN
Built 1901 by Junge, Wewelsfleth,
Germany
Original owners Cuxhavener
Uberseelotsen
Propulsion Sail, schooner rig
Tonnage 36 gross
Length 118.5ft/36.1m
Breadth 20.3ft/6.18m
Original use Pilot vessel
Condition In sailing condition
Present owners Forderverein Atalanta
Location Wismar, Germany

Andreas

August

History Sailing pilot vessel formerly stationed at Cuxhaven at the mouth of the Elbe River. Restored to sailing condition in the 1990s.
Bibliography B13

Atlas
steam dredger

Built 1876 by Gebr Schultze, Mainz, Germany
Propulsion Non self-propelled; steam dredging machinery
Length 73.8ft/22.5m
Breadth 16.6ft/5.05m
Draught 2.6ft/0.8m
Original use Dredger
Present owners Wasser-und Schiffahrtsamt
Contact address Bismarckstrasse 133, 66121 Saarbrucken
Location Volklingen-Wehrden, Germany
History Veteran steam dredger employed on the rivers and canals of Germany. Was still in use as recently as 1997. Currently exhibited.

August
steam tug

Built 1910 by Gebr Wiemann, Brandenburg, Germany
Original owners Otto Schoning, Haren
Propulsion Steam, screw; converted to diesel
Materials Steel hull, steel and wood superstructure
Original use Tug
Condition Intact
Present owners Town of Haren
Contact address Kanalstrasse, 49733 Haren
Location Haren, Germany

History Former steam tug with somewhat modernised superstructure and stack, preserved as a floating exhibit.

Aurora
sailing drifter

Built 1934 by Franz Goetz, Rugenwalde, Germany
Propulsion Sail, cutter rig; auxiliary engine, 20hp
Tonnage 14 gross

Length 60.7ft/18.5m
Breadth 14.8ft/4.5m
Draught 5.0ft/1.5m
Materials Wood throughout
Original use Fishing
Condition In sailing condition
Present owners Heidrun Stichting
Location Flensburg, Germany
History Cutter-rigged drift net fishing vessel formerly employed in the Baltic Sea. Maintained in sailing condition as a private yacht based at Flensburg.
Bibliography A10, B13

Bärbel-Marlies
inland sailing barge

Built 1914 at Mullrose, Germany
Propulsion Sail
Length 132.3ft/40.3m
Breadth 15.3ft/4.66m
Materials Steel throughout
Original use Cargo
Condition Fully restored, in sailing condition
Present owners Berliner Schiffahrtsgesellschaft
Location Berlin, Germany
History Type of cargo barge formerly common on the inland waterways of Germany. Fitted with a single mast and spritsail for operation on board bodies of water. Maintained as a floating exhibit and active sailing vessel.

Beckum
fast minesweeper

Built 1960 by Abeking & Rasmussen, Lemwerder, Germany
Original owners German Navy
Propulsion Diesel engines. Engine built by Maybach-Viertakt
Tonnage 266 displacement
Length 155.6ft/47.4m
Breadth 22.8ft/6.96m
Draught 7.1ft/2.15m
Original use Fast minesweeper
Condition Intact
Present owners Marinekamaradschaft Busum
Location Busum, Germany
History Unaltered fast minesweeper built for the German Navy, currently serving as a clubhouse in the harbour of Busum.
Bibliography B13

Bellis
fishing ketch

Former name VESTKYSTEN
Built 1924 by Karstensen & Henriksen, Slagen, Denmark
Propulsion Sail, ketch rig; diesel auxiliary engine. Engine built by Scania
Tonnage 30 gross
Length 77.1ft/23.5m

Beckum

Breadth 15.4ft/4.7m
Draught 6.6ft/2.0m
Original use Fishing
Condition In sailing condition
Present owners Rainer Pruss
Location Flensburg, Germany
History Former ketch-rigged fishing vessel built in Denmark and maintained in sailing condition as a German private yacht based at Flensburg.
Bibliography B13

Bielenberg
steam tug

Built 1928 by H C Stulcken Sohn, Hamburg, Germany
Propulsion Steam, screw, compound, 150hp
Length 68.88ft/21.0m
Breadth 18.1ft/5.5m
Draught 9.4ft/2.85m
Materials Steel throughout
Original use Tug
Condition Intact
Present owners Wilmsen
Contact address Duffelsmuble 34, 47546 Kalkar-Niedermormter
Location Kalkar, Germany
History Steam tug originally preserved by steam enthusiasts in the Netherlands in the 1970s. Later bought by a group in Honnepel, Germany, and now an exhibit on shore near Kalkar.
Bibliography B13

Bilgenentöler II
river motor vessel

Former name HELENE
Built 1932
Propulsion Diesel engines, 37hp
Tonnage 12 displacement
Length 55.8ft/17.0m
Breadth 8.2ft/2.5m
Condition Intact
Present owners Museum fur Deutschen Binnenschiffahrt
Contact address Dammstrasse 11, 47119 Duisburg
Location Duisburg, Germany
History Small motor vessel formerly employed on the Rhine River. Preserved as an exhibit of the Inland Shipping Museum in Duisburg.

Bill
motor tug

Built 1944
Propulsion Diesel engine, 75hp
Materials Steel throughout
Original use Tug
Condition Intact

Bielenberg

Present owners Niederrheinische Kies- und Sandbaggeri Gmbh
Location Rees-Haffen, Germany
History Small motor tug displayed in a plaza near the centre of the town of Rees-Haffen. Formerly used by a local dredging firm in handling its barges of dredged material.
Bibliography B13

Borkumriff
lightship

Built 1956 by Koser & Meyer, Hamburg, Germany
Original owners West German Lighthouse Service
Propulsion Diesel engines
Tonnage 629 gross
Length 176.2ft/53.7m
Breadth 29.5ft/9.0m
Draught 14.4ft/4.4m
Materials Steel throughout
Original use Lightship
Condition Intact
Present owners Forderverein Feuerschiff Borkumriff
Contact address Deichstrasse 9a, 26757 Borkum
Location Borkum, Germany
History German North Sea lightship of the 1950s retired in 1988. Currently a floating exhibit at the Island of Borkum.

Bibliography B13

Bracki
motor launch

Former name HAFEN-AMT BREMEN II, RICK I
Built 1912 by Hamburgische Staatswerft, Germany
Propulsion Diesel engine
Length 44.1ft/13.45m
Breadth 10.4ft/3.18m
Materials Steel throughout
Original use Launch
Condition In operating condition
Present owners Schiffergilde Bremerhaven
Location Bremerhaven, Germany
History Small motor launch with enclosed cabins employed by the City of Bremen, and later by the Rickmers Shipyard in Bremerhaven. Maintained in operating condition by the ship restoration guild of Bremerhaven.

Bussard
steam buoy tender

Built 1905 by Jos L Meyer, Papenburg, Germany
Original owners Wasser und Schiffahrtsamtes Ostzee
Propulsion Steam, screw, coal-fired
Tonnage 267 gross

Length 37.54m
Breadth 7.19m
Draught 3.29m
Materials Steel throughout
Original use Buoy tender
Condition Intact
Present owners Kieler Stadt und Schiffahrtsmuseum
Contact address Am Wall 65, 24103 Kiel
Location Kiel, Germany
History Largely unaltered steam buoy tender employed along the coast of Germany for seventy years. Preserved as a floating exhibit on the shorefront of Kiel.
Bibliography A16, B13

Camilla
sailing workboat

Built c1900
Length 18.0m
Breadth 4.2m
Draught 0.8m
Present owners Kreismuseum
Contact address Schlossstrasse 1, 41541 Dormagen
Location Zons/Dormagen, Germany
History Sailing workboat built around the turn of the century, preserved as an exhibit of the district museum in Dormagen.

Cap San Diego

cargo ship

Built 1962 by Deutsche Werft, Hamburg, Germany
Original owners Hamburg Sudamerik Dampfsch Ges
Propulsion Diesel engines, 11,650hp
Tonnage 9998 gross
Length 522.0ft/159.11m
Breadth 70.5ft/21.49m
Draught 27.75ft/8.46m
Materials Steel throughout
Original use Cargo ship
Condition Intact
Present owners Stifting Hamburger Admiralitat
Location Hamburg, Germany
History Classic example of a major German cargo ship of the final pre-containerisation era. Preserved as a floating museum in the centre of Hamburg's riverfront.
Bibliography B13, D41, D175, D189

Capella

concrete motor coaster

Built 1944 by Dyckerhoff & Widmann, Ostwine, Germany
Propulsion Diesel engine
Length 141.0ft/42.93m
Breadth 23.2ft/7.08m
Draught 9.2ft/2.8m
Materials Reinforced concrete hull
Original use Cargo

Capella

Cap San Diego

Condition Intact
Present owners Schiffahrtsmuseum der Hansestadt Rostock
Location Rostock, Germany
History Reinforced concrete vessel built to carry cargo in the German coastal or Baltic trades. Currently preserved as a floating exhibit of the maritime museum in Rostock.
Bibliography B13

Carmelan

fishing ketch

Former name KRISTIAN & ENE
Built 1927 by Hjorne & Jacobsen, Frederikshavn, Denmark
Propulsion Sail, ketch rig; auxiliary diesel engine, 106hp
Tonnage 34 gross
Length 83.7ft/25.5m
Breadth 15.8ft/4.8m
Draught 7.5ft/2.3m
Materials Wood throughout
Original use Fishing
Condition In sailing condition
Present owners Hagen Wcihe, Alt-Duvenstedt
Location Flensburg, Germany
History Danish ketch-rigged sailing fishing vessel of the 1920s maintained in sailing condition as a private yacht by German owners. Based at Flensburg during the summer months and at Rendsburg during the winter.
Bibliography B13

Catarina

fishing ewer

Built 1889 by Johann Brandt, Hamburg-Neuhof, Germany
Original owners Hans Rubcke, Altenwerder
Official number ALT 287
Propulsion Sail, ketch rig; auxiliary engine
Tonnage 13 gross
Length 52.82ft/16.1m
Breadth 17.22ft/5.25m
Draught 3.94ft/1.2m
Materials Wood throughout
Original use Fishing
Condition In sailing condition
Present owners Wolfgang Friedrichsen
Location Oevelgonne, nr Hamburg, Germany
History Built as a sailing fishing vessel of the type known as a 'fishing ewer'. Fully restored to sailing condition in 1977 and currently exhibited at Oevelgonne on the Elbe River, below Hamburg.

Cerberus

steam patrol boat

Former name HAVENPOLITIE I, HAVENDIENST IV
Built 1930 by W H Jacobs, Haarlem, Netherlands
Propulsion Steam, screw, 2-cylinder
Tonnage 121 displacement
Length 68.39ft/20.85m
Breadth 15.28ft/4.66m
Draught 7.5ft/2.3m
Materials Steel throughout
Original use Police steamer
Condition Intact
Present owners Westfälisches Industriemuseum
Location Dortmund, Germany
History Former steam police patrol boat built in the Netherlands and now preserved and exhibited in the large fleet of vessels maintained by the Westphalian Museum in Waltrop.

Charlotte

sailing fishing vessel

Former name MAIBO, C JENNET, OCEAN, KIRSTIN JUUL, ADDY
Built 1925 by Ove M Christensen, Glyngore/Limfjord
Propulsion Sail, cutter rig; diesel auxiliary engine, 80hp. Engine built by Mercedes-Benz
Tonnage 20 displacement
Length 57.8ft/17.6m
Breadth 12.1ft/3.7m
Draught 5.6ft/1.7m
Materials Wood throughout
Original use Fishing
Condition In sailing condition
Present owners Dieter Grote
Location Flensburg, Germany
History Cutter-rigged Scandinavian fishing vessel formerly employed in the North Sea and the entrance to the Baltic. Maintained in sailing condition as a German private yacht based at Flensburg.
Bibliography B13

Claus D

steam tug

Former name MOORFLEET, SCHULAU
Built 1913 by Janssen & Schmilinsky, Hamburg, Germany
Original owners J N H Heymann, Hamburg
Propulsion Steam, screw, compound, 220hp
Tonnage 46 gross
Length 58.25ft/17.76m
Breadth 17.22ft/5.25m
Draught 7.74ft/2.36m

Claus D

Materials Steel hull, steel and wood superstructure
Original use Tug
Condition In operating condition
Present owners Forderkreis 'Claus D', Hamburg
Location Oevelgonne, nr Hamburg, Germany
History Steam harbour tug formerly employed in the Port of Hamburg under several owners. Maintained in operating condition based in Oevelgonne on the Elbe River below the City of Hamburg.
Bibliography B13

Cogge of Bremen

sailing trading vessel

Built c1380
Propulsion Sail, single square sail
Tonnage 140 gross
Length 77.0ft/23.47m
Materials Wood throughout
Original use Cargo
Condition Intact
Present owners Deutsches Schiffahrtsmuseum
Location Bremerhaven, Germany
History Fourteenth-century trading vessel excavated from a river mudbank in 1962. Reassembled and treated for preservation indoors at the maritime museum in Bremerhaven.
Bibliography A8, D270, D291, D439

Crossen

steam grab dredger

Built 1928 by Caesar Wollheim, Breslau, Germany
Propulsion Non self-propelled; steam dredging machinery
Length 70.52ft/21.5m
Breadth 23.62ft/7.2m
Draught 2.62ft/0.8m
Materials Steel hull
Original use Dredge
Condition Intact
Present owners Westfälisches Industriemuseum
Location Waltrop, nr Dortmund, Germany
History Former steam-powered grab dredger preserved as an exhibit of the Westphalian Industrial Museum in Waltrop.

Daggi

motor fishing vessel

Former name FRIEDRICH DAWARTZ
Built 1956 by Schiffswerft Dawartz, Tonning, Germany
Official number BUS 6
Propulsion Diesel engine, 170hp. Engine built by Henschel
Tonnage 13 gross
Length 39.8ft/12.14m
Breadth 14.3ft/4.37m
Original use Fishing

Condition Intact
Present owners Nationalparkzentrum Wilhelmshaven
Location Wilhelmshaven, Germany
History Motor fishing vessel used in catching crabs or shrimp on the North Sea coast of Germany. Exhibited on shore at Wilhelmshaven.
Bibliography B13

Danube ferry scow

Built 1954 by Josef Kainz, Niederalteich, Germany
Length 51.4ft/15.65m
Breadth 14.3ft/4.37m
Materials Wood hull
Original use Vehicle ferry
Condition Intact
Present owners Deutsches Schiffahrtsmuseum
Location Bremerhaven, Germany
History Wooden scow used to ferry vehicles across the Danube River. Preserved as an exhibit on shore at the maritime museum in Bremerhaven.
Bibliography B13

Deutsche Bucht

lightship

Former name AMRUMBANK
Built 1914 by Jos L Meyer, Papenburg, Germany
Original owners State of Schleswig

Diesbar

Draught 2.4ft/0.74m
Materials Iron or steel hull
Original use Passengers
Condition In operating condition
Present owners Sachsische
Dampfschiffahrts
Contact address Hertha-Lindner-
Strasse 10, 01067 Dresden
Location Dresden, Germany
History German Elbe River passenger
steamboat in active service over a
century. Powered by rebuilt engines of
the PILLNITZ of 1857.
Bibliography B13, B16, B43

Diessen

sidewheel lake steamer

Built 1908 by Maffei, Munich, Germany
Propulsion Steam, sidewheel; converted
to diesel-hydraulic
Length 124.8ft/38.0m
Breadth 33.1ft/10.1m
Materials Steel throughout
Original use Passengers
Condition In operation
Present owners Staatliche Schiffahrt
Contact address 79252 Stegen
Location Greifenberg (Lake
Ammersee), Germany
History Sidewheel lake steamer
converted to diesel-hydraulic
propulsion in 1974 without exterior
alterations. Operates on the Ammersee
on weekends in the summer months.
Bibliography B13, B43

Diva

racing yacht

Built 1985 by Denninger & Melle,
Netherlands
Propulsion Sail
Length 43.6ft/13.27m
Breadth 14.3ft/4.35m
Draught 7.2ft/2.2m
Original use Racing yacht
Condition Intact
Present owners Deutsches
Schiffahrtsmuseum
Location Bremerhaven, Germany
History One of the most successful
German racing yachts, winner of the
Admiral's Cup in 1985. Now preserved
as one of the exhibits of the maritime
museum in Bremerhaven.
Bibliography B13

Dresden

sidewheel river steamer

Built 1926 by Werft Laubegast,
Dresden, Germany
Propulsion Steam, sidewheel, 296hp
Tonnage 416 displacement
Length 225.5ft/68.73m
Breadth 42.33ft/12.90m
Draught 3.67ft/1.12m
Materials Steel throughout
Original use Passengers
Condition In operation
Present owners Sachsische
Dampfschiffahrts Gmbh
Location Dresden, Germany
History Largely unaltered German Elbe

Lighthouse Service
Propulsion Steam, screw; converted to
diesel, 330hp
Tonnage 630 gross
Length 172.3ft/52.5m
Breadth 26.57ft/8.1m
Materials Steel throughout
Original use Lightship
Condition Intact
Present owners City of Emden
Location Emden, Germany
History Veteran German lightship
employed off the North Sea coast for
seventy years. Preserved as a floating
museum in the harbour of Emden.
Bibliography B13

Diesbar

sidewheel river steamer

Former name PILLNITZ
Built 1884 by Werft Blasewitz, Dresden,
Germany
Propulsion Steam, sidewheel, 120hp
Length 173.0ft/52.73m
Breadth 33.0ft/10.06m

Dresden

River steamboat in regular service on day excursions out of Dresden.
Bibliography B13, B16, B43

Ebenhaezer
cargo sailing vessel

Built 1908 at Leuwaarden, Germany
Propulsion Sail, tjalk rig
Length 85.3ft/26.0m
Breadth 13.8ft/4.3m
Draught 2.3ft/0.7m
Original use Cargo
Condition Intact
Present owners Fehn- und Schiffahrtsmuseum Westrbauderfehn
Location Rhauderfehn, Germany
History Sailing vessel built to carry cargoes in the Dutch coastal trade. Maintained in sailing condition as an exhibit and training vessel.

Ed 9
steam bucket dredger

Built 1926 by Oderwerken, Stettin, Germany
Propulsion Non self-propelled; steam dredging machinery
Length 159.74ft/48.7m
Breadth 31.16ft/9.5m
Draught 8.86ft/2.7m
Materials Steel throughout
Original use Dredger
Condition Intact
Present owners Town of Papenburg
Location Papenburg, Germany
History German steam ladder dredger.

Efforts to preserve may have been unsuccessful. Floating exhibit.

Elbe
steam icebreaker

Built 1911 by Gebr Wiemann, Brandenburg, Germany
Propulsion Steam, screw, triple expansion, 240hp
Length 29.5m
Breadth 7.45m
Draught 2.55m
Materials Steel hull
Original use River icebreaker
Condition Intact
Present owners Verein Alsterdampfschiffahrt
Contact address Dorotheenstrasse 9, 22301 Hamburg
Location Hamburg, Germany
History Steam icebreaker employed on the smaller navigable rivers or canals of Germany. Undergoing restoration to steaming condition at Hamburg.
Bibliography B13, D531

Elbe 1
lightship

Former name BURGERMEISTER O'SWALD
Built 1942 by Jos L Meyer, Papenburg, Germany
Original owners Wasser und Schiffahrtsdirektion
Propulsion Diesel engines, 505hp
Tonnage 641 gross

Length 160.72ft/49.0m
Breadth 31.16ft/9.5m
Draught 14.76ft/4.5m
Materials Steel throughout
Original use Lightship
Condition Intact
Present owners City of Cuxhaven
Location Cuxhaven, Germany
History Last active manned lightship in Germany, recently retired. Maintained as a floating exhibit at Cuxhaven.
Bibliography B13

Elbe 3
lightship

Former name WESER, BREMEN
Built 1888 by Werft Johann Lange, Grohn/Weser, Germany
Propulsion Non self-propelled; diesel engine added
Tonnage 255 gross
Length 147.93ft/45.1m
Breadth 23.29ft/7.1m
Draught 12.96ft/3.95m
Materials Steel hull
Original use Lightship
Condition Intact
Present owners Museumhafen Oevelgonne
Location Oevelgonne, nr Hamburg, Germany
History Veteran German lightship formerly employed off the North Sea coast. Currently maintained as a floating exhibit at Oevelgonne on the Elbe River below Hamburg.
Bibliography B13

Elbe 3
lightship

Former name BURGERMEISTER ABENDROTH
Built 1909 by Eiderwerft, Tonning, Germany
Original owners Wasser und Schiffahrtsdirektion
Propulsion Towed to station
Tonnage 450 gross
Length 144.36ft/44.0m
Breadth 22.97ft/7.0m
Draught 8.86ft/2.7m
Materials Steel throughout
Original use Lightship
Condition Fully restored
Present owners Deutsches Schiffahrtsmuseum
Location Bremerhaven, Germany
History German North Sea lightship in service for fifty-five years. Maintained as a floating exhibit in the fleet of vessels attached to the maritime museum in Bremerhaven.
Bibliography A16, B13

Elbe 27
motor patrol boat

Built 1959 by Ernst Menzer, Geesthacht, Germany
Original owners Hamburger Wasserschutzpolizei
Propulsion Diesel engine, 230hp
Length 60.0ft/18.17m
Breadth 12.8ft/3.9m
Draught 5.0ft/1.5m
Materials Steel throughout
Original use Police launch
Condition In operating condition
Present owners Museum fur Arbeit
Location Hamburg, Germany
History Police patrol boat formerly employed on the Elbe River at Hamburg. Also carries the name ALFRED WACHHOLZ. Preserved as a floating exhibit and operating vessel at Hamburg.
Bibliography B13

Elfriede
cargo sailing coaster

Built 1904 by J Jacobs, Moorrege, Germany
Propulsion Sail, cutter rig; diesel engine installed
Tonnage 27 gross
Length 49.2ft/15.0m
Breadth 15.6ft/4.75m
Materials Steel hull
Original use Cargo
Condition Fully restored, in sailing condition

Ed 9

Present owners Altonaer Museum, Norddeutsches Landesmuseum
Location Wischhafen, Germany
History Small sailing vessel built to carry cargo in the German coastal trades. Converted to a houseboat in 1963. Fully restored to sailing condition between 1984 and 1991, and now exhibited afloat at Altona on the Elbe River below Hamburg.
Bibliography B13

Else af Sletten
fishing cutter

Former name VIKING, ELKANA
Built 1923 at Bornholm, Denmark
Propulsion Sail, cutter rig; auxiliary engine
Length 42.7ft/13.0m
Breadth 12.5ft/3.8m
Draught 3.8ft/1.15m
Materials Wood throughout
Original use Fishing
Condition In sailing condition
Present owners Ingrid and Hans-Jorgen Illias
Location Flensburg, Germany
History Cutter-rigged herring fishing boat formerly based at the Island of Bornholm in the Baltic. Maintained in sailing condition as a German private yacht based at Flensburg.
Bibliography B13

Emden
fishing ketch

Former name OLD LADY, G M DANEKER
Built 1908 at Vlaardingen, Netherlands
Official number AE 7
Propulsion Sail, ketch rig; auxiliary engine
Length 78.9ft/24.02m
Breadth 21.2ft/6.46m
Materials Wood throughout
Original use Fishing
Condition Restored
Present owners Arbeitskreis Museumlogger
Contact address Petkumer Strasse 220, 26725 Emden
Location Emden, Germany
History Wooden ketch-rigged fishing vessel built in the Netherlands for the North Sea herring fishery. Maintained as a floating exhibit near the centre of Emden.
Bibliography B13

Emden I
fireboat

Built 1953 by Hamburger

Emma

Motorenfabrik Carl Jastram, Bergedorf, Germany
Original owners City of Emden
Propulsion Diesel engines, 155hp. Engine built by Deutz
Length 53.7ft/16.35m
Breadth 12.5ft/3.8m
Draught 4.3ft/1.3m
Materials Steel throughout
Original use Fireboat
Condition Intact
Present owners Deutsches Feuerwehrmuseum
Contact address St Laurentis Strasse 3, 36041 Fulda
Location Fulda, Germany
History Small fireboat formerly stationed in the harbour of Emden. Currently preserved as an exhibit on land outside the museum of firefighting at Fulda.
Bibliography B13

Emma
inland motor barge

Built 1929 at Politz, nr Stettin, Germany
Propulsion Diesel engine
Tonnage 280 displacement
Length 135.9ft/41.4m
Breadth 16.7ft/5.1m
Draught 1.5ft/0.46m
Materials Steel throughout
Original use Cargo

Condition Intact
Present owners Deutsches Schiffahrtsmuseum
Location Bremerhaven, Germany
History Example of a once numerous type of motor barge used to carry cargoes on the rivers and canals of Germany and neighbouring countries. Preserved as one of the floating exhibits of the maritime museum in Bremerhaven.
Bibliography B13

Ems
motor inspection vessel

Built 1934 by Jos L Meyer, Papenburg, Germany
Original owners Wasser- und Schiffahrtsamt Emden
Propulsion Diesel engines
Tonnage 142 gross
Length 118.2ft/36.0m
Breadth 18.9ft/5.75m
Draught 7.9ft/2.4m
Materials Steel throughout
Original use Inspection vessel
Condition In operation
Present owners Wasser-und Schiffahrtsamt Emden
Contact address Am Eisenbahndock 3, 26725 Emden
Location Emden, Germany
History Motor inspection vessel of the 1930s largely unaltered and still in

service based at Emden.
Bibliography B13

Erich Reimler
guided missile patrol vessel

Built (date not known)
Original owners East German Navy
Official number 575
Original use Guided missile patrol vessel
Location Peenemunde, Germany
History Example of a guided missile patrol vessel of the former East German Navy preserved as an floating exhibit at a Historical Technical Information Centre. Opened to the public in July 1994.

Erna Becker
fishing ketch

Former name ANNA HELENE
Built 1892 by Hinrich Sietas, Neuenfelde, Germany
Original owners Heinrich Hulsen
Official number HF 348
Propulsion Sail, ketch rig; diesel engine added, 60hp. Engine built by Jastram
Length 42.4ft/12.92m
Breadth 16.3ft/4.97m
Draught 4.5ft/1.37m
Materials Wood throughout
Original use Fishing
Condition Intact

Present owners Naturkundemuseum und okologische Station
Contact address Neuenhof 8, 21730 Balje
Location Balje, Germany
History Ketch-rigged sailing fishing vessel formerly employed on the North Sea. First diesel auxiliary engine was installed in 1923. Preserved as an exhibit on shore at Balje.
Bibliography B13

Eule
besan ewer

Former name MELPOMENE, CHRISTINA
Built 1895 by Ernst Niemand, Boizenburg, Germany
Propulsion Sail, ketch rig; diesel engine added, 70hp
Length 19.55m
Breadth 13.4ft/4.07m
Draught 3.8ft/1.15m
Materials Steel throughout
Original use Cargo
Condition Restored to sailing condition
History Ketch rigged coastal sailing cargo vessel of the type known as a 'besan ewer'. Later reduced to a cargo barge. Restored to sailing condition as a private yacht based at Hamburg.
Bibliography B13

Express
river excursion steamer

Built 1885
Propulsion Steam, screw, 80hp
Tonnage 68 displacement
Length 95.8ft/29.2m
Breadth 16.1ft/4.92m
Materials Iron or steel hull
Original use Passengers
Condition Intact
Present owners Wedstfalisches Industriemuseum
Location Waltrop, Germany
History Former river excursion steamer largely intact externally but in need of restoration. Currently a floating exhibit of the Westphalian Industrial Museum in Waltrop.
Bibliography B13

Fehmarnbelt
lightship

Former name AUSSENEIDER
Built 1908 by G H Thyen, Brake, Germany
Original owners Wasser- und Schiffahrtsamt, Tonning
Propulsion Diesel engine installed
Tonnage 486 gross
Length 149.04ft/45.44m

Breadth 23.42ft/7.14m
Draught 12.14ft/3.7m
Materials Steel hull
Original use Lightship
Condition Intact
Present owners Feuerschiff fur Lubeck
Location Lubeck, Germany
History Lightship formerly employed off the Baltic Coast of Germany. Maintained as a floating exhibit at Lubeck.
Bibliography B13

Feuerlöschboot 1
fireboat

Built 1940 by Aug Pahl, Hamburg-Finkenwerder, Germany
Propulsion Diesel engines
Length 63.3ft/19.3m
Breadth 14.8ft/4.5m
Materials Steel throughout
Original use Fireboat
Condition In operating condition
Present owners Schiffergilde Bremerhaven
Location Bremerhaven, Germany
History Small fireboat of the 1940s formerly employed in and around the Port of Bremerhaven. Preserved afloat there in operating condition by the Bremerhaven ship restoration guild.
Bibliography B13

Fischerhutte

Fischerhütte
motor ferry

Built 1950 by Staatswerft Saatsee, Rendsburg, Germany
Original owners Wasser- und Schiffahrtsamt
Official number F 6005
Propulsion Diesel engines. Engine built by Mercedes-Benz
Length 77.1ft/23.5m
Breadth 30.0ft/9.15m
Draught 2.1ft/0.65m
Materials Steel throughout
Original use Ferryboat
Condition Intact
Present owners Wasser- und Schiffahrtsamt
Contact address Alte Zentrale 4, 25534 Brunsbuttel
Location Fischerhutte, Germany
History Double-ended motor ferryboat for vehicles, exhibited on shore beside the landing of the current ferries crossing the ship canal between the North Sea and the Baltic.

Fortuna
steam tug

Built 1909 by Gebr Wiemann, Brandenburg, Germany
Propulsion Steam, screw

Length 57.4ft/17.5m
Breadth 11.81ft/3.6m
Draught 4.59ft/1.4m
Materials Steel hull, steel and wood superstructure
Original use Tug
Condition In operating condition
Present owners Westfalisches Industriemuseum
Location Waltrop, Germany
History Steam tug employed on the German canals and rivers. Preserved as a floating exhibit and active steam vessel based at the Westphalian Industrial Museum in Waltrop.
Bibliography B13

Fortuna
tjalk

Built 1914 at Westfriesland
Propulsion Sail, tjalk
Tonnage 18 gross
Length 51.18ft/15.8m
Breadth 10.99ft/3.35m
Draught 1.97ft/0.6m
Materials Steel hull
Original use Cargo
Condition In sailing condition
Present owners Museumhafen Oevelgonne
Location Oevelgonne, Germany
History Small sailing vessel built for

trading in the coastal waters of the North Sea. Maintained in sailing condition based at Oevelgonne on the Elbe River below Hamburg.

Franz-Christian
inland barge

Built 1929 by I G Hitzler, Lauenburg, Germany
Propulsion Diesel engine
Length 141.04ft/43.0m
Breadth 16.63ft/5.07m
Draught 6.56ft/2.0m
Materials Steel hull
Original use Cargo, on rivers
Condition Intact
Present owners Westalisches Industriemuseum
Location Dortmund, Germany
History Example of a German cargo barge of the 1920s built for use on rivers. Maintained as a floating exhibit at the Westphalian Industrial Museum in Waltrop.
Bibliography B13

Friedrich
passenger ferry

Former name NORDBREMEN, SUDHAMBURG
Built 1880 by Reiherstieg-Werft, Hamburg, Germany
Propulsion Steam, screw; converted to diesel, 385hp
Tonnage 69 displacement
Length 55.3ft/16.85m
Breadth 22.0ft/6.7m
Draught 6.2ft/1.9m
Materials Iron or steel hull
Original use Passenger ferry
Condition Intact
Present owners Bremische Gesellschaft zur Erhaltung 'Friedrich'
Contact address Hermannstrasse 110, 28201 Bremen
Location Bremen, Germany
History Veteran Hamburg harbour ferry converted to diesel propulsion in 1951. Otherwise largely unaltered. Currently laid up awaiting restoration.
Bibliography B13

Friedrich
besan ewer

Built 1910 by W Ropers, Stade, Germany
Propulsion Sail, ketch rig; auxiliary engine
Tonnage 46 gross
Length 64.2ft/19.55m
Breadth 16.4ft/5.0m
Materials Steel hull

Original use Cargo
Condition In sailing condition
Present owners Karl Heinz Bolter
Location Hamburg-Finkenwerder, Germany
History Ketch-rigged sailing cargo vessel built for the North Sea coastal trades of a type known as a 'besan ewer'. Maintained in sailing condition as a private yacht based at Hamburg.
Bibliography B13

Galatea
passenger lake steamer

Former name LA BARCA, ALSTER
Built 1931 by Joh Oelkers, Hamburg, Germany
Propulsion Steam, screw, compound, 66hp
Length 75.0ft/22.85m
Breadth 14.6ft/4.45m
Draught 3.7ft/1.14m
Materials Steel throughout
Original use Passengers
Condition Intact
Present owners Holsten Brauerei
Location Hamburg, Germany
History Small passenger steamer formerly used to carry commuters between residential communities on the Alster Lake in Hamburg and the centre of the city. Maintained there in largely unaltered condition, without engines, as a floating restaurant.

Georg Breusing

Bibliography B13

Gauss
water tanker

Former name TRAVE
Built 1941 by D W Kremer Sohn, Elmshorn, Germany
Original owners German Navy
Propulsion Diesel engines, 1000hp
Tonnage 845 gross
Length 185.8ft/56.6m
Breadth 28.9ft/8.82m
Draught 13.1ft/4.0m
Materials Steel throughout
Original use Survey ship
Condition Intact, in operating condition
Present owners Leonhardt Schiffahrt
Contact address Industriestrasse 1, 22869 Hamburg
Location Lubeck, Germany
History Originally built as a water tanker for the German Navy. After the Second World War she was completely rebuilt as a survey ship. Currently maintained as a floating exhibit at Lubeck.
Bibliography B13

Gebrüder
motor fishing boat

Built 1929 by Schlomer-Werft, Oldersum, Germany

Official number AZ 5
Propulsion Diesel engine, 280hp. Engine built by Cummins
Length 50.0ft/15.15m
Breadth 16.0ft/4.85m
Original use Fishing
Present owners Sielhafenmuseum Carolinensiel
Contact address Pumphusen 3, 26409 Carolinensiel
Location Carolinensiel, Germany
History Motor fishing boat employed off the North Sea coast of Germany. Undergoing restoration at the museum in Carolinensiel.
Bibliography B13

Geheimrat Garbe
steam tug

Former name FORELLE, EINTRACHT
Built 1902 by J H N Wichhorst, Hamburg
Propulsion Steam, screw, 75hp
Tonnage 106.9 displacement
Length 71.7ft/21.85m
Breadth 14.8ft/4.5m
Draught 5.4ft/1.66m
Materials Steel throughout
Original use Tug
Condition In operating condition
Present owners Christoph Lebek
Contact address Jagerallee 15, 14469 Potsdam
Location Brandenburg, Germany
History Steam tug formerly employed on the inland waterways of Germany. Maintained in operating condition as a private yacht based in Brandenburg near Berlin.
Bibliography B13

Georg Breusing
motor rescue lifeboat

Built 1963 by Abeking & Rasmussen, Lemwerder, Germany
Propulsion Diesel engine, 100hp
Tonnage 85 displacement
Length 87.5ft/26.66m
Breadth 18.4ft/5.6m
Draught 5.3ft/1.62m
Materials Steel throughout
Original use Rescue lifeboat
Condition Intact
Present owners Forderkreis Rettungskreuzer 'Georg Breusing'
Contact address Im Ratsdelft, 26625 Emden
Location Emden, Germany
History German motor rescue lifeboat with enclosed cabin. Preserved as a floating exhibit near the centre of Emden.
Bibliography B13

Gera
motor trawler

Built 1959 by VEB Peenewerft, Wolgast, Germany
Original owners VEB Fischkombinat Rostock
Official number ROS 223
Propulsion Diesel engines
Tonnage 943 gross
Length 215.0ft/65.56m
Breadth 33.8ft/10.29m
Draught 15.25ft/4.65m
Materials Steel throughout
Original use Fishing
Condition Intact
Present owners Morgenstern Museums
Contact address Fischkai, 27572 Bremerhaven
Location Bremerhaven, Germany
History Large motor trawler used in distant offshore fisheries. Example of the type of vessel replaced by the stern ramp trawler. Preserved as a floating museum in the old fishery harbour.
Bibliography B13, D35, D442

Geversdorf
motor ferry

Built 1949 by Stader Schiffswerft, Stade, Germany
Propulsion Diesel engine, 18hp
Length 118.5ft/36.1m
Breadth 35.2ft/10.72m
Draught 1.0ft/0.3m
Materials Steel throughout
Original use Ferry
Condition Intact
Present owners Fordergesellschaft Schwebefahre Osten
Contact address Deichstrasse 1, 21756 Osten
Location Osten, Germany
History Small double-ended motor ferryboat formerly used on a German river crossing. Preserved as a floating exhibit at Osten.
Bibliography B13

Glückstadt
customs inspection launch

Former name JADE
Built 1954 by Th Buschmann, Hamburg-Wilhelmsburg, Germany
Original owners German Customs
Propulsion Diesel engine, 825hp
Tonnage 106 gross
Length 29.5m
Breadth 5.2m
Materials Steel throughout
Original use Customs launch
Condition Intact
Present owners Deutsches Zollmuseum

Contact address Alter Wandrahm 16, 20457 Hamburg, Germany
Location Hamburg, Germany
History German customs inspection launch preserved as a floating exhibit at a museum of the customs service.

Goede Verwachting
Dutch sailing barge

Built 1913 in The Netherlands
Propulsion Sail, sloop rig
Length 52.1ft/15.86m
Breadth 11.1ft/3.37m
Materials Steel hull
Original use Cargo; sailing barge
Condition Intact
Present owners Museum der Deutschen Binnenschiff-fahrt
Location Duisburg, Germany
History Dutch sailing barge used to carry various cargoes on canals and inland waterways. Has been installed as a floating exhibit fully rigged in a large tank inside a hall of the inland shipping museum in Duisburg.
Bibliography B13

Goede Wil
sailing fishing vessel

Former name GOOD WILL
Built 1940 at Ostend, Belgium

Propulsion Sail, ketch rig; diesel auxiliary, 50hp. Engine built by Ford
Tonnage 25 gross
Length 46.6ft/14.2m
Breadth 13.5ft/4.1m
Materials Wood throughout
Original use Fishing
Condition Restored to sailing condition
Present owners Hartmut Hanss
Contact address Kapellenstrasse 6, 65193 Wiesbaden
Location Oevelgonne, Germany
History Ketch rigged fishing vessel built in Belgium for the North Sea fisheries. Maintained in sailing condition as a private yacht based at the 'museum harbour' at Oevelgonne on the Elbe River below Hamburg.
Bibliography B13

Goethe
sidewheel passenger steamer

Built 1913 by Gebr Sachsenberg, Cologne, Germany
Original owners Koln-Dusseldorfer Deutsche Rheinschiffahrt
Propulsion Steam, sidewheel, compound diagonal, 750hp
Tonnage 522 displacement
Length 260.0ft/79.25m
Breadth 52.0ft/15.84m
Draught 4.92ft/1.5m

Materials Steel throughout
Original use Passengers
Condition In operation
Present owners Koln-Dusseldorfer Deutsche Rheinschiffahrt
Contact address Frankenwerft 15, 50667 Cologne
Location Cologne (home port), Germany
History Only active sidewheel passenger steamer on the Rhine service between Cologne and Mainz. Converted from coal to oil fuel in 1955.
Bibliography B13, B16, B43, D100a

Goliath
salvage vessel

Built 1941 by Deschimag, Werk Seebeck, Wesermunde, Germany
Propulsion Diesel engines, 940hp. Engine built by Daimler-Benz Maybach
Tonnage 143 gross
Length 102.6ft/31.25m
Breadth 23.1ft/7.03m
Draught 5.4ft/1.65m
Materials Steel throughout
Original use Tug and salvage vessel
Condition Intact
Present owners Schiffergilde Bremerhaven
Contact address Hans-Scharoun-Platz,

Glückstadt

Goliath

27568 Bremerhaven
Location Bremerhaven, Germany
History Salvage vessel with hoisting gear forward also fitted for towing. Maintained in operating condition as a floating exhibit by the ship restoration guild of Bremerhaven.
Bibliography B13

Gorch Fock
sail training vessel

Built 1958 by Blohm & Voss, Hamburg, Germany
Original owners German Navy
Propulsion Sail, barque rig; diesel engine, 800hp. Engine built by MAN
Tonnage 1870 displacement
Length 266.0ft/81.0m
Breadth 39.0ft/12.0m
Draught 15.5ft/4.8m
Materials Steel throughout
Original use Training
Condition In sailing condition
Present owners German Navy
Location Kiel, Germany
History Still in use as a training vessel.

Gräbendorf
inland barge

Built 1920
Propulsion Non self-propelled
Length 75.5ft/23.0m
Materials Steel hull
Original use Cargo, lighter barge
Present owners Wassermuseum
Location Grabendorf, Germany
History Example of a type of barge used to carry cargo on the inland waterways of Germany. Maintained afloat as an exhibit at Grabendorf.
Bibliography B13

Gorch Fock

Gredo
steam tug

Built 1916 by Bodan Werft, Kressbronn, Germany
Propulsion Steam, screw, 62hp
Length 51.2ft/15.6m
Breadth 10.7ft/3.25m
Materials Steel throughout
Original use Tug
Condition In operating condition
Present owners Hans Werner Dorich
Contact address Pfordtenwingert 4, 63457 Hanau
Location Gemunden, Germany
History Small steam tug formerly employed towing barges on inland waterways of Germany. Employed as a private yacht and on excursions with limited seating on deck at the stern.
Bibliography B13

Greta
sailing fishing vessel

Built 1904 by Joachim Behrens, Finkenwerder, Germany
Official number HF 452
Propulsion Sail and auxiliary diesel engine, 40hp
Tonnage 4.8 gross
Length 42.7ft/13.0m
Breadth 11.7ft/3.55m
Draught 2.6ft/0.8m
Original use Fishing
Condition Fully restored to sailing condition
Present owners Eignergemeinschaft 'Greta', Kiel, Germany
Location Laboe, Germany
History Small fishing boat formerly employed under sail and power in the North Sea off the Elbe River. Preserved as an exhibit at Laboe near Kiel.
Bibliography B13

Greundiek
motor coaster

Former name RITA DOLLING, TRINCHEN BEHRENS
Built 1950 by Rickmers Werft, Bremerhaven, Germany
Propulsion Diesel engines. Engine built by Deutz
Tonnage 348 gross
Length 153.2ft/46.68m
Breadth 25.4ft/7.73m
Draught 10.6ft/3.23m
Materials Steel throughout
Original use Cargo
Condition Intact
Present owners Verein 'Alter Hafen'
Contact address c/o D Bohlmann,

H-11347

Bremervorder Str 3, 21682 Stade
Location Stade, Germany
History Small motor vessel built to carry cargo in the coastal trades. Maintained as a floating exhibit in the harbour of Stade.
Bibliography B13

Grönland
polar exploration vessel

Built 1867 by Tollef Tollefsen, Matre, Norway
Original owners German North Pole Expedition 1868
Propulsion Sail, sloop rig; auxiliary engine
Tonnage 50 gross
Length 84.64ft/25.8m
Breadth 19.68ft/6.0m
Draught 9.84ft/3.0m
Materials Wood throughout
Original use Polar exploration
Condition Fully restored
Present owners Deutsches Schiffahrtsmuseum
Location Bremerhaven, Germany
History Vessel employed in the first German North Pole expedition of 1868. Later operated as a cargo carrier in the coastal trades. Exhibited afloat in sailing condition at the maritime museum in Bremerhaven.
Bibliography A14, A16, B13, B46

Grossherzogin Elizabeth
trading schooner

Former name ARIADNE, SAN ANTONIO
Built 1909 by J Smit, Alblasserdam, Netherlands
Propulsion Sail, 3-masted schooner rig;

diesel auxiliary
Tonnage 463 gross
Length 216.6ft/66.0m
Breadth 27.3ft/8.32
Draught 11.5ft/3.5m
Materials Steel hull
Original use Cargo, later training
Condition In operation
Present owners Schulschiffverein 'Grossherzogin Elizabeth'
Contact address Reederei H W Janssen, Rathausplatz 7, 26931 Elsfleth
Location Elsfleth, Germany
History Built as a cargo-carrying schooner for operation under the Dutch flag. Restored to sailing condition as a passenger cruise vessel and later acquired by present owners for use as a training vessel for young people.
Bibliography A10, A15, B13, D123

Gustav
steam tug

Former name AUGUSTE
Built 1908 by Gebr Wiemann, Brandenburg, Germany
Original owners Reederei Schmeil & Friedrich, Hamburg
Propulsion Steam, screw, triple-expansion, 250hp
Length 87.0ft/26.5m
Breadth 16.6ft/5.06m
Materials Steel throughout
Original use Tug
Condition Intact
Present owners Hans Noritz
Contact address Streitstrasse 1-4, 13587 Berlin
Location Berlin, Germany
History Steam tug formerly employed

towing barges on the inland waterways of Germany. Lying afloat at Berlin, intact but undergoing restoration.
Bibliography B13

H-11347
lighter barge

Built 1912 by I P W Lutgens, Hamburg, Germany
Propulsion None
Length 69.86ft/21.3m
Breadth 17.38ft/5.3m
Draught 5.48ft/1.67m
Materials Iron hull
Original use Lighter barge
Condition Intact
Present owners Museum der Arbeit, Hamburg
Location Oevelgonne, nr Hamburg, Germany
History Example of a type of lighter barge used to carry various cargoes in the Port of Hamburg early in the century. Preserved as a floating exhibit there.
Bibliography B13

Hansa
motor fishing boat

Former name MÖWE
Built 1938 at Stolpmunde, Germany
Propulsion Diesel engine
Tonnage 43.3 gross
Length 42.7ft/13.0m
Breadth 14.8ft/4.5m
Draught 6.2ft/1.9m
Original use Fishing
Condition Intact
Present owners Fischer Brick, Stolpmunde
Location Hansapark, Sierksdorf, Germany
History Motor fishing boat formerly employed in the Baltic. Preserved as an exhibit at Sierksdorf.
Bibliography B13

Hans-Peter
steam tug

Former name DEUTSCHLAND
Built 1928 by Gebr Wiemann, Brandenburg, Germany
Propulsion Steam, screw, 212hp; converted to diesel
Tonnage 50 displacement
Length 105.0ft/32.0m
Breadth 18.5ft/5.64m
Materials Steel throughout
Original use River towboat
Condition Intact
Present owners Landesmuseum fur Technik und Arbeit

Contact address Museumstrasse, 68165 Mannheim
Location Mannheim, Germany
History Steam tug formerly employed towing barges on the inland waterways of Germany. Maintained as a floating exhibit of the Mannheim museum of technology.
Bibliography B13

Havel
motor fishing vessel

Built 1956 by VEB Schiffbau- und Reparaturwerft, Stralsund, Germany
Propulsion Diesel engine. Engine built by VEB Schwermaschinenbau 'Karl Liebnecht'
Tonnage 132 gross
Length 86.6ft/26.45m
Breadth 22.0ft/6.71m
Materials Steel throughout
Original use Fishing
Condition Intact
Present owners Sassnitzer Fischerei- und Hafenmuseum
Contact address Rugener Ring 27, 18545 Sassnitz
Location Sassnitz, Germany
History Motor fishing boat formerly based on the Baltic Coast of East Germany. Maintained as a floating exhibit in the harbour of Sassnitz.
Bibliography B13

Heimat
motor fishing vessel

Built 1955 by Bultjer & Sohne, Ditzum, Germany
Propulsion Diesel engine, 120hp
Tonnage 19 gross
Length 44.0ft/13.38m
Breadth 14.3ft/4.35m
Original use Fishing
Condition Intact
Present owners Sielhafenmuseum
Location Carolinensiel, Germany
History Motor fishing boat formerly employed off the North Sea coast of Germany. Preserved as one of the exhibits of the maritime museum in Carolinensiel.

Heinrich Von Der Lühe
besan ewer

Built 1910 by Sietas, Neuenfelde, Germany
Propulsion Sail, ketch rig
Length 60.0ft/18.15m
Breadth 14.1ft/4.3m
Original use Cargo
Condition In sailing condition
Present owners Gudrun Schleif

Location Stade, Germany
History Ketch rigged sailing cargo vessel employed in the German coastal trade of the type known as a 'besan ewer'. Maintained in sailing condition as a private yacht based at Stade.
Bibliography B13

Helmut
motor tug

Built 1925 by Caesar Wollheim, Cosel, Schlesien, Germany
Propulsion Diesel engine installed in 1972
Tonnage 10.29 gross
Length 62.65ft/19.1m
Breadth 15.12ft/4.61m
Draught 3.67ft/1.12m
Materials Steel hull
Original use Tug
Condition Intact
Present owners Deutsches Schiffahrtsmuseum
Location Bremerhaven, Germany
History Small harbour tug of the 1920s preserved as a floating exhibit at the maritime museum in Bremerhaven.
Bibliography B13

Hemmoor 3
barge

Built pre-1960
Propulsion Towed
Length 85.3ft/26.0m
Materials Steel throughout
Original use Cement barge
Condition Intact
Present owners Freilichtmuseum
Location Hemmoor, Germany
History Barge formerly used to transport cement. Preserved on shore in an 'open air museum' at Hemmoor.
Bibliography B13

Herbert
motor launch

Built 1923 by Ernst Menzer, Bergedorf, Germany
Propulsion Diesel engine, 60hp
Length 43.4ft/13.22m
Breadth 10.5ft/3.2m
Draught 2.9ft/0.89m
Materials Steel throughout
Original use Covered launch
Condition In operating condition
Present owners Westfalisches Industriemuseum
Location Waltrop, Germany
History Motor launch with enclosed cabin used to transport workers in the

Helmut

Port of Hamburg. Preserved as one of the floating exhibits of the Westphalian Industrial Museum in Waltrop.

Hermann
besan ewer

Built 1905 by Claus Witt, Wewelsfleth, Germany
Propulsion Sail, ketch rig
Tonnage 24.67 gross
Length 47.89ft/17.15m
Breadth 14.66ft/4.47m
Draught 4.59ft/1.4m
Materials Wood throughout
Original use Cargo
Condition Intact
Present owners City of Itzehoe
Location Itzehoe, Germany
History Example of a type of German coastal sailing cargo vessel known as a 'besan ewer'. Preserved as an exhibit on shore at Itzehoe.
Bibliography A11, B13, D267

Hermine
trading schooner

Former name EMMA, WEGA
Built 1904 by J Behrens, Hamburg-Finkenwerder, Germany
Original owners Hinrich Bardenhagen, Cranz
Propulsion Sail, schooner rig
Length 83.64ft/25.5m
Breadth 22.14ft/6.75m
Materials Wood throughout
Original use Cargo
Present owners Cuxhaven Shipwreck Museum
Location Cuxhaven, Germany
History Last surviving wooden schooner built at Hamburg. Was being converted to a sail training vessel but was damaged by ice and sank at Finkenwerder. Raised and moved to Cuxhaven to serve as an onshore exhibit.
Bibliography B13

Hindenburg

motor rescue lifeboat

Built 1944 by A Pahl, Finkenwerder,
Germany
Original owners German lifesaving
service
Propulsion Diesel engines, 150hp
Tonnage 60 displacement
Length 57.4ft/17.5m
Breadth 16.4ft/5.0m
Draught 5.58ft/1.7m
Materials Steel throughout
Original use Rescue lifeboat
Condition Intact
Present owners Kiel Schiffahrtsmuseum
Location Kiel, Germany
History German motorised lifeboat of
the 1940s with enclosed cabin.
Maintained as a floating exhibit at Kiel.

Hitzacker

customs patrol launch

Former name LIPPE
Built 1956 by Schless Werft, Wesel-am-
Rhein, Germany
Original owners German customs
service
Propulsion Diesel engine, 150hp. Engine
built by Mercedes
Tonnage 14.85 displacement
Length 56.3ft/17.15m
Breadth 6.04ft/1.83m
Draught 3.2ft/0.96m
Materials Steel throughout
Original use Customs launch
Condition Intact
Present owners Town of Hitzacker
Location Hitzacker, Germany
History German customs patrol launch
employed on the Rhine River and later
the Elbe. Maintained in operating
condition as a floating exhibit at
Hitzacker.
Bibliography B13

Hoher Göll

electric passenger launch

Built 1911 by Fr Lurssen, Vegesack,
Germany
Propulsion Electric motor
Length 61.4ft/18.72m
Breadth 11.2ft/3.4m
Draught 3.1ft/0.95m
Original use Passengers
Condition Intact
Present owners Deutsches Museum
Location Munich, Germany
History Electric launch formerly used
to carry passengers on the Konigsee.
After retirement she was acquired to
serve as an exhibit of the German
Museum in Munich.

'Iltis' class

Hoop op Welvaart

Dutch sailing barge

Former name VIER GEBROEDERS
Built 1883 by van Duivendijk,
Lekkerkerk, Netherlands
Propulsion Sail, sloop rig; diesel
auxiliary, 60hp
Tonnage 25.0 displacement
Length 42.7ft/13.0m
Breadth 11.8ft/3.61m
Materials Iron or steel hull
Original use Cargo
Condition Fully restored to sailing
condition
Present owners Dr Rainer Thonnessen
Contact address Elbchaussee 187, 22605
Hamburg
Location Oevelgonne, nr Hamburg,
Germany
History Leeboard sailing vessel built to
carry cargo on the inland waterways of
the Netherlands. Last employed as a
garbage scow. Fully restored 1991-93 to
sailing condition as a private yacht
owned in Hamburg.
Bibliography B13

'Iltis' class

torpedo boat

Built 1963-66 by Peenewerft, Wolgast,
East Germany
Original owners East German Navy
Propulsion Petrol engine
Tonnage 16.8 displacement
Length 48.87ft/14.9m
Breadth 11.15ft/3.4m
Draught 3.3ft/1.05m
Materials Steel throughout
Original use Torpedo boat
Condition Intact
Present owners Rostock Maritime

Museum
Contact address Liegeplatz Schmarl,
18016 Rostock
Location Rostock, Germany
History 'Iltis' class light torpedo boat
number 923 built for the East German
Navy in the 1960s. Preserved as an
onshore exhibit at the maritime
museum in Rostock.
Bibliography B13

Immanuel

Dutch tjalk

Former name DE JONGE PIETER
Built 1912 by Barkmeijer, Dokkum,
Netherlands
Propulsion Sail, tjalk rig; diesel
auxiliary, 80hp
Tonnage 12.0 gross
Length 54.0ft/16.46m
Breadth 11.5ft/3.5m
Original use Cargo
Condition Restoration in progress
Present owners Seilhafenmuseum
Carolinensiel
Location Carolinensiel, Germany
History Sailing cargo vessel employed
in the Dutch inland waterways trades
of the type known as a 'tjalk'.
Undergoing restoration to sailing
condition to serve as a floating exhibit
and active vessel based at
Carolinensiel.
Bibliography B13

Jantina

Dutch tjalk

Built 1900 at Dokkum, Netherlands
Propulsion Sail, tjalk
Tonnage 28.73 displacement
Length 48.81ft/14.88m

Breadth 10.99ft/3.35m
Original use Cargo
Condition Intact
Present owners Moor- und
Fehnmuseum, Elisabethfehn
Location Elisabethfehn, Germany
History Dutch sailing cargo vessel of
the 'tjalk' type formerly employed in
coastal waters and inland waterways.
Maintained as an exhibit at
Elisabethfehn.

Johanna

sailing coaster

Former name INGEBORG, HERTHA
Built 1903 by Jos Thormahlen,
Elmshorn, Germany
Propulsion Sail, ketch rig
Tonnage 37 gross, 61.0 displacement
Length 57.55ft/17.15m
Breadth 15.94ft/4.86m
Draught 3.94ft/1.2m
Materials Steel hull, wood masts
Original use Cargo
Condition In sailing condition
Present owners J von Walterhausen
Location Oevelgonne, nr Hamburg,
Germany
History Leeboard ketch built as a
sailing cargo vessel for use in the
coastal trades. Later employed as a
cargo vessel. Fully restored to sailing
condition 1973-78 and now exhibited at
Oevelgonne on the Elbe River below
Hamburg.
Bibliography B13

Jonas Von Friedrichstadt

sailing coaster

Former name TANJA, ANJA, WALTER
Built 1911 by Gebr van Diepen,

Waterhuizen, Netherlands
Propulsion Sail, ketch rig; auxiliary engine, 120hp. Engine built by Mercedes
Tonnage 69.0 gross
Length 98.5ft/30.0m
Breadth 18.1ft/5.5m
Draught 4.9ft/1.5m
Materials Steel hull
Original use Cargo
Condition In sailing condition
Present owners John von Eitzen
Contact address Alte Schule/Herrenhalling, 25840 Koldendbuttel
Location Friedrichstadt, Germany
History Ketch-rigged sailing vessel with leeboards built to carry cargo on the North Sea coast of the Netherlands. Currently maintained in sailing condition as a training vessel for young people, based at Friedrichstadt.
Bibliography B13

Junger Pionier
sidewheel river steamer

Former name KARLSBAD, SACHSEN
Built 1898 by Werft Blasewitz, Dresden, Germany
Propulsion Steam, sidewheel, 138hp
Tonnage 252 displacement
Length 183.0ft/55.78m
Breadth 34.17ft/10.42m
Draught 4.58ft/1.4m
Materials Steel throughout, except deck planking
Original use Passengers
Condition Intact, laid up
Present owners Sachsische Dampfschiffahrt Gmbh
Contact address Lingner Allee 3, 01609 Dresden
Location Dresden, Germany
History Intact Elbe River steamboat currently laid up on shore at the company's shipyard near Dresden.
Bibliography B16, B43

Kaiser Friedrich
passenger steamer

Built 1889 by Oderwerke Maschinenfabrik und Schiffsbauwerft AG, Grabow
Propulsion Steam, two compound engines, 65hp
Length 99.7ft/30.4m
Breadth 15.8tt/4.8m
Draught 4.7ft/1.42m
Materials Iron or steel throughout
Original use Passengers
Condition Fully restored to operating condition
Present owners Museum fur Verkehr

Kaiser Wilhelm

und Technik
Location Berlin, Germany
History Passenger steamer built to operate on the inland waterways of Germany. Completely rebuilt and re-engined and returned to service under steam in 1994, based in Berlin.
Bibliography B13, D532

Kaiser Wilhelm
sidewheel river steamer

Built 1900 by Dresdner Maschinebau & Schiffswerft, Dresden, Germany
Original owners Upper Weser Steamship Co
Propulsion Steam, sidewheel, compound diagonal, 168hp
Tonnage 86 displacement
Length 155.0ft/47.24m
Breadth 27.5ft/8.38m
Draught 3.02ft/0.92m
Materials Steel throughout

Original use Passengers
Condition In operating condition
Present owners Lauenburger Elbschiffahrtsmuseum
Location Lauenburg, Germany
History Sidewheel passenger steamer built for service on the Weser River. Rebuilt and lengthened in 1910. Taken off original run in 1970. Now fully restored to operating condition and making excursions on the river out of Lauenburg.
Bibliography B13, B16, B43, D135

Kapitän Meyer
steam buoy tender

Built 1950 by Seebeck Shipyard, Seebeck, Germany
Original owners Wasser und Schiffahrtsdirektion, Kiel
Propulsion Steam, screw, two triple-expansion, 1000hp
Tonnage 555 gross
Length 170.89ft/52.1m
Breadth 29.52ft/9.0m
Draught 10.82ft/3.3m
Materials Steel throughout
Original use Buoy tender
Condition Intact
Present owners Segelkamaradschaft 'Klaus Stortebeker'
Contact address Kniprodestr 93, 26388 Wilhelmshaven
Location Wilhelmshaven, Germany
History Last active steam buoy tender in West Germany when retired. Maintained in operating condition as a floating exhibit and active steam vessel based at Wilhelmshaven.
Bibliography B13

Kapitän Meyer

Kranich

Karl Friedrich Steen
floating crane

Built 1928 by Deutsche Werft, Finkenwerder, Germany
Original owners Hamburg Hafen- und Lagerhaus, Hamburg
Propulsion Diesel engine
Length 86.59ft/26.4m
Breadth 49.86ft/15.2m
Draught 5.25ft/1.6m
Materials Steel hull
Original use Floating crane
Condition Intact
Present owners Museum fur Hamburgische Geschichte
Location Oevelgonne, nr Hamburg, Germany
History Large floating crane formerly employed in the Port of Hamburg. Preserved by volunteers as a floating exhibit at the 'museum harbour' at Oevelgonne on the Elbe River.
Bibliography B13

Kiel
fireboat

Built 1941 by A Pahl, Finkenwerder, Germany
Original owners City of Kiel
Propulsion Diesel engines
Tonnage 54 gross
Length 62.32ft/19.0m
Breadth 13.5ft/4.1m
Draught 4.92ft/1.5m
Materials Steel hull
Original use Fireboat
Condition Intact
Present owners Kieler Stadt- und Schiffahrtsmuseum
Location Kiel, Germany

History Fireboat formerly stationed in the Port of Kiel. Currently maintained afloat there as an exhibit of the maritime museum.
Bibliography B13

Koralle
motor fishing boat

Built by Bootswerft Bultjer, Ditzum, Ostfriesland, Germany (date not known)
Propulsion Diesel engine, 150hp
Tonnage 20 gross
Length 49.2ft/15.0m
Breadth 15.0ft/4.57m
Draught 4.8ft/1.46m
Materials Wood throughout
Original use Fishing
Condition Intact
Present owners Museum fur Wattenfischerei
Contact address Wurster Landstrasse 118, 27638 Wremen
Location Wremen, Germany
History Motor fishing boat formerly based in the Port Wremen. Preserved on shore, fully fitted out, as an exhibit of the local fisheries museum.
Bibliography B13

Kranich
torpedo boat

Built 1958 by Fr Lurssen, Vegesack, Germany
Original owners West German Navy
Propulsion Four diesel engines, 12,000hp. Engine built by Mercedes-Benz
Tonnage 163 displacement
Length 137.79ft/42.0m
Breadth 24.93ft/7.6m
Draught 4.92ft/1.5m
Materials Wood hull, aluminium superstructure
Original use Torpedo boat
Condition Intact
Present owners Deutsches Schiffahrtsmuseum
Location Bremerhaven, Germany
History High-speed torpedo boat built for the navy of West Germany. Maintained afloat at Bremerhaven as an exhibit of the maritime museum.
Bibliography A16, B13, B46

Krippen
sidewheel river steamer

Former name TETSCHEN
Built 1892 by Werft Blazewitz, Dresden, Germany
Propulsion Steam, sidewheel, 110hp
Length 179.3ft/54.64m
Breadth 32.7ft/9.95m
Materials Steel hull
Original use Passengers
Condition In active service

Krippen

Present owners Historische
Dampfschiffs-Reederei Meissen
Contact address Siebeneichener Strasse
29a, 01662 Meissen
Location Frankfurt, Germany
History Sidewheel steamer built to
carry passengers on the Elbe River.
Originally owned in Dresden, where a
fleet of similar vessels still operates.
Currently making cruises out of
Frankfurt from May to October.
Bibliography B13, B43

Kurort Rathen
sidewheel river steamer

Former name BASTEI
Built 1896 by Werft Blascwitz, Dresden,
Germany
Propulsion Steam, sidewheel, 140hp
Tonnage 256 displacement
Length 187.6ft/57.15m
Breadth 33.5ft/10.2m
Draught 3.1ft/0.94m
Materials Steel hull
Original use Passengers
Condition In operation
Present owners Sachsische
Dampfschiffahrts Gmbh
Contact address Hertha-Lindner-
Strasse 10, 01067 Dresden
Location Dresden, Germany
History Elbe River steamboat, fully
restored in 1992-94, employed on
regular day excursions out of Dresden.
Bibliography B13, B16, B43

Kurt-Heinz
steam tug

Former name FORTUNA
Built 1901 by Gebr Maass, Neustrelitz,
Germany
Original owners Transport-
Genossenschaft, Berlin
Propulsion Steam, screw, 167hp
Length 65.8ft/20.06m
Breadth 13.58ft/4.14m
Materials Steel throughout
Original use Tug
Condition In operating condition
Present owners Kurt and Heinz Siebert
Location Berlin, Germany
History Steam tug formerly employed
on the inland waterways of Germany.
Maintained in operating condition by
private owners based in Berlin.
Bibliography B13

KW-19
river patrol boat

Built 1952 by Fr Schweers, Bardenfleth,
Germany
Original owners West German Navy

Kurort Rathen

Official number KW-19
Propulsion Diesel engine, 1000hp.
Engine built by Mercedes-Benz
Tonnage 70 displacement
Length 97.74ft/29.8m
Breadth 16.07ft/4.9m
Draught 5.25ft/1.6m
Materials Steel throughout
Original use Patrol vessel
Condition Intact
Present owners Marinekamaradschaft
Panzerkreuzer Yorck
Contact address 26434 Wangerland-
Horumersiel
Location Horumersiel, Germany
History German Navy patrol boat
formerly used on the Weser River.
Maintained on shore as an exhibit at
Horumersiel.
Bibliography B13

Laesö Rende
lightship

Former name FYRSKIB XV
Built 1887 by Royal Navy Yard,
Copenhagen, Denmark
Original owners Danish Lighthouse
Service
Propulsion Towed to station
Tonnage 130 displacement
Materials Wood hull
Original use Lightship
Condition Intact, afloat
Present owners Heikendorfer Yacht

Club
Location Heikendorf, nr Kiel, Germany
History Veteran Danish lightship
unaltered from her last appearance
when in service. Maintained afloat as a
yacht clubhouse in the harbour of
Heikendorf, Germany.
Bibliography B13

Landrath Küster
fishing ketch

Built 1889 by Hinrich Sietas, Cranz-
Neuenfelde, Germany
Original owners Heinrich and Hinrich
Wulf
Official number HF 231
Propulsion Sail, ketch rig; diesel
auxiliary, 150hp. Engine built by Volvo
Tonnage 39 gross
Length 71.54ft/21.8m
Breadth 19.6ft/5.96m
Draught 6.6ft/2.0m
Materials Wood throughout
Original use Fishing
Condition Restored to sailing condition
Present owners Jugend in Arbeit
Hamburg eV
Contact address Kutterhafen
Finkenwerder, Hamburg
Location Hamburg, Germany
History Ketch-rigged fishing vessel
formerly employed in the North Sea
off the coast of Germany. Recently
restored to sailing condition based at

the old harbour of Finkenwerder,
Hamburg.
Bibliography B13, D279

Langeness
motor tug

Built 1959 by Schiffwerft J Braun,
Speyer, Germany
Propulsion Diesel engine, 340hp; Voith-
Schneider system propulsion
Tonnage 46.51 displacement
Length 51.44ft/15.67m
Breadth 16.6ft/5.06m
Draught 7.9ft/2.08m
Materials Steel throughout
Original use Tug
Condition Intact
Present owners City of Wilhelmshaven
Location Wilhelmshaven, Germany
History Harbour tug that uses vertical
vanes instead of a propeller.
Maintained as a floating exhibit in the
Port of Wilhelmshaven.
Bibliography B13

Langeoog
motor rescue lifeboat

Built 1944 by A Pahl, Finkenwerder,
Germany
Original owners Deutsche Gesellschaft
zur Rettung, Bremen
Propulsion Diesel engine, 150hp
Tonnage 35.0 displacement
Length 45.9ft/14.0m
Breadth 14.8ft/4.5m
Draught 4.6ft/1.4m
Original use Rescue lifeboat
Condition Intact
Present owners Gemeinde Langeoog
Location Langeoog, Germany
History German motor rescue lifeboat
of the 1940s with enclosed cabin.
Currently preserved as a floating
exhibit at Bremen.
Bibliography B13

Langer Heinrich
floating crane

Built 1890 by F Schichau, Danzig,
Germany
Original owners Schichau Werft,
Danzig
Propulsion Non self-propelled
Tonnage 1595 displacement
Length 96.92ft/29.55m
Breadth 67.08ft/20.45m
Draught 9.71ft/2.96m
Materials Iron throughout
Original use Floating crane
Condition Intact
Present owners Rostock Maritime
Museum

Location Rostock, Germany
History Large floating crane maintained afloat as an exhibit at the Rostock maritime museum devoted to the history of the local shipbuilding industry.
Bibliography B13, D404

Leipzig
sidewheel river steamer

Built 1929 by Werft Laubegast, Dresden, Germany
Propulsion Steam, sidewheel, 325hp
Tonnage 397 displacement
Length 230.0ft/70.05m
Breadth 42.0ft/12.8m
Draught 2.9ft/0.89m
Materials Steel throughout, except deck planking
Original use Passengers
Condition In operation
Present owners Sachsische Dampfschiffahrts Gmbh
Contact address Hertha-Lindner-Strasse 10, 01067 Dresden
Location Dresden, Germany
History Largely unaltered German Elbe River steamboat in regular service on day excursions out of Dresden. Served as a hospital ship in the Second World War and was sunk in 1945, returning to service in 1949.
Bibliography B13, B16, B43

'Libelle' class

'Libelle' class
torpedo boat

Built 1976 by Peenewerft, Wolgast, East Germany
Original owners East German Navy
Propulsion Diesel engines
Tonnage 26.65 displacement
Length 62.4ft/18.96m
Breadth 14.5ft/4.42m
Draught 5.7ft/1.74m
Materials Light metal construction
Original use Torpedo boat
Condition Intact
Present owners Militarhistorisches Museum
Contact address Olbrichtplatz 3, 01099 Dresden
Location Dresden, Germany
History 'Libelle' class light torpedo boat number 961. Currently used as an onshore exhibit.
Bibliography B13

'Libelle' class
torpedo boat

Built 1976 by Peenewerft, Wolgast, East Germany
Original owners East German Navy
Propulsion Diesel engines
Tonnage 26.65 displacement
Length 62.19ft/18.96m
Breadth 14.76ft/4.5m
Draught 4.92ft/1.5m
Materials Steel throughout
Original use Torpedo boat
Condition Intact
Present owners Rostock Maritime Museum
Contact address Liegeplatz Schmarl, 18016 Rostock
Location Rostock, Germany
History 'Libelle' class fast torpedo boat built for the East German Navy. Preserved as an onshore exhibit at the maritime museum in Rostock.
Bibliography B13

Line Hinsch
auxiliary coasting ketch

Former name WATERHUIZEN
Built 1928 by Gebr van Diepen, Waterhuizen, Netherlands
Propulsion Diesel engine, 130hp; sail, ketch rig. Engine built by Bussing
Tonnage 100 gross
Length 96.8ft/29.5m
Breadth 18.0ft/5.5m

Line Hinsch

Draught 3.94ft/1.2m
Materials Steel throughout
Original use Cargo
Condition In operating condition
Present owners Bremerhavener
Schiffergilde eV
Location Bremerhaven, Germany
History Motor cargo vessel built in
Netherlands fitted with ketch rig.
Currently maintained by the ship
restoration guild of Bremerhaven.
Bibliography B13

Lodsen Rønne
sailing pilot vessel

Former name WINDSBRAUT
Built 1916 by Peter Hansen, Svaneke,
Bornholm
Original owners Rønne Pilots
Propulsion Sail, cutter rig. Engine built
by Volvo-Penta
Tonnage 6.0 gross
Length 49.0ft/14.9m
Breadth 9.8ft/3.0m
Draught 6.0ft/1.8m
Original use Pilot cutter
Condition In sailing condition
Present owners Gisela Klug and Dieter
Pogoda
Contact address Im Dorf 2, 27798 Hude
Location Oldenburg, Germany
History Former sailing pilot vessel
based at Ronne on the Island of
Bornholm in the Baltic Sea.
Maintained in sailing condition as a
private yacht based at Oldenburg.
Bibliography B13

Ludwig Fessler
sidewheel lake steamer

Built 1926 by Theodor Hitzler,
Regensburg, Germany
Propulsion Steam, sidewheel,
compound diagonal; converted to
diesel
Length 174.0ft/53.0m
Breadth 38.1ft/11.6m
Materials Steel throughout
Original use Passengers
Condition In operation
Present owners Chiemsee Schiffahrt
Contact address 83209 Prien am
Chiemsee
Location Prien am See (on Chiemsee)
History Former lake passenger steamer
converted to diesel hydraulic
propulsion in 1973. Apart from modern
wheelhouse otherwise largely
unaltered. Remains in regular service
connecting with a unique 'steam tram'
at the Chiemsee landing of Prien
Stock.
Bibliography B13, B43

Ludwig Fessler

Luise
sailing coaster

Built 1906 by Gebr G & H Bodewes,
Martenshoek, Netherlands
Original owners Erich Knuth,
Kleinhagen
Propulsion Sail, sloop rig; auxiliary
engine
Tonnage 43.25 gross
Length 63.8ft/19.45m
Breadth 15.84ft/4.83m
Draught 2.17ft/0.66m
Materials Steel hull
Original use Cargo
Condition Intact
Present owners Monchgutmuseum
Contact address Strandstrasse, 18586
Gohren, Rugen
Location Gohren, Germany
History Small sailing vessel formerly
used to carry cargo in the German
coastal trades. Preserved as an exhibit
at Gohren.
Bibliography B13

LV-13
lightship

Built 1952 by Philip & Sons,
Dartmouth, England
Original owners Trinity House

Propulsion Towed to station
Tonnage 550 displacement
Length 137.8ft/42.0m
Breadth 25.0ft/7.6m
Draught 10.8ft/3.3m
Materials Steel throughout
Original use Lightship
Condition Intact
Present owners Wulf Hoffmann
Location Hamburg, Germany
History Former British lightship largely
unaltered externally serving as a
floating restaurant on the harbour
front of the city of Hamburg.
Bibliography B13

M.Pk.86
cargo lighter

Built 1926 by Schiffswerft Pape,
Bodenwerder, Germany
Original owners Wasserstrassen-
Maschinenamt, Minden
Propulsion Non self-propelled
Length 62.86ft/17.0m
Breadth 11.68ft/3.56m
Original use Cargo; lighter barge
Condition Intact
Present owners Westfalisches
Industriemuseum
Location Dortmund, Germany
History Example of a type of barge

once used to store and transport coal.
Maintained as one of the floating
exhibits of the Westphalian Industrial
Museum in Waltrop.

Mannheim
sidewheel river steamer

Former name MAINZ
Built 1929 by Chr Ruthof, Mainz,
Germany
Original owners Koln-Dusseldorfer
Deutsche Rheinschiffahrt
Propulsion Steam, sidewheel,
compound diagonal, 900hp
Tonnage 586 displacement
Length 272.0ft/82.91m
Breadth 52.5ft/16.0m
Draught 4.92ft/1.5m
Materials Steel throughout
Original use Passengers
Condition Intact
Present owners City of Mannheim
Location Mannheim, Germany
History Former Rhine River sidewheel
passenger steamer maintained as a
floating museum at Mannheim.
Bibliography B13, B16, B43

Maria
fishing ketch

Built 1880 by Hinrich Sietas, Cranz-
Neuenfelde, Germany
Original owners August Bahde,
Finkenwerder
Official number HF 31
Propulsion Sail, ketch rig
Tonnage 35.9 gross
Length 44.94ft/13.7m
Breadth 19.55ft/5.96m
Draught 5.9ft/1.8m
Materials Wood throughout
Original use Fishing
Condition Intact
Present owners Deutsches Museum
Location Munich, Germany
History German sailing fishing vessel of
the late-1800s preserved as an exhibit
inside the German Museum in
Munich, fully rigged with one side
partially opened to show the interior
arrangement.
Bibliography A16, B13, D54

Marie
coasting ketch

Built 1898 by R Moller, Faaborg,
Denmark
Propulsion Sail, ketch rig
Tonnage 33 gross
Length 59.05ft/18.0m
Breadth 16.4ft/5.0m
Materials Wood throughout

Original use Cargo
Condition In sailing condition
Location Altona, nr Hamburg, Germany
History Built as a sailing cargo vessel for the Danish coastal and Baltic trades. Maintained in sailing condition by a private owner, based on the Elbe River below Hamburg.

Meersburg
motor ferry

Built 1928 by Bodan-Werft, Kressbronn
Propulsion Diesel engine, 90hp
Tonnage 140 displacement
Length 105.0ft/32.0m
Breadth 30.9ft/9.4m
Draught 7.2ft/2.2m
Materials Steel throughout
Original use Ferry
Condition Restoration in progress
Present owners Verein 'Rettet die Meersburg'
Contact address Klaus Kramer, Heilgenbronner Strasse 47, Schramberg
Location Konstanz, Germany
History Double-ended ferryboat used to carry vehicles and foot passengers across Lake Constance. Currently being restored at Constance for use as a floating exhibit.
Bibliography B13, D456a

Meissen
sidewheel river steamer

Former name KONIG ALBERT, SACHSEN
Built 1885 by Werft Blasewitz, Dresden, Germany
Propulsion Steam, sidewheel, 226hp
Tonnage 331 displacement
Length 211.08ft/64.34m
Breadth 37.0ft/11.28m
Draught 2.9ft/0.89m
Materials Steel throughout, except planked deck
Original use Passengers
Condition In operation
Present owners Sachsische Dampfschiffahrts Gmbh
Contact address Hertha-Lindner-Strasse 10, 01067 Dresden
Location Dresden, Germany
History German Elbe River steamboat in active service over a century. Engine was compounded in 1914. Used to evacuate civilians from Dresden during the Allied bombing attacks of 1943.
Bibliography B13, B16, B43

Moewe

Minden
dredger

Built 1882 by Gebr Schultz, Mainz, Germany
Original owners Imperial German Waterways Administration
Propulsion Non self-propelled; steam dredging machinery, coal fired
Length 76.42ft/23.3m
Breadth 20.27ft/6.18m
Draught 3.6ft/1.1m
Materials Iron or steel hull
Original use Dredger
Condition Intact
Present owners Museum fur Deutschen Binnenschiffahrt
Location Duisberg, Germany
History Small 'ladder' dredger formerly used on the German rivers. Maintained afloat as an exhibit at the inland shipping museum in Duisburg.

Moewe
coasting ketch

Former name ROVER
Built 1907 by Heinrich Fack, Itzehoe, Germany
Propulsion Sail, ketch rig; diesel auxiliary, 29hp. Engine built by Bohn & Kahler
Tonnage 31 gross
Length 58.07ft/17.7m
Breadth 13.45ft/4.1m
Draught 3.0ft/0.9m
Materials Steel hull
Original use Cargo
Condition In sailing condition
Present owners Bernd Alm, Tangstedt, Rade
Location Oevelgonne, nr Hamburg, Germany
History Coastwise sailing vessel originally built to carry cement in bulk. Later a motor lighter. Fully restored to sailing condition in 1977 and now based at the 'museum harbour' at Oevelgonne on the Elbe River below Hamburg.
Bibliography B13

Minden

Mytlius
fishing cutter

Former name HARMATTAN, ALICE
Built 1939 by Dawartz, Tonning,
Denmark
Propulsion Sail, cutter rig; diesel
auxiliary, 50hp
Length 46.3ft/14.12m
Breadth 12.9ft/3.92m
Materials Wood throughout
Original use Fishing
Condition In sailing condition
Present owners Verein zur Erhaltung
und Nutzung
Contact address Koppel 94, 20099
Hamburg
Location Oevelgonne, nr Hamburg,
Germany
History Former sailing fishing vessel
maintained in sailing condition based
at the 'museum harbour' at
Oevelgonne on the Elbe River below
Hamburg.
Bibliography B13

Nixe
passenger steamer

Built 1939 by Werft Nobiskrug,
Rendsburg, Germany
Propulsion Steam, screw
Length 79.7ft/24.3m
Breadth 14.92ft/4.55m
Draught 2.79ft/0.85m
Materials Steel hull
Original use Passengers
Condition Intact
Present owners Westfalisches
Industriemuseum
Location Waltrop, Germany
History Small towing and passenger
steamer formerly employed on the
German inland waterways. Preserved
afloat as an exhibit of the Westphalian
Industrial Museum in Waltrop.
Bibliography B13

Norden
sailing coaster

Built 1879 Skonevig, Norway
Propulsion Sail, cutter rig; diesel
engine, 150hp
Length 93.5ft/28.5m
Breadth 19.4ft/5.9m
Original use Cargo
Present owners Peter Fleck
Contact address Stockelsdorfer Weg 54,
23611 Bad Schwartau
Location Lubeck, Germany
History Norwegian-built cutter-rigged
sailing vessel formerly used to carry
cargo. Maintained in sailing condition
by a private owner based at Lubeck.
Bibliography B13

Nordstern
steam tug

Built 1902 by Gebr Wiemann,
Brandenburg, Germany
Original owners Golsch & Kahle,
Brandenburg
Propulsion Steam, screw, triple-
expansion, 260hp
Length 85.28ft/26.0m
Breadth 17.2ft/5.25m
Materials Steel throughout
Original use Tug
Condition In operation
Present owners Lothar Bischoff
Contact address Florastr 25, 14641
Nauen
Location Berlin, Germany
History Built as a steam towboat for
operation on the Havel River between
Berlin and Brandenburg. Maintained
in operating condition carrying
passengers on the same waterway.
Largely unaltered apart from seating
on deck.
Bibliography B13, D458

Nydam Ship, 'Viking' ship

Built c400
Propulsion Rowed
Length 74.8ft/22.8m
Breadth 10.8ft/3.3m
Draught 3.6ft/1.1m
Materials Wood throughout
Condition Intact
Present owners Archaologisches
Landesmuseum
Contact address Schloss Gottorf, 24837
Schleswig
Location Schleswig, Germany
History Archaeological relic discovered
in 1963. Upper hull is a conjectural
restoration. Housed in a new building
in 1996 where it can be viewed by the
public.
Bibliography B13

Oscar Huber
sidewheel steam tug

Former name WILHELM VON OSWALD,
FRITZ THYSSEN
Built 1922 by Ewald Berninghaus,
Duisburg, Germany
Propulsion Steam, sidewheel, 1550hp
Tonnage 200 displacement
Length 246.0ft/75.0m
Breadth 67.9ft/20.7m
Draught 5.08ft/1.55m
Materials Steel throughout
Original use River tug
Condition Intact
Present owners Museum fur Deutschen
Binnenschiffahrt
Location Duisburg, Germany
History Example of a type of large
sidewheel steam towboat once
common on the Rhine River.
Maintained afloat as an exhibit of the
museum of inland shipping in
Duisburg.
Bibliography B13, B16

Ostara
towed barge

Built 1926 by De Haan en Orlemans,
Heusden, Netherlands
Propulsion Non self-propelled
Length 219.76ft/67.0m
Breadth 15.09ft/4.5m
Draught 7.68ft/2.34m
Materials Steel hull
Original use Cargo; river and canal
Condition Intact
Present owners Westfalisches
Industriemuseum
Location Waltrop, Germany
History Example of a type of towed
barge formerly used to carry cargoes
on German rivers and canals.
Preserved as one of the exhibits of the
Westphalian Industrial Museum in
Waltrop.

Otto Lauffer
steam police launch

Former name HAFENPOLIZEI VI
Built 1928 by H C Stulcken & Sohn,
Hamburg, Germany
Original owners Finanzdeputation,
Hamburg
Propulsion Steam, screw, 2-cylinder,
47hp

Oscar Huber

Otto Lauffer

Tonnage 33.6 gross
Length 55.78ft/17.0m
Breadth 12.73ft/3.88m
Draught 6.1ft/1.86m
Materials Steel throughout
Original use Police launch
Condition In operating condition
Present owners Museum fur
Hamburgische Geschichte
Location Oevelgonne, nr Hamburg,
Germany
History Intact steam police launch
formerly used to patrol German port
areas. Preserved as a floating exhibit
and active steamer by the Hamburg
City Museum, based at Oevelgonne on
the Elbe River below Hamburg.
Bibliography B13, B16

Passat

trading barque

Built 1911 by Blohm & Voss, Hamburg,
Germany
Original owners F Laeisz, Hamburg
Propulsion Sail, 4-masted barque rig;
auxiliary engine added
Tonnage 3100 gross
Length 321.0ft/97.84m
Breadth 47.0ft/14.33m
Draught 22.0ft/6.71m
Materials Steel throughout except
decks and charthouse
Original use Cargo
Condition Intact, some interior
alterations
Present owners City of Lubeck
Contact address 23570 Travemunde,
Priwall
Location Travemunde, nr Lubeck,
Germany
History One of the world's largest
sailing vessels, built to carry nitrate
from northern Chile to Europe around
Cape Horn. Sold to Finnish owners in

the 1930s to carry grain from Australia
to Europe. Made one of the last
roundings of Cape Horn with cargo.
Bought back by German owners in the
1950s and retired to stationary use later
in that decade. Later used as a floating
summer camp for young people.
Bibliography C52, D57, 141, 192, 310, 479

Paul Kossel

launch tug

Built 1920 by Rolandwerft, Bremen,
Germany
Propulsion Diesel engine, 25hp. Engine
built by Rohol-Gluhkopf
Tonnage 13 gross
Length 46.92ft/14.3m
Breadth 9.94ft/3.03m

Passat

Draught 3.54ft/1.08m
Materials Reinforced concrete hull and
part of superstructure
Original use Launch and tug
Condition Intact, superstructure
restored
Present owners Deutsches
Schiffahrtsmuseum
Location Bremerhaven, Germany
History Small launch built of
reinforced concrete, including the
cabin. Preserved on shore at the
maritime museum in Bremerhaven.
Bibliography B13

Phenol

inland steam tanker

Built 1904 by N V Wilton's
Machienefabriek, Schiedam,
Netherlands
Propulsion Steam, screw, triple
expansion, 162.5hp
Tonnage 261.7 displacement
Length 142.68ft/43.5m
Breadth 19.91ft/6.07m
Draught 3.51ft/1.07m
Materials Steel hull
Original use Cargo, bulk liquid
Condition Intact
Present owners Westfalisches
Industriemuseum
Location Waltrop, Germany
History Small steam tank vessel
employed on inland waterways and
harbours of Germany. Preserved as one
of the exhibits of the Westphalian
Industrial Museum in Waltrop.

Pillnitz

sidewheel river steamer

Former name WELTFRIEDEN, KONIGIN
CAROLA
Built 1886 by Werft Blasewitz, Dresden,
Germany
Propulsion Steam, sidewheel,
compound, 226hp
Tonnage 279 displacement
Length 210.75ft/64.24m
Breadth 37.08ft/11.3m
Draught 3.5ft/1.07m
Materials Steel throughout, except
planked decks
Original use Passengers
Condition In operation
Present owners Sachsische
Dampfschiffahrt Gmbh
Contact address Hertha-Lindner-
Strasse 10, 01067 Dresden
Location Dresden, Germany
History German Elbe river steamboat
in regular service making day
excursions out of Dresden. Engine was
compounded in 1912, almost doubling

Pillnitz

its horsepower.
Bibliography B16

Pirna
sidewheel river steamer

Former name KONIG ALBERT
Built 1898 by Werft Blasewitz, Dresden, Germany
Propulsion Steam, sidewheel, 140hp
Tonnage 241 displacement
Length 180.5ft/55.02m
Breadth 33.92ft/10.34m
Draught 3.75ft/1.14m
Materials Steel throughout, except planked deck
Original use Passengers
Condition In operation
Present owners Sachsische Dampfschiffahrts Gmbh
Contact address Hertha-Lindner-Strasse 10, 01067 Dresden
Location Dresden, Germany
History German Elbe River steamboat in service over a century. Underwent a thorough overhaul and conversion to oil fuel 1992-1994. Currently in regular service making day excursions out of Dresden.
Bibliography B13, B16, B43, D194a

Porta
steam ladder dredger

Built 1925 by Caesar Wollheim, Cosel, nr Breslau, Germany
Original owners Wasser- und Schiffahrtsamt, Hannoversch-Munden
Propulsion Apparently non self-propelled; steam dredging machinery
Length 78.72ft/24.0m
Breadth 20.3ft/6.19m
Draught 2.69ft/0.82m
Materials Steel throughout
Original use Dredger
Condition Intact
Present owners Westfalisches Industriemuseum
Location Waltrop, Germany
History Steam ladder dredger formerly used in the canals and rivers of Germany. Preserved afloat as one of the exhibits of the Westphalian Industrial Museum in Waltrop.

Präsident Freiherr Von Maltzahn
fishing ketch

Built 1928 by J J Seitas, Cranz-Neuenfelde, Germany
Original owners Paul A Fock & H R Holst, Finkenwerder
Official number HF 294
Propulsion Sail, ketch rig; diesel

Präsident Freiherr von Maltzahn

auxiliary, 120hp
Tonnage 44 gross
Length 72.18ft/22.0m
Breadth 21.65ft/6.6m
Draught 8.2ft/2.5m
Materials Wood throughout
Original use Fishing
Condition In operating condition
Present owners Museumhafen
Oevelgonne
Contact address Oevelgonne 42, 22605
Hamburg
Location Oevelgonne, nr Hamburg,
Germany
History Sailing fishing vessel formerly
employed in the North Sea based at
Cuxhaven. Converted to a yacht in 1967
and fully restored to sailing condition.
Now based at the 'museum harbour' of
Oevelgonne on the Elbe River below
Hamburg.
Bibliography B13

Rakel
fishing ketch

Built 1896 at Larvik, Norway. Designed
by Colin Archer
Propulsion Sail, ketch rig; diesel
auxiliary
Length 91.9ft/28.0m
Breadth 17.4ft/5.3m
Draught 9.2ft/2.8m
Materials Wood throughout
Original use Fishing
Condition In sailing condition
Present owners Falk Pfau, Bremen,
Germany
Location Bremerhaven, Germany
History Ketch-rigged Norwegian
fishing vessel designed by Colin
Archer. Maintained in sailing
condition by a private owner, based at
Bremerhaven.
Bibliography B13

Rau IX
steam whale catcher

Built 1939 by Deschimag, Werk
Seebeck, Bremerhaven, Germany
Original owners Walfang
Aktiengesellschaft, Berlin
Propulsion Steam, screw, triple
expansion, 1600hp
Tonnage 380 gross
Length 151.28ft/46.11m
Breadth 26.9ft/8.2m
Draught 13.12ft/4.0m
Materials Steel throughout
Original use Whale catcher
Condition Intact
Present owners Deutsches
Schiffahrtsmuseum
Location Bremerhaven, Germany

History Intact, fully outfitted steam
whale catcher preserved as one of the
floating exhibits of the maritime
museum in Bremerhaven.
Bibliography A16, B13, B46

Recknitz
steam tug

Built 1953 by Schiffswerft Rosslau,
Rosslau, Germany
Propulsion Diesel engine
Tonnage 138.28 gross
Length 92.82ft/28.3m
Breadth 20.57ft/6.27m
Draught 10.79ft/3.29m
Materials Steel hull
Original use Tug
Condition Intact
Present owners
Binnenschiffahrtsmuseum
Location Oderberg, Germany
History Former steam harbour tug
preserved as an exhibit at Oderberg.

Regina
tug

Built 1966 by Bremer Vulkan, Vegesack,
Germany
Propulsion Diesel engine, Voith-
Schneider propulsion system, 600hp
Length 57.4ft/17.5m
Breadth 20.66ft/6.3m
Draught 9.02ft/2.75m
Materials Steel throughout
Original use Tug
Condition Intact
Present owners Maritime Tradition
Contact address Weserstrasse 18, 28757
Bremen
Location Vegesack, Germany
History Example of an early harbour
tug propelled by the Voith-Schneider
(vertical vane) system. This propulsion
was adopted to provide maximum
manoeuvrability in all directions when
guiding ships through the crowded
docks of Bremen and Bremerhaven.
Preserved on shore as an exhibit at
Vegesack.

Renate-Angelika
cargo lighter

Built 1910 at Usti, Oberelbe
Propulsion Towed
Length 152.4ft/46.42m
Breadth 21.7ft/6.6m
Materials Steel throughout
Original use Cargo
Condition Intact
Present owners Berliner
Schiffahrtsgesellschaft eV
Contact address Bamberger Str 58,

Rickmer Rickmers

10777 Berlin
Location Berlin, Germany
History Example of a type of cargo
barge employed on the canals and
rivers of Germany. Preserved afloat as
an exhibit at Berlin.
Bibliography B13

Renzo
steam tug

Built 1931 by Lucchese, Venice, Italy
Original owners A Vianello

Propulsion Steam, screw, 122hp (1912
engine)
Tonnage 48 gross
Length 63.96ft/19.5m
Breadth 14.85ft/4.52m
Draught 4.26ft/1.3m
Original use Tug
Condition Intact
Present owners Deutsches Museum
Location Munich, Germany
History Former Italian steam tug
preserved as an exhibit in Munich.

Rickmer Bock
motor rescue lifeboat

Former name HEINRICH GERLACH
Built 1944 by Aug Pahl, Finkenwerder,
Germany
Propulsion Diesel engine, 150hp
Tonnage 35 displacement
Length 46.0ft/14.0m
Breadth 14.8ft/4.5m
Draught 4.6ft/1.4m
Materials Steel throughout
Original use Rescue lifeboat
Condition Intact
Present owners Deutsche Gesellschaft
zur Rettung
Location Bremen, Germany
History German motorised rescue
lifeboat of the 1940s with enclosed
cabin. Maintained afloat as an exhibit
at Bremen.
Bibliography B13

Rickmer Rickmers
trading barque

Former name SAGRES, FLORES, MAX
Built 1896 by R C Rickmers,
Bremerhaven, Germany
Original owners R C Rickmers & Co
Propulsion Sail, barque rig (auxiliary
engine as SAGRES)
Tonnage 1980 gross
Length 259.25ft/79.02m
Breadth 40.42ft/12.32m
Draught 19.67ft/6.0m
Materials Steel hull, steel and wood
spars
Original use Cargo
Condition Intact, restored
Present owners Windjammer fur
Hamburg
Location Hamburg, Germany
History Sailing vessel built for trade
with the Far East. Later converted to a
Portuguese Naval training ship. After a
number of years laid up in a navy yard
near Lisbon, was brought back to
Hamburg and externally restored as a
floating exhibit. The former hold area
contains exhibit galleries and a
restaurant.
Bibliography A15, B13, C96, D67, D191,
D549

Riesa
sidewheel river steamer

Former name HABSBURG
Built 1897 by Werft Blasewitz, Dresden,
Germany
Original owners Sachsisch-Bohmische
Dampschiffahrt
Propulsion Steam, sidewheel,
compound oscillating, 140hp

Tonnage 94 displacement
Length 184.0ft/56.1m
Breadth 33.0ft/10.2m
Draught 2.5ft/0.76m
Materials Steel throughout
Original use Passengers
Condition Intact
Present owners
Binnenschiffahrtsmuseum
Contact address Hermann-Seidel-Str
44, 16248 Oderberg
Location Oderberg, Germany
History Sidewheel steamer built to
carry passengers on the Elbe River.
Formerly based at Dresden. Currently
maintained as a museum at Oderberg.
Bibliography B13, B16

Rigmor
sailing customs patrol vessel

Former name ANNA CHRISTINA
Built 1855 by J P Schroder, Gluckstadt,
Germany
Propulsion Sail, cutter rig
Length 53.5ft/16.3m
Breadth 12.2ft/3.72m
Draught 4.8ft/1.45m
Materials Wood throughout
Original use Customs cutter
Condition Restoration in progress
Present owners Forderverein RIGMOR

von Gluckstadt
Location Gluckstadt, Germany
History Sailing customs patrol vessel of
the 1850s. During the late 1990s was
undergoing restoration to sailing
condition at Tonning, Germany.
Bibliography B13

Rosinante
sailing coaster (aak)

Built 1909 at Moerdijk, Netherlands
Propulsion Sail, sloop rig (aak type);
auxiliary engine, 52hp
Tonnage 39 gross
Length 59.0ft/18.0m
Breadth 13.1ft/4.0m
Draught 2.0ft/0.6m
Materials Steel hull
Original use Cargo
Condition In sailing condition
Present owners Peter Hofrichter
Contact address Keplerstr 10, 22765
Hamburg
Location Oevelgonne, nr Hamburg,
Germany
History Sloop-rigged leeboard sailing
cargo vessel built in the Netherlands
for the coastal and inland waterways
trade. Maintained in sailing condition
by a private owner in Germany.
Bibliography B13

Ruth
sailing barge

Built 1926
Propulsion Sail, sloop rig (sailing
barge)
Tonnage 321 gross
Length 136.5ft/41.6m
Breadth 16.7ft/5.1m
Materials Steel throughout
Original use Cargo
Condition In sailing condition
Present owners Deutsche
Binnenreederei Gmbh
Location Berlin, Germany
History Type of barge employed on the
canals and rivers of Germany. Fitted
with a single folding mast setting a
large sprit-rigged sail. Maintained fully
rigged as a floating exhibit and active
sailing vessel.
Bibliography B13

Ruthof
sidewheel steam tug

Former name EREKCSANAD
Built 1922 by Ruthof Werft,
Regensburg, Germany
Original owners Bayerischer Lloyd,
Regensburg
Propulsion Steam, sidewheel, 800hp

Ruthof

Sachsenwald

Tonnage 505 displacement
Length 198.32ft/60.45m
Breadth 54.53ft/16.62m
Draught 4.49ft/1.37m
Materials Steel throughout
Original use River towing
Condition Intact
Present owners Arbeitskreis
Schiffahrtsmuseum
Contact address Werftstrasse, 93018
Regensburg
Location Regensburg, Germany
History Sidewheel steam towboat of a
type once common on the larger rivers
of Germany. Now preserved as a
floating exhibit at Regensburg.
Bibliography B13

Saatsee
steam floating crane

Former name SIMSON
Built 1920 by Schiffs-und-
Maschinenbau, Mannheim, Germany
Original owners Kaiserliches Kanalamt
Propulsion Non self-propelled; steam
hoisting machinery
Length 73.64ft/22.45m
Breadth 44.12ft/13.45m
Draught 4.92ft/1.5m
Materials Steel throughout
Original use Floating crane
Condition Intact

Present owners Museum der Arbeit
Contact address Maurienstr 19, 22305
Hamburg
Location Hamburg, Germany
History Large steam floating harbour
crane preserved as an exhibit at
Hamburg.
Bibliography B13

Sachsenwald
steam tug

Built 1914 by Gebr Wiemann,
Brandenburg, Germany
Original owners G Helmeke,
Altenplatow
Propulsion Steam, screw, 220hp
Length 82.0ft/25.0m
Breadth 16.73ft/5.1m
Draught 3.94ft/1.2m
Materials Steel throughout
Original use River towing
Condition Intact
Present owners Bernd Frenzl
Contact address Am Hausberg 1, 01796
Pirna
Location Pirna, Germany
History Steam towboat formerly
employed on the rivers of Germany.
Currently an excursion vessel based at
Potsdam near Berlin, without
significant alterations.
Bibliography B13

Sampo
sailing pilot vessel

Former name MAAGEN, GUSTAV
KRUGER
Built 1896 by Gebr Ihms, Kiel,
Germany
Propulsion Sail, ketch rig; diesel
auxiliary, 65hp
Tonnage 19.5 gross
Length 68.9ft/21.0m
Breadth 14.8ft/4.5m
Materials Wood throughout
Original use Pilot cutter, later cargo
Condition In sailing condition
Present owners Eignergemeinschaft
'Sampo'
Location Kiel, Germany
History Originally built as a sailing
pilot vessel for the Elbe River pilots.
Later served as a cargo vessel under the
Danish flag. Returned to German
ownership in the 1990s and currently
maintained in sailing condition there
rigged as a ketch.
Bibliography B13

Saturn
steam tug

Former name GEBR WULFF 4
Built 1907 by Janssen & Schmilinsky,
Hamburg, Germany

Original owners Gebr Wulff, Hamburg
Propulsion Steam, screw, compound,
140hp
Tonnage 26 displacement
Length 52.61ft/16.04m
Breadth 16.4ft/5.0m
Draught 6.66ft/2.03m
Materials Steel throughout
Original use Tug
Condition Intact
Present owners Rostock Maritime
Museum
Contact address Traditionsschiff,
Liegeplatz Schmarl, 18106 Rostock
Location Rostock, Germany
History German steam harbour tug
preserved on shore at the Rostock
maritime museum.
Bibliography B13

Schaarhörn
yacht/inspection steamer

Built 1908 by Schiffswerft &
Maschinefabrik, Hamburg, Germany
Original owners Hamburg State
Council
Propulsion Steam, triple expansion,
600hp
Tonnage 140 gross
Length 117.0ft/37.0m
Breadth 22.45ft/6.8m
Draught 9.8ft/3.0m
Materials Steel throughout
Original use State yacht
Condition In operation
Present owners Freunde des
Dampfschiffs 'Schaarhörn' eV
Contact address Geschaftsstelle
Hollandweg 54, 25241 Pinneberg
Location Hamburg, Germany
History Yacht and inspection steamer
for the State of Hamburg. Owned in
Great Britain in the 1970s as a private
yacht. Eventually returned to Germany
and fully restored there. Based at the
'museum harbour' at Oevelgonne on
the Elbe River below Hamburg.
Bibliography D456, D573

Schmilka
sidewheel river steamer

Former name HOENZOLLERN, MEISSEN,
SACHSEN
Built 1897 by Werft Blasewitz, Dresden,
Germany
Propulsion Steam, sidewheel, 138hp
Tonnage 255 displacement
Length 183.92ft/56.06m
Breadth 33.42ft/10.19m
Draught 3.83ft/1.17m
Materials Steel throughout, except
deck planking
Original use Passengers

Condition Intact, laid up
Present owners Sachsische Dampfschiffahrt Gmbh
Contact address Lingner Allee 3, 01609 Dresden
Location Dresden, Germany
History Veteran German Elbe River steamboat that survives laid up on shore at the company shipyard near Dresden. Has not operated since her boiler was condemned in 1977.
Bibliography B16, B43

Schulschiff Deutschland
sail training ship

Built 1927 by J C Tecklenborg, Bremerhaven, Germany
Original owners Deutscher Schulschiff Verein
Propulsion Sail, full-rigged ship
Tonnage 1257 gross
Length 221.5ft/67.51m
Breadth 39.0ft/11.89m

Draught 16.5ft/5.03m
Materials Steel throughout
Original use Training vessel
Condition Intact
Present owners Deutscher Schulschiff Verein
Contact address Auf dem Dreieck 5, 28197 Bremen
Location Vegesack, Germany
History Full-rigged ship built as a training vessel for future officers in the German merchant marine. Since the Second World War has been used as a floating school, with rig intact, moored near the Port of Bremen.
Bibliography A14, B13, C26, C96

Schulte
cargo lighter

Built 1913
Propulsion Towed
Length 74.5ft/22.71m
Breadth 18.5ft/5.64m

Schaarhorn

Schulschiff Deutschland

Materials Steel throughout
Original use Cargo lighter barge
Present owners Museum of Labor, Hamburg
Location Hamburg, Germany
History Example of a type of lighter barge formerly employed in the Port of Hamburg. Preserved as a floating exhibit at Barmbek, Hamburg.

Sea Cloud
luxury yacht

Former name ANTARNA, PATRIA, ANGELITA, HUSSAR
Built 1931 by Friedrich Krupp, Kiel, Germany
Original owners E F Hutton, New York
Propulsion Sail, 4-masted barque rig, diesel engines
Tonnage 2323 gross

Length 253.3ft/77.21m
Breadth 49.0ft/14.94m
Draught 16.5ft/5.03m
Materials Steel throughout
Original use Yacht
Condition In operation
Location Germany (registered in Cayman Islands)
History World's only luxury yacht built as a 4-masted barque. Owned by American millionairess Marjorie Hutton, who loaned her to the United States Coast Guard during the Second World War. Later the presidential yacht of the Dominican Republic, and a training ship for young people operating out of Miami. Fully restored by German owners to operate as a luxury cruise ship, primarily in the Mediterranean and the Caribbean.
Bibliography D42, D325, D347, D373

Seefalke

ocean tug

Built 1924 by J C Tecklenborg,
Geestemunde, Germany
Propulsion Diesel engines, 3000hp
Tonnage 619 gross
Length 191.93ft/58.5m
Breadth 29.53ft/9.0m
Draught 14.44ft/4.4m
Materials Steel throughout
Original use Ocean towing
Condition Intact
Present owners Deutsches
Schiffahrtsmuseum
Location Bremerhaven, Germany
History Veteran German seagoing tug
employed in long ocean tows and
salvage. Now maintained as one of the
floating exhibits of the maritime
museum in Bremerhaven.
Bibliography B13, B46, D398

Seehund type

midget submarine

Built 1945
Original owners Germany Navy
Propulsion Diesel engines
Tonnage 12.5 displacement
Length 39.69ft/12.1m
Breadth 4.26ft/1.3m
Draught 5.08ft/1.55m
Materials Steel throughout
Original use Midget submarine
Condition Intact
Present owners Cuxhaven Wreck
Museum
Location Cuxhaven, Germany
History Example of a numerous class
of midget submarine built for the
German Navy during the Second
World War. Exhibited on shore at
Cuxhaven.

Seehund type

midget submarine

Built 1945
Original owners German Navy
Propulsion Diesel engines, 25hp
Tonnage 12.5 displacement
Length 39.69ft/12.1m
Breadth 4.26ft/1.3m
Draught 5.08ft/1.55m
Materials Steel throughout
Original use Midget submarine
Condition Intact
Present owners Auto & Technik-
Museum
Contact address Obere Au 2, 74889
Sinsheim
Location Sinsheim, Germany
History Example of a numerous class
of midget submarines built for the

Seefalke

German Navy during the Second
World War. Preserved as an exhibit on
shore in Sinsheim.

Seehund type

midget submarine

Built 1944
Original owners German Navy
Propulsion Diesel and electric motors
Tonnage 14.9 displacement
Length 39.1ft/11.86m
Breadth 5.7ft/1.68m
Draught 4.11ft/1.55m
Materials Steel throughout
Original use Midget submarine
Condition Intact
Present owners Deutsches
Schiffahrtsmuseum
Contact address Van-Ronzelen-Strasse,
27568 Bremerhaven
Location Bremerhaven, Germany
History Two-man midget submarine
built for use in the Second World War.
Fitted to carry two torpedoes
externally. Preserved as an exhibit
inside the maritime museum in
Bremerhaven.

Seehund type

midget submarine

Built 1944
Original owners German Navy
Propulsion Diesel and electric motors
Tonnage 14.9 displacement
Length 39.1ft/11.86m
Breadth 5.7ft/1.68m
Draught 4.11ft/1.55m
Materials Steel throughout
Original use Midget submarine
Condition Intact
Present owners Wehrtechnische

Type XXVIIB 'Seehund'

Seute Deern, ex-Elizabeth Bandi

Studiensammlung
Contact address Mayener Str 85-87, 56070 Koblenz
Location Koblenz, Germany
History Two-man midget submarine built for use in the Second World War. Fitted to carry two torpedoes externally. Preserved as an exhibit in Koblenz.

Seehund type
midget submarine

Built 1944
Original owners German Navy
Propulsion Diesel and electric motors
Tonnage 14.9 displacement
Length 39.1ft/11.86m
Breadth 5.7ft/1.68m
Draught 4.11ft/1.55m
Materials Steel throughout
Original use Midget submarine
Condition Intact

Present owners German Navy
Location Wilhelmshaven, Germany
History Two-man midget submarine built for use in the Second World War. Fitted to carry two torpedoes externally. Preserved as an exhibit in Wilhelmshaven.

Seima
steam tug

Former name EINTRACHT
Built 1908 by Gebr Wiemann, Brandenburg, Germany
Propulsion Steam, screw, 110hp
Tonnage 120 displacement
Length 65.4ft/19.92m
Breadth 14.7ft/4.48m
Materials Steel throughout
Original use Tug
Condition In operation
Present owners Deutsche Binnenreederei

Contact address Abt Technik, Alt Stralau 55-58, 10245 Berlin
Location Berlin, Germany
History Originally built as a tug. Currently used for passenger cruises.
Bibliography B13

Seute Deern
trading schooner

Former name ELIZABETH BANDI
Built 1919 by Gulfport Shipbuilding Co, Gulfport, Mississippi, USA
Original owners Marine Co, Mobile
Propulsion Sail, 4-masted schooner; later auxiliary barque
Tonnage 814 gross
Length 178.58ft/54.43m
Breadth 36.17ft/11.02m
Draught 14.76ft/4.5m
Materials Wood throughout originally; later steel deckhouse and masts
Original use Cargo
Condition Intact, in stationary use
Present owners Deutsches Schiffahrtsmuseum
Location Bremerhaven, Germany
History Built on the American Gulf of Mexico coast as a 4-masted schooner for carrying various cargoes in the Atlantic coastal trade. Converted to a training ship for the merchant marine in Germany in the 1930s with addition of a steel deckhouse and barque rig. Since the Second World War has served as refugee housing, a floating school in the Netherlands, and currently as a floating restaurant in Bremerhaven.
Bibliography A14, B13, B46, C96

Seute Deern
trading ketch

Former name HAVET
Built 1939
Propulsion Sail, ketch rig; diesel auxiliary, 165hp. Engine built by Alpha
Tonnage 105 gross
Length 118.2ft/36.0m
Breadth 23.5ft/7.15m
Draught 10.5ft/3.2m
Materials Wood throughout
Original use Cargo
Condition In operation
Present owners 'Clipper' Deutsches Jugendwerk zur See eV
Location Bremerhaven, Germany
History Ketch-rigged sailing vessel built to carry cargo in the coastal and Baltic Sea trades. Maintained in sailing condition as a youth training vessel based at Bremerhaven.
Bibliography B13

Spökenkieker
fishing ketch

Former name MARTHA
Built 1935 by Dawartz, Tonning
Original owners Fritz Lorenzen, Husum
Propulsion Sail, ketch rig; diesel auxiliary, 100hp
Tonnage 15.0 displacement
Length 49.2ft/15.0m
Breadth 13.1ft/4.0m
Materials Wood throughout
Original use Fishing
Condition In sailing condition
Present owners Helmut Janecke
Location Wismar, Germany
History Sailing fishing vessel built in the 1930s. Maintained in sailing condition as a private yacht.
Bibliography B13

St Georg
passenger steamer

Former name FALKE
Built 1875 by Reiherstieg-Werft, Hamburg, Germany
Original owners H E Justus, Hamburg, Germany
Propulsion steam, screw, 2-cylinder, 116hp
Tonnage 36.48 gross
Length 79.2ft/24.12m
Breadth 13.8ft/4.2m
Materials Iron hull
Original use River passenger steamer
Condition Restored to steam in 1994, in operation
Present owners Verein Alsterdampfschiffahrt
Contact address Dorotheenstrasse 9, 22301 Hamburg
Location Hamburg, Germany
History Commuter steamer formerly employed on the large lake around which many of the residential suburbs of Hamburg are located. Brought back to Hamburg and fully restored to operating condition with an appropriate steam engine. Currently employed on weekend excursions/dinner cruises.

St Georg
sailing fishing vessel

Built 1923 in the Netherlands
Propulsion Sail, cutter rig
Length 52.5ft/16.0m
Breadth 14.8ft/4.5m
Draught 2.6ft/0.8m
Materials Steel hull
Original use Fishing
Condition Intact
Present owners St Nikolaus-

Schifferverein
Contact address Kaiser-Heinrich-Str 25,
56220 Urmitz
Location Urmitz, Germany
History Cutter-rigged vessel built in the
Netherlands. Preserved as an exhibit
on shore beside the Rhine River, fully
rigged.
Bibliography B13

Stadt Wehlen
sidewheel river steamer

Former name DRESDEN, MUHLBERG
Built 1879 by Werft Blasewitz, Dresden
Propulsion Steam, sidewheel, 140hp.
Engine built by Rushton & Co, Prague
Tonnage 271 displacement
Length 194.3ft/59.21m
Breadth 34.25ft/10.44m
Draught 3.0ft/0.88m
Materials Steel throughout, except
planked decks
Original use Passengers
Condition In operation
Present owners Sachsische
Dampfschiffahrts Gmbh
Contact address Hertha-Lindner-
Strasse 10, 01067 Dresden
Location Dresden, Germany
History The oldest operating German
Elbe River steamboat. Powered by the
1857 engine of a previous steamer
named DRESDEN. In regular service
making day excursions out of Dresden.
Bibliography B13, B16, B43

Stettin
steam icebreaker

Built 1933 by Stettiner Oderwerke,
Stettin, Germany
Original owners Stettin Industrie und
Handelskammer
Propulsion Steam, screw, triple
expansion, 2200hp, coal-fired
Tonnage 836 gross
Length 169.78ft/51.75m
Breadth 4406ft/13.43m
Draught 17.72ft/5.4m
Materials Steel throughout
Original use Icebreaker
Condition In operating condition
Present owners Forderverein Eisbrecher
'Stettin'
Contact address Kapt Manfred Fraider,
Kielmannseggstr 98, 22043 Ham
Location Travemunde, Germany
History German steam icebreaker in
active use until 1981. Maintained in
operating condition based at
Travemunde during the summer
months and at Oevelgonne on the Elbe
River below Hamburg the remainder
of the year.

Stettin

Bibliography B13, B16, D414

Stier
motor tug

Built 1954 by Jade Werft,
Wilhelmshaven, Germany
Original owners Hapag Lloyd,
Bremerhaven
Propulsion Diesel engines, Voith
Schneider system, 350hp
Tonnage 76 gross
Length 65.12ft/19.85m
Breadth 20.34ft/6.2m
Draught 10.33ft/3.15m
Materials Steel throughout
Original use Tug
Condition Intact
Present owners Deutsches
Schiffahrtsmuseum
Location Bremerhaven, Germany
History First tug built with the Voith
Schneider system which uses vertical
vanes rather than a propeller. System
was adopted for guiding ships through
the congested docks of Bremen and
Bremerhaven because it gives full
manoeuvrability in every direction.
Now preserved as an outdoor exhibit
on shore at the maritime museum in

Bremerhaven.
Bibliography B13, B46

Stralsund
steam railway ferry

Built 1890 by Schichau, Elbing,
Germany
Original owners Deutsche Reichsbahn
Propulsion Steam, screw, 225hp
Length 123.0ft/37.5m
Breadth 32.14ft/9.8m
Materials Steel throughout
Original use Railway ferry
Condition In operation
Present owners Deutsche Reichsbahn,
Berlin
Location Wolgast, Germany
History Small steam railway ferry built
to operate between Stralsund and the
Island of Rugen in northeastern
Germany. Recently retired, and now
serving as an exhibit afloat at Wolgast.
Bibliography B13, B16

Taucher Flint III
cargo barge (tjalk)

Former name WELVAART
Built 1910 in the Netherlands

Propulsion Sail, tjalk rig; converted to
work barge with steam engine
Tonnage 69 gross
Length 81.4ft/24.08m
Breadth 16.1ft/4.9m
Draught 6.8ft/2.06m
Materials Steel throughout
Original use Cargo, later work barge
Condition In operation
Present owners Reyner Biermann
Location Peckfitz, Germany
History Dutch cargo-carrying 'tjalk'
floated by a Hamburg company after
being wrecked near Cuxhaven in 1910,
and converted to their own use as a
salvage vessel with steam engine and
hoisting gear. Now preserved afloat as
a historic exhibit.
Bibliography B13

Teniers
steam tug

Built 1909 by P Smit Jun, Rotterdam,
Netherlands
Propulsion Steam, screw, 145hp
Length 79.31ft/24.18m
Breadth 15.74ft/4.8m
Draught 4.76ft/1.45m
Materials Steel hull

Original use Tug
Condition Intact
Present owners Westfalisches
Industriemuseum
Location Dortmund, Germany
History Steam harbour tug built in the
Netherlands. Currently maintained as
one of the floating exhibits of the
Westphalian Industrial Museum in
Waltrop.
Bibliography B13

Thea-Angela
motor river barge

Built 1929 by Wolthuis & Zoon,
Veendam, Netherlands
Propulsion Diesel engine
Tonnage 258 displacement
Length 111.6ft/34.0m
Breadth 19.8ft/6.02m
Draught 6.4ft/1.95m
Materials Steel throughout
Original use Cargo, river motor barge
Condition Intact
Present owners Schiffahrtsmuseum
Haren
Contact address Kanalstrasse, 49733
Haren
Location Haren, Germany
History Originally built as a cargo river
barge. Now preserved as a floating
exhibit.
Bibliography B13

Teniers

Theodor Heuss
rescue lifeboat

Former name H H MEIER
Built 1960 by Fr Schweers, Bardenfleth,
Germany
Original owners German lifeboat
service
Propulsion Diesel engine
Tonnage 30 gross
Length 76.1ft/23.2m
Breadth 17.4ft/5.3m
Draught 4.7ft/1.42m
Materials Steel throughout
Original use Rescue lifeboat
Condition Intact
Present owners Deutsches Museum
Contact address Museumsinsel, 80306
Munich
Location Munich, Germany
History Currently on exhibit.
Bibliography B13

Tiger
steam harbour tug

Built 1910 by Janssen & Schmilinsky,
Hamburg, Germany
Original owners Jurgen Hinrich
Steffen, Hamburg
Propulsion Steam, screw, 420hp
Tonnage 38 gross
Length 52.43ft/15.98m
Breadth 15.75ft/4.8m

Draught 5.91ft/1.8m
Materials Steel throughout
Original use Tug
Condition In operating condition
Present owners Museumhafen
Oevelgonne
Location Oevelgonne, nr Hamburg,
Germany
History Steam harbour tug built to
operate in the harbour of Hamburg.
Has wheelhouse that lowers for passing
under the city's bridges. Maintained as
an operating steam vessel based at the
'museum harbour' at Oevelgonne on
the Elbe River below Hamburg.
Bibliography B13, B16, D116

Traditionsschiff
motor cargo vessel

Former name DRESDEN
Built 1957 by Warnowwerft,
Warnemunde, Germany
Original owners VEB Deutsche
Seereederei
Propulsion Diesel engines, 1800hp
Tonnage 6527 gross, 10,000
displacement
Length 518.35ft/157.99m
Breadth 65.5ft/19.96m
Draught 27.5ft/8.38m
Materials Steel throughout
Original use Cargo
Condition Intact
Present owners Rostock
Schiffbaumuseum
Contact address Liegeplatz Schmarl,
18106 Rostock
Location Rostock, Germany
History Large cargo vessel built in East
Germany during the 1950s. Serves as a
floating museum containing exhibits
on Rostock shipbuilding from
medieval times to the present. Also
serves as headquarters for a fleet of
museum craft displayed in the water
and on shore.

U-1
submarine

Built 1906 by Germaniawerft, Kiel,
Germany
Original owners Imperial German
Navy
Propulsion Kerosine engines and
electric motors
Tonnage 238 displacement
Length 138.75ft/42.4m
Breadth 12.5ft/3.8m
Draught 10.5ft/3.2m
Materials Steel throughout
Original use Submarine
Condition Intact, partly cut open
Present owners Deutsches Museum

Location Munich, Germany
History First submarine of the German
Navy. Primarily used for tests and
training. Retired in 1919 and given to
present owners two years later.
Exhibited inside the museum with one
side cut open to show the interior
layout.
Bibliography A6, B13

U-9
submarine

Built 1966 by Howaldtswerke AG, Kiel,
Germany
Original owners German Navy
Official number U-9
Propulsion Diesel and electric motors
Tonnage 455 displacement
Length 152.8ft/46.57m
Breadth 15.1ft/4.59m
Draught 14.0ft/4.26m
Materials Steel throughout
Original use Submarine
Condition Intact
Present owners Wehrtechnische
Studiensammlung
Contact address Geibstrasse, 67346
Speyer
Location Speyer, Germany
History On exhibit.
Bibliography B13

U-10
submarine

Built 1967 by Howaldtswerke AG, Kiel,
Germany
Original owners German Navy
Official number U-10
Propulsion Diesel and electric motors
Tonnage 455 displacement
Length 152.8ft/46.57m
Breadth 15.1ft/4.59m
Draught 14.0ft/4.26m
Materials Steel throughout
Original use Submarine
Condition Intact
Present owners Freizeit in
Wilhelmshaven Gmbh
Location Wilhelmshaven, Germany
History On exhibit.
Bibliography B13

U-995
submarine

Built 1941 by Blohm & Voss, Hamburg,
Germany
Original owners German Navy
Propulsion Diesel and electric motors,
3200hp
Tonnage 769 displacement
Length 220.0ft/67.06m
Breadth 20.0ft/6.1m

Draught 15.0ft/4.57m
Materials Steel throughout
Original use Submarine
Condition Intact
Present owners Deutscher Marinebund
Contact address Strandstrasse 92, 24233 Laboe
Location Laboe, nr Kiel, Germany
History German U-boat that served in the Second World War. Later operated by the Norwegian Navy as the KAURA. Returned to Germany and now installed on shore as a museum and monument to the crew of submarines lost during the war.
Bibliography A6, B13, D233

Undine

trading schooner

Former name NORDSTRAND I
Built 1931 by Gebr Niestern, Delfsijl, Netherlands
Propulsion Sail, schooner rig
Tonnage 96 gross
Length 121.4ft/37.0m
Breadth 19.0ft/5.8m
Materials Steel hull
Original use Cargo
Condition Restored to sailing condition
Present owners Joachim Kaiser
Contact address Reichenstrasse 30, 25348 Gluckstadt
Location Hamburg, Germany
Bibliography B13, D266

Valdivia

schooner yacht

Former name VANADIS
Built 1868 by Sodra Varvet, Stockholm, Sweden
Propulsion Sail, schooner rig; diesel auxiliary added
Tonnage 27 gross, 50 displacement
Length 95.2ft/29.0m
Breadth 16.7ft/5.1m
Draught 9.2ft/2.8m
Original use Yacht
Condition In sailing condition
Present owners Uwe Kutzner
Location Flensburg, Germany
Bibliography B13

Vampyr II

steam tug

Former name WALTERSHOF, HUGO STINNES V
Built 1911 in the Netherlands
Propulsion Steam, screw
Length 72.5ft/22.1m
Breadth 18.2ft/5.56m
Materials Steel throughout
Original use Tug

Undine

Condition Intact
Present owners Verein Alsterdampfschiffahrt
Contact address Bansenstrasse 11, 21075 Hamburg
Location Hamburg, Germany
History Restored steam vessel.
Bibliography B13

Vegesack

fishing ketch

Built 1895 by Bremer Vulkan, Bremen, Germany
Official number BV 2
Propulsion Sail, ketch rig
Tonnage 74 gross, 55 displacement
Length 116.2ft/35.4m
Breadth 17.8ft/5.42m
Materials Steel hull
Original use Fishing
Condition Intact
Present owners Maritime Tradition
Contact address Weserstrasse 18, 28757

Bremen
Location Vegesack, Germany
History Sailing fishing vessel formerly employed in the North Sea fisheries. Fully restored to sailing condition and her original appearance. Maintained as a floating exhibit and an active sailing vessel based at Vegesack.
Bibliography B13

Volldampf

steam tug

Former name ELSE OTTO
Built 1896 by Stettiner Vulcan, Stettin, Germany
Propulsion Steam, screw; converted to diesel
Tonnage 72 displacement
Length 58.71ft/17.9m
Breadth 13.78ft/4.2m
Draught 4.92ft/1.5m
Materials Steel hull
Original use Tug
Condition Intact
Present owners Deutsches Technik Museum
Contact address Trebbiner Str 9, 10963 Berlin
Location Berlin, Germany
History Steam tug formerly employed on the inland waterways of Germany. Preserved afloat as an exhibit in Berlin.
Bibliography B13

Wal

steam icebreaker

Built 1938 by Stettiner Oderwerke, Stettin, Germany
Original owners Wasserstrassen-

Wal

Walter Havernick

Maschinenamt, Rendsburg
Propulsion Steam, screw, 1200hp
Tonnage 662 gross
Length 164.0ft/50.0m
Breadth 40.34ft/12.3m
Draught 17.22ft/5.25m
Materials Steel throughout
Original use Icebreaker
Condition Intact
Present owners Museumsschiff Dampf-
Eisbrecher 'Wal'
Location Bremerhaven, Germany
History German steam icebreaker
maintained in operating condition and
exhibited at Bremerhaven.
Bibliography B13, D389

Walter
river lighter

Former name FRITZ
Built 1901 by Droescher, Rathenow,
Germany
Propulsion Towed
Tonnage 558 displacement
Length 197.7ft/60.25m
Breadth 20.4ft/6.23m
Materials Steel throughout
Original use Cargo, river barge
Condition Intact
Present owners Museumshafen Lubeck
Contact address c/o Rolf Buttner,
Kronsforder Allee 19a, 23560 Lubeck
Location Lubeck, Germany
History Preserved as a floating exhibit.
Bibliography B13

Walter Hävernick
fireboat

Former name FEUERWEHR IV,
OBERBAURAT SCHMIDT
Built 1930 by A Pahl, Finkenwerder,

Germany
Propulsion Diesel engine, 120hp
Tonnage 27 displacement
Length 54.12ft/16.5m
Breadth 11.81ft/3.6m
Draught 4.59ft/1.4m
Materials Steel throughout
Original use Fireboat
Condition Intact
Present owners Museum fur
Hamburgische Geschichte
Location Oevelgonne, nr Hamburg,
Germany
History Fireboat formerly stationed in
the Port of Hamburg. Maintained in
operating condition based at the
'museum harbour' at Oevelgonne on
the Elbe River below Hamburg.
Bibliography B13

Wehlen-Bastei

Wasserboot II
fresh water tanker

Built 1928 by Joh Oelkers, Hamburg,
Germany
Propulsion Steam, screw; converted to
diesel
Tonnage 240 displacement
Length 77.08ft/23.5m
Breadth 19.02ft/5.8m
Materials Steel throughout
Original use Water boat
Condition Intact
Present owners Museumshafen
Oevelgonne
Location Oevelgonne, nr Hamburg,
Germany
History Steam tanker formerly used to
supply fresh water to ships in the Port
of Hamburg. Maintained in operating
condition based at the 'museum
harbour' at Oevelgonne on the Elbe
River below Hamburg.

Wasserschutzpolizei 10
police boat

Built 1957 by Schiffswerft Ernst
Wilhelm, Eberbach, Neckar, Germany
Propulsion Diesel engine, 240hp. Engine
built by Daimler-Benz
Tonnage 10.5 displacement
Length 43.3ft/13.2m
Breadth 10.5ft/3.2m
Draught 3.0ft/0.9m
Materials Steel throughout
Original use Police boat
Condition Intact
Present owners Landesmuseum fur
Technik und Arbeit
Contact address Museumstrasse, 68165
Mannheim
Location Mannheim, Germany
History Preserved as a floating exhibit.
Bibliography B13

WBR-7
inshore minesweeper

Built 1943 by Abeking & Rasmussen,
Lemwerder, Germany
Original owners German Navy
Propulsion Diesel engines, 2550hp
Tonnage 140 displacement
Length 128.5ft/39.17m
Breadth 18.75ft/5.71m
Draught 5.0ft/1.52m
Materials Wood throughout
Original use Minesweeper
Condition Intact
Present owners Marinekamaradschaft
von 1895
Location Frankfurt, Germany
History German minesweeper built for
use in the Second World War.
Maintained in operating condition as a
training vessel based at Frankfurt.

Wehlen-Bastei
steam passenger ferry

Built 1925 by Werft Laubegast, Dresden,
Germany
Propulsion Steam, screw, compound,
45hp
Tonnage 23.5 gross
Length 47.56ft/14.5m
Breadth 11.48ft/3.5m
Draught 2.3ft/0.7m
Materials Steel throughout
Original use Pedestrian ferry
Condition In active service
Present owners Oberelbische
Verkehrsgesellschaft Pirna-Sebnitz, Pirna
Location Wehlen, Germany
History The last operating steam
pedestrian ferry in Germany. Operating
on the Elbe River in the eastern part of
the country.

Weilheim
minesweeper

Built 1958 by Burmester, Bremen,
Germany
Original owners West German Navy
Propulsion Two diesel engines, twin
screw, 4000hp. Engines built by
Maybach
Tonnage 465 displacement
Length 154.5 ft./43.5m
Breadth 26.5 ft./8.0m
Draught 8.25 ft./2.5m
Materials Wood throughout
Original use Minesweeper
Condition Intact, recently retired
Present owners City of Wilhelmshaven
Location Wilhelmshaven, Germany
History West German 'Lindau' class
coastal minesweeper based on
American MSC design. Official
number M1077. Retired in 1995 and
turned over to the City of
Wilhelmshaven in 1997 for use as a
floating exhibit.

Wels
dredger

Built 1936 by Lubecker Maschinenbau
Gesellschaft, Lubeck, Germany
Length 67.0ft/20.42m
Breadth 15.6ft/4.76m
Draught 2.6ft/0.8m
Original use Dredger
Present owners Museumshafen Lubeck
Contact address c/o Rolf Buttner,
Kronsforder Allee 19A, 23560 Lubeck
Location Lubeck, Germany
History Preserved as an exhibit.
Bibliography B13

Weser
lightship

Former name NORDERNEY I
Built 1907 by A G Weser, Bremen,
Germany
Original owners Wasser und
Schiffahrtsamt, Bremerhaven
Propulsion Steam, screw; replaced with
diesel engine, 330hp
Tonnage 382 gross, 532 displacement
Length 172.3ft/52.5m
Breadth 26.25ft/8.0m
Draught 15.09ft/4.6m
Materials Steel throughout
Original use Lightship
Condition Intact
Present owners City of Wilhelmshaven
Location Wilhelmshaven, Germany
History Veteran German lightship
formerly stationed off the North Sea
coast. Superstructure and light were
modernised during active career.

Windsbraut

Maintained as a floating museum at
Wilhelmshaven.
Bibliography B13

Wilhelm Bauer
submarine

Former name U-2540
Built 1945 by Blohm & Voss, Hamburg,
Germany
Original owners German Navy
Propulsion Diesel and electric motors
Tonnage 1621 displacement
Length 251.64ft/76.07m
Breadth 21.65ft/6.6m
Materials Steel throughout
Original use Submarine
Condition Intact
Present owners Deutsches
Schiffahrtsmuseum
Location Bremerhaven, Germany
History German submarine completed
at the end of the Second World War.
Maintained as one of the floating
exhibits of the maritime museum in
Bremerhaven.
Bibliography B13

Wilhelmine Von Stade
trading ketch

Former name WILHELMINE
Built pre-1912
Propulsion Sail, ketch rig; diesel
auxiliary, 60hp
Length 82.1ft/25.0m
Breadth 13.5ft/4.1m
Materials Iron or steel hull
Original use Cargo
Condition In sailing condition
Present owners Town of Stade
Contact address Rathaus, 21682 Stade
Location Stade, Germany
Bibliography B13

Woltman

Willi
motor barge

Built 1909 in Deest, Netherlands
Propulsion Diesel engine. Engine built
by Mercedes-Benz
Tonnage 370 displacement
Length 128.0ft/39.0m
Breadth 16.6ft/5.07m
Draught 6.9ft/2.1m
Materials Iron hull
Original use Cargo, motor barge
Condition Intact
Present owners Landesmuseum fur
Technik und Arbeit
Contact address Museumstrasse, 68165
Mannheim
Location Mannheim, Germany
History Preserved as an exhibit.
Bibliography B13

Windsbraut
trading ketch

Built 1911 by D Ropers, Stade, Germany
Propulsion Sail, ketch rig
Tonnage 127 gross
Length 88.0ft/26.75m
Breadth 16.4ft/5.0m
Materials Steel hull
Original use Cargo
Condition In sailing condition
Present owners Windsbraut eV
Contact address Postfach 1504, 21655
Stade
History Active sailing vessel and
exhibit.
Location Stade, Germany

Wismar
motor fishing boat

Built 1949 by VEB Boddenwerft,
Damgarten
Original owners FPG Inselfisch,
Karlshagen
Official number KAR 45
Propulsion Diesel engine, 80hp
Tonnage 31.09 gross
Length 57.73ft/17.6m
Breadth 16.4ft/5.0m
Draught 7.8ft/2.38m
Materials Wood throughout
Original use Fishing
Condition Intact
Present owners Rostock Maritime
Museum
Location Rostock, Germany
History Example of a German Baltic
motor fishing boat of the 1940s.
Preserved as an exhibit on shore at the
maritime museum in Rostock.
Bibliography B13

Woltman
steam harbour tug

Built 1904 by Gebr Sachsenburg,
Rosslau, Germany
Propulsion Steam, screw, 240hp
Tonnage 103 displacement
Length 65.6ft/20.0m
Breadth 16.73ft/5.1m
Draught 7.87ft/2.4m
Materials Steel hull, steel and wood
superstructure
Original use Tug
Condition In operating condition
Present owners Forderverein
Schleppdampfer Woltman eV
Contact address Muggenkampstr 31a,
20257 Hamburg
Location Oevelgonne, nr Hamburg
History Steam harbour tug in
operating condition formerly
maintained by steam enthusiasts in the
Netherlands. Acquired in Germany
and now based at Oevelgonne on the
Elbe below Hamburg.
Bibliography B13

WSS-10
experimental hydrofoil

Built 1953 by H C Stulcken Sohn,
Hamburg, Germany
Propulsion Petrol engines, 140hp
Length 30.18ft/9.2m
Breadth 6.56ft/2.0m
Draught 6.89ft/2.1m
Materials Steel hull
Original use Experimental
Condition Intact

WSS-10

Present owners Deutsches
Schiffahrtsmuseum
Location Bremerhaven, Germany
History Early experimental hydrofoil.
Preserved as an outdoor exhibit on
land at the maritime museum in
Bremerhaven.
Bibliography A16, B13

Württemburg
sidewheel steam towboat

Built 1908 by Gebr Sachsenburg,
Rosslau, Germany
Original owners Neue Deutsche
Bohmische Elbschiffahrt
Propulsion Steam, sidewheel
Length 209.26ft/63.8m
Breadth 23.71ft/7.23m
Draught 2.72ft/0.83m
Materials Steel throughout
Original use River towing
Condition Intact
Present owners Magdeburg State
Museum
Contact address Heinrich-Heine-Platz,
39114 Magdeburg
Location Magdeburg, Germany
History Large sidewheel steam towboat
of a type once common on the larger
German rivers. Preserved on shore as a
museum at Magdeburg.
Bibliography A16, B13

Württemburg

Great Britain

No nation has had a greater impact on world maritime development than Great Britain. This is particularly true from the birth of the Industrial Revolution in the British Isles in the 1700s to well into the twentieth century. That 'revolution' brought a dramatic increase in the demand for shipping, to bring raw materials to feed the new industries and to transport the finished products to ever-expanding markets. Britain developed a far-flung colonial empire, a merchant marine for worldwide trading that was unrivalled, and a navy larger than the combined fleets of any two potential opponents. Great Britain was one of the earliest nations to become seriously involved in maritime historic preservation. In fact, it can probably claim the earliest documented example. When Sir Francis Drake returned from the first British circumnavigation of the globe with his ship GOLDEN HINDE filled with treasure taken from Spain, Queen Elizabeth decreed that the vessel should be preserved permanently in a berth near London. It survived there well into the seventeenth century. Among the many vessels preserved in Britain today are several that embody actual milestones in the evolution of ships. Leading examples are the GREAT BRITAIN, pioneer transatlantic steamer that demonstrated the practicality of both iron construction and the propeller; the WARRIOR, first armoured warship with an iron hull; and TURBINIA, the yacht that first demonstrated steam turbine propulsion.

198
steam picket boat

Built 1911 by J Samuel White, East Cowes, Isle of Wight, England
Original owners British Royal Navy
Propulsion Steam, screw, compound. Engine built by A G Mumford, Colchester
Length 50.0ft/15.24m
Breadth 9.75ft/2.97m
Draught 3.75ft/1.14m
Materials Wood hull, steel and wood cabin
Original use Navy launch
Condition In operating condition
Present owners Royal Naval Museum
Location Portsmouth, England
History Preserved as a floating exhibit.
Bibliography B27

296
steam launch

Built 1942 by Hancocks Shipbuilding Co, Pembroke Dock, Wales
Original owners British Royal Navy
Propulsion Steam, screw, compound. Engine built by LNER, Glasgow, Scotland
Length 52.5ft/16.0m
Breadth 13.5ft/4.1m
Draught 5.25ft/1.6m
Materials Wood hull
Original use Navy launch
Condition In operating condition

Present owners West Wales Maritime Heritage Society
Location Milford Haven, Wales

376
steam launch

Built 1944 by Hancock Shipbuilding Co, Pembroke Dock, Wales
Original owners British Royal Navy
Propulsion Steam, screw, compound, 75hp. Engine built by W Sisson, Gloucester
Length 54.0ft/16.46m
Breadth 13.6ft/4.15m
Draught 5.25ft/1.6m
Materials Wood throughout
Original use Navy launch
Condition Undergoing restoration indoors
Present owners Chatham Historic Dockyard Trust
Location Chatham, England
Bibliography B27

1262
RAF launch

Built 1942 by Walton Yacht Slip, Walton-on-Thames, England
Original owners Royal Air Force
Original use Pinnace (launch)
Condition Intact; some alterations during active service
Present owners Scottish Maritime Museum, Irvine, Scotland

Location Irvine, Scotland
History Launch built during the Second World War for the use of the British Royal Air Force. Currently on exhibit with the fleet of the Scottish Maritime Museum.

Admiral Beatty
canal boat

Built 1896
Propulsion Towed by horses
Materials Wood throughout
Original use Cargo (canals)
Present owners The Black Country Museum
Contact address Tipton Road, New Wolverhampton Road, Dudley
Location Dudley, England
History Canal boat formerly employed on the inland waterways of England and preserved as an exhibit.

Advance
river barge

Former name D T Co ADVANCE
Built 1926 by P K Harris & Sons, Appledore, North Devon, England
Original owners Devon Trading Co, Exeter, England
Propulsion Towed; also engine, 15hp
Tonnage 20 gross
Length 48.1ft/14.66m
Breadth 15.2ft/4.63m
Depth 4.4ft/1.34m

376

Materials Wood throughout
Original use Cargo
Condition Aground, largely intact
Present owners Captain P M Herbert
Contact address Hartland Terrace,
Bude, Cornwall, England
Location River Torridge, England
History Built to carry sand and gravel
in sheltered waters on the north coast
of Devon. Survives aground in the
River Torridge between Appledore and
Bideford. Proposed exhibit.
Bibliography B29, D34

Alaska
passenger steamer

Built 1883 by J S & W J Horsham,
Bourne End, England
Original owners J S & W J Horsham
Propulsion Steam, screw, 2-cylinder
Tonnage 16 gross
Length 60.0ft/18.29m
Breadth 10.0ft/3.05m
Materials Wood throughout
Original use Passengers
Condition In operating condition

Present owners J M Yanaghas
Location Great Britain
History Fully restored nineteenth
century steam passenger launch, later
used as a yacht.
Bibliography B27

Albion
Norfolk wherry

Former name PLANE
Built 1898 by William Brighton, Lake
Lothing, Suffolk, England
Original owners W D & A E Walker,
Bungay, Suffolk
Propulsion sail, single mast, gaff-rigged
loose-footed mainsail
Length 58.0ft/17.68m
Breadth 15.0ft/4.57m
Draught 4.5ft/1.37m
Materials Wood throughout
Original use Cargo; inland waterways
Condition In operation
Present owners Norfolk Wherry Trust
Contact address Miss P J Oakes, 14
Mount Pleasant, Norwich NR2 2DG
Location Ludham, Norfolk, England

Albion sailing on Breydon Water in 1951

Alliance

History Type of sailing vessel called a
wherry used to carry cargo on inland
waterways of eastern England. Fully
restored to sailing condition in 1949 as
one of the first British efforts to
preserve a former working vessel. Used
for educational cruises.
Bibliography B49, C10, C57, D275

Aleida I
motor tug

Built 1930 by Rowhedge Iron Works,
Colchester, England
Original owners Great Ouse Catchment
Board
Propulsion Diesel engine. Engine built
by Widdop
Length 33.0ft/10.05m
Breadth 9.33ft/2.84m
Draught 3.75ft/1.14m
Materials Iron hull
Original use Tug
Condition Intact
Present owners The Boat Museum
Location Ellesmere Port, England
History Preserved as an exhibit.

Alfred Corry
sailing rescue lifeboat

Built 1893 by Breeching Brothers, Great
Yarmouth, England
Original owners Royal National
Volunteer Lifeboat Institution
Propulsion Sail, ketch rig
Length 44.0ft/13.41m
Materials Wood throughout
Original use Rescue lifeboat
Condition Intact
Present owners International
Boatbuilding Centre
Location Lowestoft, England
History Preserved as an exhibit.

Alliance
submarine

Former name HMS ALLIANCE
Built 1945 by Vickers-Armstrong,
Barrow, England
Original owners Royal Navy
Propulsion Diesel and electric motors
Tonnage 1620 displacement
Length 281.67ft/85.85m
Breadth 22.25ft/6.78m
Draught 17.0ft/5.18m
Materials Steel throughout
Original use Submarine
Condition Intact
Present owners Royal Navy Submarine
Museum, Gosport, Hants, England
Location Gosport, England
History British submarine built at the
end of the Second World War,
preserved on shore as an exhibit of a
museum devoted to the history of
submarines in the Royal Navy.
Bibliography A6, B24, D293

Amy Howson
Humber sloop

Former name SOPHIA, I KNOW
Built 1914 by Joseph Scarr & Sons,
Beverly, England
Original owners Mr Scaife
Propulsion Sloop rig
Length 68.0ft/20.73m
Breadth 17.0ft/5.18m
Draught 8.0ft/2.44m
Materials Steel hull, wood mast and
spars
Original use Cargo, inland waterways
Condition In operation
Present owners Humber Keel and Sloop
Preservation Society
Contact address c/o D Robinson, 135
Waterside Road, Barton-on-Humber

Location South Ferriby, Lincolnshire, England
History Example of a type of sailing vessel used to move cargo on the rivers of Yorkshire and Lincolnshire known as a Humber sloop. Fully restored and maintained in sailing condition.

Anglia
spritsail barge

Built 1898 by H Shrubsall, Ipswich, England
Original owners E A Hibbs
Propulsion Spritsail ketch rig
Tonnage 54 gross
Length 282.3ft/25.1m
Breadth 20.3ft/6.2m
Draught 5.6ft/1.7m
Materials Wood throughout
Original use Cargo; sailing barge
Condition Intact
Present owners G Reeves
Location Hoo, England
History Sailing barge built to carry cargo on the rivers and estuaries of eastern England. Later maintained as a private yacht, and currently serving as a houseboat fully rigged.

Antares
motor fishing boat

Built 1965 by J & G Forbes, Sandhaven
Original owners Eyemouth Fisherman's Mutual Association
Propulsion Diesel engine
Length 55.0ft/16.8m
Materials Wood hull
Original use Fishing
Condition Intact
Present owners Scottish Maritime Museum, Irvine, Scotland
Location Irvine, Scotland
History Example of a type of motor fishing boat employed off the coast of Scotland in the 1960s. Exhibited as part of the fleet of the Scottish Maritime Museum.

Arctic Corsair
motor fishing boat

Built 1960 by Cook, Welton & Gemmell, Beverly, England
Original owners Boyd Line, Hull
Propulsion Diesel engine, 1800hp. Engine built by Mirlees, Bickerton & Day
Tonnage 764 gross
Length 191.5ft/58.3m
Breadth 34.0ft/10.4m
Materials Steel throughout
Original use Fishing
Condition Intact

Present owners Hull City Council
Location Kingston-on-Hull, England
History Example of a British fishing boat of the 1960s preserved for use as a floating museum on the fishing industry of eastern England.

Ardwina
spritsail barge

Built 1909 by Orvis & Fuller, Ipswich, England
Propulsion Spritsail ketch rig
Tonnage 66 gross
Length 85.0ft/26.0m
Breadth 21.1ft/6.4m
Draught 6.4ft/2.0m
Materials Wood throughout
Original use Cargo, sailing barge
Condition In operation
Present owners Ardwina Ltd
Location St Katherine's, London, England
History Sailing barge built to carry cargo on the rivers and estuaries of eastern England. Now fitted to carry passengers on charters out of St Katherine's Dock next to the Tower of London.

Aries
canal boat

Built 1935 by Walker Brothers, Rickmansworth, England
Original owners Grand Union Canal

Carrying Co
Propulsion Diesel engine, 18hp. Engine built by Russell Newbury
Length 72.0ft/21.94m
Breadth 7.0ft/2.13m
Draught 3.0ft/0.91m
Materials Wood throughout
Original use Cargo; later canal maintenance
Condition Intact
Present owners Graham Warwick
Location Ellesmere Port, England
History Preserved as a floating exhibit.

Aspull
icebreaking barge

Built Date not known
Original owners British Waterways Board
Length 48.5ft/14.78m
Breadth 7.5ft/2.29m
Materials Wood hull
Original use Canal icebreaker
Condition Intact
Present owners National Waterways Museum
Contact address Ellesmere Port, England L65 4EF
Location Ellesmere Port, England
History Icebreaking barge formerly used on the Leeds and Liverpool Canal in central England, now preserved afloat as part of a large museum fleet at Ellesmere Port.
Bibliography B4

Atrato
spritsail barge

Built 1898 by Forrest & Son, Wivenhoe, England
Propulsion Spritsail ketch rig
Tonnage 63 gross
Length 84.4ft/25.7m
Breadth 18.6ft/5.7m
Draught 6.0ft/1.8m
Materials Steel hull, wood mast and spars
Original use Cargo, sailing barge
Condition Undergoing restoration
Present owners Rupert Ashmore
Location Battersea, London
History Built as a sailing barge to carry cargo on the rivers and estuaries of eastern England. Later converted to a motor barge. Currently being restored to sailing condition.

Auld Reekie
steam coaster

Former name VITAL SPARK, VIC 27
Built 1943 by Isaac Pimblott & Sons, Northwich, Cheshire, England
Original owners Ministry of War
Propulsion Steam, compound
Tonnage 96 gross
Length 66.75ft/20.35m
Breadth 18.42ft/5.61m
Draught 9.5ft/2.9m
Materials Steel throughout
Original use Cargo, harbour

Antares

Auld Reekie

Condition In operation
Present owners Land Sea and Air Youth Club
Location Oban, Scotland
History Small steamer built to carry cargo in harbour areas during the Second World War. Based on the 'Clyde puffer', a type used before the war to carry cargo around the west coast of Scotland via the Crinan Canal. Used as a club tender and for cruises. Maintained in operating condition in the region once served by the puffers.
Bibliography B27

B.A.S.P.
rescue lifeboat

Built 1924 by White, Cowes, Isle of Wight, England
Original owners Royal National Lifeboat Institution
Propulsion Motor
Length 45.0ft/13.5m
Breadth 12.5ft/3.75m
Draught 4.3ft/1.3m
Materials Wood hull
Original use Rescue lifeboat
Condition Intact
Present owners Royal National Lifeboat Collection
Location Chatham, England
History Preserved as an indoor exhibit.

Bacup
motor canal barge

Built 1951 by W J Yarwood, Northwich, England
Propulsion Engine. Engine built by Widdop

Length 62.0ft/18.9m
Breadth 15.0ft/4.57m
Materials Steel throughout
Original use Cargo, canals
Condition Intact
Present owners National Waterways Museum
Contact address Ellesmere Port, Cheshire, England L65 4EF
Location Ellesmere, England
History Motor barge formerly used to carry cargo on the Leeds and Liverpool Canal in central England. Preserved afloat as an exhibit, as part of a very large fleet of preserved coastal and inland waters craft.
Bibliography B4

Balmoral
passenger ferry

Built 1949 by J I Thornycroft, Southampton, England
Original owners Southampton, Isle of Wight Steam Packet Co
Propulsion Diesel engine
Tonnage 688 gross
Length 203.46ft/62.03m
Breadth 32.01ft/9.76m
Draught 6.63ft/2.02m
Materials Steel throughout
Original use Passenger ferry
Condition In operation
Present owners Craig Inns Ltd
Location Southampton, England
History Built as a ferry to operate between the Isle of Wight and the mainland of England. Used for passenger excursions during the summer months.
Bibliography D238, D239

Banshee
steam yacht

Built 1880 by H McIntyre & Co, Paisley, Scotland
Original owners Sir W B Forwood
Propulsion Steam, screw, compound, 75hp (current). Engine built by John Ashton (current)
Length 44.5ft/13.6m
Breadth 7.5ft/2.3m
Materials Iron hull, wood cabin
Original use Yacht
Condition Fully restored to operating condition
Present owners Anthony Goddard
Location River Medina
History Classic Victorian clipper-bow steam yacht, fully restored to operating condition in 1989 with steam engine and boilers built in 1971.

Barnabas
lugger

Built 1881 by Henry Trevorrow, St Ives, Cornwall, England
Original owners Thomas Family
Propulsion Two-masted lug rig
Tonnage 12 gross
Length 39.2ft/11.95m
Breadth 11.5ft/3.51m
Draught c6.0ft/1.83m

Barnabas

Materials Wood throughout
Original use Fishing
Condition Intact
Present owners Cornish Maritime Trust
Location Penryn, Falmouth, England
History Last surviving example of a Cornish two-masted lugger preserved as an exhibit afloat at Falmouth.

Basuto
cargo canal steamer

Built 1902 by William Jacks & Co, Port Dundas, Glasgow, Scotland
Propulsion Steam, screw, twin compound
Length 66.0ft/20.12m
Breadth 16.5ft/5.03m
Draught 9.0ft/2.74m
Materials Iron with steel additions
Original use Cargo, Forth & Clyde Canal
Condition Intact
Present owners Boat Museum Trust
Contact address Dockyard Road, Ellesmere Port, Cheshire L65 4EF, England
Location Ellesmere Port, England
History Small steamer used to carry

Basuto

cargo on the no longer extant Forth and Clyde Canal in Scotland. Later used as a barge, but was restored to steam power by a private owner and is now an exhibit afloat at Ellesmere Port.
Bibliography B4, B27

Belfast
cruiser

Former name HMS BELFAST
Built 1938 by Harland & Wolff, Belfast, Northern Ireland
Original owners Royal Navy
Propulsion Geared turbines. Engine built by Parsons
Tonnage 13,175 displacement
Length 579.0ft/176.48m
Breadth 66.0ft/20.12m
Draught 22.47ft/6.95m
Materials Steel throughout
Original use Cruiser
Condition Intact
Present owners Imperial War Museum
Contact address Lambeth Road, London SE1, England
Location London, England
History Last surviving British heavy cruiser, and a veteran of the Second World War. Preserved afloat in the Thames River near the Tower of London as a museum and a Naval memorial.
Bibliography A8, B24, B49, D562,570,571

Belfast

Blossom

Beric
spritsail barge

Built 1896 by Cann, Harwich
Original owners Cranfield Brothers
Official number 105421
Propulsion Spritsail ketch rig
Tonnage 63 gross
Materials Wood throughout
Original use Cargo
Condition Intact
Present owners Licensing Solutions Ltd
Location St Katherine's Dock, London
History Built as a sailing barge to carry cargo on the rivers and estuaries of eastern England. Restored to sailing condition as a charter vessel, but currently lies rigged at the yacht harbour at St Katherine's Dock in London where she is used for receptions.

Bessie
canal boat

Built 1917
Materials Iron hull
Original use Cargo, canals
Condition Intact
Present owners The Black Country Museum
Contact address Wolverhampton Road, Dudley, West Midlands, England
Location Dudley, England
History Example of a canal boat used

to carry various cargoes on the inland waterways of England preserved as an exhibit.

Bigmere
canal barge

Built 1948 by W J Yarwood & Sons, Northwich, England
Original owners Bridgewater Canal
Propulsion Towed by tug
Length 71.0ft/21.64m
Breadth 14.5ft/4.42m
Draught 6.0ft/1.83m
Materials Steel throughout
Original use Cargo, canal barge
Condition Intact
Present owners North Western Museum of Inland Navigation
Location Ellesmere Port, England
History Steel canal barge of a type built in the 1940s for use on the Bridgewater Canal. Preserved as one of the many floating exhibits of the maritime museum in Ellesmere Port.
Bibliography B4

Birchills
canal barge

Built c1914 by Braithwaite and Kirk, West Bromwich, England
Original owners Fellows, Morton & Clayton
Propulsion Diesel engine. Engine built

by Gardner
Length 57.0ft/17.37m
Breadth 7.0ft/2.13m
Draught 2.5ft/0.76m
Materials Iron sides, wood bottom
Original use Cargo
Condition Intact
Present owners David Heap
Location Ellesmere Port, England
History Preserved as a floating exhibit.

Black Prince
Fenland barge

Built Date not known
Length 45.0ft/13.72m
Materials Wood throughout
Original use Cargo, Fenland barge
Condition Largely intact hull
Present owners Museum of Technology
Contact address Cheddars Lane, Cambridge, England
Location Cambridge, England
History Type of flat-bottomed barge once used on the waterways of the Fenland region of eastern England. Excavated from a clay pit near Ely in 1974 and now preserved indoors at Cambridge.

Blossom
fishing lugger

Built 1887 at Berwick, Northumberland, England

Propulsion Single masted lug rig
Tonnage c9 gross
Length 33.4ft/10.18m
Breadth 9.0ft/2.74m
Materials Wood throughout
Original use Fishing
Condition Intact
Present owners Tyne and Wear Museums
Location Newcastle upon Tyne, England
History Fishing craft of a type similar to the 'coble' of northeast England, preserved as a museum exhibit in Newcastle.

Box Boat 337
canal barge

Built in England, date not known
Original owners National Coal Board
Propulsion Towed by horses or tug
Length 60.0ft/18.29m
Breadth 6.83ft/2.08m
Draught 2.0ft/0.61m
Materials Wood hull
Original use Cargo; coal
Condition Intact
Present owners The Boat Museum
Location Ellesmere Port, England
History Preserved as a floating exhibit.

Branksome
steam launch

Former name THE LILY
Built 1896 by G Brockbank, Bowness-on-Windermere, England
Original owners Mrs E Howarth, Windermere
Propulsion Steam, compound. Engine built by Sissons, Gloucester
Tonnage 18 gross
Length 50.0ft/15.24m
Breadth 9.0ft/2.74m
Materials Wood throughout
Original use Yacht
Condition Intact, in operation
Present owners Windermere Nautical Trust
Contact address Beresford Road, Windermere, England
Location Windermere, England
History Elegant Victorian steam launch with aft cabin preserved in operating condition in a museum boathouse at Windermere.
Bibliography B27

Brent
steam harbour tug

Former name TID 159
Built 1945 by W Pickersgill & Sons, Sunderland, England

Brent

Length 92.99ft/28.35m
Breadth 27.09ft/8.26m
Materials Steel throughout
Original use Tug
Condition Intact
Present owners Merseyside Maritime Museum
Location Liverpool, England
History Preserved as a floating exhibit.
Bibliography B56

Bronington
coastal minesweeper

Former name HMS BRONINGTON
Built 1953 by Cook, Welton & Gemmell, Beverly, England
Original owners Royal Navy
Propulsion Diesel engines, 2500hp
Tonnage 425 displacement
Length 152.0ft/46.33m
Breadth 28.75ft/8.76m
Draught 8.25ft/2.5m
Materials Hull wood over aluminium frames, superstructure wood
Original use Minesweeper
Condition Intact
Location Manchester, England
History Preserved as an exhibit; the first independent command of Prince Charles when a serving naval officer.
Bibliography D84

Brunel Drag Boat
dredger

Former name Nickname said to have been BERTHA
Built 1844 (and designed) by I K Brunel, Bristol, England
Original owners Bridgewater Dock Co
Propulsion Steam, chain hauling
Tonnage 63.6 displacement

Original owners Ministry of Transport
Propulsion Steam, compound
Tonnage 54 gross
Length 65.0ft/19.81m
Breadth 17.0ft/5.18m
Depth 7.33ft/2.23m
Materials Steel throughout
Original use Tug
Condition Intact
Present owners Ron L Hall, Maldon, Essex, England
Location Maldon, Essex, England
History Standard British steam harbour tug built during the Second World War and now maintained in operating condition by a private owner.
Bibliography B27, D217

Britannia
tug

Former name T B HEATHORNE
Built 1893 at Gainsborough, England
Original owners South Metropolitan Gas Co
Propulsion Steam, screw; converted to diesel
Length 74.0ft/22.55m
Breadth 16.0ft/4.88m
Draught 10.0ft/3.05m
Materials Iron hull, steel and wood superstructure
Original use Tug
Condition Intact
Present owners Douglas Steven and

Partners
Location London, England
History Preserved as an exhibit.
Bibliography D515

Britannia
royal yacht

Built 1953 by John Brown Ltd, Clydebank, Scotland
Original owners Queen Elizabeth II
Propulsion Steam turbines, 12,000hp
Tonnage 4715 displacement
Length 412.3ft/125.67m
Breadth 55.0ft/16.76m
Draught 15.6ft/4.75m
Materials Steel throughout
Original use Royal yacht
Condition Intact
Location Leith, Scotland
History Royal yacht built to replace the VICTORIA AND ALBERT of 1901. Intended for King George VI but commissioned after his death. Now preserved as a floating exhibit.
Bibliography C15, C40, D398a, D399

Britannia
motor fishing vessel

Built 1904, Porthleven, England
Official number LN224
Propulsion Diesel engine
Materials Wood throughout
Original use Fishing
Condition Intact as a motor vessel

Present owners National Fishing Heritage Centre
History Restoration proposed.
Location Grimsby, England

Brocklebank
tug

Built 1965 by W J Yarwood & Sons, Northwich, England
Original owners Alexandra Towing Co, Liverpool
Propulsion Diesel engines
Tonnage 172 gross

Brunel Drag Boat

Length 54.0ft/16.46m
Breadth 13.75ft/4.19m
Draught 3.0ft/0.91m
Materials Iron throughout, except planked decks
Original use Dredging, dock
Condition Intact
Present owners Bristol Industrial Museum
Location Bristol, England
History The world's oldest steam powered craft still afloat. Designed by Brunel to clean mud and silt out of the locks and basins of harbours, hauling itself along by chains. Employed in the docks of Bridgewater, England, but similar to one used in Bristol, where she is now exhibited.
Bibliography B27, B29

Cabby
spritsail barge

Built 1928 by Gill, Rochester, England
Original owners LRTC
Official number 160687
Propulsion Spritsail ketch rig and auxiliary engine
Tonnage 76 gross
Materials Wood throughout
Original use Cargo, sailing barge
Condition Intact, in operation
Location Strood, England
History Built as a sailing barge to carry cargo on the rivers and estuaries of eastern England. Took part in the Dunkirk evacuation of the Second World War. Currently maintained in sailing condition as a charter vessel.
Bibliography B5, C74

Calshot
liner tender

Former name GALWAY BAY
Built 1930 by J I Thorneycroft, Southampton, England
Original owners Southampton, Isle of Wight Steam Packet Co
Propulsion Steam, screw; converted to diesel
Tonnage 684 gross
Length 147.0ft/44.81m
Breadth 33.0ft/10.06m
Draught 12.0ft/3.66m
Materials Steel hull, steel and wood superstructure
Original use Liner tender, used to take passengers out to ships at anchor
Condition Intact
Present owners Southampton Museum
Location Southampton, England
History Preserved as a floating exhibit.
Bibliography B16, C11

Cambria in her heyday

Calshot as Galway Bay

Calshot Spit
lightship

Built 1914 by J I Thorneycroft, Southampton, England
Original owners Trinity House
Propulsion Towed to station
Tonnage 140 displacement

Materials Iron throughout
Original use Lightship
Condition Intact
Present owners Ocean Village
Location Southampton, England
History Formerly marked the entrance to the Port of Southampton. Preserved as an onshore exhibit.

Cambria
spritsail barge

Built 1906 by William Everard, Greenhithe, England
Original owners F T Everard & Sons
Propulsion Spritsail ketch rig
Tonnage 109 gross
Length 91.0ft/27.74m
Breadth 22.0ft/6.71m
Materials Wood throughout
Original use Cargo, sailing barge
Condition Laid up, in need of re-restoration
Present owners The Cambria Trust
Location Sittingbourne, England
History Built as a sailing barge to carry cargo on the rivers and estuaries of eastern England. Was the last British vessel carrying cargo under sail when retired around 1970. Preserved for a number of years by the British Maritime Trust, and was on display in St Katherine's Dock near the Tower of London. Currently stored on a steel barge at Sittingbourne in poor condition awaiting restoration.
Bibliography B49, D341

Canning

steam tug

Built 1954 by Cochrane & Sons, Ltd, Selby, Yorkshire, England
Original owners Alexandra Towing Co
Propulsion Steam, triple expansion
Tonnage 200 gross
Length 94.0ft/28.65m
Breadth 28.0ft/8.53m
Draught 12.0ft/3.66m
Materials Steel throughout
Original use Tug
Condition Intact
Present owners Maritime and Industrial Museum
Contact address South Dock, Swansea, Wales
Location Swansea, Wales
History Steam tug originally employed in the Port of Liverpool, and later at Swansea, Wales. Was the last steam tug active in south Wales. Now preserved as a floating exhibit at Swansea.
Bibliography B27

Cariad

sailing pilot cutter

Built 1904 by E Rowles, Pill, Somersetshire, England
Original owners Thomas Richards, Cardiff, Wales
Propulsion Cutter rig, auxiliary engine added in 1922
Tonnage 18 gross
Length 47.5ft/14.48m
Breadth 12.75ft/3.89m
Draught 8.17ft/2.49m
Materials Wood throughout
Original use Pilot vessel
Condition Intact
Present owners Newport Maritime Trust
Location Newport, England
History Built as a pilot vessel serving port on the Bristol Channel. Operated for many years as a private yacht, and now maintained as a floating exhibit.

Carola

steam yacht

Built 1898 by Scott & Co, Bowling, Scotland
Original owners C W & J Scott
Propulsion Steam, compound. Engine built by Ross & Duncan, Motherwell, Scotland
Tonnage 40 gross
Length 70.9ft/21.59m
Breadth 13.1ft/3.99m
Draught 7.5ft/2.29m
Materials Steel hull, steel and wood deckhouses

Caroline

Original use Yacht
Condition Intact, in operation
Location Irvine, Scotland
History Unaltered steam yacht of the turn of the century maintained in operating condition, based at the Scottish Maritime Museum in Irvine.

Caroline

Naval light cruiser

Built 1914 by Cammell Laird, Birkenhead, England
Original owners Royal Navy
Propulsion Steam turbines, 40,000hp. Engine built by Parsons
Tonnage 3750 displacement
Length 446.0ft/135.94m
Breadth 41.5ft/12.65m
Draught 14.5ft/4.42m
Materials Steel throughout
Original use Light cruiser
Condition In use, largely unaltered
Present owners Royal Navy Reserve
Location Belfast, Northern Ireland
History British light cruiser that took part in the night actions following the Battle of Jutland in the First World War. Has served as a floating Naval drill hall since prior to the Second World War. Apart from some additions to the superstructure she remains virtually unaltered.
Bibliography B24, B49, D6

Cavalier

destroyer

Former name HMS CAVALIER
Built 1944 by Samuel White, Cowes, Isle of Wight, England
Original owners Royal Navy

Cavalier at Newcastle in 1989

Propulsion Steam turbines. Engine built by Parsons
Tonnage 1710 displacement
Length 362.75ft/110.57m
Breadth 35.67ft/10.87m
Draught 16.0ft/4.88m
Materials Steel throughout
Original use Destroyer
Condition Intact, undergoing refurbishment
Present owners Cavalier Maritime Trust
Location Chatham, England
History Only surviving British destroyer that saw action in the Second World War. Recently in danger of scrapping or sale overseas, but now appears to have a secure future at the historic Naval dockyard in Chatham.
Bibliography B49, D416

Cedar
canal float/deck scow

Built Date not known
Original owners Manchester Ship Canal
Propulsion Towed by horses or mules
Tonnage c62 gross
Length 72.0ft/21.95m
Breadth 14.58ft/4.44m
Draught 4.0ft/1.22m
Materials Wood throughout
Original use Cargo, canals
Condition Undergoing restoration
Present owners Boat Museum Trust
Contact address Ellesmere Port, Cheshire L65 4EF, England
Location Ellesmere Port, England
History Float or deck scow used to carry cargoes on the wider canals of England, now preserved as part of the very large fleet of former working craft at the museum in Ellesmere Port.
Bibliography B4

Centaur
canal barge

Built c1899 by Bantock, Wolverhampton, England
Propulsion Towed by horses
Length 72.0ft/21.95m
Breadth 7.0ft/2.13m
Draught 3.5ft/1.07m
Materials Hull wood and iron
Original use Cargo, canals
Condition Intact
Present owners The Boat Museum
Location Ellesmere Port, England
History Canal boat formerly used to carry cargo on the Birmingham canals in central England. Now preserved as one of a large fleet of former working craft at the museum in Ellesmere Port.
Bibliography B4

Centaur
spritsail barge

Built 1895 by Cann Brothers, Harwich, England
Original owners Charles Stone
Official number 99460
Propulsion Spritsail ketch rig
Tonnage 61 gross
Length 85.6ft/26.1m
Breadth 19.5ft/5.9m
Draught 6.2ft/1.9m
Materials Wood throughout
Original use Cargo, sailing barge
Condition Intact
Present owners Thames Sailing Barge Club
Location Maldon, Essex, England
History Built as a sailing barge to carry cargoes on the rivers and estuaries of eastern England. Currently maintained in sailing condition as a charter vessel.
Bibliography C74

Cervia
steam tug

Former name EMPIRE RAYMOND
Built 1946 by Alexander Hall & Co Ltd, Aberdeen, Scotland
Original owners Ministry of War Transport
Propulsion Steam, triple expansion. Engine built by Alexander Hall & Co
Tonnage 233 gross
Length 112.83ft/34.39m
Breadth 27.08ft/8.25m
Draught 11.65ft/3.55m
Materials Steel throughout
Original use Tug
Condition Intact
Present owners East Kent Maritime
Trust
Contact address c/o Ramsgate Maritime Museum, Clock House, Royal Harbour
Location Ramsgate, England
History Intact steam tug retired in the early 1980s preserved as a floating exhibit.
Bibliography B27, D76

Chalk barge

Built 1948 by Hillyard, Littlehampton, England
Original owners Arun Navigation Co
Propulsion Towed
Length 58.0ft/17.68m
Breadth 10.83ft/3.3m
Materials Wood hull
Original use Cargo; chalk
Condition Intact
Present owners The Boat Museum
Location Ellesmere Port, England
History Preserved as a floating exhibit.

Challenge
steam tug

Built 1946 by Alexander Hall & Co Ltd, Aberdeen, Scotland
Original owners Elliott Steam Tug Co Ltd
Propulsion Steam, triple expansion
Tonnage 212 gross
Length 100.0ft/30.48m
Breadth 26.0ft/7.92m
Draught 13.5ft/4.11m
Materials Steel throughout
Original use Tug
Condition Intact, restoration in progress
Present owners The Dunkirk Little

Ships Restoration Trust
Location Tilbury, England
History Last steam tug to operate in the Port of London. Was exhibited for a number of years in St Katherine's Dock there, but has now been moved to Tilbury, a former dock for ocean liners near the mouth of the Thames.
Bibliography B27, D425

Chiltern
powered canal barge

Built 1946 by Fellowes, Morton & Clayton, Uxbridge, England
Original owners Fellows, Morton & Clayton
Propulsion 27hp engine
Length 71.0ft/21.64m
Breadth 7.0ft/2.13m
Materials Wood throughout
Original use Cargo, canals
Condition Intact
Present owners The Boat Museum
Contact address Ellesmere Port, Cheshire L65 4EF, England
Location Ellesmere Port, England
History Motorised canal boat formerly used to carry cargoes on the inland waterways of central England. Now preserved in the large fleet of former working craft at the museum in Ellesmere Port.
Bibliography B4

City of Adelaide
composite sailing ship

Former name CARRICK
Built 1864 by W Pile, Jr, Sunderland, England
Original owners Devitt & Moore

City of Adelaide

Propulsion Ship rig
Tonnage 860 gross
Length 176.67ft/53.85m
Breadth 33.25ft/10.13m
Depth 18.5ft/5.64m
Draught 18.5ft/5.64m
Materials Hull wood over iron frames
Original use Cargo and passengers
Condition Undergoing restoration
Present owners Scottish Maritime
Museum
Location Irvine, Scotland
History Built to carry cargo and
passengers between the British Isles
and Australia. Later used as a floating
hospital, an accommodation hulk, and
a Naval Reserve clubhouse at Glasgow.
Has now been moved to Irvine and
placed ashore for full restoration to her
original appearance.
Bibliography A14, D256, D257, D369,
D397

City of Edinboro
sailing fishing boat

Former name WILLIAM MCCANN,
FRIDA, CITY OF EDINBURGH
Built 1884 by William McCann, Hull,
England
Original owners George Bowman &
Richard Simpson
Propulsion Sail, ketch rig; diesel
auxiliary added
Tonnage 83.42 gross
Length 110.0ft/33.53m
Breadth 20.0ft/6.1m
Draught 10.75ft/3.28m
Materials Wood throughout
Original use Fishing
Condition In sailing condition
Present owners Humber Sailing Trawler
Society
Location Hull, England
History Used for cruises.
Bibliography B29

CMB-4
coastal motor boat

Built 1916 by J I Thornycroft,
Hampton, England
Original owners Royal Navy
Official number CMB 4
Propulsion V/12 motor; 250hp. Engine
built by Thornycroft
Tonnage 4 displacement
Length 40.0ft/12.19m
Breadth 8.5ft/2.59m
Materials Wood throughout
Original use Torpedo boat
Condition Intact
Present owners Imperial War Museum
Contact address Lambeth Road,
London SE1

CMB-103

Location Duxford, England
History Fast torpedo boat built during
the First World War. Sank the Russian
Bolshevik cruiser OLEG in 1919.
Preserved on land at the Duxford
Airfield in Cambridgeshire, England.

CMB-103
coastal motor boat

Built 1921 by Camper & Nicholson,
Gosport, England
Original owners Royal Navy
Official number CMB 103
Propulsion 18-cylinder motors; 450hp.
Engine built by Green
Tonnage 24 displacement
Length 72.5ft/22.1m
Breadth 14.0ft/4.27m
Materials Wood throughout
Original use Torpedo boat
Condition Undergoing restoration
Present owners Imperial War Museum
Contact address Lambeth Road,
London SE1
Location Chatham, England
History Fast torpedo boat also
designed for high-speed minelaying
built just after the First World War.
Displayed indoors at the former
Chatham Dockyard while awaiting
restoration.

Compton Castle
sidewheel river steamer

Built 1914 by Cox & Co, Falmouth,
England
Original owners River Dart Steamboat
Co

Propulsion Steam, sidewheel, inclined
compound
Tonnage 97 gross
Length 108.0ft/32.92m
Breadth 28.0ft/8.53m
Draught 3.0ft/0.91m
Materials Steel throughout
Original use Passengers
Condition Laid up, some structures
added, engine in a museum
Location Truro, Cornwall
History Built to carry passengers on the
Dart River in southwest England.
Converted to a floating restaurant in
1964. Engines are preserved in a
museum on the Isle of Wight. The
similar KINGSWEAR CASTLE has been
restored to operation in the east of
England.
Bibliography B29

Comrade
Humber keel

Former name WANDA, ADA CARTER
Built 1923 by Warrens Shipyard, New
Holland, Lincolnshire, England
Original owners Turner Carmichael,
John Taylor, Schofield Family
Propulsion Single mast; two square sails
Length 61.5ft/18.75m
Breadth 15.0ft/4.57m
Draught 8.0ft/2.44m
Materials Steel hull, wood spars
Original use Cargo
Condition In sailing condition
Present owners Humber Keel and Sloop
Preservation Society
Contact address 135 Waterside Road,
Barton-upon-Humber, England
Location Beverly Beck, Yorkshire

Concrete canal boat

History Steel sailing barge of a type known as a Humber keel used to carry cargoes on the rivers of Yorkshire and Lincolnshire. Restored to sailing condition as a passenger cruise vessel.
Bibliography C95, D215

Concrete barge

Built 1944 by Waites Construction, Barrow in Furness, England. Designed by Mouchel & Partners
Original owners Ministry of War Transport
Propulsion Towed by tugs
Length 90.0ft/27.42m
Breadth 23.0ft/7.13m
Draught 8.0ft/2.46m
Materials Reinforced concrete hull
Original use Cargo, barge
Condition Intact
Present owners National Waterways Museum, Gloucester
Location Gloucester, England
History Preserved as a floating exhibit.

Concrete canal boat

Built 1918 by A H Guest, Stourbridge, England
Propulsion Towed by horses
Tonnage 16 displacement
Length 70.0ft/21.34m
Breadth 7.0ft/2.13m
Draught 3.5ft/1.07m
Materials Concrete hull
Original use Cargo, canals
Condition Hull intact
Present owners National Waterways Museum
Location Gloucester, England
History Canal boat built out of concrete to conserve steel during the First World War period. Now a floating exhibit at the waterways museum created in old warehouses of the Gloucester Docks.

Constable
Stour river barge

Built 1830
Propulsion Towed barge
Length 47.0ft/14.33m
Draught 3.0ft/0.91m
Materials Wood throughout
Original use Cargo
Present owners River Stour Trust
Contact address 30 Normandy Way, Bures, Suffolk
Location Sudbury, Suffolk
History Only surviving example of a River Stour barge. Was used as lead barge of a pair, linked with the house barge. Preserved as an exhibit.

Creole
luxury yacht

Former name MAGIC CIRCLE, VIRA
Built 1927 by Camper & Nicholson, Southampton, England. Designed by Charles Nicholson
Original owners Alexander Smith Cochran
Propulsion Sail, 3-masted schooner rig; auxiliary engine, 1780hp
Tonnage 525 displacement
Length 191.0ft/58.22m
Breadth 31.0ft/9.44m
Draught 17.5ft/5.35m
Materials Wood throughout
Original use Yacht
Condition Fully restored in 1984-86
Present owners Estate of Maurizio Gucci
Location Great Britain(flag)
History Large luxury yacht rigged as a 3-masted schooner. Owned after the Second World War by a Greek shipping magnate, and later served as a training vessel for young people based in Denmark. Has been fully restored as a yacht.
Bibliography A1

Cuddington
motor coaster

Built 1948 by Yarwoods, Northwich, England
Original owners Imperial Chemical Industries
Propulsion Diesel engine; 265hp
Tonnage 300 gross
Length 102.0ft/31.09m
Breadth 20.0ft/6.1m
Materials Steel throughout
Original use Cargo
Condition Intact
Present owners The Boat Museum, Ellesmere Port, England
Location Ellesmere Port, England
History Small motor cargo vessel formerly employed in the area of Liverpool and the Irish Sea. Preserved as a floating exhibit at Ellesmere Port.
Bibliography B4

Cutty Sark
tea clipper

Former name MARIA DO AMPERO, FERREIRA
Built 1869 by Scott & Linton; completed by Denny Bros, Dumbarton, Scotland. Designed by Hercules Linton
Original owners John Willis
Propulsion Full-rigged ship rig
Tonnage 963 gross
Length 212.0ft/64.62m
Breadth 36.0ft/10.97m
Draught 21.0ft/6.4m
Materials Hull wood over iron frames
Original use Cargo
Condition Fully restored
Present owners Cutty Sark Maritime Trust
Contact address 16 Elbury Street, London SW1
Location Greenwich, London, England
History The trade in tea between China and the West inspired the building of the first clipper ships in the mid-1840s, and was to remain the mainstay of these vessels until their era ended in the 1870s. CUTTY SARK was one of the last tea clippers built, and is today the only clipper ship of any type surviving intact. She was designed to be very fast in order to win the premium paid to the ship bringing home the first tea of the season. The Suez Canal opened the

Creole

year she was built, and by the following year the premium was being paid to steamers taking advantage of this shorter route. CUTTY SARK remained in the tea trade through the 1870s and then spent a few years in general trading. Her last years under the British flag were spent carrying wool between Australia and England. In 1895 she was sold to Portuguese owners. She was reduced in rig to a barquentine following a dismasting in 1916. Captain W.H. Dowman of Falmouth, England, saw her in a British port and decided she should be preserved. In 1922 he bought the ship and made her part of a floating nautical school he was operating. After his death, his widow in 1938 presented the ship to the Thames Nautical Training School at Greenhithe who made her a floating annexe to their schoolship WORCESTER. They maintained the ship until 1952 when the Cutty Sark Preservation Society was formed under the leadership of Frank Carr, Director of the National Maritime Museum, and the patronage of HRH the Duke of Edinburgh. The ship was permanently installed in a stone drydock at Greenwich on the Thames, and fully restored to her appearance as an active sailing vessel.
Bibliography C59, D21, 71-2, 245, 296, 315, 322

Cygnet
spritsail barge

Built 1881 by Curel, Frindsbury, England
Original owners Walter Wrinch, Ewarton
Official number 84028
Propulsion Spritsail rig
Tonnage 16 gross
Materials Wood throughout
Original use Cargo
Condition In sailing condition
Present owners Mica Brown
Location Pin Mill, England
History Built as a sailing barge to carry cargoes on the rivers and estuaries of eastern England. Currently maintained in sailing condition as a private yacht.

Daniel Adamson
canal tug/inspection vessel

Former name RALPH BROCKLEBANK
Built 1903 by Tranmere Bay Development Co, Birkenhead, England
Original owners Shropshire Union Canal Co
Propulsion Steam, compound, 500hp
Length 110.00ft/33.53m

Cutty Sark

Breadth 24.5ft/7.47m
Draught 8.67ft/2.64m
Materials Steel throughout
Original use Passenger carrying tug
Condition Intact, afloat
Present owners The Manchester Ship Canal Co
Location Ellesmere Port, England
History Ship canal tug and inspection vessel. Transferred to the Manchester Ship Canal Co and renamed in 1922. Now exhibited afloat in operating condition at the museum in Ellesmere Port near the outlet of the Canal.
Bibliography B4, B16, B27, D87

Dannebrog
spritsail barge

Built 1901 by McLearon, Harwich, England
Propulsion Spritsail; former ketch
Materials Wood throughout
Original use Cargo
Condition Undergoing restoration
Location Hoo, England
History Built as a sailing barge to carry cargoes on the rivers and estuaries of eastern England. Currently being restored to sailing condition by a private owner.

Dawn
spritsail barge

Built 1897 by Cook, Maldon, England
Official number 105902
Propulsion Spritsail

Daniel Adamson

Tonnage 54 gross
Materials Wood throughout
Original use Cargo
Condition In need of restoration
Present owners Dawn Sailing Barge
Trust
Location Hoo, England
History Built as a sailing barge to carry
cargoes on the rivers and estuaries of
eastern England. Used as a training
vessel. Laid up in the early 1990s. An
effort is currently underway to restore
her to sailing condition.

Daybreak
Humber keel

Built 1934 by Dunston's, Thorne,
England
Propulsion Sail, single-mast square-
rigged, or towed; engine added 1939
Materials Steel hull
Original use Cargo
Condition In sailing condition
Present owners Tony and Sally
Woodward
Location Thames River, England
History Sailing barge known as a
'Humber keel' built to carry grain from
the docks of Hull, England, to flour
mills. Diesel engine added in 1939.
Restored to sailing rig by present
owners.

De Wadden
coasting schooner

Built 1917 by Gebroeders van Diepen,
Waterhuizen, Netherlands
Propulsion Schooner, three masts;
diesel auxiliary
Tonnage 239 gross
Length 116.75ft/35.59m
Breadth 24.6ft/7.5m
Draught 10.5ft/3.2m
Materials Steel hull, wood masts
Original use Cargo
Condition Restored
Present owners Merseyside Maritime
Museum
Location Liverpool, England
History Dutch-built coastal schooner
that operated for many years under the
British flag. Now an exhibit in a stone
graving dock near the Maritime
Museum in Liverpool. Restoration was
underway in 1998, possibly for return
to sailing condition.
Bibliography B56, D126, D484

Decima
spritsail barge

Built 1899 by Day, Southampton,
England

De Wadden

Original owners E J & W Goldsmith
Ltd
Official number 110055
Propulsion Spritsail
Tonnage 67 gross
Materials Steel hull
Original use Cargo
Condition Restored, but currently laid
up
Present owners Jeremy Taunton
Location Faversham, England
History Built as a sailing barge to carry
cargoes on the rivers and estuaries of
eastern England. Restored to sailing
condition as a charter vessel, but laid
up since 1996.

Demon
gunboat

Former name HMS DEMON,
HMS SNAPPER, HMS HANDY
Built 1883 by Armstrong, Whitworth &
Co, Newcastle, England
Original owners Royal Navy
Propulsion Steam, screw
Tonnage 508 displacement
Length 115.0ft/35.05m
Breadth 37.0ft/11.28m
Materials Iron hull
Original use Gunboat
Condition Remains of hull with part of
engine
Present owners H G Pounds,

Shipbreakers
Contact address 225 Southampton
Road, Paulsgrove, Cosham, Hampshire
Location Portsmouth, England
History Last surviving Victorian steam
gunboat of its type. Currently beached
and kept in a scrapyard.

Discovery
exploration ship

Built 1901 by Stevens Yard, Dundee,
Scotland
Original owners British National
Antarctic Expedition
Propulsion Steam, triple expansion,
450hp
Tonnage 736 gross
Length 171.0ft/52.12m
Breadth 33.83ft/10.31m
Draught 15.75ft/4.8m
Materials Wood throughout
Original use Polar exploration
Condition Fully restored
Present owners Dundee Heritage Trust
Location Dundee, Scotland
History The wooden-hulled auxiliary
barque DISCOVERY was built in 1901 for
the 1901 Antarctic expedition of the
British Royal Geographical Society.
Her design was based on an earlier
DISCOVERY, a whaling ship that had
been used on an 1875 expedition
towards the North Pole. DISCOVERY
was given a massively reinforced hull
for survival in ice, and screw and
rudder that could be hoisted into
vertical shafts to avoid ice damage. Her
interior was fully fitted out with
laboratories, including a magnetic
observatory. Manned by a crew of
volunteers under Commander Robert
Falcon Scott, she sailed from New
Zealand in December 1901, returning
to England in September 1904 after
spending a summer frozen in the ice.
She was subsequently sold to the
Hudson's Bay Company to supply their
outposts in northern Canada. In 1914
she was chartered by the French
Government to carry military aid to
Russia. In 1923 she was again fitted out
in England for research in the
Antarctic. Her last such expedition
took place in 1931 under the leadership
of Sir Douglas Mawson. She was then
turned over to the British Boy Scouts
for use as a stationary training ship
moored in the centre of London. In
1955 responsibility for the ship was
assumed by the London Division of
the Royal Naval Reserve. DISCOVERY
was turned over to the Maritime Trust
in April 1979 for restoration and
conversion to a floating museum of

Discovery

polar exploration. During the restoration the ship was moored at St Katherine's Dock in London where she was kept open to the public. The City of Dundee on the west coast of Scotland, where the ship had originally been built, subsequently offered to provide a permanent berth for her.
Bibliography A14, B49, D455

Dolly
steam launch

Built 1850 near Windermere, England
Original owners Alfred Fildes
Propulsion Steam, single cylinder
Length 41.0ft/12.5m
Breadth 6.5ft/1.98m
Materials Wood throughout
Original use Yacht
Condition Fully restored, operational
Present owners G H Pattinson
Contact address Windermere
Steamboat Museum, Windermere, England
Location Windermere, England
History Mid nineteenth-century steam launch with cabin that sank in Ullswater in 1895 and was raised almost intact in 1962. Restored to operating condition with original

engine. Currently preserved afloat in a museum boathouse at Windermere.
Bibliography B27

Donola
steam launch

Former name LODONA
Built 1893 by Kingdom Yacht, Launch & Engineering Works, Teddington, England
Original owners Alfred Palmer
Propulsion Steam, compound, 3hp
Tonnage 16 gross
Length 58.0ft/17.68m
Breadth 7.75ft/2.36m
Materials Steel hull
Original use Yacht
Condition Intact
Present owners National Maritime Museum
Contact address Greenwich, London SE10
Location Greenwich, England
History Elegant Victorian steam launch preserved as an indoor exhibit at the National Maritime Museum.
Bibliography B27

Edith May
spritsail barge

Built 1906 by Cann, Harwich, England
Propulsion Spritsail
Tonnage 64 gross
Materials Wood throughout
Original use Cargo
Condition In sailing condition
Present owners Roger Angus
Location London, England
History Built as a sailing barge to carry cargoes on the rivers and estuaries of eastern England. Currently based at St Katherine's Dock in London as either a yacht or charter vessel.

Edme
spritsail barge

Built 1898 by Cann, Harwich, England
Original owners F W Horlock
Official number 105425
Propulsion Spritsail ketch rig, no engine
Tonnage 50 gross
Materials Wood throughout
Original use Cargo, sailing barge
Condition In sailing condition
Present owners Harman-Harrison Consortium

Location St Osyth, England
History Built as a sailing barge to carry cargoes on the rivers and estuaries of eastern England. Restored to sailing condition by present owners in 1992.

Edmund Gardner
pilot vessel

Built 1953 by Philip & Son, Dartmouth, England
Original owners Mersey Docks & Harbour Board
Propulsion Diesel engines
Tonnage 701 gross
Length 177.5ft/54.1m
Breadth 31.75ft/9.68m
Draught 14.74ft/4.5m
Materials Steel throughout
Original use Pilot vessel
Condition Intact
Present owners Merseyside Marine Museum, Canning Dock, Liverpool
Location Liverpool, England
History Former pilot vessel for the Port of Liverpool. Currently open to the public resting in a graving dock near the maritime museum there.
Bibliography B56

Edward Bridges
rescue lifeboat

Built 1975 by W M Osborne
Original owners Royal National Lifeboat Institution
Propulsion Diesel engines, 920hp
Length 54.0ft/16.2m
Breadth 17.0ft/5.1m
Draught 4.5ft/1.35m
Original use Rescue lifeboat
Condition Intact
Present owners Royal National Lifeboat Collection
Location Chatham, England
History Preserved as an indoor exhibit.

Egremont
motor ferry

Built 1952 by Philip & Son, Dartmouth, England
Original owners Wallesey Corporation
Propulsion Diesel engines
Tonnage 566 gross
Length 147.0ft/44.8m
Breadth 34.0ft/10.4m
Draught 7.33ft/2.2m
Materials Steel throughout
Original use Ferry
Condition Intact, in use
Present owners Island Cruising Club
Contact address Island Street, Salcombe, Devon TQ8 8DR
Location Salcombe, England
History Currently a floating headquarters and accommodations.

Elswick II
lighter

Built 1913 at Bill Quay, England
Original owners Vickers
Propulsion None as built; engine
Tonnage 50 displacement
Length 57.0ft/17.37m
Breadth 23.66ft/7.21m
Materials Wood throughout
Original use Cargo; river lighter
Condition Restored in 1980s
Present owners Tyne and Wear Museums
Location Newcastle-on-Tyne, England
History Example of a type of clinker-planked lighter barge once used to carry cargo on the Tyne River. Now preserved on shore as an exhibit.

Elswick II

Ena
spritsail barge

Built 1906 by W B McLearon, Harwich, England
Original owners R & W Paul Ltd
Propulsion Spritsail; Rushton engine added 1949
Tonnage 73 gross
Length 88.2ft/26.9m
Breadth 20.6ft/6.3m
Depth 6.9ft/2.1m
Materials Wood throughout
Original use Cargo
Condition In sailing condition
Present owners Paul & White Ltd, Social & Sports Club
Location Ipswich, England
History Built as a sailing barge to carry cargoes on the rivers and estuaries of eastern England. Currently maintained in sailing condition by a sports club.
Bibliography A10, B5

Enterprise
Hastings lugger

Built 1909
Propulsion Two-masted lug rig
Materials Wood throughout
Original use Fishing
Condition Intact
Present owners The Fisherman's Museum
Contact address Rock-a-Nore Road, Hastings, East Sussex, England
Location Hastings, England
History Example of a Hastings lugger used to fish off the beaches of Sussex. Preserved as an exhibit in a boathouse in Hastings.

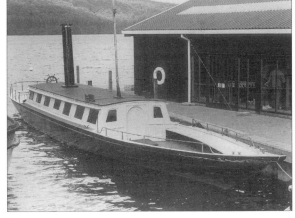
Esperance

Esperance
steam launch

Built 1869 by T B Sheath & Co, Rutherglen, Scotland
Original owners H W Schneider
Propulsion Steam, screw; later petrol engine
Length 65.0ft/19.81m
Breadth 10.0ft/3.05m
Draught 4.5ft/1.37m
Materials Iron hull, wood deck and deckhouse
Original use Yacht
Condition Intact, afloat
Present owners Windermere Nautical Trust
Contact address Beresford Road, Windermere, Cumbria, England
Location Windermere, England
History Early Victorian steam launch with cabin exhibited afloat at the Windermere Steamboat Museum.
Bibliography C20

Edmund Gardner

Ethel

powered canal barge

Built 1952 at Mirfield, England
Original owners Calder Carrying Co
Propulsion Diesel engine. Engine built
by Lister
Tonnage 60 gross
Length 57.5ft/17.53m
Breadth 14.0ft/4.27m
Draught 6.0ft/1.83m
Materials Wood throughout
Original use Cargo
Condition In need of restoration
Present owners The Boat Museum
Contact address Dockyard Road,
Ellesmere Port, South Wirral, Cheshire
Location Ellesmere Port, England
History Motorised wooden barge
known as a 'keel' used to carry coal on
the Calder and Hebble Navigation.
Currently preserved as part of the large
fleet of former working craft at the
museum in Ellesmere Port.
Bibliography B4

Ethel

Ethel Ada

spritsail barge

Built 1903 by Shuttlewood, Paglesham,
England
Original owners G & A Underwood
Official number 118352
Propulsion Spritsail
Tonnage 49 gross
Length 82ft/25.0m
Breadth 19.1ft/5.8m
Depth 5.4ft/1.6m
Materials Wood throughout
Original use Cargo
Condition Apparently in sailing
condition
Present owners Geoffrey Mellor
Location Orwell, England
History Built as a sailing barge to carry
cargoes on the rivers and estuaries of
eastern England. Now maintained in
sailing condition as a yacht based at
Snape Maltings on the Ore River.

Eva

iron steam yacht

Built 1874 by J I Thorneycroft,
Chiswick, England
Propulsion Steam, screw, 42hp
Length 42.0ft/13.72m
Breadth 6.15ft/1.87m
Materials Iron hull, wood deckhouse
Original use Yacht
Condition Fully restored, in use
Present owners G E Lindsay
Location Thames River, England
Bibliography B27

Excelsior

fishing ketch

Former name SVINOR
Built 1921 by John Chambers & Co,
Lowestoft, England
Original owners Wood Greaves &
Associates
Propulsion Sail, ketch rig; diesel
auxiliary added
Tonnage 55.36 gross
Length 77.0ft/23.47m
Breadth 19.25ft/5.87m
Materials Wood throughout
Original use Fishing
Condition In sailing condition
Present owners Excelsior Trust
Contact address Riverside Road,
Lowestoft NR33 0TU
Location Lowestoft, England
History Survivor of the last British
sailing fishing fleet which was based at
Lowestoft, later used for training.

Explorer

steam fishery research vessel

Built 1955 by Alexander Hall & Co,
Aberdeen, Scotland
Original owners Department of
Agriculture & Fisheries for Scotland
Propulsion Steam, screw, triple
expansion, 1300hp
Tonnage 831 gross
Length 202.0ft/61.57m
Breadth 32.75ft/9.98m
Draught 14.16ft/4.32m
Materials Steel throughout
Original use Fishery research
Condition Intact
Location Leith, Scotland
History Built as an ocean trawler
adapted to fisheries research. Preserved
as a floating exhibit.
Bibliography B27

FCB-18

lighter

Built 1940s
Original owners Manchester Ship
Canal Co
Propulsion Towed by tug
Length 80.0ft/24.6m
Breadth 18.0ft/5.5m
Draught 3.5ft/1.07m
Materials Concrete hull
Original use Cargo
Condition Intact
Present owners The Boat Museum
Location Ellesmere Port, England
History Preserved as a floating exhibit.

Excelsior

Freshspring

Felix
spritsail barge

Built 1893 by Cann, Harwich, England
Original owners Robert Smith
Official number 97686
Propulsion Spritsail
Tonnage 68 gross
Length 82.3ft/25.1m
Breadth 19.8ft/6.0m
Depth 6.8ft/2.1m
Materials Wood throughout
Original use Cargo
Condition Apparently in sailing
condition
Present owners Kevin Symonds
Location London, England
History Built as a sailing barge to carry
cargoes on the rivers and estuaries of
eastern England. Restored to sailing
condition as a yacht and reception
facility and now based at St Katherine's
Dock next to the Tower of London.

Flying Buzzard
steam tug

Former name HARECRAIG II
Built 1951 by Ferguson Brothers, Port
Glasgow, Scotland

Original owners Clyde Shipping Co
Propulsion Steam, screw, compound,
1180hp. Engine built by Ferguson
Brothers
Tonnage 261 gross
Length 109.0ft/33.22m
Breadth 27.0ft/8.23m
Draught 13.0ft/3.96m

Materials Steel throughout
Original use Tug
Condition Intact
Present owners Maryport Town
Council
Contact address 18 Grange Road,
Bushey, Hertfordshire, England
Location Maryport, England
History Steam tug maintained as a
floating exhibit in the old harbour of
Maryport.
Bibliography B27

Frederica Johanna
inland motor barge

Built 1931 by H & J Peters,
Dedemsvaart, Netherlands
Propulsion Diesel engine
Length 103.0ft/31.5m
Materials Steel throughout
Original use Cargo, inland motor barge
Condition Intact, acquired in 1997
Present owners Sandwich Sailing and
Motor Boat Club
Location Sandwich, England
History Inland motor barge acquired in
1997 for use as a clubhouse and
floating exhibit.

Freshspring
steam water carrier

Built 1947 by Lytham Shipbuilding and
Engineering, Lytham, England
Original owners Royal Navy
Propulsion Steam, screw, triple
expansion, 450hp
Tonnage 285 gross
Length 121.0ft/36.88m
Breadth 24.5ft/7.47m
Draught 10.5ft/3.2m
Materials Steel hull, steel and wood

superstructure
Original use Water carrier
Condition Intact
Present owners Oswald Burgess
Location Bristol, England
History Built for transporting water to
ships within a Naval base. Currently
being restored as an operating steam
vessel by a private owner.
Bibliography B27, B29, D81

Friendship
canal barge

Built 1925 by Sephtons, Sutton Stop,
England
Original owners Joseph and Rose
Skinner
Propulsion Towed by horses
Tonnage 22 gross
Length 71.5ft/21.79m
Breadth 7.0ft/2.13m
Draught 3.75ft/1.14m
Materials Wood throughout
Original use Cargo, canals
Condition Intact
Present owners The Boat Museum
Location Ellesmere Port, England
History Narrow boat employed in the
coal trade on the Oxford Canal until
1959. Preserved afloat at
Ellesmere Port
Bibliography B4

Gannet
composite screw sloop

Former name MERCURY,
HMS PRESIDENT, HMS GANNET
Built 1878 by Sheerness Dockyard,
Sheerness, England
Original owners Royal Navy
Propulsion Steam, screw, 2-cylinder,

Gannet

100hp; barque rig
Tonnage 1230 displacement
Length 170.0ft/51.82m
Breadth 36.0ft/10.97m
Draught 15.0ft/4.57m
Materials Wood throughout
Original use Cruising sloop
Condition Hull largely intact
Present owners Chatham Historic
Dockyard Trust
Location Chatham, England
History Victorian sail and steam
warship built to patrol remote areas of
the British Empire. Later served as a
Naval Reserve drill ship and as a
floating annexe to a school training
boys for careers at sea. Now on show in
a graving dock at the former Chatham
Dockyard, where she is to be restored
to her original appearance.
Bibliography A15, B24, B49, D185

Garlandstone
trading ketch

Built 1909 by James Goss, Calstock,
England
Original owners Captain John Russan
Propulsion Ketch rig
Tonnage 75 gross
Length 76.0ft/23.16m
Breadth 20.17ft/6.15m
Materials Wood throughout
Original use Cargo
Condition Undergoing restoration
Location Calstock, England
History Trading ketch employed
carrying cargo in the British coastal
trade. Currently being restored to her
original appearance for exhibit at the
site of her original construction.
Bibliography D204

Garnock
harbour tug

Built 1956 by George Brown & Co,
Greenock, Scotland
Original owners Irvine Harbour Co
Propulsion Diesel engine
Tonnage 78 gross
Length 71.75ft/21.87m
Breadth 21.92ft/6.68m
Draught 8.2ft/2.5m
Materials Steel throughout
Original use Tug
Condition Intact
Present owners Scottish Maritime
Museum
Location Irvine, Scotland
History British harbour tug of the
1950s preserved afloat as an exhibit at
Irvine, Scotland.

Gay Crusader
motor yacht

Built 1935 by Gibbs, Teddington,
England
Propulsion Petrol engine. Engine built
by Gray
Tonnage 11.59 displacement
Length 35.0ft/10.9m
Breadth 9.0ft/2.7m
Draught 3.0ft/0.9m
Materials Wood throughout
Original use Motor yacht
Present owners Dunkirk Little Ships
Restoration Trust
Location Southampton, England
History Currently undergoing
restoration.

GD-101
canal dredger

Built Date not known
Original owners Manchester Ship
Canal Co
Propulsion Diesel engine. Engine built
by Dorman
Length 48.0ft/14.63m
Breadth 14.5ft/4.42m
Draught 5.0ft/1.52m
Materials Steel throughout
Original use Dredging, canals
Condition Intact
Present owners The Boat Museum

George
canal barge

Built 1910 by Wigan Coal and Iron Co
Original owners National Coal Board
Propulsion Pulled by horses or mules
Length 62.0ft/18.9m
Breadth 14.25ft/4.34m
Draught 3.75ft/1.14m
Materials Iron and wood hull
Original use Cargo

Location Ellesmere Port, England
History Preserved as a floating exhibit.

General Jenkins
passenger launch

Former name KATHLYN
Built 1942 by Leo Robinson,
Tewkesbury, England
Original owners British Admiralty
Propulsion Steam, screw, compound
Length 64.0ft/19.51m
Breadth 13.0ft/3.96m
Draught 5.25ft/1.6m
Materials Wood throughout
Original use Passenger launch
Condition In operating condition
Present owners A Theobald & R B
Richmond-Dodd
Location Great Britain
History In use as a yacht.
Bibliography B27

Condition Intact
Present owners Northwest Museum of
Inland Navigation
Contact address Dockyard Road,
Ellesmere Port, South Wirral, Cheshire
Location Ellesmere Port, England
History Canal boat formerly employed
carrying cargoes on the Leeds and
Liverpool Canal. Now exhibited afloat
in the collection of preserved working
craft at Ellesmere Port.
Bibliography B4

George Smeed
spritsail barge

Built 1882 by Smeed Dean & Co,
Murston, England
Original owners Smeed Dean & Co
Official number 84430
Propulsion Spritsail
Tonnage 59 gross
Materials Wood throughout
Original use Cargo
Condition Undergoing restoration, to
be rerigged
Location Maldon, England
History Built as a sailing barge to carry
cargoes on the rivers and estuaries of
eastern England. Later used as a
houseboat at Heybridge, England, and
now being restored to sailing condition
at Maldon.

Garnock

Gifford

towed narrowboat

Built 1926 by William Nurser, Braunston, England
Original owners Thomas Clayton Ltd
Propulsion Towed by horses or mules
Length 71.5ft/21.79m
Breadth 7.0ft/2.13m
Materials Wood throughout
Original use Cargo, canals
Condition Intact
Present owners The Boat Museum Society
Location Ellesmere Port, England
History Narrow canal boat built to carry liquid cargoes on the canals of central England. Now exhibited afloat with the large fleet of former working craft preserved at Ellesmere Port.
Bibliography B4, D394

Gipsey Moth IV

circumnavigation yacht

Built 1966 by Camper & Nicholson, Gosport, England
Original owners Sir Francis Chichester
Propulsion Ketch rig; auxiliary diesel engine. Engine built by Perkins
Tonnage 16 gross
Length 54.0ft/16.46m
Breadth 10.5ft/3.2m
Draught 7.75ft/2.36m
Materials Wood hull, aluminium masts
Original use Yacht for circumnavigation
Condition Intact
Present owners The Cutty Sark Maritime Trust
Contact address 16 Ebury Street, London SW1, England
Location Greenwich, England
History Yacht designed for the single-handed rounding of the globe for which Sir Francis Chichester received a knighthood. Preserved on shore at Greenwich near the clipper ship CUTTY SARK.
Bibliography B49, D78

Gladys

spritsail barge

Built 1901 by Cann Brothers, Harwich, England
Original owners William T Whitmore
Propulsion Sail, spritsail ketch rig; diesel engine added. Engine built by Kelvin
Tonnage 68 gross
Length 84.0ft/25.6m
Breadth 22.0ft/6.71m
Materials Wood throughout
Original use Cargo, sailing barge

Gladys

Condition In sailing condition
Present owners Mardorf Peach Ltd
Location London, England
History Built as a sailing barge to carry cargoes on the rivers and estuaries of eastern England. Restored to sailing condition for use as a corporate yacht in 1974, and currently based at St Katherine's Dock next to the Tower of London.
Bibliography C74

Glenlee

trading barque

Former name GALATEA, CLARASTELLA, ISLAMOUNT
Built 1896 by A Rodger & Co, Port Glasgow, Scotland
Original owners R Ferguson & Co, Port Glasgow
Propulsion Sail, barque rig
Tonnage 2758 gross
Length 245.63ft/74.87m
Breadth 38.91ft/11.86m
Draught 17.72ft/5.4m
Materials Steel hull, steel and wood masts
Original use Cargo
Condition Undergoing restoration to original appearance
Present owners Clyde Maritime Trust
Location Glasgow, Scotland
History Preserved as a floating exhibit.
Bibliography A14, C96, D73, D559

Glenway

spritsail barge

Built 1913 by Little, Rochester, England
Original owners John Wilks
Propulsion Spritsail

Tonnage 82 gross
Materials Wood throughout
Original use Cargo
Condition Being restored to sailing condition
Present owners Hugh Poore
Location Sittingbourne, England
History Built as a sailing barge to carry cargoes on the rivers and estuaries of eastern England. Later served as a yacht and houseboat before being abandoned at Maldon. Present owner brought her to Sittingbourne, where he is doing major restoration work on the hull.
Bibliography B5

Golden Cross

tug

Built 1955 by Scott & Sons, Bowling, Great Britain
Original owners Tees Towing Co
Propulsion Diesel engines, 750hp. Engine built by Crossley Brothers
Tonnage 132 gross
Length 83.25ft/25.4m
Breadth 24.0ft/7.3m
Draught 10.33ft/3.1m
Materials Steel throughout
Original use Tug
Condition Intact
Present owners Canary Wharf
Location London, England
History Preserved as a floating exhibit.

Goleulong 2000 Lightship

Former name HELWICK
Built Date not known
Original owners Trinity House
Official number LV No 14
Propulsion Towed to station
Tonnage 550 displacement
Length 137.0ft/41.7m
Materials Steel throughout
Original use Lightship
Condition Intact, in use
Present owners Goleulong 2000 Lightship
Contact address Harbour Drive, Cardiff CF1 5PA
Location Cardiff, Wales
History Used as a floating centre for religious activities.

Gondola

steam launch

Built 1859 by Jones, Quiggin & Co, Liverpool, England
Original owners Furness Railway Co
Propulsion Steam screw, 2-cylinder, 16hp
Length 86.0ft/26.21m

Gondola

Breadth 14.0ft/4.27m
Draught 4.66ft/1.42m
Materials Iron hull, wood cabin
Original use Passengers
Condition Totally restored; largely new steel hull & engine
Present owners The National Trust
Contact address 42 Queen Anne's Gate, London SW1, England
Location Coniston Water, England
History Very elegant steam launch of the mid-nineteenth century with cabin and gilded figurehead. Engine is a replica of the original, and the vessel herself has been extensively rebuilt. Makes excursions under steam on Coniston Water in the English Lake District.
Bibliography B27, C20

Grace Darling
rescue lifeboat

Built 1954 by Groves & Gutteridge
Original owners Royal National Lifeboat Institution
Propulsion Diesel engines. Engine built by Ferry
Length 35.5ft/10.6m
Breadth 10.7ft/3.2m
Draught 2.5ft/0.75m
Materials Wood hull
Original use Rescue lifeboat
Condition Intact
Present owners Royal National Lifeboat Collection
Location Chatham, England
History Preserved as an indoor exhibit.

Grace Darling

Great Britain
transatlantic passenger steamer

Built 1843 by I K Brunel, Bristol, England
Original owners Great Western Steamship Co
Propulsion Steam screw, 4-cylinder; later sail, full-rigged ship
Tonnage 3443 gross
Length 285.0ft/86.87m
Breadth 50.5ft/15.39m
Draught 18.0ft/5.49m
Materials Iron hull, wood over iron beam decks, iron and wood masts
Original use Passengers
Condition Largely restored externally
Present owners Great Britain Project
Contact address Great Western Dock, Bristol, England
Location Bristol, England
History Regular steamship service across the North Atlantic was begun in 1838 employing wooden vessels propelled by sidewheels. Five years later the Great Western Steamship Company placed in service a vessel that was revolutionary in virtually every respect. She was far larger than any previous steamer, was driven by a propeller, and had an iron hull with clipper lines. The strength of this hull was soon dramatically proven when the GREAT BRITAIN spent almost a year aground off the coast of Ireland and was refloated with no serious damage. From 1852 to 1876 she was operated very successfully in the passenger trade between England and Australia. Her engines were then removed and in 1882 she was returned to service as the world's largest sailing cargo vessel. In

Great Britain

May 1886 she arrived at Port Stanley in the Falklands partially dismasted and was condemned and converted to a storage hulk, mostly for wool. She served in this capacity lying at anchor there until 1937. In that year her almost century-old hull was beached in a nearby cove and abandoned. In the late 1960s interest in salvaging and preserving the GREAT BRITAIN developed in both the United States and England. In 1970 she was temporarily refloated, placed on a giant barge, and transported back to the British Isles. At Bristol, she was refloated again for a 6 mile trip up the River Avon, and eased into the same stone drydock in which she had been built 130 years before. Since then she has been undergoing restoration back to her appearance when first completed in 1843. Restoration of her exterior is now largely complete, and work is now advancing on recreation of her interiors and replicas of her

original engines.
Bibliography D25, 39, 99, 171, 183, 198-9, 207

Greta
spritsail barge

Built 1892 by Stone, Brightlingsea, England
Official number 98324
Propulsion Spritsail barge
Tonnage 46 gross
Length 80.0ft/24.4m
Breadth 18.7ft/5.7m
Depth 5.6ft/1.7m
Materials Wood throughout
Original use Cargo
Condition In sailing condition
Present owners Steve Norris
Location Faversham, England
History Built as a sailing barge to carry cargoes on the rivers and estuaries of eastern England. Currently maintained in sailing condition as a private yacht.
Bibliography B5

Hathor
wherry yacht

Built 1905 by D S Hall, Reedham, England
Original owners Misses E & H Colman
Propulsion Sail, single-masted wherry rig
Tonnage 23 gross
Length 56.0ft/17.07m
Breadth 14.2ft/4.33m
Materials Wood throughout
Original use Yacht
Condition In sailing condition
Present owners Wherry Yacht Charter
Location Wroxham, England
History One of two surviving wherries built for use as pleasure craft on the rivers of eastern England. Available for charter.
Bibliography C57

Haven
lightship

Former name SPURN
Built 1959 by Cook, Wetton and Gemmell, Beverly, England
Original owners Humber Conservancy Board
Propulsion Towed to station
Tonnage 590 displacement
Length 114.0ft/34.75m
Breadth 26.0ft/7.92m
Draught 12.0ft/3.66m
Materials Steel throughout
Original use Lightship
Condition Intact
Location Milford Haven, Wales
History Formerly employed off the east coast of England. Preserved as a floating exhibit.
(The current name refers to its present location. It never served on a 'Haven' station.)

Helwick
lightship

Former name HUMBER
Built 1937 by Philip and Son, Dartmouth, England
Original owners Trinity House
Official number No 91
Propulsion None, towed to station
Tonnage 300 gross
Length 118.0ft/35.97m
Breadth 28.0ft/8.53m
Draught 10.5ft/3.2m
Materials Steel throughout, except planked decks
Original use Lightship
Condition Intact
Present owners Industrial and Maritime Museum
Location Swansea, Wales
History Veteran British lightship preserved as one of the floating exhibits of the maritime museum in Swansea.

Henry
spritsail barge

Built 1904 by Goldsmiths Yard, Grays, England
Original owners Cole and Lecquire Ltd
Propulsion Spritsail
Tonnage 44 gross
Length 76.3ft/23.2m
Breadth 18.1ft/5.5m
Depth 5.1ft/1.6m
Materials Wood throughout
Original use Cargo
Condition Undergoing restoration and rerigging
Present owners Steve and Jan Downer
Location Faversham, England
History Built as a sailing barge to carry cargoes on the rivers and estuaries of eastern England. Has spent many years

Helwick

as a houseboat at Sittingbourne and Faversham. Reportedly being restored and rerigged to sail.

Herbert Leigh
rescue lifeboat

Built c1951 in Great Britain
Original owners Royal National Lifeboat Institution
Propulsion Diesel engine
Length 47.0ft/14.3m
Original use Rescue lifeboat
Condition Intact
Present owners The Dock Museum
Location Barrow-in-Furness, England
History Preserved as an exhibit.

Hispania
racing yacht

Built 1909 by Astilleros Karrpard, Pasages, Spain
Original owners King Alphonso XIII of Spain
Propulsion Sail, cutter rig
Length 63.5ft/19.3m
Breadth 13.7ft/4.2m
Materials Wood throughout
Original use Yacht
Condition In need of restoration
Location Hamble River, England
History Former racing yacht built for the King of Spain. Efforts are underway to restore her to sailing condition.

HMAFV-2757
high-speed rescue vessel

Built 1956 by Vospers, Southampton, England
Original owners Royal Air Force
Propulsion Twin petrol engines. Engines built by Rolls Royce
Length 68.0ft/20.73m
Original use Fast air-sea rescue vessel
Condition Intact
Present owners Royal Air Force Museum
Contact address Grahame Park Way, London NW9, England
Location London, England
History High-speed craft stationed near military airfields to rescue aviators whose aircraft went down in the water. Preserved as an exhibit of the Royal Air Force Museum.

Holland I
submarine

Built 1901 by Vickers, Son & Maxim, Barrow-in-Furness, England. Designed by John P Holland

Holland I

Original owners Royal Navy
Propulsion Surface; petrol engine. Submerged; electric motor
Tonnage 105 displacement
Length 63.5ft/19.35m
Breadth 11.0ft/3.35m
Draught 5.5ft/1.68m
Materials Steel throughout
Original use Submarine
Condition Largely intact
Present owners Royal Navy Submarine Memorial Museum, Gosport, Hants
Location Gosport, England
History First submarine built for the Royal Navy. Designed by the American inventor John P Holland. Sunk off Plymouth, England, early in the century and raised almost intact in the 1980s. Exhibited on shore at a museum devoted to the history of submarines in the Royal Navy.
Bibliography A6, D92

Hoshi
sailing yacht

Built 1909 by Camper & Nicholson, Gosport, England
Original owners J Oswald
Propulsion Schooner rig, auxiliary engine. Engine built by Lister Blackstone
Tonnage 32 gross
Length 72.0ft/21.95m
Breadth 14.17ft/4.32m
Draught 7.75ft/2.36m
Materials Wood throughout
Original use Yacht
Condition Intact, in sailing condition
Present owners Island Cruising Club

Humber

HSL-102

Contact address Island Street,
Salcombe, Devon
Location Salcombe, England
History Turn of the century sailing
yacht maintained in sailing condition.
Used for sailing cruising out of
Salcombe.
Bibliography A10, D417

HSL-102
air-sea rescue launch

Built 1941
Original use Aviation rescue launch
Condition Fully restored to 1941
appearance
Location Southampton, England
History Fast motor launch stationed at
military airfields to rescue aviators
who crashed in the water. Restored to
original appearance as a floating
exhibit.

Humber
motor launch

Built 1946 by British Power Boat Co,
Southampton, England
Propulsion Two diesel engines; 260hp.
Engine built by Perkins
Length 44.5ft/13.6m
Breadth 13.5ft/4.1m
Draught 2.75ft/0.8m
Materials Wood hull
Original use Motor launch
Condition Intact, fully restored
Location Portsmouth, England
History Preserved as an onshore exhibit.

Hydrogen
spritsail barge

Built 1906 by Gill, Rochester, England
Official number 123640
Propulsion Spritsail
Tonnage 98 gross
Materials Wood throughout
Original use Cargo
Condition In sailing condition
Location Maldon, England
History Built as a sailing barge to carry
cargoes on the rivers and estuaries of
eastern England. Maintained in sailing
condition as a charter vessel based at
Maldon.

Irene
coasting ketch

Built 1907 by J F Carver and sons,
Bridgewater, England
Original owners Symons of
Bridgewater
Propulsion Ketch rig, auxiliary engine
added, diesel, 100hp

Irene

Tonnage 97 gross
Length 85.0ft/25.91m
Breadth 21.0ft/6.4m
Draught 9.0ft/2.74m
Materials Wood throughout
Original use Cargo
Condition Intact, in sailing condition
Present owners Dr L Morrish
Contact address Bishop's Lodge, Oakley
Green, Windsor, Berkshire
Location Gloucester, England
History Ketch built to carry cargo in
the British coastal trades. Maintained
in sailing condition as a charter vessel
sailing out of various ports on the west
coast of England.
Bibliography D368, D506

Ironsides
spritsail barge

Built 1900 by Clarke & Stanfield, West
Thurrock, England
Official number 112710
Propulsion Spritsail ketch rig
Tonnage 78 gross
Length 85.0ft/25.6m
Breadth 20.33ft/6.2m
Depth 6.4ft/2.0m
Materials Iron hull
Original use Cargo, sailing barge
Condition In sailing condition
Present owners Mark Towers
Location Maldon, England
History Built as a sailing barge to carry
cargoes on the rivers and estuaries of
eastern England. Maintained in sailing
condition as a charter vessel based in
Maldon.

Ivy May
canal maintenance craft

Built 1934 by Neath Canal Co, Neath
Canal, Wales
Original owners Neath Canal Co
Propulsion Towed
Length 58.5ft/17.83m
Breadth 9.5ft/2.9m
Draught 3.0ft/0.91m
Materials Wood hull
Original use Canal maintenance, weed
cutter
Condition Intact
Present owners Welsh Industrial and
Maritime Museum
Contact address Bute Street, Cardiff,
Glamorgan, Wales
Location Cardiff, Wales
History Maintenance craft used to cut
weeds in the Neath Canal in south
Wales. Was on exhibit ashore at the
Industrial Museum in Cardiff, but the
vessels of that museum have now been
either scrapped or dispersed.

Ironsides

J G Graves of Sheffield
rescue lifeboat

Built 1958 by W M Osborne
Original owners Royal National
Lifeboat Institution
Propulsion Diesel engines
Length 37.0ft/11.1m
Breadth 11.5ft/3.4m
Draught 3.5ft/1.1m
Materials Wood hull
Original use Rescue lifeboat
Condition Intact
Present owners Royal National Lifeboat
Collection
Location Chatham, England
History Preserved as an indoor exhibit.

Jacinta FD-159
motor fishing boat

Built 1972 by Clelands Shipbuilding
Co, Wallsend-on-Tyne, England
Original owners J Marr & Son
Official number 341758
Propulsion Diesel engine, 1900bhp
Tonnage 599 gross
Length 143.0ft/43.6m
Breadth 32.0ft/9.8m
Materials Steel throughout
Original use Fishing
Condition Engine inoperable,
otherwise intact
Location Fleetwood, England
History Motor fishing boat preserved
as an example of a type that once
operated out of Fleetwood.

Janet
naval steam pinnace

Former name No 236
Built 1892 by J Samuel White Ltd,
Cowes, Isle of Wight, England
Original owners British Admiralty
Propulsion Steam, screw, compound,
30hp. Engine built by J Samuel White
Ltd
Length 40.0ft/12.2m
Breadth 9.5ft/2.9m
Materials Wood throughout
Original use Naval pinnace
Condition Fully restored in 1992
Present owners Geoffrey St John
Location Severn River, England
History Former Royal Navy steam
pinnace attached to series of
battleships until retired in 1912.
Purchased for conversion to a yacht in
Ireland. Fully restored to steaming
condition 1988-92 with original engine.

Jesse Lumb
rescue lifeboat

Built c1939 in Great Britain
Original owners Royal National
Lifeboat Institution
Propulsion Diesel engine
Length 46.0ft/14.0m
Original use Rescue lifeboat
Condition Intact
Present owners Imperial War Museum
Location Duxford, England
History Preserved as an onshore
exhibit.

Jock
spritsail barge

Built 1907 by R & W Paul, Ipswich,
England
Official number 122975
Propulsion Spritsail, auxiliary engine
added in 1948
Tonnage 86 gross
Length 90.7ft/27.6m
Breadth 21.5ft/6.6m
Depth 7.1ft/2.2m
Materials Wood throughout
Original use Cargo
Condition Intact, in sailing condition
Location London, England
History Built as a sailing barge to carry
cargoes on the rivers and estuaries of
eastern England. Was maintained in
sailing condition making corporate
cruises out of St Katherine's Dock in
London. Now lying at Gravesend Yacht
Basin on the lower Thames and
apparently no longer sailing.

John H Amos
paddle tug

Former name HERO
Built 1931 by Bow Mclachlan & Co, Paisley, Scotland
Original owners River Tees Conservancy
Propulsion Steam, sidewheel, two diagonal compound, 127hp
Tonnage 202 gross
Length 110.0ft/33.53m
Breadth 42.0ft/12.8m
Materials Steel hull, steel and wood superstructure
Original use Tug
Condition Intact, in need of restoration
Present owners Medway Maritime Museum
Contact address Martin Stevens, Cellar Hill Farm, Teynham, Sittingbourne
Location Chatham, England
History Last intact sidewheel tug in the British Isles. Currently lying at the former Naval Dockyard in Chatham, in an area not open to the public, in need of restoration. Proposal to exhibit and return to operating condition.
Bibliography B27

John H Amos

John King
harbour tug

Former name DURDHAM, PETER LEIGH
Built 1935 by Charles Hill & Sons, Bristol, England
Original owners C J King & Sons
Propulsion Diesel engine, 337hp. Engine built by Petter; currently Lister
Tonnage 49 gross
Length 68.5ft/21.0m
Breadth 17.0ft/5.25m
Draught 8.5ft/2.62m
Materials Steel hull
Original use Tug
Condition Intact
Present owners Bristol Industrial Museum
Location Bristol, England
History British harbour tug, veteran of D-Day invasion, preserved as a floating exhibit at the quay in front of the City of Bristol's Industrial Museum.

Jolie Brise
sailing pilot cutter

Built 1913 by Paumelle, Le Havre, France
Original owners Cherbourg Pilot Service
Propulsion Sloop rig
Tonnage 23 gross
Length 56.17ft/17.12m
Breadth 15.83ft/4.82m

Draught 7.5ft/2.29m
Materials Wood throughout
Original use Pilot cutter
Condition In sailing condition
Contact address The Quay, Exeter, Devon
Location Exeter, England
History French sailing pilot cutter later converted to a British yacht. Was based at Exeter, England, as a sail training vessel and exhibit, but the maritime museum there has been closed and the preserved vessels dispersed, with most going to either Bristol or Lowestoft.
Bibliography A10, D40, D345, D349

Kathleen & May
coasting schooner

Former name LIZZIE MAY
Built 1900 by Ferguson & Baird, Connahs Quay, Wales
Original owners Captain John Coppack
Propulsion Three-masted topsail schooner rig; auxiliary engine added
Tonnage 136 gross
Length 98.33ft/29.97m
Breadth 23.17ft/7.06m
Draught 10.08ft/3.07m
Materials Wood throughout
Original use Cargo
Condition In need of restoration
Present owners S E L Clarke, Bideford
Location Gloucester, England
History In April 1900 a three-masted

Kathleen & May

topsail schooner took the water from Ferguson & Baird's Yard at Connah's Quay near Chester, England. She was built to the order of Captain John Coppack and named, as was the widespread practice in those days, after his two daughters Lizzie and May. Until 1908 she was employed taking cargoes such as cement, coal, pitch and clay anywhere between Oban, Scotland, and the Channel Islands off France. In that year she was purchased by M J Fleming of Youghal in southern Ireland, renamed KATHLEEN & MAY, and placed in the coal trade between the Bristol Channel and Ireland, carrying oats or pit-props on the return passages. In 1931 she was purchased by Captain Tommy Jewell, a well-known coasting skipper from Appledore, England. In order to meet growing competition from motor vessels, KATHLEEN & MAY was fitted with an 80hp auxiliary engine. At the same time, her topmasts were shortened and all sails above the lowermasts were done away with. Tommy Jewell operated the vesssel until 1961, after which she had a series of owners until finally retired in 1966. In 1970 she was acquired by the Maritime Trust through the generosity of Sir Yue-Kong Pao, Chairman of the World-Wide Shipping Group. The Trust fully restored KATHLEEN & MAY at Plymouth, England, with her original topsail schooner rig, and exhibited her there until 1978. In July of that year she was moved to St Katherine's Dock in London to join several other Trust vessels exhibited there. The Maritime Trust fleet has since been dispersed to several locations around the British Isles. Again in need of restoration, she has been transferred to a private owner who intends to make her an exhibit at Bideford.
Bibliography A14, B49, D48, D460

Katie Ann
North Sea beam trawler

Former name THYME
Built 1921 by S Richards & Co, Lowestoft, England
Original owners W J Garner
Propulsion Sailing trawler, converted to diesel. Engine built by Gardner
Length 70.0ft/21.34m
Breadth 17.75ft/5.41m
Draught 7.67ft/2.34m
Materials Wood throughout
Original use Fishing
Condition Intact

Present owners Maritime and Industrial Museum
Location Swansea, Wales
History North Sea beam trawler that once fished out of Swansea on the south coast of Wales. Now preserved as one of the floating exhibits of the maritime and industrial museum in Swansea.

Kennet
river tug/inspection launch

Built 1931 by James Pollock Sons & Co
Original owners Thames Conservancy
Propulsion Petrol engine, 72hp. Engine built by Crossley
Length 35.33ft/10.77m
Breadth 9.0ft/2.74m
Draught 4.5ft/1.37m
Materials Steel throughout
Original use Tug and inspection launch
Condition Intact
Present owners Star Tug & Marine Co, London
Location Gloucester, England
History Preserved as an exhibit.

Kent
motor tug

Built 1948 by Richards Ironworks, Lowestoft, England
Original owners J P Knight, Rochester
Propulsion Diesel engine, 880bhp. Engine built by British Polar Atlas
Length 88.0ft/26.8m

Materials Steel throughout
Original use Tug
Condition Intact, undergoing renovation
Present owners South East Tug Society
Location Chatham Dockyard; Chatham, England
History Intact tug of the 1940s maintained by an enthusiast group who moor her in one of the basins of the former Chatham Dockyard.

Kenya Jacaranda
fishing ketch

Former name TORBAY LASS
Built 1923 by R Jackman & Sons, Brixham, England
Propulsion Sail, ketch rig; two diesel engines
Tonnage 80.4 displacement
Length 77.1ft/23.5m
Breadth 18.1ft/5.5m
Draught 8.5ft/2.6m
Materials Wood throughout
Original use Fishing
Condition In sailing condition
Present owners The Mayflower Sail Training Society
Location Tilbury, England
History Used for sail training.

Kerne
naval steam tug

Former name VIKING, TERRIER
Built 1913 by Montrose Shipbuilding

Co, Montrose, Scotland
Original owners Chatham Naval Dockyard
Propulsion Steam, triple expansion, 400hp
Length 75.0ft/22.86m
Breadth 18.5ft/5.64m
Draught 10.0ft/3.05m
Materials Steel throughout
Original use Tug
Condition In operating condition
Present owners North Western Steamship Co
Contact address 48 Heygarth Road, Eastham, Wirral, Cheshire, England
Location Wirral, England
History Former Naval dockyard steam tug maintained in operating condition by a group of steam enthusiasts based at Wirral, near Liverpool.
Bibliography B27, B56, D276, D483

Kindly Light
sailing pilot cutter

Former name THEODORA
Built 1911 by Armour Brothers, Fleetwood, England
Original owners Lewis Alexander
Propulsion Cutter rig
Tonnage 20 gross
Length 52.0ft/15.85m
Breadth 14.5ft/4.42m
Draught 8.5ft/2.59m
Materials Wood throughout
Original use Pilot cutter
Condition Undergoing restoration

Kent

Kindly Light

deckhouse wood
Original use Passengers on river
Condition In operation
Present owners Paddle Steam
Navigation Co
Contact address 10 Crescent Rise,
Crescent Road, London N3 1HS
Location Rochester, England
History Built to carry passengers on the
Dart River in southwest England.
Engine dates from 1904. Fully restored
to operating condition in 1984 and
currently making excursions out of
Rochester and Chatham Dockyard on
the Medway River in southeast
England.
Bibliography B27, B43, B49

Kittiwake
steam launch

Built 1898 by T W Hayton, Bowness,
England
Original owners W G Groves,
Windermere
Propulsion Steam, screw, triple
expansion
Length 40.0ft/12.19m
Breadth 7.0ft/2.13m
Materials Wood throughout
Original use Yacht
Condition In operating condition
Present owners Windermere Steamboat
Museum
Location Windermere, England

Kittiwake

Location Gweek, Cornwall, England
History Formerly a sailing pilot vessel
serving ports on the Bristol Channel.
Preserved for a number of years on
shore beside an industrial museum in
Cardiff, Wales. The vessels exhibited
there have been displaced by a
development project, and she has been
moved to Cornwall where she is being
restored to sailing condition.
Bibliography B40, C89

Kingswear Castle
river excursion steamer

Built 1924 by Philip & Son, Dartmouth,
England
Original owners River Dart Steamboat
Co
Propulsion Steam, sidewheel,
compound diagonal, 130hp. Engine
built by Cox & Co, Falmouth
Tonnage 94 gross
Length 108.0ft/32.92m
Breadth 28.0ft/8.53m
Draught 3.0ft/0.91m
Materials Steel hull, decks and part of

Kingswear Castle

History Elegant steam launch from the turn of the century. Converted to diesel propulsion in 1951, but restored with original steam engine in 1984.

Kitty
spritsail barge

Built 1895 by Cann Brothers, Harwich, England
Original owners F W Horlock
Official number 105418
Propulsion Spritsail
Tonnage 65 gross
Materials Wood throughout
Original use Cargo
Condition In sailing condition
Present owners Roger Marriott
Location Portsmouth, England
History Built as a sailing barge to carry cargoes on the rivers and estuaries of eastern England. Restored to sailing condition in 1964 for charter use and now based at Ocean Village, Portsmouth, on the south coast.

Knocker White
steam tug

Former name CAIRNROCK
Built 1924 by T van Duivendijk, Lekkerkerk, Netherlands
Original owners Harrisons Lighterage Co, London
Propulsion Steam, screw; converted to diesel

Tonnage 90 gross
Length 77.2ft/23.53m
Breadth 20.0ft/6.1m
Materials Steel throughout
Original use Tug
Condition Intact
Present owners Museum of London
Location London, England
History Example of a typical London lighterage tug of the 1920s. Preserved as a floating exhibit.

Kyles
steam coaster

Built 1872 by J Fullerton & Co, Paisley, Scotland
Propulsion Steam, screw, compound
Tonnage 122 gross
Length 82.25ft/25.07m
Breadth 18.17ft/5.54m
Materials Iron and steel hull
Original use Cargo
Condition Intact
Present owners Scottish Maritime Museum
Location Irvine, Scotland
History The oldest surviving British steam coaster. Preserved as a floating exhibit.
Bibliography D115

Lady Daphne
spritsail barge

Built 1923 by Short Brothers, Rochester,

England
Original owners Mrs Lillian Bradley
Official number 127276
Propulsion Sail, spritsail ketch rig
Tonnage 117 gross
Length 90.8ft/27.68m
Breadth 21.5ft/6.55m
Materials Wood throughout
Original use Cargo, sailing barge
Condition In sailing condition
Present owners Taylor Woodrow Ltd
Location London, England
History Built as a sailing barge to carry cargoes on the rivers and estuaries of eastern England. Restored to sailing condition in 1974 as a corporate yacht and currently based at St Katherine's Dock next to the Tower of London.
Bibliography C74

Lady Jean
spritsail barge

Former name SIR ALAN HERBERT
Built 1923 by Short Brothers, Rochester, Kent
Original owners Mrs Lillian Bradley, Rochester
Propulsion Spritsail
Tonnage 86 gross
Length 91.2ft/27.8m
Breadth 21.67ft/6.61m
Materials Wood throughout
Original use Cargo
Condition In sailing condition
Present owners Iden Wickens

Location Maldon, England
History Built as a sailing barge to carry cargoes on the rivers and estuaries of eastern England. Maintained in sailing condition as a yacht based at Maldon.
Bibliography C74

Lady of the Lea
spritsail barge

Built 1931 by Hyam & Oliver, Rotherhithe, England
Original owners British War Department
Propulsion Sail, spritsail ketch rig
Length 72.0ft/21.9m
Breadth 13.0ft/4.0m
Materials Wood throughout
Original use Cargo; explosives
Condition In sailing condition
Present owners Brian Pain
Location Faversham, England
History Small sailing barge built to carry explosives. Maintained in sailing condition as a yacht based at Standard Quay, Faversham
Bibliography C74

LCT-7074
landing craft tank

Built 1944 in Great Britain
Original owners Royal Navy
Official number LCT-7074
Propulsion Diesel engines, 1000hp. Engines built by Paxman
Tonnage 640 displacement
Length 192.0ft/58.52m
Breadth 31.0ft/9.45m
Draught 5.6ft/1.65m
Materials Steel throughout
Original use Landing craft
Location Birkenhead, England
History Landing craft built for the Second World War, designed to carry tanks and troops. Possibly the last survivor of her type of vessel. Recently acquired to serve as an exhibit at Birkenhead, across the Mersey River from Liverpool.

Leader
fishing ketch

Former name LORNE LEADER
Built 1892 by A W Gibbs, Galmpton, England
Propulsion Sail, ketch rig; auxiliary engine added
Length 79.0ft/24.1m
Breadth 19.0ft/5.8m
Draught 10.25ft/3.1m
Materials Wood throughout
Original use Fishing
Condition In sailing condition

Kyles

Location Dartmouth, England
History Used for charter.
Bibliography A10, D93a

Lincoln Castle
sidewheel river ferry

Built 1940 by A & J Inglis, Glasgow, Scotland
Original owners London & North Eastern Railway
Propulsion Steam, sidewheel, triple expansion diagonal, 850hp. Engine built by Ailsa Shipbuilding Co, Troon
Tonnage 598 gross
Length 199.58ft/60.83m
Breadth 57.0ft/17.37m
Draught 4.5ft/1.37m
Materials Steel throughout
Original use Ferry across river estuary
Condition Intact, in use
Present owners Colin Johnson
Location Grimsby, England
History Sidewheel steam ferryboat built to carry vehicles and foot passengers across the Humber River in northeast England. Retired on completion of the Humber Bridge in 1979. Now serves as a floating restaurant and bar at Alexandra Dock, Grimsby.
Bibliography B16, B43, B58, C22

Lydia Eva
steam drifter

Former name WATCHMOOR
Built 1930 by Kings Lynn Slipway, Kings Lynn, England
Original owners Harry Eastick
Propulsion Steam, triple expansion. Engine built by Crabtree & Co
Tonnage 138 gross
Length 95.0ft/28.96m
Breadth 20.5ft/6.25m
Draught 9.67ft/2.95m
Materials Steel throughout
Original use Fishing; Herring drifter
Condition Intact
Present owners The Lydia Eva & Mincarlo Charitable Trust
Location Lowestoft, England
History British North Sea steam herring drifter restored by the Maritime Trust in 1970 and exhibited by them at Great Yarmouth and later London. Transferred to the present owners by the Trust around 1990, for further use as a floating exhibit.
Bibliography B27, B49, D224, D342

M-33
monitor

Former name HMS MINERVA

Lydia Eva

M-33

Built 1915 by Workman Clark, Belfast, Ireland
Original owners Royal Navy
Propulsion Steam, screw, triple expansion
Tonnage 580 displacement
Length 177.25ft/54.03m
Breadth 31.0ft/9.45m
Materials Steel throughout
Original use Monitor
Condition Undergoing restoration
Present owners Treadgold Museum & Hampshire County Council
Location Portsmouth, England
History Preserved as an exhibit.
Bibliography D105

Maid of the Loch
sidewheel lake steamer

Built 1953 by A & J Inglis, Glasgow, Scotland
Original owners British Transport Commission
Propulsion Steam, sidewheel, compound diagonal, 900hp. Engine built by Rankin & Blackmore, Greenock
Tonnage 555 gross
Length 191.0ft/58.22m
Breadth 51.0ft/15.54m
Draught 7.08ft/2.16m
Materials Steel hull, aluminium superstructure

Original use Passengers
Condition Intact. Laid up
Present owners Alloa Brewery Co
Location Loch Lomond, Scotland
History The last sidewheel steamer built for service on Loch Lomond. Laid up in 1981, but now undergoing extensive restoration for a return to steaming condition.
Bibliography A17, B16, B27, B43, D408

Mannin 2
dredger

Built 1936 by Lobnitz & Co, Renfrew, Scotland
Original owners Isle of Man Harbour Commissioners
Propulsion Steam, screw, 2-cylinder, 150hp
Tonnage 127 gross
Length 100.65ft/30.68m
Breadth 23.0ft/7.01m
Materials Steel throughout
Original use Dredger
Condition Intact
Present owners P Bird, Essex
Location Ellesmere Port, England
History Preserved as a floating exhibit.
Bibliography B4, B27

Marbury
canal icebreaker

Built Date not known
Propulsion Towed
Length 41.0ft/12.7m
Breadth 6.8ft/2.1m
Draught 2.0ft/0.61m
Materials Wood hull sheathed with iron
Original use Canal icebreaker
Condition Intact
Present owners Shropshire Union Canal Society
Location Ellesmere Port, England
History Preserved as a floating exhibit.
Bibliography B4

Marie May
spritsail barge

Built 1920 by Huston's, Maidstone, England
Propulsion Sail; spritsail ketch
Length 86.0ft/26.2m
Breadth 22.0ft/6.7m
Materials Wood throughout
Original use Cargo; sailing barge
Condition Hull restoration underway since December 1995
Present owners Geoff Lynch
Location Woolston, Southampton, England
History Sailing barge built to carry

Maid of the Loch

cargo in the rivers and estuaries of eastern England. Currently being restored by a private owner.

Mariette
sailing yacht

Built 1915 by Nat Herreshoff, Bristol, Rhode Island, USA
Original owners Frederick J Brown
Propulsion Schooner rig; auxiliary engine
Length 138.0ft/42.0m
Breadth 23.5ft/7.2m
Draught 14.5ft/4.4m
Materials Wood throughout
Original use Yacht
Condition Fully restored; in sailing condition
Present owners Tom Perkins
Location Great Britain (flag)
History Sailing yacht designed and built early in the century by the leading yacht building yard in the United States. Fully restored in Great Britain by a private owner.
Bibliography A1, D410

Marigold
sailing yacht

Built 1892 by Charles Nicholson, Gosport, England
Original owners W R Martin
Propulsion Cutter rig
Tonnage 38 displacement
Length 59.1ft/18.0m
Breadth 12.2ft/3.71m
Draught 8.7ft/2.66m
Materials Wood throughout
Original use Yacht

Condition Fully restored, in sailing condition
Present owners Greg Powlesland
Location Great Britain
History Victorian sailing yacht produced by a leading British designer and builder. Recently restored to sailing condition and original appearance.
Bibliography D114, D413

Marjorie
spritsail barge

Built 1902 by Orvis, Ipswich, England
Original owners R & W Paul Ltd
Propulsion Spritsail
Tonnage 56 gross
Length 84.0ft/25.6m
Breadth 19.3ft/5.9m
Depth 6.2ft/1.9m
Materials Wood throughout
Original use Cargo
Condition In sailing condition
Present owners Simon Devonshire
Location Hoo, England
History Built as a sailing barge to carry cargoes on the rivers and estuaries of eastern England. Maintained in sailing condition as a yacht or charter vessel based at Hoo.

Marsa
steam lighter

Former name VIC 85
Built 1944 by Dunston's Yard, Thorne, Lincolnshire, England
Original owners British Admiralty
Propulsion Steam, screw; converted to diesel

Tonnage 145 gross
Length 85.0ft/25.9m
Breadth 18.0ft/5.5m
Draught 8.66ft/2.6m
Materials Steel hull
Original use Cargo
Condition Undergoing restoration
Location Irvine, Scotland
History Small steam cargo lighter built for harbour service during the Second World War, on the lines of the 'Clyde puffers' used before the war on the west coast of Scotland. Being restored by a private owner at the former shipyard that is now part of the Scottish Maritime Museum.

Mary Joseph
fishing lugger

Built 1877 by William Paynter, Kilkeel, Ireland
Original owners Patrick Collins
Propulsion Lugger rig, converted to motor vessel
Tonnage 21 gross
Length 51.5ft/15.7m
Breadth 15.0ft/4.57m
Draught 6.0ft/1.83m
Materials Wood throughout
Original use Fishing
Condition Intact
Present owners Ulster Folk & Transport Museum
Contact address Cultra Manor, Holywood, County Down
Location Holywood, Northern Ireland
History Built as a sailing fishing boat and later converted to a motor vessel. Preserved as an onshore exhibit; appearance as when last in service.

Mary Rose

Henry VIII of England, and foundered with the King himself watching while sailing out to meet a French force threatening to land on the Isle of Wight in 1545. She went down apparently for much the same reasons the VASA did in 1628 – too much weight on board and open gunports too close to the water. Some cannons were salvaged from the wreck using primitive diving methods, but her actual location was eventually lost. After years of searching, she was rediscovered in 1979 completely buried in the bottom silt. This silt was found to have not only completely preserved the wooden structure of the ship that sank into it, but also artifacts made from virtually every material from metal to cloth and leather. The ship remains, consisting of most of one side and the ship's bottom and lower stern, were raised in one piece in 1982 and placed in a covered graving dock in the Portsmouth Dockyard for treatment and exhibition. A museum nearby displays examples from the full range of weapons and personal effects found in the ship, including the archers' longbows and arrows, and their leather armlets with distinct tooled designs.
Bibliography C59, D447

Massey Shaw
fireboat

Built 1935 at Cowes, Isle of Wight, England
Original owners London County Council
Propulsion Steam, screw, triple expansion, 400hp; converted to diesel
Tonnage 51 gross
Length 75.0ft/22.86m
Breadth 12.6ft/3.84m
Materials Steel throughout
Original use Fireboat
Condition Intact
Present owners Massey Shaw Perservation Society
Location Millwall, England
History Veteran London steam fireboat that took part in the Dunkirk troop evacuation during the Second World War. Preserved afloat at Millwall, near London.
Bibliography B5

Mary Rose
sixteenth-century warship

Built 1510 by Portsmouth Royal Dockyard, Portsmouth, England
Original owners King Henry VIII
Propulsion Ship rig; four masts
Tonnage 1150 displacement
Length 105ft/32.0m(keel)
Breadth 39.0ft/11.89m
Draught 14.0ft/4.27m
Materials Wood throughout
Original use Warship
Condition One side survives largely complete down to keel
Present owners The Mary Rose Trust
Contact address Old Bond Store, 48 Warblington Street, Portsmouth PO1
Location Portsmouth, England
History Since the raising of the Swedish seventeenth-century warship VASA in 1961, the most remarkable similar retrieval of a sunken historic vessel has been the raising of much of the intact hull of the sixteenth-century MARY ROSE off Portsmouth, England, in 1982. This ship is the earliest known to have mounted guns within the hull firing through gunports in the vessel's side. She was originally built as a 'carrack' in 1510. When twenty-five years old she was rebuilt with the more modern system of armament. MARY ROSE served as the flagship of the Navy of

Mayflower in service on the Sharpness Canal about 1922

May
spritsail barge

Built 1891 by Cann, Harwich, England
Original owners Cranfield Brothers
Official number 97680
Propulsion Spritsail
Tonnage 57 gross
Materials Wood throughout
Original use Cargo
Condition In sailing condition
Present owners Tate & Lyle
Location London, England
History Built as a sailing barge to carry cargoes on the rivers and estuaries of eastern England. Maintained as a corporate yacht and charter vessel based at St Katherine's Dock next to the Tower of London.
Bibliography D169

Mayflower
steam tug

Built 1861 by Stothert & Marten, Bristol, England
Original owners T Hadley
Propulsion Steam, screw, compound (not original). Engine built by W Sisson & Co, Gloucester (current)
Tonnage 45 displacement
Length 63.25ft/19.28m
Breadth 12.0ft/3.66m
Draught 7.0ft/2.13m
Materials Iron throughout
Original use Tug
Condition Restored to operating condition
Present owners Bristol Industrial Museum
Location Bristol, England
History The world's oldest tug in steaming condition. Was fully restored 1982-87 with an engine dating from 1898. Can usually be seen moored beside the Industrial Museum in Bristol.
Bibliography B27, B29, D272, D352

Medway Queen
river excursion steamer

Former name HMS MEDWAY QUEEN
Built 1924 by Ailsa Shipbuilding Co, Troon, Scotland
Original owners New Medway Steam Packet Co
Propulsion Steam, sidewheel, compound, 900hp. Engine built by Ailsa Shipbuilding Co
Tonnage 316 gross
Length 179.75ft/54.79m
Breadth 49.0ft/14.94m
Draught 7.67ft/2.34m
Materials Steel throughout

Medway Queen

Original use Passengers
Condition Restoration in progress
Present owners Medway Queen Restoration and Preservation Ltd
Contact address 23 Milton Road, Gravesend, Kent, England
Location Great Britain
History Built to carry passengers on the Medway River in southeast England. One of the makeshift fleet of vessels that rescued British troops from the beaches of Dunkirk, France, in the Second World War. Used as a clubhouse at a marina on the Isle of Wight 1964-84. Since then has been the subject of a struggling restoration effort. Has sunk several times, most recently in 1998.
Bibliography B5, 43, 49, D93, 500, 502, 555

Mendip
powered canal barge

Built 1948 by W J Yarwood & Sons, Northwich, England
Original owners Fellowes, Morton & Clayton
Propulsion Diesel engine, 9hp. Engine built by Lister
Length 72.0ft/22.2m
Breadth 7.0ft/2.1m
Draught 3.5ft/1.07m
Materials Steel sides and wood bottom
Original use Cargo, canals
Condition Intact

Present owners The Boat Museum
Location Ellesmere Port, England
History Preserved as a floating exhibit.
Bibliography B4

Merak
canal barge

Built 1936 by W H Walker & Bros, Rickmansworth, England
Original owners Grand Union Canal Carrying Co
Propulsion Towed by motor boat
Length 71.0ft/22.0m
Breadth 7.0ft/2.2m
Draught 3.5ft/1.1m
Materials Wood throughout
Original use Cargo, canals
Condition Intact
Present owners The Boat Museum
Location Ellesmere Port, England
History Preserved as a floating exhibit.
Bibliography B4

Merope
powered canal barge

Former name GERTRUDE, SANDRA
Built 1936 by W H Walker, Rickmansworth, England
Original owners Grand Union Canal Carrying Co
Propulsion Diesel engine. Engine built by Bolinder
Length 71.5ft/21.79m
Breadth 7.0ft/2.13m

Draught 3.25ft/0.99m
Materials Wood throughout
Original use Cargo
Condition Intact
Present owners The Boat Museum
Location Ellesmere Port, England
History Preserved as a floating exhibit.

MGB-60
motor gunboat

Former name HMS MGB-60
Built 1940 by Hythe, Southampton, England. Designed by Scott Paine
Original owners Royal Navy
Official number MGB-60
Propulsion Diesel or petrol engines
Length 72.0ft/21.9m
Materials Wood throughout
Original use High-speed gunboat
Condition Largely intact
Location Lowestoft, England
History Veteran of the Second World War. Served as a houseboat at Woodbridge, England, for around 40 years. Currently being restored at Lowestoft.

Mincarlo
motor fishing boat

Built 1962 by Brooke Marine Ltd, Lowestoft, England
Original owners Diesel Trawlers Ltd
Official number LT 412
Propulsion Diesel engines

Tonnage 166 gross
Length 98.0ft/29.9m
Breadth 22.5ft/6.9m
Draught 9.5ft/2.9m
Materials Steel throughout
Original use Fishing
Condition Intact
Present owners The Lydia Eva and
Mincarlo Charitable Trust
Location Lowestoft, England
History Preserved as a floating exhibit.

Mirosa
spritsail barge

Former name READY
Built 1892 by John Howard, Maldon,
England
Original owners Charles Gurreridge
Propulsion Spritsail
Tonnage 49 gross
Original use Cargo
Condition In sailing condition
Present owners Peter Dodds
Location Faversham, England
History Built as a sailing barge to carry
cargoes on the rivers and estuaries of
eastern England. Maintained in sailing
condition as a private yacht; one of the
few remaining spritsail barges without
an auxiliary engine. A regular
participant in the annual sailing barge
races.

ML-293
naval motor launch

Built 1941 by Hamworthy, Poole,
England
Original owners Royal Navy
Propulsion Petrol engines, 1120hp
Tonnage 85.6 displacement
Length 112.0ft/34.14m
Breadth 18.33ft/5.59m
Draught 4.75ft/1.45m

MTB-71

Mossdale

Materials Wood throughout
Original use Fast gunboat
Condition Intact, in operating
condition
Present owners R G Morley
Location Bristol, England
History Used for sea scout training.

Monarch
steam narrowboat

Built 1908 by Fellows, Morton &
Clayton Ltd, Saltley, England
Original owners Fellows, Morton &
Clayton Ltd
Propulsion Steam, screw, compound;
replaced by diesel engine
Tonnage 23 gross
Length 72.0ft/21.95m

Breadth 7.0ft/2.13m
Draught 3.75ft/1.14m
Materials Iron sides and wood bottom;
wood cabin
Original use Cargo, canals
Condition Intact, in active use
Present owners A Millward and P
Kirkbride
Contact address c/o North Western
Museum of Inland Navigation
Location Ellesmere Port, England
History Narrowboat built to carry
cargoes on the canals of central
England. Maintained as a private yacht
and a floating exhibit at a canal
museum when not cruising.

Mossdale
Mersey flat

Former name RUBY
Built c1865 by John Smith, Liverpool,
England
Original owners Shropshire Union
Railway & Canal Co
Propulsion Towed by horses or mules
Length 72.0ft/21.95m
Breadth 14.25ft/4.34m
Draught 5.5ft/1.68m
Materials Wood throughout
Original use Cargo
Condition Intact
Present owners The Boat Museum
Contact address Dockyard Road,
Ellesmere Port, Cheshire L65 4EF
Location Ellesmere Port, England
History Type of river and canal barge
known as a Mersey flat, preserved on
shore as an exhibit with the large fleet

of working craft at the museum in
Ellesmere Port.
Bibliography B4

MTB-71
motor torpedo boat

Built 1940 by Vosper
Original owners Royal Navy
Propulsion Petrol engines, 1000hp.
Engines built by Isotta-Fraschini
Tonnage 22 displacement
Length 60.0ft/18.3m
Breadth 15.5ft/4.7m
Materials Wood throughout
Original use Torpedo boat
Condition Largely restored
Present owners Hampshire County
Council
Location Portsmouth, England
History Torpedo boat built in Great
Britain for the Norwegian Navy but
not delivered due to the outbreak of
the Second World War. Saw action
during the war as a British vessel.
Served as a houseboat near Chichester,
England, for many years before being
acquired for restoration to her Second
World War appearance. Currently
exhibited on shore in the Portsmouth
Dockyard.

MTB-102
motor torpedo boat

Built 1937 by Vospers Ltd, Portsmouth,
England
Original owners Royal Navy
Propulsion Petrol engines; 3000hp;

MTB-102 as built

replaced by diesel engines. Engines built by Isotta-Fraschini
Length 68.0ft/20.73m
Breadth 14.75ft/4.5m
Draught 3.17ft/0.97m
Materials Wood throughout
Original use Torpedo boat
Condition Intact, in operating condition
Present owners MTB 102 Trust
Contact address Hilltop, Castle Street, Wroxham, Norfolk NR12 8AB
Location Lowestoft, England
History Prototype fast torpedo boat built for the Royal Navy shortly before the Second World War. Original engines replaced with diesel engines in 1948. Maintained in operating condition as a Sea Scout vessel.
Bibliography B5, D246, D255

Nellie
spritsail barge

Built 1901 by Charles Cremer, Faversham, England
Official number 114452
Propulsion Spritsail
Tonnage 43 gross
Length 79.3ft/24.2m
Breadth 17.5ft/5.3m
Original use Cargo
Condition Restored to sailing condition in 1994
Present owners Dr Diane Montgomery

Location Maldon, England
History Built as a sailing barge to carry cargoes on the rivers and estuaries of eastern England. Maintained in sailing condition as a private yacht.

Norada
wherry

Former name LADY EDITH
Built 1912 by Ernest Collins, Wroxham, England
Original owners Ernest Collins Ltd
Propulsion Sail, single-masted wherry rig
Tonnage 15.4 gross
Length 53.0ft/16.15m
Breadth 12.0ft/3.66m
Draught 3.75ft/1.14m
Materials Wood throughout
Original use Charters
Condition In sailing condition
Present owners Wherry Yacht Charters (R D Matthews)
Location Wroxham, England
History Used for charter.

Nore
lightship

Built 1936 by Samuel White, East Cowes, Isle of Wight, England
Original owners Corporation of Trinity House
Official number LV No 87

Propulsion None, towed to station
Tonnage 186 gross
Length 86.0ft/26.21m
Breadth 21.5ft/6.55m
Draught 9.5ft/2.9m
Materials Steel throughout
Original use Lightship
Condition Intact, laid up, in need of renovation

Present owners Mark Stowe
Location Hoo, England
History Veteran British lightship formerly employed on the world's oldest lightship station dating from the 1730s. First used as a floating exhibit at St Katherine's Dock in London. Later transferred to a private owner who moved her to Hoo.

North Carr
lightship

Built 1933 by A & J Inglis, Glasgow, Scotland
Original owners Northern Lighthouse Board
Propulsion None, towed to station
Tonnage 250 displacement
Length 101.0ft/30.78m
Breadth 26.0ft/7.92m
Materials Steel throughout, except planked decks
Original use Lightship
Condition Intact
Location Dundee, Scotland
History Lightship formerly employed off the coast of Scotland. Serves as a museum alongside in Dundee.
Bibliography D328

North Foreland
rescue lifeboat

Built 1951 by White, Cowes, Isle of Wight, England
Original owners Royal National Lifeboat Institution

North Carr

Northwich and Oak

Propulsion Diesel engines, 80hp.
Engines built by Ferry
Length 46.75ft/14.0m
Breadth 12.75ft/3.8m
Draught 4.25ft/1.3m
Materials Wood hull
Original use Rescue lifeboat
Condition Intact
Present owners Royal National Lifeboat
Collection
Location Chatham, England
History Preserved as an indoor exhibit.

Northwich
towed narrowboat

Built 1898 by Fellows, Morton &
Clayton, Birmingham, England
Original owners Fellows, Morton &
Clayton
Propulsion Towed by horses
Tonnage 35 gross
Length 70.67ft/21.54m
Breadth 7.17ft/2.19m
Draught 4.21ft/1.28m
Materials Iron sides and wood bottom;
wood cabin
Original use Cargo
Condition Intact
Present owners National Waterways
Museum
Location Gloucester, England
History Narrowboat built to carry
cargoes on the canals of England.
Currently a floating exhibit moored at

the National Waterways Museum
housed in a converted warehouse in
the Gloucester docks.

Nuneham
river steam launch

Built 1898 by Edwin Clark & Co,
Brimscombe, England
Original owners Salter Brothers
Propulsion Steam, screw, triple
expansion, 55hp (current). Engine built
by Sissons (current)
Tonnage 31 displacement
Length 86.0ft/26.2m

Oakdale

Breadth 13.5ft/4.1m
Draught 3.0ft/0.9m
Materials Steel hull, steel and wood
deckhouse
Original use Passengers
Condition Fully restored to operating
condition
Present owners Thames Steam Packet
Boat Co
Location Thames River, England
History Late Victorian steam launch
with enclosed cabin built to carry
passengers on the Thames River.
Converted to diesel propulsion in 1948.
Fully restored 1995-98 with an

appropriate steam engine dating from
1921. Used for charter.
Bibliography D357

Oak
motorised canal boat

Built 1934 by Charles Hill
Original owners Severn & Canal
Carrying Co
Propulsion Diesel engine, 9hp. Engine
built by Petter
Length 71.0ft/21.64m
Breadth 7.0ft/2.13m
Materials Steel sides and wood bottom
Original use Cargo, canals
Condition Intact
Present owners National Waterways
Museum
Location Gloucester, England
History English narrowboat formerly
operated on the canals between
Gloucester and Birmingham. Fully
restored in 1988 and preserved as a
floating exhibit.

Oakdale
Mersey flat

Built 1951 by Richard Abel & Sons,
Runcorn, England
Original owners Richard Abel & Sons
Propulsion Towed; engine added by
present owner
Tonnage 66 gross
Length 72.5ft/22.1m
Breadth 15.75ft/4.8m
Materials Wood throughout
Original use Cargo barge
Condition Intact
Present owners David Keenan
Location Liverpool, England
History Example of a type of bulk
cargo barge known as a 'Mersey flat'
formerly employed on the Mersey
River and Liverpool Bay. Restored by a
private owner, but displayed afloat at
Liverpool as an 'associate vessel' of the
Merseyside Maritime Museum.
Bibliography B56

Ocean Mist
steam yacht

Former name ARIES, OCEAN ROVER,
SAMUEL GREEN
Built 1919 by G Brown & Co Ltd,
Greenock, Scotland
Propulsion Steam, screw, triple
expansion, 500hp. Engine built by
McKie & Baxter Ltd, Paisley
Tonnage 383 gross
Length 125.5ft/38.2m
Breadth 23.5ft/7.2m
Draught 9.1ft/2.8m

Materials Steel throughout
Original use Yacht
Condition Intact
Location Leith, Scotland
History Intact steam yacht with
original engines and boilers. Was
brought to Leith under own power in
1987 for conversion to floating
restaurant.

Ocelot
submarine

Former name HMS OCELOT
Built 1962 by Chatham Dockyard,
Chatham, England
Original owners Royal Navy
Propulsion Diesel and electric motors,
6000hp
Tonnage 2140 displacement
Length 290.25ft/88.5m
Breadth 26.5ft/8.1m
Draught 18.25ft/5.6m
Materials Steel throughout
Original use Submarine
Condition Intact
Present owners Chatham Dockyard
Trust
Location Chatham, England
History One of the last submarines
built at Chatham Dockyard. Preserved
there as a floating exhibit.

Olga
sailing pilot cutter

Built 1909 by J Bowden, Porthleven,
Cornwall, England
Original owners Pilot H C Edmunds,
Barry, Wales
Propulsion Cutter rig; now has 4.236
Perkins diesel engine
Tonnage 35 gross
Length 56.0ft/17.07m
Breadth 13.5ft/4.11m
Draught 8.5ft/2.59m
Materials Wood throughout
Original use Pilot vessel
Condition Intact
Present owners Maritime and
Industrial Museum
Location Swansea, Wales
History Built as a sailing pilot vessel
serving ports on the Bristol Channel.
Now a floating exhibit at the maritime
and industrial museum in Swansea.
Bibliography C89

Olive
sailing wherry

Built 1909 by Ernest Collins, Wroxham,
England
Original owners Ernest Collins Ltd
Propulsion Sail, single-masted wherry

Olga

Tonnage 21.15 gross
Length 46.8ft/14.26m
Breadth 13.75ft/4.19m
Materials Wood throughout
Original use Charters
Condition In sailing condition
Present owners Wherry Yacht Charters
Location Wroxham, England
History Wherry yacht built for cruising
charters on the rivers of eastern
England. Available for charter.

Onyx
submarine

Former name HMS ONYX
Built 1966 by Cammell Laird,
Birkenhead, England
Original owners Royal Navy
Propulsion Diesel and electric motors,
6000hp
Tonnage 1610 displacement
Length 290.25ft/88.5m
Breadth 26.5ft/8.1m
Draught 18.25ft/5.6m
Materials Steel throughout
Original use Submarine
Condition Intact
Present owners Warship Preservation
Trust
Location Birkenhead, England
History Preserved as a floating exhibit
at the port of Birkenhead where she
was originally launched.

Onyx (Ocelot is same class)

Osprey

Orinoco
spritsail barge

Built 1895 by Hughes, East Greenwich, England
Propulsion Sail, spritsail barge; auxiliary engine added
Tonnage 70 gross
Materials Wood throughout
Original use Cargo
Condition In sailing condition
Present owners Robert Deards
Location Hoo, England
History Built to carry cargoes under sail on the rivers and estuaries of southeast England. Refitted as a private yacht in 1990, and currently based at Hoo, England.

Osprey
lake steamer

Built 1902 by Neil Shepherd, Windermere, England
Propulsion Steam, screw, compound. Engine built by W Sisson & Co, Gloucester
Tonnage 8 gross
Length 45.0ft/13.72m
Breadth 8.0ft/2.44m
Draught 3.5ft/1.07m
Materials Wood throughout (teak)
Original use Yacht
Condition Fully restored
Present owners Windermere Nautical Trust
Contact address Windermere Steamboat Museum, Rayrigg Road, Windermere
Location Windermere, England
History Elegant turn of the century steam launch with aft cabin built for use on the English lakes. Preserved in operating condition in a museum boathouse in Windermere. The 1901 engine was formerly in the steam launch WATER VIPER.
Bibliography B27, C20

Otto
steam launch

Former name GREBE
Built 1896 by Forrest & Sons, Wivenhoe, Essex, England
Original owners J M Sladen
Propulsion Steam, triple expansion, 100hp. Engine built by W Sisson & Co, Gloucester
Length 43.5ft/13.26m
Breadth 6.58ft/2.01m
Materials Steel hull
Original use Yacht
Condition Fully restored
Present owners Ben Black, Skelmersdale, Lancashire
Location Windermere, England
History Late Victorian steam launch maintained in operating condition in museum boathouse at Windermere.
Bibliography B27

Pascual Flores
trading schooner

Built 1919 by Antonio Mari, Porrevivja, Spain
Propulsion Sail, 3-masted schooner rig; diesel auxiliary
Tonnage 150 gross
Length 96.0ft/29.26m
Breadth 28.0ft/8.53m
Materials Wood throughout
Original use Cargo
Condition Undergoing restoration
Present owners Nova Trust, Bristol, England
Location Milford Haven, Wales
History Built to carry cargo under sail in the Spanish Mediterranean and coastal trade. Proposed for use as a sail training vessel.
Bibliography B29

Peggy
sailing yacht

Built 1791 at Castletown, Isle of Man, UK
Original owners Quayle Family, Castletown
Propulsion Schooner rig
Length 26.42ft/8.05m
Breadth 7.5ft/2.29m
Materials Wood throughout
Original use Yacht
Condition Intact, virtually as built
Present owners The Nautical Museum
Contact address Grellings Hill, Castletown, Isle of Man
Location Castletown, Isle of Man
History One of the oldest intact sailing craft in the world. Was sealed up in a stone boathouse on the Isle of Man in the early 1800s. Boathouse and vessel are now part of the Castletown Museum.
Bibliography D205, D206, D387

Pelican
harbour maintenance boat

Built 1956 by Isaac Pimblott, Northwich, England
Original owners Manchester Ship Canal Co
Propulsion Diesel engine. Engine built by Gardner
Length 71.0ft/21.64m
Breadth 15.5ft/4.72m
Draught 5.0ft/1.52m
Materials Steel throughout
Original use Maintenance; harbour facilities
Condition Intact, in working order
Present owners The Boat Museum
Location Ellesmere Port, England
History Preserved as a floating exhibit.

Perseverance
floating crane/dredger

Built 1934 by J Pollock, Son & Co, Faversham, England
Original owners Grand Union Canal Co
Propulsion Non-self propelled; steam hoisting machinery. Engine built by Grafton & Co, Bedford, England
Tonnage 70 displacement
Length 70.0ft/21.34m
Breadth 13.75ft/4.19m
Draught 3.75ft/1.14m
Materials Steel throughout
Original use Floating crane, dredger
Condition Intact
Present owners Surrey & Hampshire Canal Society
Location Ellesmere Port, England
History Steam floating crane built to maintain English canals. Preserved as an onshore exhibit.
Bibliography B27

Petrel
lightship

Built 1915 by Dublin Drydock Ltd, Dublin, Ireland
Original owners Irish Lighthouse Service
Propulsion Towed to station

Tonnage 400 gross
Length 102.0ft/31.09m
Breadth 24.0ft/7.32m
Draught 13.5ft/4.11m
Materials Iron hull, steel deckhouse
Original use Lightship
Condition Intact, in use
Present owners Down Cruising Club
Contact address 60 Ballydown Road,
Killinchy Anchorage, Newtownards
Location Strangford Lough, Northern
Ireland
History Former Irish lightship intact
except for some interior spaces
converted to social areas for clubhouse.
Maintained afloat at Stangford Lough
in Northern Ireland.

Phoebe
towed canal barge

Built in England (date not known)
Propulsion Towed by horses or tug
Length 72.0ft/22.1m
Breadth 7.0ft/2.1m
Draught 3.0ft/0.99m
Materials Iron hull
Original use Cargo, canals
Condition Intact
Present owners The Boat Museum
Location Ellesmere Port, England
History Preserved as a floating exhibit.
Bibliography B4

Planet
lightship

Former name BAR
Built 1960 by Philips, Dartmouth,
England
Original owners Mersey Harbour
Board
Official number LV 23
Propulsion Towed to station
Materials Steel throughout
Original use Lightship
Condition Intact
Location Birkenhead, England
History Preserved as a floating exhibit.

Plymouth
anti-submarine frigate

Former name HMS PLYMOUTH
Built 1959 by Devonport Dockyard,
Devonport, England
Original owners Royal Navy
Propulsion Steam turbines, 30,000hp
Tonnage 2560 displacement
Length 370.0ft/112.78m
Breadth 41.0ft/12.5m
Draught 17.0ft/5.18m
Materials Steel throughout
Original use Frigate
Condition Intact

Plymouth when in service

Present owners Warship Preservation
Trust
Location Birkenhead, England
History A Falklands War veteran
preserved as a floating exhibit.

Portlight
spritsail barge

Built 1925 by Horlock, Mistley, England
Official number 145405
Propulsion Spritsail barge
Tonnage 68 gross
Materials Steel hull
Original use Cargo
Condition In sailing condition
Present owners L Tester
Location Hollowshore, nr Faversham,
England
History Built as a sailing barge to carry
cargoes on the rivers and estuaries of
eastern England. Maintained in sailing
condition as a private yacht based near
Faversham, England.

Portwey
steam tug

Built 1926 by Harland & Wolff, Govan,
Glasgow, Scotland
Original owners Channel Coaling Co,
Weymouth
Propulsion Steam, twin screw,
compound, 330hp. Engine built by D &
W Henderson & Co, Partick, Scotland
Length 80.5ft/24.54m
Breadth 18.17ft/5.54m
Draught 9.0ft/2.74m
Materials Steel hull, steel and wood
superstructure
Original use Tug
Condition Intact, in operating
condition
Present owners The Maritime Trust; on
loan to Tug Portwey Association
Contact address 16 Ebury Street,
London SW1
Location London, England
History Twin screw steam tug formerly

employed at Weymouth and Falmouth
on the south coast of England.
Exhibited by the Maritime Trust at St
Katherine's Dock, London, in the
1980s. Now on loan by the Trust to a
group that maintains her in steaming
condition based in West India Dock,
London.
Bibliography B27, D97

President
convoy sloop

Former name HMS PRESIDENT,
HMS SAXIFRAGE
Built 1917 by Lobnitz and Co Ltd,
Renfrew, Scotland
Original owners Royal Navy
Propulsion Steam, 4-cylinder triple
expansion
Tonnage 1290 displacement
Length 262.67ft/76.2m
Breadth 35.0ft/10.67m
Draught 13.67ft/4.17m
Materials Steel throughout except
wood decks
Original use Escort vessel and decoy
ship
Condition Altered to stationary
training vessel
Location London, England
History Built during the First World
War as an escort vessel with merchant
ship profile to mislead enemy
submarines. For many years a moored
Naval Reserve training ship alongside
the embankment in the centre of
London, now retired.

President
steam canal barge

Built 1909 by Fellows, Morton &
Clayton, Saltley, England
Original owners Fellows, Morton &
Clayton
Propulsion Steam, screw, 2-cylinder
Length 71.5ft/21.79m
Breadth 7.0ft/2.13m
Draught 3.15ft/0.96m
Materials Iron sides, wood bottom
Original use Cargo, canals
Condition Intact
Present owners Black Country Museum
Location Dudley, England
History Steam narrowboat used to
carry cargo on the English canals.
Preserved as a floating exhibit.
Bibliography D362

Prince Frederick's Barge
oared royal barge

Built 1732 by John Hall, London,
England

Original owners Frederick, Prince of
Wales
Propulsion Rowed
Length 63.33ft/19.3m
Breadth 7.62ft/2.32m
Materials Wood throughout
Original use Royal barge
Condition Intact
Present owners National Maritime
Museum
Location Greenwich, England
History Very ornate eighteenth-century
Royal barge. Preserved as an indoor
exhibit.
Bibliography D28

Provident
fishing ketch

Built 1924 by Sandes, Galmpton,
Devon, England
Original owners William Pillar,
Brixham
Propulsion Ketch rig
Tonnage 39 gross
Length 70.0ft/21.34m
Breadth 18.0ft/5.49m
Draught 9.5ft/2.9m
Materials Wood throughout
Original use Fishing
Condition In sailing condition
Present owners Island Trust
Location Salcombe, Devon, England
History Sailing fishing boat of the
Brixham trawler type formerly based
on the south coast of England. Used as
a training ship. Now maintained in
sailing condition converted to a
cruising yacht.
Bibliography D98, D113

Provident

President moored on the Thames Embankment

Pudge
spritsail barge

Built 1922 by London & Rochester,
Frindsbury, England
Propulsion Spritsail barge; auxiliary
engine added
Tonnage 68 gross
Length 82.0ft/24.99m

Breadth 24.0ft/7.3m
Materials Wood throughout
Original use Cargo
Condition In sailing condition
Present owners Thames Barge Sailing
Club
Location London, England
History Built as a sailing barge to carry
cargoes on the rivers and estuaries of
eastern England. Rerigged in 1968 for
operation under sail by club members.
Bibliography B5, C74

Pyronaut
fireboat

Built 1934 by Charles Hill, Bristol,
England
Original owners City of Bristol
Propulsion Diesel engine
Length 57.0ft/17.37m
Breadth 13.0ft/4.0m
Draught 3.0ft/0.9m
Materials Steel throughout
Original use Fireboat
Condition Intact
Present owners Bristol Industrial
Museum
Location Bristol, England
History Small fire boat called a 'fire
float' based for many tears in the Port
of Bristol. Preserved as a floating
exhibit.

Queen Galadriel
coasting ketch

Former name ELSE
Built 1937 by Ring Andersen,
Svendborg, Denmark
Original owners Captain Jensen,
Svendborg
Propulsion Sail, ketch rig; diesel engine,
200hp
Tonnage 86 gross
Length 78.1ft/23.8m
Breadth 21.0ft/6.4m
Draught 8.33ft/2.54m
Materials Wood hull, steel and wood
masts
Original use Cargo
Condition In sailing condition
Present owners The Cirdan Trust,
Chelmsford
Location Ipswich, England
History Danish ketch built for the
coastal and Baltic trades. Used for sail
training.

Queen Mary II
passenger steamer

Former name QUEEN MARY
Built 1933 by W Denny Brothers,
Dumbarton, Scotland
Original owners London, Midland &
Scottish Railway

Propulsion Three steam turbines, 3800hp, twin screw. Engine built by W Denny Brothers
Tonnage 1014 gross
Length 263.33ft/80.26m
Breadth 37.0ft/11.28m
Draught 7.5ft/2.29m
Materials Steel throughout
Original use Passengers
Condition Intact; adapted to restaurant use
Present owners Bass Charrington Ltd
Location London, England
History Built as a passenger steamer to run between Glasgow, Scotland, and points on the Clyde Estuary. Retired in 1977 and briefly slated to become a floating museum at Glasgow. Sold for use as a floating restaurant and now moored in the Thames near the centre of London. Was named QUEEN MARY II at the time of the building of the Cunard Liner QUEEN MARY.
Bibliography B16, B58, D436

Queen Mary II

Raven
lake steamer

Built 1871 by T B Seath & Co, Rutherglen, Scotland
Original owners Furness Railway Co
Propulsion Steam, single cylinder. Engine built by A Campbell & Co, Glasgow
Length 71.0ft/21.64m
Breadth 14.5ft/4.42m
Materials Iron throughout
Original use Cargo
Condition Intact
Present owners Windermere Nautical Trust
Contact address Beresford Road, Windermere, Cumbria
Location Windermere, England

History Built to carry cargo on Lake Windermere. Fully restored and refitted. Normally a floating exhibit moored at the Boat Museum in Windermere.
Bibliography B27

Reaper
Scottish fifie

Former name SHETLANDER
Built 1901 by J & G Forbes, Sandhaven, Scotland
Propulsion Two-masted lugger rig
Length 72.0ft/21.95m
Materials Wood throughout
Original use Fishing
Condition Fully restored
Present owners Scottish Fisheries Museum

Reaper

Raven

Contact address St Ayles, Harbourhead, Anstruther
Location Anstruther, Scotland
History Example of a Scottish herring drift net fishing vessel of the 'fifie' type. Fully restored as a floating exhibit at the Scottish Fisheries Museum.

Reminder
spritsail barge

Built 1929 by Horlock, Mistley, England
Original owners Fred Horlock
Propulsion Spritsail barge
Tonnage 79 gross
Materials Steel hull
Original use Cargo
Condition In sailing condition
Present owners Anglian Yacht Services
Location Maldon, England
History Built as a sailing barge to carry cargoes on the rivers and estuaries of eastern England. Maintained in sailing condition as a charter vessel based at Maldon.

Renfrew Ferry
steam ferry

Former name ERSKINE FERRY
Built 1935 by Fleming & Ferguson, Paisley, Scotland
Propulsion Steam, chain hauling, triple expansion
Length 68.0ft/20.73m
Breadth 48.0ft/14.63m
Materials Steel throughout
Original use Ferry
Condition Intact, deck enclosed for museum
Present owners Renfrew District Council
Location Renfrew, Scotland
History Ferryboat for vehicles and pedestrians on the River Clyde. Preserved as a floating exhibit.
Bibliography B16

Repertor
spritsail barge

Built 1924 by Horlock, Mistley, England
Original owners M R Horlock
Propulsion Spritsail barge
Tonnage 69 gross
Materials Steel hull
Original use Cargo
Condition In sailing condition
Present owners David Pollack
Location Faversham, England
History Built as a sailing barge to carry cargoes on the rivers and estuaries of eastern England. Maintained in sailing condition as a private yacht.

Result
coasting schooner

Built 1893 by Robert Kent & Co, Carrickfergus, Northern Ireland
Original owners Thomas Ashburner & Co, Barrow, England
Propulsion Three-masted topsail schooner rig; later ketch
Tonnage 122 gross
Length 102.0ft/31.09m
Breadth 21.67ft/6.61m
Draught 9.58ft/2.29m
Materials Steel hull, wood decks and masts
Original use Cargo
Condition Undergoing restoration
Present owners Ulster Folk & Transport Museum
Contact address Cultra, Holywood, County Down
Location Holywood, Northern Ireland
History Built to carry cargo under sail in the British coastal trades. Later converted to a ketch with auxiliary engine for further trading. Transported overland to her present location for restoration to original appearance as a land exhibit.
Bibliography A15, D353

Robin
steam coaster

Former name MARIA
Built 1890 by MacKenzie, MacAlpine & Co, Blackwall, England
Original owners Arthur C Ponsonby, Newport

Robin as restored

Propulsion Steam, triple expansion, coal-fired
Tonnage 366 gross
Length 143.0ft/43.59m
Breadth 22.0ft/6.71m
Draught 13.0ft/3.96m
Materials Steel throughout
Original use Cargo
Condition Fully restored
Present owners The Cutty Sark Maritime Trust
Contact address 16 Ebury Street, London SW1
Location London, England
History Only restored example of a British steam coaster of the late 1800s. Last operated under the Spanish flag in the 1960s. Restored by the Maritime Trust and exhibited afloat at St Katherine's Dock in London. Currently laid up in West India Dock, London.
Bibliography B27, D464

Ryde Queen
steam sidewheel ferry

Former name RYDE
Built 1937 by William Denny & Bros, Dumbarton, Scotland
Original owners Southern Railway

Ryde Queen

Propulsion Steam, sidewheel, triple
expansion, 133hp. Engine built by
William Denny & Bros
Tonnage 603 gross
Length 216.0ft/65.84m
Breadth 29.08ft/8.86m
Draught 10.0ft/3.05m
Materials Steel throughout
Original use Passengers
Condition Intact, but needs restoration
Present owners Island Harbour Marina
Location Nr Newport, Isle of Wight,
England
History Steam sidewheel ferry built to
operate to the Isle of Wight off the
south coast of England. Grounded in a
mud berth near Newport, Isle of
Wight, for use as a pub and restaurant
at a marina. Intact, but no longer in
use and reportedly derelict.
Bibliography B43

Sabrina 5
towed barge

Built 1944 by Charles Hill, Bristol,
England
Original owners British Transport
Commission
Propulsion Towed by tugs
Tonnage 90 gross
Length 90.0ft/27.4m
Breadth 18.0ft/5.5m
Materials Steel hull, steel and wood
wheelhouse
Original use Cargo
Condition Intact
Present owners National Waterways
Museum
Location Gloucester, England
History Barge formerly used to carry
goods between Bristol Channel ports
and inland docks on the River Severn.
Preserved as a floating exhibit.

Saira
coasting ketch

Former name SARAH
Built 1899 by Hunt and Flower,
Kingston-on-Hull, England
Propulsion Ketch rig
Length 71.0ft/21.6m
Materials Steel hull
Original use Cargo
Location Penrhyn, Cornwall, England
History Steel-hulled ketch built to
carry cargo in the coastal trades.
Currently in need of restoration and
reportedly for sale.

Sapphire
canal coal barge

Built 1952
Original owners T & S Element
Propulsion Towed
Length 72.0ft/21.95m
Breadth 7.0ft/2.13m
Materials Wood throughout
Original use Cargo on canals
Condition Intact
Present owners The Boat Museum
Location Ellesmere Port, England
History Birmingham Canal day boat
used to carry coal from the Cannock
coal fields to Black Country industries.
Exhibited afloat at the museum.
Bibliography B4

Scorpio
coal transporter barge

Former name HELENA
Built 1890
Original owners Wigan Coal & Iron Co
Propulsion Towed
Tonnage 70 gross
Length 72.0ft/21.95m
Breadth 14.5ft/4.42m
Draught 3.75ft/1.14m
Materials Hull iron and wood
Original use Cargo
Condition Restored
Present owners North Western Museum
of Inland Navigation
Contact address Dockyard Road,
Ellesmere Port, Cheshire
Location Ellesmere Port, England
History Dumb barge used on the
canals around the estuary of the
Mersey River to carry coal direct from
collieries to power stations. Retired in
1971 and now exhibited afloat at the
museum in Ellesmere Port.
Bibliography B4

Seiont II
steam harbour dredger

Built 1937 by W J Yarwood, Northwich,
England
Original owners Caernarfon Harbour
Commissioners
Propulsion Steam, compound
Length 86.67ft/26.42m
Breadth 20.0ft/6.1m
Materials Steel hull, wood
superstructure
Original use Dredger
Condition Intact
Present owners National Museum of
Wales
Location Caernarfon, Wales
History Steam grab harbour dredger,
retired in 1978. Preserved as a floating
exhibit at Caernarfon, North Wales.
Bibliography B27, D82

Severn Progress
motor tug

Former name PROGRESS
Built 1932 by Charles Hill, Bristol,
England
Original owners Severn & Canal
Carrying Co
Propulsion Diesel engine, 100hp.
Engine built by Lister
Length 46.0ft/14.0m
Breadth 11.5ft/3.5m
Draught 4.0ft/1.22m
Materials Iron hull, steel wheelhouse
Original use Towing, rivers
Condition In operating condition
Present owners National Waterways
Museum, Gloucester
Location Gloucester, England
History Maintained as an operating
vessel. Exhibited.

Shieldhall

Shad
motorised narrowboat

Built 1936 by Yarwoods, Northwich,
England
Original owners Fellows, Morton &
Clayton
Propulsion Diesel engine. Engine built
by Lister
Length 71.0ft/21.64m
Breadth 7.0ft/2.13m
Draught 3.5ft/1.07m
Materials Steel sides and wood bottom
Original use Cargo
Condition Intact
Present owners The Boat Museum
Location Ellesmere Port, England
History Motorised narrowboat
formerly used to carry cargo on the
canals of central England. Preserved as
a floating exhibit at the museum in
Ellesmere Port.
Bibliography B4

Shamrock
sailing barge

Built 1899 by Frederick Hawke,
Plymouth, England
Original owners Tom Williams
Propulsion Ketch rig
Tonnage 37 gross
Length 57.0ft/17.37m
Breadth 18.17ft/5.54m
Draught 6.17ft/1.88m
Materials Wood throughout
Original use Cargo
Condition Fully restored
Present owners Cotehele Quay Museum
Location Cotehele Quay, England
History Sailing barge formerly
employed carrying cargoes on the
Tamar river and estuary in southwest
England. Fully restored in the 1970s for
exhibition afloat at Cotehele Quay.
Bibliography B29, D5, D556

Shieldhall
steam sludge tanker

Built 1955 by Lobnitz & Co, Renfrew,
Scotland
Original owners Glasgow Corporation
Propulsion Steam, screw, triple
expansion, 1600hp. Engine built by
Lobnitz & Co
Tonnage 1753 gross
Length 268.0ft/81.69m
Breadth 44.6ft/13.59m
Draught 13.33ft/4.06m
Materials Steel throughout
Original use Sludge tanker
Condition In operating condition
Present owners Solent Steam Packet Ltd
Location Southampton, England

History Maintained as an active steam vessel. Exhibited.
Bibliography B27, D83, D331

Sir Walter Scott
lake excursion steamer

Built 1899 by W Denny & Brothers, Dumbarton, Scotland
Original owners Loch Katrine Steamboat Co
Propulsion Steam, triple expansion, 140hp. Engine built by M Paul & Co, Dumbarton
Length 110.0ft/33.53m
Breadth 19.0ft/5.79m
Draught 5.0ft/1.52m
Materials Steel throughout
Original use Passengers
Condition In operation
Present owners Strathclyde Regional Council
Location Loch Katrine, Scotland
History Lake steamboat in service for a century on Loch Katrine in western Scotland. Operates on excursions each year from May to September.
Bibliography B16, B27, D46, D424

SND No 4
steam dredger

Built 1925 by N V de Klop, Sliedrecht, Netherlands
Original owners Sharpness New Dock & Gloucester Navigation
Propulsion Non-self propelled; steam dredging machinery. Engine built by N V de Klop
Length 85.0ft/25.91m
Breadth 25.0ft/7.62m
Materials Steel throughout
Original use Dredger
Condition Intact
Present owners National Waterways Museum
Location Gloucester, England
History Preserved as a floating exhibit.

Solace
sailing wherry

Built 1903 by Hall, Reedham, England
Propulsion Sail, single-masted wherry rig
Tonnage 40.06 gross
Length 68.0ft/20.73m
Breadth 16.0ft/4.88m
Draught 4.25ft/1.29m
Materials Wood throughout
Original use Yacht
Condition In sailing condition
Present owners John R Rudd, Maidenhead, England
Location Norfolk, England

Solace

History Traditional working sailing craft of the rivers of eastern England maintained as a sailing yacht.

Sotero
Portuguese river lighter

Built c1950 at Montejo, Portugal
Propulsion Sloop rig
Length 64.17ft/19.56m
Breadth 14.83ft/4.52m
Draught 2.5ft/0.76m
Materials Wood throughout
Original use River lighter
Condition Intact
Present owners International Sailing Craft Association
Location Oulton Broad, England
History Type of sailing lighter employed in carrying cargo on the Tagus river in the area of Lisbon, Portugal. Acquired as part of a collection of sailing craft from around the world. First exhibited at Exeter in the southwest of England, and now at Oulton Broad, nr Lowestoft, England.

Souvenir d'Antan
river steam launch

Former name ATALANTA
Built 1901 by Alfred Burgoine, Kingston-on-Thames, England
Propulsion Steam, screw

Length 45.0ft/13.7m
Draught 2.0ft/0.6m
Materials Wood throughout
Original use Yacht
Condition In operating condition
Location Great Britain
History Classic steam launch with cabin at stern built for use on the River Thames. Restored in the late 1980s with original engine and boiler.

S Paio, 'Xavega'
fishing boat

Built at Aveiro Lagoon, Portugal
Propulsion Rowed
Length 52.83ft/16.1m
Breadth 14.33ft/4.37m
Draught 1.5ft/0.46m
Materials Wood throughout
Original use Fishing
Condition Intact
Present owners International Sailing Craft Association
Location Oulton Broad, England
History Portuguese four-oared 'Xavega' used to fish for sardines with trawl nets off the beaches. Acquired as part of an extensive collection of watercraft from around the world. First exhibited at Exeter on the south coast of England, and now housed at Oulton Broad, near Lowestoft, on the east coast.

Spartan
steam lighter

Former name VIC 18
Built 1940 by J Hay & Sons, Bowling, Scotland
Original owners Ministry of War Transport
Propulsion Steam, screw; later diesel
Tonnage 97 gross
Length 66.7ft/20.33m
Breadth 18.5ft/5.64m
Materials Steel throughout
Original use Cargo
Condition Intact
Present owners Scottish Maritime Museum
Location Irvine, Scotland
History Steam lighter built during the

Spartan

Second World War to move cargo within a harbour. Based on the 'Clyde Puffer' used prior to the war on the west coast of Scotland via the Crinan Canal. Preserved as a floating exhibit at the Scottish Maritime Museum.

Speedwell
canal grain barge

Built by Dapdune Yard (date not known)
Original owners William Stevens, Guildford
Propulsion Towed
Length 74.0ft/22.56m
Breadth 15.0ft/4.57m
Materials Wood throughout
Original use Cargo
Condition Intact
Present owners The Boat Museum
Location Ellesmere Port, England
History Wooden barge formerly employed carrying grain on the Wey river. Currently a floating exhibit at the museum in Ellesmere Port.
Bibliography B4

Spry
Severn trow

Built 1894 by William Hurd, Chepstow, Wales
Original owners William Davis, Chepstow
Propulsion Sloop rig (Severn trow type)
Length 73.0ft/22.25m
Materials Wood throughout
Original use Cargo
Condition Fully restored
Present owners Upper Severn Navigation Trust, Ironbridge
Location Blists Hill, England
History Last surviving example of a sailing cargo vessel known as a 'Severn Trow'. Completely rebuilt as an active sailing vessel and exhibit at the Blists Hill Open Air Museum on the upper Severn river in the late 1980s.

Spurn
lightship

Former name BULL
Built 1927 by Goole Shipbuilding & Repairing Co, Goole, England
Original owners Humber Conservancy Board
Propulsion Towed to station
Tonnage 200 gross
Length 81.0ft/24.69m
Breadth 22.0ft/6.71m
Draught 12.33ft/3.76m
Materials Steel throughout

Spry at Ironbridge Gorge Museum 1985

Original use Lightship
Condition Intact
Present owners Hull City Council
Location Kingston on Hull, England
History British lightship in active use until 1975, now preserved as a floating exhibit in the centre of the old docks of Hull.

SRN-1
experimental hovercraft

Built 1959 by Saunders-Roe, Cowes, Isle of Wight, England
Original owners Cockerill
Propulsion Aircraft engine, 435hp. Engine built by Alvis
Original use Experimental hovercraft
Condition Intact
Present owners Montague Motor Museum
Location Beaulieu, England
History First experimental hovercraft built. Preserved as an onshore exhibit.

St Cybi
rescue lifeboat

Built 1950 by White, Cowes, Isle of Wight, England
Original owners Royal National Lifeboat Institution
Propulsion Diesel engines, 120hp. Engine built by Ferry
Length 52.0ft/15.6m
Breadth 13.5ft/4.2m
Draught 4.55ft/1.3m
Materials Wood hull
Original use Rescue lifeboat
Condition Intact
Present owners Royal National Lifeboat

Collection
Location Chatham, England
History Preserved as an indoor exhibit.

Stickleback
midget submarine

Former name HMS STICKLEBACK, SPIGGEN
Built 1954 by Vickers Armstrong, Barrow, England
Original owners Royal Navy
Official number X-51
Propulsion Diesel engine, 50hp. Engine built by Perkins
Tonnage 36 displacement
Length 53.83ft/16.41m
Breadth 6.25ft/1.91m
Materials Steel throughout
Original use Midget submarine
Present owners Imperial War Museum
Location Duxford, England
History Intended prototype for a series of midget submarines based on the X-class of the Second World War. Loaned to the Swedish Navy 1958-1976. Preserved on shore at Duxford Airfield in Cambridgeshire.
Bibliography A6

Streatley
passenger steamer

Built 1905 by Salter Brothers, Oxford, England
Original owners Salter Brothers
Propulsion Steam, screw. Engine built by Sisson
Length 85ft/25.9m
Materials Steel hull and wood deckhouse

Original use Passengers
Condition In operating condition
Present owners Steamship Streatley Ltd.
Location Thames River, England
History Classic single-deck passenger steamer that has spent its career on the Thames River based in the Oxford area. Converted to diesel propulsion in 1958, and since 1994 fully restored with its original 1905 steam engine. In operation for passenger cruises.

Sundowner
naval steam launch

Built 1912 by British Admiralty
Original owners Royal Navy
Propulsion Steam, screw; converted to diesel, 72hp
Length 52.0ft/15.85m
Breadth 12.5ft/3.81m
Draught 5.0ft/1.52m
Materials Wood throughout
Original use Naval launch, converted to yacht
Condition Intact, in operating condition
Present owners East Kent Maritime Trust
Contact address c/o Ramsgate Maritime Museum
Location Ramsgate, England
History British naval steam pinnace converted to a motor yacht. Formerly owned by Herbert Lightoller, the only officer to survive the sinking of the TITANIC. Took part in the Dunkirk evacuation of the Second World War. Preserved as a floating exhibit and operating vessel.
Bibliography B5, D389a

Susan Ashley
rescue lifeboat

Built 1948 by Groves & Gutteridge
Original owners Royal National
Lifeboat Institution
Propulsion Diesel engine
Length 41.0ft/12.3m
Breadth 11.7ft/3.5m
Materials Wood hull
Original use Rescue lifeboat
Condition Intact
Present owners Royal National Lifeboat
Collection
Location Chatham, England
History Preserved as an indoor exhibit.

Swallow
steam launch

Built 1911 by Neil Shepherd, Bowness,
England
Original owners W Warburton,

Tattershall Castle

Windermere
Propulsion Steam, triple expansion.
Engine built by W Sisson & Co
Tonnage 14 gross
Length 45.33ft/13.82m
Breadth 8.0ft/2.44m
Draught 3.0ft/0.9m
Materials Wood throughout
Original use Yacht
Condition In operating condition
Present owners Windermere Nautical
Trust
Location Windermere, England
History Elegant Edwardian steam
launch with cabin preserved in
operating condition in a museum
boathouse in Windermere.
Bibliography B27

Swan
fishing lugger

Built 1900 by Hay & Co, Lerwick,
Scotland
Propulsion Sail, two-masted lugger rig
Tonnage 57 gross
Length 67.83ft/20.67m
Breadth 19.67ft/5.99m
Draught 9.0ft/2.74m
Materials Wood throughout
Original use Fishing
Condition In need of restoration
Present owners The Swan Trust
Location Great Britain
History Last surviving sailing fishing
vessel of the 'fifie' type that was built
and operated out of the Shetland
Islands. Proposed exhibit and active
sailing vessel.

Tattershall Castle
steam sidewheel ferry

Built 1934 by William Gray & Co, West
Hartlepool, England
Original owners British Rail
Propulsion Steam, sidewheel, inclined
triple expansion, coal fired. Engine
built by Central Marine Engine Works,
Hartlepool
Tonnage 556 gross
Length 209.58ft/63.88m
Breadth 57.0ft/17.37m
Draught 4.5ft/1.4m
Materials Steel throughout
Original use Vehicle and passenger
ferry
Condition Intact, outwardly unaltered
Present owners Scottish & Newcastle
Retail
Location London, England
History Steam sidewheel ferry built to
carry vehicles and foot passengers
across the Humber river in northeast
England. Currently a floating
restaurant and nightclub moored at
the Thames embankment near the
centre of London.
Bibliography B16, B27, B43, C22

TGB
rescue lifeboat

Built c1940s in Great Britain
Original owners Royal National
Lifeboat Institution
Propulsion Diesel engine
Length 47.0ft/14.3m
Original use Rescue lifeboat
Condition Intact
Present owners Scottish Maritime

Swallow (with Branksome astern)

Museum
Location Irvine, Scotland
History Preserved as an exhibit.

Thalatta
spritsail barge

Built 1906 by W B McLearon, Harwich, Essex
Original owners R & W Paul, Ipswich
Official number 116179
Propulsion Spritsail ketch rig. Engine built by Ruston
Tonnage 67 gross
Length 88.9ft/27.1m
Breadth 20.6ft/6.3m
Depth 7.1ft/2.2m
Materials Wood throughout
Original use Cargo, sailing barge
Condition In sailing condition
Present owners East Coast Sail Trust
Location Maldon, England
History Built as a sailing barge to carry cargoes on the rivers and estuaries of eastern England. Maintained in sailing condition as a sail training vessel for young people based at Maldon.
Bibliography C74

The Three Brothers
fishing coble

Built 1912 by Baker & Percy Sidall, Bridlington, England
Propulsion Sail, dipping lug rig
Length 40.0ft/12.19m
Materials Wood throughout
Original use Fishing
Condition Intact
Present owners Bridlington Sailing Coble Preservation Society
Location Bridlington, England
History Preserved as an exhibit.

Thistle
spritsail barge

Built 1895 by Hamilton, Port Glasgow, Scotland
Official number 105727
Propulsion Spritsail barge; auxiliary engine (Kelvin) installed 1948
Tonnage 82 gross
Materials Steel hull
Original use Cargo
Condition In sailing condition
Location Ipswich, England
History Built as a sailing barge to carry cargo on the rivers and estuaries of eastern England. Later a houseboat, but rerigged in 1988. Maintained in sailing condition by a private owner based on the Orwell river.

TID-164

TID-164
harbour steam tug

Former name HERCULES
Built 1945 by William Pickersgill, Southwick, England
Original owners Ministry of War Transport
Propulsion Steam, compound, 220hp. Engine built by John Dickinson, Sunderland
Tonnage 68 gross
Length 68.0ft/20.73m
Breadth 17.5ft/5.33m
Draught 7.3ft/2.21m
Materials Steel throughout
Original use Cargo
Condition Intact, in need of restoration
Present owners Martin Stevens
Location Chatham, England
History Survivor of a group of steam tugs built for harbour and dockyard use in the Second World War. Currently laid up intact in an area of the historic dockyard at Chatham not open to the public.
Bibliography B27

TID-172
harbour steam tug

Former name PALLION
Built 1946 by H Scarr Ltd, Hessle, England
Original owners Ministry of War Transport
Propulsion Steam, screw, compound. Engine built by J Dickinson & Sons, Sunderland
Tonnage 54 gross
Length 74.0ft/22.55m
Breadth 17.5ft/5.33m
Draught 8.0ft/2.44m
Materials Steel throughout
Original use Tug
Condition In operating condition
Present owners Albert Groom
Location River Stour, England
History Serves as a yacht.
Bibliography B27

Tollesbury
spritsail barge

Built 1901 by H Felton, Sandwich, England
Propulsion Sail, spritsail yawl
Length 84.2ft/25.7m
Breadth 20.4ft/6.2m
Draught 6.6ft/2.0m
Materials Wood throughout
Original use Cargo, sailing barge
Condition Intact, in use
Present owners Albert Barnes
Location London, England
History Built as a sailing barge to carry cargoes on the rivers and estuaries of eastern England. Participated in the evacuation of British troops from Dunkirk during the Second World War. Fully restored though no longer sailing; used as a floating bar. Present owner was a crew member during the Dunkirk evacuation.

Tovaritsch
naval sail training ship

Former name GORCH FOCK
Built 1933 by Blohm & Voss, Hamburg, Germany
Original owners German Navy
Propulsion Sail, barque rig; diesel auxiliary engine
Tonnage 1760 displacement
Length 242.0ft/73.76m
Breadth 39.35ft/11.99m
Draught 17.0ft/5.18m
Materials Steel throughout
Original use Training ship
Condition Intact, laid up in a British port
Location Great Britain
History Built as a training ship for the German Navy. Awarded to Russia after the Second World War and renamed. Remained in service until the breakup of the Soviet Union, and was then laid up in England while on a training cruise. Has been condemned by the British authorities for further use without major renovation. There are proposals to restore her to sail again in England.
Bibliography A10, A14, C25, C96, D302

Trincomalee undergoing restoration at Hartlepool in 1996

Trincomalee
sailing frigate

Former name FOUDROYANT,
HMS TRINCOMALEE
Built 1817 by Wadia Shipyard, Bombay,
India
Original owners Royal Navy
Propulsion Full-rigged ship rig
Tonnage 1066 displacement
Length 180.0ft/54.86m
Breadth 40.25ft/12.27m
Draught 13.5ft/4.11m
Materials Wood throughout
Original use Frigate
Condition Afloat, undergoing
restoration
Present owners The Trincomalee Trust
Location Hartlepool, England
History Oldest surviving frigate of the
British Navy and the only one to see
active service under sail. Also the
oldest warship of the Royal Navy still
afloat. Spent many years moored at
Portsmouth, England, as the stationary
training vessel FOUDROYANT. A
complete restoration to her original
appearance is nearing completion at
Hartlepool, where she will be
permanently moored as a floating
exhibit.
Bibliography A14, B24, D241, 330, 343,
575

Tube Boat No 39
canal barge

Built c1920
Original owners Stewarts & Lloyds
Propulsion Towed by tug
Length 71.0ft/21.64m
Breadth 7.0ft/2.1m
Materials Wood throughout
Original use Cargo; steel tubes
Condition Intact
Present owners The Boat Museum
Location Ellesmere Port, England
History Preserved as a floating exhibit.

Turbinia
steam turbine demonstrator

Built 1894 by Brown & Hood, Wallsend
on Tyne, England
Original owners Charles Parsons
Propulsion Steam turbines. Engines
built by Charles Parsons
Tonnage 44.5 displacement
Length 103.25ft/31.47m
Breadth 9.0ft/2.74m
Draught 3.0ft/0.91m
Materials Steel hull, steel
superstructure
Original use Demonstration yacht
Condition Intact

Turbinia

Present owners Tyne & Wear County Council Museums
Location Newcastle on Tyne, England
History Boat used by William Parsons, the inventor of the marine steam turbine, to test and demonstrate his system of propulsion. Fastest vessel in the world when completed. Preserved indoors as an exhibit in Newcastle.
Bibliography A17, C40, D208, D473

U-457

submarine

Built 1967 in Russia
Original owners Soviet Navy
Length 300.0ft/91.4m
Materials Steel throughout
Original use Submarine
Condition Intact
Location Folkstone, England
History Russian conventionally-powered submarine of the Cold War period known to NATO as the FOXTROT class. Originally exhibited by a private firm at the Thames Barrier below London, and later exhibited at Folkstone on the south coast of England.

U-534

submarine

Built 1942 by Deutsche Werft, Hamburg, Germany
Original owners German Navy
Official number U-534
Propulsion Diesel and electric motors

Tonnage 1247 displacement
Length 287.5ft/76.7m
Breadth 24.5ft/6.86m
Draught 15.5ft/4.7m
Materials Steel throughout
Original use Submarine
Condition Intact, recently raised from

North Sea
Present owners Warship Preservation Trust
Location Birkenhead, England
History German Second World War Type IXC submarine raised from where it was lying sunk in the North

Sea. Currently exhibited on shore at Birkenhead.

Unicorn

uncompleted sailing frigate

Former name HMS UNICORN II, HMS CRESSY, HMS UNICORN
Built 1824 by Chatham Dockyard, Chatham, England
Original owners Royal Navy
Propulsion Full-rigged ship rig (intended)
Tonnage 1084 gross, 1077 displacement
Length 166.0ft/50.6m
Breadth 39.92ft/12.17m
Draught 13.08ft/4.0m
Materials Wood throughout
Original use Frigate (never completed)
Condition Intact hull, never rigged
Present owners Unicorn Preservation Society
Location Dundee, Scotland
History One of two surviving sailing frigates of the Royal Navy. Was never commissioned as a seagoing vessel. Spent entire career as a stationary drill ship. Present owners had intended to rig the vessel but apparently now plan to preserve her in her present configuration.
Bibliography A14, B24, B49, D401, D496, F23

The stern of the Unicorn

VIC-32

Vagrant
schooner yacht

Former name QUEEN MAB
Built 1910 by N G Herreshoff, Bristol,
Rhode Island, USA
Original owners Harold Vanderbilt
Propulsion Sail, schooner rig
Tonnage 63 gross
Length 76.0ft/23.16m
Breadth 17.5ft/5.33m
Draught 10.67ft/3.25m
Materials Wood throughout
Original use Yacht
Condition In sailing condition
Present owners Peter de Savary
Location Great Britain
History Fully restored American
schooner yacht built by that country's
top designer of the type. Available for
charter.

VIC-32
steam lighter

Built 1943 by Richard Dunston,
Thorne, England
Original owners Ministry of War
Transport
Propulsion Steam, compound. Engine
built by Crabtree, Great Yarmouth
Tonnage 95 gross
Length 66.5ft/20.27m
Breadth 18.42ft/5.61m
Draught 8.0ft/2.4m
Materials Steel throughout
Original use Cargo
Condition In operation
Present owners Nick Walker
Location Crinan, Scotland
History Steam lighter of a series built
during the Second World War to carry
cargo within harbours. Based on the

'Clyde puffer' used prior to the war on
the west coast of Scotland via the
Crinan Canal. Maintained in steaming
condition as an overnight cruise vessel
operating in the same waters as the
original puffers.
Bibliography B27, C17

VIC-56
cargo steamer

Built 1946 by J Pollock & Sons,
Faversham, England
Original owners Ministry of War
Transport
Propulsion Steam, screw, compound,
140hp. Engine built by Crabtree, Great
Yarmouth
Length 85.0ft/25.9m
Breadth 20.0ft/6.1m
Draught 8.66ft/2.64m
Materials Steel throughout
Original use Cargo
Condition In operating condition
Present owners Henry Cleary
Location Rotherhithe, England
History Steam harbour lighter of a
series built for the Second World War
based on the design of the traditional
'Clyde puffer'. Acquired for
preservation by aprivate owner in 1979.
In use as an operating steamer.
Bibliography B27, C17

VIC-96
cargo steamer

Former name C668
Built 1945 by R Dunston & Co, Thorne,
South Yorkshire, England
Original owners Ministry of War
Transport
Propulsion Steam, compound, 140hp.

Engine built by Crabtree, Great
Yarmouth
Length 85.0ft/25.9m
Breadth 18.0ft/5.49m
Draught 8.66ft/2.64m
Materials Steel throughout
Original use Cargo, harbour
Condition Intact
Present owners Maryport Town
Council
Location Maryport, England
History Small steam cargo vessel built
during the Second World War for use
in harbours, based on the 'Clyde
puffer' used before the war on the west
coast of Scotland and the Crinan
Canal. Preserved as a floating exhibit
in Maryport on the west coast of
England.
Bibliography B27, C17

Victor
coasting ketch

Built 1895 by Shrubsall, Ipswich,
England
Official number 105762
Propulsion Sail, spritsail ketch rig
Tonnage 56 gross

Length 82.2ft/25.0m
Breadth 20.3ft/6.2m
Materials Wood throughout
Original use Cargo
Condition In sailing condition
Present owners N Briggs
Location Southampton, England
History Available for charter.

Victory HMS
ship-of-the-line

Built 1765 by Chatham Dockyard,
Chatham, England
Original owners Royal Navy
Propulsion Full-rigged ship rig
Tonnage 3500 displacement
Length 226.0ft/68.88m
Breadth 51.83ft/15.8m
Draught 19.67ft/6.0m
Materials Wood throughout
Original use Ship-of-the-Line
Condition Fully restored
Present owners Royal Navy
Location Portsmouth, England
History Apart from the Swedish VASA
of the seventeenth century, the only
surviving example is HMS VICTORY
built at Chatham, England, in 1765. She

Victory

served as the British flagship at the Battle of Trafalgar in 1805, and was the ship in which Admiral Lord Horatio Nelson died. Prior to Trafalgar VICTORY had seen twenty-seven years of active service, taking part in numerous engagements and serving as the flagship of Admiral Jervis at the Battle of Cape St Vincent in 1797. She ceased operational service in 1812 and from then until 1922 was moored in Portsmouth harbour, where she served intermittently as flagship of the local naval command. She remained there until 1922 when concern over deterioration of her hull led to her being placed in the Dockyard's No 2 graving dock. A campaign was begun by the Society for Nautical Research to raise funds for the ship's repair, and her restoration to the appearance she had in 1805. This was so successful it was possible to complete the work by July 1928. The Society also created, close by the ship, a museum, which has become the Royal Naval Museum. During intensive German bombing of the Dockyard during the Second World War, VICTORY's massive oak sides withstood one of a stick of bombs which fell between the dockside and the bow. HMS VICTORY is maintained in No 2 Drydock, HM Naval Base, as the oldest commissioned warship of any navy. Fully restored to her appearance at the time of Trafalgar and open to the public by guided tour.
Bibliography A8, A14, B24, C59, D66, D314

Vigilance
Brixham sailing trawler

Built 1930s by Uphams
Official number BM-76
Propulsion Sail, ketch rig
Materials Wood throughout
Original use Fishing; 'Brixham trawler'
Condition In sailing condition
Present owners Syndicate based in Brixham
Location Brixham, Devon, England
History Preserved as a floating exhibit and for charter.
Bibliography Classic Boat, March 1998

Vigilant
Customs cruiser

Former name EILEEN SIOCHT
Built 1902 by Cox and Co, Falmouth, England
Original owners Commissioners of HM Customs

Propulsion Steam, screw
Tonnage 140 displacement
Length 100.0ft/30.48m
Breadth 16.0ft/4.88m
Materials Steel hull, wood deckhouses and masts
Original use Customs cruiser
Condition Restoration proposed
Present owners The Vigilant Trust
Location Shoreham, England
History Steam patrol vessel built for the British customs service at the turn of the century. Converted to a private yacht in 1920, and later converted to a houseboat. Efforts to preserve and restore the vessel began in 1989.

Vigilant
spritsail barge

Built 1904 by Orvis & Fuller, Ipswich, England
Official number 116176
Propulsion Sail, spritsail ketch rig
Tonnage 73 gross
Materials Wood throughout
Original use Cargo
Condition In sailing condition
Present owners Dawes, Thomas and Martin
Location Maldon, England
History In use as a sailing yacht.

Warrior
ironclad frigate

Former name HMS VERNON III, HMS WARRIOR
Built 1860 by Ditchburn & Mare, Blackwall, England
Original owners Royal Navy
Propulsion Steam, screw, 1250hp
Tonnage 9210 displacement
Length 389.0ft/118.57m
Breadth 58.33ft/17.78m
Materials Iron hull, iron and wood masts
Original use Armoured steam frigate
Condition Fully restored
Present owners Warrior Preservation Trust
Location Portsmouth, England
History We are fortunate in having a number of surviving ships that excellently represent important stages in the evolution of naval architecture and shipbuilding. WARRIOR, however, represents far more. She is the actual vessel that ushered in a new age in naval warfare. Her construction was a response to the French building of the wooden armoured steam frigate LA GLOIRE, the first armoured warship apart from some floating batteries employed in the Crimean War. In

Warrior

building WARRIOR the British Navy took the evolution of the warship several steps further. She was much larger and more powerful than LA GLOIRE, and her hull was built of iron. Overnight she made all other warships in the world obsolete. The great strength of the fleet of British ironclads that she initiated undoubtedly played a role in keeping peace in Europe for the next half-century. WARRIOR herself was never to see action. After 1881 she served a number of stationary uses, including training ship and torpedo depot. In 1929 she was taken to Pembroke Dock in southwest Wales and converted to a moored landing stage as a fuel depot. Her restoration

was announced as one of the aims of the Maritime Trust when it was formed in the late 1960s. WARRIOR was transferred from the Royal Navy in 1979 and towed to Hartlepool on England's northeast coast. There the ship was totally restored to her appearance as a seagoing warship of the 1860s. Local industries provided support, and the engineering training programme of a local college provided some of the labour. When completed, the ship was towed to the Portsmouth Naval Dockyard where she is exhibited afloat near HMS VICTORY and the remains of the MARY ROSE.
Bibliography D64, D147, D292, D478, D568

Waverley operating in 1981

Water Viper
steam launch

Built 1907 by Borwick & Son, Windermere, England
Propulsion Steam, screw; converted to petrol engine. Engine built by Sissons; currently Morris
Tonnage 7 gross
Length 42.5ft/12.95m
Breadth 7.0ft/2.13m
Draught 3.0ft/0.91m
Materials Wood throughout
Original use Yacht
Condition Fully restored
Present owners J R M Pilling; loaned to Windermere Steamboat Museum
Location Windermere, England
History Elegant Edwardian steam launch converted to petrol engine propulsion on loan to the museum in Windermere, where she is exhibited in operating condition in the museum's boathouse.

Waterlily
steam launch

Built 1866 by J I Thornycroft, Chiswick, England
Original owners Thomas Thornycroft
Propulsion Steam, screw, 8hp. Engine built by J I Thornycroft
Tonnage 10 gross
Length 42.0ft/12.8m
Breadth 7.0ft/2.13m
Draught 2.0ft/0.61m
Materials Iron hull, wood cabin
Original use Yacht
Condition Intact
Present owners J Thornycroft; on loan to National Maritime Museum
Location Greenwich, London, England
History Victorian steam launch with cabin, restored by apprentices of the firm that built her 110 years before. Loaned to the National Maritime Museum in Greenwich for exhibition.
Bibliography B27

Watkin Williams
rescue lifeboat

Built 1956
Original owners Royal National Lifeboat Institution
Length 42.0ft/12.8m
Original use Rescue lifeboat
Condition Intact
Present owners Welsh Industrial and Maritime Museum
Location Cardiff, Wales
History Preserved as an exhibit (museum closing).

Waverley
sidewheel excursion steamer

Built 1946 by A & J Inglis, Glasgow, Scotland
Original owners London & North Eastern Railway
Propulsion Steam, sidewheel, inclined triple expansion, 2100hp. Engine built

by Ranking & Blackmore
Tonnage 693 gross
Length 239.5ft/73.0m
Breadth 57.25ft/17.45m
Draught 6.5ft/1.98m
Materials Steel throughout
Original use Passengers
Condition In operation
Present owners Waverley Steam Navigation Co
Location Glasgow, Scotland
History Launched in October 1946, the sidewheel passenger steamer WAVERLEY was the last such vessel built to operate out of Scotland's River Clyde. She replaced the WAVERLEY of 1899 which had been sunk during the Dunkirk evacuation of the Second World War. During her first twenty-seven years she was employed mainly as a summer pleasure steamer, but also undertook ferry services in winter months. When the CALEDONIA was retired in 1970 she became the last

seagoing paddlewheel steamer in the world. Her owners, Caledonian MacBrayne Ltd, decided to retire the vessel in 1973 rather than undertake costly repairs. WAVERLEY was offered to the Paddle Steamer Preservation Society for the sum of one pound. The Society spent two years restoring the vessel to return to active service, depending heavily on donations of materials and volunteer labour. In 1975 the Waverley Steam Navigation Company was established to manage her operation. Through an imaginative programme of cruises and goodwill from the public it was possible to successfully operate WAVERLEY once again as a Clyde excursion vessel. Because the Clyde season is short, attempts were made to find out-of-season employment on other waters. In 1977 a group of successful excursions was made out of Liverpool. This experience led to trips further afield to the Solent, Thames and Bristol Channel. WAVERLEY has become something of a national institution, and is now a regular visitor welcomed annually at ports around the British Isles. One of her main attractions is her 66-inch stroke triple-expansion inclined engine whose operation may be viewed by passengers from either side of the open engineroom.
Bibliography B16, B27, B43, D104, 329, 558

Wellington

Wellington
escort sloop

Former name HMS WELLINGTON
Built 1934 by Devonport Dockyard, Plymouth, England
Original owners Royal Navy
Tonnage 990 displacement
Length 266.0ft/81.08m
Breadth 34.0ft/10.36m
Draught 8.75ft/2.67m
Materials Steel throughout
Original use Escort sloop, GRIMSBY class
Condition Intact
Present owners Honourable Company of Master Mariners
Location London, England
History Veteran of service in the Second World War, converted to a floating clubhouse for master mariners, moored at the Thames Embankment in central London. Has been at this location since 1947. Engines have been removed and interiors altered.
Bibliography B49

Will
spritsail barge

Former name WILL EVERARD
Built 1925 by Fellows, Yarmouth, England
Original owners F T Everard & Co
Propulsion Sail, spritsail ketch rig
Tonnage 150 gross
Materials Steel hull
Original use Cargo
Condition In sailing condition
Present owners Sue Harrison
Location Rochester, England
History Used as a sailing yacht.

Will and Fanny Kirby
rescue lifeboat

Built 1963 by W M Osborne
Original owners Royal National Lifeboat Institution
Propulsion Diesel engine
Length 37.0ft/11.1m
Breadth 11.5ft/3.4m
Draught 3.5ft/1.1m
Materials Wood hull
Original use Rescue lifeboat
Condition Intact
Present owners Royal National Lifeboat Collection
Location Chatham, England
History Preserved as an indoor exhibit.

William Gammon
rescue lifeboat

Built 1947
Original owners Royal National Lifeboat Institution
Length 46.75ft/14.25m
Original use Rescue lifeboat

Condition Intact
Present owners Industrial and Maritime Museum
Location Swansea, Wales
History Preserved as a floating exhibit.

Wincham
motor cargo vessel

Built 1948 by Yarwoods, Northwich, England
Original owners Imperial Chemical Industries, Liverpool
Propulsion Diesel engines
Tonnage 201 gross
Length 105.5ft/31.9m
Breadth 23.75ft/7.19m
Draught 10.0ft/3.03m
Materials Steel throughout
Original use Cargo
Condition Intact

Present owners Wincham Preservation Society
Location Liverpool, England
History Small motor cargo vessel built to carry commodities in bulk on the west coast of England. Maintained in operating condition by an enthusiast group that usually moors her at the maritime museum in Liverpool.
Bibliography B56

Windsor Belle
river passenger steamer

Built 1901 by Edward Burgoine, Windsor, England
Original owners A Jacobs
Propulsion Steam, screw, compound, 20hp. Engine built by McKie & Baxter
Tonnage 23 gross
Length 59.5ft/18.14m

William Gammon

Breadth 11.5ft/3.51m
Materials Wood throughout
Original use Passengers
Condition In operating condition
Present owners Windsor Belle Ltd
Location Hurley, England
History In operation as a passenger
steamer.
Bibliography B27

Wingfield Castle
steam sidewheel ferry

Built 1934 by William Gray & Co, West
Hartlepool, England
Original owners London & North
Eastern Railway
Propulsion Steam, sidewheel, triple
expansion, 1500hp. Engine built by
Central Marine Engine Works, West
Hartlepool
Tonnage 550 gross
Length 209.0ft/63.9m
Breadth 57.0ft/17.4m
Draught 7.75ft/2.29m
Materials Steel hull, steel and wood
superstructure
Original use Vehicle and passenger
ferry
Condition Largely restored
Present owners Hartlepool Borough
Council

Location Hartlepool, England
History Steam sidewheel ferry built to
carry vehicles and foot passengers
across the Humber river in northeast
England. Restored at Hartlepool in
1987-1992 for her present use as an
exhibit/restaurant/conference centre.
Bibliography B16, B27, B43, C22

Worcester
motor canal tug

Built 1908 by Isaac Abdela & Mitchell,
Brimscombe, England
Original owners Sharpness New Docks
Co
Propulsion Oil engine, 30hp. Engine
built by Bolinder
Length 45.0ft/13.72m
Breadth 7.0ft/2.13m
Draught 3.75ft/1.14m
Materials Iron throughout
Original use Canal tug
Condition Intact
Present owners The Boat Museum
Location Ellesmere Port, England
History Motor tug used to tow barges
and canal boats on the narrow canals
of central England. Preserved afloat as
an exhibit at the museum in Ellesmere
Port.
Bibliography B4

Wye
canal barge

Built 1959 by Thomas Launch Works
Original owners British Waterways
Transport
Propulsion Towed
Length 72.0ft/21.95m
Breadth 7.0ft/2.1m
Materials Steel throughout
Original use Cargo, canal boat
Condition Intact
Present owners National Waterways
Museum, Gloucester
Location Gloucester, England
History Preserved as a floating exhibit.

Wyvenhoe
spritsail barge

Built 1898 at Wyvenhoe, England
Propulsion Sail, spritsail ketch rig
Tonnage 45 gross
Materials Iron hull, wood masts
Original use Cargo, sailing barge
Condition In sailing condition
Present owners Wyvenhoe Trust
Location London
History Used for charter cruises.
Bibliography C74

XE-8
midget submarine

Former name HMS EXPUNGER
Built 1945 by Thomas Broadbent &
Sons Ltd, Huddersfield, England
Original owners Royal Navy
Propulsion Diesel engine, 30hp. Engine
built by Gardner
Tonnage 30 displacement
Length 53.17ft/16.21m
Breadth 5.83ft/1.78m
Materials Steel throughout
Original use Midget submarine
Condition Needs some restoration
Present owners Imperial War Museum
Contact address Lambeth Road,
London SE1 6HZ
Location Chatham, England
History Midget submarine of the type
used by the Royal Navy to disable the
battleship TIRPITZ during the Second
World War. Sank off the south coast of
England while serving as a target in
1952 and was raised in 1973. Exhibited
indoors at the former Naval Dockyard
in Chatham while awaiting restoration.
Bibliography A6

Xylonite
spritsail barge

Built 1926 by F W Horlock, Mistley,
England
Official number 145408
Propulsion Sail, spritsail ketch rig
Tonnage 68 gross
Materials Iron hull, wood masts
Original use Cargo, sailing barge
Condition In sailing condition
Present owners Cirdan Trust
Location Maldon, England
History Used for charter cruises.

Ysolt
steam yacht

Built 1893 by Simpson Strickland,
Dartmouth, England
Propulsion Steam, quadruple
expansion 50ihp. Engine built by
Simpson, Strickland
Length 53.0ft/16.1m
Breadth 7.5ft/2.3m
Materials Wood throughout (teak)
Original use Yacht
Condition Intact
Present owners Reg W Dean
Contact address 18 Ardenconnel Way,
Rhu, Helensburgh, Scotland G84 8RZ
Location Helensburgh, Scotland
History Intact late nineteenth-century
steam yacht maintained by private
owner.

Wingfield Castle in the Jackson Dock, Hartlepool

Greece

Greek seafaring in ancient times has been a major focus of modern marine archaeology since it was developed shortly after the Second World War. Thus far, the remains of vessels studied, and in a few cases brought to the surface, have been incomplete. Exploration of one of the deepest points in the Mediterranean has now led to the discovery of the first ancient vessels in what is described as a virtually intact state. Small wooden sailing vessels of traditional design were operated under the Greek flag well into this century.

Later in the century, a handful of Greek shipping magnates created one of the world's largest merchant fleets, specialising in tanker operation, but also involved in the general cargo and passenger trades.

Eugene Eugenides

Eugene Eugenides
schooner yacht

Former name FLYING CLIPPER, SUNBEAM II
Built 1929 by W Denny Bros, Dumbarton, Scotland
Original owners Sir Walter Runciman
Propulsion Three-masted topsail schooner rig, diesel engine
Tonnage 634 gross
Length 195.0ft/59.44m
Breadth 30.0ft/9.14m
Draught 17.42ft/5.31m
Materials Steel hull, steel and wood masts
Original use Yacht
Condition In operation
Present owners National Mercantile Marine Academy
Location Piraeus, Greece
History Built as a yacht for extended cruising under sail. Converted to a training vessel by a Swedish shipping company, and later sold to Greece where she serves as the training ship of the national merchant marine academy.
Bibliography A14, C96

Evangelistria
trading schooner

Built 1939 by Mavrikos & Sons, Syros, Greece
Original owners Captain Antonios K Bonis
Propulsion Sail, two-masted schooner rig
Tonnage 90 gross
Length 65.6ft/20.15m
Breadth 20.93ft/6.4m
Materials Wood throughout
Original use Cargo
Condition Intact
Present owners Aegean Maritime Museum
Location Myconos Island, Greece
History Example of traditional Greek sailing craft used to carry cargoes in the Aegean. In active use until 1978. Preserved as a floating exhibit.

Giorgios Averof

Giorgios Averof
armoured cruiser

Built 1910 by Cantieri Orlando, Livorno, Italy
Original owners Hellenic Navy
Propulsion Steam reciprocating engines; 19,000hp
Tonnage 10,000 displacement
Length 459.31ft/140.0m
Breadth 68.9ft/21.0m
Draught 24.61ft/7.5m
Materials Steel throughout
Original use Armoured cruiser
Condition Intact
Present owners Hellenic Navy
Location Piraeus, Greece
History Only surviving armoured cruiser of the early twentieth century. Served in wars with Turkey in 1912-1913, and with the Allied forces during the Second World War. Preserved as a floating museum at Piraeus.
Bibliography D203

Panaghiotis
motor coaster

Former name SAINT BEDAN
Built 1937 by Scott & Sons, Bowling, Great Britain
Propulsion Diesel engines. Engines built by Polar
Tonnage 452 gross
Materials Steel throughout
Original use Cargo
Condition Intact, but derelict
Location Island of Zakynthos, Greece
History Picturesque wreck on a beach.

Thalis O Milissios
cable layer

Former name JOSEPH HENRY
Built 1908 by Newport News Shipbuilding & Drydock Co, Newport News, Virginia, USA
Original owners US Army Signal Corps
Propulsion Steam reciprocating, compound
Tonnage 601 gross
Length 167.5ft/51.05m
Breadth 32.0ft/9.75m
Depth 16.33ft/4.98m
Materials Steel hull
Original use Cable ship
Condition Intact
Present owners Aegean Maritime Museum
Location Piraeus, Greece
History Steam cable laying vessel built for the US Army. The oldest cable layer in the world with its original engines. Preserved as a floating exhibit.
Bibliography D178

Guatemala

The northernmost and largest of the countries of Central America, Guatemala has coastline on both the Caribbean and the Pacific. Her only deepwater ports are located on the shorter Caribbean coast, the largest being Puerto Barrios from which the country exports its leading products, coffee, bananas, and exotic woods. Guatemala maintains a small navy of patrol craft to police its coastlines, and several navigable rivers and lakes.

Tikal
naval patrol boat

Built c1963 in the United States
Original owners Probably US Coast Guard
Official number P401
Propulsion Diesel engine
Length 40.0ft/12.2m
Materials Steel throughout
Original use Navy patrol boat
Condition Intact
Present owners Guatemalan Navy
Contact address Base Naval de Pacifico, Puerto Quetzal
Location Puerto Quetzal, Guatemala
History Small patrol boat either formerly operated by the US Coast Guard, or built as a copy of a standard Coast Guard design. Displayed on land at the entrance to a military base.

Hungary

Prior to its defeat in the First World War, Hungary was a semi-autonomous kingdom, linked to Austria to form the Austro-Hungarian Empire, with access to the sea through control of the Croatian coast of the Adriatic. Since 1918 it has been landlocked, its only navigable waters the Danube River and its tributaries, and Lake Balaton. Unfortunately, the last operating Hungarian sidewheel steamer was retired in 1986. The KOSSUTH survives at Budapest somewhat defaced with signage for an onboard bar or restaurant, though owned by the City's excellent land-based museum of technology and transport. The PETÖFI is reportedly intact somewhere in the vicinity of Budapest, and may eventually return to service, and Austria is supposed to be refitting the Budapest-built SCHÖNBRUNN for further service on the Danube which should include visits to Hungary.

Helka
lake steamer

Built 1891 by Schoenichen & Hartmann, Budapest, Hungary
Propulsion Steam, screw; converted to diesel

Length 115.46ft/35.2m
Breadth 16.07ft/4.9m
Materials Steel hull
Original use Passengers
Condition Intact
Present owners Hungarian Transport Museum
Location Balatonfured, Hungary
History First passenger steamboat on Lake Balaton. Original engines are preserved by the Budapest Transport Museum. Vessel herself is preserved on shore as an exhibit near the lake.
Bibliography B16

Kelén
passenger steamer

Built 1891 by Schoenichen & Hartmann, Budapest, Hungary
Propulsion Steam, screw; converted to diesel
Length 115.46ft/35.2m
Breadth 16.07ft/4.9m
Materials Steel hull
Original use Passengers
Condition In operating condition
Present owners MAHART
Location Siofok, Hungary
History Sistership of the HELKA. Operating as a passenger vessel (reserve boat for route).
Bibliography B16

Kossuth
sidewheel steamer

Former name FERENCZ FERDINAND FOHERCZEG, RIGO, LEANYFALU
Built 1914 by Ganz Danubius, Budapest, Hungary

Kossuth

Propulsion Steam, sidewheel, compound diagonal, 580hp
Length 197.0ft/60.05m
Breadth 51.0ft/15.54m
Materials Steel hull
Original use Passenger steamer
Condition Intact
Present owners Hungarian Transport Museum, Budapest, Hungary
Location Budapest, Hungary
History Sidewheel steamer built to operate on the Danube river. Preserved afloat at Budapest as a restaurant and museum.
Bibliography B16, B43

Leitha
river monitor

Former name FK201, LAJTA
Built 1872 by Pest Machineworks, Pest, Austria-Hungary
Original owners Austro-Hungarian Navy
Propulsion Steam, screw
Tonnage 310 displacement
Length 164.1ft/50.0m
Breadth 26.3ft/8.0m
Materials Iron throughout
Original use River monitor
Condition Armoured hull survives
Present owners Hungarian Military History Museum
Location Hungary
History Oldest surviving river monitor. Currently undergoing restoration at a military facility near Budapest for eventual exhibition.
Bibliography D12, D465

Petöfi
sidewheel steamer

Former name SZENT LASZLO
Built 1920 by Werft MFTR, Komarom, Hungary
Propulsion Steam, sidewheel, compound diagonal, 580hp
Length 197.0ft/60.05m
Breadth 51.0ft/15.54m
Materials Steel hull
Original use Passenger steamer
Condition Intact, undergoing restoration
Present owners Magyar Hajozasi R T, Budapest, Hungary
Location Budapest, Hungary
History Sidewheel steamer built to operate on the Danube river. Was the last day steamer operating out of Budapest when retired in 1984. Currently being restored to operating condition at a yard near Budapest.
Bibliography B16, B43

Reckeve Floating Mill
moored flour mill

Built Date not known
Propulsion Non-self propelled; moored in one location
Length 42.31ft/12.9m
Breadth 29.52ft/9.0m
Materials Wood throughout
Original use Flour mill
Condition Intact
Present owners Museum of the Island of Szentendre
Location Island of Szentendre, Hungary
History Moored current-operated mill built on two hulls with a mill wheel between. Preserved as a floating exhibit.

India

India has often been described by travel writers as a 'land of contrasts'. This is no less true in the maritime field. Wooden craft of traditional design and traditional methods of construction are still numerous in coastal waters, and on the larger navigable rivers. The country also has modern merchant ships engaged in world trade, and a modern navy maintaining its balance of power with neighbour Pakistan, with whom it has unresolved territorial disputes. The last fleet of square-rigged vessels in the world carrying cargoes were a group of brigs, brigantines and barkentines copied after European designs which were transporting rice across the Bay of Bengal well into the second half of the twentieth century. None is known to survive today. Steam or diesel-propelled paddlewheel boats, built when India was still a British colony, are occasionally reported on the larger rivers, but it is difficult to determine how many are actually in service since they are usually treated as local transportation and not advertised for tourist travel.

Benares
sidewheel river steamer

Former name PRINCE OF WALES
Built Date not known
Propulsion Steam, sidewheel, inclined
Materials Steel hull
Original use Passengers
Condition Intact, in operating condition
Location Munger, India
History Large sidewheel river steamer, probably built in the British Isles between 1930 and 1950. Laid up at Munger in the State of Bihar, and apparently available for steaming on special occasions.

Bhopal
sidewheel river steamer

Built 1945 by Denny, Dumbarton, Scotland
Original owners Rivers Steam Navigation Co

Propulsion Steam, sidewheel, diagonal triple-expansion, coal fired
Tonnage 500 gross
Length 200.0ft/60.9m
Breadth 31.0ft/9.4m
Draught 8.8ft/2.7m
Materials Steel throughout
Original use Passengers, cargo & towing
Condition Currently in use
Location Nr Calcutta, India
History The first paddlewheel steamer built in Great Britain after the Second World War. One of four sisters completed by the builders in 1945 for use on the rivers of India. Currently survives as a stationary training facility for a maritime school.

River Ganga
sidewheel river steamer

Built 1946
Propulsion Diesel, paddlewheel
Materials Steel hull
Original use Passengers and cargo
Condition Intact
Location Calcutta, India
History Paddlewheel river steamer, probably built in the British Isles for use in India, now serving as a floating museum at Calcutta.

Vikrant
aircraft carrier

Former name HMS HERCULES
Built 1945 by Vickers Armstrong, Walker, Newcastle on Tyne, England
Original owners British Royal Navy
Propulsion Steam turbines
Tonnage 14,000 displacement
Length 630.0ft/192.0m
Breadth 80.0ft/24.4m
Materials Steel throughout
Original use Aircraft carrier
Condition Intact
Present owners Indian Navy
Location Mumbai (formerly Bombay), India
History Built for the British Royal Navy for use in the Second World War but incomplete when the war ended. Laid up unfinished and eventually transferred to India. Completed by the Harland and Wolff Shipyard in Belfast, Ireland, in 1961. Modernised with new engines and boilers in 1979, and fitted with 'ski ramp' for Harrier aircraft in 1989. Retired from active service in September 1997. Proposed as a museum.

Indonesia

The vast archipelago of Indonesia covers much of the area between the south coast of Asia and the north coast of Australia. It was a colony of the Netherlands for centuries, but little evidence of that chapter in its past survives today. Traditional craft abound, ranging from colourfully decorated sailing outrigger canoes launched from beaches to wooden inter-island motor vessels that still carry some sail set from tall, gaff-rigged masts and long bowsprits. Future officers in the Indonesian merchant marine train on board a steel barkentine of western design which has visited ports in Europe and North America on some of its longer voyages.

Dewarutji
sail training ship

Built 1952 by Stulckenwerft, Hamburg, Germany
Original owners Indonesian Government
Propulsion Sail, barquentine rig; diesel engine. Engine built by MAN
Materials Steel hull, steel and wood masts
Original use Training ship
Condition In operation
Present owners Indonesian Government
Location Jakarta, Indonesia
History Built as a training vessel for the Indonesian merchant marine. Was the first Indonesian vessel to circumnavigate the globe in 1964 on a voyage that included participating in the first Operation Sail in New York harbour. In use for training.

Dewarutji

Iraq

During the First World War, Great Britain fought to end Turkish rule over Mesopotamia, the fertile region drained by the Tigris and Euphrates Rivers. After putting down an Arab revolt that followed the war the British created the Kingdom of Iraq encompassing much of the region, under their mandate. That mandate was ended in 1932 to allow Iraq to enter the League of Nations as an independent nation, but close ties with Britain were maintained by treaty. During the Second World War the allies occupied the region to guard its rich oilfields and use it as a staging point for supplying Russia. Petroleum is by far the leading export of the country, currently severely reduced in volume by a United Nations embargo in response to Iraq's attempt to annex its neighbour Kuwait by military force. Iraq has important seaports on its very limited coastline at the head of the Persian Gulf, and its two great rivers have served as avenues of commerce, and on occasion as routes for naval expeditions.

Name unknown
river gunboat

Built 1937 by John Thornycroft & Co, Southampton, England
Original owners Navy of Iraq
Propulsion Two diesel engines, twin screw, 380hp
Tonnage 67 displacement
Length 100ft/30.5m
Breadth 17ft/5.1m
Draught 3ft/0.9m
Materials Steel throughout
Original use River gunboat
Condition Afloat, intact, apparently little altered
Present owners Navy of Iraq
Location Basrah, Iraq
History One of four sisterships built in England for the Iraqi Navy shortly before the Second World War. Outwardly unaltered from her original appearance. Laid up, apparently a museum; there are some historical exhibits on board, but it is not known how accessible she may be to the general public.

Israel

Formerly Palestine, a region under the control of the Ottoman Empire and later Great Britain, Israel struggled to gain its independence, finally succeeding in 1947, and since has had to fight several wars with its neighbours for its survival. It has several seaports on the Mediterranean, and one port on the Gulf of Aqaba, an arm of the Red Sea. Israel has established a merchant fleet for worldwide trading, and a modern navy, but the most dramatic chapter in its maritime history remains the period from the Second World War to 1947 when a makeshift fleet of vessels of all ages and origins attempted to smuggle thousands of Jewish refugees, many of them survivors of concentration camps, into the future nation through a determined British blockade.

Af-Al-Pi-Chen
tank landing craft

Built 1944 in Great Britain
Original owners Royal Navy
Propulsion Diesel engines
Tonnage 640 displacement
Length 192.0ft/58.52m
Breadth 31.0ft/9.45m
Draught 5.4ft/1.65m
Materials Steel throughout
Original use Landing craft
Condition Intact
Present owners Haifa Maritime Museum
Location Haifa, Israel
History Second World War tank landing craft later used in an attempt to bring Jewish refugees to Palestine. Preserved as an onshore exhibit.

Italy

Italians have been seafarers since the days of Ancient Rome. Early in this century giant galleys attributed to the Emperor Caligula were found largely intact on the bottom of Lake Nemi. They were placed on exhibit in a building beside the Lake but were destroyed by fire there at the end of the Second World War. Recent explorations of the deepest areas of the Mediterranean are reportedly turning up extremely well-preserved shipwrecks that include early Roman trading vessels. In the modern era, Italy has sent to sea the full range of merchant vessels and warships. Larger sailing ships, including Italian-built steel ships and barks, were employed in worldwide trade, but apparently no examples survive today. Smaller wooden brigantines and barkentines were used for trading in the Mediterranean well into this century. The brigantine EBE is an interesting approach to maritime preservation, installed as an exhibit at the Science Museum in Milan far from the sea, in a specially-built building she shares with a portion of the superstructure of the Italian transatlantic luxury liner CONTE BIANCAMANO. Three magnificent lakes in the Italian Alps are home to a group of surviving sidewheel steamers, some in service and others serving stationary roles which may some day be restored to service.

Af-Al-Pi-Chen

Amerigo Vespucci

Amerigo Vespucci
naval sail training ship

Built 1931 by Royal Shipyard,
Castellamare di Stabia, Italy
Original owners Italian Navy
Propulsion Full-rigged ship rig; two
diesel engines, 1900hp
Tonnage 3550 displacement
Length 269.0ft/81.99m
Breadth 50.8ft/15.48m
Draught 21.5ft/6.55m
Materials Steel throughout
Original use Training ship
Condition In active service
Present owners Accademia Navale
Location Livorno (home port), Italy
History Steel full-rigged ship built to
resemble the wooden ships of the line
of the early 1800s. Designed as a
training vessel for the Italian naval
academy at Livorno and still in service.
Her near-sistership CRISTOFORO
COLOMBO was given to Russia after the
Second World War, but eventually
scrapped.
Bibliography A10, A14, C25, C96

Bragozzo d'Altura
fishing lugger

Built at Chioggia, Italy
Propulsion Sail, two-masted lugger rig
Length 44.61ft/13.6m
Breadth 13.78ft/4.2m
Materials Wood throughout
Original use Fishing
Condition Intact, on exhibit
Present owners Cesenatico Maritime
Museum
Location Cesenatico, Italy
History Example of type of sailing
fishing vessel formerly employed along
the Dalmatian coast. Preserved as a
floating exhibit.
Bibliography B34

CB-22
midget submarine

Built 1943 by Caproni, Milan, Italy
Original owners Italian Navy
Propulsion Diesel and electric motors
Tonnage 44.3 displacement
Length 49.15ft/14.98m
Breadth 6.85ft/2.09m

Draught 6.65ft/2.03m
Materials Steel throughout
Original use Midget submarine
Condition Intact
Present owners Trieste War Museum
Location Trieste, Italy
History Midget submarine of the
Second World War preserved as an
onshore exhibit.

Concordia
lake steamer

Former name XXVIII OTTUBRE
Built 1927 by N Odero fu Aless, Como,
Italy
Original owners Soc Lariana
Propulsion Steam, sidewheel, 3-cylinder
diagonal, 600hp. Engine built by N
Odero
Tonnage 286 displacement
Length 176.1ft/53.66m
Breadth 38.0ft/11.58m
Materials Steel throughout
Original use Passengers
Condition In active service
Present owners Gestione Gov Nav
Laghi Maggiore di Garda di Como

Location Como (home port), Italy
History Sidewheel steamer built to
operate on Lake Como. Renamed
CONCORDIA in 1943 because original
name commemorated Mussolini's
march on Rome in 1922. Additional
passenger lounge added aft during
1970s. In service making limited
excursion trips during summer.
Bibliography B16, B43

Ebe
trading brigantine

Former name SAN GIORGIO
Built 1921 by Benetti, Viareggio, Italy
Propulsion Sail, brigantine rig
Tonnage 600 gross
Length 179.0ft/54.56m
Breadth 31.5ft/9.6m
Depth 30.0ft/9.14m
Materials Wood throughout
Original use Cargo; later training ship
Condition Reassembled inside museum
building
Present owners Science Museum of
Milan
Contact address Via S Vittore 29, Milan,

Italy
Location Milan, Italy
History Brigantine built to carry cargo in the Mediterranean. Later converted to a naval training vessel. In the 1960s was cut into sections and transported to Milan for reassembly and rerigging inside a specially built building behind the Science Museum, as an exhibit.
Bibliography A14, D143

Florette
trading brigantine

Built 1922 by Fratelli Picchiotti, La Tinaia, Italy
Propulsion Sail, brigantine rig; auxiliary engine added. Engine built by Fiat Aifo
Tonnage 120 gross
Length 118.2ft/36.0m
Breadth 23.0ft/7.0m
Draught 8.5ft/2.6m
Materials Wood hull
Original use Cargo
Condition In sailing condition; modern rigging
Present owners Florette Diving and Sailing Club
Location S Stefano, Italy
History Originally built for the Italian marble trade rigged as a brigantine. Converted to carry passengers. Currently has a modern rig that approximates her original one. Available for charter.

G Zanardelli
sidewheel lake steamer

Former name GIUSEPPE ZANARDELLI
Built 1904 by Escher-Wyss & Cie, Zurich, Switzerland
Original owners Soc Navigarda
Propulsion Steam, sidewheel; converted to diesel-hydraulic, 600hp
Tonnage 278 gross
Length 154.0ft/46.94m
Breadth 38.0ft/11.58m
Draught 5.5ft/1.68m
Materials Steel throughout
Original use Passengers
Condition In active service
Present owners Nav Lago di Garda
Contact address Via Ariosto 21, Milan, Italy
Location Peschiera, Lake Garda, Italy
History Former sidewheel steamer built to operate on Lake Garda. Damaged by grounding in fog in October 1977. Returned to operation with steam engine replaced by diesel-hydraulic propulsion. Primarily used for charters.
Bibliography B43

Giovanni Pascoli
sailing lugger

Built 1936 at Cattolica, Italy
Propulsion Sail, two-masted lugger rig
Tonnage 61.21 gross
Length 67.24ft/20.5m
Breadth 20.66ft/6.3m
Draught 6.89ft/2.1m
Materials Wood throughout
Original use Cargo
Condition Intact
Present owners Cesenatico Maritime Museum
Location Cesenatico, Italy
History Example of a 'trabaccolo' formerly used for carrying cargo on the Adriatic coast of Italy. Preserved as a floating exhibit.
Bibliography B34

Italia
sidewheel lake steamer

Built 1909 by Odero fu Aless, Genoa, Italy
Original owners Soc Navigarda
Propulsion Steam, sidewheel; converted to diesel-hydraulic, 600hp. Engine built by Haggluns (current)
Tonnage 371 gross, 304 displacement
Length 171.3ft/52.5m
Breadth 38.0ft/11.58m
Draught 5.5ft/1.68m
Materials Steel throughout
Original use Passengers
Condition In active service
Present owners Nav Lago di Garda
Contact address Via Ariosto 21, Milan
Location Peschiera, Lake Garda, Italy
History Former sidewheel steamer built for operation on Lake Garda. Converted to diesel-hydraulic propulsion in 1970s. Upper deck altered by addition of passenger lounges and moving pilothouse forward. Making limited excursions during the summer.
Bibliography B43

Lombardia
sidewheel lake steamer

Built 1908 by N Odero fu Aless, Genoa, Italy
Propulsion Steam, sidewheel, compound diagonal
Length 170.7ft/52.0m
Materials Steel throughout
Original use Passengers
Condition Largely intact, engine removed
Location Arona, Lake Maggiore, Italy
History Preserved as a floating restaurant.

MAS-15
torpedo boat

Built 1917 by Naval Dockyard, Venice, Italy
Original owners Italian Navy
Propulsion Petrol engines, 450hp
Tonnage 16 displacement
Length 52.5ft/16.0m
Breadth 8.65ft/2.64m
Draught 3.95ft/1.2m
Original use Torpedo boat
Condition Intact
Present owners Museo delle Bandiere
Location Rome, Italy
History First World War torpedo boat which sank the Austro-Hungarian battleship SVENT ISTVAN in 1918. Preserved as an onshore exhibit.

MAS-96
torpedo boat

Built 1917 by Orlando, Leghorn, Italy
Original owners Italian Navy
Propulsion Petrol engines, 500hp
Tonnage 12.4 displacement
Length 52.85ft/16.11m
Breadth 9.15ft/2.79m
Draught 4.25ft/1.29m
Original use Torpedo boat
Condition Intact
Present owners Vittoriale
Location Gardone, Italy
History Torpedo boat that saw service in the First World War. Preserved as an indoor exhibit.

MS-472
torpedo boat

Built 1942 by Cantieri Riuniti Dell'Adriatico, Monfalcone, Italy
Original owners Italian Navy
Propulsion Petrol engines, 3450hp
Tonnage 62.4 displacement
Length 91.83ft/27.99m
Breadth 14.08ft/4.29m
Draught 5.08ft/1.55m
Materials Wood hull, aluminium superstructure
Original use Torpedo boat
Condition Intact
Location Ravenna, Italy

MS-473
fast gunboat

Former name MS-613, MS-31
Built 1942 by Cantieri Riuniti dell' Adriatico, Monfalcone, Italy
Original owners Italian Navy
Propulsion Petrol engines, 3450hp
Tonnage 63 displacement
Length 91.83ft/27.99m
Breadth 14.08ft/4.29m
Draught 5.08ft/1.55m
Materials Wood hull, aluminium superstructure, steel masts
Original use Fast gunboat
Condition Intact
Present owners Museo Storico Navale
Contact address 2148 Riva degli Schiavoni, Venice, Italy
Location Venice, Italy
History Italian fast gunboat that served in the Second World War exhibited on shore in the old dockyard of Venice.

Palinuro
fishing barquentine

Former name COMMANDANT LOUIS RICHARD
Built 1934 by Dubigeon, Nantes, France
Propulsion Sail, barquentine rig; diesel auxiliary. Engine built by Fiat
Tonnage 858 gross
Length 190.0ft/57.91m
Breadth 33.0ft/10.06m
Draught 16.0ft/4.88m
Materials Steel throughout
Original use Fishing
Condition In active service
Present owners Italian Navy
Location La Maddalena, Sardinia, Italy
History Built as a mother ship for codfishing from dories on the Grand Banks off Newfoundland. Acquired from French owners by the Italian Navy for conversion to a naval sail training vessel and still in service.
Bibliography A14

Patria
sidewheel lake steamer

Former name SAVOIA
Built 1926 by N Odero fu Aless, Como, Italy
Original owners Soc Lariana
Propulsion Steam, sidewheel, diagonal triple expansion, 600hp. Engine built by N Odero
Tonnage 276 gross, 286 displacement
Length 170.0ft/51.82m
Breadth 38.0ft/11.58m
Materials Steel throughout
Original use Passengers
Condition Largely intact, out of service
Present owners Gov Nav Lago di Como
Contact address Via Ariosto 21, Milan
Location Como, Italy
History Sidewheel steamer built for operation on Lake Como. Withdrawn from service in 1990 for hull repairs. Hull work has been completed but the need for further renovation is holding up her return to service.
Bibliography B16, B43

Piemonte
sidewheel lake steamer

Former name REGINA MADRE
Built 1904 by Escher-Wyss & Cie, Zurich, Switzerland
Original owners Soc Subalpina
Propulsion Steam, sidewheel, compound diagonal, 440hp. Engine built by Escher-Wyss
Tonnage 301 gross, 273 displacement
Length 168.0ft/51.2m
Breadth 38.0ft/11.58m
Materials Steel throughout
Original use Passengers
Condition In active service
Present owners Nav Lago di Maggiore
Contact address Via Ariosto 21, Milan, Italy
Location Arona, Lake Maggiore, Italy
History Sidewheel steamer built for operation on Lake Maggiore. Maintained in operating condition but makes only limited public cruises and charters during summer months.
Bibliography B16, B43

Pietro Micca
steam tug

Former name DILWARA
Built 1895 by Rennoldson and Son, South Shields, England
Propulsion Steam, screw, triple expansion. Engine built by Rennoldson and Son
Tonnage 134 gross
Length 95.5ft/29.11m
Materials Steel hull
Original use Tug
Condition Intact, renovation needed
Present owners Associazione Amici delle Navi a Vapore G Spinelli
Location Fiumicino, Rome, Italy
History Proposed for restoration to active steamer.

Plinio
sidewheel lake steamer

Built 1903 by Escher-Wyss, Zurich, Switzerland
Propulsion Steam, sidewheel, diagonal compound
Length 167.4ft/51.0m
Materials Steel throughout
Original use Passengers
Condition Intact, engine removed
Present owners Club Nautico Lario
Location Colico, Lake Como, Italy
History In use as a club boat and restaurant.
Bibliography B43

Palinuro

Williamsburg

Europeans first visited Japan in the 1500s, but it was not until the mid-1800s that the country finally emerged from its self-imposed isolation and began to adopt western technology. Within a short time the Japanese had created shipyards capable of building iron-hulled steamships based on European designs. In the latter half of the twentieth century Japan became the leading shipbuilding country in the world, but it has now been eclipsed by its neighbours South Korea and Taiwan. Throughout this period wooden craft of traditional construction continued to be used for coastal trading and inshore fishing, powered by sail and later by diesel engines. Some of these smaller traditional craft are now preserved as exhibits in museums of Japanese folk culture and rural life, while the larger historic ships surviving in the country all reflect strong western influence.

Puritan
schooner yacht

Built 1931 by Electric Boat Co, Groton, Connecticut, USA. Designed by John Alden
Original owners Henry J Bauer
Propulsion Sail, schooner rig; auxiliary engine
Length 102.75ft/31.32m
Breadth 22.9ft/6.7m
Draught 9.0ft/2.74m
Materials Steel hull
Original use Yacht
Condition Fully restored
Present owners Feruzzi Family
Location Italy (nation of owners)
History Two-masted schooner yacht built in the United States early in the century. Recently fully restored for private owners in Italy.
Bibliography A1

Quattro Fratelli
fishing lugger

Former name BIGHELLONE
Built 1925 by Pietro Terenzi, Cattolica, Italy
Propulsion Sail, two-masted lugger rig
Length 42.84ft/13.06m
Breadth 12.14ft/3.7m
Materials Wood throughout
Original use Fishing
Condition Intact
Present owners Cesenatico Maritime Museum
Location Cesenatico, Italy
History Example of a 'trabaccolo' formerly used for carrying cargo on the Adriatic coast of Italy. Preserved as a floating exhibit.
Bibliography B34

Williamsburg
motor yacht

Former name ANTON BRUUN
Built 1930 by Bath Iron Works, Bath, Maine
Original owners Hugh J Chisholm
Propulsion Diesel engines
Tonnage 1332 gross
Length 243.75ft/74.3m
Breadth 36.0ft/10.97m
Draught 15.0ft/4.57m
Materials Steel hull, steel and wood superstructure
Original use Yacht
Condition Laid up, awaiting restoration
Location Italy
Bibliography C18

5 Fukuryu Maru
motor fishing boat

Former name HAYABUSA MARU, KOTOSHIRO MARU 7
Built 1946 by Koza Shipbuilding, Wakayama, Japan
Original owners Kadoichi Nishikawa
Propulsion Diesel engines, 250hp
Tonnage 140.86 gross
Length 93.68ft/28.56m
Breadth 19.35ft/5.9m
Materials Wood hull
Original use Fishing
Condition Intact
Present owners Dai 5 Fukuryu Maru Museum
Location Tokyo, Japan
History Japanese fishing vessel that was caught in the radioactive fallout from the American 1954 hydrogen bomb test in the Pacific. Preserved as an indoor exhibit.
Bibliography D294

Hikawa Maru
passenger liner

Built 1930 by Yokohama Dock Co, Yokohama, Japan
Original owners Nippon Yusen K K

Propulsion Diesel engines, 2187hp
Tonnage 11,622 gross
Length 521.5ft/158.95m
Breadth 66.0ft/20.12m
Depth 41.0ft/12.5m
Materials Steel throughout
Original use Passengers
Condition Intact
Location Yokohama, Japan
History Last surviving Japanese pre-Second World War passenger liner. Served as a hospital ship during the war. Preserved as a floating museum at Yokohama.

'Kairyu' type
midget submarine

Built 1945 in Japan
Original owners Japanese Imperial Navy
Propulsion Diesel and electric motors, 85hp
Tonnage 18.97 displacement
Length 56.67ft/17.27m

Hikawa Maru

Breadth 4.25ft/1.29m
Draught 4.25ft/1.29m
Materials Steel throughout
Original use Midget submarine
Condition Intact
Present owners Marineakademie
Location Etajima, Japan
History Preserved as an onshore exhibit.

Kaiwo Maru
sail training ship

Built 1930 by Kawasaki Dockyard Co, Kobe, Japan
Original owners Japanese Ministry of Transport
Propulsion Sail, four-masted barque; diesel auxiliary
Tonnage 2285 gross, 4343 displacement
Length 307.0ft/93.57m
Breadth 42.5ft/12.95m
Draught 22.5ft/6.86m
Materials Steel throughout
Original use Training ship
Condition Intact, retired as seagoing vessel
Location Tokyo, Japan
History Built as a training ship for the Japanese merchant marine. Sistership of the Nippon Maru (I). Has now been replaced by a similarly rigged vessel of the same name. Moored at Tokyo as a stationary training ship.
Bibliography A14, C96, D512a

Kaiwo Maru

Kojima

naval escort vessel

Former name SHIGA
Built 1944 by Sasebo Navy Yard, Sasebo, Japan
Original owners Imperial Japanese Navy
Propulsion Diescl engines, 4200hp
Tonnage 940 displacement
Length 256.0ft/78.0m
Breadth 29.75ft/9.1m
Draught 10.0ft/3.1m
Materials Steel throughout
Original use Escort vessel
Condition Intact
Present owners City of Chiba
Location Chiba, Japan
History Preserved as a floating exhibit.

Kyo Maru No 2

whale catcher

Built 1946 by Kawasaki Jukogo, Kobe, Japan
Propulsion Diesel engine, 950hp. Engine built by Kawasaki Jukogo
Tonnage 285 gross
Length 127.7ft/38.9m
Breadth 23.6ft/7.2m
Depth 13.1ft/4.0m
Materials Steel hull
Original use Whale catcher
Location Taiji, Japan
History Japanese whale catcher preserved as a museum exhibit.

Meiji Maru

lighthouse tender

Built 1874 by Robert Napier, Glasgow, Scotland
Original owners Japanese Lighthouse Service
Propulsion Steam, screw; later rigged as full-rigged ship
Tonnage 1038 gross
Length 249.3ft/75.99m
Breadth 28.0ft/8.53m
Depth 25.0ft/7.62m
Materials Iron hull
Original use Lighthouse tender; training
Condition Intact
Present owners Mercantile Marine University
Location Tokyo, Japan
History Built for the Japanese Government as the Royal Yacht. Later served as a lighthouse tender and, with current rig, as a training ship. Eventually retired to serve as a stationary drill ship. Now a museum permanently embedded in the shore.
Bibliography A14, C96

Meiji Maru

Mikasa

pre-Dreadnought battleship

Built 1900 by Vickers, Sons and Maxim, Barrow, England
Original owners Imperial Japanese Navy
Propulsion Steam, reciprocating; 15,000hp
Tonnage 15,140 displacement
Length 432.0ft/131.67m
Breadth 76.0ft/23.16m
Depth 27.0ft/8.23m
Materials Steel throughout
Original use Pre-Dreadnought battleship
Condition Intact
Present owners Mikasa Preservation Society
Location Yokosuka, Japan
History World's only surviving pre-Dreadnought battleship. Flagship at the Japanese naval victory in the Battle of Tsushima Strait, during the Russo-Japanese War of 1905. Preserved as a relic of that war embedded in the shore at the Yokosuka naval base.
Bibliography A8, D504

Nippon Maru

sail training ship

Built 1930 by Kawasaki Dockyard, Kobe, Japan
Original owners Japanese Ministry of

Mikasa with statue of Admiral Togo

Nippon Maru

Transport
Propulsion Sail, four-masted barque rig; diesel engines
Tonnage 2285 gross
Length 307.0ft/93.57m
Breadth 42.5ft/12.95m
Draught 22.5ft/6.86m
Materials Steel throughout
Original use Training ship
Condition Intact
Location Yokohama, Japan
History Built as a training ship for the Japanese merchant marine. Sistership of the KAIWO MARU (I). Replaced in the 1980s by a vessel of similar rig with the same name. Moored at Yokohama as a floating museum.
Bibliography A14, C25, C96, D512a

Shibaura Maru
steam tug

Built 1926 by Asano Shipyard, Kawasaki, Japan
Original owners Metropolitan Government of Tokyo
Propulsion Steam, screw
Tonnage 37.74 gross
Length 59.99ft/18.29m

Breadth 14.07ft/4.29m
Draught 6.0ft/1.83m
Materials Steel throughout
Original use Tug
Condition Intact

Present owners Metropolitan Government of Tokyo
Location Tokyo, Japan
History Preserved as an onshore exhibit.

Soya
cargo/research vessel

Former name CHIRYO MARU
Built 1938 by Tatsunami-Shosen Co
Original owners Maritime Safety Agency
Propulsion Diesel engines
Tonnage 2736 gross
Length 254.36ft/77.53m
Breadth 51.84ft/15.8m
Depth 30.51ft/9.3m
Materials Steel throughout
Original use Cargo; Antarctic research
Condition Intact
Present owners Museum of Maritime Science
Contact address 3-1 Highashi-Yashio, Shinagawa-ku, Tokyo 135, Japan
Location Tokyo, Japan
History Originally built as a cargo vessel. Converted first to a lighthouse tender and later to Antarctic research vessel. Maintained as a floating exhibit next to the large maritime museum at Tokyo.

Stella Polaris
cruise vessel

Built 1927 by A/B Gotaverken, Gothenburg, Sweden
Original owners Rederi A/B Clipper, Malmo
Propulsion Diesel engines, 3500hp

Tonnage 5105 gross
Length 360.0ft/109.73m
Breadth 50.5ft/15.39m
Draught 18.0ft/5.49m
Materials Steel throughout
Original use Passenger cruises
Condition Intact
Location Nr Tokyo, Japan
History Last passenger vessel with a clipper bow. Built as a cruise ship, and now maintained as a floating hotel moored in Tokyo Bay.
Bibliography D327, D578

Unyo Maru
sail training ship

Built 1909 by Osaka Iron Foundry, Osaka, Japan
Original owners Japanese Ministry of Agriculture and Forests
Propulsion Sail, barque rig; steam auxiliary, triple expansion, 303hp
Tonnage 448 gross
Length 150.5ft/45.87m
Breadth 26.5ft/8.08m
Draught 12.0ft/3.66m
Materials Steel throughout
Original use Training ship
Condition Intact
Present owners Institute for Fisheries Research
Location Tokyo, Japan
History Built as a sailing training ship for the Japanese fishing fleet. Later moved ashore to serve as a stationary drill ship. Preserved ashore where it was last used for training and as a museum.
Bibliography A14, C96

Stella Polaris

Kenya

The boundaries of this East African nation are the result of a protectorate established by Great Britain in the 1890s. Kenya received its independence in 1963, around the same time as its neighbours Tanganyika (now Tanzania), and Uganda. It has coastline on the Indian Ocean with one major port, Mombasa, and two lesser ones, Malindi and Lamu. All three ports have been important destinations for the seasonal fleets of sailing dhows based in the Persian Gulf. Part of Kenya's western boundary is formed by the coastline of Africa's largest lake, Victoria, which has been navigated by steamers or motor vessels since the turn of the century.

Kavirondo
steam tug

Built 1913 by Fleming & Ferguson, Paisley, Scotland (pre-fabricated). Designed by Kisumu, Kenya
Original owners Uganda Railway
Propulsion Steam, screw, 400hp
Tonnage 200 displacement
Length 100.0ft/30.5m
Breadth 21.0ft/6.4m
Draught 7.0ft/2.1m
Materials Steel throughout
Original use Tug
Condition In service
Present owners Kenya Railway
Location Lake Victoria, Kenya
History Steam tug transported overland for assembly on the shore of Lake Victoria. Used to move lighter barges on the lake. Served as a gunboat with the British forces on the lake during the First World War. Still in use on the lake by the Kenya Railways.
Bibliography C20a

Malawi

This landlocked country in the centre of Africa has as much of its eastern border the west shore of Lake Nyasa. Treaties between Britain and local chieftains led in 1891 to the creation of the Protectorate of Nyasaland, which adopted the name Malawi when it gained its independence in 1964. Missionaries from the British Isles had become active in the region two decades before the Protectorate was formed. Malawi's historic ship bears the name of a prominent Bishop of Likoma, a port on the Lake, and was originally used for missionary activities.

Chauncey Maples
mission steamer

Built 1899 by Alley & MacLellan, Glasgow, Scotland (shipped in sections). Designed by Alexander Johnson
Original owners Universities' Mission to Central Africa
Propulsion Steam; converted to diesel
Length 127.0ft/38.7m
Breadth 20.0ft/6.1m
Draught 6.0ft/1.8m
Materials Steel hull
Original use School and Mobile Mission
Condition In operation; altered and re-engined
Present owners Malawi Railways
Location Lake Malawi, Malawi
History Former mission steamer used as a lake Army transport during the First World War. Returned to use as a motor vessel carrying passengers and cargo.
Bibliography D187

Malaysia

Malaysia occupies much of the Malay Peninsula that lies between the Straits of Malacca and the South China Sea, as well as the former territories of North Borneo and Sarawak on the north coast of the island of Borneo. The portion on the Malay Peninsula was colonised by Portugal in 1511, taken away by the Dutch in 1641, and ceded by them to the British in 1824. It received its independence in 1957, and merged with the territories on Borneo in 1960. The small island of Singapore at the tip of the Malay Peninsula, site of one of the world's major seaports, was initially part of this merger but left in a few years to become a nation on its own. The British introduced steamships for coastal and inter-island trading, but traditional wooden boats, sailing and later motorised, continued to carry on some of these trades as well as inshore fishing, and Malaysia is one of the first countries in the region to preserve examples of these craft in a maritime museum setting.

Kemajuan
sailing fishing boat

Built Date not known
Propulsion Sail; perahu rig
Materials Wood throughout
Original use Fishing or cargo
Condition Intact
Present owners Terengganu Museum
Location Terengganu, Malaysia
History Example of a type of local traditional sailing craft preserved as an exhibit.

Sabar
sailing fishing boat

Built Date not known
Propulsion Sail; perahu rig
Materials Wood throughout
Original use Fishing or cargo
Condition Intact
Present owners Terengganu Museum
Location Terengganu, Malaysia
History Example of a local traditional sailing craft preserved as an exhibit.

Sri Trengganu
motor patrol vessel

Built 1961 by Vosper, Portsmouth, England
Original owners Royal Malaysian Navy
Propulsion Diesel engines, 3500hp. Engines built by Bristol Siddeley
Tonnage 96 displacement
Length 103.0ft/31.4m
Breadth 19.9ft/6.0m
Draught 5.6ft/1.7m
Materials Steel throughout
Original use Patrol vessel
Condition Intact, last used for training
Present owners Malacca Museum Corporation
Location Malacca, Malaysia
History Patrol vessel built in Great Britain for the Malaysian Navy. Currently preserved as a floating exhibit.

Malta

The three islands that make up this tiny nation are rocky and largely treeless. Since the sixteenth century Malta's primary importance has been its strategic location roughly midway between Gibraltar and Suez, and between Italy to the north and Africa to the south. At Valetta it has one of the finest harbours and natural naval bases in the world. Centuries ago the Maltese developed two distinctive local craft, the luzza used for fishing, once lateen-rigged and now motorised, and the DJASSA, used as a water taxi or ferry in the Grand Harbour of Valetta, which is usually rowed. Both are colourfully decorated, and seldom exceed thirty feet in length. Ship repair has become a major industry in Malta, which now has drydocks that can accommodate some of the largest supertankers. Smaller yards serve the international yachting community, which has found the islands a convenient place to have major work done on either steel or wood hulls.

Amazon
steam yacht

Built 1885 by Tankerville Chamberlayne, Southampton, England
Original owners Tankerville Chamberlayne
Propulsion Steam, screw, compound; replaced by diesel in 1937
Tonnage 58.06 gross
Length 91.2ft/27.79m
Breadth 15.1ft/4.6m
Draught 8.0ft/2.4m
Materials Wood planked over iron and wood frames
Original use Steam yacht
Condition Intact, restoration in progress
Present owners Mr & Mrs E Morgan-Busher
Contact address PO Box 85, Valletta CMR 01, Malta GC
Location Malta

Mexico

This country has two long coastlines, and little in the way of navigable internal waterways. Various types of fishing craft operate in coastal waters, and a small fleet of merchant shipping is employed primarily in the coastal trade. There is a museum of technology and transportation in the capital, Mexico City, which apparently has no boats among its collections. The only Mexican entry in this Register is an island steamer from southern California which is the subject of a last-ditch effort at preservation based in that State.

Catalina
passenger steamer

Built 1924 by Los Angeles Shipbuilding & Dry Dock Co, Los Angeles, California
Original owners Wilmington Transportation Co
Propulsion Steam, screw, triple expansion, 3600hp
Tonnage 1766 gross
Length 285.2ft/86.93m
Breadth 52.1ft/15.88m
Materials Steel throughout
Original use Passengers
Condition Poor; virtually abandoned
Location Ensenada, Mexico
History Built to ferry passengers and freight between San Pedro, California, and Catalina Island. Laid up; proposed for renovation as a floating restaurant.
Bibliography B44

Myanmar

Formerly the Kingdom of Burma, this country became a British colony in the nineteenth century, gaining its independence after the Second World War. The current military government, which came into power in the early 1990s, has done little to encourage modernisation of the country or to promote tourism but there are signs this may be changing. The major internal waterway of Myanmar is the Irrawaddy River, on which can be seen a wide variety of wooden craft. Dugout canoes are still plentiful, and some larger boats employ sail. Even larger motor vessels on the river have wooden hulls, and some have distinctive bow or stern designs that must go back centuries. The British introduced steamboats to the river, eventually placing in service several generations of large paddlewheel boats with iron or steel hulls produced by shipyards in England or Scotland.

Pandaw
sternwheel river steamer

Built 1947, by Yarrow, Scotstoun, Scotland
Original owners Irrawaddy Flotilla Co
Propulsion Steam, sternwheel, triple-expansion; now diesel screw
Tonnage 500 gross
Length 200.0ft/60.9m
Breadth 32.0ft/9.8m
Draught 7.6ft/2.3m
Materials Steel throughout
Original use Passengers and cargo
Condition In operation
Present owners Irrawaddy Flotilla Co
Location Mandalay, Myanmar

Catalina at Catalina Island, California, in 1975.

Netherlands

The Netherlands may well lead the world in the number of surviving historic vessels per square mile. For every example restored to sailing or steaming condition there are probably several more unrestored hulls serving as houseboats moored along the country's numerous rivers and canals. When large fleets of sailing craft are seen out on one of the lakes or bays of the Netherlands, they are as likely to be traditional vessels as modern yachts. Two of the oldest surviving steam warships, the turreted rams BUFFEL and SCHORPIOEN, are now floating museums in the Netherlands. The preservation in working condition of small steam tugboats for recreational use, by small groups of private individuals, seems to have originated in this country and later spread elsewhere in northern Europe, most notably to Sweden and Finland. The Netherlands has the oldest museum devoted to tugboats, both inland and oceangoing. The latter, several examples of which are now being preserved, represent a specialisation in deep-sea towing and salvage in which the Dutch take particular pride. The Netherlands has also led the way in the preservation of examples of the more prosaic harbour craft, from dredgers to floating grain elevators.

Abraham Crijnssen

Aaltje
tjalk

Built 1903 by Van Aller, Hasselt
Original owners Bosman, Hasselt
Propulsion Sail, sloop rig
Tonnage 129 gross
Length 85.4ft/25.65m
Breadth 16.0ft/4.82m
Draught 3.0ft/0.9m
Materials Steel hull
Original use Cargo
Condition In sailing condition
Present owners H Dijk
Location The Hague, Netherlands
History 'Tjalk' built to carry cargo in the Dutch coastal and inland waters trades. Operated until 1977. Restored to

sailing condition and converted to carry sailing parties 1993-94. Active during the summer months.

Abraham Crijnssen
minesweeper

Built 1936 by Gusto Shipyard, Schiedam, Netherlands
Original owners Royal Netherlands Navy
Official number A 925
Propulsion Steam turbines 1690ihp
Tonnage 450 displacement
Length 186.0ft/56.7m
Breadth 25.5ft/7.8m
Draught 6.9ft/2.1m
Materials Steel throughout
Original use Minesweeper
Condition Intact
Present owners Den Helder Marinemuseum
Location Den Helder, Netherlands
History Largely unaltered Dutch minesweeper of the 1930s. Was able to escape from the Dutch East Indies to Australia when the islands were invaded by the Japanese. Preserved as a floating exhibit.

Adelaar
steam tug

Built 1925 by Hubertina, Haarlem, Netherlands
Propulsion Steam, screw, 150hp

Length 67.7ft/20.62m
Breadth 17.4ft/5.3m
Draught 5.9ft/1.8m
Materials Steel hull, steel and wood superstructure
Original use Tug
Condition In operating condition
Location Beverwijk, Netherlands
History Steam tug employed for its first forty years in the harbour of Rotterdam. Maintained in operating condition by a private owner.

Advance
cargo steamer

Former name VIC 24
Built 1942 by Richard Dunston, Thorne, Yorkshire, England
Original owners British Royal Navy
Propulsion Steam, screw, compound, 110hp
Length 66.5ft/20.27m
Breadth 19.0ft/5.79m
Draught 8.5ft/2.59m

Adelaar

Materials Steel throughout
Original use Cargo
Condition In operating condition
Present owners Nigel Boston
Location Dordrecht, Netherlands
History Employed by the British Royal Navy at Scapa Flow, and later Portsmouth, transporting stores and ammunition. Restored to working condition by a private owner since 1983. Preserved as an active steamer.

Albatros
coasting ketch

Built 1899 by Kalkman, Capelle a d Ijssel, Netherlands
Propulsion Sail, ketch rig; engine added, 160hp
Tonnage 127 gross
Length 97.7ft/29.78m
Breadth 19.75ft/6.02m
Draught 7.02ft/2.14m
Materials Steel hull, wood masts
Original use Cargo
Condition In operating condition
Present owners Ton Brouwer, Edam, Netherlands
Location Amsterdam, Netherlands (based in Malta)
History Example of a Dutch 'Noordzeeklipper'. Cargo-carrying, under sail.

Alida
trading sloop

Former name ANTONIE, GERLI, NOOIT VOLMAAKT
Built 1903 by Draaisma Franeker, Netherlands
Propulsion Sail, sloop rig
Tonnage 15 gross
Length 42.77ft/13.04m
Breadth 9.8ft/2.98m
Draught 2.1ft/0.65m
Materials Steel throughout
Original use Cargo
Condition Intact
Present owners Noordelijk Scheepvaart Museum
Location Groningen, Netherlands
History Example of a Dutch 'Friese tjalk' formerly employed on the inland waterways of the Netherlands. Preserved as an onshore exhibit.

Alles Heeft Een Tijd
hagenaar

Former name AN GODS ZEGEN IS ALLES GELEGEN
Built 1914 by De Bock & Meier, Oude Wetering, Netherlands
Propulsion Sail, sloop rig, 'hagenaar'

Albatros

type
Tonnage 59 gross
Length 62.4ft/19.0m
Breadth 12.6ft/3.85m
Draught 1.1ft/0.35m
Materials Steel throughout
Original use Cargo
Condition Intact
Present owners Stichting Maritiem Buitenmuseum, Leuvehaven, Rotterdam
Location Rotterdam, Netherlands
History Example of a Dutch 'hagenaar' formerly employed on the inland

waterways of the Netherlands. Preserved as a floating exhibit.

Andries Jacob
fishing sloop

Former name DRIE GEBROEDERS, VROUWE ANTHONIE
Built 1900 by Dirk van Duivendijk, Tholen, Netherlands
Original owners Jan Bliek, Veere
Official number YE 36
Propulsion Sail, sloop rig
Length 48.72ft/14.85m

Breadth 16.08ft/4.9m
Draught 2.3ft/0.7m
Materials Wood throughout
Original use Fishing
Condition In sailing condition
Present owners Stichting Behoud Hoogaars
Contact address Postbus 480, 4380 AL Vlissingen
Location Veere-Sluis/Middelburg, Netherlands
History Example of a Dutch 'hoogaar' formerly used in the river estuaries of southwest Holland. Currently active.

Anita Jacoba
Zeeuwse klipper

Former name RISICO, EMANUEL, EBENHAEZER, LIA
Built 1892 by Ruitenberg, Waspik, Netherlands
Propulsion Sail, sloop rig
Tonnage 123 gross
Length 80.0ft/24.0m
Breadth 17.8ft/5.35m
Draught 4.4ft/1.1m
Materials Iron hull, wood mast
Original use Cargo
Condition In sailing condition
Present owners Rob van het Hof
Location Schiedam, Netherlands
History Type of sailing cargo vessel formerly employed in the coastal and inland waters trade known as a 'Zeeuwse klipper'. Converted to carry sailing parties and restored to her original rig in 1970-71.

Anke Langenberg
steam tug

Former name RONNY
Built 1949 by Biesbosch, Dordrecht, Netherlands
Propulsion Steam, screw
Length 136.2ft/41.5m
Original use Tug
Condition Undergoing restoration
Location Dordrecht, Netherlands
History Proposed as an active steam vessel.

Anna
klipper

Built 1896
Propulsion Sail, sloop rig; 'klipper' type
Original use Cargo
Condition In sailing condition
Location Dordrecht, Netherlands
History Currently an active sailing vessel.

Annigje
hassalter aak

Built 1908 by Van Goot, Kampen, Netherlands
Original owners G Hutton, Kampen
Propulsion Sail, sloop rig; 'hassalter aak' type
Tonnage 108 gross
Length 74.52ft/22.72m
Breadth 15.65ft/4.77m
Draught 4.5ft/1.38m
Materials Iron hull
Original use Cargo
Condition Intact
Present owners Stichting Maritiem

Annigje

Buitenmuseum, Leuvehaven, Rotterdam
Location Rotterdam, Netherlands
History Example of a Dutch 'hassalter aak', formerly used on the inland waterways of The Netherlands. Preserved as a floating exhibit.
Bibliography D132

Arbeid Adelt
stevenaak

Built 1884
Propulsion Sail, ketch rig; 'stevenaak' type
Original use Cargo
Condition In sailing condition
Location Groningen, Netherlands
History Currently an active sailing vessel.

Balder
logger

Former name ZEEAREND, OCEAAN I
Built 1912 by A de Jong, Vlaardingen, Netherlands
Original owners Visserij Mij 'Mercurius', 'Vlaardingen'
Official number VL 92
Propulsion Sail, ketch rig
Tonnage 105 gross

Balder

Bonaire at Den Helder for restoration

Length 78.08ft/23.8m
Breadth 21.65ft/6.6m
Draught 10.17ft/3.1m
Materials Steel hull, wood deckhouse
Original use Fishing
Condition Fully restored
Present owners Ver Nederlandisch
Scheepvaart Museum
Contact address Kattenburgerplein 1,
1018K Amsterdam, Netherlands
Location Amsterdam, Netherlands
History Type of Dutch sailing vessel
known as a 'logger' formerly used in
the North Sea fisheries. Fully restored
for exhibition afloat at Amsterdam
beside the maritime museum.
Bibliography D131

Bisschop Van Arkel
coasting schooner

Former name ANTJE ADELHEIT,
ADELHEIT
Built 1900 by J J Pattje, Waterhuizen,
Netherlands
Original owners Located in Idafehn,
Germany
Propulsion Sail, schooner rig; diesel
engine added, 200hp
Tonnage 79 gross
Length 88.09ft/26.85m
Breadth 18.37ft/5.6m

Draught 6.36ft/1.94m
Materials Steel hull, wood masts
Original use Cargo
Condition In sailing condition
Present owners Gerrit van der Veer
Location Kampen, Netherlands
History Example of a Dutch coastal
schooner with flat bottom and
leeboards. Restored in 1979-84.
Currently used for charter.

Bonaire
cruising gunboat

Former name ABEL TASMAN
Built 1877 by Wilton Fijenoord,
Rotterdam, Netherlands
Original owners Royal Netherlands
Navy
Propulsion Sail, barquentine rig; steam
auxiliary
Tonnage 837 displacement
Length 176.0ft/53.64m
Breadth 29.5ft/8.99m
Draught 12.67ft/3.86m
Materials Iron hull wood sheathed
Original use Cruising gunboat
Condition Hull survives; undergoing
restoration
Present owners Stichting 'Bonaire'
Delfzeil
Location Den Helder, Netherlands

History Built as a cruising gunboat for
the Dutch Navy. Served for many years
as floating classrooms for a school in
Delfzijl, housed over without rig. Has
now been moved to Den Helder for
exhibit during restoration to original
appearance.
Bibliography A14

Bracksand
klipper

Former name SUZA
Built 1899 at Groningen, Netherlands
Propulsion Sail, ketch rig; auxiliary
engine, 225hp. Engine built by
Mercedes (1952)
Length 118.3ft/36.05m
Breadth 21.7ft/6.6m
Draught 4.1ft/1.24m
Original use Cargo
Condition In sailing condition
Present owners Rederij Zierikzee BV
Location Zierikzee, Netherlands
History Two-masted 'klipper' formerly
used in coastal trading from Denmark
to Portugal. Now used for charters on
inland waters of the Netherlands.

Buffel
seagoing turret ram

Former name HR MS BUFFEL
Built 1867 by Napier, Glasgow, Scotland
Original owners Royal Netherlands
Navy
Propulsion Steam, screw, twin
compound, 2200hp
Tonnage 2261 displacement
Length 205.71ft/62.7m
Breadth 40.22ft/12.26m
Depth 24.93ft/7.6m
Draught 4.72m
Materials Iron hull
Original use Ram and seagoing turret
ship
Condition Restored, without original
engines or armament
Present owners Prins Hendrik Museum
Location Rotterdam, Netherlands
History Coast-defence turret ram
which served for many years as a
stationary training hulk in the
Amsterdam navy yard. Fully restored
as a museum ship at Rotterdam.
Bibliography D336

Buffel

De Vier Gebroeders

Christiaan Brunings
waterways inspection steamer

Built 1900 by Jan F Meursing, Amsterdam, Netherlands
Original owners Rijkswaterstaat
Propulsion Steam, screw, coal fired, 375hp
Tonnage 51.8 gross
Length 95.8ft/29.2m
Breadth 20.5ft/6.25m
Draught 9.2ft/2.8m
Materials Steel hull, wood and steel superstructure
Original use Waterways inspection
Condition Excellent, in operating condition
Present owners Nederlands Scheepvaart Museum
History Fully restored and exhibited as an operating steam vessel.
Location Amsterdam, Netherlands

De Drie Gebroeders
fishing sloop

Former name HD305, LE7, WR76, UK14
Built 1894 by U Zwolsman, Workum, Netherlands
Original owners P Vlaming Bzn
Official number TX 11
Propulsion Sail, sloop rig
Length 47.56ft/14.5m
Materials Wood throughout
Original use Fishing

Condition Preserved in poor condition
Present owners Maritime Museum at Oudeschild
Location Oudeschild, Netherlands
History Example of a Dutch 'blazer', a type of sailing fishing vessel formerly employed in the coastal waters of The Netherlands. Preserved as an onshore exhibit.

De Hoop
trading sloop

Built 1890 by Fernhout, Smilde, Netherlands
Propulsion Sail, sloop rig
Tonnage 96.2 gross
Length 68.01ft/20.73m
Breadth 15.91ft/4.82m
Draught 1.8ft/0.54m

Materials Steel hull
Original use Cargo
Condition Intact
Present owners Stichting Maritiem Buitenmuseum, Leuvehaven, Rotterdam
Location Rotterdam, Netherlands
History Example of a Dutch 'dektjalk' formerly employed on the inland waterways of The Netherlands. Preserved as an onshore exhibit.

De Hoop
trading sloop

Former name NOOIT VOLMAAKT
Built 1901 by G J van Goor, Meppel, Netherlands
Original owners Arend van Oosten
Propulsion Sail, sloop rig
Tonnage 42.8 gross
Length 58.38ft/17.8m
Breadth 12.96ft/3.95m
Materials Steel hull
Original use Cargo
Condition In sailing condition
Present owners Zuiderzeemuseum
Location Enkhuizen, Netherlands
History Example of a Dutch 'boierpraam' formerly employed on the inland waterways of The Netherlands. Currently exhibited.

De Koningssloep
royal barge

Built 1818 by Rijkswerf, Rotterdam, Netherlands
Original owners King Willem I
Propulsion Rowed

De Koningssloep

Tonnage 6 displacement
Length 55.94ft/17.05m
Breadth 8.73ft/2.66m
Materials Wood throughout (oak)
Original use Royal barge
Condition Fully restored
Present owners Royal Netherlands Navy
Location Amsterdam, Netherlands
History Barge last used for the Royal
Wedding in October 1962. Fully
restored in 1986. Preserved as an
indoor exhibit.

De Nederlander
sidewheel steam ferry

Former name WESTERSHELDE
Built 1905 by J & K Smit, Kinderdijk,
Netherlands
Original owners Provinciale
Stoomboot Dienst, Middelburg
Propulsion Steam, sidewheel, inclined
(now compound), 140hp
Length 168.92ft/51.5m
Breadth 37.7ft/11.5m
Draught 7.3ft/2.22m
Materials Steel throughout
Original use Ferry
Condition In operation
Present owners Nederlandse
Raderstoomboot Maatschappij
Location Rotterdam, Netherlands
History Steam sidewheel ferryboat
reduced to a bunkering landing stage
without engines and boilers in 1933.
Restored since 1988 with an engine
built in 1923. Currently used for
charter.
Bibliography B43, C6a

De Tukker
Schoeneraak

Built 1912
Propulsion Sail, ketch rig; 'Schoeneraak'
type
Original use Cargo
Condition In sailing condition
Location Enschede, Netherlands
History Currently an active sailing
vessel.

De Vier Gebroeders
trading sloop

Built 1890 by Ruytenberg, Waspik,
Netherlands
Propulsion Sail, sloop rig
Tonnage 110 gross
Length 68.07ft/20.7m
Breadth 16.5ft/5.03m
Draught 6.88ft/2.1m
Materials Iron hull
Original use Cargo
Condition Intact
Present owners Zuiderzeemuseum
Location Enkhuizen, Netherlands
History Example of a Dutch 'hektjalk',
formerly employed on the inland
waterways of The Netherlands.
Preserved as a floating exhibit.

Dockyard V
steam tug

Built 1947 by Rotterdam Drydock Co,
Rotterdam, Netherlands
Propulsion Steam, screw, 500hp. Engine
built by Lentz
Length 82.2ft/25.06m

Dockyard V

Breadth 20.7ft/6.31m
Draught 9.51ft/2.9m
Materials Steel hull, steel and wood
superstructure
Original use Tug
Condition Intact
Present owners Maritiem
Buitenmuseum
Location Rotterdam, Netherlands
History Preserved as a floating exhibit.

Dockyard IX
steam tug

Built 1939 by Rotterdam Drydock,
Rotterdam, Netherlands
Propulsion Steam, screw, 500hp
Tonnage 230 gross
Length 82.1ft/25.0m
Breadth 20.8ft/6.35m

Draught 9.9ft/3.0m
Materials Steel hull, steel and wood
superstructure
Original use Tug
Condition In operating condition
Present owners Maritiem
Buitenmuseum, Leuvehaven
Location Rotterdam, Netherlands
History Currently an operating steam
vessel.

Drie Gebroeders
sailing coaster

Built c1900
Propulsion Sail
Tonnage 20 gross
Length 37.7ft/11.5m
Breadth 11.2ft/3.4m
Draught 1.0ft/0.3m

De Nederlander

Original use Cargo
Condition Intact
Present owners Maritiem
Buitenmuseum
Location Rotterdam, Netherlands
History Preserved as an exhibit.

Ebenhaezer
bolschip

Built 1928 by Velthuis, Groningen,
Netherlands
Propulsion Sail, sloop rig; 'bolschip'
type
Tonnage 64.5 gross
Length 68.8ft/20.95m
Breadth 13.6ft/4.14m
Draught 2.2ft/0.68m
Original use Cargo
Condition On exhibit
Present owners Veenkolonial Museum
Location Veendam, Netherlands
History Preserved as an exhibit.

Elfin
torpedo recovery vessel

Former name TCA 1, HOM 7,
DROOGDOK 18
Built 1933 by J Samuel White, East
Cowes, Isle of Wight, England
Original owners British Royal Navy
Propulsion Steam, screw, two
compound engines, 250hp
Length 108.0ft/32.9m
Breadth 24.9ft/7.6m
Draught 7.5ft/2.3m
Original use Torpedo recovery vessel
Condition Restoration proposed
Present owners Stichting tot Behoud
van het Stoomschip
Location Wormerveer, Netherlands
History Proposed as an active steamer.

Emma
sontvaarder

Built 1931
Propulsion Sail, ketch rig; 'sontvaarder'
type
Original use Cargo
Condition In sailing condition
Location Lelystad, Netherlands
History Currently an active sailing
vessel.

Engelina
koftjalk

Built 1909
Propulsion Sail, ketch rig; 'koftjalk' type
Original use Cargo
Condition In sailing condition
Location Staveren, Netherlands
History Currently active.

Elfin

Familietrouw
trading sloop

Built 1894 at Stadskanaal, Netherlands
Propulsion Sail, sloop rig
Tonnage 32.5 gross
Length 54.2ft/16.5m
Breadth 13.2ft/4.02m
Draught 1.6ft/0.49m
Original use Cargo
Condition Intact
Present owners Veenkolonial Museum
Location Nieuwe Pekela, Netherlands
History Preserved as a floating exhibit.

Finland
steam tug

Former name DELFSHAVEN, HERCULES,
ARABE
Built 1921 by De Groot & van Vliet,
Sukkerveer
Propulsion Steam, screw, triple
expansion, 225hp, coal-fired
Length 73.73ft/22.48m
Breadth 17.3ft/5.27m
Draught 8.2ft/2.5m
Materials Steel hull, steel and wood
superstructure
Original use Tug
Condition In operating condition

Present owners D Vastenhout
Location Rotterdam, Netherlands
History Currently an operating steam
vessel maintained by steam enthusiasts
at Rotterdam.

Friesland
dredger

Built 1936 by Holthuis, Veendam,
Netherlands
Propulsion Non-self propelled
Tonnage 15 gross
Length 84.4ft/25.72m
Breadth 22.63ft/6.9m
Draught 4.9ft/1.5m
Materials Steel throughout
Original use Dredger
Condition Intact
Present owners Stichting
Stoombaggermolen
Contact address Boskalis Westminster,
Sliedrecht
Location Sliedrecht, Netherlands
History Preserved as a floating exhibit.

Furie
seagoing steam tug

Former name HOLMVIK, HOLMEN III,
GEBR BODEWES VI
Built 1916 by G & H Bodewes,
Martinshoek, Netherlands
Original owners G & H Bodewes
Propulsion Steam, screw, 450hp
Length 99.32ft/30.28m
Breadth 19.91ft/6.07m
Draught 10.17ft/3.1m

Furie

Geertruida

Materials Steel throughout
Original use Seagoing tug
Condition In operating condition
Present owners Stichting Hollands Glorie
Location Maasluis, Netherlands
History Oldest Dutch seagoing tugboat. Preserved as an exhibit and operating steam vessel.

Gabrielle
steam tug

Former name AMELIE, ODETTE, RACHAEL, WILLY
Built 1903 by Gebr Wiemann, Brandenburg, Germany
Propulsion Steam, screw, 125hp
Length 64.0ft/19.5m
Breadth 14.3ft/4.35m
Draught 5.6ft/1.7m
Materials Steel hull, steel and wood superstructure
Original use Tug
Condition In operating condition
Location De Woude, Netherlands
History Currently an operating steam vessel.

Gebroeders Bever
steam tug

Former name DOCKYARD III
Built 1941 by Rotterdamse Droogdok Maatschappij, Rotterdam, Netherlands
Propulsion Steam, screw, 500hp. Engine built by Lentz
Length 82.2ft/25.06m

Breadth 20.7ft/6.31m
Draught 8.7ft/2.65m
Materials Steel hull, steel and wood superstructure
Original use Tug
Condition In operating condition
Location Dordrecht, Netherlands
History Currently an operating steam vessel.

Geertruida
towed lighter

Built 1906 by Gebr Boot, Leiderdorp, Netherlands
Original owners H Maas, Bergen op Zoom
Propulsion Towed by steam tugs; diesel engine since 1956, 110hp
Tonnage 424 gross
Length 142.84ft/43.55m
Breadth 24.0ft/7.3m
Draught 7.2ft/2.19m
Materials Steel hull, steel and wood superstructure
Original use Cargo
Condition Intact
Present owners Maritiem Buitenmuseum, Leuvehaven, Rotterdam
Location Rotterdam, Netherlands
History Example of the type of towed barge known as a 'sleepkastje' used on the River Rhine and connecting waterways. Preserved as a floating exhibit.

Gruno
trading sloop

Built 1899 by Barkmeijer, Sneek, Netherlands
Propulsion Sail, sloop rig
Tonnage 120 gross
Length 73.8ft/22.5m
Breadth 15.8ft/4.8m

Draught 1.8ft/0.55m
Materials Steel hull
Original use Cargo
Condition Intact
Present owners Maritiem Buitenmuseum, Leuvehaven, Rotterdam
Location Rotterdam, Netherlands
History Example of a 'Groninger tjalk' used to carry cargo on the coastal and inland trades of The Netherlands. Preserved as a floating exhibit.

Gudsekop
trading sloop

Former name FRIESLAND
Built 1908 by Akke van der Zee, Joure, Netherlands
Propulsion Sail, sloop rig
Tonnage 18.5 gross
Length 43.14ft/13.15m
Breadth 9.91ft/3.02m
Draught 3.51ft/1.07m
Materials Steel hull
Original use Cargo
Condition In sailing condition
Present owners Stichting Gudsekop, Utrecht
Location Akkrum, Netherlands
History Example of a type of working sailing vessel known as a 'skutsje' formerly used on the inland waterways of Friesland and Groningen originally built to transport potatoes. In use as a training vessel.

Gudsekop

Havendienst 20

motor tug

Built 1941 by Gebr Paans, Rodevaart, Netherlands
Propulsion Diesel engine, 240hp. Engine built by Schraube
Tonnage 10 gross
Length 60.2ft/18.33m
Breadth 14.7ft/4.47m
Draught 6.2ft/1.9m
Materials Steel throughout
Original use Tug
Condition Intact
Present owners Buitenmuseum
Location Rotterdam, Netherlands
History Preserved as a floating exhibit.

Heaven

lightship

Former name LIGHTVESSEL No 8, SMITH KNOLL
Built in Great Britain
Original owners Trinity House
Propulsion Towed to station
Materials Steel throughout
Original use Lightship
Condition Intact, in use
Location Rotterdam, Netherlands
History In use as a discoteque.

Heiltje

hagenaar

Built 1895
Propulsion Sail, sloop rig; 'hagenaar' type
Original use Cargo
Condition In sailing condition
Location Amsterdam, Netherlands
History Currently an active sailing vessel.

Helena

sailing coaster

Built 1876 by Jonker, Kinderdijk, Netherlands
Original owners W F Frommand
Propulsion Sail
Materials Iron hull
Original use Cargo
Condition Hull has survived as a barge, unrigged
Present owners Stichting Rotterdamse Zeilschip
Location Rotterdam, Netherlands
History Currently undergoing restoration.

Hercules

steam tug

Former name FREMAD, GEBR BODEWES

Holland

Built 1915 by Bodewes, Martenshoek, Netherlands
Propulsion Steam, screw, compound, 225hp
Length 71.2ft/21.7m
Breadth 18.2ft/5.56m
Draught 7.5ft/2.3m
Materials Steel hull
Original use Tug
Condition In operating condition
Present owners Stichting Calorische Werktuigen te Schiedam
Location Schiedam, Netherlands
History Currently an operating steam vessel.

Holland

motor salvage tug

Built 1949 by J Smit & Son, Foxhol, Netherlands
Original owners Doeksen Salvage, Terschelling, Netherlands
Propulsion Diesel engine, 2100hp
Tonnage 547.77 gross
Length 191.7ft/57.56m
Breadth 31.6ft/9.5m
Materials Steel throughout
Original use Salvage tug
Condition Intact; last used as research vessel
Present owners Stichting Vriendenkring
Location Den Helder, Netherlands
History Proposed as a floating exhibit.

Houtepen

minesweeper

Built 1961 by De Noord, Alblasserdam, Netherlands
Original owners Royal Netherlands Navy
Official number M 882
Propulsion Diesel engine, 1100hp
Length 108.6ft/33.08m
Breadth 22.5ft/6.87m
Draught 5.9ft/1.8m
Original use Minesweeper
Condition Intact
Present owners Mariniers Museum
Location Rotterdam, Netherlands
History Preserved as a floating exhibit.

Hudson

seagoing motor tug

Former name EBRO
Built 1939 by Smit Shipyard, Rotterdam, Netherlands

Hugo

Hydrograaf

Hugo
steam tug

Former name HUGO HEDRICH
Built 1929 by Botje & Ensing,
Groningen, Netherlands
Propulsion Steam, screw, compound,
150hp
Length 60.7ft/18.5m
Breadth 17.1ft/5.2m
Draught 7.7ft/2.35m
Materials Steel hull
Original use Tug
Condition In operating condition
Location Zaandam, Netherlands
History Currently an operating steam
vessel.

Original owners Smit Towing Co
Propulsion Diesel engines, 600hp
Tonnage 294 gross
Length 115.7ft/37.55m
Breadth 24.4ft/7.4m
Draught 12.9ft/3.5111
Materials Steel throughout
Original use Seagoing tug
Condition Restoration in progress
Present owners Stichting Help De
Hudson
Contact address Mer Gijzenstraat 29,
4681 BN NW-Vossemeer
Location Rotterdam, Netherlands
History Dutch seagoing tug employed
in worldwide towing. Currently being
restored to serve as a floating exhibit.

Hydrograaf
steam survey ship

Built 1910 by Wilton Fijenoord,
Rotterdam, Netherlands
Original owners Royal Netherlands
Navy
Propulsion Steam, screw; converted to
diesel
Tonnage 209 gross
Length 134.69ft/40.45m
Breadth 22.31ft/6.7m
Materials Iron hull, iron and wood
superstructure
Original use Hydrographic surveying
Condition Intact, in operation,
outwardly unmodernised
Present owners Reederij De Hydrograaf
BV Bilthoven
Location Amsterdam, Netherlands
History Currently available for charter.

Ideaal
Friese maatkast

Built 1926
Propulsion Sail, sloop rig; 'Friese
maatkast' type
Original use Cargo
Condition In sailing condition
Location Beneden-Rijn, Netherlands
History Currently an active sailing
vessel.

Insulinde
rescue lifeboat

Built 1926 by Gebr Niestern, Delzijl,
Netherlands
Original owners Dutch lifeboat service
Propulsion Diesel engine
Length 61.66ft/18.8m
Breadth 13.3ft/4.05m
Draught 4.3ft/1.3m
Materials Steel throughout
Original use Rescue lifeboat

Condition Intact
Present owners Nederlands Scheepvaart
Museum
Location Amsterdam, Netherlands
History World's first motorised self-
righting and self-bailing lifeboat.
Preserved as a floating exhibit.
Bibliography A16

Jacob Langenberg
steam tug

Former name VON BOTTICHER
Built 1902 by Schichau AG, Elbing,
Germany
Propulsion Steam, screw
Length 87.8ft/26.75m
Breadth 21.8ft/6.63m
Draught 10.5ft/3.2m
Materials Steel hull
Original use Tug
Condition In operating condition
Present owners Stichting tot Behoud
van het Stoomschip te Medem
Location Medemblik, Netherlands
History Currently an operating steam
vessel.

Jan De Sterke
steam tug

Former name HENDRINA II, MARIETTE
Built 1913 by v Straaten en v d Brink,
S'Gravenhage, Netherlands
Propulsion Steam, screw, 65hp
Length 47.2ft/14.37m
Breadth 12.8ft/3.9m
Draught 5.4ft/1.65m
Materials Steel hull, steel and wood
superstructure
Original use Tug
Condition In operating condition

Insulinde

Present owners Stichting 'De Compound'
Location Gorinchem, Netherlands
History Currently an active steam vessel.

Jan Van Der Heyde
motor fireboat

Built 1930 by A Pahl, Hamburg, Germany
Propulsion Petrol engines. Engines built by Maybach
Length 55.8ft/17.0m
Breadth 12.3ft/3.75m
Draught 4.1ft/1.25m
Materials Steel throughout
Original use Fireboat
Condition Intact
Present owners Nationaal Brandweermuseum, Hellevoetsluis
Location Rotterdam, Netherlands
History Preserved as a floating exhibit.

Jantina
trading sloop

Built 1895 by Vermeulen, Woerden, Netherlands
Propulsion Sail, sloop rig; auxiliary engine added in 1942
Tonnage 34 gross
Length 59.04ft/18.0m
Breadth 11.3ft/3.45m
Draught 1.1ft/0.34m

Jan de Sterke

Materials Steel hull
Original use Cargo
Condition Undergoing restoration to 1942 appearance
Present owners Maritiem Buitenmuseum, Leuvehaven, Rotterdam
Location Rotterdam, Netherlands
History Example of a Dutch 'bok' formerly employed on the inland waterways of The Netherlands. Preserved as floating exhibit.

Johannes
steam tug

Former name SCHILL
Built 1908 by Wollheim, Cosel, nr Breslau, Germany
Original owners Berliner Lloyd
Propulsion Steam, screw, compound, 120hp, coal fired
Length 51.5ft/15.7m
Breadth 14.43ft/4.4m
Draught 5.08ft/1.55m
Materials Steel hull
Original use Tug
Condition In operating condition, passenger cabin added aft
Present owners Simon Visser
Contact address Zuideinde 212, Westzaan, Netherlands
Location Westzaan, Netherlands
History German steam tugboat acquired by Dutch owners in 1973. In use as an excursion steamer.
Bibliography D68

Jonge Pieter
westlander

Built 1911
Propulsion Sail, sloop rig; 'westlander' type
Original use Cargo
Condition In sailing condition
Location Ter Aar, Netherlands
History Currently an active sailing vessel.

Johannes

Joris II
floating crane

Built 1937 by De Klop, Sliedrecht, Netherlands
Propulsion Diesel hoisting engine
Length 56.0ft/17.05m
Breadth 24.3ft/7.4m
Draught 1.6ft/0.5m
Materials Steel throughout
Original use Floating crane
Condition Intact
Present owners Maritiem Buitenmuseum
Location Rotterdam, Netherlands
History Preserved as a floating exhibit.

Kapitein Kok
sidewheel steamer

Former name REEDERIJ OP DE LEK 6
Built 1912 by J & K Smit, Krimpen an den Lek, Netherlands
Original owners Stoomboot Reederij op de Lek, Schoonhoven
Propulsion Steam, sidewheel, compound; converted to diesel
Length 189.85ft/57.88m
Breadth 44.77ft/13.65m
Draught 8.86ft/2.7m
Materials Steel throughout
Original use Passengers
Condition In operation
Present owners Raderboot Kapitein Kok BV
Location Amsterdam, Netherlands
History Built to operate on the River Lek out of Rotterdam. Sold to German owners in 1950 and used as a floating restaurant on the Rhine. Returned to The Netherlands and restored to passenger service.
Bibliography B16, B43, C6a

L-9512
landing craft

Built 1962 by Rijkswerf, Den Helder, Netherlands
Original owners Royal Netherlands Navy
Official number L-9512
Propulsion Diesel engine, 200hp
Length 47.4ft/14.45m
Breadth 11.8ft/3.6m
Draught 4.6ft/1.4m
Original use Landing craft
Condition Intact
Present owners Mariniers Museum
Location Rotterdam, Netherlands
History Preserved as a floating exhibit.

Lena
trading sloop

Former name EERSTE ZORG, JAN, NICO, NOOITEGEDACHT, VROUW WILH
Built 1878 by van der Giessen, Krimpen a d Ijssel, Netherlands
Original owners D Westerduin, Rotterdam
Propulsion Sail, sloop rig
Tonnage 60 gross
Length 66.14ft/20.16m
Breadth 12.24ft/3.73m
Draught 1.4ft/0.43m
Materials Iron hull
Original use Cargo
Condition Intact
Present owners Buitenmuseum
Location Rotterdam, Netherlands
History Example of a type of working sailing vessel known as a 'kraak'. Preserved as an exhibit.

Lichtschip No 10
lightship

Former name TEXEL
Built 1952 by Rijkswerf Willemsoord, Den Helder, Netherlands
Original owners Netherlands lighthouse service
Propulsion Towed to station
Length 149.0ft/45.4m
Breadth 26.0ft/7.9m
Draught 10.0ft/2.93m
Materials Steel throughout
Original use Lightship
Condition Intact
Present owners St Kustverlichting
Location Den Helder, Netherlands
History Preserved as a floating exhibit.

Lichtschip No 12
lightship

Former name NOORDHINDER
Built 1963 by Zaltbommel, De Waal, Netherlands
Original owners Netherlands lighthouse service
Propulsion Towed to station
Length 151.0ft/46.0m
Breadth 26.3ft/8.0m
Draught 9.8ft/3.0m
Materials Steel throughout
Original use Lightship
Condition Intact
Location Hellevoetsluis, Netherlands
History Preserved as a floating exhibit.

Lightvessel No 12
lightship

Former name OUTER GABBARD
Built c1968 in Great Britain
Original owners Trinity House
Propulsion Towed to station
Materials Steel throughout
Original use Lightship
Condition Intact, unconverted
Location Dordrecht, Netherlands
History Proposed floating restaurant.

Loodsschoener Nr 1
pilot vessel

Former name SILVER SPRAY
Built 1916 by Piet Smit Jr, Rotterdam, Netherlands
Original owners Netherlands State Pilotage Service
Propulsion Sail, schooner rig
Tonnage 99 gross
Length 92.0ft/28.04m
Breadth 20.7ft/6.31m
Draught 5.15ft/1.57m
Materials Steel hull
Original use Pilot vessel
Condition Hull survived intact; current status unknown
Location Rotterdam, Netherlands

Maarten
steam tug

Built 1926 by Gebr v d Werf, Nijmegen, Netherlands
Propulsion Steam, screw, triple expansion, 150hp. Engine built by I A Kreber, Vlaardingen
Length 63.9ft/19.46m
Breadth 15.4ft/4.7m
Draught 6.9ft/2.1m
Materials Steel hull, steel and wood superstructure
Original use Tug
Condition In operating condition
Present owners Stichting Stoomboot Maarten

Kapitein Kok

Location Leeuwarden, Netherlands
History Currently an operating steam vessel.

Maashaven
steam tug

Built 1915 at Rotterdam
Original owners Nederlandse Stoomsleepdienst van P Smit Jr
Propulsion Steam, screw; converted to diesel
Tonnage 5.486 gross
Length 39.53ft/12.05m
Breadth 10.86ft/3.31m
Draught 4.76ft/1.45m
Materials Steel throughout
Original use Tug
Condition Intact
Present owners Maritime Buitenmuseum
Location Rotterdam, Netherlands
History Veteran diesel tug formerly steam-powered. Served under a number of owners. Acquired in 1998 for exhibition by the musuem.

Mercuur
minesweeper

Former name HR HS MERCUUR, HR HS ONVERSCHROKKEN, AM-483
Built 1953 by Peterson Builders Inc, Sturgeon Bay, Wisconsin
Original owners United States Navy
Official number A 856
Propulsion Diesel engines, 1600hp
Tonnage 735 displacement
Length 172.0ft/52.43m
Breadth 36.0ft/10.97m
Draught 10.7ft/3.25m
Materials Wood throughout
Original use Minesweeper
Condition Intact
Present owners Stichting Behoud Maritieme Monumenten, Den Haag
Location Scheveningen, Netherlands
History Non-magnetic wooden minesweeper built for the US Navy and later transferred to The Netherlands. Preserved as a floating exhibit.

Merula
tug

Built 1907
Length 67.0ft/20.4m
Breadth 10.2ft/3.1m
Materials Steel hull, steel and wood superstructure
Original use Tug
Condition Intact
Location Kijkduin, Netherlands

Maarten

History Preserved as an onshore exhibit.

Mijl Op Zeven
westlandse pram

Built c1916
Propulsion Non-self-propelled
Tonnage 10 displacement
Length 36.1ft/11.0m

Breadth 7.5ft/2.3m
Draught 0.7ft/0.2m
Original use Cargo barge; 'westlandse praam'
Condition Intact
Present owners Maritiem Buitenmuseum
Location Rotterdam, Netherlands
History Preserved as a floating exhibit.

Mijn Genoegen
river klipper

Former name NOOIT VOLMAAKT, VAN KINSBERGEN
Built 1899 at Geertruidenberg, Netherlands
Propulsion Sail, sloop rig; 'river klipper' type
Tonnage 159 displacement
Length 70.8ft/21.57m
Original use Cargo
Condition Intact
Present owners Stichting Museumhaven Zierikzee
Location Zierikzee, Netherlands
History Preserved as a floating exhibit.

MK-63
sailing fishing boat

Built 1912 by De Haas, Monnikendam, Netherlands
Original owners Jan Uithuisje, Marken
Official number MK-63
Propulsion Sail, cutter rig
Tonnage 15 gross
Length 43.3ft/13.5m
Breadth 14.0ft/4.2m
Draught 3.3ft/1.0m
Materials Wood throughout
Original use Fishing
Condition In sailing condition

Mercuur

MK-63

Present owners Peter Dorleijn
Location Hoorn, Netherlands
History Currently an active sailing vessel.

Neeltje
motor fishing boat

Built 1939 by v d Beldt, West-Graftdijk, Netherlands
Official number WR 103
Propulsion Diesel engine, 140hp
Length 83.3ft/25.39m
Breadth 14.1ft/4.3m
Draught 3.3ft/1.0m
Original use Fishing
Condition Intact
Present owners Delta-Expo
Location Oosterscheldedam, Netherlands
History Preserved as an onshore exhibit.

Neerlandia
koftjalk

Built 1910
Propulsion Sail, sloop rig; 'koftjalk' type
Original use Cargo
Condition In sailing condition
Location Kampen, Netherlands
History Currently an active sailing vessel.

Nescio
klipper sloop

Former name TRUUS DELTA-8
Built 1903 by Werf 'De Hoop', Leiden, Netherlands
Original owners R Zuurmondt
Propulsion Sail, sloop rig, kerosene engine, 20hp
Length 77.6ft/23.2m
Breadth 16.0ft/4.83m
Draught 3.8ft/1.15m
Materials Steel hull, wood spars
Original use Cargo
Condition In sailing condition
Present owners H J Hollander
Location Swartsluis, Netherlands
History 'Klipper' sloop formerly employed on the inland waterways of the Netherlands. Converted to a tanker in 1965. Restored to original condition in 1984 with passenger accommodations.

Nieuwe Zorg
Friese tjalk

Built 1901 by Van de Werf, Drachten, Netherlands
Propulsion Sail, sloop rig
Tonnage 86 gross
Length 74.4ft/22.35m
Breadth 16.0ft/4.78m

Draught 3.7ft/1.1m
Materials Steel hull, wood mast
Original use Cargo
Condition In sailing condition
Present owners Veldhuis
Location Kampen, Netherlands
History Type of sailing cargo vessel known as a 'Friese tjalk' formerly employed in the Dutch coastal and inland waters trades. Converted to carry sailing parties and restored to original rig in 1985.

No 19
floating grain elevator

Built 1926 by Chantier Naval J Cockerill, Hoboken, Belgium
Original owners Located in Port of Antwerp, Belgium
Propulsion Non-self-propelled; steam-powered machinery
Tonnage 560 gross, 560 displacement
Length 100.0ft/30.46m
Breadth 34.3ft/10.46m
Materials Steel throughout
Original use Floating grain elevator
Condition Intact, machinery in working condition
Present owners Maritiem Buitenmuseum, Leuvehaven, Rotterdam
Location Rotterdam, Netherlands
History Preserved as a floating exhibit.

Noord Holland
sailing yacht

Built 1905 by Scheepswerf Gebr Boot, Leiderdorp, Netherlands
Original owners Netherlands State Waterways Department
Propulsion Sail, sloop rig; diesel engine, 45hp
Length 75.44ft/23.0m
Breadth 16.4ft/5.0m
Draught 7.22ft/2.2m
Materials Steel hull, wood deckhouses and masts
Original use Yacht
Condition In sailing condition; deckhouse altered
Present owners Netherlands State Waterways Department
Location Lelystad, Netherlands
History Built as a private yacht and acquired by the State Waterways

Noord Holland

Noordzee

Original use Cargo
Condition In sailing condition
Present owners Rob Peetoom
Location Delft, Netherlands
History Example of a type of working
vessel known as a 'Zeeuwse Paviljoen
Tjalk' formerly employed on the inland
waterways of the Netherlands.
Restored to sailing condition in 1970,
and converted in 1987 to carry sailing
parties.

Pieter Bel
sailing fishing boat

Built 1917
Propulsion Sail, sloop rig; 'kwak' type
Original use Fishing
Condition In sailing condition

Location The Hague, Netherlands
History Currently an active sailing
vessel.

Pieter Boele
river tug

Former name SPECULANT, DIREKTOR
JOH KNIPSCHER, MATHILDE
Built 1893 by Wed Boele, Slikkeveer,
Netherlands
Original owners Rhederei Hucttner,
Duisberg, Germany
Propulsion Steam, screw, triple
expansion, 450hp
Tonnage 33.2 displacement
Length 101.52ft/30.95m
Breadth 19.6ft/5.97m
Draught 6.56ft/2.0m

Department in 1915. Now used as an
inspection vessel.

Noordzee
steam tug

Former name NOORDSEE, TAUCHER
SIEVERS IV, B & V XII
Built 1922 by Janssen & Schmilinsky,
Hamburg, Germany
Original owners Blohm & Voss
Shipyard
Propulsion Steam, screw, triple
expansion, 320hp
Tonnage 71 gross
Length 74.8ft/22.8m
Breadth 18.9ft/5.75m
Draught 9.5ft/2.9m
Materials Steel hull, steel and wood
superstructure
Original use Tug
Condition In operating condition
Present owners C P Jongert
Contact address Zuiderweg 01, 1676 GN
Twisk, Netherlands
Location Medemblik, Netherlands
History Steam tug originally employed
by the major shipyard in Hamburg,
Germany. Maintained in operating
condition by a private owner in the
Netherlands.

Oosterschelde
trading schooner

Former name SYLVAN, FUGLEN,
FUGLEN II
Built 1918 by H Appelo & Son,
Zwartsluis, Netherlands
Original owners Hollandsche
Algemeene Atlantische
Scheepvaartmaat
Propulsion Sail, three-masted schooner;
auxiliary engine

Tonnage 260 gross
Length 119.16ft/36.33m
Breadth 24.7ft/7.53m
Draught 10.79ft/3.29m
Materials Steel hull, steel and wood
masts
Original use Cargo
Condition In sailing condition
Present owners B V Reederij
Oosterschelde
Location Rotterdam, Netherlands
History Dutch auxiliary cargo schooner
later converted to a motor vessel.
Restored to original sailing rig for the
races for the 1992 Columbus
celebrations. Currently used as a sail
training vessel.
Bibliography D9, D316

P-6398
fishing ketch

Built Date not known
Propulsion Sail, ketch rig
Materials Wood throughout
Original use Cargo or fishing
Condition Intact
Present owners Ermelo Jachthaven
Location Ermelo, Netherlands
History Preserved as an onshore
exhibit.

Parodie
tjalk

Built 1898 by Van der Adel at
Papendrecht, Netherlands
Propulsion Sail, sloop rig, auxiliary
engine, 103hp
Tonnage 51 gross
Length 65.72ft/20.03m
Breadth 15.09ft/4.6m
Draught 4.92ft/1.5m
Materials Steel hull, wood spars

Oosterschelde

Pieter Boele

Prins Der Nederlanden
sidewheel river steamer

Former name RUDESHEIM, RHEINLAND
Built 1926 by Gebr Sachsenberg,
Cologne, Germany
Original owners Köln-Dusseldorfer
Deutsche Rheinschiffahrt
Propulsion Steam, sidewheel,
compound diagonal, 750hp. Engine
built by Gebr Sachsenberg, Rosslau
Tonnage 536 displacement
Length 260.0ft/79.1m
Breadth 49.0ft/14.9m
Draught 4.92ft/1.5m
Materials Steel throughout
Original use Passengers
Condition Undergoing restoration
Present owners Nederlandse
Raderstoomboot Maatschappij
Location Rotterdam, Netherlands
History Sidewheel passenger steamer
built for German owners for operation
on the Rhine river. Has been taken to
the Netherlands where she is to be
restored to steaming under the name
MAJESTEIT.
Bibliography B16, B43

Materials Steel hull, steel and wood
superstructure
Original use River towing
Condition In operating condition
Present owners Maritiem
Buitenmuseum, Leuvehaven,
Rotterdam
Location Rotterdam, Netherlands
History Currently an active steamer.

Pollux
stationary training vessel

Built 1940 by Vershure, Amsterdam,
Netherlands
Original owners Matrozen-Instituut,
Amsterdam
Propulsion None; stationary use
Tonnage 746.89 gross
Length 201.45ft/61.4m
Breadth 36.3ft/11.06m
Draught 2.0ft/0.61m
Materials Steel throughout
Original use Stationary training
Condition Intact; in use
Present owners International Maritime
Training Institute, Amsterdam
Location Ijmuiden, Netherlands
History Stationary flat-bottomed
barge. In use training seamen in safety
at sea.
Bibliography A14, C96

Pollux

Prins Hendrik
rescue lifeboat

Built 1950 by Scheepsbouw Maatschappy H Schouten, Muiden, Netherlands
Original owners Royal Netherlands Lifesaving Service
Propulsion Diesel engine. Engine built by Volvo Penta
Length 66.83ft/20.37m
Breadth 13.28ft/4.05m
Draught 4.66ft/1.42m
Materials Steel hull
Original use Rescue lifeboat
Condition In operating condition
Present owners Royal Netherlands Lifesaving Service
Location Den Helder, Netherlands
History Motor lifeboat credited with saving 728 people. Currently on loan to the National Lifesaving Museum in Den Helder as a floating exhibit and for excursions.

Reddingboot I
rescue lifeboat

Built 1948 by J Samuel White & Co, Cowes, Isle of Wight, England
Original owners Netherlands lifeboat service
Propulsion Diesel engines, 40hp. Engine built by Ferry
Tonnage 25 displacement
Length 46.6ft/14.2m
Breadth 12.7ft/3.88m
Draught 4.3ft/1.32m
Original use Rescue lifeboat
Condition Intact
Present owners Reddingmuseum 'Jan Lels'
Location Hoek van Holland, Netherlands
History British-built motorised rescue lifeboat formerly employed by the Dutch lifesaving service. Preserved as an exhibit at Hoek van Holland, main entrance to the Port of Rotterdam.

Roek
steam tug

Former name JACOMIEN
Built 1930 by Gebr van de Windt, Vlaardingen, Netherlands
Original owners Fa Fransen, Dordrecht
Propulsion Steam, screw, triple expansion, coal fired, 165hp
Length 66.42ft/20.25m
Breadth 16.0ft/4.89m
Draught 6.56ft/2.0m
Materials Steel hull, steel & wood superstructure
Original use Tug
Condition In operating condition
Present owners Joop Mos, 'Hawser

Samenwerking

Holland'
Location Enkhuizen, Netherlands
History Currently in use as an operating steamer.

Rosalie
steam tug

Former name WILLEM IV, WILLEM III, JACOBA, NIEUWE ZORG
Built 1873 by F Smit, Kinderdijk, Netherlands
Original owners Royal Netherlands Army Corps
Propulsion Steam, screw, compound, coal fired, 95hp
Length 62.32ft/19.0m
Breadth 13.78ft/4.2m
Draught 5.91ft/1.8m
Materials Iron hull, iron and wood superstructure
Original use Tug
Condition In operating condition
Present owners Joop Mos, 'Hawser Holland'
Location Netherlands
History Currently in use as an operating steamer.

Samenwerking
trading sloop

Built c1900 at Sliedrecht, Netherlands
Propulsion Sail, sloop rig
Tonnage 30 gross
Length 38.3ft/11.5m
Breadth 8.6ft/2.6m
Draught 1.65ft/0.5m
Materials Iron Hull, wood mast
Original use Cargo
Condition In sailing condition
Present owners Paul Versteege and Peter Jansen
Location Wijk, Duurstede, Netherlands
History Currently in use as an active sailing vessel.

Scheelenkuhlen
steam tug

Built 1927 by Johann Oelkers, Hamburg, Germany
Propulsion Steam, screw, compound, 220hp
Length 70.2ft/21.4m
Breadth 18.1ft/5.61m
Draught 5.9ft/1.8m

Materials Steel hull, steel & wood superstructure
Original use Tug
Condition In operating condition
Location Zaandam, Netherlands
History In use as an operating steamer.

Schorpioen
coast defence turret ram

Built 1868 by Soc des Forges et Chantiers, Toulon, France
Original owners Royal Netherlands Navy
Propulsion Steam, screw, 2225hp; brig rig
Tonnage 2140 displacement
Length 205.0ft/62.48m
Breadth 39.0ft/11.89m
Draught 16.0ft/4.88m
Materials Iron throughout
Original use Coast defence ram/turret ship
Condition Externally restored; lacks original engines/guns
Present owners Den Helder Marinemuseum
Location Den Helder, Netherlands

Bibliography D440
History Used for many years as a training and accommodation hulk at Den Helder. Restored and preserved as a floating exhibit.

Simson
floating crane

Built 1958 by Smit, Kinderdijk, Netherlands
Propulsion Non-self-propelled
Materials Steel throughout
Original use Floating crane
Condition Intact
Present owners Maritiem Buitenmuseum
Location Rotterdam, Netherlands
History Preserved as a floating exhibit.

Succes
steam tug

Former name SUCCES I, SLEIPNER
Built 1897 by Huiskens en v Dijk, Dordrecht, Netherlands
Propulsion Steam, screw, diagonal, 250hp

Length 126.0ft/38.4m
Breadth 23.3ft/7.11m
Draught 6.6ft/2.0m
Materials Steel hull, steel and wood superstructure
Original use Tug; converted to passenger use
Condition In operating condition
Location Enkhuizen, Netherlands
History Currently in use as a passenger vessel.

Succes
steam river tug

Built 1909 by Huiskens en v Dijk, Dordrecht, Netherlands
Propulsion Steam, screw, 275hp
Length 70.6ft/21.5m
Breadth 15.8ft/4.82m
Draught 7.2ft/2.2m
Materials Steel hull
Original use River tug
Condition In operating condition
Location Maasbracht, Netherlands
History Currently an active steam vessel.

Succes

Tecla
fishing ketch

Former name GRAAF VAN LIMBURG STIRIUM
Built 1915 by Albert de Jong, Vlaardingen, Netherlands

Original owners Nick Parleviet
Propulsion Ketch rig
Length 80.25ft/24.45m
Breadth 20.66ft/6.3m
Draught 10.2ft/3.1m
Materials Iron hull
Original use Fishing
Condition Restored to sailing vessel
Present owners Janny Pierik and Jaap Vleeken
Contact address Groot Lageland 23, 8064 Zwartsluis, Netherlands
Location Zwartsluis, Netherlands
History Ketch-rigged fishing vessel restored to original appearance externally and maintained in sailing condition as a charter vessel.
Bibliography D346

Thor
steam tug

Former name Y8262, PAULINE
Built 1918 at The Hague, Netherlands
Propulsion Steam, screw
Materials Steel hull, steel and wood superstructure
Original use Tug, later minesweeper
Condition Intact, cabin added aft
Location Zwolle, Netherlands
History Currently a floating restaurant.

Tonijn
submarine

Built 1965 by Wilton-Fijenoord, Rotterdam, Netherlands
Original owners Royal Netherlands Navy
Propulsion Diesel and electric motors 4400hp
Tonnage 1494 displacement
Length 261.0ft/79.5m
Breadth 26.0ft/7.9m

Schorpioen

Draught 16.0ft/4.9m
Materials Steel throughout
Original use Submarine
Condition Intact
Present owners Den Helder Naval
Museum
Contact address c/o Havenplein 3, NL-
1780 CA Den Helder, Netherlands
Location Den Helder, Netherlands
History Dutch submarine of the 1960s
preserved as an onshore exhibit and
naval memorial.

Trix
motor fishing boat

Former name MACHIEL
Built 1903 by Vuyk, Capelle a d Ijssel,
Netherlands
Propulsion Diesel engine, 425hp
Tonnage 100 gross
Length 91.1ft/27.75m
Breadth 21.8ft/6.65m
Draught 9.4ft/2.87m
Original use Fishing
Condition Undergoing restoration
Present owners Stichting 'De Nieuwe
Aanpak'
Location Scheveningen, Netherlands

Trui
sailing fishing boat

Built 1875
Propulsion Sail, sloop rig; 'botter' type
Original use Fishing
Condition In sailing condition
Location Delft, Netherlands
History Currently an active sailing
vessel.

Twenthe
rescue lifeboat

Built 1942 by Witsen, Alkmaar,
Netherlands
Original owners Royal Netherlands
Lifesaving Service
Propulsion Diesel engines, 80hp
Tonnage 25 displacement
Length 49.2ft/14.98m
Breadth 11.8ft/3.6m
Draught 3.6ft/1.1m
Original use Rescue lifeboat
Condition Intact
Present owners Nationaal
Reddingmuseum
Location Den Helder, Netherlands
History Preserved as an indoor exhibit.

TX-58
sailing fishing boat

Built 1902
Propulsion Sail, sloop rig; 'Wieringer

Tonijn

aak' type
Original use Fishing
Condition In sailing condition
Location Delft, Netherlands
History Currently an active sailing
vessel.

U-111
submarine

Built 1965 at Sudomekh, Russia
Original owners Russian Navy
Propulsion Diesel and electric motors,
6000hp
Tonnage 1950 displacement
Length 300.3ft/91.5m
Breadth 26.3ft/8.0m
Draught 20.0ft/6.1m
Materials Steel throughout
Original use Submarine
Condition Intact
Location Den Helder, Netherlands
History Russian non-nuclear
submarine of the Cold War era open to
the public as a floating exhibit.

Utrecht Ship
medieval trading vessel

Built c1100
Propulsion Probably single square sail
Tonnage 10.4 displacement
Length 58.38ft/17.8m
Breadth 12.46ft/3.8m
Materials Wood throughout
Original use Cargo
Condition Largely intact hull excavated
in 1930
Present owners Centraal Museum,
Utrecht
Location Utrecht, Netherlands

History Preserved as an indoor exhibit.

Vertrouwen
motor fishing boat

Built c1948 at Amsterdam, Netherlands
Propulsion Diesel engine, 150hp
Length 59.1ft/18.0m
Materials Steel throughout
Original use Fishing
Condition Intact
Present owners Delta-Expo
Location Oosterscheldedam,
Netherlands
History Preserved as an onshore
exhibit.

Volharding I
steam tug

Former name HARMONIE VI
Built 1930 by De Hoop Shipyard, Neder
Hardinxveld, Netherlands
Original owners NV Sliedrecht Mij
Harmonie, Vreeswijk
Propulsion Steam, screw, triple
expansion, 175hp, coal fired. Engine
built by Vlaardingsche Machinefabrik
Length 66.43ft/20.25m
Breadth 16.04ft/4.89m
Draught 7.22ft/2.2m
Materials Steel hull, steel and wood
superstructure
Original use Tug
Condition In operating condition
Present owners Maritiem
Buitenmuseum, Leuvehaven,
Rotterdam
Location Rotterdam, Netherlands
History Preserved as a floating exhibit
and operating steamer.

Voorwaarts
motor coaster

Built 1906 by De Dageraad Shipyard,
Woubrugge, Netherlands
Original owners Fa Karsemeier,
Naarden
Propulsion Oil engine. Engine built by
Rennes
Tonnage 60 gross
Length 65.27ft/19.9m
Breadth 12.6ft/3.85m
Draught 2.0ft/0.6m
Materials Steel hull
Original use Cargo
Condition Intact
Present owners Buitenmuseum
Maritiem Museum
Location Rotterdam, Netherlands
History Preserved as a floating exhibit.

Voorwaarts Voorwaarts
trading ketch

Former name SUDFALL, SAHLENBURG,
OSTE, VORWARTS
Built 1899 by J & G Verstockt,
Martenshoek, Netherlands
Original owners J H Puister
Propulsion Sail, ketch rig
Tonnage 105 gross
Length 88.29ft/26.91m
Breadth 17.68ft/5.39m
Draught 7.55ft/2.3m
Materials Steel hull, wood masts
Original use Cargo
Condition In operating condition
Present owners Stichting Behoud 2-
mast koftjalk VV anno 1899
Location Groningen, Netherlands
History Example of a Dutch 'koftjalk', a

type formerly employed in the European coastal tardes. Currently an operating sailing vessel.

Vrouw Elisabeth
sailing fishing vessel

Built 1909 by Baas Kater, Durgerdam, Netherlands
Official number RD 28
Propulsion Sail, sloop rig; auxiliary diesel engine, 39hp
Tonnage 18.7 gross
Length 41.7ft/12.7m
Breadth 12.8ft/3.9m
Draught 3.0ft/0.9m
Original use Fishing
Condition In sailing condition
Present owners Stichting Beheer Ransdorp
Contact address 28, Vogelzand 2106, 1788 GL Den Helder
Location Den Helder, Netherlands
History Currently active.

Y-8017
harbour tug/icebreaker

Built 1957 by Rijkswerf, Den Helder, Netherlands
Propulsion Diesel engine, 300hp
Length 54.4ft/16.58m
Breadth 15.2ft/4.63m
Original use Harbour tug and icebreaker
Location Den Helder, Netherlands

Y-8122
steam tug

Former name SLEEPDIENST 2
Built 1936 by Rijkswerf, Willemsoord, Netherlands
Propulsion Steam, screw, 115hp (1909 engine)
Tonnage 20.54 displacement
Length 63.3ft/19.29m
Breadth 16.3ft/4.97m
Draught 4.7ft/1.42m
Materials Steel hull
Original use Tug
Condition Intact, undergoing refurbishment
Present owners Stichting Nautische Monumenten te Den Helder
Location Den Helder, Netherlands
History Proposed as an exhibit.

Zeemeeuw
motor coaster

Built 1937 by Noord Nederlandse Scheepswerven, Groningen, Netherlands
Propulsion Diesel engine, 190hp.

Voorwaarts Voorwaarts

Engine built by Klockner
Tonnage 199.99 gross
Length 117.7ft/35.85m
Breadth 21.0ft/6.4m
Draught 8.0ft/2.43m
Materials Steel hull
Original use Cargo
Condition Intact
Present owners Maritiem

Buitenmuseum
Location Rotterdam, Netherlands
History Preserved as a floating exhibit.

Zuiderzee
trading schooner

Former name GENIUS, ENIGKEIT, KLAUS HEINRICH KARSTENS, PIRAT

Built 1909 by J J Pattje & Son, Waterhuizen, Netherlands
Propulsion Sail, two-masted schooner
Materials Steel hull
Original use Cargo
Condition In sailing condition
Location Netherlands
History Currently used for charters.
Bibliography A10

Zeemeeuw

New Zealand

The two islands that would become New Zealand were first mapped by Captain Cook in the 1770s, and frequented by whalers in the early 1800s. Great Britain had established its first colony in Australia in 1788, but was reluctant to accept responsibility for these distant islands across the Tasman Sea until the early 1830s, when France began showing interest in them. Britain then reversed its policy of discouraging settlement and sent out its first administrator. The islands had a sizeable native Maori population, until recently cannibals, who were skilled in lodge building, intricate woodcarving, and the construction of large dugout canoes. The new arrivals adapted western designs to local needs, creating distinct variations on European or North American vessel types. The scow schooner, with shallow draught and squared-off hull lines, became popular for navigating New Zealand estuaries with little depth of water. Very narrow river steamers were developed that could shoot rock-filled rapids when bound downstream, and winch themselves upstream against rushing currents.

African Queen
river launch

Former name WAIREKA
Built 1908 by Yarrow & Co, Glasgow, Scotland (pre-fabricated)
Original owners A Hatrick & Co
Propulsion Motor, screw, 40hp
Tonnage 6.3 gross
Length 62.9ft/19.12m
Breadth 6.6ft/1.98m
Draught 1.0ft/0.3m
Materials Steel hull, wood superstructure
Original use Cargo and passengers
Condition In operation
Present owners Waireka Tours
Location Taupo, New Zealand
History Currently used for cruises.
Bibliography C8

Alma
trading schooner

Built 1902 by G T Nicol, Auckland, New Zealand
Original owners Ada Beatrice Nicol
Propulsion Sail, two-masted schooner rig; diesel auxiliary added
Tonnage 63.02 gross
Length 79.6ft/24.26m
Breadth 25.6ft/7.8m
Draught 3.6ft/1.09m
Materials Wood throughout
Original use Cargo
Condition Undergoing restoration
Location Hokianga, New Zealand
History Classic example of square-bilged scow dating from early 1900s. Deck scow with no hold space. Used to carry general cargo between Auckland and Waiheke Island in Hauraki Gulf. Laid up in early 1960s. Currently being restored to an active sailing vessel.
Bibliography C44

Earnslaw
steam passenger/cargo vessel

Built 1912 by J McGregor & Co, Dunedin, New Zealand
Original owners New Zealand Government Railways
Propulsion Steam, screw, two triple expansion engines, coal fired
Tonnage 330 gross
Length 165.6ft/50.47m
Breadth 24.0ft/7.32m

Draught 6.6ft/1.98m
Materials Steel throughout
Original use Passengers and cargo
Condition In operating condition
Present owners Fiordland Travel
Location Queenstown, New Zealand
History Largest and only survivor of a line of nine steamships built to carry passengers on Lake Wakatipu in New Zealand's South island. Currently used for passenger cruises.
Bibliography B3, D51, D360

Echo
auxiliary trading schooner

Built 1905 by W Brown & Sons, Kaipara River, New Zealand
Original owners Karamea Steamship Co
Propulsion Sail, two-masted schooner rig, auxiliary oil engine. Engine built by Hercules
Tonnage 132 gross
Length 104.0ft/31.7m
Breadth 26.0ft/7.92m
Draught 6.1ft/1.85m
Materials Wood throughout
Original use Cargo
Condition Large deckhouse added, in need of restoration
Present owners Timothy Copeland Dare
Location Picton, New Zealand
History Currently used as an onshore clubhouse.
Bibliography B3, C44

Edwin Fox
full-rigged sailing ship

Built 1853 by William Henry Foster, Sukeali, Bengal, India
Original owners Thomas Reeves
Propulsion Sail, full-rigged ship rig
Tonnage 747 gross
Length 144.8ft/44.14m
Breadth 29.8ft/9.08m
Draught 20.0ft/6.1m
Materials Wood throughout
Original use Cargo and passengers
Condition Hull survives without decks
Present owners Edwin Fox Restoration Society
Location Picton, New Zealand
History Built by native shipwrights at Sukeali, Bengal, the EDWIN FOX spent most of the 1850s as a British troopship, first in the Crimean War, and later in the Indian Mutiny of 1858. She was then employed carrying emigrants between the British Isles and Australia and New Zealand. On one voyage her passengers were convicts being deported to the Antipodes, making her the last surviving vessel to have participated in this trade. In 1885 she arrived in Port Chalmers, New Zealand, from London fully fitted out as a floating freezing plant for meat. Reduced to a hulk, she was employed as a freezing plant at several New Zealand ports, the last one Picton near the north point of South Island. In 1900 she was converted to a coal

Earnslaw

storage hulk there when a new freezing plant was built on shore. She was employed in this capacity until the 1950s. After retirement, her hull was towed into a bay near Picton and beached there. Her interior was open to the weather, but her lower hull, largely sheathed in layers of planking and copper sheeting, survived very well. Beginning in the 1960s, there were several efforts to rescue the ship and preserve her. None was successful until 1986 when she was finally refloated and moved to a berth near the centre of Picton. EDWIN FOX has now been thoroughly recorded by teams of archaeologists, and plans are underway to at least partly restore the vessel as a floating museum. Today she represents the only intact hull of a wooden deepwater sailing ship built to British specifications surviving in the world outside the Falkland Islands.
Bibliography A14, B3, D86, D151

Jane Gifford
trading ketch

Built 1908 by D M Darroch, Omaha, New zealand
Original owners Coromandel Granite Co
Propulsion Sail, ketch rig
Tonnage 45 gross
Length 67.1ft/20.45m
Breadth 18.6ft/5.67m
Draught 2.6ft/0.75m
Materials Wood throughout
Original use Cargo
Condition Restored to sailing condition
Present owners Waiuku Museum Society
Location Waiuku, New Zealand
History New Zealand's only example of a scow-hulled ketch in operational condition. Currently an active sailing vessel.

Kopu
sidewheel tug

Built 1897 by John Young, Thames, New Zealand
Original owners Northern Steamship Co
Propulsion Steam, sidewheel, 2-cylinder, 5hp
Length 60.0ft/18.29m
Breadth 24.0ft/7.32m
Materials Wood throughout
Original use Towing
Condition Poor; as raised after long period underwater
Present owners Historical Maritime Park

Kopu

Location Paeroa, New Zealand
History Steam sidewheel towboat built for use on a river in northern New Zealand. Raised in 1980 after a number of years sunk in shallow water there. Exhibited grounded.

Koura
harbour defence motor launch

Former name HMNZS KOURA, P3564, HDML 1350
Built 1943 by Ackerman Boat Works, Los Angeles, California, USA
Original owners Royal Navy
Propulsion Diesel engines, twin screw
Tonnage 47 displacement

Length 72.0ft/21.95m
Breadth 15.8ft/4.82m
Draught 5.3ft/1.62m
Materials Wood hull
Original use Harbour defence launch
Condition Intact
Present owners Paeroa Maritime Historic Park
Location Paeroa, New Zealand
History Second World War harbour defence motor launch which spent her entire working life in New Zealand waters. Sold to Paeroa Maritime Historic Park and displayed as a floating exhibit.
Bibliography C61

Kuparu
harbour defence motor launch

Former name HMNZS KUPARU, P3563, HDML 1348
Built 1944 by Ackerman Boat Works, Los Angeles, California, USA
Original owners Royal New Zealand Navy
Propulsion Diesel engines, twin screw
Tonnage 47 displacement
Length 72.0ft/21.95m
Breadth 15.8ft/4.82m
Draught 5.3ft/1.62m
Materials Wood hull
Original use Harbour defence launch (HDML type)
Condition Intact, stored on shore under cover
Present owners Royal New Zealand Navy
Location Devonport, New Zealand
History Proposed as a future exhibit at the Naval Museum in Devonport, Auckland.
Bibliography C61

Lyttelton
steam tug

Former name CANTERBURY
Built 1907 by Ferguson Brothers, Port Glasgow, Scotland
Original owners Lyttelton Harbour Board
Propulsion Steam, screw, two compound engines, 800hp, coal fired

Lyttelton

Settler

Tonnage 292 gross
Length 125.0ft/38.1m
Breadth 25.0ft/7.62m
Draught 11.5ft/3.51m
Materials Steel hull, steel and wood
superstructure
Original use Tug
Condition In operating condition
Present owners Lyttelton Tug
Preservation Society
Location Lyttelton, New Zealand
History Steam harbour tug formerly
employed at Lyttleton, New Zealand.
Preserved as a floating exhibit and
active steamer.
Bibliography B3

Manawanui
motor tug/diving tender

Former name YTL 622
Built 1945 by United Shipbuilders,
Auckland, New Zealand
Original owners United States Navy

Propulsion Diesel engines, 320hp
Tonnage 74 gross
Length 75.8ft/22.9m
Breadth 18.25ft/5.6m
Draught 8.0ft/2.4m
Materials Steel throughout
Original use Tug, later diving tender
Condition Intact
Present owners Paeroa Historical
Maritime Park
Location Paeroa, New Zealand
History Reportedly built for the US
Navy at the end of the Second World
War. Employed by the New Zealand
Navy as a diving tender. Preserved as a
floating exhibit.
Bibliography C61

Ongarue
river launch

Built 1903 by Yarrow & Co, London,
England (pre-fabricated)
Original owners A Hatrick & Co,

Wanganui
Propulsion Screw, oil engine; converted
to diesel
Tonnage 13.37 gross
Length 60.1ft/18.31m
Breadth 8.4ft/2.56m
Draught 1.0ft/0.3m
Materials Steel hull, wood
superstructure
Original use Passengers and cargo
Condition Intact
Present owners New Zealand
Department of Conservation
Location Pipiriki, New Zealand
History Pre-fabricated in England and
assembled in New Zealand to carry
passengers and freight on river
between Wanganui and Pipiriki. Laid
up in 1958 and preserved as an onshore
exhibit.
Bibliography C8

Owhiti
trading ketch

Built 1925 by D M Darrock & Sons,
Stanley Bay, New Zealand
Original owners A W Bryant Ltd,
Auckland
Propulsion Sail, ketch rig
Length 71.5ft/21.79m
Breadth 22.0ft/6.71m
Draught 3.67ft/1.12m
Materials Wood throughout
Original use Cargo
Condition In sailing condition
Present owners David Skyrme
Location Auckland, New Zealand
History Scow-hulled coastal trader.
Currently an active sailing vessel.

Rapaki
floating crane

Built 1926 by Fleming & Ferguson,
Paisley, Scotland

Propulsion Steam powered crane
Tonnage 762 gross
Length 170.0ft/51.82m
Breadth 52.3ft/15.96m
Materials Steel throughout
Original use Floating crane
Condition Intact, afloat
Present owners Auckland Maritime
Museum
Location Auckland, New Zealand
History Large steam-powered floating
crane formerly based in the harbour of
Lyttelton, New Zealand. Now
preserved as a museum exhibit at
Auckland.

Settler
trade/passenger steamer

Built 1905 by C Bailley Jr, Auckland,
New Zealand
Original owners Captain L T Kitching,
Dargaville
Propulsion Steam, screw; converted to
diesel
Length 50.0ft/15.24m
Breadth 13.0ft/3.96m
Draught 4.0ft/1.22m
Materials Wood throughout
Original use Passengers and cargo
Condition In operating condition
Present owners New Zealand Maritime
Trust
Location Paeroa, New Zealand
History Built to carry passengers and
freight on rivers in northern New
Zealand. Round bilged as distinct from
scow hull. Preserved as a floating
exhibit and excursion vessel.

Taioma
steam tug

Former name EMPIRE JANE
Built 1944 by Alexander Hall & Co,
Aberdeen, Scotland
Original owners British Ministry of
War Transport
Propulsion Steam, screw, triple-
expansion, 900hp
Tonnage 232 gross
Length 105.2ft/32.06m
Breadth 27.15ft/8.27m
Draught 11.7ft/3.56m
Materials Steel throughout
Original use Tug
Condition Intact
Present owners Tauranga Historic
Village Museum
Location Tauranga, New Zealand
History British-built steam tug which
spent over 30 years working in
Wellington Harbour. Preserved as an
onshore exhibit.
Bibliography D371

Te Aroha
auxiliary trading schooner

Built 1909 by T M Lane & Son,
Auckland, New Zealand
Original owners Wairoa and Mohaka
Steamship Co, Napier
Propulsion Diesel engines; schooner rig
Tonnage 104.65 gross
Length 86.4ft/25.33m
Breadth 24.0ft/7.31m
Draught 6.4ft/1.95m
Materials Wood hull
Original use Cargo
Condition In operation
Present owners Aotea Shipping Co
Location Auckland, New Zealand
History Currently used for cargo and
passengers.

Te Toki A Tapiri
Maori war canoe

Built pre-1869 by Maori canoe builders
in New Zealand
Propulsion Paddles
Length 82.0ft/25.0m
Materials Wood throughout
Original use War canoe
Condition Intact
Present owners The Auckland Museum
Location Auckland, New Zealand
History Preserved as an indoor exhibit.

Toroa
steam ferry

Built 1925 by George Niccol, Auckland,
New Zealand
Original owners Devonport Steam
Ferry Co
Propulsion Steam, screw, 51hp
Tonnage 309 gross
Length 131.0ft/39.93m
Breadth 31.0ft/9.45m
Draught 9.9ft/3.0m
Materials Hull wood over steel frames,
superstructure wood
Original use Ferryboat
Condition In operating condition
Present owners Toroa Preservation
Society, Birkenhead
Location Auckland, New Zealand
History Last steam ferry built for
Auckland harbour. Complete with
original machinery and thus possibly
unique in the world. Currently used
for charters.
Bibliography C4

Tuhoe
auxiliary trading schooner

Built 1919 by George T Niccol,
Auckland, New Zealand
Original owners Northern Steamship
Co

Propulsion Sail, schooner rig; diesel
engine, 240hp
Tonnage 192.47 gross
Length 97.8ft/29.76m
Breadth 24.7ft/7.49m
Draught 6.5ft/2.0m
Materials Wood throughout
Original use Cargo
Condition In sailing condition
Present owners MV Tuhoe Preservation
Society
Location Kaiapoi, New Zealand
History Restored 1980 and currently
used for cruises.

Undine
trading sloop

Built 1887 by Fuller Brothers, Keriken,
New Zealand
Original owners Fuller Brothers
Propulsion Sail, sloop rig; diesel
auxiliary engine, 10hp. Engine built by
Bukh
Tonnage 6 gross
Length 35.0ft/10.67m
Breadth 9.6ft/2.93m
Draught 3.3ft/1.01m
Materials Wood throughout
Original use Cargo
Condition In sailing condition
Present owners J Duder & B Marler
Location Auckland, New Zealand

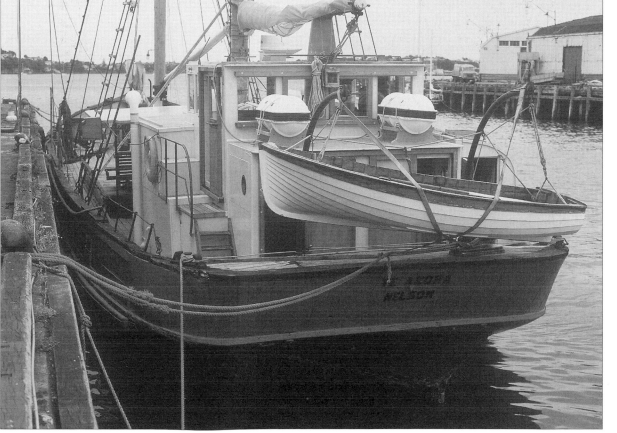

Te Aroha

William C Daldy

The half of the Korean Peninsula still under a communist government remains a very difficult region from which to obtain information. Small warships have tended to be the favoured subject of preservation efforts in communist countries, but the only preserved vessel in North Korea of which we have any reports is a United States Navy surveillance ship seized in peacetime near the boundary of Korean territorial waters. There is also reportedly a sidewheel steamer on a North Korean river, but she is a recent reproduction of the DRESDEN of the 1920s, a vessel which is still in operation based at the city of that name in what was formerly East Germany.

History Farmers' workboat, used as a fishing boat until rescued off the beach in 1980 and restored. Currently an active sailing vessel.

Waimarie
sidewheel river steamer

Former name AOTEA
Built 1900 by Yarrow & Co, London, England (pre-fabricated)
Original owners Wanganui Settlers River Steamship Co
Propulsion Steam, sidewheel, two diagonal engines
Tonnage 80.23 gross
Length 102.0ft/31.09m
Breadth 16.0ft/4.88m
Draught 1.5ft/0.46m
Materials Steel hull, wood deckhouse with steel frame
Original use Cargo and passengers
Condition Undergoing restoration indoors
Present owners Wanganui Riverboat Restoration & Navigation Trust
Location Wanganui, New Zealand
History First ship to be registered in Wellington port. Last paddle steamer to operate in New Zealand 1900-49; sunk at berth in 1952, currently

undergoing restoration indoors.
Bibliography C8

Wairua
river steamer

Built 1904 by Yarrow & Co, London, England (pre-fabricated)
Original owners A Hatrick & Co, Wanganui
Propulsion Steam, screw, 66hp
Tonnage 9.6 gross
Length 65.0ft/19.8m
Breadth 8.0ft/2.44m
Draught 1.0ft/0.31m
Materials Steel hull, wood deckhouse
Original use Cargo and passengers
Condition Restoration in progress
Present owners Wanganui Riverboat Services
Location Wanganui, New Zealand
History An example of Yarrow's famous raised propeller boats which used tunnel drive and were active on the Wanganui river. Sunk at wharf in 1950, currently under restoration.
Bibliography C8

William C Daldy
steam tug

Built 1935 by Lobnitz & Co, Renfrew, Scotland
Original owners Auckland Harbour Board
Propulsion Steam, twin-screw, two triple expansion, 1500hp, coal fired
Tonnage 354.94 gross
Length 119.0ft/36.27m
Breadth 32.15ft/9.8m
Draught 13.9ft/4.23m
Materials Steel hull, steel and wood superstructure
Original use Tug
Condition In operating condition
Present owners William C Daldy Preservation Society
Location Auckland, New Zealand
History Worked in Auckland Harbour 1936-1977, when rescued from the breakers and preserved as a floating exhibit and operating steamer.
Bibliography B3, D227, D242

Pueblo
surveillance vessel

Former name USS PUEBLO
Built 1944 by Kewaunee Shipbuilding and Engineering, Kewaunee, Wisconsin, USA
Original owners United States Army
Official number FP-344
Propulsion Diesel engines, 1000hp
Tonnage 560 gross, 850 displacement
Length 176.5ft/53.8m
Breadth 32.0ft/9.8m
Draught 9.25ft/2.8m
Materials Steel throughout
Original use Supply ship
Condition Intact
Present owners North Korean Navy
Location Wonsan, North Korea
History Built during the Second World War as a small US Navy supply ship. Later converted to a surveillance vessel and eventually seized by the North Korean Navy while operating off the coast of that country in January 1968. Now preserved in a museum.
Bibliography D312

Norway

Surviving evidence of Norway's long seafaring heritage includes two largely intact Viking ships of the period AD 900-1000 excavated in the late 1800s and now on exhibit in a suburb of Oslo. The country's mountainous coastline, with its magnificent fjords, made land transportation very difficult, forcing the Norwegians to rely on sailing ships, and later steamers, for travel between the major cities, all of which lie on arms of the sea. During the final era of the deepwater sailing ship, Norway maintained a large fleet of these vessels trading around the world. The only restored veteran of this fleet is the Scottish-built bark ELISSA now based in Galveston, Texas, which was once owned in Norway as the FJELD. The modern whaling industry, with factory ships and shore stations, and steam whale catchers, was largely developed by Norwegians. Maritime historic preservation in Norway has focused on smaller vessels, sail and steam, formerly employed in coastal waters, fjords, and lakes. One lake steamer, the SKIBLADNER of 1856 on Lake Mjosa, is the oldest operating paddlewheel steamer in Europe.

Aarvak
motor sealing boat

Built 1912 by Kristian Dekke, Bergen, Norway
Original owners A/S Bergen Saelfangsderselskab
Propulsion Diesel engines
Tonnage 122.3 gross
Length 104.4ft/31.82m
Breadth 22.8ft/6.19m
Materials Wood throughout
Original use Sealing
Condition Intact
Present owners Hareid Historical Soc
Location Hareid, Norway
History Preserved as an exhibit.

Adella
sailing coaster

Former name GISKE, MISJONAER SKREFSRUD
Built 1864, probably in Norway

Propulsion Sail, sloop rig; later ketch; later motor vessel
Tonnage 61.56 gross
Length 72.4ft/22.07m
Breadth 21.4ft/6.52m
Draught 7.8ft/2.38m
Materials Wood throughout
Original use Cargo
Condition Restoration in progress
Present owners Tarald Glastad
Location Farsund, Norway
History Sailing cargo vessel formerly employed transporting fish between the Lofoten Islands and the mainland of Norway. Being restored to an active sailing vessel.

Ammonia
steam railway ferry

Built 1929 by Moss Vaerft, Moss, Norway
Original owners Norsk Transport AS-Rjukanbanen
Propulsion Steam, screw, two triple expansion, 450hp
Tonnage 929 gross
Length 230.6ft/70.3m
Breadth 35.1ft/10./m
Materials Steel throughout
Original use Railway ferry
Condition Intact, out of service

Present owners Norsk Transport AS
Location Lake Tinn, Norway
History Built to carry railway freight cars on a 38km route on Lake Tinn between Mael and Tinnoset. This was the scene of the Second World War commando sinking of another railway ferry carrying heavy water produced for German atomic bomb development. The AMMONIA was used to represent that ferry in the 1964 film *Heroes of Telemark*. Currently laid up.

Anna Af Sand
sailing coaster

Built 1848 by Staumberg Brothers, Ryfylke, Norway
Propulsion Sail, sloop rig; auxiliary engine added
Tonnage 24 gross
Length 50.0ft/15.24m
Breadth 16.0ft/4.88m
Draught 9.0ft/2.74m
Materials Wood throughout
Original use Cargo
Condition In sailing condition
Present owners Stavanger Museum
Location Stavanger, Norway
History Preserved as an exhibit and active sailing vessel.

Anna Kristina
sailing coaster

Former name DYREFJELD
Built 1889 at Kristiansand, Norway
Propulsion Sail, ketch rig; diesel auxiliary
Tonnage 80 gross
Materials Wood throughout
Original use Cargo
Condition In sailing condition
Present owners Hans van de Vooren
Location Hardanger, Norway
History Winner of an award from the Norwegian Maritime Heritage Society for best restored vessel of its type. Currently an active sailing vessel.

Anna Rogde
trading schooner

Built 1868 by Bangsunds Skibsveerft, Namsos, Norway
Propulsion Sail, schooner rig; auxiliary engine added
Tonnage 92 gross
Length 80.0ft/24.38m
Breadth 21.58ft/6.58m
Draught 9.67ft/2.95m
Materials Wood throughout
Original use Cargo

Anna af Sand

Condition In sailing condition
Present owners Magne and Aage Indahl
Location Asker, Norway
History believed to be the oldest surviving schooner built in Norway. Currently in use as a sailing yacht.

Bilfergen
ferry

Built 1921 by Johan T Nerhus, Hardanger, Norway
Original owners Aalesunds Faergeselskat A/S
Propulsion Diesel engine; 96hp
Tonnage 34 gross
Length 63.5ft/19.35m
Breadth 16.67ft/5.08m
Draught 7.33ft/2.23m
Materials Wood throughout
Original use Ferry
Condition In operation
Present owners Sondeled Veteranskibsklubb
Location Sondeled, nr Risor, Norway
History Small wooden ferryboat built to carry five cars athwartships. Currently used for excursions.

Bjoren
tugboat

Built 1867 by Kristiansands Mek. Verksted, Kristiansand
Propulsion Steam, screw
Length 68.9ft/21.0m
Original use Tugboat
Condition In operation
Present owner Town of Bygland
Location Bygland, Norway
History Employed as a tugboat until around 1950. Now operated on cruises and charters on the Bygland Fjord.

Borgenes
convoy escort trawler

Former name T-276, CAILIFF
Built 1942 by Collingwood Shipyards, Georgian Bay, Ontario, Canada
Original owners British Royal Navy
Propulsion Steam, screw, triple expansion, 850hp
Tonnage 770 displacement
Length 164.0ft/50.0m
Breadth 27.66ft/8.4m
Draught 14.0ft/4.3m
Materials Steel throughout
Original use Trawler-type convoy escort vessel
Condition Restoration in progress
Present owners Olaf T Engvig, Oslo
Location Hitra, Norway
History Small escort vessel which took part in the Battle of the Atlantic in the

Børøysund

Second World War. Being restored as an exhibit and active steamer.
Bibliography D160,163

Børøysund
coastal steamer

Former name HYMA, SKJAERGAR, ODIN
Built 1908 by Trondhjems Mek Verksted, Trondheim, Norway
Original owners Trondheim Laegterkompagni
Propulsion Steam, screw, triple expansion, 256hp, coal fired
Tonnage 179 gross
Length 108.59ft/33.1m
Breadth 18.27ft/5.57m
Draught 8.6ft/2.62m
Materials Steel hull, steel and wood superstructure
Original use Passengers and cargo
Condition In operating condition
Present owners Norsk Veteranskibsklub
Location Oslo, Norway
History Last coal-burning steamer in Norway. Currently in use as an active

steamer.
Bibliography B14, B16

Christiania
sailing rescue lifeboat

Built 1895. Designed by Colin Archer
Length 45.0ft/13.7m
Materials Wood throughout
Original use Sailing rescue lifeboat
Condition Intact, but was sunk over a year
Present owners Carl Emil and Johan Peterson
Location Brevik, Norway
History Was in sailing condition when she sank in September 1997. Raised in May 1999. Owners currently restoring her to sail again.
Bibliography Classic Boat, July 1999

Christian Radich
sail training vessel

Built 1937 by Framnaes Mek Verksted, Sandefjord, Norway
Original owners Ostlandets Skoleskib
Propulsion Sail, full-rigged ship; diesel auxiliary engine
Tonnage 676 gross
Length 192.09ft/58.55m
Breadth 32.0ft/9.75m
Draught 15.98ft/4.87m
Materials Steel hull, steel and wood masts
Original use Training vessel

Christian Radich

Fram with additional deck added aft, 1897-98

Condition In operation
Present owners Ostlandets Skoleskib
Location Oslo, Norway (home port)
History Still in use as a sail training vessel.
Bibliography A10, A14, C25, C96

Colin Archer
rescue lifeboat

Built 1893 by Colin Archer Yard, Larvik, Norway
Original owners Norwegian Lifeboat Institution
Propulsion Sail, ketch rig; auxiliary engine added
Length 45.6ft/13.9m
Breadth 15.26ft/4.65m
Draught 7.55ft/2.3m
Materials Wood throughout
Original use Rescue lifeboat
Condition In sailing condition
Present owners Norsk Sjofartsmuseum
Location Oslo, Norway
History Prototype for sailing rescue vessels formerly employed on the coast of Norway. Preserved as a floating exhibit.
Bibliography A10, C51

Engebret Soot
steam launch

Built 1861
Propulsion Steam, screw

Tonnage 32 gross
Materials Iron hull
Original use Launch
Location Oslo, Norway
History Preserved as an exhibit.

Fram
polar exploration vessel

Built 1892 by Colin Archer Yard, Larvik, Norway
Original owners Fridjof Nansen
Propulsion Sail, three-masted schooner rig; steam, screw, 220hp
Tonnage 402 gross
Length 127.95ft/39.0m
Breadth 36.09ft/11.0m
Draught 15.58ft/4.75m
Materials Wood throughout
Original use Polar exploration
Condition Intact
Present owners Norsk Sjofartsmuseum
Location Oslo, Norway
History The first vessels employed in polar exploration were converted from other uses. FRAM was one of the first to be built specifically for that purpose. Since her owner Fridtjof Nansen hoped to reach the North Pole by being carried there on currents in the Arctic Sea, her designer Colin Archer had to create a hull that would withstand being frozen in the polar ice for two winters or more. FRAM was given

sides 28 to 32 inches thick, and her hull was divided into three watertight compartments. There were 68 diagonal timber braces below the main deck to counteract inward pressure, and both the screw and the rudder could be raised into vertical shafts in the hull when in danger of being damaged by the ice. Most importantly, the hull was shaped in such a way that it would tend to be pushed upward out of the ice as pressure increased, instead of being trapped and crushed. Many of these features were adopted by subsequent polar research vessels. Nansen's 1893 expedition did not reach the North Pole, but it set a record that still stands for the farthest north attained by a surface vessel. Between 1898 and 1902 FRAM was used by Otto Sverdrup in exploring the waters between Northern Canada and Greenland, spending four more winters in the ice above the Arctic Circle. In 1911 she was employed by Norway's most famour polar explorer, Roald Amundsen, for the successful expedition to the Antarctic on which he became the first man to reach the South Pole. FRAM has been preserved as a historic vessel since 1929. Today she rests in a building built for her on the shore of Oslo Harbour, not far

from Amundsen's GJOA in which he conquered the Northwest Passage.
Bibliography A14, C51, D155, D453

Frøia
sailing coaster

Built 1857 at Hardanger, Norway
Propulsion Sail, sloop rig; converted to schooner with auxiliary engine
Tonnage 40 displacement
Length 55.76ft/17.0m
Breadth 18.04ft/5.5m
Materials Wood throughout
Original use Cargo
Condition In sailing condition
Present owners Norway Yacht Charters
Location Oslo, Norway
History Built to carry cargo in the Norwegian coastal trade. Interior altered to accommodate passengers. Currently in use for charters.

Gamle Rogaland
coastal passenger steamer

Former name STAUPER, TUNGENES, ROGALAND
Built 1929 by Stavanger Stob & Dok, Stavanger, Norway
Propulsion Diesel engines. Engines built by General Motors
Tonnage 851 gross
Length 188.5ft/57.43m
Breadth 31.2ft/9.5m
Materials Steel throughout
Original use Coastal passenger steamer
Condition In operation since 1991
Present owners Stiftelsen Veteranskipslaget Rogaland
Location Stavanger, Norway
History Coastal passenger vessel largely unaltered in appearance. Converted to a repair ship. Has now been returned to carrying passengers, making cruises on the fjords out of Stavanger, Norway.

Gjøa
sailing coaster

Built 1873 by Knut Johanneson Skaale, Hardanger, Norway
Propulsion Sail, sloop rig; auxiliary engine added
Tonnage 67 gross
Length 69.0ft/21.03m
Breadth 20.5ft/6.25m
Draught 9.0ft/2.74m
Materials Wood throughout
Original use Cargo, later polar voyage
Condition Intact
Present owners Norsk Sjofartsmuseum
Location Oslo, Norway

History Built to carry cargo under sail in the Norwegian coastal trade. Used by Amundsen for the first transit of the Northwest Passage in 1903-06. Presented to the City of San Francisco where it was displayed in a park for many years. Returned to Norway in 1974. Preserved as an onshore exhibit.
Bibliography D8, D22, D158, D209, D378

Gokstad Ship
Viking ship

Built c850, probably in Norway
Original owners Probably Olav of Geirstadr
Propulsion Sail, single square sail, oars
Length 78.74ft/24.0m
Breadth 20.5ft/6.25m
Draught 2.79ft/0.85m
Materials Wood throughout
Original use Cargo
Condition Intact
Present owners The Viking Ship Museum
Location Oslo, Norway
History Largely intact Viking ship used for the burial of a local chieftain near the present town of Sandefjord. Excavated 1980. Preserved as an indoor exhibit.
Bibliography A8, C7, D386

Granvin
coastal cargo/passenger vessel

Built 1931
Propulsion Diesel engine; Bolinger 150hp replaced in 1968
Tonnage 115.0 gross
Length 89.9ft/27.4m
Breadth 18.4ft/5.6m
Depth 9.5ft/2.9m
Materials Steel hull; steel and wood deckhouse
Original use Cargo and passengers
Condition Restored, in operation
Present owners Hardanger Sunnhordlandske Dampskipsselskap
Contact address Strandgt 191, Bergen, Norway
Location Bergen, Norway
History Norwegian motor vessel formerly used to carry passengers and cargo in the fjords of the west coast and now making fjord excursions.

Hansteen
survey ship

Former name IVAR ELIAS, HAAREK
Built 1866 by Nylands Verksted, Oslo, Norway
Original owners Norges Geografiske

Opmaaling
Propulsion Steam, screw, 125hp, coal fired; schooner rig
Tonnage 114 gross
Length 101.5ft/30.94m
Breadth 16.33ft/4.98m
Draught 7.42ft/2.26m
Materials Iron hull, wood superstructure
Original use Survey ship
Condition Intact, fully restored
Present owners Olaf T Engvig
Location Oslo, Norway
History One of the oldest hydrographic survey vessels in existence. Later employed as a cargo vessel. Preserved as a floating exhibit.
Bibliography B16, D161

Hekkingen
lighthouse tender

Built 1913 by Moss Shipyard, Moss, Norway
Original owners Norwegian Lighthouse Service
Propulsion Steam, triple expansion; 64hp (removed)
Tonnage 165 gross
Length 108.8ft/33.2m
Breadth 21.4ft/6.5m

Depth 11.1ft/3.4m
Materials Steel hull
Original use Lighthouse tender
Condition Hull restored
Present owners Olaus Ottesen
Contact address Oevermarka 46, N-8800 Sandness Joen, Norway
Location Norway
History Veteran Norwegian steam-powered lighthouse tender. Currently undergoing restoration to an active steam vessel. A replacement for the original engine was being sought in 1998.

Heland
motor fishing boat

Built 1937 at Vestnes, Romsdal, Norway
Original owners Severin Roald, Alesund
Propulsion Petrol engine; 140hp
Length 63.0ft/19.2m
Breadth 16.0ft/4.88m
Draught 10.9ft/3.32m
Materials Wood throughout
Original use Fishing
Condition Intact
Present owners Sunnmore Museum, Alesund

Location Borgund, nr Alesund, Norway
History Fishing vessel that ran the German blockade in the Second World War. Preserved as a floating exhibit.

Hestmanden
steam coaster

Former name VEGAFJORD
Built 1911 by Laxevaag Maskin & Jernskibsbyggeri, Bergen, Norway
Original owners A/S Vesteraalens Dampskibsselskab, Stokmarknes
Propulsion Steam, screw, triple expansion, 475hp
Tonnage 755 gross
Length 195.0ft/59.44m
Breadth 30.0ft/9.14m
Draught 15.0ft/4.57m
Materials Steel throughout
Original use Cargo
Condition Intact
Present owners Norsk Veteranskibsklub Trondheim
Location Trondheim, Norway
History Veteran Norwegian steam cargo vessel, operated by Great Britain during the Second World War. Restored in the 1980s. Preserved as a floating exhibit.
Bibliography B14, D159

Hansteen on the Trondheimsfjord in summer 1990

Hitra
submarine chaser

Former name SC-718
Built 1943 by Fisher Boat Works, Detroit, Michigan
Original owners United States Navy
Propulsion Diesel engines, twin screw
Tonnage 148 displacement
Length 110.0ft/33.53m
Breadth 17.0ft/5.18m
Draught 6.5ft/1.98m
Materials Wood hull reinforced with steel
Original use Submarine chaser
Condition Fully restored
Present owners Norwegian Navy
Location Oslo, Norway
History Transferred from the US Navy to the free Norwegian forces during the Second World War and used to run the blockade. Preserved as a floating exhibit and operational vessel.
Bibliography D503, D526

Kvaernes
steamer

Built 1895
Propulsion Steam
Condition Undergoing restoration to 1895 appearance
Location Kristiansund, Norway

Kysten I
coastal cargo/passenger steamer

Former name ASKAAS, KYSTEN
Built 1909 by Trondhjems Mek Verksted, Trondheim, Norway
Original owners Namsos Dampskibsselskab, Namsos
Propulsion Steam, screw, triple expansion, 383hp
Tonnage 377 gross
Length 148.1ft/45.14m
Breadth 21.1ft/6.43m
Draught 15.39ft/4.69m
Materials Steel throughout
Original use Passengers and cargo
Condition In operating condition
Present owners Jubileumsskipet A/S KystenI, Husoysund
Location Tonsberg, Norway
History Currently in use for charters.
Bibliography B16

Loyal
trading brigantine

Built 1877 at Hardanger, Norway
Propulsion Sail, brigantine rig
Length 121.39ft/37m
Original use Cargo
Condition Restored by present owner

The Oseberg Viking ship

Present owners John Havsberg
Location Korsfjorden, Norway
History Traded worldwide and rounded Cape Horn. Made a record run from New York to Haugsund in 18.5 days fully loaded. Once used for smuggling between USA and Africa.

Oline
coasting sloop

Former name EIDFJORD
Built c1865 at Hardanger, Norway
Propulsion Sail, sloop rig; auxiliary engine added, 30hp
Length 45.0ft/13.72m
Breadth 16.0ft/4.88m
Materials Wood throughout
Original use Cargo
Condition In sailing condition
Location Norway
History Small 'Hardanger sloop' built for use in the Norwegian coastal trade or fishing. Fully restored in 1985 when

she was awarded a prize for the best restored vessel over 30ft in length. Preserved as an exhibit and active sailing vessel.

Opreisningen
femboring

Built c1900 in Norway
Propulsion Sail, large square sail and topsail
Length 44.0ft/13.4m
Materials Wood throughout
Original use Ferry and fishing vessel
Condition Intact
Present owners Norske Sjofartsmuseum
Location Oslo, Norway
History Sailing craft called a 'femboring', with small cabin at stern, related in design and construction to the Viking ships of almost 1000 years earlier. Exhibited indoors at the maritime museum in Oslo.

Oseberg Ship
Viking ship

Built c800, probably in Norway
Original owners Probably Queen Aasa
Propulsion Sail, single square sail, oars
Length 72.18ft/22.0m
Breadth 16.4ft/5.0m
Draught 2.46ft/0.75m
Materials Wood throughout
Original use Royal barge
Condition Intact
Present owners The Viking Ship Museum
Location Oslo, Norway
History Ornate Viking ship apparently used by royalty. Later used in the burial of two noblewomen. Excavated largely intact in 1994. Upper stem and stern restored. Preserved as an indoor exhibit.
Bibliography A8, C7, C59

Oster
coastal cargo/passenger steamer

Former name VAKA
Built 1908 by Kristiansands M/V, Kristiansand, Norway
Original owners Indre Nordhordlandske Dampskibsselskab
Propulsion Steam, screw, triple expansion, 54hp
Tonnage 167 gross
Length 106.1ft/32.2m
Breadth 21.7ft/6.6m
Materials Steel throughout
Original use Passengers and cargo
Condition Restoration in progress
Location Norway
History Small steamer built to operate in the Norwegian fjords. Was the last coal-burning vessel based at Bergen when converted to diesel in 1964. Currently being restored as an active steam vessel using the engine from the British dredge CLEARWAY.

Rap
torpedo boat

Former name MAELSTROM (during delivery)
Built 1872 by J I Thorneycroft, Chiswick, England
Original owners Norwegian Navy
Propulsion Steam, screw, compound, 100hp
Tonnage 10 displacement
Length 59.7ft/18.2m
Breadth 7.87ft/2.4m
Draught 2.95ft/0.9m
Materials Steel throughout
Original use Torpedo boat
Condition Intact

Present owners Norwegian Navy
Location Horten, Norway
History World's first vessel to launch self-propelled torpedoes. Preserved as an onshore exhibit.
Bibliography D1

Rjaanes
car ferry

Built 1936
Original use Car ferry
Condition Undergoing restoration
Location Kristiansund, Norway

Skibladner
sidewheel steamer

Built 1856 by Motala Verksted A/B, Motala, Sweden
Original owners A/S Oplandske Dampskibsselskab
Propulsion Steam, sidewheel, triple expansion, 606hp (1888). Engine built by Akers Mek Verksted
Tonnage 264 gross
Length 164.47ft/50.13m
Breadth 16.8ft/5.12m
Draught 8.2ft/2.5m
Materials Iron hull, iron and wood superstructure
Original use Passengers
Condition In operation
Present owners A/S Oplandske Dampskibsselskab
Location Lillehammer, Norway

History World's oldest passenger steamer still in operation. Engines date from 1888. In use as a passenger steamer.
Bibliography A17, B16, B43, D118, D237

Sørlandet
sail training ship

Built 1927 by P Hoivolds Mek Verksted, Kristiansand, Norway
Original owners Sorlandets Skoleskib
Propulsion Sail, full-rigged ship; auxiliary engine added
Tonnage 568 gross
Length 186.0ft/56.69m
Breadth 29.07ft/8.86m
Draught 15.98ft/4.87m
Materials Steel hull, steel and wood masts
Original use Training ship
Condition In operation
Present owners Municipality of Kristiansand
Location Kristiansand, Norway
History Last major European sail training ship to operate without an engine. One was finally installed in 1960. In use as a sail training vessel.
Bibliography A10, A14, C25, C96, D219

Southern Actor
whale catcher

Former name ITAXA III, POLARBRIS 8
Built 1950 by Smith's Dock Co,

Southern Actor

Middlesborough, England
Original owners Chr Salvesen & Co (South Georgia Co)
Propulsion Steam, triple expansion 1800ihp. Engine built by NE Marine Engine Co
Tonnage 439 gross
Length 158.9ft/48.4m
Breadth 27.5ft/8.4m
Draught 14.0ft/4.3m
Materials Steel throughout
Original use Whale catcher
Condition Recently restored, in operating condition
Present owners Foundation; managed by Sandefjord Whaling Museum
Location Sandefjord, Norway
History Norwegian steam whale catcher restored to operating condition as floating exhibit and travelling ambassador of the Sandefjord Museum.
Bibliography D23, D376

Sorlandet

Statsraad Lehmkuhl on a visit to New York

Statsraad Lehmkuhl

sail training ship

Former name GROSSHERZOG
FRIEDRICH AUGUST
Built 1914 by J C Tecklenborg,
Geestemunde, Germany
Original owners Deutsche Schulschiff
Verein
Propulsion Sail, barque rig; auxiliary
engine
Tonnage 1701 gross
Length 258.17ft/78.69m
Breadth 41.47ft/12.64m
Materials Steel hull, steel and wood
masts
Original use Training ship
Condition In operating condition

Present owners Stiftelsen Seilshipet
Statsraad Lehmkuhl
Location Bergen, Norway
History Built as a sail training vessel for
the German merchant marine. After
1922 served as a sail training ship for
the Norwegian merchant marine based
at Bergen. In use for youth sail
training.
Bibliography A10, A14, C25, C26, C96

Stavenes

coastal steamer

Built 1904 by Bergens M/V, Bergen,
Norway
Propulsion Steam, triple expansion;
converted to diesel, 350hp

Stavenes

Tonnage 187 gross
Length 111.5ft/34.02m
Breadth 20.1ft/6.1m
Draught 9.8ft/3.0m
Materials Steel hull
Original use Fjord passenger and cargo steamer
Location Kaupanger, Norway
History Small steamship employed in the fjords of Norway until retired in 1972. Was initially sold to a British owner for conversion to a yacht. Spent a number of years laid up in North Wales awaiting restoration, and has now been returned to Norway.

Stord I
coastal steamer

Former name O T MOE, STORD
Built 1913 by Laxevaag Maskin & Jernskibsbyggeri, Laxevaag, Norway
Original owners Hardanger Sunnhordlandske Co
Propulsion Steam, screw, triple expansion, 500hp
Tonnage 469 gross
Length 155.2ft/47.31m
Breadth 33.8ft/10.3m
Materials Steel hull
Original use Passengers and cargo
Condition Undergoing restoration after fire
Present owners Veteranskipslaget Fjordabaten
Location Bergen, Norway
History Proposed as an active steam vessel.
Bibliography B16

Styrbjørn
steam tug

Former name ATLET
Built 1910 by Gotaverken, Gothenburg, Sweden
Original owners Trafiktiebolaget, Grangesberg-Oselsund
Propulsion Steam, screw, 550hp, coal fired
Tonnage 167 gross
Length 93.25ft/28.42m
Breadth 22.33ft/6.81m
Draught 12.5ft/3.81m
Materials Steel hull, steel and wood superstructure
Original use Tug
Condition In operating condition
Present owners Norsk Veteranskibsklub
Location Oslo, Norway
History Preserved as an exhibit and active steamer.
Bibliography B16

Suldal
passenger steamer

Built 1885 by Stavanger Stoberi & Dock, Stavanger, Norway
Propulsion Steam, screw, compound, 150hp (present engine)
Tonnage 39 gross
Length 63.9ft/19.48m
Breadth 14.2ft/4.38m
Materials Iron or steel hull, wood superstructure
Original use Passengers
Condition Restored to operating condition
Present owners Foreningen Suldalsdampen
Location Suldalsvatn, Norway
History Preserved as an exhibit and active steamer.
Bibliography B16

Svanen
sail training ship

Former name SMART, JASON
Built 1916 by J Ring Andersen Yard, Svendborg, Denmark
Original owners A/S Aino, Arendal, Norway
Propulsion Sail, three-masted schooner rig; auxiliary engine
Tonnage 102 gross
Length 98.39ft/29.99m
Breadth 22.5ft/6.86m
Draught 8.5ft/2.59m
Materials Wood throughout
Original use Cargo
Condition In sailing condition
Present owners Stiftelsen Svanen
Location Oslo, Norway
History In use for youth sail training.
Bibliography A11, A15

Thorolf
steam coaster

Built 1911 by Skaaluren, Hardanger, Norway
Original owners O A Devold
Propulsion Steam, screw, compound, 75hp
Tonnage 27 gross
Length 60.0ft/18.29m
Breadth 14.42ft/4.4m
Materials Wood hull, steel and wood superstructure

Original use Cargo
Condition In operating condition
Present owners Foreningen til Dampskipet Thorolf
Location Alesund, Norway
History Currently in use for charters.
Bibliography B16

Tjeld
motor torpedo boat

Built 1960 by Boatservice Ltd, Oslo, Norway
Original owners Norwegian Navy
Propulsion Diesel engines, 6200hp
Tonnage 70 displacement
Length 80.33ft/24.5m
Breadth 24.5ft/7.5m
Draught 6.75ft/2.1m
Original use Torpedo boat
Condition Intact
Present owners Marinemuseet
Contact address Postboks 21, 3191 Horten, Norway
Location Horten, Norway
History Norwegian torpedo boat of the 1960s preserved as an exhibit at the Naval Base in Horten.

Vaerdalen

Vaerdalen
coastal passenger/cargo steamer

Built 1891 by Trondheims Mek
Vaerksted, Trondheim, Norway
Original owners Vaerdalsbruket A/S
Propulsion Steam, screw, compound;
converted to diesel, 220hp
Tonnage 49.7 gross, 112 displacement
Length 82.25ft/25.1m
Breadth 16.0ft/4.9m
Draught 6.0ft/1.8m
Materials Iron and steel hull, wood
superstructure
Original use Passengers and cargo
Condition Restoration in progress
Present owners Olaf T Engvig, Oslo
Location Trondheim, Norway
History Norwegian coastal and fjord
steamer in active service for 86
years.Proposed as an active steamer.
Bibliography D162

Wyvern
sailing yacht

Former name Havfruen III
Built 1896 by Porsgrund Baadbyggeri,
Porsgrund, Norway. Designed by Colin
Archer
Original owners Frederick Croft
Propulsion Sail, cutter rig; auxiliary
engine
Tonnage 42.84 gross
Length 59.7ft/18.2m
Breadth 17.71ft/5.4m
Draught 10.66ft/3.25m
Materials Wood throughout
Original use Yacht
Condition In sailing condition
Present owners Stavanger Maritime
Museum
Location Stavanger, Norway
History Preserved as an exhibit and
active sailing vessel.

Oman

Oman has existed under a series
of Arab dynasties since the
seventh century. Maritime
commerce has been a major
activity of this land, which has a
number of seaports on the
Arabian Sea and the Gulf of
Oman, the approach to the
Persian Gulf. Arab dhows, of
traditional wooden construction
and a type of lateen rig, have
carried on much of the country's
trade right up to the present,
making seasonal voyages as far
afield as Kenya and Tanzania on
the coast of Africa. A small navy is
maintained to patrol Oman's long
coastline, which includes the
south side of the strategic Strait
of Hormuz at the entrance to the
Persian Gulf.

Al Hadir
traditional sailing dhow

Built Date not known
Propulsion Sail, dhow rig; auxiliary
engine
Tonnage 300 displacement
Materials Wood throughout
Original use Cargo; later armed vessel
Condition Intact
Present owners Armed Forces Museum
Location Bait al Falaj Fort, Oman
History Traditional sailing dhow of the
Persian Gulf converted to a small Naval
vessel. Now retired and maintained as
an exhibit in the nation's Naval
Museum.

Al Mansur
naval patrol vessel

Built 1973 by Brooke Marine,
Lowestoft, England
Original owners Royal Navy of Oman
Propulsion Two diesel engines 4800hp
Tonnage 153 displacement
Length 123.0ft/37.5m
Breadth 22.5ft/6.9m
Draught 5.5ft/1.7m
Materials Steel throughout
Original use Patrol vessel
Condition Intact
Present owners Armed Forces Museum
Location Bait Al Falaj Fort, Oman
History Retired Naval patrol vessel
maintained as an exhibit of the
nation's Naval Museum.

Pakistan

Strife in India between Moslem
and Hindu following the granting
of independence in 1947
eventually led to partitioning of
the country and the creation of
the largely Moslem nation of
Pakistan with territory both in
the region of the Arabian Sea and
the Bay of Bengal. East Pakistan
on the Bay of Bengal eventually
seceded, forming Bangladesh. The
remaining nation of Pakistan on
the Arabian Sea has one major
seaport, Karachi, and maintains a
navy primarily aimed at India with
whom it has a long-standing
territorial dispute over the region
of Kashmir.

Mujahid
minesweeper

Former name USS MSC-261
Built 1956 by Hodgdon Brothers, East
Boothbay, Maine
Original owners Navy of Pakistan
Propulsion Diesel engines, twin screw,
1200hp
Tonnage 320 displacement
Length 141.1ft/43.0m
Breadth 26.1ft/7.95m
Draught 8.4ft/2.55m
Materials Wood throughout
Original use Minesweeper
Condition Intact
Present owners Pakistan Maritime
Museum Centre
Location Karachi, Pakistan
History Preserved as a floating exhibit
in the museum lagoon.

SX-404 Type
midget submarine

Built c1973 by Cosmos, Leghorn, Italy
Original owners Navy of Pakistan
Propulsion Probably diesel and electric
motors
Tonnage 40 displacement
Length 52.4ft/16.0m
Breadth 6.6ft/2.0m
Materials Steel throughout
Original use Midget Submarine
Condition Intact
Present owners Pakistan Maritime
Museum Centre
Location Karachi, Pakistan
History Preserved as a floating exhibit
in the museum lagoon.

Panama

The Isthmus of Panama, then
under the control of Colombia,
became an important world
thoroughfare in the mid-1800s
after the discovery of gold in
California. Travellers seeking a
shorter sea route could go there
by steamer, cross from sea to sea
by mule train and later railway,
and take a second steamer from
there to San Francisco. Panama is
best known as the location of the
isthmian canal linking Atlantic and
Pacific Oceans which eliminated
the long voyage around South
America. Construction of the
canal was begun by the French in
the 1880s. When they suspended
the project, they abandoned
much of their equipment where it
was lying. Some of the dredgers
and tugs were returned to
service when the United States
resumed construction shortly
after the turn of the century, but
apparently none of these vessels
survives today.

Hercules
floating crane

Built 1913 at Duisburg, Germany
Original owners Panama Canal Co
Propulsion Towed
Tonnage 4000 gross
Length 150.0ft/45.7m
Breadth 88.5ft/27.0m
Depth 16.66ft/5.1m
Materials Steel hull
Original use Floating crane
Condition In active service
Present owners Panama Canal Co
Location Gamboa, Panama
History Giant floating crane dating
from the final years of construction of
the Panama Canal. Has been
maintained in operating condition
since that time, but is now due for
replacement by more modern
equipment.

Peru

This South American country has several seaports on the Pacific Ocean, and access to the Atlantic through Iquitos, a port on the upper Amazon River 2300 miles from the sea. Its most interesting group of vessels is the small collection of venerable steamers and former steamers based at Puno at the north end of landlocked Lake Titicaca, 12,500ft above sea level. These vessels traded with the Bolivian port of Guaqui at the south end of the Lake, which was eventually linked by rail with the port of Arica on the Pacific. All were pre-fabricated in shipyards in the British Isles between 1862 and 1931, and the earliest were transported to the lake in pieces over an arduous mountain track by mule train. There have been sightings of abandoned steamboat remains in Peru's Amazon region, and one former steamer, the RIO AMAZONAS built in the British Isles in 1897, was making excursions out of Iquitos in the late 1980s as a somewhat altered motor vessel.

America
river gunboat

Built 1904 by Tranmere Bay Development Co, Birkenhead, England
Original owners Marina de Guerra del Peru
Propulsion Steam, screw, coal fired
Tonnage 240 displacement
Length 133.3ft/40.63m
Breadth 20.5ft/6.25m
Draught 5.0ft/1.52m
Materials Steel throughout
Original use Gunboat
Condition Intact
Present owners Marina de Guerra del Peru
Contact address Teniente Primero Manuel Clarero Naval Station
Location Amazon River, Peru
History River gunboat built to operate on the upper Amazon and its tributaries. Took part in the Battle of Pedrera in the war with Colombia in 1911. Preserved as a floating exhibit.

Coya
lake steamer

Built 1893 by Denny & Co, Dumbarton, Scotland (pre-fabricated)
Original owners The Peruvian Government
Propulsion Steam, screw, compound
Tonnage 546 gross

Coya

Length 170.0ft/51.82m
Breadth 26.0ft/7.93m
Draught 12.0ft/3.66m
Materials Steel hull, steel and wood superstructure
Original use Passengers and cargo
Condition Intact, out of service, laid up/beached
Present owners Empresa Nacional de Ferrocarriles del Peru
Location Puno, Lake Titicaca, Peru
Bibliography B19

Ollanta
lake steamer

Former name GRAN MARISCAL ANDRES DE SANTA CRUZ
Built 1931 by Earle's Shipbuilding & Engineering Co, Hull, England (pre-fabricated)
Original owners Empresa Nacional de Ferrocarriles del Peru
Propulsion Steam, twin screw
Length 260.0ft/79.25m
Breadth 35.6ft/10.85m

America

Materials Steel hull, steel and wood superstructure
Original use Passengers and cargo
Condition Out of service, apparently in good condition, laid up
Present owners Empresa Nacional de Ferrocarriles del Peru
Location Puno, Lake Titicaca, Peru
Bibliography B19, D561

Puno
lake steamer

Former name YAPURA
Built 1862 by James Watt & Co and The Thames Iron Works, Poplar, England (pre-fabricated)
Original owners The Peruvian Corporation
Propulsion Steam, screw; converted to diesel. Engine built by Paxman-Ricard (current)
Tonnage 200 gross
Length 128.0ft/39.01m
Breadth 20.0ft/6.1m
Draught 8.0ft/2.44m
Materials Iron hull, iron and wood superstructure
Original use Passengers and cargo
Condition In operation
Present owners Marina de Guerra del Peru
Location Puno, Lake Titicaca, Peru
History Currently a hospital ship.
Bibliography B19

Yavari
lake steamer

Former name CHUCUITO
Built 1862 by James Watt & Co and the Thames Iron Works, Poplar, England (pre-fabricated)
Original owners The Peruvian Corporation
Propulsion Steam, screw; converted to semi-diesel engine. Engine built by Bolinder
Tonnage 240 gross
Length 150.0ft/41.15m
Breadth 17.0ft/5.18m
Draught 10.0ft/2.44m
Materials Iron hull, iron and wood superstructure
Original use Passengers and cargo
Condition Laid up; funds for restoration being sought
Present owners La Asociacion Yavari
Location Puno, Lake Titicaca, Peru
Bibliography B19, D295

Philippines

This nation, made up of a large number of islands of various sizes, lies between the China Sea and the Pacific Ocean. It spent centuries as a colony of Spain until taken from that country by the United States in 1898. The latter nation kept the islands as its foothold in Asia, until they were invaded by Japan in 1942. The Philippines finally achieved full independence in 1946. Small, traditional sailing craft have been employed in fishing throughout the islands. Steam vessels were developed for inter-island trading during the early years of this century, to be replaced by motor vessels in the years following the Second World War. The independent Philippines remained staunch allies of the United States through the era of the Cold War, and the fleets of their Navy and Coast Guard have been largely composed of vessels that first served in the Navy and Coast Guard of that country.

Quezon
minesweeper and patrol vessel

Former name USS VIGILANCE
Built 1943 by Associated Shipbuilding in Seattle, Washington, USA
Original owners United States Navy
Propulsion Diesel engines, 2880hp by General Motors
Tonnage 1250 tons displacement
Length 221.0ft/67.41m
Breadth 32.0ft/9.8m
Draught 10.75ft/3.28m
Materials Steel throughout
Original use Minesweeper and escort vessel
Condition Unaltered; was brought out of lay-up and refitted in 1996
Present owners Philippine Navy
Location Manila, Philippines
History Built for the United States Navy during the Second World War. Was in the thick of action during landings at Okinawa. Transferred to the Philippine Navy in 1967.

Rajah Humabon
destroyer escort

Former names HATSUHI, USS ATHERTON
Built Federal Shipbuilding at Kearney, New Jersey, USA
Original owners United States Navy
Propulsion Diesel engines, twin screw, 6000hp by General Motors
Tonnage 1602 tons displacement
Length 306.0ft/93.27m
Breadth 36.5ft/11.15m
Draught 10.5ft/3.2m
Materials Steel throughout
Original use Destroyer escort
Condition Unaltered; brought out of lay-up and refitted in 1996
Present owners Philippine Navy
Location Manila, Philippines
History Destroyer escort that saw action with the United States Navy during the Second World War. Transferred to Japanese Self-Defense Force in 1955, and to the Philippine Navy in 1976.

Poland

The modern nation of Poland came into existence at the end of the First World War. Following the Second World War its boundaries were re-drawn. Poland has several seaports on the Baltic, some of which were formerly German, and an extensive internal network of navigable rivers and canals. During the period of the Cold War, Poland became one of the major shipbuilding centres of the communist bloc nations. A fleet of paddlewheel steamers was formerly operated on the Vistula River between Warsaw and the port of Gdansk. The last were apparently retired in the 1970s. Several were still in existence in the late 1980s, in a derelict state, but not beyond restoration.

Batory
Customs patrol boat

Former name HEL, LISTOPADA, DZIERSYNSKI, KP-1
Built 1932 by Stocznia Modlinska, Modlin, Poland
Original owners Polish Frontier Guard
Propulsion Diesel engines
Tonnage 28 displacement
Length 69.54ft/21.2m
Breadth 11.81ft/3.6m
Draught 4.43ft/1.35m
Materials Steel throughout
Original use Customs patrol boat
Condition Intact
Present owners Hel Naval Base
Location Hel, Poland
History Took part in the defence of Poland at the beginning of the Second World War, later escaping to Sweden. Preserved as an onshore exhibit.
Bibliography D288

Blyskawica
destroyer

Built 1936 by Samuel White & Co, Cowes, Isle of Wight, England
Original owners Polish Navy
Propulsion Steam turbines, 54,000hp
Tonnage 2144 displacement
Length 374.0ft/114.0m
Breadth 37.0ft/11.28m
Draught 10.25ft/3.12m
Materials Steel throughout

Original use Destroyer
Condition Intact
Present owners Polish Navy
Location Gdynia, Poland
History Served with the Allied forces in the Second World War. Preserved as a floating exhibit.
Bibliography C48, D337

Dar Pomorza
sail training vessel

Former name POMORZE, COLBERT, PRINZESS EITEL FRIEDRICH
Built 1909 by Blohm & Voss, Hamburg, Germany
Original owners German Schoolship Association
Propulsion Sail, full-rigged ship; auxiliary diesel engine, 430hp
Tonnage 1561 gross
Length 298.58ft/91.01m
Breadth 41.33ft/12.6m
Draught 18.75ft/5.72m
Materials Steel hull, steel and wood masts
Original use Training vessel
Condition Intact
Present owners Polish State Sea School
Location Gdynia, Poland

Blyskawica while still in service, 1955

History Built as a sail training ship for the German merchant marine. Acquired by Poland in 1929. Retired in 1981. Preserved as a floating exhibit.
Bibliography C25, C26, C96, D265

Samarytanka
medical launch

Built 1931 by Stocznia Gdynska, Gdynia, Poland
Original owners Urzad Morski
Tonnage 28 gross
Length 49.2ft/15.0m
Breadth 42.5ft/12.96m
Draught 4.92ft/1.5m
Materials Steel throughout
Original use Medical launch
Condition Intact
Present owners Stosznia Gdynska im Komuny Paryskiez
Location Gdynia, Poland
History First vessel built at Gdynia shipyard. Preserved as an onshore exhibit.

Soldek
steam collier

Built 1949 by Zjednoczenie Stoczni Polskich, Gdansk, Poland
Original owners Polish Steamship Co
Propulsion Steam, screw, 4-cylinder compound
Tonnage 2005 gross
Length 284.17ft/86.62m
Breadth 40.5ft/12.34m
Draught 17.67ft/5.39m
Materials Steel throughout
Original use Cargo
Condition Intact
Present owners Centralnie Muzeum Morskie
Location Gdansk, Poland
History First vessel built in Poland after the Second World War. Preserved as a floating exhibit.

Soldek

Portugal

Portuguese navigators were the first to chart some of the world's most important routes of maritime commerce, including the passage around the Cape of Good Hope to Asia. Portugal once had an extensive colonial empire in Africa, Asia, and South America, but by the late-1800s this had been reduced to Angola and Mozambique in southern Africa, and small outposts like Goa in India, and Macao on the coast of China. The coastal and inland waters of Portugal itself have been home to a variety of traditional craft used for fishing, gathering seaweed, and transporting goods, including port wine. The Portuguese until quite recently maintained one of the last fleets of seagoing sailing vessels, a group of wood and steel barkentines and large schooners employed in seasonal dory fishing for cod on the Grand Banks off Newfoundland. Largely unaltered survivors of this fleet are the wooden barkentine GAZELA OF PHILADELPHIA now owned in the United States, and the steel four-masted schooner CREOULA refitted in Portugal as a training vessel.

A Pombinha
Tagus sailing lighter

Built in Portugal (date not known)
Propulsion Sail, sloop rig
Length 64.71ft/19.73m
Breadth 15.74ft/5.4m
Materials Wood throughout
Original use Cargo
Condition Intact
Present owners Commune de Moita
Location Moita, Portugal
History Preserved as a floating exhibit.
Bibliography B30

Baia Do Seixal
Tagus sailing lighter

Built Date not known
Propulsion Sail, sloop rig
Length c65.0ft/20.0m
Breadth c16.0ft/5.0m
Materials Wood throughout
Original use Cargo
Condition In sailing condition

Present owners Commune de Seixal
Location Seixal, Portugal
History Preserved as a floating exhibit.
Bibliography B30

Bergantim Real
royal barge

Built 1778 in Portugal
Original owners Portuguese Royal Family
Propulsion Rowed
Length 96.13ft/29.3m
Breadth 13.06ft/3.98m
Materials Wood throughout
Original use Royal barge
Condition Intact
Present owners Museu de Marinha
Location Lisbon, Portugal
History Preserved as an indoor exhibit.

Boa Viagem
Tagus sailing lighter

Built 1930 in Portugal
Propulsion Sail, sloop rig
Length 65.27ft/19.9m

Breadth 17.71ft/5.4m
Materials Wood throughout
Original use Cargo
Condition In sailing condition
Present owners Commune de Moita
Location Moita, Portugal
History Preserved as a floating exhibit.

Creoula
sail fishing boat

Built 1937 by Cia Uniao Fabril, Lisbon, Portugal
Original owners Parceia Geal de Pescaras
Propulsion Sail, four-masted schooner rig; diesel engine, 600hp
Tonnage 655 gross
Length 207.67ft/63.3m
Breadth 32.48ft/9.9m
Materials Steel throughout
Original use Fishing
Condition In sailing condition
Present owners Portuguese Government
Location Lisbon, Portugal
History Built for the Portuguese Grand

Banks dory codfishing fleet. Converted to a sail training ship in the 1980s and remains in use as such.

Dom Fernando II e Gloria
sailing frigate

Built 1843 by Naval Dockyard, Damao, Portuguese India
Original owners Portuguese Navy
Propulsion Sail, full-rigged ship
Tonnage 1850 displacement
Length 160.0ft/48.77m
Breadth 42.0ft/12.8m
Draught 20.0ft/6.1m
Materials Wood throughout
Original use Frigate
Condition Fully rebuilt in 1990s
Present owners Portuguese Navy
Location Lisbon, Portugal
History Oldest surviving Portuguese warship. Badly damaged by fire in 1963 while in use as a stationary training ship near Alfeite. Salvaged in 1992 and restored. Preserved as a floating exhibit.
Bibliography D235, D446

Creoula

Fragata Do Tejo
sailing lighter

Built in Portugal (date not known)
Propulsion Sail, sloop rig
Tonnage 100 gross
Length 72.18ft/22.0m
Breadth 20.01ft/6.1m
Draught 9.84ft/3.0m
Materials Wood throughout
Original use Cargo
Condition Intact
Present owners Museu de Arte Popular
Location Lisbon, Portugal
History Preserved as an onshore exhibit.

Fregata do Tejo

Leao Holandes
trading schooner

Former name TAHITI, SEPHA VOLLAARS, MARIE HILCK, MARTHA AHRENS
Built 1910 by G & H Bodewes, Martenshoek, Netherlands
Original owners Captain Dehle, Blitzfleth, Germany
Propulsion Sail, three-masted schooner rig; diesel auxiliary
Tonnage 101.7 gross
Length 144.32ft/44.0m
Breadth 20.17ft/6.15m
Draught 10.5ft/3.2m
Materials Wood throughout
Original use Cargo
Condition In sailing condition
Present owners Dirk-Willem & Joanne Gesink, Netherlands
Location Olhao, Portugal
History Built to carry cargo under the German flag. Currently in use for cruises.
Bibliography C53

Sagres
sail training ship

Former name GUANABARA, ALBERT LEO SCHLAGETER
Built 1937 by Blohm & Voss, Hamburg, Germany
Original owners German Navy
Propulsion Sail, barque rig; diesel engine, 750hp
Tonnage 1869 displacement
Length 266.75ft/81.31m
Breadth 30.5ft/9.3m
Draught 24.75ft/7.54m
Materials Steel throughout
Original use Training ship
Condition In operation
Present owners Portuguese Navy
Location Alfeite, Portugal
History Built for the German Navy, serving after the Second World War with the Brazilian Navy. Acquired by Portugal in 1962. Currently used as a training ship.
Bibliography A14, C25, C96

Sagres

WORLD SHIP TRUST

Patron HM King Bhumibol Adulyadej of Thailand

Founded by Frank G G Carr CB CBE FSA

202 Lambeth Road, LONDON, SE1 7JW
Telephone 0171-261 9535 Fax 0171-401 2537
Registered Charity Number 277751

THE WORLD SHIP TRUST is a Registered UK Charity, founded in 1979, to advance the education of the international public in the importance of the world's maritime heritage by urging governments and other bodies to preserve historic ships and associated artefacts. The Trust is managed by an international Council and currently has members in more than thirty countries. As well as sponsoring this Register, it publishes a Review three time a year which provides an on-going update of the world's ship preservation scene. Its Maritime Heritage Award, presented periodically to worthy preserved ships and usually presented on the Trust's behalf by Heads of States, is the most coveted award of its kind. The plates which follow feature most of these award-winners. Anyone interested in helping to further the Trust's aims should write to the above address.

The first award to a ship was made to the recovered and restored Vasa. It was presented on 3 April 1982 by King Carl Gustav XVI of Sweden to Mr Tore Tallroth, Chairman of the Sea History Museums Council.

Shown here being sprayed to stabilise the timbers, the MARY ROSE won the third award. It was presented at Buckingham Palace on 28 October 1983 by HM Queen Elizabeth II, and was received by HRH Prince Charles, as President of the Mary Rose Trust.

The USS CONSTITUTION was given the Trust's fifth
award. It was presented on 17 December 1987 by
President Ronald Reagan to Commander David
M Cashman, USN, Commanding Officer.

Two awards were made in 1988, the first to HMS WARRIOR (1860). It was presented on 24 March of that year by HRH Prince Philip to Sir John Smith CBE for his unstinted contribution to the ship's preservation.

The second 1988 award went to POLLY WOODSIDE (left and opposite) in Australia, and was presented on 17 October by Dr Davis McCaughy, Governor of Victoria, to Commander Michael Parker CVO, Chairman of Melbourne Maritime Museum.

The SUBANAHONGSA, a Royal Barge of Thailand, received an award which was presented on 4 June 1992 by HM King Bhumibol Adulyadej to the Director of Thailand's National Fine Arts Department.

The Dutch BUFFEL was the recipient of the tenth award, presented on 8 September 1995 by Vice Admiral J A L Van Aalst, Inspector of the Royal Netherlands Armed Forces, to Mr Lex Kater, Director of the Prins Hendrik Maritime Museum, Rotterdam.

The 1996 award went to the Brunel's iron ship
GREAT BRITAIN, and was presented on 15 October by
HRH Prince Philip to Sir Richard Gaskell, Chairman
of the Great Britain Project.

The award to the HUASCAR was made on
15 November 1995 by the Chilean Minister of State
and received by Admiral Jorge Balaresque Walbaum,
Commander-in-Chief Second Naval Zone, Chilean Navy.

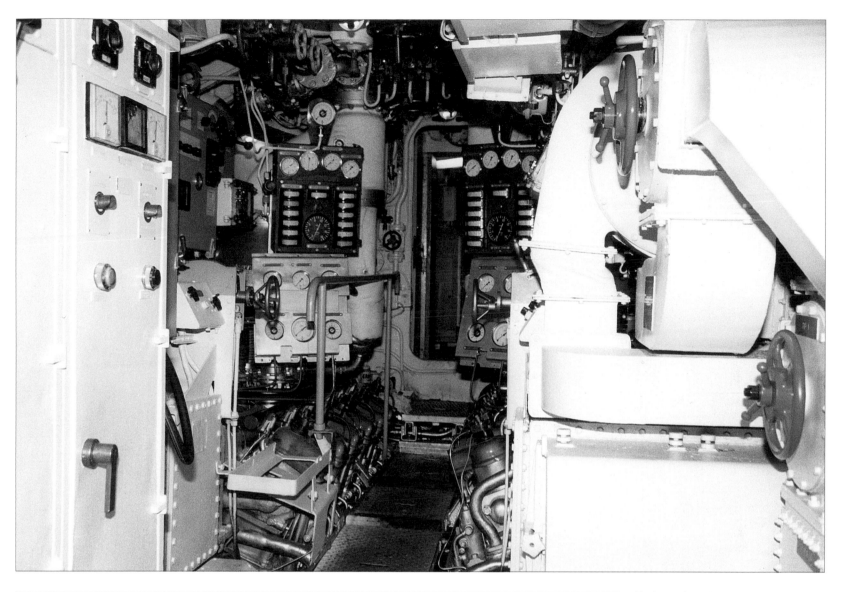

The fourteenth award went to the French submarine
Argonaute. It was presented to M Jacques Chauveau,
President of AMERAMI, by M Christian Poncelet,
President du Senat.

Portugal received the first of two awards to date
for the royal barge BERGANTIM REAL. It was presented
on 20 November 1997 by Senhor Jorge Sampaio,
President of Portugal, to Admiral Nuno Gonçalo
Vieira Matias, Chief of Naval Staff, Portuguese Navies.

Portugal's second award went to the DOM FERNANDO II E GLORIA.
It was presented on 11 March 1999 by Senhor Jorge Sampaio,
President of Portugal, to Admiral Nuno Gonçalo Vieira Matias,
Chief of Naval Staff, Portuguese Navies.

The next presentation will be a joint award to the two preserved American Liberty ships JEREMIAH O'BRIEN (above) and JOHN W BROWN.

The award for the Millenium Year will go to the tea clipper CUTTY SARK, now restored to her original appearance at Greenwich in south-east London.

Overleaf
The most recent award was to the barque STAR OF INDIA, presented on 28 April 1999 by President Gerald S Ford to Mr Bob Dysart, President of the San Diego Maratime Museum.

Romania

This country came into existence in 1857 through the merging of the principalities of Moldavia and Walachia, which had been freed from Russian rule by the Treaty ending the Crimean War. Its southern boundary is formed by the Danube River, whose delta at the Black Sea makes up much of Romania's fairly short coastline. This stretch of the Danube was once navigated by many passenger steamers and steam towboats. The TUDOR VLADIMIRESCU built as a towboat in 1854 but converted to carry passengers in 1958, is one of the oldest operating steam vessels in the world. There are reports that the former Romanian royal yacht LIBERTATEA, originally privately owned in England, has now been bought by interests in London who probably intend to return her to England and restore her to operating condition.

Borcea
sidewheel river tug

Built 1913 at Turnu Severin, Romania
Original owners Navigatia Fluviala Romana
Propulsion Steam, sidewheel, compound diagonal, 190hp. Engine built by Gebruder Saschsenberg
Length 124.7ft/38.0m
Breadth 21.3ft/6.5m
Materials Steel hull
Original use Towboat; later passengers
Condition In operation
Present owners Navigatia Maritimadi Fluviala Romina
Location Galati, Romania
History Currently used as a passenger steamer.
Bibliography B43

Libertatea
steam yacht

Former name LUCEAFERAL, NAHLIN
Built 1930 by John Brown Ltd, Clydebank, Scotland
Original owners Lady Yule
Propulsion Steam turbines, 4000hp
Tonnage 1574 displacement
Length 300.0ft/91.44m
Breadth 36.0ft/10.97m
Draught 14.8ft/4.51m

Materials Steel hull, steel and wood superstructure
Original use Yacht
Condition Intact, in use
Present owners Government of Romania
Location Galati, Romania
History Built for a British owner. Later became the royal yacht of King Carol of Romania, later used as a passenger vessel. Currently in use as a floating restaurant.
Bibliography B16, C15, C40, D471, D541a

Mircea
sail training ship

Built 1938 by Blohm & Voss, Hamburg, Germany
Original owners Government of Romania
Propulsion Sail, barque rig; diesel engine, 1100hp
Tonnage 1760 displacement
Length 242.0ft/73.76m
Breadth 39.5ft/12.04m
Draught 17.0ft/5.18m
Materials Steel hull, steel and wood masts
Original use Training ship
Condition In operation

Present owners Government of Romania
Location Constanta, Romania
History Currently in use as a training ship.
Bibliography A14, C96

Priboesti-Maramures
floating mill

Built Date not known
Propulsion Stationary
Length 42.0ft/12.8m
Breadth 43.3ft/13.2m
Materials Wood throughout
Original use Floating mill
Condition Intact
Present owners Popular Science Museum
Location Sibiu, Romania
History Example of type of moored floating mill once common on Eastern European rivers. Preserved as a floating exhibit.

Tudor Vladimirescu
sidewheel river tug

Former name GRIGORE MANU, SARMISEGETUZA, CROATIA
Built 1854 by Altofen Shipyard, Budapest, Hungary

Original owners DDSG
Propulsion Steam, sidewheel, oscillating, 600hp. Engine built by Escher Wyss
Length 215.84ft/65.8m
Breadth 47.23ft/14.4m
Materials Iron hull
Original use Towboat, later passengers
Condition Intact, out of service, laid up
Present owners NAVROM
Location Galati, Romania
History Built as a sidewheel towboat for use on the Danube. Later converted to passenger service. Currently laid up.
Bibliography B16, B43

Mircea at New York during Operation Sail, 1976

Russia

Occupying a vast area extending across both Europe and Asia, Russia was during its early history more concerned with internal commerce than with foreign trade. Peter the Great introduced western shipbuilding techniques, and created a navy in the western European tradition, in the early 1700s. During the nineteenth century sailing ships flying the Russian flag engaged in world trade were usually built and owned in Russian-controlled Finland. In the early 1930s the communist government embarked on a major shipbuilding effort aimed at creating one of the world's largest merchant fleets of steam and motor-powered vessels. This effort to compete in the world shipping industry was resumed following the interruption of the Second World War. Russia's European coastlines are linked by systems of navigable rivers and modern canals. Craft employed there included both Russian-built steam tugs and passenger boats, and others confiscated on rivers like the Danube at the end of the war, some of which may survive to be put back into service if tourism on these waterways continues to expand.

Aurora

Angara
lake steamer

Former name ZARIST
Built 1899 by Armstrong-Whitworth, Newcastle, England (pre-fabricated) at Lake Baikal, Siberia, Russia
Propulsion Steam, screw, triple-expansion, 1215hp
Length 199.95ft/60.96m
Breadth 35.0ft/10.67m
Draught 20.99ft/6.4m
Materials Steel throughout
Original use Passengers and cargo
Condition Intact
Present owners Irkutsk Museum
Location Lake Baikal, Siberia, Russia
History Icebreaking passenger steamer pre-fabricated in England and assembled in Siberia for use on Lake Baikal. Was the scene of historic events during the Russian Civil War. Had been lying half sunk but intact on the

shore of the lake. Now serving as an exhibit and museum.
Bibliography B16

Aurora
cruiser

Built 1900 by Galerni Island Shipyard, St Petersburg, Russia
Original owners Imperial Russian Navy
Propulsion Steam, screw, triple expansion, 11,600hp
Tonnage 6630 displacement
Length 416.0ft/126.8m
Breadth 55.0ft/16.76m
Draught 21.0ft/6.4m
Materials Steel throughout
Original use Cruiser
Condition Intact
Present owners Russian Government
Location St Petersburg, Russia
History Cruiser of the pre-dreadnought era that played a central

role in the Bolshevik Revolution of 1917. Served as an anti-aircraft battery during the seige of Leningrad during the Second World War. Preserved in immaculate condition as a naval museum and memorial.
Bibliography A8, D286

E-8
steam tug

Built Date not known
Propulsion Apparently steam, screw
Materials Steel throughout
Original use Tug
Condition Intact
Location Lake Ladoga, Russia
History Tug, apparently steam-powered, formerly employed on Russian rivers. Currently an exhibit on shore at a maritime museum beside Lake Ladoga.

Gasetel
towing steamer

Former name TSAREV
Built 1901
Propulsion Steam, screw
Length 120.38ft/36.7m
Breadth 20.11ft/6.13m
Materials Steel throughout
Original use Towing
Condition Intact
Location Volgagrad, Russia
History Veteran towing steamer preserved on shore as an exhibit at a museum at Volgagrad.

K-21
submarine

Built 1938 by Ordzhonikidze Shipyard, Russia
Original owners Russian Navy
Official number S-21

Propulsion Diesel and electric motors
Tonnage 2600 displacement
Length 320.33ft/97.65m
Breadth 24.25ft/7.4m
Draught 14.8ft/4.51m
Materials Steel throughout
Original use Submarine
Condition Intact
Location Severomorsk, Russia
History Russian submarine that saw action in the Second World War, and at one point made an unsuccessful attack on the German battleship TIRPITZ. Used for stationary training after 1959, and now on shore as an exhibit and memorial at Severomorsk.

Krasnyi Vyimpel
official yacht

Former name ADMIRAL ZAVOYKO
Built 1910
Original owners Governor-General of Kamchatka
Propulsion Steam, screw
Length 192.21ft/58.6m
Breadth 27.88ft/8.5m
Materials Steel throughout
Original use Official yacht
Condition Intact
Present owners Pacific Fleet Museum

Krassin

Location Vladivostok, Russia
History Government yacht that took part in the Bolshevik Revolution of 1917 in the Pacific. Preserved afloat as a naval museum and memorial in Vladivostock.

Krassin
steam icebreaker

Former name LEONID KRASSIN, SVYATOGOR
Built 1917 by Armstrong-Whitworth & Co, Newcastle on Tyne, England
Original owners Russian Government
Propulsion Steam, triple screw, triple expansion, 10,000hp. Engine built by Schlieker Werft, Hamburg (current)
Tonnage 10,620 displacement
Length 323.25ft/98.5m
Breadth 71.0ft/21.6m
Draught 30.0ft/9.1m
Materials Steel throughout
Original use Icebreaker
Condition Intact, apparently in operating condition
Present owners International Fund for the History of Science, Murmansk, Russia
Location St Petersburg, Russia
History Veteran Russian icebreaker, re-engined but apparently still steam-powered. Visited the United States in 1941 when it was thought she would be loaned to the US Coast Guard for use in eastern Greenland, but was never transferred. Superstructure has been modernised and two original stacks have been replaced. In use for training and exhibited.

Kronverk
sail training/research vessel

Former name SIRIUS
Built c1949 in Finland
Original owners Soviet Government
Propulsion Sail, barquentine rig; diesel engine
Tonnage c626 displacement
Length 123.0ft/37.49m
Breadth 29.0ft/8.84m
Draught 11.5ft/3.51m
Materials Wood throughout
Original use Sail training or research
Condition Intact
Location St Petersburg, Russia
History One of a series of wooden sailing vessels built in Finland in the late 1940s as Second World War reparations payment to Russia. Apparently employed as a research vessel. Now retired and moored as an exhibit in one of the canals of the City of St Petersburg.
Bibliography A15

Krasnyi Vyimpel at Vladivostock with the submarine S-56 in the background

Kruzenshtern
trading barque

Former name PADUA
Built 1926 by J C Tecklenborg,
Wesermunde, Germany
Original owners F Laeisz & Co,
Hamburg
Propulsion Sail, four-masted barque
rig; auxiliary diesel engine added
Tonnage 3545 gross
Length 319.5ft/97.38m
Breadth 46.0ft/14.02m
Materials Steel throughout
Original use Cargo
Condition In operation
Present owners Russian Ministry of
Fisheries
Location Kaliningrad, Russia
History Last major sailing ship built in
the world to carry cargoes on long
voyages. Awarded to Russia after the
Second World War and converted to a
training vessel with auxiliary engines.
Had been a training vessel for the
Russian fishing fleet based at Talinn,
Estonia. Home port has now been
moved to Kaliningrad, Russia.
Bibliography A10, A15, C25

N V Gogol
river steamer

Built 1911, Nizhni Novgorod, Russia
Propulsion Steam, sidewheel
Materials Steel throughout
Original use Passengers
Condition In operating condition
Location Archangel, Russia
History Russian river steamer
refurbished for cruises on the
Severnaya Dvina river. Cruises out of
Archangel were advertised briefly in
1998 by the Russian tourist service
Intourist.

Narodovolec
submarine

Former name D-2
Built 1929 by Ordzhonikidze Shipyard,
St Petersburg, Russia
Original owners Soviet Navy
Propulsion Diesel and electric motors
Tonnage 1354 displacement
Length 249.33ft/76.0m
Breadth 21.33ft/6.5m
Draught 12.5ft/3.8m
Materials Steel throughout
Original use Submarine
Condition Intact
Present owners Russian Navy
Location St Petersburg, Russia
History Russian submarine that saw
action in the Second World War. Used

Kruzenshtern

Narodovolec

No 302

for stationary training after 1958, and currently preserved on shore in St Petersburg.

Nicolai Knipovich
Arctic research vessel

Built Date not known
Propulsion Sail, ketch rig; diesel engine
Materials Wood throughout
Original use Arctic research
Condition Intact
Location Archangel, Russia
History Ketch-rigged motor vessel formerly employed in the Russian Arctic region. Currently preserved as an exhibit at the maritime museum in Archangel.

No 302
armed motor launch

Built c1940
Original owners Soviet Navy
Official number 302
Propulsion Diesel engine
Tonnage 30 displacement
Length c80.0ft/24.38m
Breadth c14.0ft/4.27m
Original use Armed motor launch
Condition Intact
Present owners City of Khabarovsk
Location Khabarovsk, Russia
History Small armed motor launch of the Second World War period preserved as an exhibit and naval memorial on shore.

Ost
steam sidewheel ferry

Built c1900 in Russia
Propulsion Steam, sidewheel
Length 195.6ft/59.6m
Breadth 43.0ft/13.1m
Original use Ferry
Condition Intact
Location Siberia, Russia
History Intact steam sidewheel ferryboat preserved on shore in Siberia. Was apparently the boat that carried Lenin across a river into exile in 1900.

S-56
submarine

Built 1939 by Dalzavod Shipyard, Vladivostok, Russia
Original owners Soviet Navy
Propulsion Diesel and electric motors
Tonnage 1090 displacement

Sedov

Length 255.0ft/77.72m
Breadth 21.0ft/6.4m
Draught 13.33ft/4.06m
Materials Steel throughout
Original use Submarine
Condition Intact
Present owners Pacific Fleet Museum
Location Vladivostok, Russia
History Russian submarine that saw action in the Second World War, preserved on shore at Vladivostock as an exhibit and naval memorial.
Bibliography A6, A16

Sedov
auxiliary trading barque

Former name KOMMODORE JOHNSEN, MAGDALENE VINNEN
Built 1921 by Germania Werft, Kiel, Germany
Original owners F A Vinnen, Bremen
Propulsion Sail, four-masted barque; diesel auxiliary engine
Tonnage 3476 gross, 5300 displacement
Length 328.8ft/100.22m
Breadth 48.0ft/14.63m
Materials Steel throughout
Original use Cargo
Condition In operation
Location Russia
History Built on the lines of a sailing cargo vessel, but was always fitted with an auxiliary engine. Converted to a cargo-carrying training ship in the 1930s. Awarded to Russia after the Second World War and refitted for training use only. Still in active service. Some cadet berths are available to paying trainees of any nation.
Bibliography A10, A14, C96, D305

Sviatitel Nicolai
sidewheel river steamer

Built 1887
Propulsion Steam, sidewheel
Length 194.18ft/59.2m
Breadth 50.41ft/15.37m
Draught 4.1ft/1.25m
Materials Iron or steel hull
Original use Passengers
Condition Intact
Present owners Shushenskoe Historic Village
Location Shushenskoe, Siberia, Russia
History Veteran Yenesei river paddlewheel steamer that carried Lenin into exile at Shushenskoe in 1897. Preserved afloat as a museum.

TO-215
submarine chaser

Built c1942
Original owners Russian Navy
Propulsion Diesel engine
Materials Steel throughout
Original use Submarine chaser
Condition Intact
Location Lake Ladoga, Russia
History Russian submarine chaser, probably a veteran of the Second World War, exhibited on shore at a maritime museum beside Lake Ladoga.

Vityaz
motor cargo ship

Former name EKVATER, EMPIRE FORTH, MARS
Built 1939 by Seebeck, Geestemunde, Germany
Original owners Neptun Steamship Co, Bremen
Propulsion Diesel engines, 3000hp
Tonnage 5700 displacement
Length 352.27ft/107.4m
Breadth 48.54ft/14.8m
Draught 15.42ft/4.7m
Materials Steel throughout
Original use Cargo
Condition Intact
Present owners Kaliningrad Maritime Museum
Location Kaliningrad, Russia
History German cargo ship confiscated by Great Britain after the Second World War but later transferred to Russia. Used by Russia as a cargo vessel and later as a research vessel. Preserved afloat as a museum at Kaliningrad.

Zapad
trading schooner

Built 1949 in Finland
Original owners Soviet government
Propulsion Sail, three-masted schooner; diesel engine
Tonnage 322 gross
Length 126.93ft/38.66m
Breadth 29.16ft/8.89m
Draught 9.16ft/2.79m
Materials Wood throughout
Original use Cargo
Condition In operation
Location Home port Archangel, Russia
History One of the large series of wooden sailing vessels built in Finland in the late 1940s as Second World War reparations payments to Russia. Employed as a training vessel based at Archangel in northern Russia.

Seychelles

Composed of 115 islands scattered across the Indian Ocean northeast of Madagascar, the Seychelles were first settled by the French in the 1750s. Great Britain took the islands from France in 1794, and granted them their independence in 1976. Schooners were employed here in the inter-island trade well after they had gone out of use elsewhere in the world. The one surviving example is a steel-hulled vessel that is laid up intact but un-maintained, and is not currently the subject of any preservation efforts.

Isle of Farquhar
trading schooner

Former name LA PERLE
Built 1909 at Groningen, Netherlands
Propulsion Sail, three-masted schooner rig; diesel auxiliary engine. Engine built by Blackstone
Tonnage 176 gross
Length 102.0ft/31.1m
Materials Steel throughout
Original use Cargo
Condition Intact, but unmaintained, laid up
Location Nr Mahe, Seychelles
Bibliography C92

Singapore

When Malaysia gained its independence from British colonial rule, Singapore, located on an island at the southern tip of the Malay Peninsula, to which it is linked by a causeway, chose to remain politically separate. Its busy seaport created from a small fishing village in the early 1800s had quickly become a major crossroads for shipping due to its location at the meeting point of the Malay Straits, the straits between Sumatra and Borneo, and the China Sea. Few ports have seen such a variety of shipping, including quite recently the larger traditional sailing craft of such regions as the Malay coast, the islands of Indonesia, Indochina, and even China. In the last decade Singapore has grown dramatically in importance, handling during some years of the 1990s a larger volume of trade than any other port in the world.

Vietnamese refugee boat

Built Date not known
Condition Intact
Location Singapore
History Small Vietnamese cargo or fishing boat used by refugees fleeing that country during the Communist takeover of the early 1970s. Preserved as an onshore exhibit.

Additional small naval vessels preserved in Russia as monuments or relics

Location	Type	Pennant number
Azov	torpedo boat	TKA-001
Baltysk	torpedo boat	36
Blagoveschensk	river monitor	BK-905
Bisk	river monitor	BKA- 162
Murmansk	torpedo boat	TKA-12
Novorossiisk	torpedo boat	TKA-341
	armed launch	
Perm	river monitor	BKA-181
Petropavllovsk	torpedo boat	TK-456
Pinsk	river monitor	BKA-92
Severomorsk	torpedo boat	
St Petersburg	torpedo boat	
Taganrog	armed launch	KTSC-772
Vladivostok	torpedo boat	123
	armed fishing boat	MPC-80
Zelenodolsk	river monitor	BK-234

Slovak Republic

Formerly the eastern portion of the Republic of Czechoslovakia created after the First World War, Slovakia declared its independence in July 1992, which became official as of January 1993. Slovakia has no coastline, and little in the way of navigable waterways aside from a stretch of the Danube River, which forms part of its southern border with Hungary, and passes through its capital city, Bratislava. This industrial centre has been an important port on the river since the days of the Austro-Hungarian Empire in the late nineteenth century.

Devin
sidewheel steam ferry

Former name DUNAJ, MAGYER, TABAU
Built 1911 at Regensburg, Germany
Propulsion Steam, sidewheel, compound diagonal, 110hp, coal fired
Length 109.9ft/33.5m
Breadth 25.3ft/7.7m
Materials Steel throughout
Original use Ferry
Condition Largely unaltered, in use
Location Bratislava, Slovak Republic
History Small steam sidewheel ferryboat formerly used at a river crossing in Bratislava. Retired in 1966. Served for a time as a floating clubhouse, and is now a floating restaurant still largely unaltered in appearance.
Bibliography B43

South Africa

The first permanent European colony at the Cape of Good Hope was established by the Dutch in 1652. Great Britain occupied the Cape twice during the Napoleonic Wars, and finally bought the Colony from the Netherlands in 1814. Britain fought the Boer War which ended in 1902, consolidating its control over the region, but in 1910 allowed the creation of the Union of South Africa whose early political leaders had been Boer military commanders. The leading ports on the Cape's otherwise inhospitable coastline are Cape Town, Durban, Port Lincoln, and Port Elizabeth. There are no major navigable rivers, and most lakes large enough for boating are man-made. South Africa has been one of the last strongholds of steam power, keeping steam trains in use until quite recently on major routes and still preserving a few in operation for tourists and enthusiasts. The South African ports were some of the last to be served by steam tugs. The last of these have now been retired, but some fine examples now make up a good part of the country's preserved historic vessels.

Alwyn Vintcent
steam tug

Built 1959 by Cantieri Navali e Officiene Meccaniche, Venice, Italy
Original owners South African Railways & Harbours
Propulsion Steam, screw, triple expansion, coal fired
Tonnage 111 gross
Length 82.67ft/25.2m
Breadth 20.08ft/6.12m
Draught 10.5ft/3.2m
Materials Steel hull, steel and wood superstructure
Original use Tug
Condition In operating condition
Present owners South African Maritime Museum
Location Cape Town, South Africa
History Served as a tug and as a tender to liners in Algoa and Mossel Bays, where passengers were lowered to the tug in large baskets. Preserved as a floating exhibit.
Bibliography C80

Cable Restorer
steam cable ship

Former name RETRIEVER
Built 1944 by Swan Hunter, Wallsend, England
Original owners Cable & Wireless, London
Propulsion Steam, twin screw, triple expansion
Tonnage 1506 gross
Length 251.97ft/76.82m
Breadth 41.0ft/12.5m

Materials Steel throughout
Original use Cable ship
Condition In operation
Present owners South Atlantic Cable Co
Location Cape Town, South Africa
History Steam submarine cable laying and maintenance vessel built during the Second World War.

Durban
minesweeper

Former name SAS DURBAN
Built 1957 by Camper & Nicholson, Southampton, England
Original owners South African Navy
Propulsion Diesel engines, 3000hp
Tonnage 360 displacement
Length 152.0ft/46.6m
Breadth 28.75ft/8.5m
Draught 8.25ft/2.51m
Materials Hull wood over aluminium frames, superstructure aluminium
Original use Minesweeper
Condition Intact
Present owners Natal Maritime Museum
Location Durban, South Africa
History Preserved as a floating exhibit.

J E Eaglesham
steam tug

Built 1958 by Cantieri Navali e Officiene Meccaniche, Venice, Italy
Original owners South African Railways & Harbours Administration
Propulsion Steam, screw, triple expansion, coal fired
Tonnage 111 gross

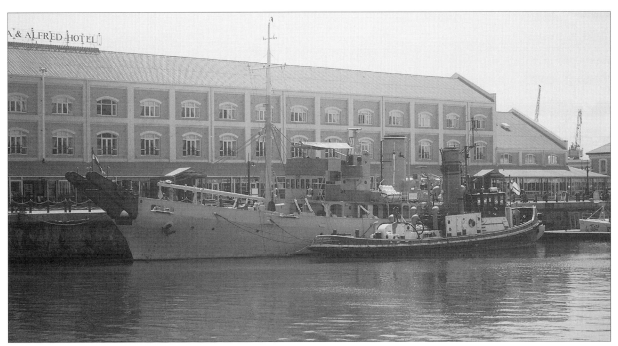

Alwyn Vintcent lying outboard of Somerset at Cape Town

J R More (left) and Ulundi at Durban

Length 82.67ft/25.2m
Breadth 20.08ft/6.12m
Draught 10.5ft/3.2m
Materials Steel hull, steel and wood
superstructure
Original use Tug
Condition Intact
Present owners Natal Parks, Game &
Fish Preservation Board,
Pietermaritzburg
Location Howick, South Africa
History Preserved as an onshore
exhibit, 60 miles inland from the port
of Durban.
Bibliography C80

J R More
steam tug

Built 1961 by Ferguson Brothers, Port
Glasgow, Scotland
Original owners South African
Railways and Harbours Administration
Propulsion Steam, screw, triple
expansion
Tonnage 805 gross
Length 172.28ft/53.73m
Breadth 37.11ft/11.31m
Draught 16.24ft/4.95m
Materials Steel hull
Original use Tug
Condition Intact

Present owners Natal Maritime
Museum
Location Durban, South Africa
History Last survivor of a very large
class of steam tugs operated in South
African harbours. Preserved as a
floating exhibit and for cruises.
Bibliography C80

Pretoria
minesweeper

Former name SAS PRETORIA,
HMS DUNKERTON
Built 1954 by Goole Shipbuilding Co,
Goole, England
Original owners British Royal Navy
Propulsion Diesel engines, 3000hp
Tonnage 440 displacement
Length 152.0ft/46.6m
Breadth 28.75ft/8.5m
Draught 8.25ft/2.51m
Materials Hull wood over aluminium
frames, superstructure aluminium
Original use Minesweeper
Condition Intact
Present owners Charles Bates
Location Hout Bay, South Africa
History Sold by the South African Navy
in 1987 for use as a privately-owned
maritime museum. Preserved as a
floating exhibit.

Somerset
boom tender

Former name SAS SOMERSET,
HNS BARCROSS
Built 1941 by Blyth Dry Dock &
Shipbuilding Co, Blyth, England
Original owners British Royal Navy
Propulsion Steam, screw, triple
expansion, 850hp
Tonnage 750 displacement
Length 182.0ft/55.47m
Breadth 32.25ft/9.83m
Draught 11.5ft/3.5m
Materials Steel throughout
Original use Boom tender
Condition Intact
Present owners South African Maritime
Museum
Location Cape Town, South Africa
History Built during the Second World
War to tend anti-submarine nets
protecting British harbours.
Transferred to the South African Navy
in 1951 and donated to the maritime
museum at Capetown in the 1980s.
Preserved as a floating exhibit.
Bibliography D201, D466

Ulundi
steam tug

Built 1927 by Henry Robb Ltd, Leith,
Scotland
Original owners Messina Brothers, Port
Elizabeth
Propulsion Steam, screw, coal fired
Tonnage 87 gross
Length 75.33ft/22.96m
Breadth 18.08ft/5.51m
Draught 9.75ft/2.97m
Materials Steel hull, steel and wood
superstructure
Original use Tug
Condition Intact
Present owners Natal Maritime
Museum
Location Durban, South Africa
History Preserved as an onshore
exhibit.
Bibliography C80

William Weller
steam tug

Built 1958 by Cantieri Navali e
Officiene Meccaniche, Venice, Italy
Original owners South Africa Railways
and Harbours Administration
Propulsion Steam, screw, triple
expansion, coal fired
Tonnage 111 gross
Length 82.67ft/25.2m
Breadth 20.08ft/6.12m
Draught 10.5ft/3.2m
Materials Steel hull, steel and wood
superstructure
Original use Tug
Condition In operating condition
Present owners Naval Cadets
Location Port Elizabeth, South Africa
History Used as a training vessel.
Bibliography C80

South Georgia

This remote, mountainous island in the South Atlantic has throughout this century been administered by Great Britain. During the same period, it has served as the site for several whaling factories primarily operated by Norwegian companies. The whaling factories are now abandoned, and the only year-round inhabitants of the island are scientists and a small British military contingent. Norwegian industrial archeologists have begun studying the abandoned factories, but as yet there has been no attention given to the vessels abandoned with them, primarily steam whale catchers, and coaling hulks that were converted from nineteenth-century sailing vessels. There have been proposals to return one or more of the whale catchers, some of which were still afloat until fairly recently, to Norway for preservation. The former hulks BRUTUS and BAYARD are now among the more intact remains of unrestored nineteenth-century sailing vessels anywhere in the world.

Albatros
whale catcher

Built 1921 by Bokeroens Skibs, Svelvik, Norway
Propulsion Steam, screw, triple expansion
Tonnage 210 gross
Length 113.0ft/34.4m
Breadth 21.5ft/6.6m
Draught 13.0ft/4.0m
Materials Steel throughout
Original use Whale catcher
Condition Intact, sunk alongside pier, abandoned
Present owners Crown receiver of wrecks
Location Grytviken, South Georgia

Bayard
trading barque

Built 1864 by T Vernon, Liverpool, England
Original owners R Alexander & Co, Liverpool
Propulsion Sail, barque rig
Tonnage 1319 gross
Length 219.7ft/66.96m
Breadth 36.5ft/11.13m
Materials Iron hull, iron and wood masts
Original use Cargo
Condition Aground, hull and lowermasts intact, abandoned
Present owners British crown wreck
Location Ocean Harbour, South Georgia
History Cargo ship converted to coal storage hulk at South Georgia.
Bibliography B25

Brutus
full-rigged trading vessel

Former name SIERRA PEDROSA
Built 1883 by J Reid & Co, Port Glasgow, Scotland
Original owners Thompson, Anderson & Co, Liverpool, England
Propulsion Sail, full-rigged ship
Tonnage 1686 gross
Length 249.0ft/75.9m
Breadth 38.1ft/11.61m
Materials Steel hull, steel and wood masts
Original use Cargo
Condition Aground, hull and lowermasts largely intact, abandoned
Present owners British crown wreck
Location Prince Olaf Harbour, South Georgia
Bibliography B25

Dias
whale catcher

Former name KAPDUEN, VIOLA
Built 1906 by Cook, Welton & Gemmell, Beverly, England
Propulsion Steam, screw, triple expansion
Tonnage 167 gross
Length 108.5ft/33.1m
Breadth 21.5ft/6.6m
Materials Steel throughout
Original use Whale catcher
Condition Intact, lying sunk beside pier, abandoned
Present owners Crown receiver of wrecks
Location Grytviken, South Georgia

Petrel
whale catcher

Built 1928 by Nylands Vaerksted, Oslo, Norway
Original owners Compania Argentina de Pesca, Buenos Aires
Propulsion Steam, screw, triple expansion
Tonnage 245 gross
Length 115.0ft/35.05m
Breadth 23.0ft/7.01m
Materials Steel throughout
Original use Whale catcher
Condition Sunk alongside pier, largely intact, abandoned
Present owners British crown wreck
Location Grytviken, South Georgia
Bibliography B25

Polar 4
whale catcher

Former name KARRAKATTA
Built 1912 by Akers Mek Verksted, Oslo, Norway
Original owners Western Australian Whaling Co Ltd
Propulsion Steam screw
Tonnage 179 gross
Length 104.6ft/31.9m
Breadth 21.5ft/6.6m
Depth 12.3ft/3.7m
Materials Steel throughout
Original use Whale catcher
Condition Virtually intact, abandoned on shore
Location Husvik, South Georgia
History Intact steam whale catcher abandoned on the marine railway of a small shipyard in South Georgia near the extensive remains of a whaling shore factory.
Bibliography B25, D419

Polar 4

Spain

Having sponsored both Columbus' discovery of the 'New World' and Magellan's first circumnavigation of the globe, Spain assembled the earliest European colonial empire primarily in the Americas. By the end of the nineteenth century this empire had been reduced to the Canary Islands off Africa and a few outposts on that continent. Spain occupies much of the Iberian Peninsula between the Atlantic Ocean and the Mediterranean, with seaports on both coasts. Historically, its most enterprising port has been Barcelona on the Mediterranean, which is today the home of the country's leading maritime museum. Thus far, historic vessels preserved in the country have tended to reflect its recent naval past, fishing industry, or coastal and Mediterranean trades under sail.

Altair
schooner yacht

Built 1931 by William Fife & Sons Fairlie, Scotland. Designed by William Fife III
Original owners Guy H MacCaw
Propulsion Sail, schooner rig; auxiliary engine
Tonnage 161 displacement
Length 107.66ft/39.52m
Breadth 20.33ft/6.2m
Draught 13.1ft/4.0m
Materials Wood throughout
Original use Yacht
Condition Fully restored 1985-1987
Location Spain
History Schooner yacht designed and built by a leading British firm. Fully restored to her original appearance and sailing condition by owners in Spain.
Bibliography A1

Isla Ebusitana
trading schooner

Built 1856 at Palma de Mallorca, Spain
Propulsion Sail, schooner rig
Materials Wood throughout
Original use Cargo

Condition Restored to sailing condition
Location Spain
History Mediterranean trading schooner built in Spain and based in Ibiza. Later reduced to a ketch-rigged motor vessel. Has been restored to schooner rig and fitted to carry passengers on cruises or charters in the Mediterranean.

Jaizkibel
harbour dredger

Built 1933
Original use Dredger
Present owners San Sebastian Museum
Location San Sebastian, Spain
History Harbour dredger of the 1930s preserved as a museum exhibit.

Juan Sebastian De Elcano
sail training ship

Built 1928 by Astilleros Echevarrieta, Cadiz, Spain
Original owners Spanish Navy
Propulsion Sail, four-masted topsail schooner rig; diesel engine, 500hp
Tonnage 3750 displacement
Length 308.72ft/94.1m
Breadth 42.98ft/13.1m

Draught 22.24ft/6.78m
Materials Steel throughout
Original use Training ship
Condition In operation
Present owners Spanish Navy
Location Cadiz, Spain
History Still in use as a training ship.
Bibliography A14, C25, C96

Lagun Artean
Hake fishing boat

Built 1969
Original use Hake Fishing boat
Present owners San Sebastian Museum
Location San Sebastian, Spain
History Example of a type of fishing vessel once common in ports of the north coast of Spain. Now preserved as a museum exhibit.

Peral
submarine

Built 1888 by Carraca, Cadiz, Spain
Original owners Spanish Navy
Propulsion Electric motor
Tonnage 87 displacement
Length 70.0ft/21.34m
Breadth 8.5ft/2.59m
Materials Steel throughout
Original use Submarine
Condition Intact
Present owners Spanish Navy
Location Cartagena, Spain
History Second submarine built for Spain and the oldest surviving. Preserved as an onshore exhibit.
Bibliography A6

Rafael Verdera
coastal sailing vessel

Built 1841 in Spain
Propulsion Sail, currently ketch-rigged
Materials Wood throughout
Original use Cargo
Condition In sailing condition
Location Spain
History Small coastal or Mediterranean Sea sailing cargo vessel whose history can be traced back to 1841. Currently making cruises or charters under the Spanish flag rigged as a ketch.
Bibliography D542

SA-42
midget submarine

Former name F-II
Built 1957 at Cartagena, Spain
Original owners Spanish Navy
Propulsion Diesel and electric motors
Tonnage 20 displacement
Length 45.41ft/13.84m

Juan Sebastian De Elcano

Breadth 6.0ft/1.83m
Draught 5.0ft/1.52m
Materials Steel throughout
Original use Midget submarine
Condition Intact
Present owners Spanish Navy
History One of two midget subamrines
built for the Spanish Navy based on
the German 'Seehund'. Preserved as an
onshore exhibit.
Location Cartagena, Spain

Sayremar I
trading schooner

Former name CALA SANT VICENC,
PUERTO DE PALMA, CARMEN FLORES
Built 1918 by Antoni Mari Aguirre,
Torrevieja, Spain
Original owners Pascual Flores
Benavente
Propulsion Sail, schooner rig; engine
added
Tonnage 166.87 gross
Length 100.0ft/30.45m
Breadth 28.0ft/8.5m
Draught 11.5ft/3.5m
Materials Wood throughout
Original use Cargo
Condition Rig removed, converted to
motor vessel
Present owners Barcelona Maritime
Museum
Location Barcelona, Spain
History Built as a schooner to carry
cargo in the Spanish Mediterranean
trade. Later converted to a motor
vessel, and currently maintained as a
floating exhibit as such.
Bibliography D545

Sudan

A largely land-locked region in
tropical Africa, the Republic of
Sudan has one major seaport on
the Red Sea which is linked to
the capital, Khartoum, by highway
and rail. The navigable internal
waterways are limited to
portions of the upper Nile River
and the two rivers that join to
form it at Khartoum, the Blue
Nile and the White Nile. Sudan
was conquered in the early
nineteenth century by Egypt, then
a part of the Ottoman Empire. It
was lost in 1885 to followers of
the Mahdi, a charismatic Moslem
leader, while being administered
on behalf of Egypt by an
Englishman, General Charles
Gordon. The British took the
country by military force in 1898,
and a joint protectorate was set
up with Egypt. Egypt demanded
full control following the Second
World War, but after the fall of
the monarchy in that country
agreed to Sudanese independence
in the early 1950s. Sudan is
currently in the midst of a lengthy
civil war. The two historic vessels
surviving in the country are relics
of the fighting in 1885 and 1898.

Bordein
sidewheel river steamer

Built 1869 by Bulaq Dockyard, Egypt
Original owners Sir Samuel Baker
Propulsion Steam, sidewheel
Materials Iron hull
Original use Exploration ship
Condition Intact hull with paddleboxes
Present owners River Transport
Corporation
Location Khartoum, Sudan
History Built for Sir Samuel Baker's
expedition to the upper Nile in 1869.
Later used by General Gordon in the
Sudanese War of 1884. Preserved as an
onshore exhibit.

Melik
river gunboat

Built 1897 by J I Thornycroft, Chiswick,
England
Original owners Egyptian Navy
Propulsion Steam, twin screw, 600hp
Tonnage 140 displacement
Length 145.0ft/44.2m
Breadth 24.5ft/7.47m
Draught 2.0ft/0.61m
Materials Steel hull
Original use Gunboat
Condition Hull intact, converted to
clubhouse
Present owners Khartoum Sailing
Club
Location Khartoum, Sudan
History Built for General Kitchener's
successful campaign to retake the
Sudan. Currently preserved as a
clubhouse across the Nile from the city
of Khartoum.

Sweden

The Scandinavian countries have
enthusiastically embarked on the
restoration of their surviving
coastal sailing vessels, and coastal
and inland steamers. Like Finland,
Sweden has a fleet of passenger
steamboats, many of which had
never been converted to motor
vessels. The majority belong to
the 'white fleet' based at
Stockholm, which served
communities on the complex
waterways of the surrounding
archipelago. Sweden has some
large, navigable lakes that are
linked by the Gota Canal, a
waterway built in the early
nineteenth century that extends
from Gothenburg on the west
coast to Stockholm on the east.
A number of the passenger
steamers and log-handling
tugboats that once operated on
the lakes have been restored to
operating condition, and a fleet of
vintage former steamers carries
passengers on cruises through
the canal. All the latter are now
powered by diesel engines and
have had their superstructures
somewhat modernised. Many of
Sweden's restored sailing vessels
are based in Stockholm, whose
miles of urban shoreline are lined
with as fascinating an array of
craft as can be seen anywhere.

Af Chapman
full-rigged trading vessel

Former name G D KENNEDY,
DUNBOYNE
Built 1888 by Whitehaven Shipbuilding
Co, Whitehaven, England
Original owners Charles E Martin &
Co, Dublin
Propulsion Sail, full-rigged ship; diesel
auxiliary
Tonnage 2300 displacement
Length 256.89ft/78.3m
Breadth 37.42ft/11.41m
Draught 18.33ft/5.59m
Materials Iron hull, iron and wood
masts
Original use Cargo
Condition Intact, in use
Present owners City of Stockholm

Af Chapman

Location Stockholm, Sweden
History British-built cargo ship later used as a Swediah naval sail training ship. In current use as a youth hostel.
Bibliography A14, C96, D120

Alma Af Stavre
steam passenger launch

Built 1873 by William Lindbergs, Stockholm, Sweden
Propulsion Steam, screw, compound, 80hp
Length 56.7ft/17.27m
Breadth 12.4ft/3.78m
Materials Iron hull
Original use Passenger launch
Condition In operating condition
Present owners Angbatsforeningen Alma af Stavre
Location Stavre, Sweden
History In use for cruises.

Amalia
coasting ketch

Built 1899 at Viken, Sweden
Propulsion Sail, ketch rig; diesel engine added
Tonnage 36 gross
Length 59.04ft/18.0m
Breadth 19.19ft/5.85m
Draught 6.23ft/1.9m
Materials Wood throughout
Original use Cargo
Condition In sailing condition
Present owners Ulf Busch
Location Nynashamn, Sweden
History Coastal and Baltic sailing trader in use as a yacht.

Astrid Finne
sail rescue vessel

Former name OSTERGARN
Built 1937 by Johan Anker, Vollen, Norway
Original owners Norwegian Lifesaving Service
Propulsion Sail, ketch rig; diesel engine added, 200hp
Tonnage 44.5 gross
Length 60.68ft/18.5m
Breadth 17.71ft/5.4m
Draught 9.18ft/2.8m
Materials Wood throughout
Original use Rescue vessel
Condition In sailing condition
Present owners Mot Battre Vetande Bratterbergsskolan
Location Ockero, Sweden
History Sailing rescue cutter later converted to a private yacht. Currently in use for sail training.

Atene

Astrid Finne

Atene
trading schooner

Built 1909 at Svendborg, Denmark
Propulsion Sail, schooner rig; diesel engine added
Tonnage 61 gross
Length 75.44ft/23.0m
Breadth 18.37ft/5.6m
Draught 8.86ft/2.7m
Materials Wood throughout
Original use Cargo
Condition In sailing condition
Present owners Foreningen NS Atene
Location Tjorn, Sweden
History In use for sail training.
Bibliography A11

Blidösund
coastal passenger steamer

Built 1911 by Eriksbergs Mek Verkstad, Gothenburg, Sweden
Original owners Angfartyg A/B Stockholm-Blidosund
Propulsion Steam, screw, compound, 320hp, coal fired
Tonnage 167 gross
Length 115.78ft/35.29m
Breadth 22.97ft/7.0m
Draught 8.89ft/2.71m
Materials Iron hull
Original use Passengers
Condition In operation
Present owners Roslagens Skeppslag

Bohuslän

Location Stockholm, Sweden
History Steamboat built to carry
passengers in the channels of the
Stockholm archipelago. In service.
Bibliography B16

Bohuslän
coastal passenger steamer

Built 1914 by Eriksbergs Mek Verksted,
Gothenburg, Sweden
Original owners Marstrands Nya
Anfartygs A/B
Propulsion Steam, screw, triple
expansion, 700hp
Tonnage 327 gross
Length 139.17ft/42.42m
Breadth 23.81ft/7.26m
Draught 10.17ft/3.1m
Materials Steel hull, steel and wood
superstructure
Original use Passengers
Condition In operation
Present owners Sallskapet Angbatan
Location Gothenburg, Sweden
History Steamer built to carry
passengers on the west coast of Sweden
north of Gothenburg. In service
between Gothenburg and Marstrand
and also on evening cruises.
Bibliography B16, D7

Bore
icebreaker

Built 1894 by Kockums, Malmo,
Sweden
Propulsion Steam, screw, compound,
605hp
Tonnage 374 gross
Length 130.54ft/39.8m
Breadth 29.18ft/8.9m
Materials Steel hull
Original use Icebreaker
Condition In operation
Present owners Swecox International
A/B
Location Vasteras, Sweden
History Steam harbour icebreaker
converted for cruising. In use for
cruises.
Bibliography B16

Boxholm II
coastal passenger/towing steamer

Built 1904 by Ljungrens Mek Verkstad,
Kristianstad, Sweden
Original owners Boxholms Aktiebolag
Propulsion Steam, screw, compound,
85hp, wood fired
Tonnage 37 gross
Length 65.71ft/20.03m
Breadth 14.63ft/4.46m
Draught 6.14ft/1.87m
Materials Steel hull, steel and wood
superstructure

Original use Passengers and towing
Condition In operation
Present owners R Hektor & S-O
Sjoberg, Boxholm
Location Lake Sommen, Sweden
History The last wood-burning
passenger steamer in Europe. Cruises
on Lake Sommen between Tranas and
Malexander.
Bibliography B16

Bremon
minesweeper

Built 1940 by Eriksbergs Mek Verkstad,
Gothenburg, Sweden
Original owners Swedish Navy
Propulsion Steel throughout
Tonnage 460 displacement
Length 186.0ft/56.59m
Breadth 25.0ft/7.6m
Draught 6.56ft/2.0m
Materials Steel throughout
Original use Minesweeper
Condition Intact
Present owners Naval Museum
Location Karlskrona, Sweden
History Survivor of a class of twelve
minesweepers employed by the
Swedish Navy during the Second
World War. Preserved as a floating
exhibit.
Bibliography D11

Dan Brostrom
motor ferry

Built 1963 by Broderna Larsson Varv
och Mek Verkstad, Kristinehamn,
Sweden
Propulsion Diesel engines
Materials Steel throughout
Original use Ferry
Condition Intact
Present owners Goteborgs Maritima
Centrum
Location Gothenburg, Sweden
History Preserved as a floating exhibit.

Deodar
fishing ketch

Former name RIGMOR
Built 1911 at Brixham, England
Propulsion Sail, ketch rig; diesel engine
added, 185hp
Tonnage 53 gross
Length 78.72ft/24.0m
Breadth 19.02ft/5.8m
Draught 8.86ft/2.7m
Materials Wood throughout
Original use Fishing
Condition In sailing condition
Present owners Thomas Hellstrom
Location Stockholm, Sweden
History British-built fishing vessel of
the 'Brixham trawler' type. Now
maintained as a yacht.
Bibliography B69

Djurgården 3
steam ferry

Former name NYBRON I,
STADSGARDEN I
Built 1893 by Brodins Varvet, Gavel,
Sweden
Propulsion Steam, screw, compound,
55hp
Length 68.55ft/20.9m
Breadth 17.71ft/5.4m
Materials Steel throughout
Original use Ferry
Condition In operation
Present owners Stiftelsen
Skargardsbaten
Location Stockholm, Sweden
History Steam harbour ferryboat
retired in 1969 but restored in the
1980s. In use for cruises.
Bibliography B16

Drottningholm
coastal passenger steamer

Former name NYA STROMMA KANAL,
VALKYRIAN
Built 1909 by Motala Verkstad, Motala,
Sweden
Original owners Stockholms Angslups
A/B
Propulsion Steam, screw, compound,
85hp
Tonnage 128 gross
Length 76.64ft/22.75m
Breadth 17.55ft/5.35m
Materials Steel throughout
Original use Passengers
Condition Angfartygs A/B Stromma
Kanal
Location Stockholm, Sweden
History Small passenger steamer in
service in Stockholm.
Bibliography B16

Ejdern
coastal passenger steamer

Built 1880 by Goteborgs Mek Verkstad,
Gothenburg, Sweden
Propulsion Steam, screw, compound,
65hp
Tonnage 38 gross
Length 70.6ft/21.52m
Breadth 13.98ft/4.26m
Draught 5.58ft/1.7m
Materials Iron hull, iron and wood
superstructure
Original use Passengers
Condition In operation
Present owners Museiforeningen
Angfartyg Ejdern
Location Sodertalje, Sweden
History Retired from service in the
Stockholm Archipelago in 1957 but

Djurgården 3

restored in 1974 with her original
engine which had been preserved in a
museum. In operation.
Bibliography B16

Ejdern
pilot vessel

Built 1895 by Lundberg and Carlssons,
Gothenburg, Sweden
Original owners Swedish Royal Pilot
Board
Propulsion Sail, cutter rig. Engine built
by Volvo (current)
Tonnage 17 gross
Length 39.5ft/12.0m
Breadth 14.6ft/4.45m
Draught 6.2ft/1.9m
Materials Wood throughout
Original use Pilot vessel
Condition Fully restored 1991-94
Present owners Foreningen
Lotsbaten
Location Groto, Sweden
History In use as an active sailing
vessel.

Elfdalen
tugboat

Built 1888 by Sodra Varvet, Stockholm
Propulsion Steam, screw
Length 70.2ft/21.4m
Original use Tugboat
Condition In operating condition

Present owner Olle Nordesjo
Location Leksand, Sweden
History Built as a log warping tug to
handle timber on the Swedish lakes.
Currently maintained in steaming
condition by a private owner, based on
Lake Siljan.

Ellen
trading ketch

Former name WILLIAM
Built 1898 at Thuro, Denmark
Propulsion Sail, ketch rig; diesel engine,
95hp
Tonnage 66 gross
Length 66.26ft/20.2m
Breadth 19.78ft/6.03m
Draught 7.87ft/2.4m
Materials Wood throughout
Original use Cargo
Condition In sailing condition
Present owners Municipality of Lidingo
Location Lidingo, Sweden
History Built to carry cargo under sail
in the Danish coastal and Baltic trades.
In use for youth training.
Bibliography B69

Engelbrekt
coastal passenger steamer

Built 1866 by Motala Verkstad,
Lindholmen, Sweden
Propulsion Steam, screw, compound,

80hp (present engine from 1904)
Tonnage 58 gross
Length 79.1ft/24.1m
Breadth 14.6ft/4.45m
Draught 5.7ft/1.75m
Materials Iron hull
Original use Passengers
Condition Hull intact, restoration in
progress
Present owners Angfartygs AB
Engelbrekt
Location Insjon, Sweden

Esab IV
passenger launch

Built 1920 by Elekstriska Svetsnings
Aktiebolaget, Gothenburg, Sweden
Propulsion Screw, 210hp
Tonnage 31 gross
Length 51.82ft/15.8m
Breadth 13.12ft/4.0m
Draught 6.89ft/2.1m
Materials Steel throughout
Original use Passenger launch
Condition Intact
Present owners Gothenburg Maritime
Centre
Location Gothenburg, Sweden
History One of the world's earliest
welded-hull vessels and probably the
oldest surviving today. Preserved as an
exhibit.
Bibliography B50, D37

Finngrundet

Falken
sail training vessel

Built 1947 by Royal Naval Dockyard, Stockholm, Sweden. Designed by Captain Tore Herlin
Original owners Royal Swedish Navy
Propulsion Sail, schooner rig; diesel auxiliary, 128hp. Engine built by Scania
Tonnage 220 displacement
Length 112.5ft/34.3m
Breadth 23.6ft/7.2m
Draught 13.8ft/4.2m
Materials Steel throughout
Original use Training
Condition In sailing condition
Present owners Royal Swedish Navy
Location Karlskrona, Sweden
History In use for training.

Färjan 4
steam ferry

Built 1920 by Motala Verkstad, Motala, Sweden
Propulsion Steam, screw, compound, 86hp, coal fired
Tonnage 94 gross
Length 67.42ft/20.55m
Breadth 17.55ft/5.35m
Draught 7.51ft/2.29m
Materials Steel throughout
Original use Ferry
Condition In operating condition
Present owners Sallskapet Angbatan
Location Gothenburg, Sweden
History Served for 50 years as a ferryboat in Gothenburg harbour. In use for excursions.
Bibliography B16, B50

Finngrundet
lightship

Built 1903 by Getle Mek Verkstad, Gavle, Sweden
Original owners Swedish Ministry of Sea
Propulsion Steam, screw; converted to diesel
Length 99.77ft/30.41m
Breadth 22.47ft/6.85m
Draught 12.14ft/3.7m
Materials Steel throughout
Original use Lightship
Condition Intact
Present owners Maritime Museum
Location Stockholm, Sweden
History In use as a floating exhibit.
Bibliography A16

Fladen
lightship

Former name HAVRINGE, OLANDSREV
Built 1914 by Bergsunds Shipyard, Stockholm, Sweden
Original owners Swedish Coast Guard
Propulsion Diesel engines, 240hp
Tonnage 378 displacement
Length 107.61ft/32.8m
Breadth 25.26ft/7.7m
Draught 11.81ft/3.6m
Materials Steel throughout
Original use Lightship
Condition Intact
Present owners Gothenburg Maritime Centre
Location Gothenburg, Sweden
History Preserved as floating exhibit.
Bibliography B50

Flodsprutan II
fireboat

Former name BRANDBAT II
Built 1931 by Lindholmen Motala A/B, Gothenburg, Sweden
Original owners City of Gothenburg
Propulsion Diesel engines, 480hp
Tonnage 136 gross
Length 85.28ft/26.0m
Breadth 19.02ft/5.8m
Draught 6.89ft/2.1m
Materials Steel throughout
Original use Fireboat
Condition Intact
Present owners Gothenburg Maritime Centre
Location Gothenburg, Sweden
History Formerly employed in Gothenburg Harbour. Preserved as an exhibit.
Bibliography B50

Flottisten
Inspection vessel

Built 1890 by Hernosands Mek. Verkstad, Hernosand
Propulsion Steam, screw, compound, 110hp. Engine by builders
Length 123.9ft/37.78m
Breadth 61ft/18.6m
Draught 13.3ft/4.06m
Materials Steel hull
Original use Inspection vessel and excursions
Condition In operating condition
Present owners Helen and Karl-Erik Olsson
Location Leksand, Sweden
History Built as an inspection vessel on the Swedish lakes and also used for excursions. Later employed as a log warping tug. Fully restored and maintained in steaming condition on Lake Siljan by private owners.

Fortuna
steam tug

Former name FORT UNNA
Built 1857 at Dellenlakes, Helsingland, Sweden
Propulsion Steam, screw
Length 53.14ft/16.2m
Materials Iron hull, wood superstructure
Original use Tug
Condition In operating condition
Location Hudiksvall, Sweden
History Possibly the world's oldest steam tug. Engine dates from 1915. In use as an active steamer.

Freja Af Fryken
passenger lake steamer

Former name FREJA, KALMARSUND NR 3
Built 1868 by Motala Verkstad, Motala, Sweden
Propulsion Steam, screw, 15hp
Tonnage 40 gross
Length 66.8ft/20.36m
Breadth 13.6ft/4.15m
Original use Passengers
Condition Fully restored after lying sunk 1896-1994
Present owners Angbatsforeningen Freja
Location Lake Fryken, Sweden
History Small passenger steamer built for use on the Baltic but later moved to Lake Fryken in western Sweden. Foundered in a squall in 1896. Was rediscovered in 1976 in 52m of water and eventually raised in 1994. Damaged by fire during restoration,

but finally re-launched in 1997. Returned to operation with her original engine and boiler.

Fryken
motor coaster

Former name ISVANIA, SVANO
Built 1938 by Aalborg Vaerft, Aalborg, Denmark
Original owners Brostrom Line
Propulsion Diesel engines, 800hp
Tonnage 1024 gross
Length 216.3ft/63.4m
Breadth 33.1ft/10.1m
Draught 14.37ft/4.38m
Materials Steel hull, steel and wood superstructure
Original use Cargo
Condition Intact
Present owners Gothenburg Maritime Centre
Location Gothenburg, Sweden
History Preserved as a floating exhibit.

Gerda
steam launch

Built 1865 by Lindholmens, Gothenburg, Sweden
Propulsion Steam, screw, 10hp
Length 44.3ft/13.5m
Breadth 10.8ft/3.3m
Materials Iron hull
Original use Passenger launch
Condition In operating condition
Present owners Faktorimuseet
Location Eskilstuna, Sweden
History Early steam launch restored to operating condition for excursions in 1996.

Gerda
passenger ferry

Former names HANEBERG, GERDA
Built 1865 by Lindholmens Shipyard, Gothenburg
Propulsion Steam, screw; converted to diesel; converted back to steam
Length 44.6ft/13.6m
Original use Passenger ferry
Condition In operating condition
Present owner Town of Eskilstuna
Location Eskilstuna, Sweden
History Small steam passenger ferry employed in Stockholm area and later between Haneberg and Balgviken. Converted to motor vessel in 1915. Restored to a steam vessel in the 1990s using a Finnish engine dating from c1900. Preserved as an exhibit and active steamer.

Gladen
sail training vessel

Built 1946 by Royal Naval Dockyard, Stockholm, Sweden. Designed by Captain Tore Herlin
Original owners Royal Swedish Navy
Propulsion Sail, schooner rig; diesel auxiliary, 128hp. Engine built by Scania
Tonnage 220 displacement
Length 112.5ft/34.3m
Breadth 23.6ft/7.2m
Draught 13.8ft/4.2m
Materials Steel throughout
Original use Training
Condition In sailing condition
Present owners Royal Swedish Navy
Location Karlskrona, Sweden

Göteborgspram
lighter

Built Date not known
Propulsion Towed
Length 52.15ft/15.9m
Breadth 17.06ft/5.2m
Draught 5.9ft/1.8m
Materials Wood throughout
Original use Cargo, lighter barge
Condition Intact
Present owners Gothenburg Maritime Centre
Location Gothenburg, Sweden
History Example of open lighter barge used to move cargo in Gothenburg Harbour until the 1960s. Preserved as an exhibit.

Gratitude
fishing ketch

Former name OSTANVAG
Built 1907 at Porthleven, England
Propulsion Sail, ketch rig; diesel engine, 184hp
Tonnage 63 gross
Length 77.74ft/23.7m
Breadth 19.55ft/5.96m
Draught 9.18ft/2.8m
Materials Wood throughout
Original use Fishing
Condition In sailing condition
Present owners Svenska Kryssarklubbens Seglarskola
Location Gothenburg, Sweden
History In use for sail training.
Bibliography A10, B69

Gunhild
fishing ketch

Built 1936 by Halso Shipyard, Sweden
Propulsion Sail, ketch rig; heavy oil engine, 150hp
Tonnage 42 gross
Length 53.79ft/16.4m
Breadth 18.7ft/5.7m
Draught 6.56ft/2.0m
Materials Wood throughout
Original use Fishing
Condition Intact
Present owners Gothenburg Maritime Centre
Location Gothenburg, Sweden
History One of a very few of these

vessels still fitted with its original hot-bulb type engine. Preserved as a floating exhibit.
Bibliography B50

Gustavsberg VII
coastal passenger steamer

Former name SAXAREN
Built 1912 by Oskarshamns Mekaniska Verkstad, Oskarshamns, Sweden
Original owners A/B Gustafsbergs Fabriks Intressenter
Propulsion Steam, screw
Tonnage 202 gross
Length 112.4ft/34.26m
Breadth 23.33ft/7.11m
Draught 8.2ft/2.5m
Materials Steel throughout
Original use Passengers
Condition In operation
Present owners Rederi AB Diana
Location Stockholm, Sweden

Hajen
submarine

Built 1904 by Stockholm Navy Yard, Stockholm, Sweden
Original owners Swedish Navy
Propulsion Oil and electric motors
Tonnage 127 displacement
Length 70.83ft/21.59m
Breadth 11.83ft/3.61m
Draught 9.83ft/3.0m
Materials Steel throughout
Original use Submarine

Ingo

Condition Intact
Present owners Karlskrona Naval Museum
Location Karlskrona, Sweden
History First submarine built for the Swedish Navy. Preserved as an exhibit.
Bibliography A6, D512

Harge
tugboat

Former names RANNICK, BLIDO, KIND, WULF, HARGE, HARGE II
Built 1907 by Wennbergs Mek. Verkstad, Karlstad
Propulsion Steam, screw
Length c65ft/20m
Original use Tug
Condition In operating condition
Present owners Mikael Bjork, Elisabeth Lidwall, and Volivi Portanen
Location Ljustero, Sweden
History Small steam tugboat much altered during its long career, but now largely restored to original appearance by private owners. Active as a yacht.

Hawila
trading ketch

Built 1935 by Lindstols, Risor, Norway
Propulsion Sail, ketch rig; diesel engine, 157hp
Tonnage 87 gross
Length 83.9/ft/25.6m
Breadth 22.99ft/6.4m
Draught 9.84ft/3.0m
Materials Wood throughout
Original use Cargo
Condition In sailing condition
Present owners Brattebergskolan
Location Ockero, Sweden
History In use for sail training.
Bibliography B69

Helene
trading schooner

Built 1916 at Ystad, Sweden
Propulsion Sail, schooner rig; diesel engine, 185hp
Tonnage 94 gross
Length 80.43ft/24.52m
Breadth 20.76ft/6.33m
Draught 9.35ft/2.85m
Materials Wood throughout
Original use Cargo
Condition In sailing condition
Present owners Anders Lonn
Location Kalmar, Sweden
History Currently in use as a yacht.
Bibliography B69

Jarramas

Herbert
passenger launch

Built 1905 by Eriksbergs Mek Verkstad, Gothenburg, Sweden
Propulsion Steam, screw, 45hp
Length 50.1ft/15.25m
Breadth 12.1ft/3.68m
Original use Passenger launch
Condition In operating condition
Present owners Mjorns Angbatsforeningen
Location Alingsas, Sweden
History In use for excursions.

Herkules
tug/icebreaker

Built 1939 by Oresunds Shipyard, Landskrona, Sweden
Original owners C L Hanssons Stuveri, Gothenburg
Propulsion Diesel engines, 765hp
Tonnage 102 gross
Length 76.85ft/23.43m
Breadth 20.37ft/6.21m
Draught 8.69ft/2.65m
Materials Steel hull, steel and wood superstructure
Original use Tug and icebreaker
Condition Intact
Present owners Foreningen Bogserbaten Herkules/Klubb Maritim
Location Gothenburg, Sweden

History Formerly employed in Gothenburg Harbour. Preserved as an exhibit.
Bibliography B50

Ingo
trading schooner

Built 1922 at Sjotorp, Sweden
Propulsion Sail, three-masted schooner rig; diesel engine, 200hp
Tonnage 139 gross
Length 91.84ft/28.0m
Breadth 22.96ft/7.0m
Draught 8.2ft/2.5m
Materials Wood throughout
Original use Cargo
Condition In sailing condition
Present owners Stiftelsen for Skonaren Ingo
Location Gothenburg, Sweden
History Preserved as a floating exhibit and active sailing vessel.
Bibliography B50, B69

Jarramas
sail training ship

Built 1900 by Naval Dockyard, Karlskrona, Sweden
Original owners Swedish Navy
Propulsion Sail, full-rigged ship
Tonnage 350 displacement
Length 128.42ft/39.14m

Breadth 27.5ft/8.38m
Draught 10.5ft/3.2m
Materials Iron hull and deckhouses, iron and wood masts
Original use Training ship
Condition Intact
Present owners City of Karlskrona
Location Karlskrona, Sweden
History Preserved as a floating exhibit.
Bibliography A14, C96, D70

Juno
passenger canal steamer

Built 1874 by Motala Verkstad, Motala, Sweden
Original owners Rederi A/B Gota Kanal
Propulsion Steam, screw; converted to diesel
Tonnage 304 gross
Length 99.38ft/30.3m
Breadth 21.98ft/6.7m
Materials Iron hull
Original use Passengers
Condition Intact, in operation
Present owners Rederi A/B Gota Kanal
Location Gothenburg, Sweden
History In use for passengers on the Gota Canal.
Bibliography B16

KBV-238
motor launch

Former name TV-238
Built 1962 in Sweden
Propulsion Diesel engine, 200hp. Engine built by Scania
Length 52.5ft/16.0m
Breadth 12.1ft/3.7m
Original use Motor launch
Condition Intact
Present owners Maritime Museum, Karlskrona
Location Karlskrona, Sweden
History Diesel launch built in Sweden in the 1960s, apparently for naval use. Preserved as an exhibit afloat at the new maritime museum in the former Karlskrona Navy Yard.

Klaback
steam tug

Former name SPANGAREN
Built 1918 by Motala Verkstad, Motala, Sweden
Original owners Royal Swedish Navy
Propulsion Steam, screw
Tonnage 167 gross
Length 90.98ft/27.73m
Breadth 22.47ft/6.85m
Draught 11.15ft/3.4m
Materials Steel hull
Original use Tug

Condition In operating condition
Present owners Sture Sjogren
Location Stockholm, Sweden
History Steam harbour tug built for the Swedish Navy, currently in use as a yacht.

Kvartsita

trading schooner

Former name BONO
Built 1945 in Raa, Sweden
Propulsion Sail, schooner rig; diesel engine
Tonnage 98 gross
Length 75.77ft/23.1m
Breadth 22.96ft/7.0m
Draught 8.86ft/2.7m
Materials Wood throughout
Original use Cargo
Condition In sailing condition
Present owners Stiftelsen Skaftokuttern
Location Skafto, Sweden
History In use for sail training.
Bibliography B69

Linnea

trading schooner

Built 1915 at Sjotorp, Sweden
Propulsion Sail, schooner rig; diesel engine, 130hp
Tonnage 97 gross
Length 83.97ft/25.6m
Breadth 23.09ft/7.04m
Draught 8.69ft/2.65m
Materials Wood throughout
Original use Cargo
Condition In sailing condition
Present owners Egil Bergstrom
Location Gamleby, Sweden
History In use for sail training.
Bibliography B69

Lord Nelson

fishing ketch

Built 1885 by Smith & Stephenson, Grimsby, England
Propulsion Sail, ketch rig; diesel engine added, 120hp
Tonnage 91 gross
Length 84.0ft/25.6m
Breadth 19.78ft/6.03m
Draught 10.17ft/3.1m
Materials Wood throughout
Original use Fishing
Condition In sailing condition
Present owners Kutterklubben Lord Nelson
Location Stockholm, Sweden
History Built as a sailing trawler on the north-east coast of England. In use for sail training.

Mariefred

Mälaren 3

steam ferry

Former name SEXAN
Built 1903 by Sodra Varvet, Stockholm, Sweden
Original owners Stockholms Angslups A/B
Propulsion Steam, screw, compound, 34hp
Tonnage 46 gross
Length 51.02ft/15.55m
Breadth 14.63ft/4.46m
Draught 5.41ft/1.65m
Materials Iron hull, iron and steel superstructure
Original use Ferry
Condition In operating condition
Present owners Angslups A/B, Stockholm
Location Beckholmen, Sweden
History The last surviving Lake Malar steam ferryboat. In use for cruises.
Bibliography B16

Malmo Redd

lightship

Built 1896
Original owners Swedish Lighthouse Service
Propulsion Towed to station

Length 66.65ft/20.32m
Breadth 21.16ft/6.45m
Draught 9.02ft/2.75m
Materials Steel throughout
Original use Lightship
Condition Intact
Present owners Malmo Maritime Museum
Location Malmo, Sweden
History Preserved as a floating exhibit.

Mariefred

coastal passenger steamer

Built 1903 by Sodra Varvet, Stockholm, Sweden
Propulsion Steam, screw, compound, 298hp
Tonnage 178 gross
Length 104.82ft/31.95m
Breadth 19.91ft/6.07m
Materials Steel throughout
Original use Passengers
Condition In operation
Present owners Gripsholms Mariefreds Angfartygs AB
Location Stockholm, Sweden
History Steamer built to operate between Stockholm and Mariefred. Still in active service.
Bibliography A17, B16, D450

Marieholm

passenger steamer

Built 1933 by A P Moeller, Odense, Denmark
Original owners Swedish American Line
Propulsion Steam, screw, 3-cylinder compound, 950hp
Tonnage 1150 gross
Length 212.0ft/64.62m
Breadth 32.5ft/9.91m
Draught 14.1ft/4.3m
Materials Steel throughout
Original use Passengers
Condition Intact, in stationary use
Present owners Anfartygs A/B Marieholm
Location Gothenburg, Sweden
History Last Swedish America Line ship surviving in Sweden. Preserved as a floating restaurant.
Bibliography B16, B50

Marité

fishing schooner

Built 1923 at Fecamp, France
Propulsion Sail, three-masted topsail schooner rig; diesel engine 450hp
Tonnage 170 gross
Length 114.8ft/35.0m

Breadth 26.24ft/8.0m
Draught 13.78ft/4.2m
Materials Wood throughout
Original use Fishing
Condition In sailing condition
Present owners H/B Ambratt
Location Stockholm, Sweden
History Built for the French North
Atlantic codfishing fleet. In use for
cruises.
Bibliography B69, D283

Mina
trading schooner

Built 1876 at Fagelo, Sweden
Propulsion Sail, schooner rig
Tonnage 99.7 gross
Length 82.66ft/25.2m
Breadth 22.8ft/6.95m
Draught 9.84ft/3.0m
Materials Wood throughout
Original use Cargo
Condition In sailing condition
Present owners Bengt Adamsson
Location Stockholm, Sweden
History Last surviving 'vanern galeass'.
In use as a yacht.
Bibliography A10, B69

Marité

Najaden of 1898

Motala Express
passenger steamer

Built 1895 by Jonkopings Mek Verkstad,
Jonkopings, Sweden
Propulsion Steam, screw, triple
expansion, 360hp, coal fired
Tonnage 186 gross
Length 117.0ft/35.66m
Breadth 22.0ft/6.71m
Draught 10.0ft/3.05m
Materials Iron or steel hull
Original use Passengers
Condition In operating condition
Present owners Rederi AB Kind
Location Akersund, Sweden
History In use for excursions.
Bibliography B16

Najaden
sail training ship

Built 1897 by Naval Dockyard,
Karlskrona, Sweden
Original owners Swedish Navy
Propulsion Sail, full-rigged ship
Tonnage 350 displacement
Length 131.42ft/40.06m
Breadth 27.5ft/8.38m
Draught 12.17ft/3.71m
Materials Wood throughout
Original use Training ship

Condition Intact
Present owners City of Halmstad
Location Halmstad, Sweden
History Sail training ship built for the Swedish Navy. Preserved as a floating exhibit.
Bibliography A14, C96

Najaden
trading schooner

Former name NORA
Built 1918 at Waterhuizen, Netherlands
Propulsion Sail, three-masted schooner rig
Length 111.52ft/34.0m
Breadth 23.06ft/7.05m
Materials Steel hull
Original use Cargo
Condition In sailing condition
Location Stockholm, Sweden
History In use for cruises.

Nell-Britt
trading schooner

Former name TRYGGO
Built 1929 at Raa, Sweden
Propulsion Sail, schooner rig; diesel engine, 125hp
Tonnage 67 gross
Length 73.9ft/22.53m
Breadth 20.14ft/6.14m
Draught 7.54ft/2.3m
Materials Wood throughout
Original use Cargo
Condition In sailing condition
Present owners Unga Ornar
Location Vastervik, Sweden
History In use for cruises.
Bibliography B69

Nordkaparen
submarine

Built 1961 by Kockums Mek Verkstad, Malmo, Sweden
Original owners Swedish Navy
Propulsion Diesel and electric motors
Tonnage 835 displacement
Length 226.5ft/69.3m
Breadth 16.75ft/5.1m
Draught 17.41ft/5.3m
Materials Steel throughout
Original use Submarine
Condition Intact
Present owners Gothenburg Maritime Centre
Location Gothenburg, Sweden
History Preserved as a floating exhibit.
Bibliography B50

Najaden of 1918

Norrskär
coastal passenger steamer

Former name SANDHAMNS EXPRESS
Built 1909 by Eriksbergs Mek Verkstad, Gothenburg, Sweden
Propulsion Steam, screw, compound, 320hp
Tonnage 236 gross
Length 109.54ft/33.39m
Breadth 22.58ft/6.88m
Draught 8.42ft/2.57m
Materials Iron hull, steel superstructure
Original use Passengers
Condition In operation
Present owners Waxholms Anfartygs A/B
Location Stockholm, Sweden
Bibliography B16

Östanå I
coastal passenger steamer

Built 1906 by Bergsunds Mek Verkstad, Stockholm, Sweden
Propulsion Steam, screw; converted to diesel
Tonnage 218 gross
Length 109.12ft/33.26m
Breadth 22.51ft/6.86m
Materials Iron hull, iron and wood superstructure
Original use Passengers
Condition In operation
Present owners Anfartygs A/B Stromma Kanal
Location Stockholm, Sweden
History Steamer built to operate in the Stockholm Archipelago. Returned to service in 1985 with diesel engine.
Bibliography A17

Östersund
passenger lake steamer

Former name LAS VEGAS
Built 1874 by Oskarshamns Mek Verkstad, Oskarshamn, Sweden
Propulsion Steam, screw, compound, 120hp. Engine built by Harnosand Mek Verkstad (current)
Length 82.7ft/25.2m
Breadth 14.8ft/4.5m
Materials Iron hull
Original use Passengers
Condition In operating condition
Present owners Foreningen Ostersunds Vanner
Location Ostersund (Lake Storsjon), Sweden
History Currently used for excursions.

Östanå I

Polstjärnan af Vänern
steam inspection vessel

Former name POLSTJÄRNAN
Built 1929 by Lindholmen,
Gothenburg, Sweden
Original owners Swedish Government
Propulsion Steam, screw, compound,
190hp
Tonnage 115 gross
Length 98.73ft/30.1m
Breadth 19.02ft/5.8m
Materials Steel throughout
Original use Inspection vessel for sea-
marks
Condition In operating condition
Present owners Angbats A/B
Polstjärnan
Location Karlstad, Sweden
History Currently used for cruises after
restoration by steam enthusiasts.
Bibliography B16

Primus
passenger steamer

Built 1875 by William Lindbergs,
Stockholm, Sweden
Propulsion Steam, screw, 65hp
Length 63.0ft/19.19m
Breadth 14.8ft/4.5m
Materials Iron hull
Original use Passengers
Condition In operating condition
Present owners Medelpads
Sjohistoriska forening
Location Sundsvall, Sweden
History Currently used for excursions.

Rex
steam tug

Built 1902 in Sweden
Propulsion Steam, screw
Length 48.6ft/14.8m
Breadth 13.0ft/3.96m
Materials Steel hull
Original use Tug
Condition Maintained in operating
condition
Location Sweden
History Steam tug built to operate
on the Stromsholms Canal.
Maintained in operating condition
by a group of Swedish steam
enthusiasts.

Robert
passenger steamer/tug

Former name HUDIK
Built 1866 at Bergsund, Sweden
Propulsion Steam, screw, compound,
coal fired (1907 engine)
Tonnage 20 displacement

Length 45.7ft/13.92m
Breadth 10.0ft/3.02m
Draught 6.0ft/1.8m
Original use Passengers, later tug
Condition Restored to steaming
condition
Present owners Olle Mannert, Anders
Westerberg, Tomas Blom
Location Sweden
History Currently an active steamer.

Saltsjön
coastal passenger steamer

Former name BJÖRKFJARDEN
Built 1925 by Eriksbergs Mek Verkstad,
Gothenburg, Sweden
Original owners Waxholms Nya
Anfartygs
Propulsion Steam, screw, compound,
383hp
Tonnage 249 gross

Sankt Erik

Length 120.03ft/37.5m
Breadth 22.97ft/7.0m
Draught 7.55ft/2.3m
Materials Steel throughout
Original use Passengers
Condition In operation
Present owners Anfartygs A/B Saltsjon-
Malaren
Location Stockholm, Sweden
Bibliography B16

Sankt Erik
icebreaker

Former name ISBRYTAREN II
Built 1915 by Finnboda Varv,
Stockholm, Sweden
Original owners Stockholm
Hamnstryelse
Propulsion Steam, screw, triple-

expansion, 4000hp
Tonnage 1616 gross
Length 200.0ft/60.96m
Breadth 55.8ft/17.0m
Draught 21.3ft/6.49m
Materials Steel throughout
Original use Icebreaker
Condition Intact
Present owners National Maritime
Museum
Location Stockholm, Sweden
History Veteran Swedish steam
icebreaker preserved as a floating
exhibit.
Bibliography D228

Sarpen
trading ketch

Former name FREJA
Built 1892 at Nykobing, Denmark
Propulsion Sail, ketch rig; diesel engine,
180hp
Tonnage 46 gross
Length 65.6ft/20.0m
Breadth 19.22ft/5.86m
Draught 6.89ft/2.1m
Materials Wood throughout
Original use Cargo
Condition In sailing condition
Present owners Simrishamns Scoutkar
Location Simrishamn, Sweden
History In use for sail training.
Bibliography A11, B69

Schebo
passenger launch

Built 1874 by Kockums, Malmo,
Sweden
Propulsion Steam, screw
Tonnage 17 displacement
Length 42.0ft/12.8m
Materials Iron hull
Original use Passenger launch
Condition In operating condition
Location Malmo, Sweden
History Currently used for excursions.

Småland
destroyer

Built 1952 by Eriksbergs Mek Verkstad,
Gothenburg, Sweden
Original owners Royal Swedish Navy
Propulsion Steam turbines, 58,000hp
Tonnage 3400 displacement
Length 397.0ft/121.0m
Breadth 41.33ft/12.6m
Draught 18.0ft/4.24m
Materials Steel throughout
Original use Destroyer
Condition Intact
Present owners Gothenburg Maritime
Centre
Location Gothenburg, Sweden

Småland

History First destroyer to be fitted with surface-to-surface missiles. Preserved as a floating exhibit.
Bibliography B50

Sölve
monitor

Former name PEGASUS
Built 1875 by Motala Warf, Norrkoping, Sweden
Original owners Royal Swedish Navy
Propulsion Steam, screw, 115hp
Tonnage 460 displacement
Length 130.48ft/39.78m
Breadth 26.31ft/8.02m
Draught 8.2ft/2.5m
Materials Iron throughout
Original use Coast defence monitor
Condition Undergoing restoration
Present owners Gothenburg Maritime Centre
Location Gothenburg, Sweden
History World's oldest surviving low-freeboard monitor of the type developed by the Swedish-American engineer John Ericsson. Proposed as an exhibit.
Bibliography B50

Spica
torpedo boat

Built 1966 by Gotaverken, Sweden
Original owners Swedish Navy
Propulsion Three gas turbines, 4250hp each. Engine built by Bristol-Proteus
Tonnage 210 displacement
Length 139.5ft/42.5m
Breadth 23.6ft/7.2m
Materials Steel throughout
Original use Torpedo boat
Condition Intact
Present owners Maritime Museum, Karlskrona
Location Karlskrona, Sweden
History Swedish torpedo boat of the 1960s preserved as an exhibit afloat at the new maritime museum in the former Karlskrona Navy Yard.
Bibliography D213

Stockvik
steam harbour tug

Former name ST CANUTE, ST KNUD, ORTHONA
Built 1931 by Frederikshavn Vaerft & Flydedok, Frederikshavn, Denmark
Original owners Odense Harbour Commissioners
Propulsion Steam, triple expansion, 500hp
Tonnage 138 gross
Length 86.1ft/26.64m

Storskär

Breadth 25.5ft/7.77m
Draught 10.5ft/3.2m
Materials Steel hull, steel and wood superstructure
Original use Tug
Condition In operating condition
Location Stockvik, Sweden
History Danish steam harbour tug used by a harbour authority for towing, icebreaking, and firefighting. Acquired by Exeter Maritime Museum for use as a floating exhibit in 1968. Sold to a Swedish owner after the museum closed. Left Exeter under her own steam in March 1999.
Bibliography B27, B29

Storm Princess
steam tug

Built 1908 by Wilhelmsbergs Mek Verkstad, Gothenburg, Sweden
Original owners Bogser A/B Stormking
Propulsion Steam, screw; converted to diesel
Tonnage 29 gross
Length 54.32ft/16.56m
Breadth 13.84ft/4.22m
Draught 7.87ft/2.4m
Materials Steel hull, steel and wood superstructure
Original use Tug
Condition In operating condition

Present owners Sallskapet Angbatan
Location Gothenburg, Sweden
History Preserved as a floating exhibit.
Bibliography B50

Storskär
coastal passenger steamer

Former name STRANGNAS EXPRESS
Built 1908 by Lindholmens Varv, Gothenburg, Sweden
Propulsion Steam, screw, triple expansion, 560hp
Tonnage 235 gross
Length 120.83ft/36.83m
Breadth 22.92ft/6.99m
Draught 9.84ft/3.0m
Materials Iron hull, iron and wood superstructure
Original use Passengers
Condition In operation
Present owners Waxholms Angfartygs A/B
Location Stockholm, Sweden
Bibliography B16

Strand
tug

Former names WULF II, LINDAS, URANUS, STRAND
Built 1890 by Bolinders Mek. Verkstad, Stockholm

Propulsion Steam, screw
Length 69.8ft/21.3m
Original use Tug
Condition In operating condition
Present owner Per Palmer
Location Gothenburg, Sweden
History Small steam tugboat employed at various locations in Sweden. Currently maintained as an operating steam vessel by private owners.

T-38
torpedo boat

Built 1951 by Kockums Mek Verkstad, Malmo, Sweden
Original owners Royal Swedish Navy
Propulsion Diesel engines, 4500hp
Tonnage 38.5 displacement
Length 75.5ft/23.0m
Breadth 18.42ft/5.6m
Draught 4.5ft/1.4m
Materials Steel throughout
Original use Torpedo boat
Condition Intact
Present owners Malmo Technical Museum
Location Malmo, Sweden
History Preserved as an onshore exhibit.
Bibliography A16

Tärnan
trading schooner

Built 1913 at Karlshamn, Sweden
Propulsion Sail, schooner rig
Tonnage 65 gross
Length 72.0ft/21.95m
Breadth 19.19ft/5.85m
Draught 7.87ft/2.4m
Materials Wood throughout
Original use Cargo
Condition In sailing condition
Present owners Per-Olof Warnholz
Location Hamburgsund, Sweden
Bibliography B69

Tärnan
passenger excursion steamer

Built 1901 by Sodra Varvet, Stockholm, Sweden
Propulsion Steam, screw, 47hp
Length 65.6ft/20.0m
Breadth 16.1ft/4.9m
Materials Steel hull
Original use Passengers
Condition In operating condition
Present owners Stiftelsen Skargardsbaten
Location Stockholm, Sweden
History In use for excursions.

Thomée
ferry

Built 1875 by Motala Mek Verkstad, Motala, Sweden

Tärnan

T-38

Propulsion Steam, screw, compound, 150hp, coal fired
Tonnage 106 gross
Length 75.88ft/23.13m
Breadth 15.91ft/4.85m
Draught 7.05ft/2.15m
Materials Iron hull
Original use Ferry
Condition In operation
Present owners City of Ostersund
Location Ostersund, Sweden
Bibliography B16, D264

Thor
passenger/cargo steam launch

Built 1887 by Bergsunds Mek Verkstad, Stockholm, Sweden
Original owners Rappe-Asa Kanalsktiebolag
Propulsion Steam, screw, single cylinder, 35hp, wood burning
Tonnage 12 gross
Length 54.07ft/16.48m
Breadth 11.81ft/3.6m
Draught 5.05ft/1.54m
Materials Steel hull

Original use Passengers and cargo
Condition In operation
Present owners Stiftelsen Smalands
Museum
Location Vaxjo, Sweden
History In use for excursions.
Bibliography A17, B16

Tomten
tug

Built 1862 by Sodra Varvet, Stockholm
Propulsion Steam, screw
Length 52.4ft/16m
Original use Tug
Condition In operating condition
Present owner Ingvar Larsson
Location Leksand, Sweden
History Built as a log warping tug to
handle timber rafts on the Swedish
lakes. Maintained in steaming
condition on Lake Siljan by private
owner.

Trafik
passenger lake steamer

Built 1892 by Bergsunds Mek Verkstad,
Stockholm, Sweden
Propulsion Steam, screw, compound,
240hp
Tonnage 129 gross
Length 103.87ft/31.66m
Breadth 20.6ft/6.28m
Draught 8.37ft/2.55m
Materials Steel throughout
Original use Passengers
Condition In operation
Present owners SS Trafik Ekonomisk
Forening
Location Hjo, Sweden
History In use for excursions.
Bibliography A17, B16

U-3

TV-253
customs patrol vessel

Built 1960 by Djupviks Yard, Tjorn,
Sweden
Original owners Swedish Customs
Propulsion Diesel engine and petrol
engines; 460hp
Tonnage 10.4 displacement
Length 49.27ft/15.02m
Breadth 12.23ft/3.73m
Draught 3.51ft/1.07m
Materials Steel throughout
Original use Customs patrol
Condition Intact
Present owners Gothenburg Maritime
Centre
Location Gothenburg, Sweden
History Swedish customs cutter built
with experimental propulsion system
consisting of a diesel engine flanked by
two petrol engines. Preserved as a
floating exhibit.
Bibliography B50

U-3
submarine

Built 1942 by Karlskrona Naval
Shipyard, Karlskrona, Sweden
Original owners Royal Swedish Navy
Propulsion Diesel and electric motors
Tonnage 367 displacement
Length 162.75ft/49.6m
Breadth 15.42ft/4.7m
Draught 12.5ft/3.8m
Materials Steel throughout
Original use Submarine
Condition Intact
Present owners Malmo Technical
Museum
Location Malmo, Sweden
History Preserved as an onshore
exhibit.
Bibliography A6

Vasa

Valborg II
sailing coaster

Former name NINA, GERD
Built 1902 by Sjotorp Shipyard, Sjotorp,
Sweden
Original owners Karl-Gustaf Mork
Propulsion Sail, schooner rig; later
ketch rig and diesel auxiliary
Tonnage 133.79 gross
Length 88.07ft/26.85m
Breadth 22.73ft/6.93m
Draught 10.92ft/3.33m
Materials Wood throughout
Original use Cargo
Condition Intact
Present owners Gothenburg Maritime
Centre
Location Gothenburg, Sweden
History Preserved as a floating exhibit.
Bibliography B50

Vasa
sailing warship

Built 1627 by Royal Dockyard,
Stockholm, Sweden
Original owners Royal Swedish Navy
Propulsion Sail, full-rigged ship
Tonnage 1300 displacement
Length 180.0ft/54.86m
Breadth 38.0ft/11.58m
Materials Wood throughout
Original use Warship

Condition Intact hull raised in 1961
Present owners National Museum of
Sweden
Location Stockholm, Sweden
History Though it took place in 1961,
the raising of the VASA remains one of
the most remarkable retrievals of a
sunken historic ship ever undertaken.
VASA had been the finest ship in the
Swedish Navy when she capsized and
foundered while leaving Stockholm
harbour on her maiden voyage in 1628.
She was found by divers in 1956 resting
upright in the bottom mud, buried to
around her normal waterline in a
remarkable state pf preservation. The
discovery was the culmination of a
search begun by marine archaeologist
Anders Franzen, who had theorised
correctly that wooden wrecks in Baltic
coastal waters would be protected from
harmful marine life by the lower salt
content of the water. VASA was raised
in stages using cables passed through
tunnels dug under the hull and
attached to salvage pontoons. On and
around the ship was found a wealth of
the carved decoration with which the
ship had been embellished, and
numerous artifacts providing
information on the life of seventeenth-
century seamen. The hull was treated
with polyetheline glycol for almost
thirty years to prevent deterioration

Viking

following its drying out. Replicas of most of the carvings have now been fitted in place, including the lion figurehead. VASA was housed in a cramped temporary structure for many years while the treatment of the wood was taking place. She has now been moved to a specially built permanent structure standing over an old stone drydock. Visitors now get a dramatic overall view of the ship as they enter the main hall. They can also approach it at close range from every level on a series of balconies. Galleries in other parts of the building tell the story of the ship and display many of the artifacts found.
Bibliography C59, D75, 179, 289a, 290, 351, F5

Viking
cargo carrying training ship

Built 1907 by Burmeister & Wain, Copenhagen, Denmark
Original owners Den Danske Handelsfaades Skoleskib
Propulsion Sail, four-masted barque rig
Tonnage 2760 gross
Length 287.58ft/87.65m
Breadth 45.58ft/13.89m
Draught 23.17ft/7.06m
Materials Steel hull and deckhouses, steel and wood masts
Original use Cargo
Condition Intact
Present owners City of Gothenburg
Location Gothenburg, Sweden
History Built for the Danish merchant marine and employed in the Australian grain trade until the 1940s. Later a maritime school at Gothenburg. Preserved as a floating exhibit.
Bibliography B50, C52, 54, 75, 96, D121, 247, 428

Warpen
coastal passenger steamer

Built 1873 by William Lindbergs, Stockholm, Sweden
Propulsion Steam, screw
Length 67.4ft/20.55m
Breadth 15.6ft/4.75m
Materials Iron hull
Original use Passengers
Condition In operating condition
Present owners Angsbaten Warpen

Aktiebolag
Location Bollnas, Sweden
History In use for excursions.

Westkust
trading schooner

Built 1932 at Sjotorp, Sweden
Propulsion Sail, three-masted schooner; diesel engine, 205hp
Tonnage 145 gross
Length 87.25ft/26.6m
Breadth 23.52ft/7.17m
Draught 10.5ft/3.2m
Materials Wood throughout
Original use Cargo
Condition In sailing condition
Present owners Orust Skolfartygsstiftelse
Location Orust, Sweden
History In use for sail training.

Whiskey Class
submarine

Built Date not known
Original owners Russian Navy
Materials Steel throughout
Original use Submarine
Condition Intact
Location Stockholm, Sweden
History Russian non-nuclear submarine of the Cold War era open to the public as a floating exhibit in Stockholm.

Westkust

Switzerland

Apart from the river port of Basel on the Rhine, large lakes surrounded by mountains are this country's only navigable waterways. Since the mid-nineteenth century, the larger passenger vessels on these lakes have been elegant sidewheel steamers. Some of the last steamers were converted to diesel propulsion, but the majority have remained steam-powered. The recent conversion of the MONTREAUX back to steam is believed to be the first in a series of such projects. The larger Swiss lakes were also home to a unique type of two-masted sailing vessel, two examples of which, the NEPTUNE and LA VAUDOISE, have been restored and are maintained in sailing condition.

Blumlisalp
sidewheel lake steamer

Built 1906 by Escher-Wyss, Zurich, Switzerland
Original owners Bern-Lotschberg-Simplon Railroad
Propulsion Steam, sidewheel, compound, 600hp
Tonnage 294 displacement
Length 198.32ft/60.45m
Breadth 43.14ft/13.5m
Materials Steel throughout
Original use Passengers
Condition In operation
Present owners Vaporama
Location Thun, Switzerland
History Built to carry passengers on Lake Thun and still in service there.
Bibliography B16, B43, D24, D381

Gallia
passenger lake steamer

Built 1913 by Escher-Wyss, Zurich, Switzerland
Original owners Schiffahrtsgesellschaft des Vierwaldstattersees
Propulsion Steam, sidewheel, compound diagonal, 1085hp. Engine built by Escher-Wyss
Tonnage 328.9 displacement
Length 206.36ft/62.9m
Breadth 45.57ft/14.5m
Materials Steel throughout
Original use Passengers
Condition In operation
Present owners Schiffahrtsgesellschaft des Vierwaldstattersees
Location Lucerne, Switzerland
History Built to carry passengers on Lake Lucerne and still in service there.
Bibliography B16, B28, B43

La Suisse
passenger lake steamer

Built 1910 by Sulzer Freres, Lausanne, Switzerland
Original owners Compagnie Generale de Navigation
Propulsion Steam, sidewheel, compound diagonal, 1400hp. Engine built by Sulzer Freres
Tonnage 518 gross
Length 256.0ft/78.03m
Breadth 52.0ft/15.85m
Draught 5.67ft/1.73m
Materials Steel throughout
Original use Passengers
Condition In operation
Present owners Compagnie Generale de Navigation, Geneva
Location Lausanne, Switzerland
History Built to carry passengers on Lake Geneva and still in service there.
Bibliography B16, B28, B43

La Vaudoise
cargo carrying lake sailing vessel

Former name LA VIOLETTE
Built 1932 by Chantier Naval, Bret-Locum, Haut Savoie, France
Original owners Eloi Giroud, Villeneuve
Propulsion Sail, two masts lateen-rigged; diesel auxiliary, 120hp
Length 55.77ft/17.0m
Breadth 20.34ft/6.2m
Draught 3.28ft/1.0m
Materials Wood throughout
Original use Cargo
Condition In sailing condition
Present owners Confrerie des Pirates D'Ouchy
Location Lausanne, Switzerland
History One of two surviving sailing vessels built to carry cargo on the Swiss lakes. Preserved as a floating exhibit and active sailing vessel.
Bibliography B42

Lotschberg
passenger lake steamer

Built 1914 by Escher-Wyss, Zurich, Switzerland
Original owners Berner Alpenbahn Gesellschaft
Propulsion Steam, sidewheel, compound diagonal, 450hp. Engine built by Escher-Wyss
Tonnage 260 displacement
Length 185.0ft/56.39m
Breadth 42.0ft/12.8m

Lotschberg

Blumlisalp

Materials Steel throughout
Original use Passengers
Condition In operation
Present owners Schiffsbetrieb BLS
Location Thun, Switzerland
History Built to carry passengers
on Lake Brienz and still in service
there.
Bibliography B16, B28, B43, D212

Montreaux
passenger lake steamer

Built 1904 by Sulzer, Winterthur,
Switzerland
Original owners Compagnie Generale
de Navigation
Propulsion Steam, sidewheel; later
diesel; to be restored to steam
Tonnage 322 displacement
Length 206.8ft/63.0m
Breadth 7.2ft/14.3m
Materials Steel throughout
Original use Passengers
Condition In operation
Present owners Compagnie Generale de
Navigation
Location Geneva, Switzerland
Bibliography B43

Neptune
cargo carrying lake sailing vessel

Built 1904 at Brigantin, France
Original owners Robert Thorens,
Geneva
Propulsion Sail, two masts lateen-
rigged; diesel engine added
Tonnage 200 gross
Length 90.0ft/27.43m
Breadth 27.67ft/8.13m
Draught 5.5ft/1.68m
Materials Wood throughout
Original use Cargo
Condition Intact
Present owners State of Geneva
Location Geneva, Switzerland
History One of two surviving sailing
vessels built to carry cargo on the
Swiss lakes. Preserved as a floating
exhibit.
Bibliography B42, D79

Rhone
passenger lake steamer

Built 1927 by Sulzer Freres, Geneva,
Switzerland
Original owners Compagnie Generale
de Navigation
Propulsion Steam, sidewheel,
compound diagonal, 900hp. Engine
built by Sulzer Freres
Tonnage 364 displacement
Length 215.0ft/65.53m

Breadth 48.0ft/14.63m
Draught 5.75ft/1.75m
Materials Steel throughout
Original use Passengers
Condition In operation
Present owners Compagnie Generale de
Navigation
Location Geneva, Switzerland
History Built to carry passengers on
Lake Geneva and still in service there.
Bibliography B16, B28, B43

Rigi
passenger lake steamer

Built 1848 by Ditchburn & Mare,

Neptune

Greenwich, England (pre-fabricated)
Original owners
Postdampfschiffahrtsges auf dem
Vierwaldstattersee
Propulsion Steam, sidewheel,
oscillating, 110hp (1894). Engine built
by Escher-Wyss (current)
Tonnage 90 displacement
Length 125.0ft/38.1m
Breadth 26.9ft/8.2m
Draught 4.45ft/1.37m
Materials Iron hull, wood
superstructure
Original use Passengers
Condition Intact
Present owners Swiss Transport

Museum
Location Lucerne, Switzerland
History Oldest surviving Swiss lake
steamer. Preserved as an onshore
exhibit.
Bibliography A17, B16, B28, B43

Savoie
passenger lake steamer

Built 1914 by Sulzer Freres, Winterthur,
Switzerland
Original owners Compagnie Generale
de Navigation
Propulsion Steam, sidewheel,
compound diagonal, 900hp. Engine
built by Sulzer Freres
Tonnage 367 displacement
Length 206.64ft/63.0m
Breadth 46.9ft/14.3m
Materials Steel throughout
Original use Passengers
Present owners Compagnie Generale de
Navigation
Location Lausanne, Switzerland
History Built to carry passengers on
Lake Geneva and still in service there.
Bibliography B16, B28, B43

Schiller
passenger lake steamer

Built 1906 by Sulzer Freres, Winterthur,
Switzerland
Original owners Schiffahrtsgesellschaft
des Vierwaldstattersees
Propulsion Steam, sidewheel,
compound diagonal, 700hp. Engine
built by Sulzer Freres
Tonnage 319.9 displacement
Length 206.69ft/63.0m
Breadth 46.92ft/14.3m
Materials Steel throughout
Original use Passengers
Condition In operation
Present owners Schiffahrtsgesellschaft
des Vierwaldstattersees
Location Lucerne, Switzerland
History Built to carry passengers on
Lake Lucerne and still in service there.
Bibliography B16, B28, B43

Simplon
passenger lake steamer

Built 1915 by Sulzer Freres, Lausanne,
Switzerland
Original owners Compagnie Generale
de Navigation
Propulsion Steam, sidewheel,
compound diagonal, 1400hp. Engine
built by Sulzer Freres
Tonnage 483 displacement
Length 256.0ft/78.05m
Breadth 52.0ft/15.85m

Present owners Zurichsee
Schiffahrtsgesellschaft
Location Zurich, Switzerland
History Built to carry passengers on
Lake Zurich and still in service there.
Bibliography B16, B28, B43

Stadt Zurich
passenger lake steamer

Built 1909 by Escher-Wyss, Zurich,
Switzerland
Original owners Zurichsee
Schiffahrtsgesellschaft
Propulsion Steam, sidewheel,
compound diagonal, 500hp. Engine
built by Escher-Wyss
Tonnage 291 displacement
Length 194.0ft/59.13m
Breadth 44.25ft/13.49m
Materials Steel throughout
Original use Passengers
Condition In operation
Present owners Zurichsee
Schiffahrtsgesellschaft
Location Zurich, Switzerland
History Built to carry passengers on
Lake Zurich and still in service there.
Bibliography B16, B28, B43

Uri

Draught 5.83ft/1.78m
Materials Steel throughout
Original use Passengers
Condition In operation
Present owners Compagnie Generale de
Navigation
Location Lausanne, Switzerland
History Largest Swiss lake steamer,
entering service in 1920.
Bibliography B16, B28, B43

Stadt Luzern
passenger lake steamer

Built 1928 by Gebruder Sachsenberg,
Rosslau, Germany
Original owners Schiffahrtsgesellschaft
des Vierwaldstattersees
Propulsion Steam, sidewheel, 3-cylinder
diagonal, 1120hp. Engine built by
Gebruder Sachsenberg
Tonnage 427 displacement
Length 208.33ft/63.5m
Breadth 49.87ft/15.2m
Materials Steel throughout
Original use Passengers
Condition In operation
Present owners Schiffahrtsgesellschaft
des Vierwaldstattersees
Location Lucerne, Switzerland
History Built to carry passengers on
Lake Lucerne and still in service there.
Bibliography B16, B28, B43

Stadt Rapperswil
passenger lake steamer

Built 1914 by Escher-Wyss, Zurich,
Switzerland
Original owners Zurichsee
Schiffahrtsgesellschaft
Propulsion Steam, sidewheel,
compound diagonal, 500hp. Engine
built by Escher-Wyss
Tonnage 249.3 displacement
Length 194.0ft/59.13m
Breadth 44.25ft/13.49m
Materials Steel throughout
Original use Passengers
Condition In operation

Thalwil
passenger lake steamer

Former name NEU-ZURICH
Built 1892
Propulsion Steam, screw; converted to
diesel in 1936
Materials Steel throughout

Stadt Rapperswil

Original use Passengers
Condition Intact
Present owners Verkehrshaus Luzern
Location Lucerne, Switzerland
History Preserved as an onshore
exhibit.
Bibliography D423

Unterwalden
passenger lake steamer

Built 1902 by Escher-Wyss, Zurich,
Switzerland
Original owners Schiffahrtsgesellschaft
des Vierwaldstattersees
Propulsion Steam, sidewheel,
compound diagonal, 650hp. Engine
built by Escher-Wyss
Tonnage 294 displacement
Length 204.0ft/62.18m
Breadth 46.0ft/14.02m
Materials Steel throughout
Original use Passengers
Condition In operation
Present owners Schiffahrtsgesellschaft
des Vierwaldstattersees
Location Lucerne, Switzerland
History Built to carry passengers on
Lake Lucerne and still in service there.
Bibliography B16, B28, B43

Uri
passenger lake steamer

Built 1901 by Sulzer Freres, Winterthur,
Switzerland
Original owners Schiffahrtsgesellschaft
des Vierwaldstattersee
Propulsion Steam, sidewheel,
compound diagonal, 650hp. Engine
built by Sulzer Freres
Tonnage 293.6 displacement
Length 203.0ft/61.87m
Breadth 44.0ft/13.41m
Draught 4.3ft/1.31m
Materials Steel throughout
Original use Passengers
Condition In operation
Present owners Schiffahrtsgesellschaft
des Vierwaldstattersees
Location Lucerne, Switzerland
History Built to carry passengers on
Lake Lucerne and still in service there.
Bibliography B16, B28, B43, D37a

Venoge
lake cargo vessel

Built 1904 by Sulzer, Winterthur,
Switzerland
Propulsion Diesel engine, 45hp (first
diesel vessel in Switzerland). Engine
built by Sulzer
Materials Steel hull
Original use Lake cargo vessel

Condition Intact, original engine
replaced
Present owners Compagnie Generale de
Navigation
Location Zurich, Switzerland
History Survives as a floating
piledriver.

Wilhelm Tell
passenger lake steamer

Built 1908 by Sulzer Freres, Winterthur,
Switzerland
Original owners Schiffahrtsgesellschaft
des Vierwaldstattersees
Propulsion Steam, sidewheel,
compound diagonal, 978hp
Tonnage 320 displacement
Length 206.69ft/63.0m
Breadth 46.9ft/14.3m
Materials Steel throughout
Original use Passengers
Condition Intact
Present owners Restaurant Wilhelm Tell
Location Lucerne, Switzerland
History Built to carry passengers on
Lake Lucerne. Now preserved as a
floating restaurant.
Bibliography B28, B43

Tanzania

Originally colonised by Germany
in the late 1800s, the land that
would later become Tanzania
came under British control at the
end of the First World War, when
it was given the name Tanganyika.
After independence in 1961, and
the establishment of a loose
federation with the nearby island
nation of Zanzibar, the name was
changed to Tanzania. Dar es
Salaam is the country's major
seaport on the Indian Ocean.
Tanzania also has coastline on
navigable Lake Victoria, Lake
Tanganyika, and Lake Nyasa, each
of which is shared with other
African nations. Steamer service
was first established on the lakes
during the German colonial
period. The LIEMBA, refitted with a
diesel engine in 1976, is
apparently the last of the German
vessels still in operation.

Liemba
river steamer

Former name GRAF VON GOETZEN
Built 1914 by Jos L Meyer, Papenburg,
Germany (pre-fabricated)
Original owners German Government
Propulsion Steam, screw, triple
expansion; converted to diesel
Tonnage 1575 displacement
Length 232.0ft/70.71m
Breadth 33.0ft/10.06m
Draught 9.0ft/2.74m
Materials Steel throughout
Original use Passengers and cargo
Condition In operation
Present owners Tanzania Railways
Location Kigoma, Tanzania
History Pre-fabricated in Germany and
assembled at Kigoma on Lake
Tanganyika. Still in use for passengers
and cargo
Bibliography D432, D480

Liemba

Thailand

The former Kingdom of Siam is the only nation in the region of Indochina that was never colonised by Europeans. Its southern region includes the Isthmus of Kra which forms the beginning of the Malay Peninsula. This isthmus gives Thailand coastline on both the China Sea and the Andaman Sea, which is an arm of the Indian Ocean. The major internal waterway is the Chao Phraya River which passes through the capital Bangkok. Though navigable for only fifty miles, it sees heavy traffic mainly consisting of motor vessels and barges transporting rice. Thailand's remarkable fleet of ceremonial barges is based on craft that would once have been used on the river in warfare. There are around thirty altogether housed in two boathouses, one of which, containing the largest and most ornate barges, can normally be visited by the public.

Anantanagaraj
ceremonial barge

Built 1914 at Bangkok, Thailand
Original owners King of Siam
Propulsion Rowed by 54 oarsmen
Length 147.11ft/44.85m
Breadth 8.46ft/2.58m
Materials Wood throughout
Original use Ceremonial barge
Condition Intact, maintained afloat under cover
Present owners Government of Thailand
Location Bangkok, Thailand
History Highly decorated barge rowed in an annual water parade by 54 oarsmen. Based on similar barges going back to the late 1700s.
Bibliography C82

Anekajatibhujonga
ceremonial barge

Built c1910 at Bangkok, Thailand
Original owners King of Siam
Propulsion Rowed by 61 oarsmen
Length 149.8ft/45.67m
Breadth 9.54ft/2.91m
Materials Wood throughout
Original use Ceremonial barge

Condition Intact, maintained afloat under cover
Present owners Government of Thailand
Location Bangkok, Thailand
History Highly decorated barge rowed in an annual water parade by 64 oarsmen. Based on similar barges going back to the late 1700s.
Bibliography C82

Subanahongsa
ceremonial barge

Built 1911 at Bangkok, Thailand
Original owners King of Siam
Propulsion Rowed by 50 oarsmen
Length 151.37ft/46.15m
Breadth 10.4ft/3.17m
Materials Wood throughout
Original use Ceremonial barge
Condition Intact, maintained afloat under cover
Present owners Government of Thailand
Location Bangkok, Thailand
History Largest of a fleet of highly decorated barges rowed in an annual water parade. Based on similar barges going back to the late 1700s.
Bibliography C82

Tahchin
patrol frigate

Former name USS GLENDALE
Built 1943 by Consolidated Steel, San Pedro, California, USA
Original owners United States Navy
Propulsion Steam turbines, 5500hp
Tonnage 1509 displacement
Length 304.0ft/92.63m
Breadth 37.5ft/11.43m
Draught 12.66ft/3.86m
Materials Steel throughout
Original use Escort vessel
Condition In commission
Present owners Royal Thai Navy
Location Based at Bangkok, Thailand
History Second World War veteran. Last surviving vessel of a class of patrol frigate escort vessels built for the United States Navy based on British frigates of the period.

Tuamotu Islands

One of the island groups within French Polynesia, the atolls of the Tuamotu are spread across over one thousand miles of the Pacific Ocean east of Tahiti. Tangaroa seems to be one of the more frequently visited. For almost a century, published accounts of globe-circling yachting voyages have been reporting calling at the island and visiting the prominent wreck of the sailing ship COUNTY OF ROXBURGH lying on beach there. She is one of three surviving iron-hulled four-masted ships, a number of which were produced, exclusively in British shipyards, in the 1870s and 1880s. The other survivors are the MUNOZ GAMERO, ex-COUNTY OF PEEBLES in Chile, and the FALLS OF CLYDE, the only restored example, in Honolulu, Hawaii.

County of Roxburgh
full-rigged trading vessel

Built 1886 by Barclay, Curle & Co, Glasgow, Scotland
Original owners R & J Craig, Glasgow
Propulsion Sail, four-masted full-rigged ship
Tonnage 2209 gross
Length 285.6ft/87.05m
Breadth 43.5ft/13.26m
Materials Iron hull, iron and wood masts
Original use Cargo
Condition Intact hull on beach with remains of masts
Present owners Government of Tuamotu Islands
Location Island of Takaroa, Tuamotu
Bibliography D271

Turkey

When the oldest historic vessel in Turkey was built during the 1600s, Istanbul was the capital of the Ottoman Empire, whose control extended from Hungary right around the east end of the Mediterranean all the way to Algeria. The empire went into decline over the following centuries, and was finally dissolved and replaced by modern Turkey after the First World War. Turkey has been a gathering place for vintage ships in this century. The British liner GERMANIC of 1874 survived as a passenger vessel under the Turkish flag until 1950. In the 1960s there was an unsuccessful effort to preserve the Turkish battlecruiser YAVUZ, which had been built prior to the Second World War as the German GOEBEN. Istanbul continues to be a stronghold of steam ferries, with a Scottish-built fleet dating from 1961. These are screw vessels that bear a strong resemblance to previous generations of sidewheel steamers. The 1911 screw steam ferry GUZELHISAR was to have become a maritime museum, but a recent photograph shows her still laid up, and not in good condition.

Burgaz
steam ferry

Built 1912 by Atel et Chantiers de Province, Port Bouc, France
Original owners Turkish State Shipping Lines
Propulsion Steam, screw, twin triple-expansion, 790hp
Tonnage 697 gross
Length 201.11ft/61.3m
Breadth 30.02ft/9.15m
Draught 8.2ft/2.5m
Materials Steel hull, steel and wood superstructure
Original use Ferry
Condition In operation
Present owners Turkish State Shipping Lines
Location Istanbul, Turkey
History Oldest Turkish steamer in active service.

Güzelhisar

Length 152.33ft/46.43m
Breadth 26.08ft/7.95m
Draught 8.17ft/2.49m
Materials Steel hull, steel and wood superstructure
Original use Ferry
Condition Intact, set aside for museum
Present owners Sehir Hatlari Isletmesi
Location Istanbul, Turkey
History Retired in 1986 and set aside for a museum.
Bibliography B16

Kadirga
royal barge

Built 1600s in Turkey
Original owners Sultan of the Ottoman Empire
Propulsion Rowed
Length 121.2ft/40.0m
Breadth 18.7ft/5.7m
Materials Wood throughout
Original use Royal barge
Condition Intact
Present owners Istanbul Maritime Museum
Location Istanbul, Turkey
History Turkish royal barge dating at least from 1671 and maybe from the 1500s. Preserved as an indoor exhibit.
Bibliography B7

Nusret
minelayer

Former name YARDIM
Built 1912 by Germania Werft, Kiel, Germany
Original owners Turkish Navy
Propulsion Steam, screw, triple

Caiques of Sultan Abdulmejit
two royal barges

Built Mid-1800s in Turkey
Original owners Sultan Abdulmejit I
Propulsion Rowed
Length 104.96ft/32.0m
Breadth 7.87ft/2.4m
Materials Wood throughout
Original use Royal barges
Condition Intact
Present owners Istanbul Maritime Museum
Location Istanbul, Turkey
History Barges built for Turkish sultan who ruled from 1839-1861. Preserved as an indoor exhibit.

Gayret
destroyer

Former name USS EVERSOLE
Built 1946 by Todd Pacific in the

United States
Original owners United States Navy
Propulsion Steam turbines, 60,000hp
Tonnage 3500 displacement
Length 390.5ft/119.0m
Breadth 41.2ft/12.6m
Draught 19.0ft/5.8m
Materials Steel throughout
Original use Destroyer
Location Izmir, Turkey
History Preserved as a museum.

Güzelhisar
steam ferry

Former name BOSPHORUS NO 68
Built 1911 by Hawthorn, Leslie & Co, Hebburn, England
Original owners Turkish State Shipping Lines
Propulsion Steam, screw, twin triple-expansion, 440hp
Tonnage 453 gross

Nusret

expansion, 1200hp
Tonnage 365 displacement
Length 132.0ft/40.23m
Breadth 22.0ft/6.71m
Draught 8.5ft/2.59m
Materials Steel throughout
Original use Minelayer
Condition Intact
Present owners Army-Navy Park
Location Chanakkale, Turkey
History The minelayer that took part in
the defence of the Dardanelles in 1915.
Preserved as an onshore exhibit.

Savarona
steam yacht

Built 1931 by Blohm & Voss, Hamburg,
Germany
Original owners Mrs E R Cadwalader
Propulsion Steam turbines; converted
to diesel, 7000hp
Tonnage 4646 gross
Length 408.5ft/124.51m
Breadth 53.0ft/16.15m
Draught 20.5ft/6.25m
Materials Steel hull, steel and wood
superstructure
Original use Yacht
Condition Fully restored 1989-1992,
operational
Present owners Government of Turkey,
leased to Kahraman Sadikoglu
Location Istanbul, Turkey
History Probably the largest steam
yacht ever built. Later used as
presidential yacht of Turkey. In use for
charters.
Bibliography C40, D426

TA-1
torpedo boat

Built c1952 in the former Soviet Union
Original owners Navy of Cyprus
Propulsion Diesel engines, 2400hp
Tonnage 25 displacement
Length 72.16ft/21.99m
Breadth 15.42ft/4.7m
Draught 4.92ft/1.5m
Materials Aluminium hull
Original use Torpedo boat
Condition Intact
Present owners Turkish Navy
Location Golauk, Turkey
History Captured in the 1974 invasion
of Cyprus. Preserved as an onshore
exhibit.

Ukraine

Under Russian control since the
time of Catherine the Great, this
large region north of the Black
Sea first declared its
independence at the end of the
First World War but was soon
absorbed into the Soviet Union. It
finally achieved full independence
after the dissolution of the Soviet
Union in 1991. The Ukraine
controls the northwest coastline
of the Black Sea, from the delta of
the Danube to that sea's
northern extension, the Sea of
Azov. Its major internal waterway
is the Dnieper River, which
extends from the Black Sea north
through the nation's capital Kiev
to its northern boundary, a
distance of over 600 miles. In the
early 1800s canals were built
linking the Dnieper to the Baltic
through Latvia, Poland, and
Germany. After the break-up of
the Soviet Union Russia and the
Ukraine contested control of the
very large naval force, the Black
Sea Fleet, based in the Ukrainian-
controlled harbour of Sebastopol
on the island of Crimea. A
division of the fleet was finally
agreed upon, and Russia was
allowed to lease the Crimean
base. During the Soviet period
the region of the Ukraine also
adopted the Russian penchant for
preserving small warships
mounted on pedestals as
monuments or memorials.

M-305
submarine

Former name M-256
Built Date not known
Original owners Soviet Navy
Propulsion Diesel and electric motors
Materials Steel throughout
Original use Submarine
Condition Intact
Location Odessa, Ukraine
History Former Russian submarine
apparently built around the Second
World War period. Superstructure may
have been modernised at a later date.
Preserved on shore as an exhibit and
naval memorial.

Zhelesniakov
river gunboat

Built c1939 by Leninskaya Kruznica
Yard, Kiev, Ukraine
Original owners Soviet Navy
Propulsion Diesel engines, 300hp
Tonnage 240 displacement
Length 157.50ft/48.01m
Breadth 25.0ft/7.62m
Draught 4.5ft/1.37m
Materials Steel throughout
Original use River gunboat
Condition Intact
Present owners City of Kiev
Location Kiev, Ukraine
History Sole survivor of a class of six
monitors that saw service in the
Second World War in the Russian
Dnieper River Flotilla. Preserved on
shore at Kiev as a war memorial.
Bibliography A16

Additional small naval vessels preserved in the Ukraine as monuments or relics

Location	Type	Pennant number
Berdjansk	torpedo boat	Komsomoletz class
Izmail	river monitor	BKA-134
Jevpatoria	minesweeper	
Kertch	river monitor	BKA- 81
	anti-aircraft boat	
Kherson	river monitor	BKA-334
Mariupol	river monitor	BKA-44
Nikolaev	torpedo boat	
Odessa	minesweeper	T-729
Otchakov	torpedo boat	TKA-383
Sebastopol	torpedo boat	TKA-52
	torpedo boat	TKA-725
Tcherkassi	river monitor	BKA-41

M-305

United States of America

American maritime enterprise in the early years of independence seemed to know no bounds, with major involvement in the China trade, domination of the transatlantic trade under sail, and the early development of the clipper ship. Following the American Civil War, shipping in international trade went into serious decline, but protected coastal commerce on the Atlantic, Pacific, and Great Lakes prospered. The United States produced the first economically successful steam-powered vessel in 1807, and went on to produce some of the most remarkable inland steamboats the world has seen, giant 'floating palaces' for service on the Great Lakes, the Mississippi River, and various large bays, rivers, and sounds on east and west coast. None of these craft survives, and the country has thus far not been in the forefront in the restoration of working steam vessels, with the noteworthy exception of three Second World War built cargo ships. The United States in the 1940s and 1950s had the first maritime museums to take on the preservation of fleets of historic vessels, at Mystic, Connecticut, and San Francisco. The latter museum was particularly successful in gathering a fleet with a strong regional context, but the problems of maintaining large wooden vessels as static exhibits have now made the survival of some of these ships uncertain. Many countries are now preserving warships of the Second World War or later, but the United States can claim the only remaining battleships with five open to the public, and the possibility that the USS NEW JERSEY and USS IOWA may be added, in New York Harbor and at San Francisco.

A D Haynes II
river towboat

Built 1955 by Dravo, Neville Island, Pennsylvania
Official number 270550
Propulsion Diesel engines
Tonnage 1103 gross
Length 184.4ft/56.2m
Breadth 45.1ft/13.7m
Depth 11.7ft/3.6m
Materials Steel throughout
Original use River towboat
Condition Intact, recently retired
Present owners Louisville Waterfront Development Corporation
Location Louisville, Kentucky, USA
History Diesel towboat of the 1950s employed pushing large rafts of barges on the Mississippi and Ohio rivers. Acquired for conversion to a floating museum.

A J Meerwald
oyster dredger

Former name CLYDE A PHILIPS
Built 1928 by Charles H Stowman & Sons, Dorchester, New Jersey
Original owners A J Meerwald & Sons, South Dennis, New Jersey
Propulsion Sail, schooner rig; diesel engine, 100hp
Tonnage 57 gross
Length 76.3ft/23.26m
Breadth 22.1ft/6.74m
Draught 6.3ft/1.9m
Materials Wood throughout
Original use Oystering
Condition Restored to sailing condition
Present owners Delaware Bay Schooner Project
Location Dorchester, New Jersey, USA
History Currently a travelling exhibit and used for sail training.

Ada C Lore
oyster dredger

Former name KATHRYN & ELMA, EMMA L EVANS
Built 1923 at Dorchester, New Jersey
Propulsion Sail, schooner rig; later motor vessel
Tonnage 59 gross
Length 77.0ft/23.5m
Breadth 22.5ft/6.9m
Materials Wood throughout
Original use Oystering
Condition Restoration in progress
Present owners Bivalve Packing
Location Bivalve, New Jersey, USA
History Schooner built for dredging oysters in Delaware Bay. Currently being restored from motor vessel to sailing vessel. When restoration is completed she will be the first sailing oyster dredger working on the Bay in several decades.

Adirondack
steam ferry

Former name GOVERNOR EMERSON C HARRINGTON II, MOUNT HOLLY*
Built 1913 by Merrill-Stevens Shipyard, Jacksonville, Florida
Original owners Jacksonville Ferry and Land Co
Propulsion Steam, screw, 2-cylinder, 400hp; converted to diesel
Length 153.0ft/46.6m
Breadth 42.0ft/12.8m
Materials Steel throughout
Original use Ferryboat
Condition In operating condition
Present owners Champlain Lake and Canal Cruises
Contact address RD 1, Box 17, North Street, New Haven, Vermont 05472
Location Burlington, Vermont, USA
History Built as the SOUTH JACKSONVILLE* for use as a ferry on the Saint Johns River in Florida. Later used on the Delaware River north of Philadelphia, at New York City on the East River, and on the Chesapeake Bay near Annapolis. After 1953 served as a ferry across Lake Champlain. Superstructure has been altered several times. Current appearance largely dates from 1937. In use for excursions.
Bibliography D45a

Adventure
fishing schooner

Built 1926 by Everett James, Essex, Massachusetts
Original owners Captain Jeffrey F Thomas
Propulsion Sail, schooner rig; diesel auxiliary
Tonnage 130 gross
Length 107.0ft/32.61m
Breadth 24.5ft/7.47m
Materials Wood throughout
Original use Fishing
Condition In sailing condition
Present owners Gloucester Adventure Inc
Location Gloucester, Massachusetts, USA
History Last fishing schooner to sail out of the port of Boston. Later spent many years as a cruise vessel based at Camden, Maine. Preserved as a floating exhibit and active sailing vessel.
Bibliography A14, D186

Adventuress
schooner yacht

Built 1913 by Rice Brothers, East Boothbay, Maine
Original owners Jane Borden
Propulsion Sail, schooner rig; diesel engine, 225hp
Tonnage 78 gross
Length 85.5ft/26.06m
Breadth 21.4ft/6.52m

Adventure

Materials Wood throughout
Original use Yacht
Condition In sailing condition
Present owners Youth Adventure Inc
Location Seattle, Washington, USA
History Originally built for a hunting expedition to the Arctic. Served as a pilot vessel at San Francisco from 1914 to 1950. Now used for sail training.
Bibliography D20

Air-sea rescue boat

Built 1942 by Miami Shipbuilding, Miami, Florida
Original owners United States Navy
Length 63.0ft/19.2m
Materials Wood throughout
Original use Rescue craft
Condition Intact, afloat
Present owners American Patrol Boats Museum
Location Rio Vista, California, USA
History Example of high speed boats built to rescue aviators from the water near military airfields. Preserved as a floating exhibit by a group that specialises in restoring small naval craft.

Alabama
sailing pilot schooner

Former name ALABAMIAN
Built 1926 by Pensacola Shipbuilding Co, Pensacola, Florida
Original owners Mobile Bay Bar Pilots Association
Propulsion Sail, schooner rig; diesel engines, twin screw
Tonnage 70 gross
Length 88.63ft/27.01m
Breadth 21.6ft/6.58m
Materials Wood throughout
Original use Pilot vessel
Condition Undergoing restoration
Present owners Robert S Douglas
Location Vineyard Haven, Mass, USA
History Built as a pilot vessel at the entrance to Mobile Bay, Alabama. Proposed use for sailing cruises.

Alabama
battleship

Former name USS ALABAMA
Built 1942 by Norfolk Naval Shipyard, Portsmouth, Virginia
Original owners United States Navy
Official number BB-60
Propulsion Steam turbines, 130,000hp
Tonnage 38,892 displacement
Length 679.5ft/207.11m
Breadth 108.0ft/32.92m
Draught 36.0ft/10.97m
Materials Steel throughout
Original use Battleship
Condition Intact
Present owners USS Alabama Battleship Commission
Location Mobile, Alabama, USA
History Second World War battleship preserved as a floating exhibit.
Bibliography B45, C64, D317

Albacore
experimental submarine

Former name USS ALBACORE
Built 1953 by Portsmouth Naval Shipyard, Kittery, Maine
Original owners United States Navy
Propulsion Diesel engines
Tonnage 1242 displacement
Length 203.84ft/62.13m
Breadth 27.33ft/8.33m
Draught 18.58ft/5.66m
Materials Steel throughout
Original use Experimental submarine
Condition Intact
Present owners Portsmouth Submarine Memorial Association
Location Portsmouth, New Hampshire, USA
History Experimental submarine whose hull form was intended as a prototype for that of future nuclear submarines. Preserved as an onshore exhibit.
Bibliography C64

Alma
trading schooner

Built 1891 by Fred Siemer, Hunters Point, California
Original owners James Peterson
Propulsion Sail, schooner rig
Tonnage 41 gross
Length 59.0ft/17.98m
Breadth 22.6ft/6.89m
Materials Wood throughout
Original use Cargo
Condition In sailing condition
Present owners San Francisco Maritime National Historic Park
Location San Francisco, California,

Alabama

Albacore

USA
History Originally employed shipping hay to the city of San Francisco. Preserved as a floating exhibit and active sailing vessel.
Bibliography C68, D170

Aloha
motor fishing vessel

Built 1937 by Sturgeon Bay Boat Building, Sturgeon Bay, Wisconsin
Original owners Voight Brothers, Duluth, Minnesota
Propulsion Diesel engine, 60hp
Tonnage 26 gross
Length 41.4ft/12.53m
Breadth 12.2ft/3.72m
Materials Wood throughout
Original use Fishing
Condition Intact
Present owners United States National Park Service
Location Empire, Michigan, USA
History Example of type of fishing boat with fully enclosed deck used on the Great Lakes known as a 'fishing tug'. Preserved as an onshore exhibit.

Ambrose
lightship

Former name SCOTLAND, VINEYARD SOUND, RELIEF
Built 1908 by New York Shipbuilding Co, Camden, New Jersey
Original owners United States Lighthouse Establishment
Official number LS 87
Propulsion Steam, screw; converted to diesel
Tonnage 683 displacement
Length 135.75ft/41.38m
Breadth 29.0ft/8.84m
Materials Steel hull and masts, wood deckhouses
Original use Lightship
Condition Intact
Present owners South Street Seaport Museum
Location New York, USA
History The first lightship was established in 1732 to guide ships into the main channel of the broad Thames Estuary in England. By the late 1800s lightships had come into widespread use around the coasts of Europe and North America. In recent years most have been replaced by large automatic buoys. Many former lightships are now floating museums. A dozen are located in the United States, which now has no active lightships. One of the more historic is the AMBROSE, on exhibit at New York. She was built to mark the Ambrose Channel, the major ship channel into that port. Completed in 1907, this channel ensured the continued prominence of New York as the gateway to North America, making possible the giant superliners of the twentieth century. AMBROSE remained on station at the entrance to the channel until 1931, when she was made a relief ship for a district extending from the Delaware Bay to Rhode Island. In 1939 she was placed on the SCOTLAND station at the southern approach to New York. She was finally retired in 1963. During her long career the ship went through a number of changes. In 1908 her colour scheme was 'straw' with black letters. In the 1930s she had a black hull. During the Second World War she was painted grey and stationed off the port to challenge approaching ships. Since the end of that war she has had a red hull with large white letters. Her original steam engine was replaced with a diesel engine in 1931. AMBROSE had one of the first radiobeacons established in the United States to aid navigators. Her original oil-burning lamps were replaced with electric lights early in her career. AMBROSE is an exhibit of the South Street Seaport Museum in lower Manhattan.
Bibliography C27

American
fishing schooner

Former name CAPTAIN JAMES COOK, E F ZWICKER
Built 1934 by Smith & Rhuland, Lunenburg, Nova Scotia, Canada
Original owners E Fenwick Zwicker
Propulsion Sail, schooner rig; diesel engine
Tonnage 177 gross
Length 125.3ft/38.19m
Breadth 26.8ft/8.17m
Materials Wood throughout
Original use Fishing
Condition Intact, in use
Present owners The Lobster House
Location Cape May, New Jersey, USA
History Built for use as a dory fishing schooner based at Lunenberg, Nova Scotia. Later converted to a training vessel by an American seamen's union for use at a school located at Piney Point, Maryland. Currently preserved as a floating restaurant.

American Eagle
sail fishing vessel

Former name ANDREW AND ROSALIE
Built 1930 by Arthur H Boucher, Gloucester, Massachusetts
Original owners Captain Patrick Murphy, Gloucester

American Eagle

Balclutha

Propulsion Sail, schooner rig; diesel
engine, 150hp
Tonnage 70 gross
Length 76.4ft/23.29m
Breadth 19.3ft/5.88m
Materials Wood throughout
Original use Fishing
Condition In sailing condition
Present owners John Foss
Location Rockland, Maine, USA
History Restored in 1986. In use for
sailing cruises.
Bibliography D49

Angel's Gate
motor tug

Former name ST 695
Built 1944 Decatur, Alabama, USA
Original owners United States Army
Propulsion Diesel engine, 690HP
Tonnage 146 gross
Length 80.9ft/24.6m
Breadth 23.0ft/7.0m
Materials Steel throughout
Original use Tug
Condition Intact
Present owners Los Angeles Maritime

Museum
Location Los Angeles, California, USA
History Harbour tug built for the
United States Army during the Second
World War. Later employed in the Port
of Los Angeles. Currently maintained
as a floating exhibit of the Los Angeles
Maritime Museum.

Arkansas II
snagboat

Built 1940 by Bethlehem Steel Co,
Leetsdale, Pennsylvania
Original owners United States Army
Corps of Engineers
Propulsion Steam, sternwheel
Tonnage 459 displacement
Length 177.1ft/53.98m
Breadth 38.7ft/11.8m
Materials Steel hull, steel and wood
superstructure
Original use Snagboat
Condition In need of restoration
Present owners Arkansas Riverboat Co
Location North Little Rock, Arkansas,
USA
History Built for use clearing snags

(sunken trees) from the navigable
channels of the Mississippi River and
its tributaries. Later a floating
restaurant at Memphis, Tennessee.
Proposed as an exhibit.

Arthur Foss
steam tug

Former name WALLOWA
Built 1889 by Willamette Ship Building
Co, Portland, Oregon
Original owners Oregon Railway and
Navigation Co
Propulsion Steam, screw; converted to
diesel
Tonnage 214 gross
Length 111.0ft/33.83m
Breadth 23.75ft/7.24m
Materials Wood throughout
Original use Tug
Condition Intact
Present owners Northwest Seaport
Location Seattle, Washington, USA
History Veteran former steam tug
preserved afloat at Seattle, Washington.

Balclutha
full-rigged trading vessel

Former name PACIFIC QUEEN, STAR OF
ALASKA, BALCLUTHA
Built 1886 by Charles Connell & Co,
Scotstoun, nr Glasgow, Scotland
Original owners Robert McMillan,
Dumbarton, Scotland
Propulsion Sail, full-rigged ship
Tonnage 1862 gross
Length 256.3ft/78.12m
Breadth 38.5ft/11.73m
Draught 22.7ft/6.92m
Materials Steel hull and deckhouses,
steel and wood masts
Original use Cargo
Condition Intact
Present owners San Francisco Maritime
National Historic Park
Location San Francisco, California,
USA
History Built to carry cargo worldwide
under the British flag. Later sailed
under the American flag serving
salmon canneries in Alaska. Converted
to a waterfront attraction in the 1930s.
Restored to serve as a floating museum

at San Francisco in the 1950s. Preserved as a floating exhibit.
Bibliography D202, 249, 282, 361, 391, 551

Baltimore
steam tug/VIP launch

Built 1906 by Skinner Shipbuilding, Baltimore, Maryland
Original owners City of Baltimore
Propulsion Steam, screw
Tonnage 81 gross
Length 84.6ft/25.79m
Breadth 18.6ft/5.67m
Draught 8.2ft/2.5m
Materials Steel hull, wood superstructure
Original use Tug and VIP launch
Condition In operating condition
Present owners Baltimore Museum of Industry
Location Baltimore, Maryland, USA
History Preserved intact as a floating exhibit and active steamer.
Bibliography B26, D74

Barc 3-X
amphibious wheeled vehicle

Built 1952 by Pacific Coast Foundry
Original owners United States Army
Propulsion Diesel engines
Length 61.67ft/18.8m
Breadth 27.75ft/8.46m
Materials Steel throughout
Original use Troop carrier

Condition Intact
Present owners Army Transportation Museum
Location Fort Eustis, Virginia, USA
History Amphibious wheeled vehicle evolved from the DUKW of the Second World War. Preserved as an onshore exhibit.

Barnegat
lightship

Former name RELIEF, FIVE FATHOM
Built 1904 by New York Shipbuilding Co, Camden, New Jersey
Original owners United States Lighthouse Establishment
Propulsion Steam, screw; converted to diesel
Tonnage 668 displacement
Length 136.0ft/41.45m
Breadth 28.8ft/8.78m
Materials Steel hull and masts, wood deckhouses
Original use Lightship
Present owners Heritage Ship Guild of the Port of Philadelphia
Location Philadelphia, Pennsylvania, USA
History Oldest intact lightship surviving on the east coast of the United States. Modernised with diesel propulsion in the 1930s. Preserved as a floating exhibit.
Bibliography C27

Barry

Barry
destroyer

Former name USS BARRY
Built 1956 by Bath Iron Works, Bath, Maine
Original owners United States Navy
Propulsion Steam turbines
Tonnage 2780 displacement
Length 418.4ft/127.53m
Breadth 45.2ft/13.78m
Draught 20.0ft/6.1m
Materials Steel throughout
Original use Destroyer

Condition Intact
Present owners Naval Historical Museum
Location Washington, DC, USA
History American destroyer of the 1950s. Preserved as a floating exhibit.
Bibliography C64

Batfish
submarine

Former name USS BATFISH
Built 1943 by Portsmouth Navy Yard, Kittery, Maine
Original owners United States Navy
Propulsion Diesel and electric motors
Tonnage 1526 displacement
Length 311.7ft/95.01m
Breadth 27.25ft/8.31m
Draught 17.0ft/5.18m
Materials Steel throughout
Original use Submarine
Condition Intact
Present owners Muskogee War Memorial Park and Military Museum
Location Muskogee, Oklahoma, USA
History American submarine of the Second World War. Preserved as a floating exhibit.
Bibliography B45, C64, D55, D321

Becky Thatcher
river inspection vessel

Former name MISSISSIPPI
Built 1927 by Howard Shipyard, Jeffersonville, Indiana
Original owners United States Army Corps of Engineers
Propulsion Steam, sternwheel, 800hp
Tonnage 761 displacement
Length 213.25ft/65.0m
Breadth 38.0ft/11.58m

Baltimore

Becky Thatcher as Mississippi shortly after being retired by the Army Engineers

Materials Steel hull, wood
superstructure
Original use Inspection vessel
Condition Intact
Present owners Ohio Showboat Drama
Inc
Location Marietta, Ohio, USA
History The US Army Corps of
Engineers are responsible for keeping
the country's navigable waterways clear
by dredging and debris removal. This
vessel (under her former name
MISSISSIPPI) served as their inspection
steamer. Preserved as a floating
restaurant.
Bibliography B44

Becuna
submarine

Former name USS BECUNA
Built 1944 by Electric Boat Co, Groton,
Connecticut
Original owners United States Navy
Propulsion Diesel and electric motors
Tonnage 1526 displacement
Length 311.75ft/95.02m
Breadth 27.25ft/8.31m
Draught 17.0ft/5.18m
Materials Steel throughout
Original use Submarine
Condition Intact
Present owners Independence Seaport

Museum
Location Philadelphia, Pennsylvania,
USA
History American submarine of the
Second World War. Preserved as a
floating exhibit.
Bibliography B45, C64

Belisarius
sailing yacht

Built 1935 by Herreshoff
Manufacturing Co, Bristol, Rhode
Island. Designed by Nathaniel
Herreshoff
Original owners Carl Rockwell
Propulsion Sail, yawl rig
Length 56.15ft/17.1m
Breadth 14.0ft/4.3m
Draught 5.5ft/1.7m
Materials Wood throughout
Original use Yacht
Condition Intact, afloat
Present owners Charles & Helen Read
(Herreshoff Museum)
Contact address Herreshoff Marine
Museum, 7 Burnside St, Bristol 02809
Location Bristol, Rhode Island, USA
History Sailing yacht of the 1930s
exhibited afloat as an example of the
craft produced by the Herreshoff
Shipyard, site of the Herreshoff
Museum.

Belle of Louisville
sternwheel river steamer

Former name AVALON, IDELWILD
Built 1914 by James Rees & Sons,
Pittsburgh, Pennsylvania
Original owners West Memphis Packet
Co
Propulsion Steam, sternwheel, 400hp
Tonnage 260 gross
Length 157.5ft/48.0m
Breadth 36.0ft/10.97m
Materials Steel hull, wood
superstructure

Original use Passengers and cargo
Condition In operation
Present owners Belle of Louisville
Operating Board
Location Louisville, Kentucky, USA
History Last surviving Mississippi
River sternwheel packet built to carry
passengers and freight. In use as an
excursion vessel based at Louisville,
Kentucky.
Bibliography A17, B44, D27

Benson Ford
Great Lakes cargo vessel

Former name JOHN DYKSTRA
Built 1924 by Great Lakes Engineering
Works, River Rouge, Michigan
Original owners Ford Motor Co
Official number 223909
Propulsion Diesel engines, 3000hp
Tonnage 8626 gross
Length 596.7ft/181.8m
Breadth 62.0ft/18.9m
Depth 27.7ft/8.4m
Materials Steel throughout
Original use Cargo, Great Lakes
Condition Upper bow and forward
deckhouse on shore
Present owners HMS Victory Point
Location South Bass Island, Ohio, USA
History Proposed for use as a hotel.

Berkeley
steam ferry

Built 1898 by Union Iron Works, San
Francisco, California
Original owners Southern Pacific
Railway
Propulsion Steam, screw, triple
expansion, 188hp
Tonnage 1945 gross
Length 261.4ft/79.67m
Breadth 40.2ft/12.25m
Materials Steel hull, steel and wood

Berkeley

Bowfin

superstructure
Original use Ferry
Condition Intact
Present owners Maritime Museum
Association of San Diego
Location San Diego, California, USA
History Steam ferryboat built for use in
San Francisco Bay. Later a floating gift
shop at Sausalito, California. Preserved
as a floating exhibit.
Bibliography B44, C36, D33, 130, 418,
517, F9

Binghamton
steam ferry

Built 1905 by Newport News
Shipbuilding and Drydock Co,
Newport News, Virginia
Original owners Hoboken Ferry Co
Propulsion Steam, screw, 4-cylinder
compound, 1400hp
Tonnage 1462 gross
Length 187.5ft/57.15m
Breadth 43.3ft/13.2m
Materials Steel hull, steel and wood
superstructure
Original use Ferry
Condition Intact, in use
Present owners Hudson Landing Inc
Location Edgewater, New Jersey, USA
History Steam ferryboat that operated
between Hoboken, New Jersey and
Manhattan Island from 1905 until 1968.
Preserved as a floating restaurant.
Bibliography B44, C81

Blueback
submarine

Former name USS BLUEBACK
Built 1959 by Ingalls Shipbuilding
Corp, Pascagoula, Mississippi
Original owners United States Navy

Official number SS-581
Propulsion Diesel engines and electric
motors
Tonnage 2158 displacement
Length 219.0ft/66.7m
Breadth 29.0ft/8.8m
Materials Steel throughout
Original use Submarine
Condition Intact
Present owners Oregon Museum of
Science & Industry
Contact address 1945 SE Water Avenue,
Portland, Oregon 97214
Location Portland, Oregon, USA
History One of three conventional-
propulsion attack submarines built to
the experimental design of the USS
ALBACORE. Remained in active service
until the early 1980s. Now an exhibit.

Bowdoin
Arctic research vessel

Built 1921 by Hodgdon Brothers, East
Boothbay, Maine
Original owners Admiral Donald B
MacMillan
Propulsion Sail, schooner rig; diesel
engine
Tonnage 66 gross
Length 87.0ft/26.52m
Breadth 20.3ft/6.19m
Draught 9.5ft/2.9m
Materials Wood throughout
Original use Arctic research
Condition In sailing condition
Present owners Maine Maritime
Academy
Location Castine, Maine, USA
History Built for research voyages to
the Arctic. Later spent a number of
years as an exhibit at Mystic,
Connecticut. Restored in the 1980s and
currently used as a training vessel.

Bowfin
submarine

Former name USS BOWFIN
Built 1942 by Portsmouth Navy Yard,
Kittery, Maine
Original owners United States Navy
Propulsion Diesel and electric motors
Tonnage 1526 displacement
Length 311.7ft/95.0m
Breadth 27.25ft/8.31m
Draught 16.8ft/5.12m
Materials Steel throughout
Original use Submarine
Condition Intact
Present owners Pacific Fleet Submarine
Memorial Association
Location Pearl Harbor, Hawaii, USA
History American submarine of the
Second World War. Preserved as a
floating exhibit.
Bibliography B45, C64, D243, D318

Brilliant
schooner yacht

Built 1932 by Henry B Nevins, City
Island, New York. Designed by Olin
Stephens
Original owners Walter Barnum
Propulsion Sail, schooner rig, auxiliary
engine
Tonnage 38.5 displacement
Length 61.5ft/18.74m
Breadth 14.66ft/4.47m
Draught 8.9ft/2.69m
Materials Wood throughout
Original use Yacht
Condition In sailing condition
Present owners Mystic Seaport
Museum
Location Mystic, Connecticut, USA
History Classic American schooner
yacht of the 1930s. Took part in major

ocean races, and served as an anti-
submarine patrol vessel during the
Second World War. Has been a sail
training vessel operated by the Mystic
Seaport Museum since 1953.
Bibliography D188a, D547a

Buddy O
motor fishing boat

Built 1936 by Sturgeon Bay Boat Works,
Sturgeon Bay, Wisconsin
Original owners Ole Olsen, Frankfort,
Michigan
Propulsion Diesel engine, 45hp
Tonnage 17.3 gross
Length 36.0ft/10.97m
Breadth 12.0ft/3.66m
Materials Wood throughout
Original use Fishing
Condition Intact
Present owners Rogers Street Fishing
Village Museum
Location Two Harbors, Wisconsin,
USA
History Example of type of fishing boat
with enclosed deck known as a Great
Lakes 'fish tug'. Preserved as an
onshore exhibit.

Burma Queen
police launch

Former name HAFEN POLIZEI V
Built 1927 by H C Stulcken Sohn,
Hamburg, Germany
Propulsion Steam, screw, compound
Length 56.5ft/17.22m
Breadth 12.5ft/3.81m
Draught 5.68ft/1.79m
Materials Iron hull
Original use Police launch
Condition In operating condition
Present owners Robert E Blake

C A Thayer and Eureka

Location San Francisco, California, USA
History Former German steam-powered harbour police launch. In use as a yacht.
Bibliography B26

C A Thayer
trading schooner

Built 1895 by Hans Bendixsen, Fairhaven, California
Original owners E K Wood Lumber Co
Propulsion Sail, three-masted schooner rig
Tonnage 452 gross
Length 156.0ft/47.55m
Breadth 36.0ft/10.97m
Materials Wood throughout
Original use Cargo
Condition Intact
Present owners San Francisco Maritime National Historical Park
Location San Francisco, California, USA
History The schooner-rigged vessel saw its greatest development in the American coastal trades. Of the giant four-, five-, six- and seven-masters only a few deteriorated wrecks remain,

and the rerigged SEUTE DEERN lying at Bremerhaven, Germany. The largest intact examples are the three-masted C A THAYER, preserved in San Francisco, and her near-sistership WAWONA, preserved at Seattle, Washington. The leading schooner trade on the west coast, when these vessels were built, was the transport of lumber from Washington, Oregon and Northern California, for the construction of western cities and, after the earthquake of 1906, the rebuilding of San Francisco. Trading along that coast was made particularly hazardous by the prevailing westerly winds and the lack of sheltered harbours. Often lumber had to be loaded while the vessel was lying at anchor in a tiny cove or open roadstead beneath towering cliffs, where a sudden gale could trap a sailing vessel. The C A THAYER served in this trade until 1912, after which she was employed in supplying salmon canning factories in Alaska. After 1924 she was used fishing for cod in the northern Pacific. She was used as a barge by the US Army during the Second World War, returning to codfishing after the war. She made her

last working voyage under sail in 1950. For the next five years she was lying beached beside a highway in the State of Washington serving as an attraction for tourists. The State of California then acquired the C A THAYER and restored her for use as a floating exhibit on the coastal schooners berthed at San Francisco. She is currently maintained by the United States National Park Service.
Bibliography A14, D69, 262, 390, 528, 533

Cangarda
steam yacht

Former name MAGEDOMA
Built 1901 by Pusey & Jones, Wilmington, Delaware
Original owners George Canfield, Marietta, Illinois
Propulsion Steam, screw, triple expansion
Tonnage 116 gross
Length 130.0ft/39.62m
Breadth 17.83ft/5.43m
Draught 7.5ft/2.29m
Materials Steel hull, wood superstructure
Original use Yacht

Condition Under restoration
Present owners Richard C Reedy
Location Gloucester, Massachusetts, USA
History Restoration to an active steamer in progress on shore.
Bibliography B44

Captain Meriwether Lewis
steam dredger

Built 1932 by Marietta Manufacturing Co, Point Pleasant, West Virginia
Original owners United States Army Corps of Engineers
Propulsion Steam, sidewheel
Tonnage 1456 displacement
Length 269.0ft/81.99m
Breadth 85.0ft/25.91m
Draught 8.5ft/2.59m
Materials Steel hull
Original use Dredger
Condition Intact
Present owners Meriwether Lewis Foundation, Peru, Nebraska
Location Brownville, Nebraska, USA
History Built for dredging the channels of the Mississippi and Missouri Rivers. Preserved as an onshore exhibit.
Bibliography B44

Cassin Young
destroyer

Former name USS CASSIN YOUNG
Built 1943 by Bethlehem Steel
Corporation, San Pedro, California
Original owners United States Navy
Propulsion Steam turbines
Tonnage 2050 displacement
Length 376.5ft/114.76m
Breadth 39.7ft/12.1m
Draught 17.75ft/5.41m
Materials Steel throughout
Original use Destroyer
Condition Intact
Present owners United States National
Park Service
Location Boston, Massachusetts, USA
History US Navy destroyer that saw
action in the Pacific during the Second
World War.
Preserved as a floating exhibit.
Bibliography B45, C64, D221

Catawissa
ocean towing steamer

Former name TANKMASTER No 1, BETH
TANK SHIP No 2, NEW YORK
Built 1897 by Harlan & Hollingsworth,
Wilmington, Delaware
Original owners The Reading Co
Propulsion Steam, screw, triple
expansion, 1000hp
Tonnage 558 gross
Length 158.0ft/48.16m
Breadth 29.0ft/8.84m
Materials Steel throughout
Original use Ocean towing
Condition Hull and deckhouse intact,
with engines; undergoing restoration
Location Kingston, New York, USA
Bibliography D56

Cavalla
submarine

Former name USS CAVALLA
Built 1943 by Electric Boat Co, Groton,
Connecticut
Original owners United States Navy
Official number SS-244
Propulsion Diesel and electric motors
Tonnage 1526 displacement
Length 311.75ft/95.02m
Breadth 27.25ft/8.31m
Draught 15.25ft/4.65m
Materials Steel throughout
Original use Submarine
Condition Intact
Present owners US Submarine Veterans
of the Second World War
Location Galveston, Texas, USA
History American submarine of the
Second World War. Preserved as an

Cassin Young

onshore exhibit.
Bibliography B45, C64

CCB-18
river gunboat

Built c1970 in the United States
Original owners United States Navy
Original use River patrol craft
Condition Intact
Present owners American Patrol Boats
Museum
Location Rio Vista, California, USA
History Armoured river gunboat of the
Vietnam War period preserved afloat
by a group specialising in restoring
small naval craft.

CG-44300
rescue lifeboat

Built 1961 by US Coast Guard
Shipyard, Curtis Bay, nr Baltimore,
Maryland
Original owners United States Coast
Guard
Propulsion Two diesel engines, 400hp.
Engine built by General Motors
Tonnage 15.8 displacement
Length 44.1ft/13.4m
Breadth 12.66ft/3.9m
Draught 3.2ft/1.0m
Materials Steel throughout
Original use Rescue lifeboat
Condition Intact

Present owners Columbia River
Maritime Museum
Location Astoria, Oregon, USA
History Built as the prototype vessel for
her class of motor lifeboats. After
testing in various sea conditions she
was assigned to the Yaquina Bay,
Oregon station, serving there until
1981. She then spent fifteen years as a
training craft at the National Motor
Lifeboat School at Cape
Disappointment, Washington. Now an
exhibit.
Bibliography D568a

CG-52302
buoy tender

Built 1944 by Coast Guard Shipyard,
Curtis Bay, Maryland
Original owners United States Coast
Guard
Propulsion Diesel engines, 120hp
Tonnage 35 displacement
Length 52.33ft/15.99m
Breadth 15.5ft/4.72m
Draught 4.25ft/1.29m
Materials Wood throughout
Original use Buoy tender
Condition Intact
Present owners Lake Champlain
Maritime Museum
Contact address Basin Harbour,
Vermont
Location Burlington, Vermont, USA

History Formerly employed tending
buoys on Lake Champlain. Preserved
as an onshore exhibit.

Charles W Morgan
whaling vessel

Built 1841 by Jethro & Zachariah
Hillman, Fairhaven, Massachusetts
Original owners Captain Charles W
Morgan
Propulsion Sail, barque rig
Tonnage 313 gross
Length 105.6ft/32.19m
Breadth 27.7ft/8.44m
Draught 17.5ft/5.33m
Materials Wood throughout
Original use Whaling
Condition Intact
Present owners Mystic Seaport
Museum
Location Mystic, Connecticut, USA
History The fact that the CHARLES W
MORGAN enjoyed an active career
spanning eighty years reflects both the
durability of the American whaling
industry and its extreme conservatism.
When major innovations in whaling
techniques appeared they were
adopted by other countries, most
notably Norway. The MORGAN's last
voyage in 1921 marked the end of the
era of whaling in square-rigged sailing
ships. It occurred late enough to be
recorded on film footage used in the

Charles W Morgan

silent motion picture *Down to the Sea in Ships*. After a period laid up at her former home port, New Bedford, Massachusetts, the MORGAN was placed on display at the summer home of millionaire Edward Green in South Dartmouth, near New Bedford. After his death she was acquired for the growing maritime museum complex at Mystic, Connecticut, arriving there in tow in November 1941. For several decades she was preserved there aground with her lower hull filled with rock salt. A thorough restoration of the ship was begun in the early 1970s. In order to restore this ship and its other historic vessels, the Mystic Seaport Museum created a complete permanent shipyard facility, including a drydock. Since no record remained of the MORGAN's appearance when built in 1841, she was restored as she appeared in the 1870s, the period from which the earliest photographs survive. This included rerigging the vessel as a barque and eliminating the painted

port colour scheme she had borne since 1921. The MORGAN is exhibited afloat beside an appropriate New England granite pier built for her, across a cove from the little full-rigged ship JOSEPH CONRAD, surrounded by a collection of restored seaport buildings and museum exhibits.
Bibliography A8, A14, B6, D149, D303, F7

Chesapeake
lightship

Former name DELAWARE, CHESAPEAKE, FENWICK
Built 1930 by Charleston Drydock & Machine Co, Charleston, South Carolina
Original owners United States Lighthouse Service
Propulsion Diesel electric, 350hp
Tonnage 630 displacement
Length 133.6ft/40.72m
Breadth 30.0ft/9.14m
Draught 14.0ft/4.27m

Materials Steel throughout
Original use Lightship
Condition Intact
Present owners City of Baltimore
Location Baltimore, Maryland, USA
History Preserved as a floating exhibit.
Bibliography C27

Chief Uncas
motor yacht

Built 1912
Original owners Busch Family
Propulsion Electric motors; converted to diesel
Length 60.0ft/18.3m
Breadth 9.5ft/2.9m
Materials Wood throughout (mahogany)
Original use Yacht
Condition Fully restored, in operation
Present owners Classic Boat Tours
Contact address PO Box 664, Cooperstown, New York
Location Cooperstown, New York, USA
History Formerly a motor yacht

belonging to one of the estates on the shore of Otsego Lake. Now used for excursions and charters based at Cooperstown at the southern end of the lake.

Christeen
oyster dredger

Built 1883 by Glenwood Marine, Glenwood Landing, New York
Original owners Captain William W Smith, Oyster Bay
Propulsion Sail, sloop rig; petrol engine, 40hp
Tonnage 12 gross
Length 38.4ft/11.7m
Breadth 15.1ft/4.6m
Materials Wood throughout
Original use Oystering
Condition Restoration in progress
Present owners Friends of the Bay
Location Oyster Bay, New York, USA
History Proposed exhibit and active sailing vessel.

City of Clinton
river towing steamer

Former name RHODODENDRON, OMAR
Built 1936 by Dravo Contracting Co,
Pittsburgh, Pennsylvania
Original owners Ohio River Co
Propulsion Steam, sternwheel
Tonnage 581 gross
Length 171.4ft/52.24m
Breadth 34.6ft/10.55m
Draught 7.0ft/2.13m
Materials Steel throughout
Original use Towing
Condition Intact, superstructure
altered as state showboat
Present owners City of Clinton
Location Clinton, Iowa, USA
History Steam towboat used on the
Mississippi and Ohio Rivers. Preserved
as a floating exhibit.
Bibliography B44

City of Milwaukee
railway/passenger lake ferry

Built 1931 at Manitowoc, Wisconsin
Original owners Grand Trunk Railroad
Propulsion Steam, screw
Tonnage 2942 gross
Length 347.9ft/106.04m
Breadth 56.2ft/17.13m
Materials Steel hull
Original use Railway and passenger
ferry
Condition Intact
Present owners Northwest Michigan
Maritime Museum
Location Elberta, Michigan, USA
History Former Lake Michigan
passenger and railway ferry. Preserved
as a floating exhibit.
Bibliography B44

City of Norfolk
oyster dredger

Former name ALLEGHENY,
GEORGE W COLLIER
Built 1900 at Deal Island, Chesapeake
Bay
Propulsion Sail, sloop rig ('skipjack'
type)
Tonnage 9 gross
Length 45.5ft/13.87m
Breadth 15.2ft/4.63m
Materials Wood throughout
Original use Oystering
Condition In sailing condition
Present owners City of Norfolk
Location Norfolk, Virginia, USA
History Preserved as a floating exhibit
and for sail training.

Clamagore
submarine

Former name USS CLAMAGORE
Built 1945 by Electric Boat Co, Groton,
Connecticut
Original owners United States Navy
Propulsion Diesel and electric motors
Tonnage 1526 displacement
Length 311.75ft/95.02m
Breadth 27.25ft/8.31m
Draught 15.25ft/4.65m
Materials Steel throughout
Original use Submarine
Condition Intact
Present owners Patriots Point
Development Authority
Location Charleston, S Carolina, USA
History American submarine
completed too late to take part in the
Second World War. Preserved as a
floating exhibit
Bibliography B45, C64

Cobia
submarine

Former name USS COBIA
Built 1943 by Electric Boat Co, Groton,
Connecticut
Original owners United States Navy
Propulsion Diesel and electric motors
Tonnage 1526 displacement
Length 311.75ft/95.02m
Breadth 27.25ft/8.31m
Draught 15.25ft/4.65m
Materials Steel throughout
Original use Submarine
Condition Intact
Present owners Wisconsin Maritime
Museum
Location Manitowoc, Wisconsin, USA
History American submarine of the
Second World War. Used as a floating
exhibit.
Bibliography B45, C64, D495

Cod
submarine

Former name USS COD
Built 1943 by Electric Boat Co, Groton,
Connecticut
Original owners United States Navy
Propulsion Diesel and electric motors
Tonnage 1526 displacement
Length 311.75ft/95.02m
Breadth 27.25ft/8.31m
Draught 15.25ft/4.65m
Materials Steel throughout
Original use Submarine
Condition Intact
Present owners Great Lakes Historical
Society, Vermilion, Ohio
Location Cleveland, Ohio, USA
History American submarine of the
Second World War. Preserved as a
floating exhibit.
Bibliography B45, C64

Col D D Gaillard
dredger

Built 1916 by Hartmann-Greiling Co,
Green Bay, Wisconsin
Original owners United States Army
Corps of Engineers
Propulsion Towed, steam dredging
machinery
Tonnage 712 displacement
Length 116.0ft/35.36m
Breadth 41.0ft/12.5m
Draught 13.75ft/4.19m
Materials Steel hull, steel and wood
superstructure
Original use Dredger
Condition Intact
Present owners Head of the Lakes
Maritime Society
History Preserved as a floating exhibit.
Restoration to an active steamer in
progress on shore.

Columbia
passenger steamer

Built 1902 at Wyandotte,
Michigan
Original owners Detroit, Belle Isle &
Windsor Ferry Co
Propulsion Steam, screw
Tonnage 968 gross
Length 200.0ft/60.96m
Breadth 45.0ft/13.72m
Draught 12.0ft/3.66m

Cod

Materials Steel hull
Original use Passengers
Condition Intact, out of service,
laid up
Present owners International Shipping
Co
Location Detroit, Michigan, USA
Bibliography B44

Columbia
lightship

Built 1950 by Rice Brothers, East
Boothbay, Maine
Original owners United States Coast
Guard
Propulsion Diesel engines
Tonnage 617 displacement
Length 128.0ft/39.01m
Breadth 30.0ft/9.14m
Draught 11.5ft/3.51m
Materials Steel throughout
Original use Lightship
Condition Intact
Present owners Columbia River
Maritime Museum
Location Astoria, Oregon, USA
History Last lightship stationed off the
mouth of the Columbia River.
Preserved as a floating exhibit.
Bibliography C27

Commander
river excursion vessel

Built 1917 by Beele Wallace Co,
Morehead City, North Carolina
Original owners Rockaway Boat Line,
New York City
Propulsion Diesel engines
Tonnage 14 gross
Length 60.9ft/18.56m
Breadth 24.4ft/7.44m
Materials Wood throughout
Original use Passengers
Condition In operating condition

Constellation

Commander

Present owners Hudson Highlands
Cruises
Location Highland Falls, New York,
USA
History Employed for many years as a
ferry across Jamaica Bay, Long Island
between Brooklyn and Rockaway, New
York. In use for excursions.
Bibliography D576

Constellation
sailing corvette

Former name USS CONSTELLATION
Built 1855 by Norfolk Naval Shipyard,
Norfolk, Virginia
Original owners United States Navy
Propulsion Sail, full-rigged ship

Tonnage 1960 displacement
Length 203.0ft/61.87m
Breadth 41.75ft/12.73m
Draught 20.0ft/6.1m
Materials Wood throughout
Original use Corvette
Condition Hull recently restored; some
non-original methods
Present owners City of Baltimore
Location Baltimore, Maryland, USA
History Last sailing warship built for
the United States Navy and one of only
two still in existence. Later served as a
sail training ship. Since the 1950s
preserved as a floating exhibit.
Bibliography C64, D52, 77, 142a, 445,
556-7, F6a

Constitution USS
sailing frigate

Built 1797 by Edmond Hartt Shipyard, Boston, Massachusetts
Original owners United States Navy
Propulsion Sail, full-rigged ship
Tonnage 2200 displacement
Length 204.0ft/62.18m
Breadth 43.5ft/13.26m
Draught 19.7ft/6.0m
Materials Wood throughout
Original use Frigate
Condition Intact, recently restored
Present owners United States Navy
Location Boston, Massachusetts, USA
History The dramatic exploits of this ship, better known by her nickname 'Old Ironsides', have thrilled American schoolboys for generations. During the Anglo-American War of 1812-15 her series of victories in ship-to-ship duels bolstered American morale in the face of humiliating defeats ashore. The CONSTITUTION also distinguished herself in heavy fighting during the American war with the Barbary pirates of Tripoli and Algiers. In the 1830s she became the subject of the first successful American campaign to preserve a ship because of its historic importance. Inspired by Oliver Wendell Holmes' poem *Old Ironsides*, the nation responded by raising the funds to rescue her from the scrappers. In the 1860s she served as a training ship for the United States Naval Academy at Annapolis, Maryland, and, during the Civil War, at the School's temporary quarters in Newport, Rhode Island. Since then the CONSTITUTION has undergone several major rebuildings, the last in the 1990s. Following a rebuilding in the 1920s she was towed to ports on both the Atlantic and Pacific coasts of the United States. The CONSTITUTION is maintained afloat at the old Boston Navy Yard in Charlestown, Massachusetts, as a commissioned vessel of the United States Navy. Once each year she is towed through the harbour of Boston. When she returns to her berth she is moored on the opposite heading to equalise weathering of her wooden hull. A museum on shore in one of the old Navy Yard buildings tells the history of the ship and describes her construction and life on board when she was an active warship.
Bibliography C64, D4, 30, 31, 134, 196, 348

Coronet
schooner yacht

Built 1885 by C & R Poillon, Brooklyn, New York
Original owners Rufus T Bush
Propulsion Sail, schooner rig
Tonnage 161 gross
Length 133.0ft/40.54m
Breadth 27.0ft/8.23m
Draught 12.5ft/3.81m
Materials Wood throughout
Original use Yacht
Condition Intact, hull deteriorated, awaiting restoration to sailing condition
Present owners School of Yacht Restoration
Location Newport, Rhode Island, USA
History Oldest surviving unaltered schooner yacht built in the United States.
Bibliography D100, D374, D375, D520

Croaker
submarine

Former name USS CROAKER
Built 1942 by Electric Boat Co, Groton, Connecticut
Original owners United States Navy
Propulsion Diesel and electric motors
Tonnage 1526 displacement

Constitution

Length 311.75ft/95.02m
Breadth 25.25ft/8.31m
Draught 15.25ft/4.65m
Materials Steel throughout
Original use Submarine
Condition Intact
Present owners Buffalo Naval and
Servicemen's Park
Location Buffalo, New York, USA
History American submarine of the
Second World War. Preserved as a
floating exhibit.
Bibliography B45, C64

Cythera
racing yacht

Built 1937 by Kungsor Batvarv,
Kungsor, Sweden. Designed by Knud
Reimers
Propulsion Sloop rig
Length 43.0ft/13.1m
Breadth 7.5ft/2.3m
Draught 5.0ft/1.5m
Materials Wood throughout
Original use Racing yacht
Condition Largely intact, undergoing
restoration
Present owners The Museum of
Yachting
Contact address PO Box 129, Newport,
Rhode Island 02840
Location Newport, Rhode Island, USA
History Swedish-built racing yacht
undergoing restoration in the
workshop of the Museum of American
Yachting in Newport.

Day Peckinpaugh
motor canal barge

Former name RICHARD J BARNES
Built 1921 Duluth, Minnesota
Propulsion Diesel engines, 360hp
Tonnage 834 gross
Length 242.2ft/73.82m

Day Peckinpaugh

Delta King

Breadth 36.0ft/10.97m
Materials Steel throughout
Original use Cargo
Condition Intact, laid up
Location Erie, Pennsylvania, USA
History Last canal motor vessel to
operate on the Erie Canal.

Delta King
sternwheel river steamer

Built 1926 by Insherwood Shipyard,
Glasgow, Scotland (pre-fabricated).
Engine built in Stockton, California
Original owners California
Transportation Co
Propulsion Steam, sternwheel,

compound, 2000hp
Tonnage 1650 gross
Length 250.0ft/76.2m
Breadth 58.0ft/17.68m
Draught 11.5ft/3.51m
Materials Steel hull, steel and wood
superstructure
Original use Passengers and cargo
Condition Externally intact, altered
internally, no engines
Location Sacramento, California, USA
History Preserved as a floating hotel.
Bibliography D188

Delta Queen
sternwheel river steamer

Built 1926 by Isherwood Shipyard,
Glasgow, Scotland (pre-fabricated).
Engine built in Stockton, California
Original owners California
Transportation Co
Propulsion Steam, sternwheel,
compound, 2000hp
Tonnage 1650 gross
Length 250.0ft/76.2m
Breadth 58.0ft/17.68m
Draught 11.5ft/3.51m
Materials Steel hull, steel and wood
superstructure
Original use Passengers and cargo
Condition In operation
Present owners Delta Queen Steamboat
Co
Location Cincinnati, Ohio, USA
History Originally a Sacramento

River steamboat. In use for river
cruises on the Mississippi and Ohio
rivers.
Bibliography B44, D153, 188, 400, 563,
564

Derrick Boat No 8
canal derrick/dredger

Built 1925
Original owners State of New York
Propulsion Towed
Tonnage 200 displacement
Length 78.0ft/23.77m
Breadth 36.0ft/10.97m
Draught 3.0ft/0.91m
Materials Steel hull, wood
superstructure
Original use Derrick or dredger
Condition Intact
Present owners H Lee White Maritime
Museum
Location Oswego, New York, USA
History Formerly used to maintain the
New York State Barge Canal.
Preserved as an onshore exhibit.

Dipper Dredge No 3
canal dredger

Built 1927
Original owners New York State
Propulsion Towed
Length 120.0ft/36.58m
Breadth 44.0ft/13.41m
Draught 6.0ft/1.83m

Materials Steel throughout
Original use Dredger
Condition Intact, recently retired
Present owners New York State
Location New York State, USA
History Formerly used to maintain the
New York State Barge Canal.
Proposed as an exhibit.

Dorothy
steam tug

Former name JANET S, JESSE JR,
J ALVAH CLARK, N Y C NO 3
Built 1890 by Newport News,
Shipbuilding & Drydock Co, Newport
News, Virginia
Original owners New York Central
Railroad
Propulsion Steam, screw, quadruple
steeple engine
Tonnage 130 gross
Length 90.0ft/27.43m
Breadth 19.0ft/5.79m
Materials Iron throughout
Original use Tug
Condition Restored, without engine
Present owners Newport News
Shipbuilding & Drydock Co
Location Newport News, Virginia, USA
History first vessel built by the
Newport News Shipyard. Preserved as
an onshore exhibit.
Bibliography D226, D536

Dorothy A Parsons
oyster dredger

Built 1901 by B P Miles, Oriole,
Maryland
Propulsion Sail, schooner rig ('bugeye'
type)
Tonnage 19 gross
Length 62.0ft/18.9m
Breadth 17.3ft/5.27m
Draught 8.0ft/2.44m
Materials Wood throughout
Original use Oystering
Condition Intact, except cut down mast
Present owners Harry Lundeburg
School of Seamanship
Location Piney Point, Maryland, USA
History Preserved as an onshore
exhibit under cover.

Drum
submarine

Former name USS DRUM
Built 1941 by Portsmouth Naval
Shipyard, Kittery, Maine
Original owners United States Navy
Propulsion Diesel and electric motors
Tonnage 1526 displacement
Length 311.6ft/94.98m

Eagle

Breadth 27.4ft/8.35m
Draught 15.25ft/4.65m
Materials Steel throughout
Original use Submarine
Condition Intact
Present owners USS Alabama Battleship
Commission
Location Mobile, Alabama, USA
History American submarine of the
Second World War. Preserved as a
floating exhibit.
Bibliography B45, C64

Eagle
sail training vessel

Former name HORST WESSEL
Built 1936 by Blohm & Voss, Hamburg,
Germany
Original owners German Navy
Propulsion Sail, barque rig; diesel
engine, 750hp
Tonnage 1634 displacement
Length 277.0ft/84.43m
Breadth 39.3ft/11.98m
Draught 17.0ft/5.18m
Materials Steel throughout
Original use Training
Condition In operation
Present owners United States Coast
Guard
Location New London, Connecticut,
USA
History Built as a sail training vessel for
the German Navy. Awarded to the
United States as reparations after the

Second World War and refurbished to
serve as a training ship for the Coast
Guard Academy in New London,
Connecticut. In use as a training vessel.
Bibliography C25, 96, D355, 388, 420, 553

E C Collier
oyster dredger

Built 1910 by George Washington
Horseman, Deal Island, Maryland
Original owners Eddie Collier
Propulsion Sail, sloop rig ('skipjack'
type)
Tonnage 19 gross
Length 76.75ft/23.39m

Breadth 17.83ft/5.43m
Materials Wood throughout
Original use Oystering
Condition Intact
Present owners Chesapeake Bay
Maritime Museum
Location St Michael's, Maryland, USA
History Preserved as a floating exhibit.
Bibliography D406

Edmund Fitzgerald
steam tug/VIP boat

Former name JOHN WANAMAKER,
CLYDE B HOLMES
Built 1924 at Baltimore, Maryland

Edmund Fitzgerald

Original owners City of Philadelphia
Propulsion Steam, screw, 1000hp
Tonnage 292 gross
Length 112.5ft/34.29m
Breadth 25.6ft/7.83m
Materials Steel throughout
Original use Tug and VIP boat
Condition Outwardly intact, internally
converted to restaurant
Location Portsmouth, New Hampshire,
USA
History Built as a steam tug and
inspection vessel for the Port of
Philadelphia. Later the last working
steam tug on the American east coast
based at Belfast, Maine. Preserved as a
floating restaurant.

Edna E Lockwood
oyster dredger

Built 1889 by John B Harrison,
Tilghman's Island, Maryland
Original owners Daniel Haddaway
Propulsion Sail, schooner rig ('bugeye'
type)
Tonnage 10 gross
Length 53.6ft/16.34m
Breadth 15.3ft/4.66m
Materials Wood throughout
Original use Oystering
Condition Intact
Present owners Chesapeake Bay
Maritime Museum
Location St Michael's, Maryland, USA
History During the nineteenth century
oysters became an extremely popular
delicacy in the United States,
consumed in great quantities in cities
like New York, Baltimore and
Philadelphia. Over-dredging and
pollution soon eliminated the oyster
beds located near those cities. In
Maryland's Chesapeake Bay an
ordinance was passed to protect the
beds by forbidding the use of powered
vessels. As a result, the Chesapeake is
now the home of one of the last fleets
of working sailing craft in North
America. The current oyster dredgers,
which number around thirty-five
vessels, are of the sloop-rigged type
known as the 'skipjack', having a
chined, planked hull developed
primarily for ease of construction.
Earlier in this century the two-masted
'bugeye' was popular for oyster
dredging under sail. These craft were
direct descendants of the Indian
dugout canoes, and usually had hulls
shaped from three or more dugout
logs. They were traditionally painted
white, and had sharply raked clipper
stems decorated with colourful carved
trailboards ending in a small

billethead. The masts had a
pronounced rake aft and set triangular
sails with no gaffs. EDNA E LOCKWOOD
was the last bugeye in the fleet by the
1960s. After being acquired by the
Chesapeake Bay Maritime Musuem in
St Michael's, Maryland, she underwent
a thorough rebuilding. She is now
exhibited at the museum in the water
in sailing condition.
Bibliography D269

Edna G
steam tug

Built 1896 at Cleveland, Ohio
Original owners Duluth, Missabe &
Iron Range Railway Co
Propulsion Steam, screw, coal fired
Tonnage 154 gross
Length 92.5ft/28.19m
Breadth 23.0ft/7.01m
Materials Steel throughout
Original use Tug
Condition Intact
Present owners City of Two Harbors
Location Two Harbors, Minnesota,
USA
History The last working steam tug in
the United States when retired.
Preserved as a floating exhibit.

Edson
destroyer

Former name USS EDSON
Built 1958 by Bath Iron Works, Bath,
Maine
Original owners United States Navy
Propulsion Steam turbines, 70,000hp
Tonnage 4916 displacement
Length 418.5ft/127.56m
Breadth 44.92ft/13.69m
Draught 15.0ft/4.57m
Materials Steel throughout
Original use Destroyer
Condition Intact
Present owners Intrepid Museum
Foundation
Location New York City, USA
History Destroyer of the 1950s
preserved as a floating exhibit.
Bibliography C64

Elissa
trading barque

Former name ACHAEOS,
CHRISTOPHOROS, GUSTAF, FJELD
Built 1877 by Alexander Hall & Co,
Aberdeen, Washington
Original owners H F Watt, Liverpool,
England

Propulsion Sail, barque rig
Tonnage 489 gross
Length 170.5ft/51.97m
Breadth 26.4ft/8.05m
Materials Iron hull, wood deckhouse,
steel and wood masts
Original use Cargo
Condition In sailing condition
Present owners Galveston Historical
Foundation
Location Galveston, Texas
History When Alexander Hall & Sons
of Aberdeen, Scotland, launched this
little barque in their 66th year of
operation, they could hardly have
foreseen the remarkable career she
would have over the next century. She
eventually sailed under the flags of six
nations – England, Norway, Sweden,
Finland, Greece and the United States;
bore six names; and experienced four
incarnations – as a barque, a
barquentine, a three-masted schooner
and a motor vessel. In 1970 she finally
arrived at a Greek scrapyard, having
last been used in smuggling cigarettes
in the Adriatic Sea. She was found
there by marine archaeologist Peter
Throckmorton, who recognised her
original identity and bought her in the
belief that someone would eventually

Elissa

be found to preserve and restore her. His gamble proved to be a success. Four years later she was bought by the Galveston Historical Foundation which had found that the ship visited that port twice in her early career. After extensive hull replating in a Greek shipyard, she was towed to Galveston in July 1979. Her subsequent restoration, not only as an exhibit, but also as an active sailing vessel, is one of the great maritime preservation success stories. It was almost entirely accomplished by self-taught amateurs, from shipwrights to riggers, many of them dedicated volunteers. The same people formed her crew when she sailed again for the first time on 31 August 1982. Since then she has travelled as far afield as Mystic, Connecticut, and Bermuda. Several cruises are made annually in the Gulf of Mexico. The remainder of the year the ship can be visited at a berth in Galveston near a preserved section of the old commercial district.
Bibliography D449, D487, D488, D537

Ellen Ruth
lake passenger launch

Built 1932 by Joseph Dingle Boat Works, St Paul, Minnesota
Original owners Guy Hill
Propulsion Petrol engine
Length 42.0ft/12.8m
Breadth 10.0ft/3.05m
Materials Wood throughout
Original use Passengers
Condition Intact
Present owners City of Wahkon
Location Wahkon, Minnesota, USA
History Launch formerly used to carry passengers to fishing resorts on Mille Lacs Lake. Preserved as an onshore exhibit.

Elsworth
oyster dredger

Built 1901 by Hubbard, Thomas & Seward, Hudson, Maryland
Original owners Hilary Wingate
Propulsion Sail, sloop rig ('skipjack' type)
Tonnage 8 gross
Length 39.9ft/12.16m
Breadth 14.3ft/4.36m
Materials Wood throughout
Original use Oystering
Condition In sailing condition
Present owners Echo Hill Outdoor School
Location Worton, Maryland, USA
History In use for educational cruises.

Emma C Berry

Emma C Berry
sailing fishing vessel

Built 1866 by R & J Palmer, Noank, Connecticut
Original owners Captain John Henry Berry
Propulsion Sail, sloop rig; later schooner rig
Tonnage 16 gross
Length 47.0ft/14.33m
Breadth 14.6ft/4.45m
Draught 6.0ft/1.83m
Materials Wood throughout
Original use Fishing
Condition Intact
Present owners Mystic Seaport Museum
Location Mystic, Connecticut, USA
History Last example of an American wet-well smack. Converted to a yacht with schooner rig, but subsequently restored to original condition.

Preserved as a floating exhibit.
Bibliography B6, D15, D117, D133

Endeavour
racing yacht

Built 1934 by Camper & Nicholsons, Gosport, England
Original owners Sir T O M Sopwith
Propulsion Sail, cutter rig
Tonnage 125 gross
Length 129.58ft/39.5m
Breadth 22.25ft/6.78m
Draught 14.75ft/4.5m
Materials Steel hull
Original use Racing yacht
Condition Restored to sailing condition
Present owners Elizabeth Meyer
Location Newport, Rhode Island, USA
History Built as a British challenger for the Americas Cup. Restored by an American owner in the 1980s.

Bibliography A1, C50, D94, D548

Enticer
motor yacht

Former name INNISFAIL
Built 1935 by Mathis Shipyard, Camden, New Jersey. Designed by John Trumpy
Propulsion Diesel engine
Length 89.0ft/27.1m
Breadth 18.0ft/5.5m
Draught 4.5ft/1.4m
Materials Wood throughout
Original use Motor yacht
Condition In operating condition
Present owners Independence Seaport Museum
Contact address 211 S Columbus Blvd & Walnut St, Philadelphia 19106
Location Philadelphia, Pennsylvania, USA
History Motor yacht of the 1930s built by a well-known shipyard across the Delaware River from Philadelphia. Preserved in operating condition by the Independence Seaport Museum in Philadelphia.

Eppleton Hall
steam tug

Built 1914 by Hepple & Co, South Shields, England
Original owners Lambton Collieries Ltd
Propulsion Steam, sidewheel, side-lever, 500hp
Tonnage 166 gross
Length 100.5ft/30.63m
Breadth 33.25ft/10.13m
Draught 10.0ft/3.05m
Materials Steel hull, steel and wood superstructure
Original use Tug
Condition Intact
Present owners San Francisco Maritime National Historical Park
Location San Francisco, California, USA
History Only steam sidewheel tug preserved outside Europe. Preserved as a floating exhibit.
Bibliography B44, D383

Equator
trading schooner

Built 1888 by Matthew Turner, Benicia, California
Original owners Dennis Reed
Propulsion Sail, schooner rig; later steam vessel
Tonnage 72 gross
Length 66.5ft/20.27m

Breadth 22.0ft/6.71m
Materials Wood throughout
Original use Cargo
Condition Hull in poor condition
Present owners City of Everett
Location Everett, Washington, USA
History At one time chartered by the writer Robert Louis Stevenson. Later converted to a steam tug for use on the American west coast. Hull survives in poor condition; stored indoors

Ernestina

fishing schooner

Former name Effie M Morrissey
Built 1894 by Tarr & James Shipyard, Essex, Massachusetts
Original owners Captain William E Morrissey, Gloucester, Mass
Propulsion Sail, schooner rig; auxiliary engine added
Tonnage 120 gross
Length 97.0ft/29.57m
Breadth 23.0ft/7.01m
Draught 13.0ft/3.96m
Materials Wood throughout
Original use Fishing
Condition In sailing condition
Present owners State of Massachusetts
Location New Bedford, Massachusetts, USA
History During the 1890s, and the first decade of this century, a series of fast New England fishing schooners was built on what was popularly called, after an early prototype, the 'Fredonia' model. They were the last New England fishing schooners to have clipper bows. Only two survive today, the smaller inshore schooner Lettie G Howard now fully restored in New York, and the larger Ernestina, ex-Effie M Morrissey, built to fish far out in the Atlantic on the Grand Banks east of Newfoundland. The latter's involvement in the rigorous North Atlantic fishery was to be just one chapter in her remarkable history. In 1925 she was acquired by Captain Bob Bartlett, a native of Newfoundland who had been involved in Peary's expedition to the North Pole in 1909. Over the next fifteen years Bartlett took the vessel on annual expeditions to the Arctic regions of Canada and Greenland performing work for American natural history museums and zoological societies. During the Second World War the schooner was employed in the same waters doing hydrographic work for the United States Navy. In 1948 she was purchased by Henrique Mendes for use as a 'Brava Packet' linking the large Cape

Ernestina

Verdean community in southern New England with the Cape Verde Islands off Africa. Under her persent name she made annual round voyages nearly every year until 1965, spending the remaining months in the inter-island trade. Between 1976 and 1982 Ernestina was rebuilt by the Cape Verdean Government for presentation to the United States. She arrived there once more in August 1982. Today she is based in New Bedford, Massachusetts, and operated with the support of that State as a training vessel and travelling exhibit.
Bibliography C93, D26, D234

Eureka

sidewheel ferry

Former name Ukiah
Built 1890 at Tiburon, California
Original owners San Francisco and Northern Pacific Railroad
Propulsion Steam, sidewheel, beam engine, 1500hp
Tonnage 2564 gross
Length 271.0ft/82.6m
Breadth 42.0ft/12.8m
Materials Wood throughout
Original use Ferry

Condition Intact
Present owners San Francisco Maritime National Historical Park
Location San Francisco, California, USA
History Built as a ferryboat for use on San Francisco Bay. Was the last walking beam sidewheel steamer in operation in North America when retired. Preserved as a floating exhibit.
Bibliography A17, B44, C36, C87a, D111

Evelina M Goulart

fishing schooner

Built 1927 at Essex, Massachusetts
Original owners Manuel J Goulart
Propulsion Sail, schooner rig; diesel engine, 260hp
Tonnage 82 gross
Length 83.7ft/25.51m
Breadth 21.2ft/6.46m
Materials Wood throughout
Original use Fishing
Condition Hull intact in poor condition
Present owners Essex Shipbuilding Museum
Location Essex, Massachusetts, USA
History Preserved as an onshore exhibit.

Evelyn S

motor fishing vessel

Built 1939 by Sturgeon Bay Boat Works, Sturgeon Bay, Wisconsin
Original owners Charles M Anderson
Propulsion Diesel engine, 90hp
Tonnage 30 gross
Length 60.0ft/18.29m
Breadth 13.0ft/3.96m
Materials Wood throughout
Original use Fishing
Condition Intact
Present owners Lake Michigan Maritime Museum
Location South Haven, Michigan, USA
History Great Lakes 'fish tug' with enclosed deck. Preserved as an onshore exhibit.

F C Lewis Jr

oyster dredger

Built 1907 at Hopkins, Virginia
Propulsion Sail, sloop rig ('skipjack' type)
Tonnage 6 gross
Length 39.0ft/11.9m
Breadth 14.6ft/4.4m
Materials Wood throughout
Original use Oyster dredging

Condition Intact
Present owners Old Harford Town
Location USA
History Preserved as an onshore exhibit.

F D Russell
motor tug

Built 1938 at Daytona Beach, Florida
Original owners Frank D Russell
Propulsion Diesel engine, 120hp
Tonnage 13 gross
Length 42.0ft/12.8m
Breadth 13.0ft/3.96m
Materials Wood throughout
Original use Tug
Condition Intact
Present owners Ponce de Leon Inlet Lighthouse Museum
Location Ponce de Leon Inlet, Florida, USA
History Preserved as an onshore exhibit.

Falcon
sternwheel river ferry

Built at Millersburg, Pennsylvania (date not known)
Original owners Millersburg Ferry
Propulsion Sternwheel; chain drive from petrol engine
Materials Wood hull
Original use River ferryboat
Condition In operation
Present owners Millersburg Ferry Boat Association
Contact address PO Box 93, Millersburg, Pennsylvania 17061
Location Millersburg, Pennsylvania, USA
History One of last two sternwheel ferryboats in the USA. Employed in carrying automobiles and foot passengers across the Susquehanna River.

Falls of Clyde
full-rigged trading vessel

Built 1878 by Russell & Co, Port Glasgow, Scotland
Original owners Falls Line, Glasgow, Scotland
Propulsion Sail, four-masted full-rigged ship
Tonnage 1809 gross
Length 266.1ft/81.11m
Breadth 40.0ft/12.19m
Draught 21.0ft/6.4m
Materials Iron hull, iron and wood deckhouses and masts
Original use Cargo
Condition Intact

Present owners Hawaii Maritime Center
Location Honolulu, Hawaii, USA
History Preserved as a floating exhibit.
Bibliography A6, D277

Fir
lighthouse tender

Built 1939 by Moore Dry Dock Co, Oakland, California
Original owners US Lighthouse Service
Official number WLM-212
Propulsion Steam, triple expansion; converted to diesel. Engine built by Fairbanks Morse (current)
Tonnage 989.0 displacement
Length 174.9ft/53.3m
Breadth 34.0ft/10.4m
Draught 12.5ft/3.8m
Materials Steel throughout
Original use Buoy and lighthouse

Falls of Clyde

tender
Condition Intact
Present owners Friends of the FIR
Contact address PO Box 99702, Seattle, Washington 98199
Location Lake Washington, Seattle, Washington, USA
History One of the last lighthouse tenders built prior to the abolition of the United States Lighthouse Service and its replacement by the United States Coast Guard. Stationed at Seattle, Washington, throughout its active career. Preserved as a museum and staionary training ship.
Bibliography C86

Fireboat No 1
fireboat

Built 1929 by Coast Line Shipping Co, Tacoma, Washington

Original owners City of Tacoma
Propulsion Diesel engines
Tonnage 105 gross
Length 96.5ft/29.41m
Breadth 20.0ft/6.1m
Draught 6.0ft/1.83m
Materials Steel throughout
Original use Fireboat
Condition Intact
Present owners Commencement Bay Maritime Museum Foundation
Location Tacoma, Washington, USA
History First fireboat based in the Port of Tacoma, Washington. Preserved as an onshore exhibit.
Bibliography D569

Firefighter
fireboat

Built 1938 by United Shipyards, Mariners Harbor, Staten Island, New York
Original owners City of New York
Propulsion Diesel electric, twin screw, 3000hp
Tonnage 600 displacement
Length 134.0ft/40.84m
Breadth 32.0ft/9.75m
Draught 9.0ft/2.74m
Materials Steel throughout
Original use Fireboat
Condition In active service
Present owners City of New York
Location New York City, USA
History Most powerful New York fireboat since construction. Has been involved in most harbour disasters in the last fifty years, including the loss of the liner NORMANDIE. Unaltered except for the removal of a folding monitor tower.

Florence
motor fishing vessel

Built 1926 by Franklin Post Shipyard, Mystic, Connecticut
Original owners Morris Thompson, New London, Connecticut
Propulsion Diesel engines, 225hp
Tonnage 14 gross
Length 39.8ft/12.13m
Breadth 12.8ft/3.9m
Materials Wood throughout
Original use Fishing
Condition Intact
Present owners Mystic Seaport Museum
Location Mystic, Connecticut, USA
History Preserved as a floating exhibit.
Bibliography B6, D14

Fri
trading ketch

Built 1912 at Svendborg, Denmark
Propulsion Sail, ketch rig
Tonnage 56 gross
Length 107.0ft/32.61m
Breadth 20.6ft/6.27m
Draught 8.0ft/2.43m
Materials Wood throughout
Original use Cargo
Condition In sailing condition
Present owners David Moodie
Location St Augustine, Florida, USA
History Ketch rigged sailing vessel built to carry cargo in the Danish coastal and Baltic trades. Bought by an American owner who sailed her to San Francisco in 1969. Later bought by David Moodie of St Augustine, Florida, who has used her to protest nuclear testing and other threats to the environment on behalf of Greenpeace.

Gazela of Philadelphia
fishing barquentine

Former name GAZELA PRIMEIRO
Built 1901 by J M Mendes, Setubal, Portugal
Original owners Parceria Geral de Pescarias
Propulsion Sail, barquentine rig; diesel engine added
Tonnage 324 gross
Length 178.0ft/54.25m
Breadth 27.0ft/8.23m
Materials Wood throughout
Original use Fishing
Condition In sailing condition
Present owners Penn's Landing Corporation
Location Philadelphia, Pennsylvania, USA
History Last working square-rigged vessel on the Atlantic when retired in 1969. Preserved as floating exhibit and

Gazela of Philadelphia

Gerda III

active sailing vessel.
Bibliography A14, D36, D454

Geo M Verity
sternwheel towing steamer

Former name SS THORPE
Built 1927 by Dubuque Boat & Boiler Works, Dubuque, Iowa
Original owners Upper Mississippi Barge Line
Propulsion Steam, sternwheel, 1000hp
Tonnage 319 gross
Length 130.1ft/39.65m
Breadth 35.1ft/10.7m
Materials Steel throughout
Original use Towing
Condition Intact, on exhibit
Present owners Keokuk River Museum
Location Keokuk, Iowa, USA
History Preserved as an onshore exhibit.
Bibliography B44

Gerda III
lighthouse tender

Built 1926
Propulsion Motor
Materials Wood throughout
Original use Lighthouse tender
Condition Fully restored, afloat
Present owners Museum of Jewish Heritage
Contact address 342 Madison Avenue, Suite 706, New York, NY 10173
Location Mystic, Connecticut, USA
History Former small Danish lighthouse tender used to evacuate Jews from Denmark to Sweden during the Second World War. Restored at Mystic, Connecticut, for eventual exhibition at New York at the recently opened Museum of Jewish Heritage in Lower Manhattan.

Goldenrod
showboat

Built 1909 by Pope Dock Co, Parkersburg, West Virginia
Original owners W R Markle
Propulsion Towed
Tonnage 1454 gross
Length 161.0ft/49.07m
Breadth 41.5ft/12.65m
Draught 6.9ft/2.1m
Materials Steel hull, wood superstructure
Original use Showboat
Condition Intact, in use
Present owners City of St Charles Convention & Visitor Bureau
Location St Charles, Missouri, USA
History Built for use as a showboat on the Mississippi and Ohio Rivers. Wooden scow hull replaced with a steel hull around 1950.
Bibliography C32

Goldstream Dredge No 8
mining vessel

Built 1928 nr Fairbanks, Alaska
Propulsion Winched itself into position
Tonnage 1065 displacement
Length 250.0ft/76.2m
Materials Steel throughout
Original use Mining
Condition Intact, grounded exhibit
Location Nr Fairbanks, Alaska, USA
History Built as a gold mining dredger. Created the body of water in which it floated by excavating in front and filling in behind. Now sits sunk where last used, largely intact.

Governor Stone
trading schooner

Built 1877 at Pascagoula, Mississippi
Original owners C A Griner
Propulsion Sail, schooner rig
Tonnage 9 gross
Length 39.0ft/11.89m
Breadth 12.6ft/3.84m
Draught 3.0ft/0.91m
Materials Wood throughout
Original use Cargo
Condition In sailing condition
Present owners Apalachicola Maritime Institute
Location Apalachicola, Florida, USA
History Built as a sailing chandlery boat to carry supplies to ships lying off Gulf of Mexico ports of the United States. Preserved as a floating exhibit and active sailing vessel.

HA.8

Grace Bailey
trading schooner

Former name MATTIE
Built 1882 by Oliver Perry Smith, Patchogue, Long Island, New York
Original owners S Ketcham
Propulsion Sail, schooner rig
Tonnage 68 gross
Length 72.0ft/21.95m
Breadth 23.5ft/7.16m
Materials Wood throughout
Original use Cargo
Condition In sailing condition
Present owners Ray Williamson
Location Camden, Maine
History In use for cruises.
Bibliography C93, D452

Growler
submarine

Former name USS GROWLER
Built 1957 by Portsmouth Navy Yard, Kittery, Maine
Original owners United States Navy
Propulsion Diesel and electric motors
Tonnage 2174 gross
Length 317.0ft/96.62m
Breadth 27.16ft/8.28m
Draught 17.0ft/5.18m
Materials Steel throughout
Original use Submarine
Condition Intact
Present owners Intrepid Museum Foundation
Location New York City, USA
History One of the first submarines designed to carry missiles. Preserved as a floating exhibit.
Bibliography C64

HA.8
midget submarine

Built 1938 by Ourazaki Dockyard, Kure, Japan
Original owners Imperial Japanese Navy
Propulsion Electric motor, 600hp
Tonnage 46 displacement
Length 79.1ft/24.11m
Breadth 6.0ft/1.83m
Materials Steel throughout
Original use Midget submarine
Condition Intact
Present owners Submarine Force Library & Museum (US Navy)
Location Groton, Connecticut, USA
History Japanese Second World War midget submarine. Preserved as an onshore exhibit.
Bibliography A6

HA.19
midget submarine

Built 1938 by Ourazaki Dockyard, Kure, Japan
Original owners Imperial Japanese Navy
Propulsion Electric motor, 600hp
Tonnage 46 gross
Length 79.1ft/24.11m
Breadth 6.0ft/1.83m
Materials Steel throughout
Original use Midget submarine
Condition Intact
Present owners United States Navy
Location Pearl Harbor, Hawaii, USA
History Japanese midget submarine that took part in the attack on Pearl Harbor in December 1941. Later taken on a tour of the United States as part

of a war bonds drive. Preserved as an onshore exhibit.
Bibliography A6

Haida dugout canoe

Built 1878 by Haida canoe builders, British Columbia, Canada
Propulsion Paddles
Length 63.0ft/19.2m
Breadth 8.25ft/2.5m
Materials Wood throughout
Original use Ceremonial, passengers
Condition Intact
Present owners American Museum of Natural History
Location New York City, USA
History One of the world's largest dugout canoes, made from a single red cedar log. Based on war canoes of the Haida people of the Canadian Pacific Coast. When this example was built the canoes were used for ceremonial visits. This canoe has been in the collection of the American Museum of Natural History since it was built in 1878.

Hazard
minesweeper

Former name USS HAZARD,
Built 1944 by Winslow Marine Railway & Shipbuilding, Winslow, Washington
Original owners United States Navy
Propulsion Diesel engines, 2000hp
Tonnage 530 gross
Length 184.5ft/56.24m
Breadth 33.0ft/10.06m
Draught 9.75ft/2.97m
Materials Steel throughout
Original use Minesweeper
Condition Intact

Present owners Greater Omaha Military Historical Society
Location Omaha, Nebraska, USA
History Second World War American minesweeper. Preserved as a floating exhibit.
Bibliography B45, C64

Hercules
steam tug

Built 1907 by John H Dialogue & Son, Camden, New Jersey
Original owners Shipowners & Merchants Tug Co, San Francisco
Propulsion Steam, screw, 3-cylinder
Tonnage 414 gross
Length 134.9ft/41.12m
Breadth 26.1ft/7.96m
Draught 14.0ft/4.27m
Materials Steel throughout
Original use Tug
Condition Intact, some restoration in progress
Present owners San Francisco Maritime National Historical Park
Location San Francisco, California, USA
History Preserved as a floating exhibit.
Bibliography D218, D253, D530

Hiddensee
fast missile corvette

Former name RUDOLPH ENGELHOFER
Built in Russia
Original owners East German Navy
Propulsion Diesel engines
Tonnage 455 displacement
Length 185.0ft/56.4m
Breadth 36.2ft/11.0m
Draught 12.5ft/3.8m
Materials Steel throughout
Original use Guided missile corvette
Condition Intact
Present owners USS Massachusetts Memorial
Location Fall River, Massachusetts, USA
History Fast missile boat built for the East German Navy during the Cold War era. Exhibited afloat with the group of former American warships at Fall River.

Hoga
naval harbour tug

Built 1940 by Consolidated Shipbuilding Corp, Morris Heights, New York
Original owners United States Navy
Official number YT-146
Propulsion Diesel engine
Tonnage 325 displacement
Length 100.0ft/30.5m
Breadth 25.0ft/7.6m
Draught 9.55ft/2.9m
Materials Steel throughout
Original use Tug
Condition Intact, recently retired
Present owners United States Navy
Location Treasure Island, California, USA
History Navy Yard tug that was stationed at Pearl Harbor at the time of the Japanese attack in December 1941. Served through the Second World War. Loaned in 1948 to the City of Oakland, California, to serve as a fireboat and tug. Recently retired by that city. A group has been formed that hopes to preserve her as the last Navy survivor of the Pearl Harbor attack.

Hope
oyster dredger

Built 1948 by Stanley G Chard, Greenwich, Connecticut
Original owners Clarence E Chard, Bridgeport, Connecticut
Propulsion Sail, sloop rig; petrol engine
Tonnage 17 gross
Length 42.2ft/12.86m
Breadth 15.2ft/4.63m
Materials Wood throughout
Original use Oystering
Condition Intact
Present owners The Maritime Center
Location Norwalk, Connecticut, USA
History Last oystering sloop built for use on Long Island Sound. Preserved as a floating exhibit.

Hornet
aircraft carrier

Former name USS HORNET
Built 1943 by Newport News Shipbuilding & Drydock Co, Newport News, Virginia
Original owners United States Navy
Official number CVS-12
Propulsion Steam turbines, 150,000hp. Engine built by Westinghouse
Tonnage 41,200 displacement
Length 894.0ft/272.4m
Breadth 192.0ft/58.5m
Materials Steel throughout
Original use Aircraft carrier
Condition Intact
Present owners Aircraft Carrier Hornet Foundation
Contact address PO Box 460, Alameda, California 94501
Location Alameda, California, USA
History Preserved as a floating exhibit.

Hope

H T Pott
motor tug

Built 1933 at St Louis, Missouri
Propulsion Diesel engine
Tonnage 55 gross
Length 58.0ft/17.7m
Breadth 15.0ft/4.6m
Materials Steel hull, wood deckhouse
Original use Tug
Condition Intact
Present owners National Museum of Transport
Location St Louis, Missouri, USA
History Small diesel tug fitted with bow knees for pushing barges filled with sand. Now an outdoor exhibit at a general museum of various systems of transportation.

Huntington
steam tug

Built 1933 Newport News, Va
Propulsion Steam, screw; converted to diesel
Length 109.0ft/33.22m
Materials Steel throughout
Original use Tug
Condition Intact
Location Norfolk, Virginia, USA
History Dieselised harbour tug converted to bed and breakfast accommodation and also serving as a floating exhibit in front of a large modern building on the Norfolk waterfront that houses historical and technical nautical displays.

Huron
lightship

Former name NORTH MANITOU, GRAYS REEF, RELIEF
Built 1921 by Charles Seabury, Bronx, New York
Original owners United States Lighthouse Service
Propulsion Steam, screw; converted to diesel
Tonnage 302 displacement
Length 69.5ft/21.18m
Breadth 24.0ft/7.32m
Materials Steel throughout
Original use Lightship
Condition Intact
Present owners City of Port Huron
Location Port Huron, Michigan, USA
History Last surviving unaltered Great Lakes lightship. Preserved as an onshore exhibit.
Bibliography C23, C27, C97

Ingham
Coast Guard cutter

Former name USCGS INGHAM
Built 1936 by Philadelphia Navy Yard, Philadelphia, Pennsylvania
Original owners United States Coast Guard
Propulsion Steam turbines, 6200hp
Tonnage 2750 displacement
Length 327.0ft/99.67m
Breadth 41.0ft/12.5m
Draught 12.5ft/3.81m
Materials Steel throughout
Original use Coast Guard patrol
Condition Intact
Present owners Patriots Point Development Authority
Location Charleston, S Carolina, USA
History Coast Guard cutter that served as a convoy escort in the North Atlantic in the Second World War, and later as flagship for the invasion of the Philippines. Preserved as a floating exhibit.
Bibliography B45, C86, D560

International
motor excursion vessel

Built 1927 at Waterton Lake, Montana
Original owners Glacier Lake Inc
Propulsion Diesel engine, 184hp
Tonnage 56 gross
Length 73.0ft/22.2m
Breadth 17.2ft/5.2m
Materials Wood throughout
Original use Passengers
Condition In operation during summer
Present owners Glacier Park Inc

Location Waterton Lake, Montana, USA
History Built to carry excursion passengers on scenic mountain lake on the United States and Canadian border. Still in service during summer. Kept in protective boathouse during winter months.

Intrepid
aircraft carrier

Former name USS INTREPID
Built 1943 by Newport News Shipbuilding & Drydock Co, Newport News, Virginia
Original owners United States Navy
Propulsion Steam turbines, 150,000hp
Tonnage 27,100 displacement
Length 888.0ft/270.66m
Breadth 93.0ft/28.35m
Draught 29.0ft/8.84m
Materials Steel throughout
Original use Aircraft carrier
Condition Intact
Present owners Intrepid Museum Foundation
Location New York City, USA
History Second World War aircraft carrier that was later used to retrieve astronauts. Preserved as a floating exhibit.
Bibliography B45, C64, D434

Isaac H Evans
oyster dredger

Former name BOYD N SHEPPARD
Built 1886 by J Vannaman & Brother, Mauricetown, New Jersey
Original owners Sheppard Family
Propulsion Sail, schooner rig
Tonnage 52 gross
Length 58.8ft/17.92m
Breadth 19.5ft/5.94m
Draught 6.0ft/1.83m
Materials Wood throughout
Original use Oystering
Condition In sailing condition
Present owners Edward B Glaser
Location Rockland, Maine, USA
History In use for cruises.

J-3792
passenger launch

Built c1954 by Lock City Machine & Marine, Sault Ste Marie, Michigan
Original owners United States Army Corps of Engineers
Propulsion Diesel engines, 156hp
Length 46.28ft/14.11m
Breadth 12.25ft/3.73m
Materials Steel throughout
Original use Passenger launch
Condition Intact
Present owners US Army

Transportation Museum
Location Fort Eustis, Virginia, USA
History US Army 'picket boat' exhibited onshore.

J & E Riggin
oyster dredger

Built 1927 by Stowmans Shipyard, Dorchester, New Jersey
Original owners Charles Riggin
Propulsion Sail, schooner rig
Tonnage 59 gross
Length 76.4ft/23.29m
Breadth 22.3ft/6.8m
Materials Wood throughout
Original use Oystering
Condition In sailing condition
Present owners Susan P Allen
Location Rockland, Maine, USA
History In use for cruises.

Japanese midget submarine

Built 1944 in Japan
Original owners Imperial Japanese Navy
Propulsion Electric motors, 600hp
Tonnage 50 displacement
Length 81.8ft/24.93m
Breadth 6.2ft/1.89m
Draught 2.6ft/0.79m
Materials Steel throughout

Intrepid

Original use Midget submarine
Condition Intact
Present owners United States Navy
Location Agana, Guam, USA
History Captured by the Americans on Guam in 1944. Preserved as an onshore exhibit.

Jean
motor yacht

Built 1913 by Charles Allen, Red Bank, New Jersey
Original owners Charles Allen
Propulsion Diesel engine
Tonnage 19 gross
Length 47.0ft/14.33m
Breadth 11.0ft/3.35m
Draught 3.5ft/1.07m
Materials Wood throughout
Original use Yacht
Condition Intact, in use
Present owners Long Island Maritime Heritage Society
Location Riverhead, Long Island, NY, USA
History Largely unaltered early cabin motor launch. Preserved as an operating vessel.

Jean
sternwheel towing steamer

Built 1938 by Commercial Iron Works, Portland, Oregon
Original owners Western Transportation Co
Propulsion Steam, sternwheel, compound

Tonnage 533 gross
Length 140.3ft/42.76m
Breadth 40.0ft/12.19m
Materials Steel throughout
Original use Towing
Condition Intact
Present owners Hells Gate State Park
Location Lewiston, Oregon, USA
History Preserved as a floating exhibit.

Jeremiah O'Brien
Liberty type cargo ship

Built 1943 by New England Shipbuilding Corp, South Portland, Maine
Original owners War Shipping Administration
Propulsion Steam, screw, triple expansion, 2500hp
Tonnage 7176 gross
Length 417.75ft/127.33m
Breadth 57.0ft/17.37m
Draught 27.75ft/8.46m
Materials Steel throughout
Original use Cargo
Condition Intact, in operating condition
Present owners San Francisco Maritime National Historical Park
Location San Francisco, California, USA
History In order to keep supplies flowing to Allied countries and its forces overseas, the United States embarked on massive shipbuilding programmes in both world wars. In the Second World War over 2500 ships were launched from one design alone

known as the 'Liberty Ship'. The Liberty was a very basic cargo vessel intended to be produced in a short time through large-scale prefabrication. They were primarily of welded construction, and were powered by triple-expansion steam engines which, though antiquated by this time, were relatively easy to manufacture and repair. Having played a vital role in winning the war, these ships then performed further valuable service in the re-establishment of the world's merchant fleets in the immediately postwar period. In 1978 the National Liberty Ship Memorial was formed to preserve one of these vessels. Working with donated funds and volunteer labour, they were able to reactivate the JEREMIAH O'BRIEN, which had lain in reserve for thirty-three years, so that she could be steamed down San Francisco Bay to her present berth on 21 May 1980, looking much as she had the year she was built. During the war she served in both the Atlantic and Pacific, and survived bombing attacks off the Normandy beaches. Since 1980 volunteers have continued to restore the ship, reinstating her Second World War armament, and maintaining her engines so that she can make at least one cruise on San Francisco Bay under her own power each summer. Apart from serving as a memorial to the wartime merchant marine and shipbuilding industry, the JEREMIAH O'BRIEN also provides an opportunity

to see an intact pre-containerisation 'break bulk' cargo vessel.
Bibliography B45, C84, D138

John J Harvey
fireboat

Built 1931 by Todd Shipyards, Brooklyn, New York
Original owners New York City Fire Department
Propulsion Petrol engines; converted to diesel-electric, 3000hp. Engine built by Fairbanks-Morse (current)
Length 130.0ft/39.6m
Breadth 28.0ft/8.5m
Draught 9.0ft/2.7m
Materials Steel throughout
Original use Fireboat
Condition Intact, in need of some restoration
Present owners George Phillips & Association
Location New York City, USA
History Veteran New York City fireboat converted to diesel-electric propulsion in 1957. Retired in the 1990s, and acquired for preservation by a group based in New York City in March 1999.
History Preserved as a floating exhibit.

John Taxis
steam tug

Former name WILLIAM STEWART
Built 1869 by Reany, Son & Archbold, Chester, Pennsylvania
Propulsion Steam, screw, steeple; converted to diesel
Tonnage 27 gross
Length 52.5ft/16.0m
Breadth 13.2ft/4.02m
Draught 6.1ft/1.86m
Materials Wood throughout
Original use Tug
Condition Hull intact, deckhouse has been replaced
Present owners River Enterprises
Location Wilmington, N Carolina, USA
History One of the oldest surviving American tugs. Preserved as an onshore exhibit.

John W Brown
Liberty type cargo ship

Built 1942 by Bethlehem-Fairfield Shipyard, Baltimore, Maryland
Original owners War Shipping Administration
Propulsion Steam, screw, triple expansion, 2500hp
Tonnage 7176 gross
Length 422.7ft/128.84m

Jeremiah O'Brien

Joseph Conrad

merchant marine. Sailed around the world by Captain Alan Villiers in the 1930s. Later an American yacht and training vessel. Preserved as a floating exhibit.
Bibliography C96, D437, 507, 552, 554, F2-3, 12

Joseph P Kennedy Jr
destroyer

Former name USS JOSEPH P KENNEDY JR
Built 1945 by Bethlehem Steel Co, Quincy, Massachusetts
Original owners United States Navy
Propulsion Steam turbines
Tonnage 2425 displacement
Length 390.5ft/119.02m
Breadth 41.3ft/12.59m
Draught 18.5ft/5.64m
Materials Steel throughout
Original use Destroyer
Condition Intact
Present owners USS Massachusetts Battleship Memorial
Location Fall River, Massachusetts, USA
History American destroyer which saw service in the Korean War. Preserved as a floating exhibit.
Bibliography B45, C64, D181

Joy Parks
oyster dredger

Built 1936 by Bronza Parks, Parksley, Virginia
Original owners Captain Orville Parks
Propulsion Sail, sloop rig ('skipjack' type)
Tonnage 17 gross
Length 46.4ft/14.14m
Breadth 15.5ft/4.72m
Draught 2.6ft/0.79m
Materials Wood throughout
Original use Oystering
Condition Intact, except cut down mast
Present owners Seafarers International Union
Location Piney Point, Maryland, USA
History Preserved as an onshore exhibit under cover.

Jupiter
steam tug

Former name SOCONY 14, S O CO NO 14
Built 1902 by Neafie & Levy, Philadelphia, Pennsylvania
Original owners Standard Oil Co
Propulsion Steam, screw; converted to diesel, 1080hp
Tonnage 180 gross
Length 91.0ft/27.74m

Breadth 57.0ft/17.37m
Draught 27.5ft/8.38m
Materials Steel throughout
Original use Cargo
Condition In operating condition
Present owners Project Liberty Ship
Location Baltimore, Maryland, USA
History Restored example of Second World War 'Liberty' type cargo ship. Preserved as an exhibit and active steam vessel.
Bibliography B45, C84, D137, D195

Joseph Conrad
sail training ship

Former name GEORG STAGE
Built 1882 by Burmeister & Wain,

Copenhagen, Denmark
Original owners Stiftelsen Georg Stages Minde
Propulsion Sail, full-rigged ship; auxiliary steam engine; later diesel
Tonnage 203 gross
Length 118.0ft/35.97m
Breadth 25.2ft/7.68m
Draught 11.0ft/3.35m
Materials Iron hull and deckhouses, iron and wood masts
Original use Training
Condition Intact
Present owners Mystic Seaport Museum
Location Mystic, Connecticut, USA
History Built as an auxiliary sail training vessel for the Danish

Jupiter

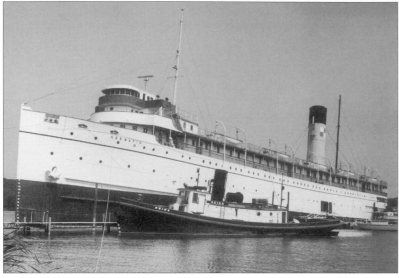

Keewatin

Breadth 22.0ft/6.71m
Materials Steel throughout
Original use Tug
Condition Intact, in operating
condition
Present owners Philadelphia Ship
Preservation Guild
Location Philadelphia, Pennsylvania,
USA
History Preserved as a floating exhibit.

Kalakala
steam ferry

Former name PERALTA
Built 1927 at Oakland, California
Propulsion Steam, screw, 3000hp
Tonnage 1417 gross
Length 265.1ft/80.8m
Breadth 53.4ft/16.3m
Materials Steel throughout
Original use Ferry
Condition Intact, needs extensive
restoration
Present owners Kalakala Foundation
Contact address 154 N 35th Street,
Seattle 98103
Location Seattle, Washington, USA
History Proposed exhibit or active
vessel.

Katahdin
passenger lake steamer

Built 1914 by Bath Iron Works (pre-
fabricated), Moosehead Lake, Maine
Original owners Coburn Steamboat Co
Propulsion Steam, screw; converted to
diesel
Tonnage 140 gross
Length 120.0ft/36.58m
Breadth 28.0ft/8.53m
Materials Steel hull, wood
superstructure

Original use Passengers
Condition Intact
Present owners Moosehead Marine
Museum
Location Greenville, Maine, USA
History Preserved as a floating exhibit.
Bibliography C56

Kathryn M Lee
oyster dredger

Built 1923 in Dorchester, New Jersey
Propulsion Sail, schooner rig
Tonnage 37 gross
Length 56.9ft/18.1m
Breadth 20.3ft/6.1m

Materials Wood throughout
Original use Oyster dredging under sail
Condition In sailing condition
Present owner James H McGlincy, Jr
Location Baltimore, Maryland USA
History Schooner built for oyster
dredging under sail in Delaware Bay.
Later employed there as a motor vessel.
Re-rigged as a schooner and currently
dredging oysters in the Chesapeake
Bay, based in Baltimore.

Keewatin
passenger/cargo lake steamer

Built 1907 by Fairfield Shipbuilding &
Engineering, Govan, Scotland
Original owners Canadian Pacific
Railway
Propulsion Steam, screw, quadruple
expansion, 3300hp, coal fired
Tonnage 3856 gross
Length 336.0ft/102.41m
Breadth 44.0ft/13.41m
Materials Steel throughout
Original use Passengers and cargo
Condition Intact
Present owners Peterson Steamship Co
Location Douglas, Michigan, USA
History Built in Scotland for use on the
Great Lakes under the Canadian flag.
Vessel was separated into two sections
to pass through the canals that bypass
the rapids of the upper St Lawrence
River. Retired in 1965. Preserved as a
grounded exhibit.
Bibliography B44

Kidd
destroyer

Former name USS KIDD
Built 1943 by Federal Shipbuilding &
Drydock Co, Kearney, New Jersey
Original owners United States Navy
Propulsion Steam turbines
Tonnage 2050 displacement
Length 376.5ft/114.76m
Breadth 39.67ft/12.09m
Draught 17.75ft/5.41m
Materials Steel throughout
Original use Destroyer
Condition Intact
Present owners Louisiana Naval War
Memorial Commission
Location Baton Rouge, Louisiana, USA
History American destroyer that saw
service in both the Second World
War and the Korean War. Preserved
as an exhibit in water on
platform.
Bibliography B45, C64, D508, D577

L A Dunton
fishing schooner

Built 1921 by Arthur D Story, Essex,
Massachusetts
Original owners Felix Hogan, Robinson
Giffon & George Nelson
Propulsion Sail, schooner rig; diesel
engine
Tonnage 134 gross
Length 123.0ft/37.49m
Breadth 25.0ft/7.62m

L A Dunton

Materials Wood throughout
Original use Fishing
Condition Intact
Present owners Mystic Seaport
Museum
Location Mystic, Connecticut, USA
History Built for fishing under sail on
the Grand Banks off Newfoundland.
Later used as a cargo vessel in eastern
Canada. Fully restored and fitted out as
a floating exhibit at the Mystic Seaport
Museum.
Bibliography B6, C93, D370, F16

L V R R (Lehigh Valley RR) No 79
harbour barge

Built 1914 by Perth Amboy Drydock,
Perth Amboy, New Jersey
Original owners Lehigh Valley Railroad
Propulsion Towed
Tonnage 454 gross
Length 89.7ft/27.34m
Breadth 30.0ft/9.14m
Materials Wood throughout
Original use Cargo; harbour barge
Condition Intact
Present owners Hudson Waterfront
Museum
Location Brooklyn, New York, USA
History Type of wooden covered
lighter barge once used in large
numbers in New York harbour,
particularly by railroads with freight
yards on the New Jersey side of the
Hudson River. Now preserved afloat
on the Brooklyn waterfront as an
exhibit and a site for events.

La Duchesse
houseboat

Built 1950s hull
Original owners George Boldt
Propulsion None
Length 100.0ft/30.5m
Materials Steel hull; two-storey wood
deckhouse from turn of century
Original use Houseboat
Condition In use; restored in 1950s with
new hull
Present owners Andrew McNally
Location Island Royal, Thousand
Islands, New York, USA
History Intact two-deck luxury
houseboat with original furnishings.
The owner built a castle on an island in
the St Lawrence River for his summer
home, and used the houseboat towed
by its own tug for excursions among
the islands and to watch powerboat
races. The current owner has willed the
houseboat to the Antique Boat
Museum in Clayton, New York.
Bibliography D323

Lettie G Howard

Lady Isabel
motor yacht

Built 1907 by Burger Boat Co
Length 43.0ft/13.1m
Materials Wood throughout
Original use Motor yacht
Condition Intact, in need of restoration
Present owners Wisconsin Maritime
Museum, Manitowoc, Wisconsin
Location Manitowoc, Wisconsin, USA
History Example of a motor yacht built
by a well-known Wisconsin boatyard.
Stored indoors pending restoration to
operating condition.

Laffey
destroyer

Former name USS LAFFEY
Built 1943 by Bath Iron Works, Bath,
Maine
Original owners United States Navy
Propulsion Steam turbines, 60,000hp
Tonnage 2200 displacement
Length 376.5ft/114.76m
Breadth 41.0ft/12.5m
Draught 19.0ft/5.79m
Materials Steel throughout
Original use Destroyer
Condition Intact
Present owners Patriots Point
Development Authority
Location Charleston, S Carolina, USA
History Warship that saw action in
both the Atlantic and the Pacific
during the Second World War.
Survived heavy damage from kamikaze
attacks during the invasion of
Okinawa. Preserved as a floating
exhibit.
Bibliography B45, C64, D29

Lane Victory
Victory type cargo ship

Built 1945 by California Shipbuilding
Corp, Los Angeles, California
Original owners United States
Maritime Commission
Propulsion Steam turbines
Tonnage 7612 gross
Length 436.5ft/133.05m
Breadth 62.0ft/18.9m
Draught 28.0ft/8.53m
Materials Steel throughout
Original use Cargo
Condition In operating condition
Present owners US Merchant Marine
Veterans of the Second World War
Location Los Angeles, California, USA
History 'Victory Ship' type of standard
cargo vessel built by the United States
in large numbers during the last years
of Second World War. Maintained in
operating condition and steamed on
special occasions by an organisation of
merchant marine veterans.
Bibliography C85, D251

Lettie G Howard
fishing schooner

Former name CAVIARE, MYSTIC C
Built 1893 by Arthur D Story, Essex,
Massachusetts
Original owners Captain Fred Howard
& Association
Propulsion Sail, schooner rig; diesel
engine added
Tonnage 60 gross
Length 74.6ft/22.74m
Breadth 21.0ft/6.4m
Draught 8.9ft/2.71m
Materials Wood throughout
Original use Fishing
Condition In sailing condition
Present owners South Street Seaport
Museum
Location New York City, USA
History Last surviving 'Fredonia
model' inshore fishing schooner. Sailed
out of Gloucester, Massachusetts, and
later Pensacola, Florida. Fully restored
to sailing condition at New York in
June 1993. Used for training.
Bibliography D59

Lewis Ark
houseboat

Built 1905 at San Francisco Bay,
California
Propulsion Stationary
Length 50.0ft/15.24m
Breadth 20.0ft/6.1m
Materials Wood throughout
Original use Houseboat

Lexington

Condition Intact, furnished
Present owners San Francisco Maritime National Historical Park
Location San Francisco, California, USA
History Type of houseboat once common on northern San Francisco Bay. Restored as an exhibit on shore on the waterfront of San Francisco.

Lewis R French
trading schooner

Built 1871 by French Brothers, South Bristol, Maine
Original owners French Brothers
Propulsion Sail, schooner rig
Tonnage 40 gross
Length 54.7ft/16.67m
Breadth 18.8ft/5.73m
Draught 7.5ft/2.29m
Materials Wood throughout
Original use Cargo
Condition In operation
Present owners Daniel Pease
Location Rockland, Maine, USA
History Built to carry cargo under sail along the coast of Maine. Fully restored in the 1970s and converted internally to carry passengers on one week cruises.
Bibliography D524

Lexington
aircraft carrier

Former name USS LEXINGTON
Built 1942 by Bethlehem Shipyard, Quincy, Massachusetts
Original owners United States Navy
Propulsion Steam turbines, 150,000hp
Tonnage 34,881 displacement
Length 872.0ft/265.78m
Breadth 147.5ft/44.95m
Draught 27.5ft/8.38m
Materials Steel throughout
Original use Aircraft carrier
Condition Intact
Present owners USS Lexington Museum on the Bay
Location Corpus Cristi, Texas, USA
History Aircraft carrier that saw service in the Second World War and later for training student pilots. Preserved as a floating exhibit.
Bibliography B45, C64, D274, D412

Lilac
lighthouse tender

Former name USLHT LILAC
Built 1933 by Pusey & Jones, Wilmington, Delaware
Original owners United States Lighthouse Service

Official number WAGL-227
Propulsion Steam, twin screw, two triple expansion engines, 1000hp
Tonnage 799 displacement
Length 172.00ft/52.43m
Breadth 32.0ft/9.75m
Draught 11.0ft/3.4m
Materials Steel throughout
Original use Lighthouse tender
Condition Intact, still has engines
Location Nr Richmond, Virginia, USA
History Proposed as an exhibit.

Ling
submarine

Former name USS LING
Built 1945 by Cramp Shipbuilding Co, Philadelphia, Pennsylvania
Original owners United States Navy
Propulsion Diesel and electric motors
Tonnage 2040 displacement
Length 312.0ft/95.1m
Breadth 27.0ft/8.23m
Materials Steel throughout
Original use Submarine
Condition Intact
Present owners Submarine Memorial Association
Location Hackensack, New Jersey, USA
History Preserved as a floating exhibit.
Bibliography B45, C64

Lionfish
submarine

Former name USS LIONFISH
Built 1943 by Cramp Shipbuilding Corp, Philadelphia, Pennsylvania
Original owners United States Navy
Propulsion Diesel and electric motors
Tonnage 1526 displacement
Length 311.75ft/95.02m
Breadth 27.25ft/8.31m
Draught 15.25ft/4.65m
Materials Steel throughout
Original use Submarine
Condition Intact
Present owners USS Massachusetts Battleship Memorial Commission
Location Fall River, Massachusetts, USA
History Submarine that saw service during the Second World War. Preserved as a floating exhibit.
Bibliography B45, C64

Little Jennie
oyster dredger

Built 1884 by J T Marsh, Solomons Island, Maryland
Propulsion Sail, schooner rig ('bugeye' type)
Tonnage 30 gross

Length 61.0ft/18.59m
Breadth 16.0ft/4.88m
Draught 3.5ft/1.07m
Materials Wood throughout
Original use Oystering
Condition Intact, in need of restoration
Present owners Long Island Maritime Heritage Society
Location Riverhead, Long Island, NY, USA
History Built for oyster dredging under sail on Chesapeake Bay. Later a yacht.

Little Rock
light cruiser

Former name USS LITTLE ROCK
Built 1944 by Cramp Shipbuilding Corp, Philadelphia, Pennsylvania
Original owners United States Navy
Propulsion Steam turbines, 100,000hp
Tonnage 10,670 displacement
Length 610.0ft/185.93m
Breadth 66.0ft/20.12m
Draught 25.0ft/7.62m
Materials Steel throughout
Original use Light cruiser
Condition Intact
Present owners Buffalo Naval and Servicemen's Park
Location Buffalo, New York, USA
History Light cruiser converted to missile cruiser in 1960. Preserved as a floating exhibit.
Bibliography C64

Logsdon
sternwheel towing vessel

Built 1941 at Beardstown, Illinois
Original owners Ray Logsdon
Propulsion Diesel, sternwheel, 200hp
Tonnage 55 gross
Length 72.0ft/21.95m
Breadth 15.0ft/4.57m
Materials Wood throughout
Original use Towing
Condition Intact
Present owners Woodward Riverboat Museum
Location Dubuque, Iowa, USA
History Preserved as an exhibit.

Lone Star
sternwheel towing steamer

Built 1922 by Lions Shipyard, Rock Island, Illinois
Original owners Builder Sand and Gravel
Propulsion Steam, sternwheel, coal fired
Tonnage 66 gross
Length 90.0ft/27.43m
Breadth 24.5ft/7.47m

Materials Wood throughout
Original use Towing
Condition Intact
Present owners Buffalo Bill Museum
Location Le Claire, Iowa, USA
History Last sternwheel towboat active on the Mississippi when retired in 1967. Preserved as an onshore exhibit.
Bibliography B44

LSM-45
landing ship medium

Former name IPOPLIARCHOS GRIGOROPOULOS
Built 1944 by Brown Brothers, Houston, Texas
Original owners United States Navy
Official number LSM-45
Propulsion Twin screw, two diesel engines, 2800hp. Engine built by Fairbanks-Morse
Tonnage 1095 displacement
Length 203.6ft/62.03m
Breadth 34.5ft/10.52m
Draught 8.3ft/2.54m

Little Rock

Materials Steel throughout
Original use Landing craft
Condition Intact
Present owners LSM Association of America
Location Omaha, Nebraska, USA
History Landing craft for personnel and vehicles built for use in the Second World War. Transferred to the Greek Navy in 1958. Laid up in the early 1990s. Towed to the United States for preservation in late 1998 or early 1999.

Luna
motor tug

Built 1930 by M M Davis, Solomons, Maryland, USA. Designed by John G Alden & Co
Original owners Boston Towboat Co
Propulsion Diesel-electric. Engine built by Winton
Tonnage 165 gross
Length 90.5ft/27.58m
Breadth 24.8ft/7.56m
Depth 11.3ft/3.44m
Materials Wood throughout

Original use Tug
Condition Largely intact but was recently sunk for over a year
Location Boston, Massachusetts, USA
History One of the first diesel-electric tugs built. Efforts to restore this vessel have recently been revived.

Madaket
motor personnel launch

Former name NELLIE C
Built 1910 by W F McDonald, Fairhaven, California
Original owners Captain Cousins
Propulsion Diesel engines
Tonnage 14 gross
Length 47.6ft/14.51m
Breadth 12.0ft/3.66m
Materials Wood throughout
Original use Passengers
Condition Intact, in operation
Present owners Humboldt Bay Maritime Museum
Location Eureka, California, USA
History Covered launch built to carry workers to local sawmills. Preserved as a floating exhibit and for excursions.
Bibliography D284

Maj Gen Wm H Hart
steam ferry

Former name HARLEM, JOHN A LYNCH
Built 1925 by Staten Island Shipbuilding Co, Mariners Harbor, Staten Island, New York
Original owners City of New York
Propulsion Steam, screw, 4-cylinder compound
Tonnage 597 gross
Length 151.0ft/46.02m
Breadth 53.0ft/16.15m
Draught 10.0ft/3.05m
Materials Steel throughout
Original use Ferry
Condition Sunk
Location Port Reading, New Jersey, USA
History Was proposed as a floating school but preservation has now been abandoned and vessel is lying sunk.
Bibliography B44

Majestic
floating theatre

Built 1923 by Thomas J Reynolds, Pittsburgh, Pennsylvania
Original owners Thomas J Reynolds
Propulsion Towed
Tonnage 168 gross
Length 135.0ft/41.15m

Breadth 40.0ft/12.19m
Materials Steel hull, wood
superstructure
Original use Floating theatre
Condition Intact, in use
Present owners City of Cincinnati
Location Cincinnati, Ohio, USA
History One of two surviving
showboats built for use on the
Mississippi and Ohio Rivers.
Bibliography C32

Major Elisha K Hanson
motor tug

Former name JOHN F NASH, MAJOR
ELISHA K HANSON
Built 1944 by Jakobsen Shipyard,
Oyster Bay, New York
Original owners United States Army
Official number LT-5
Propulsion Diesel engine 1200hp
Length 113.0ft/34.4m
Breadth 25.0ft/7.6m
Depth 14.0ft/4.3m
Materials Steel throughout
Original use Tug
Condition In operating condition
Present owners H Lee White Maritime
Museum
Location Oswego, New York
History Tug built for the United States
Army during the Second World War.
Was sent to Europe where she took
part in the Normandy invasion. Is
credited with shooting down one
German aircraft. Preserved as a
floating exhibit restored to her Second
World War Army colour scheme.

Mamie A Mister
oyster dredger

Built 1910 at Champ, Maryland
Propulsion Sail, schooner rig ('skipjack'
type)
Tonnage 26 gross
Length 56.6ft/17.2m
Breadth 18.6ft/5.7m
Materials Wood throughout
Original use Oyster dredging
Condition In sailing condition
Present owners Sail-Inn Tours
Contact address PO Box 358, Tilghman,
Maryland 21671
Location Tilghman, Maryland, USA
History One of the largest skipjacks
built for oyster dredging on the
Chesapeake Bay. The only one
currently in existence rigged with two
masts as a 'three sail bateau'. Converted
to charter use but otherwise unaltered.

Mary Murray

Maneuverboat No 3
wicket lifting scow

Built c1930
Original owners United States Army
Corps of Engineers
Propulsion Winched itself into
position, steam machinery, coal fired
Length 50.0ft/15.2m
Breadth 29.0ft/8.8m
Materials Steel throughout
Original use Dam wicket lifting scow
Condition Intact
Present owners United States Army
Corps of Engineers
Location Hannibal, Ohio, USA
History Scow with steam machinery
used to lift wickets (gates) on a dam on
the Ohio River. Now displayed on
shore at an Army Engineers operated
lock, in conjunction with exhibits
indoors.

Maple
lighthouse tender

Former name USCGS MAPLE
Built 1939 by Marine Iron &
Shipbuilding Co, Duluth,
Minnesota
Original owners United States
Lighthouse Service
Official number WAGL 234
Propulsion Diesel engines, twin screw,
430hp. Engine built by Superior

Tonnage 342 displacement
Length 122.25ft/37.2m
Breadth 27.0ft/8.2m
Draught 7.5ft/2.3m
Materials Steel throughout
Original use Lighthouse tender
Condition Intact
Present owners Great Lakes Center for
Maritime History
Location St Ignace, Michigan, USA
History Recently retired United States
Coast Guard lighthouse and buoy
tender pre-dating the Second World
War. Preserved as a floating museum at
St Ignace.

Mariette
sailing yacht

Former name GEE GEE IV,
CLEOPATRA'S BARGE II
Built 1915 by Nathaniel Herreshoff,
Bristol, Rhode Island
Original owners Frederick Brown,
Boston
Propulsion Sail, schooner rig; auxiliary
diesel engines, 370hp. Engine built by
General Motors
Tonnage 165 displacement
Length 108.1ft/33.0m
Breadth 23.5ft/7.19m
Draught 14.5ft/4.42m
Materials Steel hull
Original use Yacht
Condition Fully restored in 1995

Present owners Tom Perkins
Location USA
History Schooner yacht built early in
the century by a leading American
yard. Recently fully restored.

Marine Ship Chandlery
floating machine shop

Former name DALZELLAND,
HUGHES No 75, YR-28
Built c1919
Original owners United States Navy
Propulsion Stationary
Length 157.0ft/47.75m
Breadth 46.0ft/14.02m
Draught 7.0ft/2.13m
Materials Reinforced concrete
throughout
Original use Floating machine shop
Condition No recent information
Location New Haven, Connecticut,
USA
History Concrete workshop barge
apparently built for the Navy during
the First World War. Employed during
the Second World War as a support
facility for torpedo boats and later as a
floating machine shop for New York
tugs.

Marlin
training submarine

Former name USS MARLIN

Built 1953 by General Dynamics Corp, Groton, Connecticut
Original owners United States Navy
Propulsion Diesel and electric motors
Tonnage 347 displacement
Length 131.25ft/40.0m
Breadth 13.58ft/4.14m
Draught 12.25ft/3.73m
Materials Steel throughout
Original use Training submarine
Condition Intact
Present owners Greater Omaha Military Historical Society
Location Omaha, Nebraska, USA
History Small submarine designed for training use. One of only two built for the United States Navy. Preserved as an onshore exhibit.
Bibliography A6, C64

Martha
draketail launch

Built 1934 by Bronza Parks
Propulsion Petrol engine. Engine built by Olds
Length 43.33ft/13.2m
Breadth 8.25ft/2.5m
Materials Wood throughout
Condition Intact, fully restored
Present owners Chesapeake Bay Maritime Museum
Location St Michael's, Maryland, USA

History Example of a Hooper Island draketail launch. Donated to the Museum by the Parks Family in 1971. Now a floating exhibit.

Martha Lewis
oyster dredger

Built 1955 at Wingate, Maryland
Propulsion Sail, sloop rig ('skipjack' type)
Tonnage 8 gross
Length 46.2ft/14.1m
Materials Wood throughout
Original use Oystering
Condition In sailing condition
Location Cambridge, Maryland, USA
History Built for oyster dredging under sail on Chesapeake Bay. Maintained in sailing condition for educational programmes, including oyster dredging during the season.

Mary Murray
steam ferry

Built 1938 by United Shipyards, Mariners Harbor, Staten Island, New York
Original owners City of New York
Propulsion Steam, screw, 4-cylinder compound, 4000hp
Tonnage 2126 gross

Length 252.5ft/76.96m
Breadth 47.8ft/14.57m
Materials Steel throughout
Original use Ferry
Condition Intact, aground, laid up
Present owners George Searle
Location New Brunswick, New Jersey, USA
History Built to carry passengers and vehicles between Manhattan and Staten Island, New York. Proposed conversion to floating restaurant after retirement never took place.
Bibliography C39, C81

Mary W Somers
oyster dredger

Built 1904 by William T Young, Parksley, Virginia
Original owners Lloyd Somers
Propulsion Sail, sloop rig ('skipjack' type)
Tonnage 9 gross
Length 41.9ft/12.77m
Breadth 14.0ft/4.27m
Materials Wood throughout
Original use Oystering
Condition Intact
Present owners Havre de Grace Maritime Museum
Location Port Tobacco, Maryland, USA
History Preserved as an exhibit.

Massachusetts
battleship

Former name USS MASSACHUSETTS
Built 1941 by Bethlehem Shipyard, Quincy, Massachusetts
Original owners United States Navy
Official number BB-59
Propulsion Steam turbines
Tonnage 35,000 displacement
Length 681.0ft/207.57m
Breadth 108.15ft/32.96m
Draught 29.25ft/8.92m
Materials Steel throughout
Original use Battleship
Condition Intact
Present owners USS Massachusetts Battleship Memorial
Location Fall River, Massachusetts, USA
History Second World War battleship which saw action in the invasion of North Africa and in the Pacific. Preserved as a floating exhibit.
Bibliography B45, C64, D182

Mathilda
steam harbour tug

Built 1899 at Sorel, Quebec, Canada
Original owners Sincennes McNaughton Line, Montreal
Propulsion Steam, screw, compound

Massachusetts

Tonnage 114 gross
Length 72.0ft/21.95m
Breadth 20.0ft/6.1m
Draught 11.0ft/3.35m
Materials Steel throughout
Original use Tug
Condition Intact
Present owners Hudson River Maritime
Center
Location Kingston, New York, USA
History Small steam tug built for use in
the harbour of Montreal. Later served
as a floating exhibit at New York City.
Now preserved as an onshore exhibit.

Mayor Andrew Broaddus
floating lifesaving station

Former name USCGS LOUISVILLE
Built 1929 at Dubuque, Iowa
Original owners United States Coast
Guard
Propulsion Stationary
Length 98.0ft/29.87m
Breadth 38.0ft/11.58m
Draught 5.5ft/1.68m
Materials Wood throughout
Original use Lifesaving station
Condition Intact, in use
Present owners Belle of Louisville
Operating Board
Location Louisville, Kentucky, USA
History Last surviving floating
lifesaving station in the United States.
In use for offices.

Mclane
Coast Guard cutter

Former name USCGS MCLANE
Built 1927 by American Brown Boveri,
Camden, New Jersey
Original owners United States Coast
Guard
Official number WMEC-146
Propulsion Diesel engine
Tonnage 282.0 displacement
Length 125.0ft/38.1m
Breadth 24.0ft/7.3m
Materials Steel throughout
Original use Patrol boat
Present owners USS SILVERSIDES &
Maritime Museum
Contact address PO Box 1692,
Muskegon, Michigan 49443
Location Muskegon, Michigan, USA
History One of thirty-three Coast
Guard cutters of her class built to
combat liquor smuggling during the
'Prohibition' years. Spent the Second
World War in Alaskan waters.
Currently based at Muskegon,
Michigan, as a training vessel and
floating exhibit.
Bibliography C85

Mclane

Medea
steam yacht

Former name CORNEILLE
Built 1904 by Alexander Stephen &
Sons, Glasgow, Scotland
Original owners Captain MacAllister
Hall
Propulsion Steam, screw, compound,
30hp
Tonnage 112 gross
Length 109.7ft/33.44m
Breadth 16.65ft/5.07m
Draught 10.0ft/3.05m
Materials Steel hull, wood
superstructure
Original use Yacht
Condition Intact
Present owners Maritime Museum
Association of San Diego
Location San Diego, California, USA

History Fully restored turn-of-the-
century steam yacht preserved as a
floating exhibit.
Bibliography B44, D17, D18

Mercantile
trading schooner

Built 1916 at Deer Isle, Maine
Propulsion Sail, schooner rig
Tonnage 41 gross
Length 71.1ft/21.67m
Breadth 21.4ft/6.52m
Materials Wood throughout
Original use Cargo
Condition In operation during summer
months
Present owners Ray Williamson
Location Camden, Maine, USA
Bibliography C93

Meteor
Great Lakes whaleback steamer

Former name SOUTH PARK, FRANK
ROCKEFELLER
Built 1896 by American Steel Barge Co,
Superior, Wisconsin
Propulsion Steam, screw
Tonnage 2758 gross
Length 366.5ft/111.71m
Breadth 45.4ft/13.84m
Draught 21.8ft/6.64m
Materials Steel throughout
Original use Cargo
Condition Intact, imbedded in shore
Present owners Head of the Lakes
Maritime Society
Location Superior, Wisconsin, USA
History The whaleback steamer is
something of a maritime oddity. Only
forty-three were built between the
years 1888 and 1897, thirty-nine of

Meteor

them for use on the American Great Lakes. They were the invention of Captain Alexander McDougall, who believed that a cigar-shaped hull with a conical bow would be more seaworthy because it provided less resistance to high winds and waves. Captain McDougall built all the Great Lakes whalebacks, including the only passenger steamer CHRISTOPHER COLUMBUS of 1892, most of them in a shipyard in Superior, Wisconsin, at the west end of Lake Superior, near where the METEOR now lies. The only whaleback built outside the United States was the SAGAMORE launched at Sunderland, England, in 1893. METEOR, last survivor of the type, was built at Superior as the bulk iron ore carrier FRANK ROCKEFELLER in 1896. She was later used to carry sand, grain and automobiles. In 1943 she was converted to a tanker for further use on the Lakes. In the late 1960s the Head of the Lakes Maritime Society began a campaign to return the last whaleback to Superior to serve as a museum there. METEOR was finally retired in 1969 and donated to the Society by her last owners. She arrived at Superior under tow in September 1972. Her hull has now been imbedded in the shoreline, and doors have been cut in one side to form an entrance to exhibits installed in her former cargo tanks. Other areas of the vessel, including the bridge, engine room and living quarters for the crew, are maintained as they would have appeared when the vessel was last in active service.

Bibliography C55, C97

Milwaukee Clipper
coastal passenger steamer

Former name CLIPPER, JUNIATA
Built 1905 by American Shipbuilding Co, Cleveland, Ohio
Original owners Anchor Line
Propulsion Steam, screw, quadruple expansion, 2500hp
Tonnage 4272 gross
Length 346.0ft/105.46m
Breadth 45.0ft/13.72m
Draught 12.6ft/3.84m
Materials Steel throughout
Original use Passengers
Condition Intact, superstructure 'modernised' in 1941
Location Muskegon, Michigan, USA
History Proposed museum and convention centre.

Minnehaha
passenger lake steamer

Built 1906 at Minneapolis, Minnesota
Original owners Twin City Rapid Transit Co
Propulsion Steam, screw, triple expansion, 150hp
Length 70.0ft/21.34m
Breadth 14.84ft/4.52m
Draught 5.58ft/1.7m
Materials Wood throughout
Original use Passengers
Condition Undergoing restoration
Present owners Minnesota Transportation Museum
Location Excelsior, Minnesota, USA
History Built to carry excursionists to parks on Lake Minnetonka near Minneapolis, Minnesota. Proposed excursion vessel.

Bibliography D287

Minnesota Centenniel Showboat
floating theatre

Former name GEN JOHN NEWTON
Built 1899 by Iowa Iron Works, Dubuque, Iowa
Original owners United States Army Corps of Engineers
Propulsion Steam, sternwheel, cross compound
Length 150.0ft/45.72m
Breadth 28.0ft/8.53m
Draught 4.67ft/1.42m
Materials Steel hull
Original use Towing
Condition Converted to floating theatre.
Present owners University of Minnesota
Location St Paul, Minnesota, USA
History Built for use by the Army Engineers on the Mississippi River as a towboat and for transporting personnel and supplies.

Minnie V
oyster dredger

Built 1906 at Wenona, Maryland
Propulsion Sail, sloop rig ('skipjack' type)
Tonnage 10 gross
Length 45.3ft/13.81m
Breadth 15.7ft/4.79m
Materials Wood throughout
Original use Oystering
Condition In sailing condition
Present owners Radcliffe Maritime Museum
Location Baltimore, Maryland, USA
History Preserved as a floating exhibit and training vessel.

Miss Asia
motor yacht

Former name BING, ALALBA, LURA M II, MARGARET F
Built 1923 by Consolidated Shipbuilding, Morris Heights, NY
Original owners Lawrence P Fisher
Propulsion Petrol engines. Engines built by Palmer
Length 62.0ft/18.9m
Breadth 11.5ft/3.5m
Draught 3.5ft/1.1m
Materials Wood throughout
Original use Commuting yacht
Condition Fully restored in 1988-90
Present owners Gary Conover
Location Martha's Vineyard Island, USA
History Type of fast motor yacht used by wealthy business executives to commute between their offices in Manhattan and homes on the north shore of Long Island. Fully restored for further use as a private yacht.

Bibliography A1

Missouri
battleship

Built 1944 by New York Naval Shipyard, Brooklyn, New York
Original owners United States Navy
Propulsion Steam turbines, 212,000hp
Tonnage 57,540 displacement
Length 887.25ft/270.43m
Breadth 108.16ft/32.96m
Draught 36.17ft/11.02m

Missouri

Materials Steel throughout
Original use Battleship
Condition Intact
Present owners United States Navy
Location Pearl Harbor, Hawaii, USA
History American battleship of the
Second World War which was the site
of the Japanese surrender. Preserved as
a floating exhibit.
Bibliography B45, C64, D382, D497,
D509

Modesty
oyster dredger

Built 1923 by Wood & Chute,
Greenport, New York
Original owners Theodore Haupt
Propulsion Sail, sloop rig; petrol engine
Length 35.75ft/10.9m
Breadth 12.0ft/3.66m
Draught 2.65ft/0.81m
Materials Wood throughout
Original use Oystering
Condition Intact
Present owners Suffolk Marine
Museum
Location West Sayville, New York, USA
History Preserved as an onshore
exhibit.

Mohawk
Coast Guard cutter

Former name USCGS MOHAWK
Built 1934 by Pusey & Jones,
Wilmington, Delaware
Original owners United States Coast
Guard
Propulsion Diesel engines
Tonnage 1050 displacement
Length 153.2ft/46.7m
Breadth 36.2ft/11.03m
Draught 14.0ft/4.27m
Materials Steel throughout
Original use Coast Guard patrol
Condition Intact
Present owners Mohawk Corporation
Location Staten Island, New York,
USA
History Coast Guard cutter that
escorted convoys off Greenland in the
Second World War. Former exhibit.
Not open to the public.
Bibliography C86

Mon Lei
Chinese junk

Built 1855 at Fukien, China
Propulsion Sail, three-masted junk rig;
auxiliary engine added
Tonnage 36 gross
Length 50.0ft/15.24m
Breadth 18.0ft/5.49m

Draught 6.42ft/1.96m
Materials Wood throughout
Original use Cargo or fishing
Condition In operating condition
Present owners Alen York
Location New York City, USA
History Chinese junk converted to a
yacht.

Montgomery
sternwheel snagboat

Built 1926 by Charleston Drydock &
Machine Co, Charleston, South
Carolina
Original owners United States Army
Corps of Engineers
Propulsion Steam, sternwheel
Tonnage 411 displacement
Length 178.0ft/54.25m
Breadth 34.08ft/10.39m
Materials Steel throughout
Original use Snag removal
Condition Intact
Present owners United States Army
Corps of Engineers
Location Aliceville, Alabama, USA
History Built for removing snags
(sunken dead trees) from navigable
rivers in the southeastern United
States. Preserved as a floating exhibit.
Bibliography D380

Moshulu
trading barque

Former name DREADNOUGHT, KURT
Built 1904 by William Hamilton & Co,
Port Glasgow, Scotland
Original owners G J H Siemers,
Hamburg, Germany
Propulsion Sail, four-masted barque rig
Tonnage 3116 gross
Length 335.0ft/102.11m
Breadth 46.9ft/14.3m
Materials Steel hull and masts, wood
deckhouses
Original use Cargo
Condition Altered internally for
restaurant; windows added
Present owners Specialty Restaurants
Location Philadelphia, Pennsylvania,
USA
History Preserved as a floating
restaurant.
Bibliography C52, D90, 91, 142, 384, 385

Mount Washington
sidewheel lake steamer

Former name CHATEAUGAY
Built 1888 at Shelburne, Vermont
Original owners Champlain
Transportation Co
Propulsion Steam, sidewheel, beam

engine, 1230hp; converted to diesel.
Engine built by Fletcher, Harrison &
Co, NY/Enterprise
Tonnage 750 displacement
Length 230.0ft/70.0m
Breadth 35.0ft/10.7m
Draught 9.0ft/2.7m
Materials Iron hull
Original use Passengers
Condition In operation
Present owners Mount Washington
Steamship Corporation
Location Lake Winnipesaukee, NH,
USA
History Iron-hulled passenger
steamboat built for Lake Champlain.
Later used as a ferry. In 1940 the hull
was cut into sections and transported
overland to Lake Winnipesaukee in
New Hampshire, where it was
reassembled with a new superstructure
and diesel, screw propulsion. Hull was
lengthened by 24ft in 1982-83.

MSB-5
riverine minesweeper

Built 1952 by John Trumpy & Sons,
Annapolis, Maryland
Original owners United States Navy
Propulsion Diesel engines, 600hp
Tonnage 44 displacement

Montgomery

Length 57.25ft/17.45m
Breadth 15.84ft/4.83m
Draught 5.58ft/1.7m
Materials Wood throughout
Original use Minesweeper
Condition Intact
Present owners Pate Museum of Transportation
Location Fort Worth, Texas
History Minesweeper that took part in the Vietnam War. Preserved as an onshore exhibit.

Mustang
oyster dredger

Built 1907 at Saxis, Virginia
Propulsion Sail, schooner rig
Tonnage 11 gross
Length 45.9ft/13.99m
Breadth 10.8ft/3.29m
Materials Wood throughout
Original use Oystering
Condition Intact
Present owners Chesapeake Bay Maritime Museum
Location St Michael's, Maryland, USA
History Oyster dredger later used as a passenger vessel. Preserved as a floating exhibit.

Nantucket
lightship

Built 1936 by Pusey & Jones, Wilmington, Delaware
Original owners United States Lighthouse Service
Propulsion Steam, screw; converted to diesel, 900hp
Tonnage 900 displacement
Length 149.0ft/45.42m
Breadth 31.0ft/9.45m
Draught 16.0ft/4.88m
Materials Steel throughout
Original use Lightship
Condition Intact
Present owners HMS ROSE Foundation
Location Bridgeport, Connecticut, USA
History Built to replace a NANTUCKET lightship sunk by the liner OLYMPIC. Preserved as a floating exhibit.
Bibliography C27

Nantucket
lightship

Former name PORTLAND, BLUNT'S REEF, SAN FRANCISCO
Built 1950 by Coast Guard Shipyard, Curtis Bay, Maryland
Original owners United States Coast Guard
Propulsion Diesel engine, 550hp
Tonnage 617 displacement

Nathaniel Bowditch

Length 128.0ft/39.01m
Breadth 30.0ft/9.14m
Draught 11.0ft/3.35m
Materials Steel throughout
Original use Lightship
Condition Intact
Present owners Metropolitan District Commission, Boston
Location Quincy, Massachusetts, USA
History Lightship retired from the last active station in United States waters in 1985. Preserved as a floating exhibit.
Bibliography C27

Nantucket
lightship

Former name RELIEF, AMBROSE
Built 1952 by Coast Guard Shipyard, Curtis Bay, Maryland
Original owners United States Coast Guard
Propulsion Diesel engine, 550hp
Tonnage 617 displacement

Length 128.0ft/39.01m
Breadth 30.0ft/9.14m
Draught 11.0ft/3.35m
Materials Steel throughout
Original use Lightship
Condition Intact
Location Wareham, Massachusetts, USA
History Last lightship built in the united States and the only one with a tripod mast. Preserved as a floating exhibit.
Bibliography C27

Nathaniel Bowditch
schooner yacht

Former name LADONA, JANE DORE
Built 1922 by Hodgdon Brothers, East Boothbay, Maine. Designed by William Hand
Propulsion Sail, schooner rig; auxiliary diesel engine. Engine built by Detroit
Tonnage 54 gross

Length 90.0ft/27.4m
Breadth 21.0ft/6.4m
Draught 11.0ft/3.4m
Materials Wood throughout
Original use Yacht
Condition In sailing condition
Present owners Gib E Philbrick
Contact address Cape Rozier Inc, PO Box 459, Warren, Maine 04864
Location Rockland, Maine, USA
History Built as a yacht designed on fishing schooner lines. Served as a patrol vessel during the Second World War, and after the war was converted to a fishing vessel. Now rebuilt and employed on one-week cruises along the coast of Maine.

Nautilus
nuclear submarine

Former name USS NAUTILUS
Built 1954 by Electric Boat Co, Groton, Connecticut
Original owners United States Navy
Propulsion Nuclear power
Tonnage 3533 displacement
Length 324.0ft/99.06m
Breadth 28.0ft/8.53m
Draught 22.0ft/6.71m
Materials Steel throughout
Original use Submarine
Condition Intact
Present owners United States Navy
Location Groton, Connecticut, USA
History World's first atomic-powered warship. First vessel to reach the North Pole (submerged). Preserved as a floating exhibit.
Bibliography A6, C64, D10, D37b

Neith
sailing yacht

Built 1907 by Nathaniel Herreshoff, Bristol, Rhode Island
Original owners Ed Dunham
Propulsion Sail, cutter rig; auxiliary engine, 50hp. Engine built by Yanmar (current)
Tonnage 20.5 displacement
Length 53.5ft/16.28m
Breadth 10.5ft/3.2m
Draught 7.66ft/2.33m
Materials Wood throughout
Original use Yacht
Condition Fully restored in 1993
Present owners Jack Brown
Location USA
History Early twentieth-century racing yacht built by a leading American designer of the period. Has recently been fully restored for further use as a yacht.
Bibliography A1

Nellie & Mary
oyster dredger

Built 1891 by Rice & Brothers Shipyard, Bridgton, New Jersey
Original owners Timothy Bateman & James Peterson
Propulsion Sail, schooner rig; later motor vessel
Tonnage 22 gross
Length 49.3ft/15.03m
Breadth 17.0ft/5.18m
Materials Wood throughout
Original use Oystering
Condition Restoration in progress
Present owners Municipal Port Authority, Bridgton
Location Bridgton, New Jersey, USA
History Proposed exhibit and active sailing vessel.

Nenana
sternwheel river steamer

Built 1933 by Berg Construction Co, Nenana, Alaska
Original owners The Alaska Railroad
Propulsion Steam, sternwheel
Tonnage 1000 displacement
Length 210.0ft/64.01m
Breadth 42.0ft/12.8m
Materials Wood throughout
Original use Passengers and cargo
Condition Intact, some restoration in progress
Present owners City of Fairbanks
Location Fairbanks, Alaska, USA
History Built to carry passengers and freight on Alaskan rivers. Preserved as an onshore exhibit.
Bibliography B44

New Bedford
lightship

Former name PORTLAND, POLLOCK RIP, RELIEF, DIAMOND SHOAL
Built 1930 by Albina Iron Works, Portland, Oregon
Original owners United States Lighthouse Service
Propulsion Diesel electric, 350hp
Tonnage 630 displacement
Length 133.25ft/40.61m
Breadth 30.0ft/9.14m
Draught 13.25ft/4.04m
Materials Steel throughout
Original use Lightship
Condition Intact
Present owners City of New Bedford
Location New Bedford, Massachusetts, USA
History Preserved as a floating exhibit.
Bibliography C27

Nobska

New Way
cable maintenance schooner

Former name WESTERN UNION
Built 1939 by Elroy & Loxley, Key West, Florida
Original owners Western Union Telegraph
Propulsion Sail, schooner rig; diesel auxiliary
Tonnage 189 gross
Length 96.0ft/29.26m
Breadth 23.5ft/7.16m
Draught 7.5ft/2.29m
Materials Wood throughout
Original use Underwater cable maintenance
Condition In sailing condition
Present owners Vision Quest National
Location Philadelphia, Pennsylvania, USA
History Unique schooner-rigged undersea cable maintenance vessel built for operation on the coast of Florida. Later rebuilt to serve as a youth training vessel. In use for sail training.

No 249
canal barge

Built Date not known
Original owners Lehigh Canal Co
Propulsion Towed by horses or mules
Length 40.0ft/12.19m
Breadth 10.0ft/3.05m
Materials Wood throughout
Original use Cargo, canals
Condition Intact
Present owners Tri-Boro Sportsmen's Club
Location Northampton, Pennsylvania, USA
History Only largely-intact wooden canal boat surviving in the United States. Salvaged from flooded quarry. Preserved as an onshore exhibit.

Nobska
passenger ferry

Former name NANTUCKET
Built 1925 by Bath Iron Works, Bath, Maine
Original owners New England Steamship Co

Propulsion Steam, screw, 4-cylinder triple expansion, 1000hp
Tonnage 1082 gross
Length 210.0ft/64.01m
Breadth 50.0ft/15.24m
Materials Steel hull
Original use Passengers
Condition Undergoing restoration in drydock
Present owners Friends of the Nobska
Location Boston, Massachusetts, USA
History Built to serve as a ferryboat between Nantucket and Martha's Vineyard and the Massachusetts mainland. After retirement was taken to Baltimore, Maryland, to serve as a floating restaurant. Proposed for restoration to active steamer.
Bibliography B44, C16, C63, D395

North Carolina
battleship

Former name USS NORTH CAROLINA
Built 1940 by New York Naval Shipyard, Brooklyn, New York
Original owners United States Navy
Propulsion Steam turbines, 121,000hp
Tonnage 36,600 displacement
Length 728.75ft/222.12m
Breadth 108.35ft/33.03m
Draught 35.5ft/10.82m
Materials Steel throughout
Original use Battleship
Condition Intact
Present owners USS North Carolina Battleship Commission
Location Wilmington, N Carolina, USA
History Second World War battleship that took part in most of the campaigns of the Pacific War. Preserved as a floating exhibit.
Bibliography A8, B45, C64, D319

Northern Light
racing yacht

Built 1938
Propulsion Cutter rig
Length 70.0ft/21.3m
Materials Wood hull
Original use Racing yacht
Condition Fully restored, in operation
Present owners Seascope Systems
Contact address PO Box 119, Newport, Rhode Island 02840
Location Newport, Rhode Island, USA
History In use for charters.

Ocean Waif
schooner yacht

Built 1927 by Wilmington Boat Works, Wilmington, California

Original owners Hugh G Angelman
Propulsion Sail, schooner rig; petrol auxiliary engine
Length 44.0ft/13.41m
Breadth 13.0ft/3.96m
Draught 7.5ft/2.29m
Materials Wood throughout
Original use Yacht
Condition Intact
Present owners Los Angeles Maritime Museum
Location Los Angeles, California, USA
History Preserved as a floating exhibit.

Old Barge Café
oyster dealer vessel

Built Date not known
Propulsion Stationary
Length 68.0ft/20.73m
Breadth 16.0ft/4.88m
Materials Wood throughout
Original use Oyster dealer
Condition Intact, hull embedded in shore
Present owners John Tsilfoglou
Location New Haven, Connecticut, USA
History Last example of a type of houseboat formerly used on the waterfront of New York City by oyster wholesalers and retailers. In use as a restaurant and storage on shore.

Old Point
crab boat

Built 1909 by J G Wornom, Poquoson, Virginia
Original owners J G Wornom
Propulsion Oil engine; replaced by diesel engine
Tonnage 14 gross
Length 47.6ft/14.51m
Breadth 12.8ft/3.9m
Draught 4.0ft/1.22m
Materials Wood throughout
Original use Crabbing
Condition Intact
Present owners Chesapeake Bay Maritime Museum
Location St Michael's, Maryland, USA
History Preserved as a floating exhibit.

Olympia
protected cruiser

Former name USS OLYMPIA
Built 1892 by Union Iron Works, San Francisco, California
Original owners United States Navy
Propulsion Steam, screw, two triple expansion engines, 18,000hp
Tonnage 5586 displacement
Length 344.0ft/104.85m

Breadth 53.0ft/16.15m
Draught 21.5ft/6.55m
Materials Steel throughout
Original use Cruiser
Condition Intact
Present owners Independence Seaport Museum
Location Philadelphia, Pennsylvania, USA
History Following the end of the American Civil War the United States Navy entered a period of stagnation from which it did not emerge until the 1880s. During that decade a building programme was initiated to create a fleet of modern steel warships that would allow the country to take its place among the world's naval powers. OLYMPIA, launched at San Francisco in 1892, was a part of that building programme and is today its only survivor. She was originally rated as a cruiser, and named after the capital of the State of Washington. Her main armament consisted of four 8-inch guns in two turrets. She was also given the then popular ram bow, greatly overrated as a weapon. OLYMPIA's moment of glory came during the brief Spanish-American War of 1898, when she served as the flagship of Commodore George Dewey at the Battle of Manila Bay. This victory over a somewhat inferior naval force ensured American control of the Philippines during the period the European powers were establishing spheres of influence in the Far East. OLYMPIA brought Commodore Dewey back to New York for a victory celebration that is still one of the largest that harbour has seen. During the First World War OLYMPIA escorted convoys on the North Atlantic until April 1918 when she was sent to Murmansk to support the Allied intervention in northern Russia. The following year she was on the Adriatic Coast of the former Austro-Hungarian Empire as the Allies sought to restore order to that region She was then used to train midshipmen at the Naval Academy in Annapolis, Maryland, before being laid up at Philadelphia in 1922. After years of being preserved as a relic, she was taken over by the Cruiser Olympia Association in 1957.
Bibliography A8, C64, D157

Oscar Tybring I
sailing rescue vessel

Built 1895 by Colin Archer, Toldrodden, Norway. Designed by Colin Archer

Original owners Norwegian Society for the Rescue of the Shipwrecked
Propulsion Sail, ketch rig; diesel engine added
Length 47.0ft/14.33m
Materials Wood throughout
Original use Rescue vessel
Condition In sailing condition
Present owners Oscar Tybring Society
Location San Diego, California, USA
History Served as a Norwegian rescue vessel for forty-two years. In use as a yacht.

Overfalls
lightship

Former name BOSTON, CROSS RIP, CORNFIELD POINT
Built 1938 by Rice Brothers, East Boothbay, Maine
Original owners United States Lighthouse Service
Propulsion Diesel engine, 400hp
Tonnage 412 displacement
Length 114.75ft/34.98m
Breadth 26.0ft/7.92m
Draught 13.33ft/4.06m
Materials Steel throughout
Original use Lightship
Condition Intact
Present owners Lewes Historical Society

Olympia with Becuna inboard

Location Lewes, Delaware
History Lightship last used off the mouth of Delaware Bay. Preserved as a floating exhibit.
Bibliography C27

P A Denny
sternwheel towing vessel

Former name ROBIN D SCOTT
Built 1930 by Ward Engineering Works, Charleston, West Virginia
Original owners United States Army Corps of Engineers
Propulsion Diesel sternwheel, 460hp
Tonnage 77 gross
Length 109.0ft/33.22m
Breadth 23.0ft/7.01m
Materials Steel throughout
Original use Towing
Condition In operating condition
Present owners Charleston Festival Commission
Location Charleston, West Virginia, USA
History Built as a towboat for use assisting channel clearing work on the Ohio and Kanawha Rivers. In use for excursions.

Pampanito
submarine

Former name USS PAMPANITO
Built 1943 by Portsmouth Navy Yard, Kittery, Maine
Original owners United States Navy
Propulsion Diesel and electric motors
Tonnage 1526 displacement
Length 311.5ft/94.95m
Breadth 27.25ft/8.31m
Draught 15.25ft/4.65m
Materials Steel throughout
Original use Submarine
Condition Intact
Present owners San Francisco National Maritime Museum Association
Location San Francisco, California
History Submarine that saw action in the Pacific in the Second World War. Preserved as a floating exhibit.
Bibliography B45, C64, D45

Pardon Me
motor yacht

Built 1948 by Hutchinson, Alexandria Bay, New York
Propulsion Petrol engine 1800hp. Engine built by Packard
Length 48.0ft/14.6m
Breadth 10.5ft/3.2m
Materials Wood throughout
Original use Motor yacht
Condition Intact

Peking

Present owners Antique Boat Museum
Contact address 750 Mary Street, Clayton, New York 13624
Location Clayton, New York, USA
History Fast motor yacht claimed to be the world's largest 'runabout' cruiser, now exhibited indoors with a large number of smaller pleasure craft.

Paul Bunyan
lake tug

Built 1926 by Somers Lumber Co, Somers, Montana
Original owners Somers Lumber Co
Propulsion Diesel engine, 180hp
Length 65.0ft/19.81m
Breadth 17.0ft/5.18m
Draught 7.0ft/2.13m
Materials Wood throughout
Original use Log raft tug on Flathead Lake
Condition Intact
Present owners Miracle of America's Story Museum
Location Nr Polson, Montana, USA
History Log raft tug formerly employed on Flathead Lake. Preserved as an onshore exhibit.

PCF-1
fast patrol boat

Built 1965 by Seward Seacraft, Berwick, Louisiana
Original owners United States Navy
Official number PCF-1
Propulsion Twin screw, diesel 860hp. Engine built by General Motors
Tonnage 19 displacement
Length 50.0ft/15.3m
Breadth 13.0ft/4.0m

Draught 3.5ft/1.1m
Materials Steel throughout
Original use Patrol boat
Condition Intact
Present owners Naval Historical Center
Location Washington, DC, USA
History Prototype for a series of high speed patrol craft intended for use as small gunboats on the coast and rivers of Vietnam. Adapted from existing design for boats used to ferry crew out to oil drilling platforms in the Gulf of Mexico. Preserved as an onshore exhibit.
Bibliography C27a

Peking
trading barque

Former name ARETHUSA, HMS PEKIN, ARETHUSA
Built 1911 by Blohm & Voss, Hamburg, Germany
Original owners F Laeisz
Propulsion Sail, four-masted barque rig
Tonnage 3100 gross
Length 321.0ft/97.84m
Breadth 47.0ft/14.33m
Draught 15.35ft/4.68m
Materials Steel throughout except charthouse
Original use Cargo
Condition Intact, missing some deck fittings and interiors
Present owners South Street Seaport Museum
Location New York City, USA
History Built to carry nitrate from Chile to Europe via Cape Horn. Converted to a floating school in England in 1933. At New York since 1975. Preserved as a floating exhibit.
Bibliography A15, C96, D260

Penguin
motor fishing vessel

Built 1935 by Harvey Hurley, Wingate, Maryland
Propulsion Petrol engine
Tonnage 10 gross
Length 44.9ft/13.69m
Breadth 9.9ft/3.02m
Materials Wood throughout
Original use Fishing
Condition Intact
Present owners Calvert Marine Museum
Location Solomons Island, Maryland, USA
History Example of a type of Chesapeake Bay fishing boat known as a 'Hooper Island draketail'. Preserved as an onshore exhibit under cover.

Philadelphia

sailing/rowing gunboat

Built 1776 at Skenesborough (Whitehall), New York
Original owners Continental Navy
Propulsion Sail, single mast square-rigged
Length 53.3ft/16.25m
Breadth 15.5ft/4.72m
Draught 2.0ft/0.61m
Materials Wood throughout
Original use Gunboat
Condition Intact
Present owners Smithsonian Institution
Location Washington, DC, USA
History Early in the American War of Independence British strategists realised the rebelling colonies could be effectively cut in half by gaining control of the valley of the Hudson River and its northern extension containing Lake George and Lake Champlain. An army under General Burgoyne was organised to push south from Canada and meet a similar force coming north from New York. The plan eventually failed with Burgoyne's defeat at Saratoga before he could meet the southern force. To slow Burgoyne's southward advance the colonists hastily built a fleet of small gunboats at the south end of Lake Champlain. On 11 October 1776 this fleet engaged a British squadron in a cove behind Valcour Island. Two colonial vessels were sunk and the remainder retreated down the lake after nightfall. One of those sunk was the PHILADELPHIA, a three-gun, sloop-rigged vessel with the type of flat-bottomed hull known as a gundalow or 'gondola'. PHILADELPHIA was found by a diver in 1935 sitting on the bottom of the lake virtually intact, with her single mast still standing. She was raised using a floating crane, and displayed for many years in a shed beside the highway near Essex, New York. She toured New York State on a barge in 1940, and was later acquired by the Smithsonian Institution in Washington, DC. Today she forms a display in the naval history gallery of the Institution's Museum of American History. In spite of the lack of effective wood conservation techniques when she was raised, her hull is still remarkably intact. Most of the wood has shrunk, but retains its basic form. The cannon ball hole is clearly visible, with the cannon ball that sank her lying inside the hull.
Bibliography C64, D127, D214, D324

Pilot

pilot launch

Built 1914 at San Diego, California, USA
Original owners San Diego Pilots Association
Official number 212436
Propulsion Motor
Tonnage 19 gross
Length 52.0ft/15.8m
Breadth 13.7ft/4.2m
Materials Wood throughout
Original use Pilot launch
Condition Intact, recently retired
Present owners San Diego Maritime Museum
Location San Diego, California, USA
History Veteran San Diego pilot launch recently added to the fleet of museum vessels exhibited by the San Diego Maritime Museum.

Pilot

pilot schooner

Built 1924 by J F James & Co, Essex, Massachusetts
Original owners Boston Pilots Relief Society
Propulsion Sail, schooner rig; diesel engine, 200hp
Tonnage 140 gross
Length 116.2ft/35.42m
Breadth 25.2ft/7.68m
Materials Wood throughout
Original use Pilot vessel
Condition In sailing condition
Present owners Norman Paulsen
Location Gloucester, Massachusetts
History In use for charters.

Pioneer

trading sloop

Built 1885 by Pioneer Iron Works, Marcus Hook, Pennsylvania
Original owners Chester Rolling Mills
Propulsion Sail, sloop rig; altered to schooner; engine added
Tonnage 43 gross
Length 64.0ft/19.51m
Breadth 21.0ft/6.4m
Draught 9.0ft/2.74m
Materials Iron and steel hull
Original use Cargo
Condition In sailing condition
Present owners South Street Seaport Museum
Location New York City, USA
History In use for passenger day cruises and training.
Bibliography A15, D350

Portland

sternwheel towing steamer

Built 1947 by Northwest Marine Iron Works, Portland, Oregon
Original owners Port of Portland
Propulsion Steam, sternwheel, 1800hp
Tonnage 928 gross
Length 186.0ft/56.69m
Breadth 42.0ft/12.8m
Draught 7.0ft/2.13m
Materials Steel hull
Original use Towing
Condition Intact
Present owners Port Authority of Portland
Location Portland, Oregon, USA
History Last active sternwheel towboat on the Columbia River when retired. Preserved as a floating exhibit.
Bibliography B44, C87a, D392, D422

Portsmouth

lightship

Former name STONEHORSE, OVERFALLS, RELIEF, CAPE CHARLES
Built 1916 by Pusey & Jones, Wilmington, Delaware
Original owners United States Lighthouse Service
Propulsion Kerosine engine; converted to diesel, 315hp
Tonnage 360 displacement
Length 102.0ft/31.09m
Breadth 25.75ft/7.85m
Draught 11.35ft/3.46m
Materials Steel throughout
Original use Lightship
Condition Intact
Present owners Portsmouth Lightship Museum
Location Portsmouth, Virginia, USA

Portland

History Preserved as an onshore exhibit.
Bibliography C27, D421

Potomac
Presidential yacht

Former name CG-96002, ELECTRA
Built 1934 by Manitowoc Shipbuilding Co, Manitowoc, Wisconsin
Original owners United States Coast Guard
Propulsion Diesel engines
Tonnage 416 displacement
Length 165.0ft/50.29m
Breadth 23.75ft/7.24m
Draught 8.0ft/2.44m
Materials Steel throughout
Original use Presidential yacht
Condition Recently fully restored, operational
Present owners Potomac Association
Contact address PO Box 2064, Oakland, California 94604
Location Oakland, California, USA
History Designed as one of a series of similar Coast Guard cutters but converted to a presidential yacht soon after completion. Used as a Coast Guard patrol vessel during the Second World War. Preserved as a floating exhibit and for harbour cruises.
Bibliography C18, D252

President
sidewheel river steamer

Former name CINCINNATI
Built 1925 by Midland Barge Co, Midland, Pennsylvania
Propulsion Steam, sidewheel; now motor driven
Length 291.5ft/88.8m
Breadth 84.0ft/25.6m
Depth 7.5ft/2.3m
Materials Steel hull
Original use River passengers and cargo
Condition In operation
Present owners Gateway Riverboat Cruises
Contact address 500 N Leonor K Sullivan Blvd, St Louis, MO 63102
Location St Louis, Missouri, USA
History Large Mississippi River sidewheel 'packet' converted to an excursion vessel with diesel units replacing the paddlewheels. Currently undergoing further internal conversion to a floating casino.

Principia
motor yacht

Built 1928 by Lake Union Drydock, Seattle, Washington. Designed by L E Geary

Original owners L A Macomber
Official number 60
Propulsion Diesel engine 250hp. Engine built by Atlas Imperial
Length 96.0ft/29.3m
Breadth 18.35ft/5.6m
Draught 7.5ft/2.3m
Materials Wood hull
Original use Yacht
Condition Recently restored
Present owners Independence Seaport Museum
Contact address 211 S Columbus Blvd & Walnut St, Philadelphia 19106
Location Philadelphia, Pennsylvania, USA
History Motor yacht of the 1920s fully restored by the maritime museum in Philadelphia, and maintained by them for charters and museum events.
Bibliography A1, D53

Priscilla
oyster dredger

Built 1888 by Elisha Saxon, Patchogue, Long Island, New York
Propulsion Sail, schooner rig
Tonnage 11 gross
Length 34.2ft/10.42m
Breadth 14.0ft/4.27m
Draught 3.3ft/1.0m
Materials Wood throughout

Original use Oystering
Condition Intact
Present owners Suffolk Marine Museum
Location West Sayville, New York
History Preserved as a floating exhibit.

PT-309
motor torpedo boat

Built 1944 by Higgins Industries, New Orleans, Louisiana
Original owners United States Navy
Official number PT-309
Tonnage 56 displacement
Length 78.0ft/23.8m
Breadth 20.0ft/6.1m
Draught 5.5ft/1.7m
Original use Torpedo boat
Condition Undergoing restoration
Present owners Admiral Nimitz Museum of the Pacific War
Contact address PO Box 777, Fredericksburg, Texas 78624
Location LaPorte, Texas, USA
History Last surviving PT boat that saw action during the Second World War. Proposed as an exhibit.
Bibliography C27a

PT-617
motor torpedo boat

Built 1945 by Elco Boat Works, Bayonne, New Jersey
Original owners United States Navy
Propulsion Three petrol engines
Tonnage 55 displacement
Length 80.0ft/24.38m
Breadth 20.67ft/6.3m
Draught 5.5ft/1.68m
Materials Wood throughout
Original use Torpedo boat
Condition Intact
Present owners USS Massachusetts Memorial Commission
Location Fall River, Massachusetts
History Only restored example of an Elco-type torpedo boat of the Second World War. Preserved as an indoor exhibit.

PT-658
motor torpedo boat

Built 1945 by Higgins Industries, New Orleans, Louisiana
Original owners United States Navy
Official number PT-658
Propulsion Petrol engines
Length 78.0ft/23.8m
Breadth 20.0ft/6.1m
Draught 5.5ft/1.7m
Materials Wood throughout
Original use Torpedo boat

PTF-17

Condition Hull intact, needs extensive restoration
Present owners Oregon Museum of Science and Industry, Portland, Oregon
Location Portland, Oregon, USA
History Built for the Second World War but completed too late to be sent overseas. Employed by the Navy as a remote-controlled target. Sold for commercial use in June 1958. To be restored for exhibition as a PT boat of 1945.
Bibliography C27a

PT-695
motor torpedo boat

Built 1944 by Vosper, Annapolis, Maryland
Original owners United States Navy
Length 72.5ft/22.1m
Materials Wood throughout
Original use Torpedo boat
Condition Intact
Present owners American Patrol Boats Museum
Location Rio Vista, California, USA
History Torpedo boat built for use in the Second World War but completed too late to see action. Preserved as a floating exhibit by a group that specialises in restoring small naval vessels.

PT-796
motor torpedo boat

Built 1945 by Higgins Industries, New Orleans, Louisiana
Original owners United States Navy
Propulsion Three petrol engines
Tonnage 56 displacement
Length 78.0ft/23.77m
Breadth 20.0ft/6.1m
Draught 5.0ft/1.52m
Materials Wood throughout
Original use Torpedo boat
Condition Intact
Present owners USS Massachusetts Memorial Commission
Location Fall River, Massachusetts
History Only restored example of a Higgins-type torpedo boat of the Second World War. Preserved as an indoor exhibit.

PTF-17
motor gunboat

Built 1968 by John Trumpy & Son, Annapolis, Maryland
Original owners United States Navy
Propulsion Two diesel engines, 6200hp
Tonnage 69 displacement

Length 80.33ft/24.48m
Breadth 24.58ft/4.57m
Materials Wood throughout
Original use Gunboat
Condition Intact
Present owners Buffalo Naval and Servicemen's Park
Location Buffalo, New York
History Fast gunboat based on the PT boats of the Second World War. Preserved as an onshore exhibit.

Q-630
personnel launch/workboat

Built 1950s by Tacoma Boat Building, Tacoma, Washington
Original owners United States Army
Length 65.0ft/19.8m
Condition Intact, afloat
Present owners American Patrol Boats Museum
Location Rio Vista, California, USA
History Small launch used as a personnel ferry and general workboat by the United States Army. Preserved by a group that specialises in the restoration of small naval craft. Floating exhibit.

Queen
excursion steamer

Built 1884 by Dubuque Boiler Works, Dubuque, Iowa
Original owners Burlington, Cedar Rapids & Northern Railroad
Propulsion Steam, screw
Tonnage 35 gross
Length 75.0ft/23.37m
Breadth 15.0ft/4.57m
Materials Steel hull, wood superstructure
Original use Excursions
Condition Intact, awaiting restoration
Present owners Adventureland Amusement Park
Location Des Moines, Iowa, USA
History Small lake excursion steamer restored to original appearance in the 1980s. Laid up awaiting further restoration.

Queen Mary
transatlantic liner

Built 1936 by John Brown & Co, Clydebank, Scotland
Original owners Cunard White Star Ltd

Propulsion Steam turbines, 40,000hp
Tonnage 81,235 gross
Length 1019.0ft/310.59m
Breadth 118.6ft/36.15m
Draught 39.0ft/11.89m
Materials Steel throughout
Original use Passengers
Condition Intact, some internal alterations
Present owners City of Long Beach
Location Long Beach, California
History Until the advent of the supertankers of the 1960s, the North Atlantic passenger liners were the giants of the maritime world. When construction of the QUEEN MARY was begun in 1930 her owners, the Cunard Line, had been operating passenger steamers on the Atlantic for ninety years. International rivalry for the largest, fastest and most magnificently outfitted liner on the route had become intense after the turn of this century. QUEEN MARY surpassed the German giants BREMEN and EUROPA in size and succeeded in capturing the North Atlantic speed record, but by the time she entered service in 1936, she was slightly exceeded in size by the

Queen Mary

French NORMANDIE. Her running mate, QUEEN ELIZABETH, more than made up for this, but was unable to enter service before the outbreak of the Second World War. Both Queens performed outstanding service during the war as troopships, operating in both the Atlantic and Pacific. After the war they were both reconverted for passenger service on the North Atlantic. Finally retired in 1967, QUEEN MARY was purchased by the City of Long Beach, California, with funds raised through leases for offshore oil drilling. She is now moored permanently in the harbour of Long Beach as a floating hotel, shopping mall and maritime museum. Visitors are able to tour restored spaces that include the bridge, engineroom, main ballroom, staterooms for various classes, and reconstructed Second World War troop accommodations. An underwater tunnel takes visitors outside the hull to view one of the ship's giant propellers.
Bibliography D108, 112, 148, 156, 493, 572

Ralph J Scott
fireboat

Former name L A CITY NO 2
Built 1925 at Los Angeles, California, USA
Original owners City of Los Angeles
Propulsion Petrol engines, 1525hp
Tonnage 106 gross
Length 93.9ft/28.6m
Breadth 19.0ft/5.8m
Materials Steel throughout
Original use Fireboat
Condition Intact
Present owners Los Angeles Maritime Museum
Location Los Angeles, California, USA
History Former fireboat stationed in the Port of Los Angeles. Currently maintained as a floating exhibit of the Los Angeles Maritime Museum.

Rebecca T Ruark
oyster dredger

Built 1886 at Taylor's Island, Maryland
Propulsion Sail, sloop rig ('skipjack')
Tonnage 10 gross
Length 47.3ft/14.4m
Breadth 15.7ft/4.8m
Materials Wood throughout
Original use Oystering
Condition In sailing condition
Location Cambridge, Maryland, USA
History Built for oyster dredging under sail in Chesapeake Bay. One of a small fleet of sailing craft still engaged in this

Record

work.

Record
motor passenger/cargo vessel

Built 1914 by Stenodegard Shipyard, Vestnes, Norway
Original owners Rekord og Vigra Rutelag Co
Propulsion Diesel engine. Engine built by Burmeister & Wain (original); now Brunvoll
Tonnage 47 gross
Length 60.9ft/18.53m
Breadth 14.9ft/4.52m
Draught 10.0ft/3.05m
Materials Wood throughout
Original use Cargo and passengers
Condition Recently restored, in operating condition
Present owners Maritime & Yachting Museum
Contact address 2000 Jensen Beach Blvd, Jensen Beach, Florida 34957
Location Jensen Beach, Florida, USA
History Small Norwegian cargo vessel restored to operating condition as a yacht, and now doing charter work in Florida.

Reiss
steam tug

Former name Q A GILMORE
Built 1913 Cleveland, Ohio
Propulsion Steam, screw
Tonnage 99 gross
Length 71.0ft/21.64m
Breadth 20.0ft/6.1m
Materials Steel throughout
Original use Tug

Condition Intact
Present owners R J and Diane Peterson
Location Douglas, Michigan, USA
History Typical Great Lakes harbour tug of the turn of the century. Preserved as a floating exhibit.

Relief
lightship

Former name SAN FRANCISCO, BLUNTS REEF
Built 1904 by New York Shipbuilding Co, Camden, New Jersey
Original owners United States Lighthouse Establishment
Propulsion Steam, screw, compound
Tonnage 668 displacement
Length 129.0ft/39.32m
Breadth 29.0ft/8.8m
Draught 14.0ft/4.27m
Materials Steel hull, wood deckhouses
Original use Lightship
Condition Intact
Present owners Northwest Seaport
Location Seattle, Washington, USA
History Last surviving American lightship with original steam engine. Preserved as a floating exhibit.
Bibliography C27

Requin
submarine

Former name USS REQUIN
Built 1945 by Portsmouth Navy Yard, Kittery, Maine
Original owners United States Navy
Propulsion Diesel and electric motors
Tonnage 1854 displacement
Length 312.0ft/95.1m

Breadth 27.0ft/8.23m
Draught 17.0ft/5.18m
Materials Steel throughout
Original use Submarine
Condition Intact
Present owners The Carnegie
Location Pittsburgh, Pennsylvania, USA
History Submarine completed too late to see action in the Second World War. Preserved as a floating exhibit.
Bibliography C64, D335

Richard Robbins Sr
oyster dredger

Built 1902 by William Parsons, Greenwich, New Jersey
Propulsion Sail, schooner rig
Tonnage 30 gross
Length 49.5ft/15.09m
Breadth 18.5ft/5.58m
Draught 5.4ft/1.65m
Materials Wood throughout
Original use Oystering
Condition In sailing condition
Present owners Classic Sail Windjammer Co
Location River Edge, New Jersey, USA
History In use for cruises.

Roann
motor fishing boat

Built 1947 at Thomaston, Maine
Propulsion Diesel engine, 350hp
Tonnage 43 gross
Length 53.5ft/16.3m
Breadth 16.6ft/5.1m
Materials Wood hull
Original use Fishing

Condition Intact
Present owners Mystic Seaport Museum
Location Mystic, Connecticut, USA
History Inshore motor fishing boat of the type once common in New England. Recently acquired as part of the Mystic Seaport Museum's current policy of preserving examples of soon to disappear New England fishing craft.

Roaring Bull
sternwheel river ferry

Built at Millersburg, Pennsylvania (date not known)
Original owners Millersburg Ferry
Propulsion Sternwheel; chain drive from petrol engine
Materials Wood hull
Original use Ferryboat
Condition In operation
Present owners Millersburg Ferry Boat Association
Contact address PO Box 93, Millersburg, Pennsylvania 17061
Location Millersburg, Pennsylvania, USA
History One of last two sternwheel ferryboats in the USA. Employed in carrying automobiles and foot passengers across the Susquehanna River.

Roseway
pilot schooner

Built 1926 by J F James Shipyard, Essex, Massachusetts
Original owners Boston Pilots Relief Society
Propulsion Sail, schooner rig; diesel engine
Tonnage 97 gross
Length 94.5ft/28.8m
Breadth 24.6ft/7.5m
Materials Wood throughout
Original use Pilot vessel
Condition In sailing condition
Present owners Yankee Schooner Cruises
Location Camden, Maine, USA
History Built for use as an auxiliary pilot schooner off the port of Boston. In use for cruises.
Bibliography A15, D236

Rosie Parks
oyster dredger

Built 1955 by Bronza M Parks, Wingate, Maryland
Original owners Captain Orville Parks
Propulsion Sail, sloop rig ('skipjack' type)
Tonnage 8 gross
Length 46.2ft/14.08m
Breadth 16.7ft/5.09m
Materials Wood throughout
Original use Oystering
Condition Intact
Present owners Chesapeake Bay Maritime Museum
Location St Michael's, Maryland, USA
History Preserved as a floating exhibit.

Rumrunner II
fast motorboat

Built 1929 by Elco Corporation, Bayonne, New Jersey, USA
Propulsion Two diesel engines; 700hp (present). Engines built by Caterpillar
Length 58.0ft/17.7m
Breadth 11.5ft/3.5m
Materials Wood throughout
Original use Liquor smuggling
Condition In operation; restored as

Sabino

passenger vessel
Present owners Yankee Boat Peddlers, Newport, Rhode Island
Location Newport, Rhode Island, USA
History Built as a fast motorboat for smuggling liquor during the American period of 'Prohibition'. Fully restored as a yacht for use in excursions and charters at Newport.

Sabino
passenger river steamer

Former name TOURIST
Built 1908 by H Irving Adams, East Boothbay, Maine
Original owners Damariscotta Steamboat Co
Propulsion Steam, screw, compound, 110hp
Tonnage 25 gross
Length 57.25ft/17.45m
Breadth 15.25ft/4.65m
Draught 6.3ft/1.92m

Materials Wood throughout
Original use Passengers
Condition In operation
Present owners Mystic Seaport Museum
Location Mystic, Connecticut, USA
History Built to carry passengers between towns on the Damariscotta River in Maine. Currently an operating steamboat, used for excursions.
Bibliography B6, D107, D140, D144, D363

Sanctuary
hospital ship

Former name USS SANCTUARY
Built 1944
Original owners United States Navy
Propulsion Steam turbines
Materials Steel throughout
Original use Hospital ship
Condition Intact, externally unaltered
Present owners Project Life
Location Baltimore, Maryland, USA
History Last surviving United States hospital ship of the Second World War era. Also used in later wars. Currently being converted to temporary housing.

Savannah
nuclear cargo/passenger liner

Built 1959 by New York Shipbuilding Co, Camden, New Jersey
Original owners United States Department of Commerce
Propulsion Steam turbines, nuclear reactor
Tonnage 22,000 gross
Length 595.5ft/181.51m
Breadth 78.0ft/23.77m
Draught 29.5ft/8.99m
Materials Steel throughout
Original use Cargo and passengers
Condition Intact, in reserve fleet, laid up
Present owners United States Maritime Administration
Location Fort Eustis, Virginia, USA
History Combination passenger and cargo vessel that was the world's first nuclear-powered merchant vessel.
Bibliography D280

Scorpion
submarine

Former name POVODNAYA LODKA
Built 1973 in Russia
Original owners Soviet Navy
Official number F-540
Propulsion Diesel and electric motors

Tonnage 2475 displacement
Length 300.0ft/91.4m
Materials Steel throughout
Original use Submarine
Condition Intact
Location Long Beach, California
History Russian submarine (NATO designation 'Foxtrot') acquired during the post-Cold War reduction in the former Soviet Navy, for use as a floating exhibition in the West. Spent first two years on exhibit in Sydney, Australia, and was then taken to Long Beach in 1998 where she is moored adjacent to the passenger liner QUEEN MARY.

Seehund Type
midget submarine

Built c1945 in Germany
Original owners German Navy
Propulsion Diesel engine
Length 38.9ft/11.86m
Materials Steel throughout
Original use Midget submarine
Condition Intact
Present owners Navy Memorial Museum
Location Washington, DC, USA
History German midget submarine of the Second World War. Preserved as an indoor exhibit.

Seehund Type
midget submarine

Built c1945 in Germany
Original owners German Navy
Propulsion Diesel engine
Length 38.9ft/11.86m
Materials Steel throughout
Original use Midget submarine
Condition Intact
Present owners Submarine Force Library and Museum
Location Groton, Connecticut, USA
History German midget submarine of the Second World War. Preserved as an onshore exhibit.

Sequoia
motor yacht

Former name SEQUOIA II
Built 1925 by Mathis Yacht Building, Camden, New Jersey
Original owners Richard M Cadwalader
Propulsion Petrol engines
Tonnage 100 displacement
Length 104.0ft/31.7m
Breadth 19.0ft/5.79m
Draught 4.42ft/1.35m
Materials Wood throughout

Original use Yacht
Condition Intact, fully restored
Present owners NORSHIPCO
Location Norfolk, Virginia, USA
History Presidential yacht from 1932 until the Carter administration. In use as a corporate yacht.
Bibliography C18, D409

Sergeant Floyd
river towing/inspection vessel

Built 1932 by Howard Shipyards, Jeffersonville, Indiana
Original owners United States Army Corps of Engineers
Propulsion Diesel engines, twin screw
Tonnage 306 displacement
Length 138.0ft/42.06m
Breadth 30.0ft/9.14m
Draught 3.75ft/1.14m
Materials Steel hull, wood superstructure
Original use Towing and inspection
Condition Intact
Present owners City of Sioux City
Location Sioux City, Iowa, USA
History Employed by the Army Engineers on the Missouri River. Preserved as an onshore exhibit.

Shamrock V
racing yacht

Former name QUADRIFOGLIO
Built 1930 by Camper and Nicholson,

Shamrock V

Gosport, England
Original owners Sir Thomas Lipton
Propulsion Sail, cutter rig
Tonnage 104 gross
Length 119.83ft/36.52m
Breadth 19.67ft/6.0m
Draught 14.67ft/4.47m
Materials Wood throughout
Original use Racing yacht
Condition Fully restored, in sailing condition
Present owners Yacht Restoration School, Newport, Rhode Island
Location Newport, Rhode Island, USA
History Built as a British challenger for the America's Cup. Later a private yacht owned in Italy. Fully restored and presented to the Museum of Yachting in Newport, who later transferred her to the Yacht Restoration School. In use for cruises.
Bibliography A1, C50, D261, D462

Sherman Zwicker
fishing schooner

Built 1941 by Smith & Rhuland, Lunenburg, Nova Scotia
Original owners Zwicker & Co
Propulsion Sail, schooner rig; diesel engines
Tonnage 180 gross
Length 142.0ft/43.28m
Breadth 27.0ft/8.23m
Draught 14.0ft/4.27m
Materials Wood throughout
Original use Fishing
Condition Intact
Present owners Grand Banks Schooner Museum
Location Bath, Maine, USA
History Preserved as a floating exhibit.

Silversides
submarine

Former name USS SILVERSIDES
Built 1940 by Mare Island Navy Yard, Vallejo, California
Original owners United States Navy
Propulsion Diesel and electric motors
Tonnage 1526 displacement
Length 311.8ft/95.04m
Breadth 27.3ft/8.32m
Draught 15.0ft/4.57m
Materials Steel throughout
Original use Submarine
Condition Intact
Present owners USS Silversides and Maritime Museum
Location Muskegon, Michigan, USA
History Submarine that saw extensive action in the Second World War. Preserved as a floating exhibit.
Bibliography B45, C64, D513, D534

ST-2031
motor tug

Built Date not known
Original owners United States Army
Propulsion Diesel engine
Length 45.0ft/13.72m
Materials Steel throughout
Original use Tug
Condition Intact
Present owners US Army
Transportation Museum
Location Fort Eustis, Virginia, USA
History Small tug of the type used to
assist in dredging operations.
Preserved as an onshore exhibit.

Stanley Norman
oyster dredger

Built 1902 by Otis Lloyd, Salisbury,
Maryland
Original owners Robert L Shores, Deal
Island
Propulsion Sail, sloop rig ('skipjack'
type)
Tonnage 8 gross
Length 47.5ft/14.48m
Breadth 15.3ft/4.66m
Materials Wood throughout
Original use Oystering
Condition In sailing condition
Present owners Chesapeake Bay
Foundation
Location Annapolis, Maryland, USA
History In use for educational cruises.
Bibliography D216

Star of India
full-rigged trading vessel

Former name EUTERPE
Built 1863 by Gibson, McDonald &
Arnold, Ramsay, Isle of Man, Great
Britain
Original owners Wakefield Nash & Co,
Liverpool
Propulsion Sail, full-rigged ship; later
barque
Tonnage 1318 gross
Length 205.5ft/62.64m
Breadth 35.2ft/10.73m
Draught 21.5ft/6.55m
Materials Iron hull, wood deckhouse,
wood and iron masts
Original use Cargo and passengers
Condition Intact
Present owners Maritime Museum
Association of San Diego
Location San Diego, California, USA
History Built to carry passengers and
cargo between Great Britain and New
Zealand. Later sailed under the
American flag supporting salmon
canneries in Alaska. Preserved as a

ST-2031

floating exhibit.
Bibliography D16, 32, 248, 281, 333, 334,
431, F22

Ste Claire
excursion steamer

Built 1911 by Toledo Shipbuilding Co,
Toledo, Ohio
Original owners Detroit, Belle Isle &
Windsor Ferry Co
Propulsion Steam, screw, triple-
expansion, 2000hp
Tonnage 870 gross
Length 181.0ft/55.17m
Breadth 50.0ft/15.24m
Draught 13.0ft/3.96m
Materials Steel hull, wood
superstructure
Original use Excursions
Condition Intact, not in use, laid up
Present owners International Shipping
Co
Location Detroit, Michigan, USA
History Built to carry passengers
between Detroit, Michigan and an
amusement park and picnic grounds
on an island in the Detroit River.
Bibliography B44

Ste Genevieve
river dredger

Built 1932 by Dravo, Pittsburgh,
Pennsylvania
Original owners United States Army

Corps of Engineers
Propulsion Steam, turbine, sternwheel,
1760hp
Tonnage 1390 displacement
Length 267.0ft/81.38m
Breadth 47.1ft/14.36m
Materials Wood throughout
Original use Dredger
Condition Intact
Present owners Marine Learning
Institute, Portage des Sioux, Missouri
Location St Charles, Missouri, USA
History Steam cutterhead pipeline
dredger, formerly used to keep
navigable channels open on the
Mississippi, Ohio and Missouri Rivers.
Preserved as a floating exhibit.

Stephen Taber
trading schooner

Built 1871 by A W Vancott, Glenwood,
New York
Original owners Cox Brothers
Propulsion Sail, schooner rig
Tonnage 53.8 gross
Length 64.2ft/19.26m
Breadth 22.3ft/6.8m
Materials Wood throughout
Original use Cargo
Condition In sailing condition
Present owners Orville and Ellen
Barnes
Location Camden, Maine, USA
History Oldest American coastal
schooner still sailing that was never

substantially altered. In use for
cruises.
Bibliography A1, C93, D308

Stewart
destroyer escort

Former name USS STEWART
Built 1942 by Brown Shipbuilding Co,
Houston, Texas
Original owners United States Navy
Propulsion Diesel engines
Tonnage 1200 displacement
Length 306.0ft/93.27m
Breadth 37.0ft/11.28m
Draught 12.25ft/3.73m
Materials Steel throughout
Original use Destroyer escort
Condition Intact
Present owners State of Texas
Location Galveston, Texas, USA
History Only Second World War
destroyer escort of its type currently
being preserved. Preserved as an
onshore exhibit.
Bibliography B45, C64

Sumpter Valley Dredger
gold mining dredger

Built 1935 by the Sumpter Valley
Dredging Co, near Sumpter, Oregon
Original owners Sumpter Valley
Dredging Co
Propulsion Winched into position by
electric motors

Length 120ft/36.6m
Breadth 52ft/15.8m
Materials Wood hull, deckhouse sided with sheet metal
Original use Gold mining dredger
Condition Intact, aground
Present owners Oregon Department of Parks and Recreation
Location Near Sumpter, Oregon, USA
History Mining dredger built as a result of a 1934 increase in the price of gold. Some fittings were salvaged from two earlier dredgers active 1913-1924 whose hull remains survive nearby. Exhibited aground.

Swift of Ipswich
schooner yacht

Built 1939 by William Robinson, Ipswich, Massachusetts, USA. Designed by Howard I Chapelle
Propulsion Sail, topsail schooner rig; auxiliary engine, 165hp
Tonnage 46 gross
Length 61.9ft/18.9m
Breadth 18.0ft/5.5m
Materials Wood throughout
Original use Yacht
Condition In sailing condition
Present owners Los Angeles Maritime Museum
Location Los Angeles, California
History Sailing yacht based on the design of a privateer schooner of the

late 1700s. Product of a collaboration between marine historian and naval architect Howard Chapelle and Ipswich shipbuilder William Robinson to create 'character' yachts based on Chapelle's research. The project was interrupted by the Second World War and never revived. At one time owned by actor James Cagney, and now a youth training vessel attached to the Los Angeles Maritime Museum.

Sylvina W Beal
trading schooner

Built 1911 by Adams Shipyard, East Boothbay, Maine
Original owners Charles Henry Beal
Propulsion Sail, schooner rig; diesel engine, 80hp
Tonnage 48 gross
Length 71.7ft/21.85m
Breadth 17.2ft/5.24m
Materials Wood throughout
Original use Cargo
Condition In sailing condition
Location Boothbay Harbor, Maine, USA
History Originally built to transport sardines on the coast of Maine. In use for cruises.
Bibliography D122

Tabor Boy
pilot schooner

Former name BESTEVAER
Built 1914 by Netherlands Government, Netherlands
Original owners Netherlands Pilotage Service
Propulsion Sail, topsail schooner rig; diesel engine, 330hp
Tonnage 99 gross
Length 92.0ft/28.04m
Breadth 20.7ft/6.31m
Draught 5.15ft/1.57m
Materials Iron hull, wood deckhouses
Original use Pilot vessel
Condition In sailing condition
Present owners Tabor Academy
Location Marion, Massachusetts, USA
History Built as a Dutch North Sea pilot schooner. Acquired after the Second World War for use as a sail training vessel. In use for sail training.
Bibliography A15

Tamaroa
seagoing tug

Former name USCGS TAMAROA, USS ZUNI
Built 1943 by Commercial Iron Works, Portland, Oregon
Original owners United States Navy
Official number WMEC-166
Propulsion Diesel engine

Tonnage 1235 displacement
Length 205.0ft/62.5m
Breadth 38.5ft/11.7m
Draught 15.25ft/4.6m
Materials Steel throughout
Original use Seagoing tug
Condition Intact
Present owners Hudson River Park Conservancy
Contact address Pier 86, West 46th Street & 12th Ave, New York, NY 10036
Location New York, USA
History As the USS ZUNI served in the Pacific during the last years of the Second World War, towing barges and drydocks and assisting warships disabled by enemy action. Transferred to the Coast Guard in 1946, she spent her last active years stationed in the Port of New York. In late 1998 was being considered for use as floating headquarters for an agency creating a park along several miles of former commercial waterfront on Manhattan Island's west side.
Bibliography C64

Taney
Coast Guard cutter

Former name USCGS TANEY
Built 1936 by Philadelphia Navy Yard, Philadelphia, Pennsylvania
Original owners United States Coast Guard
Propulsion Steam turbines, twin screw, 6200hp
Tonnage 2750 displacement
Length 327.0ft/99.67m
Breadth 41.2ft/12.56m
Draught 15.3ft/4.55m
Materials Steel throughout
Original use Coast Guard patrol vessel
Condition Intact
Present owners Baltimore Maritime Museum
Location Baltimore, Maryland, USA
History Survived the Japanese attack on Pearl Harbor in December 1941. Preserved as a floating exhibit.
Bibliography B45, C86

Telco
cable maintenance vessel

Built 1938 at Sausalito, California
Original owners Pacific Telephone and Telegraph Co
Propulsion Diesel, 120hp
Tonnage 12 gross
Length 40.9ft/12.5m
Breadth 11.6ft/3.5m
Materials Wood hull

Sylvina W Beal

Original use Tug and cable
maintenance
Condition Intact, recently retired
Present owners San Francisco Maritime
National Historical Park
Location San Francisco, California,
USA
History Preserved as a floating exhibit.

Texas
battleship

Former name USS TEXAS
Built 1912 by Newport News
Shipbuilding & Drydock Co, Newport
News, Virginia
Original owners United States Navy
Propulsion Steam, screw, two
4-cylinder triple expansion, 28,100hp
Tonnage 27,000 displacement
Length 573.0ft/174.65m
Breadth 95.2ft/29.02m
Draught 29.7ft/9.05m
Materials Steel throughout
Original use Battleship
Condition Intact
Present owners State of Texas
Location San Jacinto, Texas
History The launching of
HMS DREADNOUGHT in 1906
revolutionised naval warfare.
Overnight the world's existing
warships were rendered obsolete.
Where the largest battleships up to that
time had mounted four guns in two
turrets, DREADNOUGHT mounted ten
guns in five turrets. She was also
significantly larger than any of her
predecessors. It is no wonder that she
gave her name to a whole generation of
capital ships. Following her building a
race began among the major naval
powers to produce entire battle fleets
of similar vessels. Today the only
survivor of that era is the TEXAS,
preserved by the State after which she
was named. Her active service spanned
both world wars, but she only saw
action in the second, providing
support for amphibious landings in
southern France, Normandy and the
Pacific islands. During her various
shore bombardments she fired a total
of 4278 14-inch shells from her main
armament. She was hit twice by shells
from enemy shore batteries, both times
while lying off Cherbourg, France, in
June 1944. After the war TEXAS was
decommissioned and placed in reserve
at Baltimore, Maryland. She was
turned over to the State of Texas in
1948. Her permanent berth lies beside
the ship channel leading into the Port
of Houston, at the site of the Battle of
San Jacinto in the Texan War for

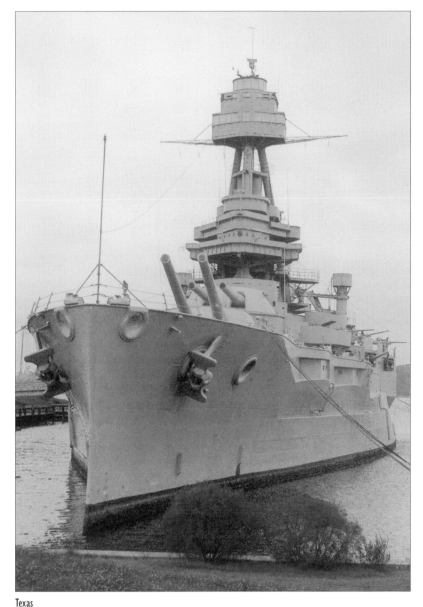
Texas

Independence. Virtually every interior
space survives unaltered, and many
may be visited by the public including
the interior of a turret mounting two
giant 14-inch guns and an engineroom
with some of the largest reciprocating
engines surviving in any vessel.
Bibliography B45, C64, D152, 320, 411,
486

Thania
motor yacht

Former name TODDY WAX
Built 1905 by Herreshoff
Manufacturing Co, Bristol, Rhode
Island
Original owners W P Hengey
Propulsion Motor
Length 53.5ft/16.3m
Breadth 10.5ft/3.2m
Draught 2.75ft/0.8m
Materials Wood throughout

Original use Motor yacht
Condition Intact; needs some
restoration
Present owners Herreshoff Marine
Museum
Contact address 7 Burnside Street,
Bristol, Rhode Island 02809
Location Bristol, Rhode Island, USA
History Motor yacht designed and built
by the Herreshoff Boatyard. Now
exhibited indoors in a museum created
in former buildings of the boatyard.

The Sullivans
destroyer

Former name USS THE SULLIVANS
Built 1943 by Bethlehem Steel Co, San
Francisco, California
Original owners United States Navy
Propulsion Steam turbines, 60,000hp
Tonnage 2100 displacement
Length 376.5ft/114.76m

Breadth 39.5ft/12.04m
Draught 18.0ft/5.49m
Materials Steel throughout
Original use Destroyer
Condition Intact
Present owners Buffalo Naval and
Servicemen's Park
Location Buffalo, New York, USA
History Destroyer that saw action in
the Second World War. Preserved as a
floating exhibit.
Bibliography B45, C64, D441

Ticonderoga
sidewheel lake steamer

Built 1906 by T S Marvel, Newburgh,
New York (pre-fabricated) and
Shelburne, Vermont
Original owners Champlain
Transportation Co
Propulsion Steam, sidewheel, beam
engine. Engine built by W & A
Fletcher, Hoboken, New Jersey
Tonnage 892 gross
Length 212.2ft/64.68m
Breadth 57.9ft/17.65m
Materials Steel hull, wood
superstructure
Original use Passengers
Condition Intact
Present owners Shelburne Museum
Location Shelburne, Vermont
History Lake Champlain on the border
between the states of New York and
Vermont was one of the first bodies of
water in the world to have regular
steam navigation. The earliest
steamboat was placed in service on its
waters in 1809, only two years after
Robert Fulton's success with a similar
craft on the Hudson River.
TICONDEROGA brought the Lake's
steamboat era to a close with her last
active season in the summer of 1953.
She had been launched forty-seven
years earlier at Shelburne Harbor,
Vermont, assembled from
prefabricated sections built in a
shipyard at Newburgh on the Hudon
River. Her walking beam sidewheel
engine was built by the W & A Fletcher
Company of Hoboken, New Jersey.
Today it is one of only two such
engines preserved in the original
vessels. The other is in the ferryboat
EUREKA, now a floating museum in
San Francisco. Following her
retirement in 1953 TICONDEROGA was
acquired by Mrs J Watson Webb for the
extensive museum village she was
creating at Shelburne, Vermont.
During the winter when the gound was
frozen, the 220ft steamboat was hauled
two miles overland to the museum on

temporary double railway lines. She sits on a rural hillside from which the Lake can only be glimpsed far in the distance. Surrounding her is a collection of typical Vermont houses and farm buildings, and an equally landlocked nineteenth-century lighthouse moved from the Lake. TICONDEROGA's gleaming white superstructure and carpeted Edwardian-era interiors have been immaculately restored. Both the steamboat and the lighthouse are used to display a collection of fine paintings and prints showing the steamboat era in the eastern United States.
Bibliography A17, B44, D231

Torsk
submarine

Former name USS TORSK
Built 1944 by Portsmouth Navy Yard, Kittery, Maine
Original owners United States Navy
Propulsion Diesel and electric motors
Tonnage 1570 displacement
Length 311.75ft/95.02m
Breadth 27.25ft/8.31m
Draught 15.5ft/4.72m
Materials Steel throughout
Original use Submarine
Condition Intact
Present owners Baltimore Maritime Museum
Location Baltimore, Maryland, USA
History Submarine that saw action in the Pacific during the Second World War. Preserved as a floating exhibit.
Bibliography B45, C64

Trieste
undersea research vessel

Built 1953 at Castellamare di Stabia, Italy
Original owners Jacques Picard
Propulsion Tethered submersible
Length 59.5ft/18.14m
Breadth 11.5ft/3.51m
Draught 18.0ft/5.49m
Materials Steel throughout
Original use Undersea research
Condition Intact
Present owners Navy Memorial Museum
Location Washington, DC, USA
History Employed in exploring the deepest areas of the oceans. Also used to search for submarines lost by the United States Navy. Preserved as an indoor exhibit.
Bibliography C64, D474

Ticonderoga

Trieste II
underwater research vessel

Built 1964 by Mare Island Naval Shipyard, Vallejo, California
Original owners United States Navy
Official number DSV-1
Propulsion Motors, multiple propellers
Tonnage 85 displacement
Length 78.0ft/23.8m
Breadth 18.0ft/5.5m
Draught 12.5ft/3.8m
Materials Steel throughout
Original use Underwater research
Condition Intact
Present owners Naval Undersea Museum
Contact address 610 Dowell Street, Keyport, Washington 98345-7610
Location Keyport, Washington, USA
History Designed for use in deep diving research, as a replacement for the original TRIESTE which was showing signs of wear after ten years of use. Continued the work done by the first TRIESTE in recovering wreckage from the USS THRESHER, and was also used in deep diving training and experiments to develop further Navy deep submergence systems. Preserved as an onshore exhibit.
Bibliography C64

Trivia
racing yacht

Built 1902 by Herreshoff Manufacturing Co, Bristol, Rhode Island, USA
Original owners Harold Vanderbilt
Propulsion Cutter rig
Length 46.0ft/14.0m
Breadth 12.0ft/3.7m
Draught 7.0ft/2.1m
Materials Wood throughout
Original use Racing yacht
Condition Intact
Present owners Herreshoff Marine Museum
Contact address 7 Burnside Street, Bristol, Rhode Island 02809
Location Bristol, Rhode Island, USA
History Racing yacht designed and built by the Herreshoff Boatyard for Harold Vanderbilt. Now an exhibit in a museum created in former boatyard buildings.

Turner Joy
destroyer

Former name USS TURNER JOY
Built 1958 by Puget Sound Bridge & Dredging Co, Seattle, Washington
Original owners United States Navy
Propulsion Steam turbines, 70,000hp
Tonnage 4200 displacement
Length 418.5ft/127.56m
Breadth 45.0ft/13.72m
Draught 22.5ft/6.86m
Materials Steel throughout
Original use Destroyer
Condition Intact
Present owners Bremerton Historic Ships
Location Bremerton, Washington, USA
History Destroyer that saw action in the Vietnam War. Preserved as a floating exhibit.
Bibliography C64

Tuscarora
passenger lake steamer

Built 1900 at Blue Mountain Lake, New York
Original owners William West Durant
Propulsion Steam, screw
Length 76.0ft/23.16m
Materials Wood throughout
Original use Passengers
Condition Awaiting restoration
Present owners Peter Halsch
Location Blue Mountain Lake, NY
History The owner hopes to restore her and put her back in the water. She no longer has her original steam engine.

Twilite
motor fishing vessel

Built 1937 by Halvor Reiter, Bayfield, Wisconsin
Original owners Hokenson Brothers
Propulsion Diesel engine
Length 38.0ft/11.6m
Materials Wood hull, metal sheathed; wood deckhouse
Original use Fishing
Condition Intact
Present owners United States National Park Service
Contact address Apostle Islands National Lakeshore, Bayfield, Wisconsin
Location Bayfield, Wisconsin
History Type of Great Lakes fishing boat known as a 'fish tug', with deckhouse extending from bow to stern for protection in winter weather. Exhibited on shore in conjunction with buildings, smaller fishing craft, and artifacts of a small family-operated fishing business.

U-484
submarine

Built in Russia (date not known)
Original owners Soviet Navy
Official number B-484
Materials Steel throughout
Original use Submarine
Condition Intact
Location Tampa, Florida, USA
History Preserved as a floating exhibit.

U-505
submarine

Built 1941 by Deutsche Werft, Hamburg, Germany
Original owners German Navy
Propulsion Diesel and electric motors
Tonnage 1144 displacement
Length 252.0ft/76.81m
Breadth 22.75ft/6.93m
Draught 15.5ft/4.72m
Materials Steel throughout
Original use Submarine
Condition Intact
Present owners Museum of Science and Industry
Location Chicago, Illinois, USA
History German submarine captured at sea in the Second World War. Preserved as an onshore exhibit.
Bibliography A6, A8, D184, D516

United States
transatlantic liner

Built 1951 by Newport News

Shipbuilding & Drydock Co, Newport News, Virginia. Designed by Charles Francis Gibbs
Original owners United States Lines
Propulsion Steam turbines, 240,000hp
Tonnage 53,329 gross
Length 990.0ft/301.6m
Breadth 101.0ft/30.8m
Materials Steel hull, steel and aluminium superstructure
Original use Passengers
Condition Intact, has not operated since late 1960s
Location Philadelphia, Pennsylvania, USA
History Largest transatlantic passenger liner built in the United States, and holder of the speed record for passenger liners for both eastbound and westbound crossings. Has been laid up almost three decades. There have been proposals for conversion either to a cruise ship or to a floating hotel. At one point she was towed to Turkey, and later Russia, to have the asbestos insulation removed.

Urger
steam canal tug

Built 1901 by Johnson Brothers, Ferrysburg, Michigan
Propulsion Steam, screw; converted to diesel
Tonnage 45 gross
Length 73.42ft/22.38m
Breadth 15.8ft/4.82m
Draught 3.42ft/1.04m

Materials Steel throughout
Original use Tug
Present owners State of New York
Location Waterford, New York, USA
History Formerly used in maintaining the channels of the New York State Barge Canal. In operating condition; travelling exhibit.

Valley Camp
Great Lakes bulk carrier

Former name LOUIS W HILL
Built 1917 by American Shipbuilding Co, Lorain, Ohio
Original owners Hanna Mining Co
Propulsion Steam, screw, triple expansion, 1800hp
Tonnage 7038 gross
Length 525.0ft/160.02m
Breadth 58.0ft/17.68m
Materials Steel throughout
Original use Cargo
Condition Intact
Present owners Le Sault de Ste Marie Historical Sites
Location Sault Ste Marie, Michigan, USA
History Typical Great Lakes bulk carrier. Exhibited in dry berth.
Bibliography C97

Vernie S
passenger steamer

Former name FOUR SISTERS
Built 1897 at Glenwood, New York
Original owners Edward Bedell

Propulsion Steam, screw; converted to diesel
Tonnage 28 gross
Length 59.2ft/18.04m
Breadth 16.7ft/5.09m
Materials Wood throughout
Original use Passengers; later lighter
Condition Intact, needs extensive restoration
Present owners Captain's Cove Marina
Location Bridgeport, Connecticut, USA
History Preserved as an onshore exhibit.

Verrazzano
steam ferry

Built 1951 by Bethlehem Shipyards, Mariners Harbor, New York
Original owners New York City
Propulsion Steam, screw, uniflow, 4800hp. Engine built by Skinner
Tonnage 2285 gross
Length 269.0ft/82.0m
Breadth 69.0ft/21.0m
Materials Steel throughout
Original use Ferry
Present owners Verrazzano Associates
Location Brooklyn, New York, USA
History Undergoing renovation for theme park in Japan.

Victory Chimes
trading schooner

Former name DOMINO EFFECT, EDWIN & MAUD
Built 1900 by John M C Moore, Bethel,

Victory Chimes

Delaware
Original owners C C Paul & Co
Propulsion Sail, three-masted schooner rig
Tonnage 208 gross
Length 126.5ft/38.56m
Breadth 23.8ft/7.25m
Materials Wood throughout
Original use Cargo
Condition In sailing condition
Present owners Captain Kip Files and Captain Paul DeGaeta
Location Rockland, Maine, USA
History Built to carry cargo on Chesapeake and Delaware Bays, passing through the locks of the canals connecting those bays. In use for cruises.
Bibliography A15, C60, C93, D145, D146

Violet
fishing ketch

Former name JOHN B MANNING, VIOLET
Built 1911 by James Noble Shipyard, Fraserburgh, Scotland
Original owners Alex Stephen
Propulsion Sail, ketch rig; auxiliary engine added. Engine built by Ford
Tonnage 24 displacement
Length 45.66ft/13.9m
Breadth 6.0ft/1.83m
Materials Wood throughout
Original use Fishing
Present owners Gary Maynard
Location USA
History Former ketch-rigged Scottish fishing boat converted to a private yacht. Restored in 1987-91, as yacht.
Bibliography A1

Virginia V
coastal passenger steamer

Built 1922 by Anderson & Co, Olalla, Washington
Original owners West Pass Transportation Co
Propulsion Steam, screw, triple expansion, 400hp
Tonnage 122 gross
Length 115.9ft/35.33m
Breadth 24.1ft/7.35m
Draught 7.0ft/2.13m
Materials Wood throughout
Original use Passengers
Condition In operating condition
Present owners Virginia V Foundation
Location Seattle, Washington, USA
History In use for excursions.
Bibliography B44, D250, D278

W O Decker
steam harbour tug

Former name SUSAN DAYTON, W O DECKER, RUSSELL I
Built 1930 by Russell Shipyard, Long Island City, Queens, New York
Original owners Newtown Creek Towing Co
Propulsion Steam, screw; converted to diesel
Tonnage 22 gross
Length 47.7ft/14.57m
Breadth 15.0ft/4.57m
Materials Wood throughout
Original use Tug
Condition In operating condition
Present owners South Street Seaport Museum
Location New York City, USA
History Preserved as a floating exhibit and used for charters.

W P Snyder Jr
sternwheel river steamer

Former name J L PERRY, W H CLINGERMAN
Built 1918 by James Rees & Sons, Pittsburgh, Pennsylvania
Original owners Carnegie Steel Co
Propulsion Steam, sternwheel, compound, 750hp
Tonnage 342 gross
Length 151.7ft/46.24m
Breadth 32.3ft/9.85m
Materials Steel hull, steel and wood superstructure
Original use Towing
Condition Intact
Present owners Ohio Historical Society
Location Marietta, Ohio, USA
History Preserved as a floating exhibit.
Bibliography A17, B44

W T Preston
sternwheel river steamer

Built 1939 by Lake Union Dry Dock, Seattle, Washington
Original owners United States Army Corps of Engineers
Propulsion Steam, sternwheel, 340hp
Tonnage 291 gross
Length 163.0ft/49.68m
Breadth 34.7ft/10.58m
Draught 3.0ft/0.91m
Materials Steel hull, wood superstructure
Original use Snag removal
Condition Intact
Present owners City of Anacortes
Location Anacortes, Washington, USA
History Used for removing snags (sunken trees) from navigable waterways of the northwestern United States. Preserved as an onshore exhibit.
Bibliography B44, D273

Wake Robin
lighthouse tender

Built 1926 by Dravo, Neville Island, Pennsylvania
Original owners United States Lighthouse Service
Propulsion Steam, sternwheel, 550hp
Length 182.0ft/55.47m
Breadth 43.0ft/13.11m
Materials Steel hull, wood superstructure
Original use River lighthouse tender
Condition Intact, in use
Present owners Bensons Inc, Covington, Kentucky
Location Warsaw, Kentucky, USA
History Last surviving lighthouse tender designed to service lights and buoys on the Mississippi and Ohio Rivers. In use as a floating restaurant.
Bibliography B44

Virginia V

Wanderbird

pilot schooner

Former name WANDERVOGEL, ELBE 2
Built 1879 by Gustav Junge,
Wevelsfleth, Germany
Original owners Imperial German
Government
Propulsion Sail, schooner rig
Tonnage 71 gross
Length 85.0ft/25.91m
Breadth 18.5ft/5.64m
Draught 10.5ft/3.2m
Materials Wood throughout
Original use Pilot vessel
Condition Fully restored to sailing
condition
Present owners Harold Sommer
Location San Francisco, California,
USA
History Built as a pilot vessel for
service in the North Sea. Later
converted and in use as a yacht.
Bibliography D194, D510, D522, D523,
D525

Wapama

steam schooner

Former name TONGASS
Built 1915 by James H Price, St Helens,
Oregon
Original owners Charles McCormick
Co
Propulsion Steam, screw, triple
expansion, 825hp
Tonnage 951 gross
Length 204.8ft/62.42m
Breadth 40.2ft/12.25m
Draught 17.0ft/5.18m
Materials Wood throughout
Original use Cargo and passengers
Condition Intact, in need of restoration
Present owners San Francisco Maritime
National Historical Park
Location Sausalito, California, USA
History Last survivor of type known as
'steam schooner'. Preserved as an
exhibit.
Bibliography A17, D356, D529

Warden Johnston

personnel launch

Built 1945 by Federal Prison Industries,
McNeil Island, Washington
Original owners Alcatraz Federal
Penitentiary
Propulsion Diesel engine, 275hp
Tonnage 58 gross
Length 64.1ft/19.54m
Breadth 16.0ft/4.88m
Materials Wood throughout
Original use Passengers
Condition In operating condition

Wavertree

Present owners San Mateo County
Council Boy Scouts
Location San Mateo, California, USA
History Built to carry passengers to and
from the Federal prison on the island
of Alcatraz, which closed in 1963. In
use for training.

Wavertree

full-rigged trading vessel

Former name DON ARIANO N,
SOUTHGATE
Built 1885 by Oswald-Mordaunt & Co,
Southampton, England
Original owners R W Leyland & Co,
Liverpool
Propulsion Sail, full-rigged ship
Tonnage 2170 gross
Length 268.5ft/81.84m
Breadth 40.2ft/12.25m

Draught 12.0ft/3.66m
Materials Iron hull, iron and wood
masts
Original use Cargo
Condition Hull intact, rig being
restored
Present owners South Street Seaport
Museum
Location New York City, USA
History The first major sailing ship
built of iron was launched in the
British Isles in 1838. Over the next four
decades iron gradually replaced wood
as the building material for deepwater
vessels. When WAVERTREE was
launched in 1885 new processes were
making steel competitive with iron as a
shipbuilding material. She was to be
one of the last, and one of the largest,
full-rigged ships built of iron. Today
she is the largest iron sailing vessel in

existence. She was originally ordered
by R W Leyland & Company of
Liverpool, but completed for
Chadwick & Pritchard of that city. Her
first voyages were made between the
Bay of Bengal and the British Isles
carrying jute for making bags and
rope. Three years after her launching
she was bought back by R W Leyland
who employed her on tramping
voyages worldwide under the name
WAVERTREE. She called at the Port of
New York on just one occasion in 1895,
discharging nitrate from the west coast
of South America and loading canned
kerosine for Culcutta. In December
1910, after being dismasted off Cape
Horn, she was condemned at Port
Stanley in the Falklands and sold for
use as a storage hulk in the Straits of
Magellan. In 1948 she was towed to
Buenos Aires, Argentina, and
converted to a sand barge. She was
acquired by the South Street Seaport
Museum in 1968 for restoration as an
example of the type of deepwater
sailing ship that visited New York's
South Street waterfront in the late
1800s. Since WAVERTREE arrived under
tow in 1970 restoration has been
underway at a South Street pier.
Projects recently completed include the
completion of a 40ft deckhouse with
quarters for twenty-four seamen and
the ship's galley.
Bibliography A8, A14, D62, D481

Wawona

trading schooner

Built 1897 by Hans Bendixsen,
Fairhaven, California
Propulsion Sail, three-masted schooner
rig
Tonnage 468 gross
Length 156.0ft/47.55m
Breadth 36.0ft/10.97m
Materials Wood throughout
Original use Cargo
Condition Intact
Present owners Northwest Seaport
Location Seattle, Washington, USA
History Preserved as a floating exhibit.
Bibliography A14, D124, D263

Wilhelm Baum

motor tug

Former name JULIE DEE, CAPTAIN
CANFIELD
Built 1923 at Baltimore, Maryland
Original owners US Army Corps of
Engineers
Propulsion Diesel engine 45hp
Length 50.0ft/15.2m

Breadth 10.0ft/3.0m
Depth 5.5ft/1.7m
Original use Tug
Condition In operating condition
Present owners Jim Bradley
Location South Haven, Michigan, USA
History Small tug formerly employed as a tender to Army Corps of Engineers harbour dredging operations. Preserved in operating condition by private owners, as the flagship of the local Coast Guard Auxiliary unit.

William A Irvin
Great Lakes bulk carrier

Built 1938 by American Shipbuilding Co, Lorain, Ohio
Original owners Pittsburg Steamship Co
Propulsion Steam turbines, 2000hp
Tonnage 8240 gross
Length 593.2ft/180.81m
Breadth 60.2ft/18.35m
Materials Steel throughout
Original use Cargo
Condition Intact
Present owners Duluth Entertainment & Convention Center
Location Duluth, Minnesota
History Typical Great Lakes bulk cargo carrier preserved as a floating exhibit.
Bibliography D3, D259

William G Mather
Great Lakes bulk carrier

Built 1925 by Great Lakes Engineering Works, River Rouge, Michigan
Original owners Cleveland-Cliffs Steamship Co
Propulsion Steam turbines, 5500hp
Tonnage 8662 gross
Length 601.0ft/183.18m
Breadth 62.0ft/18.9m
Materials Steel throughout
Original use Cargo
Condition Intact
Present owners Great Lakes Historical Society, Vermilion, Ohio
Location Cleveland, Ohio, USA
History Typical Great Lakes bulk cargo carrier preserved as a floating exhibit.
Bibliography D95

William M Black
sidewheel river dredger

Built 1934 by Marietta Manufacturing Co, Point Pleasant, West Virginia
Original owners United States Army Corps of Engineers
Propulsion Steam, sidewheel, compound, 600hp
Tonnage 1351 displacement

Length 277.0ft/84.43m
Breadth 85.0ft/25.91m
Draught 4.5ft/1.37m
Materials Steel hull, steel and wood superstructure
Original use Dredger
Condition Intact
Location Dubuque, Iowa, USA
History Hydraulic dredger formerly used in keeping open the navigable channels of the Mississippi and Ohio Rivers. Preserved as a floating exhibit.
Bibliography B44

William S Mitchell
sidewheel river dredger

Built 1934 by Marietta Manufacturing Co, Point Pleasant, West Virginia
Original owners United States Army Corps of Engineers
Propulsion Steam, sidewheel, triple expansion, 1300hp
Tonnage 1351 displacement
Length 277.0ft/84.43m
Breadth 84.75ft/25.83m
Materials Steel hull, wood superstructure
Original use Dredger
Condition Intact
Present owners Jackson County Parks & Recreation
Location Kansas City, Missouri
History Dredger formerly used in keeping open the navigable channels of the Mississippi and Ohio Rivers. Preserved as a floating exhibit.

William G Mather in active service

Willis B Boyer
Great Lakes bulk carrier

Former name COL JAMES M SCHOONMAKER
Built 1911 by Great Lakes Engineering Works, Ecorse, Michigan
Original owners Shenango Furnace Co
Propulsion Steam turbines, 4950hp
Tonnage 8603 gross
Length 590.0ft/179.83m
Breadth 64.2ft/19.57m
Materials Steel throughout
Original use Cargo
Condition Intact
Present owners City of Toledo
Location Toledo, Ohio, USA
History Typical Great Lakes bulk cargo carrier preserved as a floating exhibit.

Wm B Tennison
oyster dredger

Built 1899 by Frank Laird, Crab Island, Maryland
Original owners B P & R L Miles
Propulsion Sail, schooner rig ('bugeye' type); converted to diesel
Tonnage 18 gross
Length 60.5ft/18.44m
Breadth 17.5ft/5.33m
Materials Wood throughout
Original use Oystering, later cargo
Condition In operating condition
Present owners Calvert Marine Museum
Location Solomons Island, Maryland, USA
History Preserved as a floating exhibit and for cruises.

X-1
midget submarine

Former name USS X-1
Built 1955 by Fairchild Engine and Airplane Corporation, Farmingdale, Long Island, New York
Original owners United States Navy
Official number X-1
Propulsion Diesel engine & batteries
Tonnage 31.5 displacement
Length 49.5ft/15.0m
Breadth 7.0ft/2.1m
Draught 6.25ft/1.9m
Materials Steel throughout
Original use Experimental midget submarine
Condition Intact
Present owners US Naval Academy Museum
Contact address 118 Maryland Avenue, Annapolis, Maryland 21402-5034
Location Annapolis, Maryland, USA
History Only true midget submarine built for the United States Navy. Patterned after the British X-boats of the Second World War. She was intended as the prototype for a series of these vessels to be used in penetrating enemy harbours in wartime. Only used in experiments. No further vessels in the series were built. Preserved as an onshore exhibit.
Bibliography C77a

Yankee
coastal passenger steamer

Former name BLOCK ISLAND, HOOK MOUNTAIN, MACHIGONNE
Built 1907 by Neafie & Levy Shipyard, Philadelphia, Pennsylvania
Propulsion Steam, screw; converted to diesel, 900hp. Engine built by General Motors (current)
Tonnage 425 gross
Length 136.5ft/41.6m
Breadth 29.0ft/8.8m
Materials Steel hull, wood superstructure
Original use Passengers
Condition Largely intact, restoration in progress
Present owners James Gallagher
Location New York City, USA
History Former passenger steamer built to operate on the New England Coast. Later brought to New York and employed as an excursion boat on the Hudson River and taking visitors to the Statue of Liberty. Employed by the Government during the Second World War. Undergoing restoration by a private owner, berthed at a pier on the west side of Manhattan.

Zodiac as the pilot schooner California

Yankee Fork Gold Dredger
gold mining dredger

Built 1940. Pre-fabricated by the Bucyrus-Erie Co and assembled near Stanley, Idaho
Original owners Snake River Mining Co
Propulsion Winched into position
Tonnage 988 displacement
Length 112ft/34.1m
Breadth 54ft/16.4m
Original use Gold mining dredger
Condition Restored, open to visitors
Present owners United States Forest Service
Location Near Stanley, Oregon, USA
History Intact gold mining dredger last used in 1952. Created the water it floated in by dredging gravel in front and dumping it behind after sifting out the gold. Located aground in a historic area of ghost towns and abandoned mines jointly managed by the US Forest Service and the State of Idaho.

Yorktown
aircraft carrier

Former name USS YORKTOWN
Built 1943 by Newport News Shipbuilding & Drydock Co, Newport News, Virginia
Original owners United States Navy
Propulsion Steam turbines, 150,000hp
Tonnage 27,100 displacement
Length 872.0ft/265.79m
Breadth 93.0ft/28.35m
Draught 28.5ft/8.69m
Materials Steel throughout
Original use Aircraft carrier
Condition Intact
Present owners Patriots Point Development Authority
Location Charleston, S Carolina, USA
History Aircraft carrier that saw service in the Second World War. Preserved as a floating exhibit.
Bibliography A8, B45, C64, D430

Zapala
motor yacht

Former name SISPUD II
Built 1913 by New York Yacht, Launch & Engine Co, Morris Heights, New York
Original owners Joseph B Cousins
Propulsion Petrol engine; replaced by diesel, 350hp. Engine built by Caterpillar (current)
Length 60.0ft/18.29m
Breadth 12.0ft/3.65m
Draught 3.5ft/1.06m
Materials Wood throughout
Original use Yacht
Condition Fully restored in 1996
Present owners Earl McMillen
Location USA
History Motor yacht built early in the century by a leading New York firm. Recently fully restored for further use as a private yacht.
Bibliography A1

Zodiac
schooner yacht

Former name CALIFORNIA, ZODIAC
Built 1924 by Hodgdon Brothers, East Boothbay, Maine
Original owners R W & J S Johnson
Propulsion Sail, schooner rig, diesel engine, 275hp
Tonnage 145 gross
Length 111.4ft/33.95m
Breadth 25.2ft/7.68m
Materials Wood throughout
Original use Yacht, later pilot vessel
Condition In sailing condition
Present owners Vessel Zodiac Corp, Snohomish, Washington
Location Seattle, Washington, USA
History In use for sail training.

Uruguay

One of the smaller nations in South America, Uruguay lies to the north of the estuary of the Rio de la Plata, with the Atlantic Ocean on its east and the Uruguay River forming its western boundary. Following independence from Spain in the early 1800s, Uruguay was the object of attempts at annexation by both its much larger neighbours Argentina and Brazil. It survived several local wars through changing alliances, to finally gain full recognition of its independent status in the 1850s. The major port is Montevideo, which lies across the broad Rio de la Plata estuary from the Argentine metropolis of Buenos Aires. Other ports lie on the navigable Uruguay River. The country maintains some shipping in international trade, and a modest navy. The Navy operates as its training ship the CAPITAN MIRANDA of 1930 which, in its current configuration carrying a modern three-masted schooner rig dating from the 1960s, does not qualify for inclusion in the Register.

Salto
patrol boat

Built 1935 by Cantiere Navale di Ancona, Ancona, Italy
Original owners Uruguayan Navy
Official number 14
Propulsion Two diesel engines, twin screw, 1000hp. Engines built by General Motors
Tonnage 180 displacement
Length 137.7ft/42.0m
Breadth 19ft/5.8m
Draught 5.2ft/1.6m
Materials Steel throughout
Original use Patrol boat
Condition In operation
Present owners Uruguayan Navy
Location Based at Paysandu, Uruguay
History Small warship dating from the 1930s in largely unaltered condition. Has been used for training and as a hydrographic survey vessel, but is currently serving as a patrol vessel based at Paysandu on the Uruguay River. Two sisterships were scrapped around the 1960s.

Vanguardia
gunboat

Built 1908 at Glasgow, Scotland
Original owners Uruguayan Navy
Propulsion Steam, screw, 200hp
Tonnage 95 displacement
Materials Steel throughout
Original use Gunboat
Condition Intact, proposed exhibit
Present owners Government of Uruguay
Location Montevideo, Uruguay
History Later used as a buoy tender. Proposed as a naval museum ship.

Yemen

The present nation of Yemen was formed through the unification of South Yemen, North Yemen, and the former British colony of Aden. It occupies that portion of the coast of the Arabian Peninsula on the north side of the Gulf of Aden, and the east side of the narrows at the southern end of the Red Sea. Great Britain had acquired Aden, which now serves as Yemen's major port, as a useful coaling station for shipping, between India and the Suez Canal. Yemeni seafaring was long confined to various types of dhows, with sewn-together wooden hulls and lateen rig. Seasonal voyages taking advantage of the monsoon winds were made in these craft, south along the east coast of Africa and east to India and sometimes Indonesia. The sailing dhows were eventually replaced by motorised versions, some of which still carried the sailing rig as an auxiliary. Lately, even these have been declining in number, giving way to steel motor vessels and, in the Yemeni coastal trade, trucks on the relatively recent coastal highway. The village of Al-Hami, home to many retired seafarers, is developing into a modest-scale centre for the preservation of Yemeni maritime history.

Saiyya
cargo dhow

Built in Yemen (date not known)
Propulsion Sail, lateen dhow rig
Length c44.6ft/13.6m
Breadth c11.7ft/3.55m
Draught c3.6ft/1.1m
Materials Wood throughout
Original use Cargo
Condition Intact
Present owners Al-Hami Maritime Museum
Location Al-Hami, Yemen
History Example of a type of Yemeni dhow used in the Red Sea and Persian Gulf, preserved as an exhibit on shore.

Yugoslavia

What would later become Yugoslavia was first formed at the end of the First World War as a kingdom composed of several ethnic regions located along the arm of the Mediterranean known as the Adriatic Sea. It was reconstituted following the Second World War under a Soviet system that maintained its independence from Russian-dominated Eastern Europe. Yugoslavia began a break-up in 1991 that coincided with the one taking place in the larger Soviet Union. That year the regions of Slovenia and Croatia in the far northwest seceded, along with landlocked Macedonia in the far south. Croatia took with it the majority of Yugoslavia's Adriatic coastline and virtually all its significant seaports. In 1992 the region of Bosnia and Herzegovina also seceded, leaving within the Yugoslav federation only Serbia and Montenegro. Serbia itself has no seacoast, but a stretch of the Danube River and several of its major tributaries lie within the northern part of the country.

Jadran
sail training vessel

Former name MARCO POLO
Built 1931 by H C Stulcken Sohn, Hamburg, Germany
Original owners Yugoslavian Naval Training Association
Propulsion Sail, three-masted topsail schooner rig; diesel engine 375hp
Tonnage 700 displacement
Length 157.5ft/48.0m
Breadth 29.25ft/8.92m
Draught 13.15ft/4.0m
Materials Steel hull and deckhouses, steel and wood masts
Original use Training ship
Condition In operation
Present owners Yugoslavian Naval Academy
Location Bakar, Yugoslavia
History Built as a sail training vessel for the Yugoslav Navy. Later used by the Italians in the Second World War.
Bibliography A14, C96

Roditelj
sailing coaster

Built 1907
Propulsion Sail, schooner rig, 'trabakel' type
Materials Wood throughout
Original use Cargo
Condition In operation
Location Dubrovnik, Yugoslavia
History In use for cruises.

Split
sidewheel river steamer

Former name URFAHR, KRALJ PETAR I, CAR NIKOLA II
Built 1898 by Ruthof Shipyard, Regensburg, Germany
Original owners Srbsko Brodastko Drustvo
Propulsion Steam, sidewheel, compound diagonal, 650hp
Length 187.3ft/57.06m
Breadth 51.7ft/15.75m
Materials Steel throughout
Original use Passengers
Condition Largely unaltered in appearance, in use
Location Belgrade, Serbia
History Former Austro-Hungarian and Yugoslavian river steamer in active service over 60 years. Currently serving as a floating restaurant without major alterations.
Bibliography B43

Zanzibar

The port of Zanzibar on its island just twenty-five miles off the east coast of Africa has been important in the trade of the region since the eighth century. Arab domination of this trade eventually led to rule by an expatriate Sultan from Oman on the Persian Gulf. Great Britain acquired control of the islands of Zanzibar and Pemba in 1890 to prevent a takeover by Germany, which had established its colony Deutsche Ost Afrika on the nearby mainland. The latter became the British Colony of Tanganyika after the First World War. After Tanganyika received its independence as Tanzania in the early 1960s, Zanzibar joined it in a loose federation. Both Zanzibar and the nearby Tanzanian port of Dar es Salaam were until quite recently major stops for the fleet of dhows sailing south with the seasonal monsoon from the Persian Gulf States and Yemen. The Arab presence in Zanzibar has declined, but its heritage is still very evident in the architecture of the older buildings, including two former palaces of the Omani Sultan overlooking the harbour. The preserved barge is an interesting artifact from Britain's late-nineteenth century efforts to extend its influence in the region.

Sultan's Barge
royal barge

Built 1890s in Great Britain
Original owners Sultan of Zanzibar
Propulsion Rowed
Materials Wood throughout
Original use Royal barge
Condition Intact
Present owners Zanzibar Museum
Location Zanzibar
History Royal barge presented to the Sultan of Zanzibar by Queen Victoria. Preserved as an onshore exhibit.

Sultan's Barge

Appendix 1 Changes of status since Second Edition

ABEL TASMAN	Netherlands	renamed BONAIRE
ALEXANDRIA	United States	foundered at sea
ALVIN CLARK	United States	broken up
BERNICE J	United States	abandoned
CABOT	United States	to be broken up
CHIPCHASE	Great Britain	to be broken up
CHRYSANTHEMUM	Great Britain	broken up
CHUCUITO	Peru	renamed YAVARI
CITY OF BEAUMONT (remnant)	United States	broken up
CITY OF KEANSBURG	United States	broken up
CLARENCE CROCKETT	United States	abandoned sunk
CLEARWAY	Great Britain	to be broken up
CLIPPER	United States	renamed MILWAUKEE CLIPPER
CLYDE A. PHILLIPS	United States	renamed A. J. MEERWALD
COMANCHE	Unites States	scuttled at sea
DEVIN	Czech Republic	renamed VYSEHRAD
DIVIS	Great Britain	broken up
DRESDEN	Germany	change to TRADITIONSSCHIFF
EBRO	Netherlands	broken up
EMILY BARRETT	Great Britain	broken up
EXPLORER	Great Britain	no longer museum; for sale 1999
EXPUNGER	Great Britain	renamed XE-8
GOLDFIELD	Cayman Island	lying sunk
GRACE BOEHNER	Canada	broken up
GRAN MARISCAL ANDRES de SANTA CRUZ	Peru	renamed OLLANTA
GRANMA	Cuba	reportedly replica
GUIA	Macao	returned to commercial use
HENDRINA II	Netherlands	renamed JAN DE STERKE
HESPER (remnant)	United States	broken up
HIKITEA	New Zealand	foundered under tow
HOPEASALMI	Finland	renamed LAITIALA
HOWARD	United States	broken up
INAUGURAL	United States	sunk in flood; broken up
INCA	Peru	broken up
JOHN W. MACKAY	Great Britain	broken up
KRUZENSHTERN	Estonia	moved to Russia
LA MERCED	United States	collapsing into wreckage
L'ATALANTA	Great Britain	too small
LIGHTSHIP NO. 84	United States	lying sunk
LOODSSCHOENER NR. 1	Netherlands	project abandoned
LUTHER LITTLE (remnant)	United States	broken up
LYNN WELL LIGHTSHIP	Great Britain	broken up
LYTTELTON II	Australia	renamed VICTORIA
MARIA ASSUMPTA	Great Britain	lost by shipwreck
MARY D. HUME	United States	lying sunk
MINERVA	Great Britain	renamed M-33
NIAGARA	United States	to be broken up
PORT FAIRY	Australia	too small
PORTLAND	Australia	too small
POTSCHA WEHLEN BASTEI	Germany	change to WEHLEN BASTEI
PRINCESS MARGUERITE	Canada	broken up
PUIJO	Finland	renamed SUUR SAIMAA
RALPH T. WEBSTER	United States	abandoned sunk
RELIANT	Great Britain	no longer on exhibit
RELIEF LIGHTSHIP (1951)	United States	for sale
RUBY G. FORD	United States	broken up
RUDESHEIM	Germany	moved to Netherlands, renamed PRINS DER NEDERLANDEN
SCHWARTZBURG	Denmark	broken up
SEA ALARM	Great Britain	broken up
SEA GULL	United States	broken up
SIGSBEE	United States	broken up
SIR ALAN HERBERT	Great Britain	renamed LADY JEAN
SOOBRAZITELNYI	Russia	apparently broken up
STRELIKA	Yugoslavia	no recent information
SUSAN MAY	United States	abandoned
TANKMASTER NO. 1	United States	renamed CATAWISSA
VEGA	Estonia	moved to Finland
VORWARTS	Germany	broken up
WELTFRIEDEN	Germany	renamed PILLNITZ
WILLIAM McCANN	Great Britain	renamed CITY OF EDINBORO
YARMOUTH	Great Britain	broken up

English Sailing Barges; extant but no longer in sailing condition:

BEATRICE MAUD
BRITISH EMPIRE
BRITISH KING
CONVOY
ETHEL MAUD
MONTREAL
SCONE
SEAGULL I
SPINAWAY C
VIOLET

Appendix 2 List of vessels by type
The number of vessels in each category is shown in parentheses

Ancient or medieval vessels			(5)
Sail	square-rig	cargo or passengers	(42)
Sail	fore & aft rig	passengers	(2)
Sail	fore & aft rig	cargo	(199)
Sail	square-rig	training	(22)
Sail	fore & aft rig	training	(5)
Sail		whaling	(1)
Sail		fishing	(53)
Sail		oystering	(45)
Sail		pearling	(4)
Sail		pilot vessels	(11)
Sail		exploration and research	(6)
Sail		yachts	(28)
Sail		miscellaneous	(2)
Power	passengers	oceans	(5)
Power	passengers	coastal	(33)
Power	passengers	lakes	(73)
Power	passengers	rivers	(49)
Power	passengers	canals	(2)
Power		ferries	(35)
Power	cargo	oceans	(15)
Power	cargo	coastal	(18)
Power	cargo	harbours	(2)
Power	cargo	lakes	(9)
Power	cargo	rivers & canals	(5)
Power	cargo and towing	rivers	(8)
Power	towing	oceans	(3)
Power	towing	coastal	(3)
Power	towing	rivers, lakes and canals	(76)
Power		harbour tugs	(90)
Power		pilot vessels	(2)
Power		whaling	(4)
Power		sealing	(1)
Power		fishing	(26)
Power		yachts	(28)
Power		cable ships	(3)
Power		experimental	(5)
Power		miscellaneous	(4)
Canal boats			(26)
Canal		maintenance	(6)
Barges		rivers	(13)
Barges		harbours	(7)
Mining dredges			(4)
Floating cranes			(4)
Floating theatres			(2)
Research submersibles			(1)
Non-self propelled		miscellaneous	(5)
Rowing		royal barges	(11)
Government vessels		lightships	(46)
Government vessels		lighthouse tenders	(3)
Government vessels		surveying & research	(6)
Government vessels		inspection	(7)
Government vessels		customs patrol	(5)
Rescue craft			(27)
Government vessels		icebreakers	(8)
Government vessels		dredging and channel clearing	(23)
Government vessels		towing	(5)
Government vessels		fireboats	(8)
Government vessels		police patrol	(4)
Government vessels		coast guard patrol	(5)
Government vessels		miscellaneous	(10)
Naval	sail	ships of the line	(3)
Naval	sail	frigates	(4)
Naval	sail	corvettes	(1)
Naval	sail	gunboats	(1)
Naval	sail & steam	frigates	(2)
Naval	sail & steam	gunboats	(3)
Naval	steam	monitors	(3)
Naval	steam	seagoing monitors	(3)
Naval	steam	pre-Dreadnought battleships	(1)
Naval	steam	battleships	(5)
Naval	steam	aircraft carriers	(4)
Naval	steam	cruisers	(6)
Naval	steam	destroyers	(16)
Naval	power	submarines	(42)
Naval	power	midget submarines	(15)
Naval	power	escort vessels	(10)
Naval	power	minelayers	(1)
Naval	power	minesweepers	(15)
Naval	power	torpedo boats	(27)
Naval	power	gunboats	(11)
Naval	power	river monitors	(6)
Naval	power	submarine chasers	(1)
Naval	power	patrol boats	(7)
Naval	power	landing craft	(4)
Naval	power	launches	(5)
Naval	power	miscellaneous	(10)

ANCIENT OR MEDIEVAL VESSELS

Royal Ship of Cheops	Egypt	c.2500 BC
Oseberg Viking Ship	Norway	c.800
Gokstad Viking Ship	Norway	c.850
Utrecht Ship	Netherlands	c.1100
Cogge of Bremen	Germany	c.1380
Nydam Ship	Germany	—

SAIL – SQUARE-RIG, TWO OR MORE MASTS – CARGO OR PASSENGERS

Vicar of Bray	Falkland Islands	1841
Jhelum	Falkland Islands	1849
Edwin Fox	New Zealand	1853
Charles Cooper	Falkland Islands	1856
Santiago	Australia	1856
Egeria	Falkland Islands	1859
Star of India	USA	1863
City of Adelaide	Great Britain	1864
Bayard	South Georgia	1864
Garland	Falkland Islands	1865
Cutty Sark	Great Britain	1869
Ambassador	Chile	1869
James Craig	Australia	1874
Fleetwing	Falkland Islands	1874
Falstaff	Chile	1875
Munoz Gamero	Chile	1875
Elissa	USA	1877
Falls of Clyde	USA	1878
Lady Elizabeth	Falkland Islands	1879
Brutus	South Georgia	1883
Wavertree	USA	1885
Polly Woodside	Australia	1885
Balclutha	USA	1886
County of Roxburgh	Tuamotu	1886
Sigyn	Finland	1887
Af Chapman	Sweden	1888
Marjory Glen	Argentina	1892
Belem	France	1896
Galatea	Spain	1896
Rickmer Rickmers	Germany	1896
Suomen Joutsen	Finland	1902
Pommern	Finland	1903
Moshulu	USA	1904
Viking	Sweden	1907
Peking	USA	1911
Passat	Germany	1911
Ebe	Italy	1921
Florette	Italy	1922
Sedov	Russia	1921
Kruzenshtern	Russia	1926
Vega	Finland	1948

SAIL – FORE & AFT RIG – PASSENGERS

Olive	Great Britain	1909
Norada	Great Britain	1912

SAIL – FORE & AFT RIG, OR ONE MAST SQUARE-RIGGED – CARGO

Rafael Verdera	Spain	1841
Anna Af Sand	Norway	1848
Jensine	Denmark	1852
Ruth	Denmark	1854
Isla Ebusitana	Italy	1856
Frøia	Norway	1857
Adella	Norway	1864
Oline	Norway	c.1865
Joble	France	1866
May Queen	Australia	1867
Anna Rogde	Norway	1868
Annie Watt	Australia	1870
Stephen Taber	USA	1871
Lewis R. French	USA	1871
Isefjord	Denmark	1874
Elida	Denmark	1875
Mina	Sweden	1876
Governor Stone	USA	1877
Lena	Netherlands	1878
Norden	Germany	1879
Cygnet	Great Britain	1881
George Smeed	Great Britain	1882
Grace Bailey	USA	1882
Hoop Op Welvaart	Germany	1883
Arbeid Adelt	Netherlands	1884
Pioneer	USA	1885
Ane Catherine	Denmark	1887
Undine	New Zealand	1887
Equator	USA	1888
Anna Kristina	Norway	1889
De Hoop	Netherlands	1890
De Vier Gebroeders	Netherlands	1890
Alma	USA	1891
Anna Von Amrum	Germany	1891
May	Great Britain	1891
Anita Jacoba	Netherlands	1892
Anna Rosa	France	1892
Greta	Great Britain	1892
Les Deux Freres	France	1892
Mirosa	Great Britain	1892
Sarpen	Sweden	1892
Result	Great Britain	1893
Felix	Great Britain	1893
Spry	Great Britain	1894
De Drie Gebroeders	Netherlands	1894
Familietrouw	Netherlands	1894
Palnatoke	Denmark	1894
Eule	Germany	1895
Heiltje	Netherlands	1895

Kitty	Great Britain	1895
Defender	Australia	1895
Jantina	Netherlands	1895
Centaur	Great Britain	1895
C. A. Thayer	USA	1895
Orinoco	Great Britain	1895
Thistle	Great Britain	1895
Victor	Great Britain	1895
Angela Von Barssel	Germany	1896
Beric	Great Britain	1896
Freia	Denmark	1896
Anna	Netherlands	1896
Wawona	USA	1897
Ethel Ada	Great Britain	1897
Dawn	Great Britain	1897
Anglia	Great Britain	1898
Albion	Great Britain	1898
Atrato	Great Britain	1898
Edme	Great Britain	1898
Ellen	Sweden	1898
De Vriendschap	Netherlands	1898
Wyvenhoe	Great Britain	1898
Marie	Germany	1898
Parodie	Netherlands	1898
Shamrock	Great Britain	1899
Albatros	Netherlands	1899
Amalia	Sweden	1899
Bracksand	Netherlands	1899
Gruno	Netherlands	1899
Mijn Genoegen	Netherlands	1899
Saira	Great Britain	1899
Voorwaarts Voorwaarts	Netherlands	1899
Decima	Great Britain	1899
Victory Chimes	USA	1900
Ironsides	Great Britain	1900
Bisschop Van Arkel	Netherlands	1900
Jantina	Germany	1900
Kathleen & May	Great Britain	1900
Drie Gebroeders	Netherlands	*c.*1900
Samenwerking	Netherlands	*c.*1900
Gladys	Great Britain	1901
Hjalm	Denmark	1901
De Hoop	Netherlands	1901
Dannebrog	Great Britain	1901
Nieuwe Zorg	Netherlands	1901
Nellie	Great Britain	1901
Enterprise	Australia	1902
Valborg II	Sweden	1902
Marjorie	Great Britain	1902
Alma	New Zealand	1902
Aaltje	Netherlands	1903
Alma Doepel	Australia	1903
Alida	Netherlands	1903
Ethel Ada	Great Britain	1903
Hecla	Australia	1903
Johanna	Germany	1903
La Leone	France	1903
Nescio	Netherlands	1903
Hermine	Germany	1904
Merlandou	France	1904
Elfriede	Germany	1904
Henry	Great Britain	1904
Neptune	Switzerland	1904
Echo	New Zealand	1905
Hermann	Germany	1905
Vigilant	Great Britain	1905
Anna-Lisa Von Stade	Germany	1906
Thalatta	Great Britain	1906
Cambria	Great Britain	1906
Aron	Denmark	1906
Elinor	Denmark	1906
Hydrogen	Great Britain	1906
Anna Møller	Denmark	1906
Luise	Germany	1906
Ena	Great Britain	1906
Edith May	Great Britain	1906
Moewe	Germany	1907
Irene	Great Britain	1907
Roditelj	Yugoslavia	1907
Jock	Great Britain	1908
Annigje	Netherlands	1908
Ebenhaezer	Germany	1908
Jane Gifford	New Zealand	1908
Gudeskop	Netherlands	1908
Zuiderzee	Netherlands	1909
Garlandstone	Great Britain	1909
Engelina	Netherlands	1909
Atene	Sweden	1909
Ardwina	Great Britain	1909
Grossherzogin Elizabeth	Germany	1909
Isle of Farquhar	Seychelles	1909
Rosinante	Germany	1909
Te Aroha	New Zealand	1909
Friedrich	Germany	1910
Heinrich Von Der Lühe	Germany	1910
Leao Holandes	Portugal	1910
Neerlandia	Netherlands	1910
Sylvina W. Beal	USA	1911
Jonas von Friedrichstadt	Germany	1911
Jonge Pieter	Netherlands	1911
Brita Leth	Denmark	1911
Saint Patrick	Eire	1911
Windsbraut	Germany	1911
Wilhelmine Von Stade	Germany	*pre*-1912
Immanuel	Germany	1912
De Tukker	Netherlands	1912
Glenway	Great Britain	1913
Goede Verwachtung	Germany	1913
Tärnan	Sweden	1913
Amy Howson	Great Britain	1914
Bärbel-Marlies	Germany	1914
Bonavista	Denmark	1914
Alles Heeft Een Tijd	Netherlands	1914
Fortuna	Germany	1914
Fulton	Denmark	1915
Linnea	Sweden	1915
Svanen	Norway	1916
Helene	Sweden	1916
Principat De Catalunya	France	1916
Mercantile	USA	1916
De Wadden	Great Britain	1917
Oosterschelde	Netherlands	1918
Najaden	Sweden	1918
Sayremar I	Spain	1918
Seute Deern	Germany	1919
Marilyn Anne	Denmark	1919
Pascual Flores	Great Britain	1919
Falie	Australia	1919
Tuhoe	New Zealand	1919
Marie May	Great Britain	1920
Pudge	Great Britain	1922
Fylla	Denmark	1922
Ingo	Sweden	1922
Mjølner	Denmark	1922
Our Svanen	Australia	1922
Comrade	Great Britain	1923
Lady Daphne	Great Britain	1923
Lady Jean	Great Britain	1923
Northdown	Great Britain	1924
Repertor	Great Britain	1924
Owhiti	New Zealand	1925
Portlight	Great Britain	1925
Ideaal	Netherlands	1926
Ruth	Germany	1926
Will	Great Britain	1926
Xylonite	Great Britain	1926
Cabby	Great Britain	1928
Ebenhaezer	Netherlands	1928
Reminder	Great Britain	1929
Nell-Britt	Sweden	1929
Delphin	Germany	1930
Boa Viagem	Portugal	1930
La Vaudoise	Switzerland	1931
Lady of the Lea	Great Britain	1931
Emma	Netherlands	1931
Undine	Germany	1931
Westkust	Sweden	1932
Aurora	Germany	1934
Daybreak	Great Britain	1934
Hawila	Sweden	1935
Giovanni Pascoli	Italy	1936
Queen Galadriel	Great Britain	1937
Evangelistria	Greece	1939
Seute Deern	Germany	1939
Else Dorothea Bager	Denmark	1942
Veslets	Bulgaria	1943
Marseillois	France	1944
Carene Star	Denmark	1945
Kvartsita	Sweden	1945
Notre-Dame de Rumengol	France	1945
Pioneer	Bulgaria	1945
Helga	Finland	1948
Zapad	Russia	1949
Sotero	Great Britain	*c.*1950
Sekar Aman	Australia	—
Fragata Do Tejo	Portugal	—
A Pombinha	Portugal	—
Baia Do Seixal	Portugal	—
Al Hadir	Oman	—
Saiyya type dhow	Yemen	—

Sail – square-rig – training

Joseph Conrad	USA	1882
Presidente Sarmiento	Argentina	1897
Najaden	Sweden	1897
Jarramas	Sweden	1900
Duchesse Anne	France	1901
Unyo Maru	Japan	1909
Dar Pomorza	Poland	1909
Statsraad Lehmkuhl	Norway	1914
Sørlandet	Norway	1927
Schulschiff Deutschland	Germany	1927
Kaiwo Maru	Japan	1930
Nippon Maru	Japan	1930
Amerigo Vespucci	Italy	1931
Mercator	Belgium	1932
Danmark	Denmark	1932
Almirante Saldanha	Brazil	1933
Tovaritsch	Great Britain	1933
Georg Stage	Denmark	1935
Eagle	USA	1936
Christian Radich	Norway	1937
Sagres	Portugal	1937
Mircea	Romania	1938
Dewarutji	Indonesia	1952
Gorch Fock	Germany	1958
Gloria	Columbia	1968

Sail – fore & aft rig – training

Juan Sebastian de Elcano	Spain	1928
Jadran	Yugoslavia	1931

La Belle Poule	France	1932
L'Etoile	France	1932
Gladen	Sweden	1946
Falken	Sweden	1947
Lilla Dan	Denmark	1951
Esmeralda	Chile	1952

Sail — whaling

Charles W. Morgan	USA	1841

Sail — fishing

Mon Lei	USA	1855
Emma C. Berry	USA	1866
Trui	Netherlands	1875
Mary Joseph	Great Britain	1877
Maria	Germany	1880
Barnabas	Great Britain	1881
City of Edinboro	Great Britain	1884
Lord Nelson	Sweden	1885
Blossom	Great Britain	1887
Catarina	Germany	1889
Landrath Küster	Germany	1889
Matilda	Australia	c.1889
Erna Becker	Germany	1892
Leader	Great Britain	1892
Lettie G. Howard	USA	1893
Ernestina	USA	1894
Vegesack	Germany	1895
Rakel	Germany	1896
Swan	Great Britain	1900
Andries Jacob	Netherlands	1900
Gazela of Philadelphia	USA	1901
Reaper	Great Britain	1901
TX 58	Netherlands	1902
Astarte	Germany	1903
Greta	Germany	1904
Gratitude	Sweden	1907
Emden	Germany	1908
Enterprise	Great Britain	1909
Vrouw Elisabeth	Netherlands	1909
Deodar	Sweden	1911
Balder	Netherlands	1912
MK 63	Netherlands	1912
the Three Brothers	Great Britain	1912
Tecla	Netherlands	1914
Pieter Bel	Netherlands	1917
Marion Elizabeth	Canada	1918
Tempete	France	c.1920
L. A. Dunton	USA	1921
Excelsior	Great Britain	1921
Reginald M.	Australia	1921
Else Af Sletten	Germany	1923
Kenya Jacaranda	Great Britain	1923
Marité	Sweden	1923
Cap Lizard	France	1924
Bellis	Germany	1924
Provident	Great Britain	1924
Charlotte	Germany	1925
Quattro Fratelli	Italy	1925
Adventure	USA	1926
Carmelan	Germany	1927
Evelina M. Goulart	USA	1927
Präsident Freiherr V. Maltzan	Germany	1928
American Eagle	USA	1930
Dehel	France	1931
American	USA	1934
Palinuro	Italy	1934
Spökenkieker	Germany	1935
Julie Burgess	Australia	1936

Creoula	Portugal	1937
Belle Etoile	France	1938
Theresa E. Connor	Canada	1938
Mytlius	Germany	1939
Vigilance	Great Britain	1930s
Goede Wil	Germany	1940
Robertson II	Canada	1940
Sherman Zwicker	USA	1941
Etoile Molene	France	1954
Terima Kasih	Australia	c.1965
Tu Do	Australia	c.1968
Hong Hai	Australia	1970
Karya Sama	Australia	c.1970
Bragozzo D'altura	Italy	—
S Paio	Great Britain	—
Shin Hsun Yuan	Australia	—
Titipan	Australia	—

Sail — oystering

Little Jennie	USA	1881
Christeen	USA	1883
Isaac H. Evans	USA	1886
Rebecca T. Ruark	USA	1886
Priscilla	USA	1888
Edna E. Lockwood	USA	1889
Nellie and Mary	USA	1891
Ruby G. Ford	USA	1891
Wm. B. Tennison	USA	1899
City of Norfolk	USA	1900
Elsworth	USA	1901
Dorothy Parsons	USA	1901
Kathryn	USA	1901
Sigsbee	USA	1901
Susan May	USA	1901
Richard Robbins Sr.	USA	1902
Stanley Norman	USA	1902
Maggie Lee	USA	1903
Bernice J	USA	1904
Fannie L. Daugherty	USA	1904
Mary W. Somers	USA	1904
Virginia W	USA	1904
Hilda W. Willing	USA	1905
Ralph T. Webster	USA	1905
Minnie V	USA	1906
Ida May	USA	1906
F. C. Lewis Jr.	USA	1907
Mustang	USA	1907
Clarence Crockett	USA	1908
Howard	USA	1909
Mamie A. Mister	USA	1910
E. C. Collier	USA	1910
Flora A. Price	USA	1910
Claude W. Somers	USA	1911
Thomas W. Clyde	USA	1911
Nellie L. Bird	USA	1911
Kathryn M. Lee	USA	1923
Modesty	USA	1923
Sea Gull	USA	1924
J. & E. Riggin	USA	1927
A. J. Meerwald	USA	1928
Joy Parks	USA	1936
Wilma Lee	USA	1940
Hope	USA	1948
Rosie Parks	USA	1955

Sail — pearling vessels

Trixen	Australia	1904
Penguin	Australia	1908
Vivienne	Australia	c.1945

Ancel	Australia	1952
John Louis	Australia	1957
Sam Male	Australia	1957

Sail — pilot vessels

Wanderbird	USA	1879
Thomas F. Bayard	Canada	1880
Marie-Fernand	France	1894
Sampo	Germany	1896
Atalanta	Germany	1901
Cariad	Great Britain	1904
Olga	Great Britain	1909
Kindly Light	Great Britain	1911
Jolie Brise	Great Britain	1913
Tabor Boy	USA	1914
Lodsen Rønne	Germany	1916
Pilot	USA	1924
Roseway	USA	1926
Alabama	USA	1926

Sail — exploration and research

Grönland	Germany	1867
Gjoa	Norway	1873
Fram	Norway	1892
Discovery	Great Britain	1901
Bowdoin	USA	1921
Nicolai Knipovich	Russia	—

Sail — yachts

Peggy	Great Britain	1791
Valdivia	Germany	1868
Coronet	USA	1885
Amphitrite	Germany	1887
Akarana	Australia	1888
Marigold	Great Britain	1892
Waitangi	Australia	1894
Avel	France	1896
Wyvern	Norway	1896
Clymene	France	1901
Boomerang	Australia	1902
Trivia	USA	1902
Solace	Great Britain	1903
Maple Leaf	Canada	1904
Asgard	Eire	1905
Hathor	Great Britain	1905
Noord-Holland	Netherlands	1905
Diadem	France	1907
Hispania	Great Britain	1909
Hoshi	Great Britain	1909
Vagrant	Great Britain	1910
Calypso	France	1911
Adventuress	USA	1913
Mariette	Great Britain	1915
Nathaniel Bowditch	USA	1922
Zodiac	USA	1924
Creole	Great Britain	1927
Ocean Waif	USA	1927
Eugene Eugenides	Greece	1929
Shamrock V	USA	1930
Zaca	France	1930
Altair	Spain	1931
Puritan	Italy	1931
Sea Cloud	Germany	1931
Brilliant	USA	1932
Endeavour	USA	1934
Belisarius	USA	1935
Cythera	USA	1937
Kathleen Gillett	Australia	1939

Swift of Ipswich	USA	1939
Gipsy Moth IV	Great Britain	1966
Gretel II	Australia	1970
Parry Endeavour	Australia	1978
Australia II	Australia	1982
Diva	Germany	1985

Sail – miscellaneous

New Way (cableship)	USA	1939
Kronverk	Russia	c.1947
(training or research)		
P 6398 (cargo or fishing)	Netherlands	—
Kemajuan (cargo or fishing)	Malaysia	—
Sabar (cargo or fishing)	Malaysia	—

Power – passengers – oceans

Great Britain	Great Britain	1843
Stella Polaris	Japan	1927
Hikawa Maru	Japan	1930
Lydia	France	1931
Queen Mary	USA	1936
United States	USA	1951

Power – passengers – coastal

Robert	Sweden	1866
Warpen	Sweden	1873
Salama	Finland	1874
Primus	Sweden	1875
Ejdern	Sweden	1880
Maid of Sker	Australia	1884
Suldal	Norway	1885
Tärnan	Sweden	1901
Mariefred	Sweden	1903
Stavenes	Norway	1904
Östanå I	Sweden	1906
Yankee	USA	1907
Sabino	USA	1908
Alexandra	Germany	1908
Storskär	Sweden	1908
Børøysund	Norway	1908
Drottningholm	Sweden	1909
Norrskär	Sweden	1909
Kysten I	Norway	1909
Blidösund	Sweden	1911
Albatros	Germany	1912
Bohuslän	Sweden	1913
Kyle	Canada	1913
Stord I	Norway	1913
Skjelskor	Denmark	1915
Virginia V	USA	1922
Catalina	Mexico	1924
Helge	Denmark	1924
Nobska	USA	1925
Saltsjön	Sweden	1925
Princess Elizabeth	France	1927
Gamle Rogaland	Norway	1929
Granvin	Norway	1931
Queen Mary II	Great Britain	1933
Marieholm	Sweden	1933
Nixe	Germany	1939
Waverley	Great Britain	1946

Power – passengers – lakes

Rigi	Switzerland	1847
Skibladner	Norway	1856
Gondola	Great Britain	1859
Hjejlen	Denmark	1861
Yavari	Peru	1862
Lahtis	Finland	1865
Englebrekt	Sweden	1866
Freja	Sweden	1868
Puno	Peru	1871
Gisela	Austria	1872
Östersund	Sweden	1874
St. Georg	Germany	1875
Thomée	Sweden	1875
Queen	USA	1884
Segwun	Canada	1887
St. Josef	Austria	1887
Mount Washington	USA	1888
Kelén	Hungary	1891
Trafik	Sweden	1892
Helka	Hungary	1892
Coya	Peru	1893
Motala Express	Sweden	1895
Keenora	Canada	1897
Moyie	Canada	1898
Kaima	Finland	1898
Toimi	Finland	1898
Sir Walter Scott	Great Britain	1899
Angara	Russia	1899
Tuscarora	USA	1900
Uri	Switzerland	1901
Columbia	USA	1902
Unterwalden	Switzerland	1902
Hame	Finland	1903
Laitiala	Finland	1903
Plinio	Italy	1903
Leppävirta	Finland	1904
Boxholm II	Sweden	1904
G. Zanardelli	Italy	1904
Montreaux	Switzerland	1904
Savonlinna	Finland	1904
Piemonte	Italy	1904
Milwaukee Clipper	USA	1905
Suomi	Finland	1905
Taimi III	Finland	1905
Pohjola	Finland	1905
Karjalankoski	Finland	1905
Blumlisalp	Switzerland	1906
Heinävesi	Finland	1906
Minnehaha	USA	1906
Schiller	Switzerland	1906
Ticonderoga	USA	1906
Keewatin	USA	1907
Suur Saimaa	Finland	1907
Suvi-Saimaa	Finland	1907
Diessen	Germany	1908
Lombardia	Italy	1908
Wilhelm Tell	Switzerland	1908
Tarjanne	Finland	1908
Italia	Italy	1909
Stadt Zurich	Switzerland	1909
Thalia	Austria	1909
Ste. Claire	USA	1910
La Suisse	Switzerland	1910
Earnslaw	New Zealand	1911
Figaro	Finland	1911
Stadt Innsbruck	Austria	1911
Gallia	Switzerland	1913
Hohentweil	Austria	1913
Lokki	Finland	1913
Lotschberg	Switzerland	1914
Savoie	Switzerland	1914
Stadt Rapperswil	Switzerland	1914
Liemba	Tanzania	1914
Sicamous	Canada	1914
Katahdin	USA	1914
Simplon	Switzerland	1915
Tarahne	Canada	1917
Paul Wahl	Finland	1919
Ludwig Fessler	Germany	1926
Patria	Italy	1926
Concordia	Italy	1927
International	USA	1927
Riistavesi	Finland	1927
Rhone	Switzerland	1927
Stadt Luzern	Switzerland	1928
Galatea	Germany	1931
Ollanta	Peru	1931
Ellen Ruth	USA	1932
Norisle	Canada	1946
Norgoma	Canada	1950
Maid of the Loch	Great Britain	1953

Power – passengers – rivers

Gem	Australia	1876
Stadt Wehlen	Germany	1879
Alaska	Great Britain	1883
Diesbar	Germany	1884
Meissen	Germany	1885
Pillnitz	Germany	1886
Kaiser Friedrich	Germany	1889
Krippen	Germany	1892
Sviatitel Nikolay	Russia	c.1892
Kurort Rathen	Germany	1896
Scmilka	Germany	1897
Marion	Australia	1897
Riesa	Germany	1897
Junger Pionier	Germany	1898
Pirna	Germany	1898
Nuneham	Great Britain	1898
Kaiser Wilhelm	Germany	1900
Waimarie	New Zealand	1900
Windsor Belle	Great Britain	1901
Sudan	Egypt	1901
Ongarue	New Zealand	1903
Wairua	New Zealand	1904
Settler	New Zealand	1905
Streatley	Great Britain	1905
Ruby	Australia	1907
Waireka	New Zealand	1908
Reemere	Australia	1909
Rowitta	Australia	1909
Memnon	Egypt	1910
N. V. Gogol	Russia	1911
Schonbrunn	Austria	1912
Kapitein Kok	Netherlands	1912
Goethe	Germany	1913
Benjamin Guimaraes	Brazil	1913
Kossuth	Hungary	1914
Belle of Louisville	USA	1914
Compton Castle	Great Britain	1914
Karim	Egypt	1917
Petöfi	Hungary	1920
Keno	Canada	1922
Indiana	Egypt	1923
Kingswear Castle	Great Britain	1924
Medway Queen	Great Britain	1924
Delta King	USA	1926
Delta Queen	USA	1926
Dresden	Germany	1926
Prins Der Nederlanden	Netherlands	1926
Mannheim	Germany	1929
Leipzig	Germany	1929
Nenana	USA	1933
Klondike	Canada	1937
Vysehrad (1)	Czechoslovakia	1938

Vysehrad (2)	Czechoslovakia	1938
Stadt Wien	Austria	1939
Stadt Passau	Austria	1940
Vltava	Czechoslovakia	1940
Chickama II	Canada	1942
Pandaw	Myanmar	1946
Labe	Czechoslovakia	1949

POWER – PASSENGERS – CANALS

Juno	Sweden	1874
Thor	Sweden	1887

POWER – FERRIES

Gerda	Sweden	1865
Stralsund	Germany	1890
Eureka	USA	1890
Djurgården 3	Sweden	1893
Berkeley	USA	1898
Malaren 3	Sweden	1903
Binghampton	USA	1905
De Nederlander	Netherlands	1905
Trillium	Canada	1910
Madaket	USA	1910
Güzelhisar	Turkey	1911
Kanangra	Australia	1912
Burgaz	Turkey	1912
Lady Denman	Australia	1912
Adirondack	USA	1913
North Head	Australia	1913
Commander	USA	1917
Esab IV	Sweden	1920
Färjan 4	Sweden	1920
Bilfergen	Norway	1921
Baragoola	Australia	1922
Mön	Denmark	1923
Toroa	New Zealand	1925
Kipawo	Canada	1925
Maj. Gen. Wm. H. Hart	USA	1925
Kalakala	USA	1927
Wehlen Bastei	Germany	1927
Meersburg	Germany	1928
City of Milwaukee	USA	1931
Tattershall Castle	Great Britain	1934
Wingfield Castle	Great Britain	1934
Renfrew Ferry	Great Britain	1935
Rjaanes	Norway	1936
Ryde Queen	Great Britain	1937
South Steyne	Australia	1938
Mary Murray	USA	1938
Lincoln Castle	Great Britain	1940
Balmoral	Great Britain	1949
Geversdorf	Germany	1949
Fischerhütte	Germany	1950
Sjaelland	Denmark	1951
Verrazzano	USA	1951
Broen	Denmark	1952
Egremont	Great Britain	1952
Naomh Eanna	Eire	1958
Sprogø	Denmark	1962
Dan Brostrom	Sweden	1963
Falcon	USA	—
Roaring Bull	USA	—

POWER – CARGO – OCEANS

Hipparchus	Chile	1867
Amadeo	Chile	1884
Calderon	Ecuador	1884
Micalvi	Chile	1925

Panaghiotis	Greece	1937
Soya	Japan	1938
Fryken	Sweden	1938
Vityaz	Russia	1939
John W. Brown	USA	1942
Jeremiah O'Brien	USA	1943
Lane Victory	USA	1945
Soldek	Poland	1949
Traditionsschiff	Germany	1957
Savannah	USA	1959
Cap San Diego	Germany	1962

POWER – CARGO – COASTAL

Kyles	Great Britain	1872
Nelcebee	Australia	1883
Robin	Great Britain	1890
Vaerdalen	Norway	1891
Basuto	Great Britain	1902
Phenol	Germany	1904
Hestmanden	Norway	1911
Thorolf	Norway	1911
Record	USA	1914
Wapama	USA	1915
Line Hinsch	Germany	1929
Our Lady of Lourdes	Canada	1930
Zeemeeuw	Netherlands	1937
Spartan	Great Britain	1940
Advance	Netherlands	1942
Auld Reekie	Great Britain	1943
VIC 32	Great Britain	1943
VIC 96	Great Britain	1943
Capella	Germany	1944
Marsa	Great Britain	1944
Sabrina 5	Great Britain	1944
VIC 56	Great Britain	1946
Wincham	Great Britain	1948
Cuddington	Great Britain	1948
Greundiek	Germany	1950
Jean Yvan	Canada	1958

POWER – CARGO – HARBOURS

Vernie S	USA	1897
Wasserboot II	Germany	1928

POWER – CARGO – LAKES

Raven	Great Britain	1871
Meteor	USA	1896
Osmo	Finland	1904
Venoge	Switzerland	1904
Wenno	Finland	1907
Willis B. Boyer	USA	1911
Mikko	Finland	1914
Valley Camp	USA	1917
William G. Mather	USA	1925
William A. Irvin	USA	1938
Joe Simpson	Canada	1963

POWER – CARGO – RIVERS & CANALS

Voorwaarts	Netherlands	1906
Geertruida	Netherlands	1906
Monarch	Great Britain	1908
President	Great Britain	1909
Willi	Germany	1909
Birchills	Great Britain	c.1914
Day Peckinpaugh	USA	1921
Emma	Germany	1929
Franz-Christian	Germany	1929

Thea-Angela	Germany	1929
Frederica Johanna	Great Britain	1931
Pacifique	France	1931
Oak	Great Britain	1934
Merope	Great Britain	1936
Shad	Great Britain	1936
Chiltern	Great Britain	1946
Mendip	Great Britain	1948
Pompon-Rouge	France	1949
Bacup	Great Britain	1951
Ethel	Great Britain	1952

POWER – CARGO AND TOWING – RIVERS

Adelaide	Australia	1866
Hero	Australia	1874
Success	Australia	1877
Enterprise	Australia	1878
Colonel	Australia	1895
Australien	Australia	1897
Pyap	Australia	1897
Oscar W	Australia	1908
Pevensey	Australia	1910
Alexander Arbuthnot	Australia	1923

POWER – TOWING – OCEANS

Furie	Netherlands	1916
Thor	Netherlands	1918
Seefalke	Germany	1924
Hudson	Netherlands	1939
Holland	Netherlands	1949

POWER – TOWING – COASTAL

Catawissa	USA	1897
Hercules	USA	1907
Ivanhoe	Canada	1907

POWER – TOWING – RIVERS, LAKES, AND CANALS

Tudor Vladmirescu	Rumania	1854
Fortuna	Sweden	1857
Mayflower	Great Britain	1861
Tomten	Sweden	1862
Ahkera	Finland	1871
Bjoren	Norway	1867
Keitele	Finland	1877
Rauha	Finland	1878
Yhtiö	Finland	1878
Florrie	Australia	1880
Elfdalen	Sweden	1888
Ansio	Finland	1889
Strand	Sweden	1890
Visuvesi	Finland	1890
Vetäjä V	Finland	1891
Ahti	Finland	1892
Tippa	Finland	1892
Pieter Boele	Netherlands	1893
Halla IX	Finland	1896
Ardeche	France	1896
Volldampf	Germany	1896
Kopu	New Zealand	1897
Heikki Peuranen	Finland	1897
Metsä	Finland	1898
Enso	Finland	1899
Uitto 6	Finland	1899
Minnesota	USA	1899
Centenniel Showboat		
Keihäslahti	Finland	1900
Repola 5	Finland	1900

HURMA	Finland	1901
GASETEL	Russia	1901
KURT-HEINZ	Germany	1901
VÄNNI	Finland	1901
GEHEIMRAT GARBE	Germany	1902
NORDSTERN	Germany	1902
DANIEL ADAMSON	Great Britain	1903
LÄSÄKOSKI	Finland	1904
TAPIO	Finland	1904
TOIMI II	Finland	1904
AMANDA	Finland	1905
HAAPANIEMI	Finland	1905
PAPINNIEMI	Finland	1905
PEURA III	Finland	1905
HARGE	Sweden	1907
JANNE	Finland	1907
PASCAL	Austria	1907
JUNO	Finland	1907
WELLAMO	Finland	1907
WIPUNEN	Finland	1908
WÜRTTEMBURG	Germany	1908
JOH. PARVIAINEN	Finland	1908
HALLA XVII	Finland	1908
WORCESTER	Great Britain	1908
ARMAS	Finland	1908
GUSTAV	Germany	1908
SEIMA	Germany	1908
UURASTAJA	Finland	1908
SUCCES	Netherlands	1909
AUGUST	Germany	1910
WARKAUS	Finland	1910
KAJAANI	Finland	1911
CANAL CHAIN TUG	France	1912
BORCEA	Romania	1913
PASTEUR	France	1913
WARKAUS VII	Finland	1913
NARAMATA	Canada	1914
FREDERIC MISTRAL	Austria	1914
SACHSENWALD	Germany	1914
PARSIFAL	Finland	1915
KALLE TIHVERÄINEN	Finland	1916
W. P. SNYDER JR.	USA	1918
OBERON III	Finland	1919
OTSO	Finland	1919
VAAJAKOSKI	Finland	1920
OLLI	Finland	1920
HOVINSAARI	Finland	1921
KOUTA	Finland	1921
LONE STAR	USA	1922
OSCAR HUBER	Germany	1922
RUTHOF	Germany	1922
FELICIA	Canada	1923
PALLAS	Finland	1923
ANTERO	Finland	1924
UTRA	Finland	1925
AURE	Finland	1926
PAUL BUNYAN	USA	1926
GEO. M. VERITY	USA	1927
HANS-PETER	Germany	1928
NÄSIJÄRVI II	Finland	1929
ALEIDA I	Great Britain	1930
LAURI	Finland	1931
SEVERN PROGRESS	Great Britain	1932
H. T. POTT	USA	1933
CITY OF CLINTON	USA	1936
RADIUM KING	Canada	1937
JEAN	USA	1938
LOGSDON	USA	1941
PORTLAND	USA	1947
ANDREAS	Germany	1950
MISSINAIBI	Canada	1952
A. D. HAYNES II	USA	1955
PEGUIS II	Canada	1955

POWER – HARBOUR TUGS

JOHN TAXIS	USA	1869
ROSALIE	Netherlands	1889
ARTHUR FOSS	USA	1889
DOROTHY	USA	1890
BRITANNIA	Great Britain	1893
PIETRO MICCA	Italy	1895
EDNA G.	USA	1896
SUCCES	Netherlands	1897
LAUWERZEE	Netherlands	1898
MATHILDA	USA	1899
JACOB LANGENBERG	Netherlands	1902
JUPITER	USA	1902
GABRIELLE	Netherlands	1903
WOLTMAN	Germany	1904
BALTIMORE	USA	1906
DANIEL MCALLISTER	Canada	1907
LYTTELTON	New Zealand	1907
MERULA	Netherlands	1907
SATURN	Germany	1908
BJØRN	Denmark	1908
JOHANNES	Netherlands	1908
STORM PRINCESS	Sweden	1908
PODEROSO	Chile	1908
TENIERS	Germany	1909
FORTUNA	Germany	1909
STYRBJØRN	Norway	1910
TIGER	Germany	1910
VAMPYR II	Germany	1911
KERNE	Great Britain	1913
JAN DE STERKE	Netherlands	1913
CLAUS D	Germany	1913
REISS	USA	1913
EPPLETON HALL	USA	1914
HERCULES	Netherlands	1915
MAASHAVEN	Netherlands	1915
GREDO	Germany	1916
KLABACK	Sweden	1918
FINLAND	Netherlands	1921
NOORDZEE	Netherlands	1922
MASTER	Canada	1922
NALLE PUH	Denmark	1923
KNOCKER WHITE	Great Britain	1924
EDMUND FITZGERALD	USA	1924
FORCEFUL	Australia	1925
ADELAAR	Netherlands	1925
HELMUT	Germany	1925
PORTWEY	Great Britain	1926
SHIBAURA MARU	Japan	1926
MAARTEN	Netherlands	1926
SCHEELENKUHLEN	Netherlands	1926
ULUNDI	South Africa	1927
ROEK	Netherlands	1928
BIELENBERG	Germany	1928
ST. DENYS	France	1929
VOLHARDING I	Netherlands	1929
HUGO	Netherlands	1929
W. O. DECKER	USA	1930
LUNA	USA	1930
JOHN H. AMOS	Great Britain	1931
ST. CANUTE	Great Britain	1931
RENZO	Germany	1931
NED HANLON	Canada	1932
HUNTINGTON	USA	1933
WATTLE	Australia	1933
JOHN KING	Great Britain	1935
WILLIAM C. DALDY	New Zealand	1935
Y-8122	Netherlands	1936
F. D. RUSSELL	USA	1938
TELCO	USA	1938
VICTORIA	Australia	1939
HERKULES	Sweden	1939
DOCKYARD IX	Netherlands	1940
GEBROEDERS BEVER	Netherlands	1941
HAVENDIENST 20	Netherlands	1941
TOMMI	Finland	1943
ANGEL'S GATE	USA	1944
BILL	Germany	1944
TAIOMA	New Zealand	1944
BRENT	Great Britain	1945
FEARLESS	Australia	1945
DOCKYARD V	Netherlands	1946
CHALLENGE	Great Britain	1946
CERVIA	Great Britain	1946
TID 172	Great Britain	1946
TID 164	Great Britain	1946
KENT	Great Britain	1948
ANKE LANGENBERG	Netherlands	1949
YELTA	Australia	1949
FLYING BUZZARD	Great Britain	1951
RECKNITZ	Germany	1953
CANNING	Great Britain	1954
STIER	Germany	1954
GOLDEN CROSS	Great Britain	1955
GARNOCK	Great Britain	1956
ADMIRAL	Estonia	1956
Y-8017	Netherlands	1957
WILLIAM WELLER	South Africa	1958
J. E. EAGLESHAM	South Africa	1958
SAINT-GILLES	France	1958
ALWYN VINTCENT	South Africa	1959
LANGENESS	Germany	1959
J. R. MORE	South Africa	1961
BROCKLEBANK	Great Britain	1965
REGINA	Germany	1966

POWER – PILOT VESSEL

LADY FORREST	Australia	1900
PILOT	USA	1914
EDMUND GARDNER	Great Britain	1953

POWER – WHALING

DIAS	South Georgia	1906
POLAR 4	South Georgia	1912
ALBATROS	South Georgia	1921
PETREL	South Georgia	1928
RAU IX	Germany	1939
KYO MARU NO. 2	Japan	1946
CHEYNES II	Australia	1947
CHEYNES IV	Australia	1948
SOUTHERN ACTOR	Norway	1950

POWER – SEALING

AARVAK	Norway	1912

POWER – FISHING

ABSALON	Germany	1903
TRIX	Netherlands	1903
BRITANNIA	Great Britain	1904
ELLEN	Denmark	1906
RANGER	Australia	1909
OLD POINT	USA	1909
GOLDEN CHANCE	Falkland Islands	1914
KATIE ANN	Great Britain	1921

CLAUS SÖRENSEN	Denmark	1922
DANA	Denmark	1922
FLORENCE	USA	1926
B.C.P. 45	Canada	1927
GEBRÜDER	Germany	1929
LYDIA EVA	Great Britain	1930
MABAHISS	Egypt	1930
KRAIT	Australia	1934
PENGUIN	USA	1935
GUNHILD	Sweden	1936
LISSY	Denmark	1936
BUDDY O	USA	1936
ALOHA	USA	1937
HELAND	Norway	1937
TWILITE	USA	1937
HANNE LENE	Denmark	1938
HANSA	Germany	1938
EVELYN S	USA	1939
NEELTJE	Netherlands	1939
HELLAS	Denmark	1943
BENT II	Denmark	1944
LADY CANADIAN	Canada	1944
5 FUKURYU MARU	Japan	1946
ERON	Denmark	1947
ROANN	USA	1947
ADOLF REICHWEIN	Germany	1949
WISMAR	Germany	1949
HEIMAT	Germany	1955
DAGGI	Germany	1956
HAVEL	Germany	1956
HEMERICA	France	1957
RACLEUR D'OCEAN	France	1958
NOTRE-DAME DE ROCAMADOUR	France	1959
ARCTIC CORSAIR	Great Britain	1960
GERA	Germany	1961
CAPE SABLE	Canada	1962
MINCARLO	Great Britain	1962
ROYAL WAVE	Canada	1962
ANTARES	Great Britain	1965
LAGUN ARTEAN	Spain	1969
KOMPAS	Denmark	1971
JACINTA	Great Britain	1972
THINH VUONG	Australia	1970s
KORALLE	Germany	—
KS8-1192	Australia	—

POWER – YACHTS

DOLLY	Great Britain	1850
EL HORRIA	Egypt	1865
WATERLILLY	Great Britain	1866
ESPERANCE	Great Britain	1869
EVA	Great Britain	1874
AMAZON	Malta	1885
DONOLA	Great Britain	1893
YSOLT	Great Britain	1893
BRANKSOME	Great Britain	1896
OTTO	Great Britain	1896
CAROLA	Great Britain	1898
KITTIWAKE	Great Britain	1898
CANGARDA	USA	1901
ENA	Australia	1901
TI TU	Australia	1901
OSPREY	Great Britain	1902
MEDEA	USA	1904
THANIA	USA	1905
LADY ISABEL	USA	1907
WATER VIPER	Great Britain	1907
YENG HE	China	pre-1909
KRASNYI VYIMPEL	Russia	1910
SWALLOW	Great Britain	1911

CHIEF UNCAS	USA	1912
JEAN	USA	1913
PHOEBE	Canada	1914
WANDA III	Canada	1915
DELPHINE	Belgium	1921
PRINCIPIA	USA	1928
LIBERTATEA	Romania	1930
TIME MACHINE	Egypt	1930
WILLIAMSBURG	Italy	1930
SAVARONA	Turkey	1931
DANNEBROG	Denmark	1931
POTOMAC	USA	1934
PILAR	Cuba	1934
ENTICER	USA	1935
GAY CRUSADER	Great Britain	1935
SEQUOIA	USA	1935
PARDON ME	USA	1948
BRITANNIA	Great Britain	1954

POWER – LINER TENDERS

NOMADIC	France	1911
CALSHOT	Great Britain	1930

POWER – LAUNCHES

ENGEBRET SOOT	Norway	1861
GERDA	Sweden	1865
ALMA AF STAVRE	Sweden	1873
SCHEBO	Sweden	1874
HERBERT	Sweden	1905
BRACKI	Germany	1912
LECHALAS	France	1913
HERBERT	Germany	1923

POWER – CABLE LAYING AND MAINTENANCE

THALIS O. MILISSIOS	Greece	1908
CABLE RESTORER	South Africa	1944

POWER – EXPERIMENTAL

TURBINIA	Great Britain	1894
HYDROFOIL HD4	Canada	1914
PAUL KOSSEL	Germany	1920
WSS-10	Germany	1953
SRN 1	Great Britain	1959

POWER – MISCELLANEOUS

CHAUNCY MAPLES (school and mission)	Malawi	1899
BORDEIN (river exploration)	Sudan	1869
ETONA (floating chapel)	Australia	1899
TAUCHER (flint salvage)	Germany	1910
ELBE RIVER (icebreaker)	Germany	1911
PUHOIS (log bundling vessel)	Finland	1925
GOLIATH (salvage)	Germany	1941
PELICAN (harbor maintenance)	Great Britain	1956
VIETNAMESE (refugee boat)	Singapore	—

CANAL BOATS

SCORPIO	Great Britain	1890
ADMIRAL BEATTY	Great Britain	1896
NORTHWICH	Great Britain	1898
CENTAUR	Great Britain	1899
GEORGE	Great Britain	1900
ST. ANTONIUS	Belgium	1914
BESSIE	Great Britain	1917
CONCRETE CANAL BOAT	Great Britain	1918

TUBE BOAT No.39	Great Britain	c.1920
FRIENDSHIP	Great Britain	1925
GIFFORD	Great Britain	1926
LAURANDA	Belgium	1928
ARIES	Great Britain	1935
MERAK	Great Britain	1936
CEPHEE	Belgium	1937
BIGMERE	Great Britain	1948
FCB 18	Great Britain	1940s
SAPPHIRE	Great Britain	1952
WYE	Great Britain	—
No. 249	USA	—
BOX BOAT 337	Great Britain	—
CEDAR	Great Britain	—
PHOEBE	Great Britain	—

CANAL – MAINTENANCE

DERRICK BOAT No. 8	USA	1925
DIPPER DREDGE No. 3	USA	1927
IVY MAY (maintenance)	Great Britain	1934
PERSEVERANCE (dredger)	Great Britain	1934
ASPULL (icebreaker)	Great Britain	—
GD 101 (dredger)	Great Britain	—
MARBURY (icebreaker)	Great Britain	—

BARGES – RIVERS

CONSTABLE	Great Britain	c.1830
MOSSDALE	Great Britain	1876
ADA	Australia	1898
TP	Australia	1900
WALTER	Germany	1901
ALLISON	Australia	1907
RENATE-ANGELIKA	Germany	1910
AII	Australia	1911
VEGA	Australia	1911
DART	Australia	1912
ELSWICK II	Great Britain	1913
B22	Australia	1922
SPEEDWELL	Great Britain	1925
ADVANCE	Great Britain	1926
OSTARA	Germany	1926
D26	Australia	1926
CHALK BARGE	Great Britain	1948
HEMMOOR 3	Germany	pre-1960
BLACK PRINCE	Great Britain	—

BARGES – HARBOURS

DAEKSPRAM No. 19	Denmark	1907
H 11347	Germany	1912
SCHULTE	Germany	1913
L. V. R. R. No. 79	USA	1914
MIJL OP ZEVEN	Netherlands	c.1916
GRÅBENDORF	Germany	1920
M. PK. 86	Germany	1926
CONCRETE BARGE	Great Britain	1944
DIEU PROTEGE	France	1950
GÖTEBORGSPRÅM	Sweden	—

MINING DREDGES

GOLDSTREAM DREDGE No. 8	USA	1928
SUMPTER VALLEY DREDGE	USA	1935
YANKEE FORK GOLD DREDGE	USA	1940
DREDGE No. 4	Canada	1941

FLOATING CRANES

LANGER HEINRICH	Germany	1890

Hercules	Panama	1913
Saatsee	Germany	1920
Rapaki	New Zealand	1926
Karl Friedrich Steen	Germany	1928
Simson	Netherlands	1958

Floating theatres

Goldenrod	USA	1910
Majestic	USA	1923

Research submersibles

Trieste	USA	1953
Trieste II	USA	—

Non-self propelled — miscellaneous

Bateau Lavoir (floating laundry)	France	c.1909
Bateau Lavoir (floating laundry)	France	—
La Duchesse (houseboat)	USA	1903/1950s
Lewis Ark (houseboat)	USA	1905
Old Barge Cafe (oyster barge)	USA	—
No. 19 (grain elevator)	Netherlands	1926
Maneuverboat No.3 (dam wicket lifting scow)	USA	c.1930
Pollux (floating school)	Netherlands	1940
Priboesti-Maramures (floating mill)	Romania	—
Reckeve (floating mill)	Hungary	—
Danube (ferry scow)	Germany	1954

Rowing — royal barges

Kadirga	Turkey	1600s
Prince Frederick's Barge	Great Britain	1732
Bergantim Real	Portugal	1778
Kongechalup	Denmark	1780
Canot Imperial	France	1811
De Koningssloep	Netherlands	1818
Caiques of Sultan Abdulmejit (2)	Turkey	1800s
Sultan's Barge	Zanzibar	1800s
Anekajatibhujonga	Thailand	c.1910
Subanahongsa	Thailand	1911
Anantanagaraj	Thailand	1914

Government vessels — lightships

Fyrskib X	Denmark	1877
Fyrskib XI	Denmark	1878
Fyrskib XII	Denmark	1878
Fyrskib XIII	Denmark	1880
Laesö Rende	Germany	1887
Elbe 3	Germany	1888
Fyrskib XVII	Denmark	1895
Malmo Redd	Sweden	1896
Kemi	Finland	1901
Finngrundet	Sweden	1903
Relief	USA	1904
Barnegat	USA	1904
Weser	Germany	1907
Ambrose	USA	1907
Fehmarnbelt	Germany	1908
Elbe 3	Germany	1909
Fyrskib XXI	Denmark	1911
Havre II	France	1912
Hyöky	Finland	1912
Amrumbank	Germany	1914
Calshot Spit	Great Britain	1914
Fladen	Sweden	1914

Motorfyrskib I	Denmark	1914
Deutsche Bucht	Germany	1915
Petrel	Great Britain	1915
Portsmouth	USA	1915
Fyrskib II	Denmark	1916
C.L.S. No. 2	Australia	1918
C.L.S. No. 4	Australia	1918
Huron	USA	1921
Guillemot	Eire	1923
Spurn	Great Britain	1927
Chesapeake	USA	1930
New Bedford	USA	1930
North Carr	Great Britain	1933
Dyck	France	1935
Nantucket	USA	1936
Nore	Great Britain	1936
Helwick	Great Britain	1937
Overfalls	USA	1938
Elbe 1	Germany	1942
Scarweather	France	1947
Sandettie	France	1949
Columbia	USA	1950
L.S. no. 1	Belgium	1950
Nantucket	USA	1950
L.V. no. 13	Germany	1952
Lichtship no.10	Netherlands	1952
Nantucket	USA	1952
Borkumriff	Germany	1956
Haven	Great Britain	1959
Planet	Great Britain	1960
Lichtschip no.12	Netherlands	1963
L.V. no. 12	Netherlands	c.1968
Goleulong 2000 Lightship	Great Britain	—
Heaven	Netherlands	—
L.S. no. 2	Belgium	—
West Hinder	Belgium	—

Government vessels — lighthouse tenders

Meiji Maru	Japan	1874
Hekkingen	Norway	1913
Bradbury	Canada	1915
Gerda III	USA	1926
Wake Robin	USA	1926
Lilac	USA	1933
Ukko-Pekka	Finland	1938
Fir	USA	1939
Maple	USA	1939

Government vessels — surveying & research

Hansteen	Norway	1866
Acadia	Canada	1913
Detector	Canada	1915
Canadian Princess	Canada	1932
Explorer	Great Britain	1955
Hero	USA	1968

Government vessels — inspection

Flottisten	Sweden	1890
Saimaa	Finland	1893
Christiaan Brunings	Netherlands	1900
Lady Hopetoun	Australia	1902
Schaarhörn	Germany	1908
Becky Thatcher	USA	1927
Polstjärnan af Vänern	Sweden	1929
Kennet	Great Britain	1931
Ems	Germany	1934

Government vessels — customs patrol

Rigmor	Germany	1855
Viking	Denmark	1897
Vigilant	Great Britain	1902
Batory	Poland	1932
Gluckstadt	Germany	1954
Hitzacker	Germany	1956
TV 253	Sweden	1960

Rescue craft

City of Adelaide	Australia	1893
Alfred Corry	Great Britain	1893
Colin Archer	Norway	1893
Christiania	Norway	1895
Oscar Tybring I	USA	1895
B.A.S.P.	Great Britain	1924
Insulinde	Netherlands	1926
Queenscliffe	Australia	1926
Astrid Finne	Sweden	1937
Twenthe	Netherlands	1942
Hindenburg	Germany	1944
Langeoog	Germany	1944
Rickmer Bock	Germany	1944
William Gammon	Great Britain	1947
Reddingboot 1	Netherlands	1948
Susan Ashley	Great Britain	1948
Peinz Hendrik	Netherlands	1950
St. Cybi	Great Britain	1950
North Foreland	Great Britain	1951
Grace Darling	Great Britain	1954
Watkin Williams	Great Britain	1956
J. G. Graves of Sheffield	Great Britain	1958
Theodor Heuss	Germany	1960
CG-44300	USA	1961
Will And Fanny Kirby	Great Britain	1963
Georg Breusing	Germany	1963
Edward Bridges	Great Britain	1975

Government vessels — icebreakers

Bore	Sweden	1894
Tarmo	Finland	1907
Suur Toll	Estonia	1914
Sankt Erik	Sweden	1915
Krassin	Russia	1917
Stettin	Germany	1933
Wal	Germany	1938
Ernest Lapointe	Canada	1940
Alexander Henry	Canada	1959

Government vessels — dredging and channel clearing

Brunel Drag Boat	Great Britain	1844
Atlas	Germany	1876
Minden	Germany	1882
1 Mai	Germany	1898
D 6	France	1906
Industry	Australia	1911
Melbourne	Australia	1912
Col. D. D. Gaillard	USA	1916
S. N. D. no. 4	Great Britain	1925
Porta	Germany	1925
Ed 9	Germany	1926
Montgomery	USA	1926
Crossen	Germany	1928
Saint-Marc	France	1931
Ste. Genevieve	USA	1932
Captain Meriwether Lewis	USA	1932

WILLIAM M. BLACK	USA	1934
WILLIAM S. MITCHELL	USA	1934
MANNIN 2	Great Britain	1936
FRIESLAND	Netherlands	1936
WELS	Germany	1936
SAMSON V	Canada	1937
SEIONT II	Great Britain	1937
W. T. PRESTON	USA	1939
ARKANSAS II	USA	1940

GOVERNMENT VESSELS – TOWING

URGER	USA	1901
WARATAH	Australia	1902
WILHELM BAUM	USA	1923
P. A. DENNY	USA	1930
SERGEANT FLOYD	USA	1932
MAJOR ELISHA K. HANSON	USA	1944
ST-2031	USA	—

GOVERNMENT VESSELS – FIREBOATS

RALPH J. SCOTT	USA	1925
FIREBOAT NO. 1	USA	1929
JAN VAN DER HEYDE	Netherlands	1930
WALTER HÄVERNICK	Germany	1930
FLODSPRUTAN II	Sweden	1931
JOHN J. HARVEY	USA	1931
PYRONAUT	Great Britain	1934
MASSEY SHAW	Great Britain	1935
FIREFIGHTER	USA	1938
FEUERLÖSCHBOOT 1	Germany	1940
KIEL	Germany	1941
EMDEN 1	Germany	1953

GOVERNMENT VESSELS – POLICE PATROL

BURMA QUEEN	USA	1927
ST. ROCH	Canada	1928
OTTO LAUFFER	Germany	1928
CERBERUS	Germany	1930
WASSERSCHUTZPOLIZEI 10	Germany	1957
ELBE 27	Germany	1959

GOVERNMENT VESSELS – COAST GUARD PATROL

MCLANE	USA	1927
MHV 67	Denmark	1929
MOHAWK	USA	1934
INGHAM	USA	1936
TANEY	USA	1936
CG 52302	USA	1944

GOVERNMENT VESSELS – MISCELLANEOUS

BUSSARD (buoy tender)	Germany	1905
JOHN OXLEY (port service)	Australia	1927
MAYOR ANDREW BROADDUS (lifesaving station)	USA	1929
SAMARYTANKA (medical launch)	Poland	1931
WARDEN JOHNSTON (ferry)	USA	1945
YAMBULLA (launch)	Australia	1945
KAPITAN MEYER (buoy tender)	Germany	1949
J-3792 (picket boat)	USA	c.1954
SHIELDHALL (sludge carrier)	Great Britain	1955
FRANCE I (weather ship)	France	1958
INGOLF (fisheries inspection)	Denmark	1962

NAVAL – SAIL – SHIPS OF THE LINE

MARY ROSE	Great Britain	1510

VASA	Sweden	1627
VICTORY	Great Britain	1765

NAVAL – SAIL – FRIGATES

CONSTITUTION	USA	1797
TRINCOMALEE	Great Britain	1817
UNICORN	Great Britain	1824
DOM FERNANDO II E GLORIA	Portugal	1843

NAVAL – SAIL – CORVETTES

CONSTELLATION	USA	1855

NAVAL – SAIL – GUNBOATS

PHILADELPHIA	USA	1776

NAVAL – SAIL & STEAM – FRIGATES

JYLLAND	Denmark	1860
WARRIOR	Great Britain	1860

NAVAL – SAIL & STEAM – GUNBOATS

URUGUAY	Argentina	1874
BONAIRE	Netherlands	1877
GANNET	Great Britain	1878

NAVAL – STEAM – MONITORS

CERBERUS	Australia	1870
SÖLVE	Sweden	1875
M-33	Great Britain	1915

NAVAL – STEAM – SEAGOING MONITORS

HUASCAR	Chile	1865
BUFFEL	Netherlands	1868
SCHORPIOEN	Netherlands	1868

NAVAL – STEAM – PRE–DREADNOUGHT BATTLESHIPS

MIKASA	Japan	1900

NAVAL – STEAM – BATTLESHIPS

TEXAS	USA	1912
NORTH CAROLINA	USA	1940
MASSACHUSETTS	USA	1941
ALABAMA	USA	1942
MISSOURI	USA	1944

NAVAL – STEAM – AIRCRAFT CARRIERS

LEXINGTON	USA	1942
HORNET	USA	1943
INTREPID	USA	1943
YORKTOWN	USA	1943
VIKRANT	India	1945

NAVAL – STEAM – CRUISERS

OLYMPIA	USA	1892
AURORA	Russia	1900
GIORGIOS AVEROF	Greece	1910
CAROLINE	Great Britain	1914
BELFAST	Great Britain	1938
LITTLE ROCK	USA	1944
COLBERT	France	1956

NAVAL – STEAM – DESTROYERS

QINGDAO	China	c.1936-1940
BLYSKAWICA	Poland	1936
HAIDA	Canada	1941
CASSIN YOUNG	USA	1943
THE SULLIVANS	USA	1943
LAFFEY	USA	1943
KIDD	USA	1943
CAVALIER	Great Britain	1944
MINISTRO ZENTENO	Chile	1944
JOSEPH P. KENNEDY JR.	USA	1945
GAYRET	Turkey	1946
SMÅLAND	Sweden	1952
MAILLE-BREZE	France	1954
BARRY	USA	1956
EDSON	USA	1958
TURNER JOY	USA	1958
VAMPIRE	Australia	1959

NAVAL – POWER – SUBMARINES

PERAL	Spain	1888
HOLLAND I	Great Britain	1901
HAJEN	Sweden	1904
ALOSE	France	1904
U-1	Germany	1906
NARODOVOLEC	Russia	1929
VESIKKO	Finland	1933
LEMBIT	Estonia	1936
S-56	Russia	1939
SILVERSIDES	USA	1940
DRUM	USA	1941
U-505	USA	1941
U-995	Germany	1941
CROAKER	USA	1942
U-3	Sweden	1942
U-534	Great Britain	1942
BOWFIN	USA	1942
PAMPANITO	USA	1943
BAHIA	Brazil	1943
LIONFISH	USA	1943
COD	USA	1943
BATFISH	USA	1943
CAVALLA	USA	1943
COBIA	USA	1943
TORSK	USA	1944
BECUNA	USA	1944
WILHELM BAUER	Germany	1945
ALLIANCE	Great Britain	1945
LING	USA	1945
CLAMAGORE	USA	1945
REQUIN	USA	1945
ALBACORE	USA	1953
NAUTILUS	USA	1954
U-359	Denmark	c.1955
GROWLER	USA	1957
ARGONAUTE	France	1957
ESPADON	France	1958
BLUEBACK	USA	1959
229	China	c.1959
NORDKAPAREN	Sweden	1961
OCELOT	Great Britain	1962
SPRINGEREN	Denmark	1963
U-461	Denmark	1964
TONIJN	Netherlands	1965
U-111	Netherlands	1965
ONYX	Great Britain	1966
U-9	Germany	1966
OVENS	Australia	1967
U-10	Germany	1967

Onslow	Australia	1968
Scorpion	USA	1973
U-521	Canada	1974
Riachuelo	Brazil	1975
M-305	Ukraine	—
U-475	Great Britain	—
U-484	Finland	—
Russian Submarine	Sweden	—

Naval – power – midget submarines

Ha. 8	USA	1938
Ha. 19	USA	1938
CB-22	Italy	1943
Kairyu Type	Japan	1945
XE-8	Great Britain	1945
Stickleback	Great Britain	1945
S622	France	1945
Seehund Type	Germany	1944
Seehund Type	Germany	1944
Seehund Type	Germany	1944
Seehund Type	USA	c.1945
Seehund Type	USA	c.1945
Seehund Type	Germany	1945
Seehund Type	Germany	1945
Seehund Type	Great Britain	c.1945
Japanese	USA	c.1945
Marlin	USA	1953
X-1	USA	1955
SA 42	Spain	1957
SX-404 Type	Pakistan	c.1973

Naval – power – destroyer escorts, frigates, sloops

Wellington	Great Britain	1934
Sackville	Canada	1941
Borgenes	Norway	1942
Stewart	USA	1942
Bauru	Brazil	1943
Rajah Humabon	Philippines	1943
Tahchin	Thailand	1943
Cordoba	Colombia	1944
Kojima	Japan	1944
Diamantina	Australia	1945
Fraser	Canada	1953
Boyaca	Colombia	1957
Plymouth	Great Britain	1959
Annapolis	Canada	1963

Naval – power – minelayers

Nusret	Turkey	1912
Keihassalmi	Finland	1956

Naval – power – minesweepers

Abraham Crijnssen	Netherlands	1936
Bremon	Sweden	1940
Whyalla	Australia	1942
Castlemaine	Australia	1942
Quezon	Philippines	1943
WBR 7	Germany	1943
Hazard	USA	1944
T-729	Ukraine	1940s
Minesweeper	Ukraine	1940s
MSB 5	USA	1952
Bronington	Great Britain	1953
Mercuur	Netherlands	1953
Pretoria	South Africa	1954
Mujahid	Pakistan	1956

Durban	South Africa	1957
Oudenaarde	Belgium	1958
Weilheim	Germany	1958
Beckum	Germany	1960
Houtepen	Netherlands	1961

Naval – power – torpedo boats

Rap	Norway	1872
Derzki	Bulgaria	1905
CMB 4	Great Britain	1916
MAS 15	Italy	1917
MAS 96	Italy	1917
CMB 103	Great Britain	1921
MTB 102	Great Britain	1937
MTB 71	Great Britain	1940
MS 473	Italy	1942
MTB 472	Italy	1942
Torpedo Cutter no.3	Bulgaria	1942
PT-309	USA	1944
PT-695	USA	1944
PT 617	USA	1945
PT 796	USA	1945
TK-456	Russia	1940s
TKA-001	Russia	1940s
TKA-12	Russia	1940s
TKA-52	Ukraine	1940s
TKA-341	Russia	1940s
TKA-383	Ukraine	1940s
TKA-725	Ukraine	1940s
Torpedoboat 36	Russia	1940s
Torpedoboat 123	Russia	1940s
Torpedoboat	Russia	1940s
Torpedoboat	Russia	1940s
Torpedoboat	Ukraine	1940s
T-38	Sweden	1951
TA-1	Turkey	c.1952
Kranich	Germany	1958
Tjeld	Norway	1960
Søbjørnen	Denmark	1964
Spica	Sweden	1966
Torpedoboat	Germany	1960s
no. 925	Germany	1975
Torpedoboat	Germany	1976
Torpedoboat	Germany	1976
PT-658	USA	—
Torpedoboat	Ukraine	—

Naval – power – gunboats

Demon	Great Britain	1883
Melik	Sudan	1897
America	Peru	1904
Cartagena	Colombia	1930
River Gunboat	Iraq	1937
Zhongshan	China	pre-1938
MGB-60	Great Britain	1940
ML 293	Great Britain	1941
No. 772 & one onknown	Russia	1940s
Bras D'Or (hydrofoil)	Canada	1967
PTF-17	USA	1968
No. 3139	China	—
Hiddensee	USA	—

Naval – river monitors

Leitha	Hungary	1872
Zhelesniakov	Ukraine	1939
BKA-41	Ukraine	1940s
BKA-44	Ukraine	1940s
BKA-81	Ukraine	1940s

BKA-92	Russia	1940s
BKA-134	Ukraine	1940s
BKA-162	Russia	1940s
BKA-181	Russia	1940s
BKA-334	Ukraine	1940s
River Monitor 302	Russia	1940s

Naval – submarine chasers

Hitra	Norway	1943

Naval – patrol boats

Salto	Uruguay	1935
VMV 11	Finland	1935
Koura	New Zealand	1943
Kuparu	New Zealand	1944
KW 19	Germany	1952
Sri Trengganu	Malaysia	1961
Tikal	Guatemala	c.1962
PCF-1	USA	1965
Advance	Australia	1968
Ardent	Australia	1968
Al Mansur	Oman	1973
CCB-18	USA	—
Q-Boat	USA	—

Naval – landing craft

LCA 1825	France	1944
Af-Al-Pi-Chen	Israel	1944
Unknown	Russia	1940s
Barc 3-X	USA	1952L 9512
L9512	Netherlands	1962

Naval – launches

198	Great Britain	1911
Sundowner	Great Britain	1912
General Jenkins	Great Britain	1942
296	Great Britain	1942
1262 (Royal Air Force)	Great Britain	1942
Nottingham Castle	Canada	1943
376	Great Britain	1944
KTSC-772	Russia	1940s
Armed Launch	Russia	1940s
KBV-238	Sweden	1962

Naval – miscellaneous

Vanguardia (naval tender)	Uruguay	1908
Hydrograaf (survey ship)	Netherlands	1910
Laurindo Pitta (seagoing tug)	Brazil	1910
Marine Ship	USA	c.1919
Chandlery (workshop)		
Ondee (water carrier)	France	1935
Gauss (survey ship)	Germany	1941
HSL 102	Great Britain	1941
Somerset (boom tender)	South Africa	1941
Air Sea (rescue boat)	USA	1942
Pueblo (cargo/spy ship)	North Korea	1944
ST-8 (harbor tug)	France	1944
MPC-80 (armed fishing boat)	Russia	1940s
Anti-Aircraft Boat	Ukraine	1940s
Tamaroa (seagoing tug)	USA	1943
Sanctuary (hospital ship)	USA	1944
Manawanui (harbor tug)	New Zealand	c.1946
Freshspring (water carrier)	Great Britain	1947
Black Duck (aviation rescue)	Canada	1954
HMAFV 2757 (aviation rescue)	Great Britain	1956
Rudokop (navy tugboat)	Canada	1957

Appendix 3 Remnants of historic vessels

1 Visible remains of wrecked or abandoned ships.
2 Preserved archaeological remains.
3 Portions of ships preserved in museums.
4 Portions of ships preserved as monuments.
5 Portions of ships utilized on shore.
6 Ships serving non-museum stationary uses, with engines or other significant original features removed.

▌VISIBLE REMAINS OF WRECKED OR ABANDONED SHIPS

(Note: Readers should bear in mind that most of the remains listed below are dangerous to board, located on private property, and protected historic sites or cultural resources.)

Argentina

DUCHESS OF ALBANY – iron ship; built at Liverpool in 1884. Wrecked on the coast of Tierra del Fuego in 1893. Partly collapsed hull lies beached in Policarpo Cove.

Australia

ADOLPHE – steel four-masted barque; built at Dunquerque, France in 1902. Wrecked at entrance to Newcastle, New South Wales in 1904. Bow survives beside breakwater.
CONCORDIA – iron barque; built at Sunderland, England in 1869. Bow survives beached in Norfolk Bay, Tasmania.
ETHEL – iron barque; built at Sunderland, England in 1876. Wrecked on Yorke Peninsula in 1904. Stern lies on beach there.
FARSUND – steel barque; built at Sunderland, England in 1891. Wrecked on sand bar south of Flinders Island in 1912. Badly rusted hull still lies there.
FRANCIS PRESTON BLAIR – steel cargo vessel, Liberty type; built at Sausalito, California in 1943. Wrecked on Saumerez Reef off northeast coast of Australia in July 1945. Largely intact vessel now lies high and dry on reef.
GAYUNDAH – steel gunboat; built in Newcastle, England in 1884. Served in Queensland Navy. Hull lies beached at Redcliffe.
ITATA – iron barque; built at Liverpool in 1883. Hull lies sunk in an arm of Sydney Harbour, with part of bow visible at all stages to tide.
J-7 – submarine; built at Devonport, England in 1917. Served in Royal Australian Navy 1919-1929. Sunk as breakwater at Hampton, Victoria in 1930. Remains of hull survive there.
OTAGO – iron barque; built at Glasgow, Scotland in 1869. Bottom lies beached near Hobart, Tasmania. (see also United States)
PROTECTOR – steel gunboat; built at Newcastle, England in 1884. Served in navy

of South Australia. Hull lies beached at Heron Island, Queensland.
SVENOR – steel barque; built at Port Glasgow, Scotland in 1885. Wrecked on west coast of Tasmania in 1914. Broken up remains still lie on beach there.

Bermuda

EMILY A. DAVIES – iron ship; built at Sunderland, England in 1876. Remains of bow lie in cove across harbor from Hamilton.
NORRKOPING (ex-RUNNYMEDE) – iron barque; built at Sunderland, England in 1869. Remains of bow lie in cove across harbour from Hamilton.
TAIFUN (ex-ANCON) – steel barque; built at Greenock, Scotland in 1894. Badly rusted hull lies grounded in St. George Harbour.

Brazil

AMERICA (ex-ANDRADA, ex-BRITANNIA) – passenger liner; built at Bergen, Norway in 1890. Converted to warship by Brazilian Navy. Hull survives as a wharf at Cabo Frio, near Rio de Janeiro.

Canada

HMS CALYPSO – iron steam and sail gunboat; built at Chatham, England in 1883. Served as a stationary training ship, and later a storage hulk in Newfoundland. Hull now lies abandoned in a cove north of Lewisporte, Newfoundland.
COMET – steel four-masted barque; built at Port Glasgow, Scotland in 1901. Largely broken up hull is part of a breakwater at Royston, British Columbia.
DOUGLAS HOUGHTON – steel bulk freighter; built at Cleveland, Ohio in 1899. Sunk as a breakwater at Toronto, Ontario in the early 1970s and still largely intact there.
MELANOPE – iron ship; built at Liverpool in 1876. Largely broken up hull is part of a breakwater at Royston, British Columbia.
RAPIDS QUEEN – steel river steamer; built at Chester, Pennsylvania in 1892. Intact hull serves as a breakwater and pier at a yacht club near Toronto.
RIDGETOWN (ex-WILLIAM E. COREY) – steel bulk freighter; built at Chicago, Illinois in 1905. Grounded as a breakwater at Port Credit, Ontario (Lake Ontario) in 1974. Survives there largely intact.
RIVERSDALE – steel ship; built at Port Glasgow, Scotland in 1894. Largely broken up hull is part of a breakwater at Royston, British Columbia.

Chile

LONSDALE – steel ship; built at Londonderry, Ireland in 1889. Partially scrapped hull with bow intact lies beached

at Punta Arenas.
OLYMPIAN – steel sidewheel steamer; built at Wilmington, Delaware in 1883. Wrecked in Straits of Magellan in 1906 while under tow. Remains on beach near Cape Dungeness include engine, boilers, paddlewheels, and parts of hull.

Falkland islands

ACTAEON – wooden barque; built at Miramichi, New Brunswick in 1838. Grounded at end of wharf in Port Stanley in mid-1800s. Hull survives cut down to just above lower deck beams.
CAPRICORN – wooden barque; built at Bideford, England in 1859. Grounded at end of pier in Port Stanley in 1800s. Keel and remains of bottom lie in shallow water there.
GLENGOWAN – steel ship; built at Port Glasgow, Scotland in 1895. Burned out at Port Stanley on maiden voyage. Hull lies in shallow water at New Island where last used as a coaling hulk.
HELEN A. MILLER – wooden ship; built at Baltimore, Maryland in 1851. Burned in San Carlos Bay. Lower hull is still visible in a cove there.
MARGARET – wooden barque; built at Halifax, Nova Scotia in 1836. Grounded at end of jetty in Port Stanley in mid-1800s. Hull lies under pier there, cut down to just above lower deck beams.
ST. MARY – wooden ship; built at Phippsburg, Maine in 1890. Wrecked in Falkland Islands on maiden voyage. Broken up remains lie on beach south of Port Stanley (see also Museums; United States).
WILLIAM SHAND – wooden barque; built at Greenock, Scotland in 1839. Grounded at end of jetty in Port Stanley in mid-1800s. Hull lies there under a pier cut down to just above lower deck beams.

Finland

CHRISTINA – wooden barque built at Varnaras, Sweden in 1875. Hull lies beached at Ostervik Island, off Vardo, Aland Islands.
PEHR BRAHE – wooden barque; built at Haraldholm, Sweden in 1877. Lower hull lies in shallow cove near Mariehamn.

Great Britain

ABANA – wooden barque; built at Portland, New Brunswick in 1874. Wrecked near Blackpool, England in 1894. Portion of wreck imbedded in beach is visible at low tide.
NORNEN – wooden ship; built at Bordeaux, France in 1876. Wrecked off Berrow, England in 1897. Full length of ship's bottom is exposed on mud flats at low tide.

New Zealand

AMOKURA (ex-HMS SPARROW) – composite gunboat; built at Greenock, Scotland in 1889. Served in later years as New Zealand training ship. Hull lies sunk along shore in St. Omer Bay, South Island.
DARRA – composite barque; built at Aberdeen, Scotland in 1865. Lower hull lies beached at Quail Island off the harbour of Lyttleton, along with the remains of around fifteen other vessels.
DON JUAN – wooden ship; built in Sweden in 1857. Lower hull lies in shallow water in Deborah Bay, South Island.
FUSILIER – iron barque; built at Sunderland, England in 1860. Wrecked on west coast of North Island in 1884. Hull lies partly buried in sand dunes well inland from beach south of Wanganui.
HYDRABAD – iron ship; built at Port Glasgow, Scotland in 1865. Wrecked on the west coast of North Island in 1878. Hull lies imbedded in beach near Foxton.
OTHELLO – wooden barque (whaler); built at Fairhaven, Massachusetts in 1853. Hull lies sunk in cove at abandoned whaling station on Stewart Island, burned to waterline.
PRINCE OF WALES – wooden barque; built in Southampton, England in 1850. Used as a storage hulk in New Zealand. Lower hull now lies just off beach in Otanerau Bay, South Island.
REWA (ex-ALICE A. LEIGH) – steel four-masted barque; built at Whitehaven, England in 1889. Partially collapsed hull serves as a breakwater for a small harbour at Moturakareka Island.
TE ANAU – steel steamship; built at Dumbarton, Scotland in 1879. One of the first steamships built of mild steel. Sunk as a breakwater at Wanganui in 1924. Hull is still largely intact (see also museums).
WAVERLEY – iron steamer; built in New Zealand in 1883. Grounded as a breakwater near Blenheim in 1928. Hull, still largely intact, is now resting on beach there.

Nigeria

ALTAIR – iron four-masted barque; built at Liverpool in 1890. Grounded at mouth of Niger River in 1924. Broken up remains lie along beach there.

South Georgia

LOUISE – wooden barque; built at Freeport, Maine in 1869. Hull lies beached at abandoned whaling station at Grytviken, burned down to waterline.

United States

BASCOBEL – steel steam seagoing tugboat; built at Elizabeth, New Jersey in 1919. One of the more intact vessels among a very large collection lying sunk at a scrapyard in Rossville, New York (*see also* New Bedford).

Bendigo – steamer used to run blockade of Confederate States. Sunk in shallows off Lockwood's Folly Inlet, North Carolina in January 1864. Complete outline of hull still visible and partly above water, with remains of engines and paddlewheels.

Cora F. Cressy – wooden five-masted schooner; built at Bath, Maine in 1902. Grounded at Bremen, Maine as storage for lobsters. Hull has begun to collapse.

Frances – iron barque; built at Liverpool, England in 1861. Wrecked on Cape Cod in 1872. Bow can be seen in surf off beach near Provincetown, Massachusetts.

Lornty – iron ship; built at Sunderland, England in 1879. Partially scrapped hull lies in shallow water in Curtis Creek near Baltimore, Maryland.

New Bedford – steel coastal passenger steamer (island ferry); built at Quincy, Massachusetts in 1928. Sold to a scrapyard in Rossville, New York in 1968, but never broken up. Still lies sunk there, largely intact.

Occidental – wooden ship; built at Bath, Maine in 1874. Later used as coastwise coal barge. Hull lies sunk in shallow cove at Bayonne, New Jersey, burned to waterline.

Peter Iredale – steel four-masted barque; built at Maryport, England in 1890. Wrecked on coast of Oregon in 1906. Bow survives imbedded in beach near mouth of Columbia River.

Santiago – steel barque; built at Belfast, Ireland in 1885. Broken up remains lie on beach near Kodiak, Alaska.

2 PRESERVED ARCHAEOLOGICAL REMAINS

Canada

Nancy – wooden schooner; built in 1789. Used as a British supply ship in the War of 1812. Sunk in Lake Huron to prevent capture in 1814. Remains excavated in 1923 are now on exhibit at Wasaga Beach, Ontario under cover.

Tecumseth – wooden schooner; built in 1816. Small warship built for the War of 1812 but completed after end of War. Abandoned at Penetanguishene, Ontario on Lake Huron. Remains of hull, raised in 1953, are now displayed on shore there under cover.

China

Twin hull dugout canoe – 66 foot craft excavated in 1976. On exhibit at the Changdao Maritime Museum.

Cyprus

Kyrenia ship – wooden trading vessel of the 4th century B.C. Remains of hull raised near port of Kyrenia in 1970s displayed in a room in the Crusader castle there.

Denmark

Skudelev ships – Five wooden Viking-type ships dating from c1000 found where they had been sunk to block a channel in the Roskilde Fjord, Denmark. Believed to be two trading vessels, two warships, and a fishing vessel. Surviving remains of hulls have been reassembled and are now exhibited in the Viking Ship Hall in Roskilde.

Netherlands

Trading vessel of the mid-1600s. Bow and stern are exhibited indoors at the Ship Archeology Museum in Lelystad, along with parts of other craft of various periods found during land reclamation in the area of the former Zuiderzee.

United States

Arabia – river steamboat; built at Brownsville, Pennsylvania in 1853. Sank near Parkville, Missouri in 1856. Wreck was discovered buried 45 feet beneath a soybean field due to later changes in the course of the Missouri River. Much of the cargo and a portion of the vessel were raised in 1989 and are now on exhibit at Kansas City, Missouri.

Brown's Ferry Vessel – small wooden sailing vessel of mid-1700s. Remains of hull raised from Black River in South Carolina in 1976. Currently undergoing conservation for eventual exhibit.

USS Cairo – armoured river gunboat; built at Mound City, Illinois in 1861. Sunk by mine in the Yazoo River in December 1862. Broke up while being raised in late 1950s. Partially re-assembled remains are exhibited under cover at Vicksburg, Mississippi.

CSS Chattahoochee – wooden steam gunboat; built in 1862. Portion of lower hull raised in early 1960s is exhibited under cover at the Confederate Naval Museum in Columbus, Georgia.

CSS Muscogee – wooden armoured gunboat; built at Columbus, Georgia in 1864. Burned in April 1865. Lower hull is exhibited under cover at the Confederate Naval Museum in Columbus.

CSS Neuse – wooden armoured gunboat; built at Whitehall, North Carolina in 1863. Burned in March 1865. Lower hull is exhibited under cover near Kinston, North Carolina.

Sparrowhawk – keel and lower frames of a wooden sailing vessel found buried near Plymouth, Massachusetts. Believed to be vessel lost in 1626. Exhibited in Pilgrim Hall in Plymouth.

Ticonderoga – wooden schooner; built in 1814. American warship built for Lake Champlain squadron during War of 1812. Remains of hull raised in 1958 are displayed on shore under cover at Whitehall, New York.

175 Water Street ship – bow of a largely intact wooden vessel of the 18th century found buried in Lower Manhattan, New York City in 1982. Currently undergoing conservation treatment at the Mariners Museum in Newport News, Virginia.

3 PORTIONS OF SHIPS PRESERVED IN MUSEUMS

Australia

Shandon – iron barque; built at Port Glasgow, Scotland in 1883. Iron crew deckhouse is preserved on shore alongside the museum ship Polly Woodside in Melbourne, Australia.

Austria

U-20 – submarine; built at Pola, Austria-Hungary in 1916. Conning tower and a portion of hull are preserved in the Heeresgeschichteliches Museum in Vienna.

Canada

Cape North – wooden fishing vessel; built at Meteghan, Nova Scotia in 1945. Pilothouse and cabin are an exhibit on shore at the Fisheries Museum in Lunenburg, Nova Scotia.

Shelter Bay – steel bulk freighter; built at Cleveland, Ohio in 1907. Two storey deckhouse for pilothouse and living quarters is preserved on shore at Goderich, Ontario, where it houses a maritime museum.

Yvon Dupre Jr. – steel steam tugboat; built at Sorel, Quebec in 1946. Pilothouse is exhibited outdoors at the Port Colborne Historical and Marine Museum in Port Colborne, Ontario.

Denmark

Spaekhuggeren – submarine; built at Copenhagen, Denmark in 1957.
A portion of her interior is preserved as an exhibit in the Royal Danish Naval Museum in Copenhagen.

Finland

Herzogin Cecilie – steel four-masted barque; built at Bremerhaven, Germany in 1902. Wrecked on south coast of England in the 1930s. Salvaged living quarters for captain and officers are now an exhibit in the Maritime Museum in Mariehamn, Aland Islands.

France

Oceanor – wooden canal boat. Bow and stern are preserved as exhibits at the Musee de la Batellerie, Conflans-Saint-Honorine.

Record – steel motorized canal boat; built in Belgium in 1916. Stern with wheelhouse is preserved as an exhibit at the Musee de la Batellerie, Conflans-Sainte-Honorine.

Greece

Papamicolis – submarine; built in France in 1926. Conning tower is preserved outdoors at the Naval Museum in Piraeus.

Italy

Conte Biancamano – passenger liner; built at Glasgow, Scotland in 1925. Scrapped in Italy in 1960. Forward end of superstructure, with bridge and one passenger lounge, is an exhibit in the Science Museum in Milan.

Puglia – Cruiser; built at Taranto, Italy in 1898. Scrapped in 1923. Bow and bridge are preserved in the garden of a villa in Italy.

New Zealand

Te Anau – steel steamship; built at Dumbarton, Scotland in 1879.
Small deckhouse containing captain's stateroom is preserved as an exhibit in the Harbour Board Maritime Museum in Wellington. (see also wrecks)

Norway

Lingard – steel barque; built at Arendal, Norway in 1893. Charthouse, skylight and steering gear are now exhibited in the Norsk Sjofartsmuseum in Oslo.

Sandnaes – steel coastal passenger steamer; built at Stavanger, Norway in 1914. Scrapped in 1974. Dining saloon, stairway and stateroom are now an exhibit at the Norsk Sjofartsmuseum in Oslo.

Unknown sailing vessel – Intact crew deckhouse from a wreck found on a Norwegian beach is now an exhibit in the Norsk Sjofartsmuseum in Oslo.

Sweden

Hoppet – wooden barqueentine; built at Gefle, Sweden in 1878. Wooden crew deckhouse is an exhibit in the National Maritime Museum in Stockholm.

Amphion – wooden schooner; built in Stockholm in 1778. Former royal yacht broken up in 1885. Ornate stern and after cabin are preserved in the National Maritime Museum in Stockholm.

Switzerland

Pilatus – steel sidewheel steamboat; built in 1895. Engines, boilers and a paddlewheel are exhibited in the Transport Museum in Lucerne. Engines and feathering paddlewheel are operated by an electric motor.

United States

Australia – wooden schooner; built at Patchogue, New York in 1862. Remains of hull are exhibited indoors at the Mystic Seaport Museum in Mystic, Connecticut.

USS Balao – submarine; built at Kittery,

Maine in 1942. Conning tower is exhibited outdoors at the Navy Museum in the Washington Navy Yard in Washington, D.C.

BENJAMIN F. PACKARD – wooden ship; built at Bath, Maine in 1882. Scuttled off Eaton's Neck, New York in 1939. Aft living quarters removed before scuttling are now an exhibit at the Mystic Seaport Museum in Mystic, Connecticut.

CALCITE – steel bulk cargo vessel; built at Wyandotte, Michigan in 1912. Scrapped in 1961. Pilothouse is exhibited outdoors at Rogers City, Michigan.

CANOPUS – steel bulk cargo vessel; built at St. Clair, Michigan in 1905. Scrapped in 1961. Pilothouse has been acquired by the Great Lakes Historical Society for exhibition as an addition to their museum building in Vermilion, Ohio.

CHINA – wooden sidewheel steamship; built at New York in 1866. Scrapped near San Francisco in 1884. Wooden deckhouse containing passenger lounge was used as a summer cottage. Deckhouse has been fully restored as an exhibit at Belvidere, California.

CITY OF DETROIT III – steel sidewheel steamer; built at Wyandotte, Michigan in 1911. Scrapped in 1957. Portion of very ornate 'gothic room' is an exhibit at the Dossin Great Lakes Museum in Detroit, Michigan.

GALILEE – wooden brigantine; built at Benicia, California in 1891. Stern is exhibited outdoors at the San Francisco Maritime National Historical Park in San Francisco, California.

KAIULANI – steel barque; built at Bath, Maine in 1899. Broken up in the Philippines in 1974. Portions of bow and stern are preserved at San Francisco by the National Park Service. (Not currently on exhibit)

USS KNAPP – destroyer; built at Bath, Maine in 1943. Bridge is exhibited indoors at the Columbia River Maritime Museum in Astoria, Oregon.

NEW YORK CENTRAL NO. 31 – steel tugboat; built in Brooklyn, New York in 1923. Pilothouse is exhibited outdoors at the South Street Seaport Museum in New York.

OTAGO – iron barque; built at Glasgow, Scotland in 1869. Broken up near Hobart, Tasmania. Portion of stern is preserved at San Francisco by the National Park Service. (not currently on exhibit; see also wrecks in Australia)

USS PINTADO – submarine; built at Kittery, Maine in 1943. Conning tower is exhibited outdoors at the Admiral Nimitz State Historical Park in Fredericksburg, Texas.

Potomac

REINDEER – wooden sidewheel steamboat built at Alburg, Vermont in 1881. Pilothouse is preserved by the Lake Champlain Maritime Museum in Basin Harbour, Vermont.

Steel bay steamboat; built at Philadelphia in 1894. Reduced to a barge in 1936. Pilothouse and officers' cabins were preserved on shore at Whitestone Beach, Virginia. They have recently been acquired by the Mariners

Museum in Newport News, Virginia.

SEA FOX – wooden diesel seagoing tugboat; built at North Bend, Oregon in 1944. Portion of deckhouse including wheelhouse is exhibited outdoors at San Francisco by the Maritime National Historical Park.

SNOW SQUALL – wooden clipper ship; built at South Portland, Maine in 1851. Condemned in the Falkland Islands in 1864. Portion of bow is now preserved under cover at South Portland, Maine.

ST. MARY – wooden ship; built at Phippsburg, Maine in 1890. Wrecked in the Falkland Islands in 1891. Portion of side is part of an exhibit at the Maine State Museum in Augusta, Maine. (see also wrecks in Falkland Islands)

WALTER L. MESECK – wooden tugboat; built at Tottenville, New York in 1931. Pilothouse is exhibited under cover at the Mariners Museum in Newport News, Virginia.

WILLIAM CLAY FORD – steel bulk freighter; built at River Rouge, Michigan in 1953. Pilothouse has been placed on shore at Detroit, Michigan, where it is being restored as an exhibit of the Dossin Great Lakes Museum.

4 PORTIONS OF SHIPS PRESERVED AS NAVAL RELICS OR MONUMENTS

Belgium

HMS VINDICTIVE – light cruiser; built at Chatham, England in 1897. Sunk as a block ship at Zeebrugge in May 1918. Later raised and broken up. Portion of upper bow is displayed as a memorial at Ostend.

Chile

YELCHO – steel seagoing tugboat; built in Great Britain. Vessel that rescued men of Shackleton's Expedition from the Antarctic in 1916. Bow is preserved on shore at the naval base at Puerto Williams on the Beagle Channel.

New Zealand

RANGIRIRI – iron sternwheel river gunboat; built in the 1860s. Hull is preserved imbedded in the shore of a riverside park in Hamilton.

Singapore

MARUDU – coastal and inter-island passenger steamer; built at Belfast, Ireland in 1924. Forward portion of vessel, including bridge, is preserved on shore at Sembawang by the National Maritime Board.

Thailand

DHONBURI – steel coast defense monitor; built in Japan in 1938. Complete bridge structure, mast and turret are installed on shore at the Naval Academy in Paknam.

United States

USS ARIZONA – battleship; built at New York in 1915. Sunk at Pearl Harbour, Hawaii in December 1941. Partly visible wreck in maintained as a war memorial there.

USS FLASHER – submarine; built at Groton, Connecticut in 1943. Conning tower is preserved outdoors in a small park in Groton.

USS MICHIGAN (later WOLVERINE) – iron sidewheel gunboat; built in Erie, Pennsylvania in 1843. Scrapped in 1949. Portion of bow is preserved in a park in Erie.

USS OREGON – battleship; built at San Francisco, California in 1891. Scrapped in 1956. Large mast with gun tubs is preserved in a small park in Portland, Oregon.

USS SAILFISH (ex-SQUALUS) – submarine; built at Kittery, Maine in 1938. Sank during test dive in May 1939. Salvaged and renamed. Conning tower is preserved outdoors at the Portsmouth Navy Yard in Kittery, Maine.

USS UTAH – battleship; built at Camden, New Jersey in 1909. Sunk in Japanese attack on Pearl Harbor, Hawaii in December 1941. Wreck is maintained as a war memorial there.

5 PORTIONS OF SHIPS UTILIZED ON SHORE

Australia

JOSEPH H. SCAMMELL – wooden ship; built in Nova Scotia in 1885. Wrecked on the south coast of Australia in 1891. Wooden deckhouse is still used as part of a residence at Torquay, Australia.

Canada

OCEAN HAWK II – wooden tugboat; built at Port Greville, Nova Scotia in 1940. Serves as a restaurant lying aground on the waterfront of St. John, New Brunswick.

PRINCESS MARY – coastal passenger steamer; built at Paisley, Scotland in 1910. Converted to carry cargo in 1952. Portion of original superstructure serves as a restaurant on shore at Victoria, British Columbia.

Great Britain

MAURETANIA – passenger liner; built at Wallsend-on-Tyne, England in 1906. Scrapped in the 1930s. The second class drawing room and some of the officers' staterooms survive built into a private home in Poole, England. Portions of the Grand Saloon and Grand Staircase survive built into the Mauretania Hotel in Bristol, England.

Sweden

DROTTNINGHOLM (ex-VIRGINIAN) – steel passenger liner; built at Glasgow, Scotland

in 1905. Portions of the first class dining room and smoking lounge are built into the Henriksberg Restaurant in Gothenburg.

United States

BENSON FORD – Great Lakes bulk cargo vessel; built at River Rouge, Michigan in 1924. Upper bow and forward deckhouse have been placed on shore on South Bass Island, Ohio to serve as a hotel.

HAMPTON ROADS – steel steam ferryboat; built at Wilmington, Delaware in 1925. Retired in 1957. Placed on shore at Cambridge, Maryland for use as a restaurant. Later an antique shop, and now a real estate office.

ILLAHEE – steel turbo-electric ferryboat; built at Oakland, California in 1927. Wheelhouse and crew cabin removed during modernization serves as a beach house on the Puget Sound in Washington State.

MCKEEVER BROS. – wooden fishing vessel; built at Noank, Connecticut in 1911. Placed on shore near Salisbury, Maryland for use as a restaurant.

NEW YORK CENTRAL NO. 16 – steel steam tugboat; built at Elizabethport, New Jersey in 1924. Complete ship from waterline up installed as advertisement for a restaurant in Buzzard's Bay, Massachusetts. Engine is also preserved adjacent to vessel.

STAR OF KODIAK (ALBERT M. BOE) – steel cargo ship, Liberty type; built at South Portland, Maine in 1945. Built into shoreline for use as fish-processing plant at Kodiak, Alaska.

Appendix 4 Museums, organizations, and commercial operators owning historic ships

Note: Numbers in parentheses are city codes, which are generally preceded by 0 only when dialled within the country. Numbers preceding the parentheses are country codes.

Some important maritime museums that do not own ships have also been included.

Argentina

Armada Argentina
Comando General de la Armada
Comodoro Pyy Corbeth Uruguay
Buenos Aires
PRESIDENTE SARMIENTO
URUGUAY

Museo Naval de la Nacion
Passeo Victoria 602
1648 Tigre, Buenos Aires
54 (1) 749-0608

Australia

Aspen Pty. Ltd.
Newcastle, New South Wales
SOUTH STEYNE

Australian National Maritime Museum
G.P.O. Box 5131, 13A Union Street
Sydney 2001, New South Wales
Tel. 61 (2) 552-7777
ADVANCE
AKARANA
C.L.S. No. 4
JOHN LOUIS
KATHLEEN GILLETT
SEKAR AMAN
TU DO
VAMPIRE (loan from Australian Government)

Australian War Memorial
Canberra
KRAIT

Axel Stenross Maritime Museum
97 Lincoln Highway
Port Lincoln, South Australia 5606
Tel. 086 82 2093

Ballina Shire Council
Ballina, New South Wales
FLORRIE

Broome Shire Council
Broome, West Australia
SAM MALE

City of Port Lincoln
Port Lincoln, South Australia
CITY OF ADELAIDE

City of Sandringham
Sandringham, Victoria
CERBERUS

City of Whyalla
Whyalla, South Australia
WHYALLA

Corporation of the Town of Renmark
Renmark, South Australia
INDUSTRY

Echuca City Council
Echuca, Victoria
ADA
ADELAIDE
ALEXANDER ARBUTHNOT
ALISON
B22
D26
PEVENSEY

Flagstaff Hill Maritime Museum
Box 574
Warrnambool, Victoria
Tel. 61 (55) 64-9841
REGINALD M.
ROWITTA

Jaycees Community Foundation Inc.
Albany, West Australia
CHEYNES IV

Lady Denman Maritime Museum
8 Watt Street
Huskisson, New South Wales 2541
LADY DENMAN

Marine Board of Hobart
Hobart, Tasmania
MAY QUEEN

Maritime Trust of Australia
Melbourne, Victoria
CASTLEMAINE

Melbourne Maritime Museum
Lorimer Street East
Southbank 3006, Australia
Tel. 61 (3) 9699 9760
POLLY WOODSIDE

National Museum of Australia
Canberra
AUSTRALIA II
ENTERPRISE (steam)
HONG HAI

National Trust of South Australia
MARION

Newcastle Region Maritime Museum
Fort Scratchley,
Newcastle P.O. Box 148
Newcastle 2300, New South Wales
61 (49) 2 2588

North Head Pty. Ltd.
Hobart, Tasmania
NORTH HEAD

Northern Territory Museum of Arts & Sciences
Box 4646
Darwin, Northern Territory 0801
KS8-1192
KARYA SAMA
TERIMA KASIH
THINH VUONG
VIVIENNE

A. E. and F. O. Pointon
Mildura, Victoria
MELBOURNE

Port Arthur Historic Site Management Authority
Port Arthur, Tasmania
MATILDA

Queenscliffe Lifeboat Preservation Society Inc.
Queenscliff Maritime Center
Queenscliff, Victoria
QUEENSCLIFF

Queensland Maritime Museum
Dry Dock, 412 Stanley Street
South Brisbane, 4101 Queensland
DIAMANTINA
FORCEFUL

Reemere Steamship Co. Pty. Ltd.
Hobart, Tasmania
REEMERE

River and Riverboat Historical and Preservation Society
Mildura, Victoria
A11
SUCCESS

Rotary Club of Wentworth
Wentworth, New South Wales
RUBY

Sail and Adventure Ltd.
142 Old Eltham Road, Lower Plenty
3093 Melbourne
ALMA DOEPAL

Sea Life Center
Bicheno, Tasmania
ENTERPRISE (sail)

Signal Point River Murray Interpretive Center
Goolwa, Victoria
DART

South Australian Maritime Museum
P.O. Box 555, 119 Lipson Street
Port Adelaide, South Australia 5015
Tel. 61 (8) 240-0200
ANNIE WATT
FEARLESS
NELCEBEE
YELTA

Steamers Ltd.
Melbourne, Victoria
VICTORIA

Svanen Charters Pty. Ltd.
Sydney, New South Wales
OUR SVANEN

Swan Hill Pioneer Settlement Authority
Swan Hill, Victoria
GEM
PYAP

Sydney Historic Ships
Suite 17, 137 Pyrmont Street,
P. O. Box 140
Pyrmont 2009, New South Wales
Tel. 61 (2) 552-2011
BOOMERANG
GRETEL II
JAMES CRAIG
JOHN OXLEY
KANANGRA
LADY HOPETOUN
WARATAH

Town of Nerang
Nerang, Queensland
MAID OF SKER

Victorian Steamship Association Ltd.
Melbourne, Victoria
WATTLE

Waterview Wharf Pty. Ltd.
Sydney, New South Wales
BARAGOOLA

Western Australian Maritime Museum
Fremantle, West Australia
ANCEL
LADY FORREST
PARRY ENEDEAVOUR
TI TU
TRIXEN
YAMBULLA

Belgium

Nationaal Scheepvaartmuseum
Steenplein 1
B-2000 Antwerp
Tel. 32 (3) 232-80-50
LAURANDA
OUDENAARDE
ST. ANTONIUS

Rijn en binnevaartmuseum
c/o Dr. R. van Cleempoel
Italielei 51
2000 Antwerp
CEPHEE

Seafront
Oude Vismijn, Albertdok 1,
Vismijnstraat 12
8380 Zeebrugge
Tel. 0032 50 551415
U-480

Canada

Alberni Marine Transportation Inc.
P.O. Box 188,
Port Alberni, British Columbia v9y 7m7
Tel. 250-723-8313
Lady Rose

Assignack Historical Museum & S.S. Norisle
Heritage Park
c/o Municipal Clerk
P.O. Box 238
Manitowaning, Ontario p0p 1n0
Tel. 705-859-3196
Norisle

Bernier Maritime Museum
55 est, des Pionniers
L'Islet-sur-Mer, Quebec g0r 2b0
Tel. 418-247-5001
www.uqam.ca/musees/institutions/ins_cha
udiere/isletE.html
Bras D'or
Ernest Lapointe

The Canadian Naval Memorial Trust
H.M.C.S. Sackville
Sackville Landing
1675 Lower Water Street
Halifax b3k 2x0
Tel. 902-429-2132
learning.ns.sympatico.ca/sackville
Sackville
Open daily June to October 1100 to 1900

City of Penticton
Penticton Chamber of Commerce
185 Lakeshore Drive
Penticton, British Columbia v2a 1b7
Sicamous

Exposition Maritime
305 rue de l'Eglise, C.P.1
Saint-Joseph-de-la-Rive
Charlevoix g0a 3y0
Tel. 418-635-1131

Fisheries Museum of the Atlantic
68 Bluenose Drive
Lunenburg, Nova Scotia b0j 2c0
Tel. 902-634-4794
www.ednet.ns.ca/educ/museum/fma.html
Cape Sable
Royal Wave
Theresa E. Connor
hmcs Haida

Ontario Place Corporation
955 Lakeshore Boulevard West
Toronto, Ontario m6k 3b9
Tel. 416-314-9755
www3.simpatico.ca/hrc/haida
Haida

Ivanhoe Heritage Foundation
P. O. Box 10149
Vancouver, British Columbia v7y 1c6
Ivanhoe

The Klondike National Historic Sites
P.O. Box 390

Dawson, Yukon y0b 1g0
Tel. 403-993-5462
Keno

Maple Leaf
2087 Indian Crescent
Duncan, British Columbia v9l 5l9
Tel. 250-715-0906
Maple Leaf

Marine Museum of Manitoba
P.O. Box 7
Selkirk, Manitoba r1a 2b1
Tel. 204-482-7761
Bradbury
Chickama II
Keenora
Lady Canadian
Peguis II

Marine Museum of the Great Lakes
55 Ontario Street,
Kingston, Ontario k7l 2y2
Tel. 613-542-2261
stauffer.queensu.ca/marmus/MMuseum.ht
ml
Alexander Henry
Open January to March Monday-Friday
10.00-16.00, April to December daily
10.00-17.00

Marine Museum of Upper Canada
c/o Toronto Historical Board
Exhibition Place
Toronto, Ontario m6k 3c3
Tel. 416-392-6827
Ned Hanlon

Maritime History Archive
Henrietta Harvey Building, Room 1013
Memorial University
St. John's, Newfoundland
Tel. 709-737-8428
www.mun.ca.mha

Maritime Museum of British Columbia
28 Bastion Square
Victoria, British Columbia v8w 1h9

Maritime Museum of the Atlantic
1675 Lower Water Street,
Halifax, Nova Scotia b3j 1s3
Tel. 902-429-8210
www.ednet.ns.ca/educ/museum/mma.html
Acadia
Open daily July to October 15
09.30-17.00, Tuesdays to 20.00 and Sundays
starting at 13.00

Museum Ship Norgoma
St. Mary's River Marine Center
P.O. Box 325
Sault Ste. Marie, Ontario p6a 5l8
Tel. 705-949-9111 ext. 141
Norgoma

Northern Life Museum
P. O. Box 371
Fort Smith, Northwest Territories x0e 0p0
Radium King

Oak Bay Marina Ltd.
1327 Beach Drive,
Victoria, British Columbia v8s 2n4
Canadian Princess

Parks Canada
P. O. Box 159
Baddeck, Nova Scotia b01 1p0
Hydrofoil HD 4

Pump House Steam Museum
23 Ontario Street,
Kingston, Ontario k7l 2y2
Phoebe

Sail and Life Training Society
P.O. Box 5014, Station B
Victoria, British Columbia v8r 6n3
Tel. 250-383-6811
Robertson II

Samson V Maritime Museum
105-1005 Columbia Street
New Westminster, British Columbia V3L
4L8
Tel. 604-521-7656
www.museumsassn.bc.ca/~bcma/museums
/svm.html
Samson V
Open weekends and holidays 1200-1700

Schooner Museum
Shore Road and Cabot Trail
Margaree Harbour, Nova Scotia b0e 2b0
Tel. 902-235-2317
Marion Elizabeth

R.M.S. Segwun
P.O. Box 68
Gravenhurst, Ontario
Tel. 705-687-667
www.muskoka.com/gravenhurst/segwun/
Segwun
Wanda III

Vancouver Maritime Museum
1905 Ogden Avenue,
Vancouver, British Columbia V6J 1A3
Tel. 604-257-8300
Black Duck
St. Roch
Open daily in summer 1000-1700;
in winter closed Mondays

Chile

Museo Naval y Maritimo
Subida Artilleria s/n, Playa Ancha
Valparaiso
Tel. 56 (31) 662627

China

Zhingshan Zian Foundation
No. 23
Dushu Yuan
Wuchang District
Wuhan City
Tel. 027 8807 4280
Zhongshan

Denmark

Danmarks Faergemuseum
c/o Radhuset, Torvet
5800 Nyborg
Kong Frederik IX
Møn
Sprogø

Fiskeri og Sjofartsmuseet
Tarphagevej
6710 Esbjerg
Tel. 45 (5) 75 15 06 66
Ane Catherine
Claus Sørensen
Dana
De Tre Brodre
Eron
Hanne Lene
Hellas
Johanne
Motorfyrskib 1

Fregatten Jylland
Strandvejen 4
8400 Ebeltoft
Jylland
Fyrskib XXI
MHV 67
MRB 22

Handels-og Sofartsmuseet pa Kronborg
Kronborg Castle
DK 3000 Helsingor
Tel. 45 (2) 210685

Kystfiskerimuseet
Ndr. Strandvej
9480 Lokken
Tel. 45 () 98 99 18 4
Bent II

Langelands Museum
Jens Winthersvej 12
5900 Rudkobing
Tel. 45 () 62 51 13 47
Mjølner

Marine-Museum
Vestre Fjordvej 81
9000 Alborg
Tel. 45 () 98 11 78 03
Ingolf
Søbjørnen
Springeren

Nordsomuseet
Willemoesvej
9850 Hirtshals
Tel. 45 () 98 94 48 44
Lissy

Orlogsmuseet
Overgaden oven
Vandet 58
Copenhagen
Tel. 45 (1) 31 54 63 63
Kongechalup

Sjaelland
Kaiplads 114

nahe Christians Brygge
Copenhagen
SJAELLAND

Sofarts og Fiskerimuseet
Vestero Havnegade 5
9940 Vestero Havn/Laeso
Tel. 45 () 98 49 94 97
ELLEN

Stiftelsen Georg Stages Minde
Christianshavns Kanal 12
1406 Copenhagen
GEORG STAGE

U-359
Kai 8
Hafen
6000 Kolding
U-359

U-461
Kai 110
Kalvebod Brygge
Copenhagen
U-461

Vikingeskibshallen
Stradengen
4000 Roskilde
Tel. 45 (42) 356555
SKUDELEV VIKING SHIPS

Eire

Kilmore Quay Maritime Museum
Ballyteigue, Kilmore Quay, Co. Wexford
Tel. 353 (53) 29655
GUILLEMOT LIGHTSHIP
Open daily June to September

National Maritime Museum of Ireland
Haigh Terrace, Dun Laoghaire, Co. Dublin
Tel. 353 (1) 280 0969
www.dkm.ie/events/dublin/museums/
Open daily except Monday May to
September; Sundays and bank holidays in
October

Estonia

Eesti Riiklik Meremuuseum
(Estonian State Maritime Museum)
Pikk 70
200001 Talinn
Tel. 372 () 641 14 09
www.abc.se/~m10354/meremus.htm
LEMBIT
SUUR TOLL
open Wednesday-Sunday 10.00-18.00

Finland

Alands Sjofartsmuseum
Hamngatan 2
SF-22100 Mariehamn, Aland
Tel. 358 (28) 11-930
POMMERN

Hylkysaari Maritime Museum
Helsinki, Finland

KEMI
TARMO

Saimaa-Museum
Riihisaari
SF-57130 Savonlinna
Tel. 358 (57) 571723
MIKKO
SALAMA
SAVONLINNA

Sjohistoriska Museet vid Abo Akademi
Biskopsgatan 13
SF-20500 Abo 50
Tel. 358 (21) 65 41 52
SIGYN

Sotamuseo (War Museum)
Maurinkatu 1 00170
Helsinki 17
VESSIKO

France

A.S.C.A.N.F.E.
(Association pour la Sauvetage et la
Conservation des Anciens Navires Francais
et Etrangers
3, Quai du Port, Fort Saint-Jean
13002 Marseille
Tel. 91 91 61 44
MARSELLOIS

Association des Amis du Musee de
l'Atlantique
Musee de la Marine, Palais de Chaillot
75116 Paris
ARGONAUTE

Fondation Belem
Union Nationale de Caisses d'Epargne de
France
5 Rue Masseran
F 75007 Paris
BELEM

L'Association des Amis de la Batellerie du
Rhone
M. Tracol
5 rue Pasteur
26000 Valence
ARDECHE

Le Port-Musee
Place de l'Enfer
Douarnenez
Tel. 33 (98) 92 65 20
ST. DENYS
NORTHDOWN
SCARWEATHER

Musee de Debarquement d'Arromanches
Tel. 31 22 34 31
www.min-equp.fr/france.ocean/culture/arro
manc/arromanc.html
LCA-1825

Musee de la Marine
Palais de Chaillot
Place du Trocadero et du 11 Novembre
F 75116 Paris

Tel. 33 () 45 53 31 70
www.equipement.gouv.fr/france.ocean/cult
ure/musmar/musmar1.html
CANOT IMPERIAL
Open daily except Saturday 10.00-18.00

Musee de la Marine
Le Chateau de Brest
Brest
Tel. 33 (98) 22 12 39
www.enst-bretagne.fr:3000/anglais/musee_
mar_gb.html
LA BELLE POULE
L'ETOILE
s622

Musee de la Marine pour l'Atlantique
Face au 60, quai des Chartrons
Bordeaux
Tel. 33 (56) 44 96 11
COLBERT

Musee naval et Municipal de Balaguier
83500 La Seyne-sur-Mer
Tel. 94 94 84 72
ZACA

Germany

Altonaer Museum
Norddeutscher Landesmuseum
Museumstrasse 50,
22765 Hamburg
Tel. 49 (040) 380-74-83
ELFRIEDE

Arbeitskreis Museumsfeuerschiff
'Amrumbank'
Im Ratsdelft
26721 Emden
Tel. 49 (04921) 232-85
DEUTSCHE BUCHT

Arbeitskreis Museumslogger
Petkumer Str. 220
26725 Emden
Tel. 49 (04821) 51212
EMDEN
Open in summer Monday-Friday
10.00-13.00, 15.00-17.00
Saturday & Sunday 11.00-13.00

Arbeitskreis Schiffahrtsmuseum
Regensburg
Werftstrasse
93018 Regensburg
Tel. 49 (0941) 52510
RUTHOF

Archaologisches Landesmuseum der
Christian-Albrechts-Universitat
Schloss Gottorf
24837 Schleswig
Tel. 49 (04621) 813 300
NYDAM SHIP
Open daily March-October 09.00-17.00
November-February except Monday
09.30-16.00

Auto & Technik Museum
Obere Au 2

74889 Sinsheim-Kraichgau
Tel. 49 (07261) 61116
SEEHUND TYPE MIDGET SUBMARINE
Open daily 09.00-18.00

Berliner Schiffahrtsgesellschaft
Bamburger Str. 58
10777 Berlin
Tel. 49 (30) 213 80 41
ANDREAS
BÄRBEL-MARLIES
RENATE-ANGELIKA

Betriebsfuhrung RD Kaiser Wilhelm
Eichenweg 6
22927 Grosshansdorf
KAISER WILHELM

Reyner Biermann
Waldsiedlung
39649 Peckfitz
Tel. 49 (0390) 82 85 18
TAUCHER FLINT III

Binnenschiffahrtsmuseum Oderberg
Hermann Seidel Str. 44
16248 Oderberg
RIESA
Open daily except Monday 0900-1200 and
14.00-16.30

Lothar Bischoff
Florastr. 25
14641 Nauen
NORDSTERN

Bremische Gesellschaft zur Erhaltung der
Grossen Hafenrundfahrt
'MS. FRIEDRICH'
Hermannstr. 110
28201 Bremen
FRIEDRICH (ex-Steam)

Der Bundesminister fur Verkehr, Wasser
und Schiffahrtsamt
Am Eisenbahndock 3
26725 Emden
EMS

Cap San Diego Betriebsgesellschaft
Uberseebrucke

20459 Hamburg
Tel. 49 (040) 364209
CAP SAN DIEGO
Open daily 10.00-18.00

Chiemsee-Schiffahrt Ludwig Fessler
83209 Prien am Chiemsee
LUDWIG FESSLER

Dampfeimerkettenbagger ED 6
Erhaitungsverein e. V.
2990 Papenburg 1
Deutsche Binnenreederei Gmbh
Alt-Stralau 55-58
10245 Berlin
Tel. 49 (030) 29 38 24 00
RUTH
SEIMA

Deutsche Gesellschaft zur Rettung
Schiffbruchiger
Werderstr. 2
28199 Bremen
Tel. 49 (0421) 5 37 07 0
Rickmer Bock

Deutscher Marinebund
Strandstrasse 92
24233 Laboe
Tel. 49 (04343) 8755 56
U-995

Deutscher Schulschiff-Verein
Auf dem Dreieck 5
28197 Bremen
Schulschiff Deutschland

Deutsches Feuerwehrmuseum
St. Laurentius-Strasse 3
36041 Fulda
Tel. 49 (0661) 75017
Emden I
Open Tuesday-Sunday 10.00-17.00

Deutsches Jugendwerk zur See 'Clipper'
Jurgensallee 54
22609 Hamburg
Albatros
Amphitrite
Seute Deern (ketch)

Deutsches Museum
Museumsinsel 1
80306 Munchen
Tel. 49 (089) 2179 1
Maria
Renzo
Theodor Heuss
u-1
open daily 09.00-17.00

Deutsches Museum fur Meerskunde und
Fischerei
Katharinenberg 14-20
18439 Stralsund
Tel. 49 (03831) 29 51 35
Adolf Reichwein

Deutsches Schiffahrtsmuseum
Hans-Scharoun-Platz 1
27568 Bremerhaven
Tel. 49 (0471) 482-07-0
Danube Ferry Scow
Diva
Elbe 3
Emma
Grönland
Helmut
Kranich
Paul Kossel
Rau IX
Seefalke
Seehund Type Midget Submarine
Seute Deern (barque)
Stier
wss 10
Open daily except Monday 10.00-18.00

Deutsches Technik-Museum
Trebbiner Str. 9

10963 Berlin
Tel. 49 (040) 25 484 0
Volldampf

Deutsches Zollmuseum
Alter Wandrahm 15a-16
20457 Hamburg
Tel. 49 (040) 33 97 33 89
Glückstadt

Hans Werner Dorich
Pfordtenwingert 4
63457 Hanau
Gredo

Eignergemeinschaft Kufe
Hartmann, Schuppenbauer
Hohne, Suhr
Absalon

Eignergemeinschaft 'Sampo'
Wustenfelde 35
24147 Kiel
Tel. 49 (0431) 788 092
Sampo

Fehn- und Schiffahrtsmuseum
Westrhauderfehn
Rajen 5
26817 Rhauderfehn
Tel. 49 (045952) 80359
Ebenhaezer

Feuerschiff fur Lubeck
Postfach 11 11 50
23560 Lubeck
Tel. 49 (0451) 76068
Fehmarnbelt

Peter Fleck
Stockelsdorfer Weg 54
23611 Bad Schwartau
Norden

Fordergesellschaft zur Ehrhaltung der
Schwebefahre Osten
Deichstrasse 1
21756 Osten
Geversdorf

Forderkreis 'Claus D.'
Museumshafen Oevelgonne
Oevelgonne 42
22605 Hamburg
Claus D.

Forderkreis Rettungskreuzer 'Georg
Breusing'
Im Ratsdelft
266525 Emden
Tel. 49 (04921) 2 205 41
Georg Breusing
Open April-October 1000-1300 and
15.00-17.00

Forderverein Eisbrecher 'Stettin'
Kapt. Manfred Fraider
Kielmannseggstrasse 98
22043 Hamburg
Stettin

Forderverein Feuerschiff 'Borkumriff'
Deichstrasse 9a
26757 Borkum
Borkumriff
open daily, except Mondays

Forderverein 'Rigmor' von Gluckstadt
Am Hafen 27
25348 Gluckstadt
Tel. 49 (04124) 4618
Rigmor

Forderverein Salondampfer 'Alexandra'
Postfach 1616
24944 Flensburg
Alexandra

Forderverein Schiffahrtsgeschichte Cuxhaven
c/o Adr. Johann Voss
Grodener Chaussee 55
27472 Cuxhaven
Tel. 49 (04721) 23012
Elbe 1
Open Tuesday-Friday 13.00-17.00
Saturday 12.00-17.00, Sunday 10.00-17.00

Forderverein Schleppdampfer Woltman
Muggenkampstr. 31a
20257 Hamburg
Tel. 49 (040) 400 440
Woltman

Forderverein Zollboot 'Hitzacker'
c/o Ursula Togotzes
Vordorfsfeld I 14
29473 Gohrde/Sarenseck
Tel. 49 (058862) 1404
Hitzacker

Bernd Frenzel
Am Hausberg 1
01796 Pirna
Sachsenwald

Freunde Des Dampfschiffs 'Schaarhörn'
Geschaftstelle Hollandweg 54
25241 Pinneberg
Tel. 49 (04101) 687 68
Schaarhörn

Hansestadt Lubeck
Viermastbarque Passat
23570 Travemunde-Priwall
Tel. 49 (04502) 63 96
Passat

Harmut Hanss
Kapellenstrasse 6
65193 Wiesbaden
Goede Wil

Historisches Dampfschiffs-Reederei Meissen
Junghans & Steuer Gmbh
Siebeneichener Strasse 29a
01662 Meissen
Krippen

Peter Hofrichter
Keplerstr. 10
22765 Hamburg
Rosinante

Interessengemeinschaft
c/o Verein Alsterdampschiffahrt
Dorotheenstrasse 9
22301 Hamburg
Tel. 49 (040) 7-92-25-99
Elbe

Helmut Janecke
Bluffelstrasse 5
23966 Wismar
Tel. 49 (03841) 25 95 41
Spökenkieker

Joachim Kaiser
Reichenstrasse 30
25348 Gluckstadt
Tel. 49 (040) 752 40 36
Undine

Kieler Stadt und Schiffahrtsmuseum
Wall 65
24103 Kiel
Tel. 49 (0431) 901 3428
Bussard
Hindenburg
Kiel
Open daily, except Monday, 1000-1800
winter 10.00-17.00

Gisela Klug und Dieter Pogoda
Im Dorf 2
27798 Hude
Tel. 49 (04408) 7110
Lodsen Rønne

Koln-Dusseldorf Deutsche Rheinschiffahrt
Frankenwerft 15
50667 Koln
Goethe

Kreismuseum
Schlossstrasse 1
41541 Dormagen
Camilla
Open Tuesday-Friday 14.00-18.00

Landesmuseum fur Technik und Arbeit
Museumstrasse
68165 Mannheim
Tel. 49 (0621) 292 4730
Hans-Peter
Wasserschutzpolizei 10
Willi

Landkreis Stade
Neuenhof 8
21730 Balje
Tel. 49 (04753) 84 21 11
Erna Becker

Christoph Lebek
Jagerallee 15
14469 Potsdam
Tel. 49 (0331) 280 48 41
Geheimrat Garbe

Leonhardt Schiffahrt
Industriestr. 1
22869 Hamburg
Tel. 49 (040) 8 39 79 19
Gauss

Maritime Tradition Vegesack Nautilus
Weserstrasse 18
28757 Bremen
REGINA
VEGESACK

Mignon Segelschiffahrt
Georg-Bonne-Str. 9
22609 Hamburg
Tel. 49 (040) 822 742 11
FORTUNA (sail)

Militarhistorisches Museum der Bundeswehr
Olbrichtplatz 3
01706 Dresden
Tel. 49 (0351) 823 2800
TORPEDO BOAT

Monchgutmuseum Gohren
Strandstrasse
18586 Gohren/Rugen
LUISE

Moor und Fehnmuseum
Oldenburger Str. 1
26676 Elisabethfehn
Tel. 49 (04499) 2222
JANTINA

Museum der Arbeit
Marienstrasse 19
22305 Hamburg
Tel. 49 (040) 2984 2364
SAATSEE

Museum der Deutschen Binnenschiffahrt
Dammstrasse 11 & Apostelstrasse 84
47119 Duisburg
Tel. 49 (0203) 283 3044
BILGENTOLER II
GOEDE VERWACHTING
MINDEN
OSCAR HUBER

Museum fur Arbeit
Maurienstrasse 19
22305 Hamburg
Tel. 49 (040) 2984-2364
ELBE 27
H 11347

Museum fur Hamburgische Geschichte
Holstenwall 24
20355 Hamburg
Tel. 49 (040) 3504 2360
KARL FRIEDRICH STEEN
OTTO LAUFFER
WALTER HÄVERNICK

Museum fur Verkehr und Technik
Stern und Kreisschiffahrt Gmbh
Puschkinallee 16-17
12435 Berlin
Tel. 49 (030) 61 73 90 0
KAISER FRIEDRICH

Museum fur Wattenfischerei
Wurster Landstrasse 118
27638 Wremen
KORALLE

Museumshafen Lubeck
c/o Rolf Buttner
Kronsdorfer Allee 19a
23560 Lubeck
Tel. 49 (0451) 79 18 91
WALTER
WELS

Museumshafen Oevelgonne
Oevelgonne 42
22605 Hamburg
Tel. 49 (040) 880-73-77
ELBE 3
FORTUNA (Steam)
PRÄSIDENT FREIHERR VON MALTZAHN
TIGER

Museumsschiff Dampt-Eisbrecher 'Wal'
Van-Ronzelen Strasse 2
27568 Bremerhaven
Tel. 49 (0471) 4 45 02
WAL

Museumsschiff Gera
Morgenstern-Museums
Fischkai
27572 Bremerhaven
Tel. 49 (0471) 20138
GERA
Open April-October

Nationalparkzentrum Wilhelmshaven
Sudstrand 110 b
26382 Wilhelmshaven
Tel. 49 (04421) 91-07-0
DAGGI

Niederrheinische Kies und Sandbagerei Gmbh
Rees-Haffen
Tel. 49 (02851) 1041
BILL

Hans Noritz
Streitstrasse 1-4
13587 Berlin
Tel. 49 (030) 33 56 312
GUSTAV

Pionierbatallion 1
Medem-Kaserne
Bodenstrasse 9-11
37603 Holz-Minden
ANNA VON AMRUM

Horst Roper
Am Kanal 1
12527 Berlin
Tel. 49 (030) 67 17 858
MARIE

Sachsische Dampfschiffahrts Gmbh
Conti Elbschiffahrts Kg
Hertha-Lindner-Strasse 10
01067 Dresden
Tel. 49 (0351) 86-60-90
DIESBAR
DRESDEN
JUNGER PIONIER
KURORT RATHEN
LEIPZIG
MEISSEN

PIRNA
SCHMILKA
STADT WEHLEN

Sassnitzer Fischerei und Hafenmuseum
Rugener Ring 27
18546 Sassnitz
HAVEL
Open 10.00-17.00 (reduced days
November-March)

Schiffahrtsgeschichtliche Sammlung des
Landesmuseums fur Technik und Arbeit in
Mannheim
unterhalb der Kurpfalzbrucke
Museumsufer 1
68159 Mannheim
Tel. 49 (0621) 292 2025
MANNHEIM
Open Tuesday-Saturday 10.00-13.00 and
14.00-17.00 and Sundays 10.00-17.00

Schiffahrtsmuseum der Hansestadt Rostock
Traditionschiff
Liegeplatz Schmarl
18106 Rostock
Tel. 49 (0381) 12197 26
CAPELLA
LANGER HEINRICH
1 MAI
SATURN
TORPEDO BOAT
TORPEDO BOAT
TRADITIONSSCHIFF
WISMAR
Open daily except Monday 09.00-17.00

Schiffahrtsmuseum Haren
Kanalstrasse
49733 Haren/Ems
Tel. 49 (05932) 8225
AUGUST
THEA-ANGELA

Schiffergilde Bremerhaven
Van Ronzelen Str. 2
27568 Bremerhaven
Tel. 49 (0471) 946-46-0
ASTARTE
BRACKI
FEUERLÖSCHBOOT 1
GOLIATH
LINE HINSCH

Schulschiffverein 'Grossherzogin Elisabeth'
Reederei H. W. Janssen
Rathausplatz 7
26931 Elsfleth
Tel. 49 (04404) 2086
GROSSHERZOGIN ELISABETH

Segelkamaradschaft 'Klaus Stortebeker'
Kniprodestr. 93
26388 Wilhelmshaven
Tel. 49 (4421) 44679
KAPITAN MEYER

Seilhafenmuseum Carolinensiel
Pumphusen 3
26409 Carolinensiel/Wittmund
Tel. 49 (4464) 456

GEBRÜDER
HEIMAT
IMMANUEL

Kurt und Heinz Siebert
Stern und Kreisshiffahrt Gmbh
Sachtlebenstrasse 60
14165 Berlin
Tel. 49 (030) 8 10 004 0
KURT-HEINZ

Staatliche Schiffahrt Ammersee
79252 Stegen/Ammersee
DIESSEN

Stadt Itzehoe
Rathaus
Reichenstrasse
25524 Itzehoe
HERMANN

Stadt Stade
Schulamt
Rathaus
21682 Stade
WILHELMINE VON STADE
open Fridays 15.00-18.00

Stadtmuseum Magdeburg
Heinrich-Heine-Platz
39114 Magdeburg
WÜRTTEMBERG

Tecknikmuseum U-boat 'Wilhelm Bauer'
van-Ronzelen Strasse
27568 Bremerhaven
Tel. 49 (0471) 48 20 70
WILHELM BAUER

Dr. Rainer Thonnessen
Elbchaussee 187
22605 Hamburg
HOOP OP WELVAART

Verein Alsterdampfschiffahrt
Bansenstrasse 11
21075 Hamburg
VAMPYR II

Verein 'Alter Hafen'
D.-Th. Bohlmann
Bremervorder Str. 3
21682 Stade
Tel. 49 (04141) 83350
GREUNDIEK

Verein Alsterdampfschiffahrt
Dorotheenstrasse 9
22301 Hamburg
Tel. 49 (040) 7 92 25 99
ST. GEORG

Verein 'Angela von Barssel'
c/o Adr. Hans Berkenbeger
Marienstrasse 2
26676 Barssel
ANGELA VON BARSSEL

Verein 'Rettet die Meersburg ex-Konstanz'
c/o Klaus Kramer
Heiligenbronner Strasse 47

78713 Schramberg
Tel. 49 (07422) 660 81 13
MEERSBURG

Verein 'Windjammer fur Hamburg'
Fiete-Schmidt-Anleger
20459 Hamburg
Tel. 49 (040) 319 59 59
RICKMER RICKMERS
Open daily 10.00-18.00

Verein zur Erhaltung und Nutzung eines
Historischen Segelschiffes fur
Pfadfindergruppen
Koppel 94
20099 Hamburg
Tel. 49 (040) 249935
MYTLIUS

John von Eitzen
Alte Schule/Herrenhalling
25840 Koldenbuttel
JONAS VON FRIEDRICHSTADT

Wasser und Schiffahrtsamt
Bismarckstrasse 133
66121 Saarbrucken
Tel. 49 (0681) 60021
ATLAS

Wehrtechnische Studiensammlung des BWB
Koblenz, Leihgabe an das Technikmuseum
Speyer
Geibstrasse
67346 Speyer
U-9

Westfalisches Industriemuseum
Am Hebewerk 2
45731 Waltrop
Tel. 49 (02363) 9707 0
CERBERUS
CROSSEN
EXPRESS
FRANZ-CHRISTIAN
HERBERT
M.PK.86
NIXE
OSTARA
PHENOL
PORTA
TENIERS
Open Tuesday-Sunday 10.00-18.00

Wilmsen
Duffelsmuhle 34
47546 Kalkar-Niedermorter
BIELENBERG

'Windsbraut' e.V.
Postfach 1504
21655 Stade
Tel. 49 (04141) 63068
WINDSBRAUT

Wrackmuseum Cuxhaven
Dorfstrasse 80
27476 Cuxhaven
Tel. 49 (04721) 23341
HERMINE
SEEHUND TYPE MIDGET SUBMARINE

Great Britain

Black Country Museum
Tipton Road
Dudley DY1 4SQ
Tel. 44 (21) 557 9643
ADMIRAL BEATTY

The Boat Museum
South Pier Road
Ellesmere Port, South Wirral,
Cheshire L65 4EF
Tel. 44 (0151) 355 5017
www.british-waterways.com/museum/elles
mereport/home.htm
Open daily in summer;
Saturday-Wednesday in winter
ASPULL
BACUP
BASUTO
BIGMERE
CEDAR
CENTAUR
CHILTERN
CUDDINGTON
DANIEL ADAMSON
ETHEL
FRIENDSHIP
GEORGE
MANNIN 2
MENDIP
MERAK
MONARCH
MOSSDALE
PHOEBE
SAPPHIRE
SCORPIO
SHAD
SPEEDWELL
WORCESTER

Bristol Industrial Museum
Prince's Wharf, Prince Street
Bristol BS1 4RN
Tel. 44 (0117) 915 1470
MAYFLOWER
(museum) Open daily except Monday

Bristol Maritime Heritage Centre
Wapping Wharf, Gasferry Road
Bristol BS1 6TY
Tel. 44 (0117) 926 0680
GREAT BRITAIN
Open daily

Cambridge Museum of Technology
Riverside, Newmarket Road
Cambridge
Tel. 44 (223) 68650

Chatham Historic Dockyard Trust
The Old Pay Office, Church Lane
Chatham Historic Dockyard
Chatham ME4 4TQ
Tel. 44 (01634) 812551
CAVALIER
GANNET
OCELOT

Royal National Lifeboat Collection
Open daily April to October 10.00-17.00;

February, March and November
Wednesday, Saturday and Sunday
10.00-16.00

Cotehele Quay Museum
Cotehele Quay, St. Dominick
Saltash, Cornwall PL12 6TA
Tel. 44 (01579) 350830
www.nmm.ac.uk/tm/sis.html
SHAMROCK
Open daily April to October

Cromer RNLI Lifeboat Museum
The Gangway, Cromer, Norfolk
Tel. 44 (01263) 512503
H. F. BAILEY

The Cutty Sark Maritime Trust
16 Ebury Street
London SW1W 0LH
Tel. 44 (1) 730 0096

The Dock Museum
North Road
Barrow-in-Furness, Cumbria LA14 2PU
Tel. 44 (01229) 870871
HERBERT LEIGH
Open daily except Monday and Tuesday

Dolphin Yard Sailing Barge Museum and
Cambria Trust
Crown Quay Lane
Sittingbourne, Kent ME10 3SN
Tel. 44 (01795) 424132
CAMBRIA
Open Easter to mid-October Sundays and
bank holidays

Down Cruising Club
60 Ballydown Road, Killinchy Anchorage
Newtownards, County Down, Northern
Ireland

Dundee Heritage Trust
R.R.S. Discovery
Victoria Harbour
Dundee
Tel. 44 (382) 25282

East Coast Sail Trust
21 Butt Lane
Maldon, Essex

East Kent Maritime Trust
Ramsgate Maritime Museum
Clock House, Pier Head, Royal Harbour
Ramsgate, Kent CT11 8LS
Tel. 44 (01843) 587765
CERVIA
SUNDOWNER
Open daily April to September;
Monday-Friday October to March

The Excelsior Sailing Trust
Surrey Chambers, Surrey Street
Lowestoft, Suffolk NR32 1LJ
Tel. 44 (502) 85302

Falmouth Maritime Museum
2 Bell's Court
Falmouth

Tel. 44 (326) 318107
The Fisherman's Museum
Rock-a-Nore,
Hastings
Tel. 44 (424) 424787

Furness Museum
Ramsden Square
Barrow-in-Furness, Cumbria LA14 1LL
Tel. 44 (229) 20650

H.M.S. Belfast
Morgans Lane, Tooley Street
London SE1 2JH
Tel. 44 (0171) 407 6434
BELFAST

HMS Warrior
Victory Gate, HM Naval Base
Portsmouth, Hampshire PO1 3QX
Tel. 44 (01705) 291379
www.compulink.co.uk/~flagship/warrior.htm
WARRIOR
Open daily

Hartlepool Historic Quay
Maritime Avenue, Hartlepool Marina
Hartlepool, Cleveland TS24 0XZ
Tel. 44 (01429) 860006
www.ukonline.co.uk/UKOnline/Regional/
Northern/DO/mushar.htm
TRINCOLALEE
WINGFIELD CASTLE
Open daily

Historic Warships at Birkenhead
East Float, Dock Road
Birkenhead, Merseyside L41 1DJ
Tel. 44 (0151) 650 1573
www.liverpool.com/birkenhe/places/
warships.htm
ONYX
PLYMOUTH
Open daily

Humber Keel and Sloop Preservation
Society
c/o Glenlea
Main Road, New Ellerby
North Humberside

Imperial War Museum
Duxford Airfield
Duxford, Cambridge CB2 4QR
Tel. 44 (01223) 835000
JESSE LUMB
Open daily except 24-26 December

Island Cruising Club
Island Street
Salcombe, Devon
Tel. 44 (54 884) 3481

International Sailing Craft Association
Caldicott Road, Oulton Broad
Lowestoft, Suffolk NR32 3PH
Tel. 44 (01502) 589014
Open daily

Lydia Eva and Mincarlo Charitable Trust
Ketts Acre, Crimpcramp Lane, Wheatacre

Beccles, Suffolk NR34 0BQ
Tel. 44 (01502) 677602
Lydia Eva
Mincarlo
Open daily Easter to September or October

Mary Rose Hall and Exhibition
College Road, HM Naval Base
Portsmouth PO1 3LX
Tel. 44 (01705) 750521
www.compulink.co.uk/~mary-rose/
Mary Rose
Open daily

Maryport Maritime Museum
1 Senhouse Street, Shipping Brow
Maryport, Cumbria CA15 6AB
Tel. 44 (01900)813738
Open daily in summer

Medway Maritime Museum
Chatham Historic Dockyard
Chatham
Merseyside Maritime Museum
Albert Dock
Liverpool L3 1DN
Tel. 44 (0151) 207 0001
www.connect.org.uk/merseyworld/albert/
maritime/
Open daily

Morwellham Quay Open Air Museum
Morwellham, Tavistock, Devon PL19 8JL
Tel. 44 (01822) 832766
www.devon-cc.gov.uk/tourism/pages/
attracts/morwquay.html
Shamrock
Open daily

Museum of Science and Engineering
Blandford Square
Newcastle upon Tyne, Tyne and Wear
NE1 4JA
Tel. 44 (0191) 232 6789
www.webwork.co.uk/webwork/OnTyne/
WhatsOn/museums.html
Turbinia
Open daily

National Maritime Museum
Romney Road
Greenwich, London SE10 9NF
Tel. 44 (0181) 858 4422
Open daily except 24-26 December
10.00-17.00

The National Waterways Museum
Llanthony Warehouse, Gloucester Docks
Gloucester GL1 2EH
Tel. 44 (01452) 318054
www.british-waterways.com/museum/
home.htm
Open daily

Nautical Museum
Bridge Street
Castletown, Isle of Man
Tel. 44 (01624) 675522
Peggy
Open daily Easter through September

Norfolk Wherry Trust
63 Whitehall Road,
Norwich, Norfolk NR2 3EN

Paddle Steamer Navigation Ltd.
10 Crescent Rise, Crescent Road
London N3 1HS

R.A.F. Museum
Grahame Park Way
London NW9

Royal Naval Museum and H.M.S. Victory
HM Naval Base
Portsmouth, Hampshire PO1 3NU
Tel. 44 (01705) 727562
www.compulink.co.uk/~flagship/museum.
htm
HMS Victory
Open daily

Royal Navy Submarine Museum
Haslar Jetty Road
Gosport, Hampshire PO12 2AS
Tel. 44 (01705) 529217
www.submarine-museum.demon.co.uk/
index.html
Alliance
Holland I
Open daily except 24 December to 1 January

S.S. Great Britain
Great Western Dock, Gas Ferry Road
Bristol BS1 6TY
Tel. 44 (0117) 926 0680
Open daily

Scottish Fisheries Museum
St. Ayles, Harbourhead
Anstruther, Fife, Scotland KY10 3AB
Tel. 44 (01333) 310628
Open daily

Scottish Maritime Museum
Harbourside
Irvine, Scotland KA12 8QE
Tel. 44 (01294) 278283
T.G.B.
Open daily April to October

Seiont II Maritime Museum
Victoria Road
Caernarfon, Gwynedd, Wales
Tel. 44 (248) 600835

Ships Preservation Ltd.
The Custom House, Victoria Terrace
Hartlepool, Cleveland
Tel. 44 (429) 33051

Southampton Museums
Wool House Maritime Museum
Bugle Street
Southampton, Hampshire SO14 2AR
Tel. 44 (01703) 223941
Open daily except Mondays and bank
holidays

Spurn Lightship
Hull Marina
Castle Street

Hull, Humberside
Tel. 44 (01482) 593902
Spurn Lightship
Open daily in summer

Strathclyde Regional Council
419 Balmore Road
Glasgow G22 6NU, Scotland

Swansea Maritime and Industrial Museum
Museum Square, Maritime Quarter
Swansea, Wales SA1 1UN
Tel. 44 (01792) 650351
William Gammon
Open Daily except Mondays not bank
holidays

Trincomalee Restoration Project
Jackson Dock
Hartlepool, Cleveland TS24 0SQ
Tel. 44 (429) 223193

Ulster Folk and Transport Museum
Cultra Manor
Holywood, County Down, Northern
Ireland BT18 0EU
Tel. 44 (01232) 428428
Open daily except Christmas

Upper Severn Navigation Trust
Ironbridge Gorge Museum Trust
Ironbridge, Telford, Shropshire

VIC 32 (Nick and Rachael Walker)
c/o The Change House
Crinan Ferry, Lochgilphead, Argyll,
Scotland PA31 8QH
Tel. 44 (015465) 10232
VIC 32

The Vigilant Trust
Conrad St. John Graham
c/o HM Customs & Excise, Orpington LVO
85, The Walnuts
Orpington, Kent BR6 0TN

Waverley
Waverley Terminal, Stobcross Quay
Glasgow, Scotland
Tel. 44 (41) 423 8000

Welsh Industrial and Maritime Museum
Bute Street
Cardiff, Wales
Tel. 44 (222) 481919

Wherry Yacht Charter
P. J. A. Bower
Barton House
Hartwell Road, The Avenue
Wroxham, Norfolk NR12 8TL
Tel. 44 Wroxham 2470

Windermere Steamboat Museum
Rayrigg Road
Windermere, Cumbria LA23 1BN
Tel. 44 (015394) 45565
www.wwwebguides.com/britain/cumbria/
lakes/steam.html
open daily Easter to October

Windsor Belle
c/o 17 Boswell Road
Henley-on-Thames, Oxfordshire

Greece

Hellenic Maritime Museum
Akti Themistokleous 296
GR 185 36-Piraeus
Tel. 30 (1) 45 16 264
Thalis O. Milissios

Israel

Clandestine Immigration and Naval
Museum
204 Derekh Allenby
Haifa
Tel. 972 (4) 53 62 49
Af-Al-Pi-Chen

National Maritime Museum
P.O. Box 44855, 198 Allenby Road
Haifa 31447
Tel. 972 (4) 53 66 22

Italy

Gestione Governativa
Navigazione Laghi Maggiore di Garda di
Como
via Ariosto 21
Milano
Concordia
Patria
Piemonte

Museo Nazionale dela Scienza
Via St. Vittore 21
I-1 20123 Milano
Tel. 39 (2) 48 70 34

Ebe
Museo Storico Navale
2148 Riva degli Schiavoni
Venice
MS 473

Japan

Dai 5 Fukuryu Maru Museum
Yumenoshima, Koto-ku
Tokyo 136
5 Fukuryu Maru

Metropolitan Government
Tokyo-ko Kensetsu Jimusho
3-9-56 Konan, Minato-ku
Tokyo
Shibaura Maru

Mikasa Preservation Society
Imaokacho, Yokosuka
Kanagawa 238
Mikasa

Museum of Maritime Science
3-1 Higashi Yashio, Shinagawa-ku
Tokyo 135
Tel. (3) 528-1111
Soya

Macao

Museu Maritimo de Macau
Largo do Pagode da Barra 4, P.O. Box 47
Macao
Tel. 559922

Myanmar

Irrawaddy Flotilla Company Ltd.
Box 261
44/46 Morningside Road
Edinburgh EH10 4BF
Tel. 44 (07071) 880 638
irrawaddy-flot.demon.co.uk
Myanmar Office:
Tel. (0951) 514 944
datserco.com.mm
PANDAW

Netherlands

Ton Brouwer
William Pontstraat 41
1135 ET Edam
Tel. 31 (06) 53 14 8276
ALBATROS

Centraal Museum Utrecht
Agnietenstraat 1
Postbus 2106
3500 GC Utrecht XA **3512**
Tel. 31 (030) 236 2362
UTRECHT SHIP

A. De Leeuw
Havenstraat 5
Zaandam 1506 PG
Tel. 31 (075) 617 5945
HUGO

Delta Expo
Oosterscheldedam
4328 ZG Burg-Haamstede
Tel. 31 (01115) 27 02
NEELTJE
VERTROUVEN

Peter Dorleijn
Waterman 87
Hoorn 1622 CT
Tel. 31 (0229) 21 6507
MK 63

Van Duuren
Obe Postma Wei 12
Leeuwarden, Friesland
Tel. 31 (058) 215 9412
MAARTEN

Van. Gullik
Peelstraat 12
1944 VE Beverwijk
Tel. 31 (0251) 210942
ADELAAR

Hanzestad Compagnie
Ijsselkade 3
P.O. Box 5
Kampen 8260 AA
Tel. 31 (038) 331 6050

AALTJE

H. J. den Hollander
P.O. Box 80
Zwartsluis 8064 ZH
Tel. 31 (065) 287 0067
NESCIO

International Maritime Training Institute
Seinpostweg 15
Ijmuiden 1976 BT
Tel. 31 (0255) 53 3433
POLLUX

C. P. Jongert
Zuiderweg O.1
Twisk 1676 GN
Tel. 31 (0227) 547571
NOORDZEE

J. Koeman
De Woude 4
De Woude 1489 NB
Tel. 31 (075) 641 0455
GABRIELLE

Marinemuseum
Hoofdgracht 3
1781 AA Den Helder
Tel. 31 (0223) 657 534
www.marinemuseum.nl
ABRAHAM CRIJNSSEN
SCHORPIOEN
TONIJN

Mariniersmuseum der Koninklijke Marine
Wijnhaven 7-9
3011 WG Rotterdam ZH
Tel. 31 (010) 412 9600
HOUTEPEN
L 9512

Maritiem Buitenmuseum
Leuvehaven 50-m 72
Postbus 21191
3001 AD Rotterdam
Tel. 31 (010) 404 8072
www.buitenmuseum.demon.nl
ALLES HEEFT EEN TIJD
ANNIGJE
DE HOOP
DOCKYARD V
DOCKYARD IX
DRIE GEBROEDERS
GEERTRUIDA
GRAIN ELEVATOR NO. 19
GRUNO
HAVENDIENST 20
JANTINA
JORIS II
LENA
PIETER BOELE
SIMSON
VOLHARDING I
VOORWAARTS I
ZEEMEEUW

Maritiem Museum 'Prins Hendrik'
Leuvehaven 1
3011 EA Rotterdam
Tel. 31 (010) 4132 680

www.mmph.nl
BUFFEL

Joop Mos, Hawser Holland
Dijk 60
Enkhuizen 1601 GK
Tel. 31 (0228) 31 3366
ROEK
ROSALIE

Nationaal Reddingsmuseum
Bernhardplein 10
1781 HH Den Helder
Tel. 31 (0223) 618 320
PRINS HENDRIK
TWENTHE

Nederlands Scheepvaart Museum
Kattenburgerplein 1
1018 KK Amsterdam
Tel. 31 (020) 5232 222
www.generali.nl/scheepvaartmuseum/
BALDER
CHRISTIAAN BRUNINGS
DE KONINGSSLOEP
INSULINDE
Open Monday-Saturday 10.00-17.00;
Sundays & holidays 12.00-17.00; Closed
Mondays mid-September to mid-June

Nederlandse Raderstoomboot Mij.
Valkenstraat 62
Rotterdam 3011 VR
Tel. 31 (010) 414 6744
DE NEDERLANDER
MAJESTEIT

Noordelijk Scheepvaartmuseum
Brugstraat 24-26
9711 HZ Groningen
Tel. 31 (050) 312 2202
ALIDA

Rob Peetoom
Diepenbrock Rode
Zoetermeer 2717
Tel. 31 (079) 321 4971
PARODIE

Jenny Pierik and Jaap Vleeken
Groot Lageland 23
8064 Zwartsluis
Tel. 31 (038) 3867095
TECLA

Radersalonboot Kapitein Kok BV
Treubweg 49
Diemen 1112 BA
Tel. 31 (020) 600 7019
KAPITEIN KOK

Reederij Oosterschelde BV
Postbus 23429
Rotterdam 3001 KK
Tel. 31 (010) 436 4258
OOSTERSCHELDE

Reederij Zierikzee B.V.
Nieuwe Bogerdstraat 7
Zierikzee 4301 CV
Tel. 31 (0111) 415 318

BRACKSAND

Rijkswaterstaat
Zuiderwagenplein 2
Lelystad 8224 AD
Tel. 31 (0320) 299111
NOORD HOLLAND

Stichting Beheer Ransdorp
28, Vogelzand 2106
1788 GL Den Helder
Tel. 31 (0223) 64 4373
VROUW ELISABETH

Stichting Behoud Hoogaars
Postbus 480
Vlissingen, Zeeland 4380 AL
Tel. 31 (0118) 410045
ANDRIES JACOB

Stichting Behoud Maritieme Monumenten
Dr. Lelykade 2e Binnenhaven
P.O. Box 84071
Scheveningen 2508 AB
Tel. 31 (070) 354 0315
MERCUUR

Stichting Behoud 2-mast kofttjalk V.V. anno
1899
Tel. 31 (050) 525 7769
VOORWAARTS VOORWAARTS

Stichting Behoud van het Stoomschip
Vijfpootveld 22
Koog aan de Zaan 1541 PT
Tel. 31 (075) 617 6749
ELFIN
JACOB LANGENBERG

Stichting Calorische Werktuigen
Leliestraat 14
Schiedam 3114 NK
Tel. 31 (010) 473 7459
HERCULES

Stichting De compound
Grote Haarse Kade 49
Gorinchem 4205 VK
Tel. 31 (0183) 627 327
JAN DE STERKE

Stichting Gudsekop
Kooistukken 42
Eelde Drente 9761 JZ
Tel. 31 (050) 309 4455
GUDSEKOP

Stichting Help De Hudson
Mer. Gijzenstraat 29
4681 BN NW-Vossemeer
Tel. 31 (010) 474 3085
HUDSON

Stichting historie der Kustverlichting
Oude Rijkswerf
Den Helder
Tel. 31 (0223) 623 829
LICHTSCHIP NO. 10

Stichting Hollands Glorie
Lijsterlaan 160

Maasluis 3145 VN
Tel. 31 (010) 591 5774
FURIE

Stichting Lichtschip no. 12
Kanaalweg W.Z.
P.O. Box 1014
Hellevoetsluis 3220 BA
Tel. 31 (0181) 32 2212
LICHTSCHIP NO. 12

Stichting Maritiem Trust
Beinemastraat 2
Dordrecht 3313 CH
Tel. 31 (078) 61 40455
GEBROEDERS BEVER

Stichting Museumhaven Zierikzee
Oude Haven 16
Zierikzee 4300 AD
Tel. 31 (0111) 642 480
MIJN GENOEGEN

Stichting Nationaal Brandweermuseum
Industriehaven 8
Hellevoetsluis 3221 AD
Tel. 31 (0181) 314 479
JAN VAN DER HEYDE

Stichting Nautische Monumenten
Oude Rijkswerf
Weststraat 1 Gebouw 41
Den Helder
Tel. 31 (0223) 616100
Y 8017
Y 8122

Stichting Reddingsmuseum Jan Leis
Badweg 2b
Postbus 69
Hoek van Holland 3151 AB
Tel. 31 (0174) 383802
REDDINGSBOOT 1

Stichting Rotterdamse Zeilschip
c/o Van Anken Knuppe Damstra
Antwoordnummer 180
3001 HA Rotterdam
HELENA

Stichting Stoombaggermolen Boskalis
Westminster
Kievietlaan 1
Sliedrecht 3362 NE
Tel. 31 (0184) 420308
FRIESLAND

Stichting Vriendenkring sleepboot Holland
P.O. Box 1196
Leeuwarden 8900 CD
Tel. 31 (052) 765 3002
HOLLAND

Stichting Zr.Ms. Bonaire
Weststraat 1
Den Helder 1781 BW
Tel. 31 (0223) 616100
BONAIRE

U-111
Annie Romein Verschoorlaan 52

Den Helder 1782 TH
Tel. 31 (0223) 612 456
U-111

P. Vastenhout
A. Thijmstraat 9
Rotterdam 3027 AK

Tel. 31 (010) 462 1335
Veenkoloniaal Museum
Winkler Prinsstraat 5
9641 AP Veendam
Tel. 31 (0598) 616 393
EBENHAEZER
FAMILIETROUW

Veldhuis
Postbus 22
Zwartsluis 8064 ZG
Tel. 31 (038) 386 8721
NIEUWE ZORG

Vereeniging De Hydrograaf
Julianalaan 250
Bilthoven 3722 GW
Tel. 31 (030) 229 2272
HYDROGRAAF

Paul Versteege and Peter Jansen
Friese Steen 88
3961 XK Wijk bij duurstede
Tel. 31 (0343) 574538
SAMENWERKING

Piet Visser
Meidoornstraat 146
Zaandam 1505 TZ
Tel. 31 (075) 615 7179
SCHEELENKUHLEN

Simon Visser
Zuideinde 212
Westzaan
JOHANNES

Visserij en Jutters Museum
Barentszstraat 21
Oudeschild 1792 AD
Tel. 31 (0222) 31 4956
DE DRIE GEBROEDERS (TX11)

Zuiderzeemuseum
Wierdijk 12-22
P.O. Box 42
1600 AA Enkhuizen
Tel. 31 (0228) 351 111
www.zuiderzeemuseum.nl
DE HOOP
DE VIER GEBROEDERS

New Zealand

Fiordland Travel
P. O. Box 94
Queenstown
EARNSLAW

Historical Maritime Park
Box 153
Paeroa
Tel. 7121

New Zealand National Maritime Museum
Hobson Wharf, Eastern Viaduct
Auckland
Tel. 64 (9) 358 1019

Tauranga Historic Village
17th Avenue West,
Tauranga
Tel. 81-302
TAIOMA

William C. Daldy Preservation Society
P. O. Box 2833
Auckland
WILLIAM C. DALDY

Norway

Bergens Sjofartsmuseum
Postboks 2736, Mohlenpris
N-5026 Bergen
Tel. 47 (5) 327980

Tarald Glastad
Havneheia 7
N-4550 Farsund

Hardanger Sunnhordlandske
Dampskipsselskap
Strandgt. 191
Bergen
Tel. 47 (5) 23 87 00
GRANVIN

Jubileumsskipet A/S, S.S. Kysten I
N-3132 Husoysund

Marinemuseet
RNN Base Karl Johansvern
Horten
RAP

Norsk Sjofartsmuseum
Bygdoynesveien 37
N-0286 Oslo 2
Tel. 47 (2) 43 82 40

Norsk Veteranskibsklubb
P. O. Box 1287 Vika
Oslo 1

Norway Yacht Charters
Skippergt. 8, P.B. 91 Sentrum
0101 Oslo 1
Tel. 47 (2) 42 64 98

Ostlandets Skoleskib
Prinsensgt. 2
Oslo 1

Sondeled Veteranskibsklubb
c/o Oddvor Masdalen
N-4990 Sondeled

Stavanger Sjofartsmuseum
Musegt. 16
N-4000 Stavanger
Tel. 47 (4) 52 60 35
Sunmore Museum
N-6000 Alesund

Pakistan

Pakistan Maritime Museum
Habib Ibrahim Rehmatullah Road
Karachi
Tel. 92-21 425 1687
www.genesis-realtime.com/MUSEUM.HTM

Portugal

Museu de Marinha
Praca do Imperio, Belem
1400 Lisboa
Tel. 351 (19) 3620 012
Open daily except Monday 10.00-18.00;
winter to 17.00

Russia

Central Naval Museum
Pushkinskaya ploshchad 4
SV-199034 St. Petersburg
Tel. 218-27-01

Pacific Fleet Museum
14 Pushkin Street
Vladivostok

South Africa

Local History Museum
Old Court House, Aliwal Street
Durban 4001

South African Maritime Museum
Victoria and Albert Waterfront
Cape Town
Tel. 2721 419 2505
www.maritimemuseum.ac.za/
SOMERSET
Open daily except some holidays 10.00-17.00

Spain

Museo Maritimo de Barcelona
Puerto de la Paz 1
E-08001 Barcelona
34 (3) 301 1831
SAYREMAR I

Museo Naval de Madrid
Montalban 2
E-28014 Madrid
34 (1) 522 8530

Sweden

Anfartygs A/B, Saltsjon-Malaren
S-111 27 Stora Nygarten
45 Stockholm
BJÖRKFJÄRDEN

Angbatstrafiken Boxholm II
Rune Hektor, Fallhagsvagen 44
S-590 10 Boxholm
BOXHOLM II

Brattebergsskolan
Box 2002
430 90 Ockero

Tel. 46 (31) 78 24 20
HAWILA

For Fulla Segel
Pl. 2392 Ostersidan
450 34 Fiskebackskil
Tel. 46 (523) 226 25

Foreningen Lotsbaten
Groto, S-430 90 Ockero
www.algonet.se/~vagspel/doc2.htm
EJDERN

Goteborgs Maritima Centrum
Kajskjul 3, Lilla Bommen
411 04 Goteborg
Tel. 46 (31) 10 1290
ESAB IV
FLADEN
FLODSPRUTAN II
FRYKEN
GÖTEBORGSPRÅM
GUNHILD
INGO
NORDKAPAREN
SMÅLAND
SÖLVE
THOR
VALBORG II

Kutterklubben Lord Nelson
c/o Hakon af Malmborg
Herman Ygbergs vag 34
S-161 38 Bromma
LORD NELSON

Malmo Sjofartsmuseum
P. O. Box 406
S-201-24 Malmo
Tel. 46 (40) 733 30
MALMO REDD

Marinmuseum
Admiralitetsslattern
S-371-00 Karlskrona
Tel. 46 (455) 840 00
BREMON
HAJEN
JARRAMAS
KBV-238
SPICA

Museiangfartyget Ejdern
Per Fagerholm, Movagen 3
S-182 45 Enebyberg

Rederiaktiebolaget Gota Kanal
P. O. Box 272, Hotellplatsen 2
S-401 24 Goteborg
EJDERN

Roslagens Skeppslags Vanner
c/o Ohrqvist Laura Grubbs
Vag 22, S-183
64 Taby
BLIDÖSUND

S.S. Trafik Ekonomisk Foreningen
Box 119, S-544
00 Hjo
TRAFIK

Sallskapet Angbatan
Box 2072, S-403
12 Goteborg 2
BOHUSLAN
FARHAN 4
STORM PRINCESS

Sjofartsmuseet i Goteborg
Karl-Johansgatan 1-3
S-41459 Goteborg
Tel. 46 (31) 61 10 00

Statens Sjohistoriska Museet
Djurgardsbrunnsvagen 24, P. O. Box 27131
S-102 52 Stockholm
Tel. 46 (8) 666 4900
FINNGRUNDET
SANKT ERIK

Stiftelsen Skargardsbatan
Nybrogatan 76
S-11441 Stockholm
DJURGÅRDEN 3
MARIEFRED

Stiftelsen Smalands Museum
Box 66, S-351
02 Vaxjo
T-38

Strommakanel Angfartygs A/B
Skeppsbron 30, S-111
30 Stockholm
DROTTNINGHOLM
ÖSTANÄ I

Vasamuseet
Galavarvet, Djurgarden
Stockholm
Tel. 46 (8) 666 4800
www.vasamuseet.se/
VASA

Switzerland

Compagnie Generale de Navigation
Avenue de Rhodanie 17
1000 Lausanne 6
LA SUISSE
MONTREAUX
RHONE
SAVOIE
SIMPLON

Confrerie des Pirates D'Orchy
Case Postale 2525
1002 Lausanne
LA VAUDOISE

Schiffahrtsgesellschaft des
Vierwaldstattersees
Post Boix 855
CH-6002 Lucerne
GALLIA
SCHILLER
STADT LUZERN
UNTERWALDEN
URI

Swiss Museum of Transport and
Communications

Lidostrasse 5
6000 Lucerne
RIGI

Zurichsee-Schiffahrtsgesellschaft
Mythenquai 333
8038 Zurich
STADT RAPPERSWIL
STADT ZURICH

Turkey

Deniz Muzesi
Besiktas, Istanbul
Tel. 90 (212) 261 00 40
CAIQUES
KADIRGA
Open Friday-Tuesday 0900-1230 and 1330-1700

United States

Admiral Nimitz Museum of the Pacific War
P.O. Box 777
Fredericksburg, Texas 78624
Tel. 830-997-4379
HA-19
PT-309

Adventureland Amusement Park
P. O. Box 3355
Des Moines, Iowa 50316
Tel. 515-266-2121
QUEEN

Aircraft Carrier Hornet Museum
P. O. Box 460
Alameda, California 94501
Tel. 510-521-8448
HORNET

David & Susan Allen
P. O. Box 571
Rockland, Maine 04841
Tel. 207-594-2923
J. & E. RIGGIN

American Merchant Marine Museum
U.S. Merchant Marine Academy
Kings Point, New York 11024-1699
Tel. 516-466-9696

The Antique Boat Museum
750 Mary Street,
Clayton, New York 13624
Tel. 315-686-4104
PARDON ME

Apalachicola Maritime Institute
P. O. Box 625
Apalachicola, Florida 32320
Tel. 904-653-8708
GOVERNOR STONE

Arkansas Riverboat Company
P. O. Box 579
North Little Rock, Arkansas 72115
Tel. 501-376-4150
ARKANSAS II

Baltimore Maritime Museum
802 S. Caroline Street,

Baltimore, Maryland 21231
Tel. 410-396-3393
www.cr.nps.gov/history/maritime/ltship.html
CHESAPEAKE LIGHTSHIP
TANEY
TORSK

Baltimore Museum of Industry
1415 Key Highway
Baltimore, Maryland 21230
Tel. 301-727-4808
BALTIMORE

Orville & Ellen Barnes
70 Elm Street
Camden, Maine 04843
Tel. 207-236-3520
STEPHEN TABER

Belle of Louisville Operating Board
4th Avenue & River Road
Louisville, Kentucky 40202
Tel. 502-625-2355
BELLE OF LOUISVILLE
MAYOR ANDREW BROADDUS

Bensons, Inc.
P. O. Box 147
Covington, Kentucky 41011
Tel. 606-261-8500
WAKE ROBIN

Boston National Historical Park
Charlestown Navy Yard
Boston, Massachusetts 02129
Tel. 617-242-5601
CASSIN YOUNG

Bremerton Historic Ships Association
300 Washington Beach Avenue,
Bremerton, Washington 98337
Tel. 360-792-2457
TURNER JOY

Buffalo Bill Museum
201 River Drive North
Le Claire, Iowa 52753
Tel. 319-289-5580
LONE STAR

Buffalo & Erie County Naval &
Servicemen's Park
One Naval Park Cove
Buffalo, New York 14202
Tel. 716-847-1773
CROAKER
LITTLE ROCK
PTF-17
THE SULLIVANS

Calvert Marine Museum
P. O. Box 97
Solomons, Maryland 20688
Tel. 410-326-2042
PENGUIN
WM. B. TENNISON
Charlestown Festival Commission
P. O. Box 2749
Charleston, West Virginia 25330
Tel. 304-348-0709
P. A. DENNY

Chesapeake Bay Foundation
162 Prince George Street
Annapolis, Maryland 21401
Tel. 301-268-8816
STANLEY NORMAN

Chesapeake Bay Maritime Museum
P. O. Box 636
St. Michael's, Maryland 21663
Tel. 301-745-2916
E. C. COLLIER
EDNA E. LOCKWOOD
MUSTANG
OLD POINT
ROSIE PARKS

Christeen Oyster Sloop Corporation
West End Avenue, P.O. Box 146
Oyster Bay, New York 11771
Tel. 516-922-1098
CHRISTEEN

City of Anacortes Museum
1305 8th Street
Anacortes, Washington 98221
Tel. 206-293-1915
W. T. PRESTON

City of Bridgeton Municipal Port Authority
10 Grove
Bridgeton, New Jersey 08302
Tel. 609-455-3230
NELLIE & MARY

City of Cincinnati
644 Linn Street
Cincinnati, Ohio 45203
Tel. 513-241-6550
MAJESTIC

City of Clinton Department of Parks &
Recreation
1401 11th Avenue North
Clinton, Iowa 52732
Tel. 319-243-1260
CITY OF CLINTON

City of Everett
3002 Wetmore Avenue
Everett, Washington 98201
Tel. 206-259-0311
EQUATOR

City of New York Fire Department Marine
Division
Pier A, North River
New York, New York 10004
Tel. 212-570-4294
FIREFIGHTER

City of Norfolk
645 Church Street
Norfolk, Virginia 23510
Tel. 804-441-2222
CITY OF NORFOLK
City of Port Huron
905 7th Street
Port Huron, Michigan 48060
Tel. 313-987-6000
HURON LIGHTSHIP

City of Sioux City Department of Public
Works
P. O. Box 447
Sioux City, Iowa 51102
Tel. 712-279-6111
SERGEANT FLOYD

City of St. Charles Conventions & Visitors
Bureau
P. O. Box 745
St. Charles, Missouri 63302
Tel. 313-621-3311
GOLDENROD

City of Tacoma Fire Department
901 South Fawcett Avenue
Tacoma, Washington 98402
Tel. 206-591-5737
FIREBOAT NO. 1

City of Two Harbors
610 Second Avenue
Two Harbors, Minnesota 55616
Tel. 218-834-5631
EDNA G.

City of Wahkon Civic Association
P. O. Box 103
Wahkon, Minnesota 56386
Tel. 612-495-3441
ELLEN RUTH

Classic Boat Tours
Lake Otsego Boat Tours
Box 664,
Cooperstown, New York 13326
Tel. 607-547-5295
CHIEF UNCAS
Operates daily May 15 to October 12

Cleveland Coordinating Committee for
Cod
1089 East 9th Street,
Cleveland, Ohio 44114
Tel. 216-566-8770
www.usscod.org
COD

Clyde A. Phillips Project
P. O. Box 57
Dorchester, New Jersey 08316
Tel. 609-785-2060
A. J. MEERWALD

Columbia River Maritime Museum
1792 Marine Drive
Astoria, Oregon 97103
Tel. 503-325-2323
COLUMBIA

Delta Queen Steamboat Company
30 Robin Street Wharf
New Orleans, Louisiana 70130
Tel. 504-586-0631
DELTA QUEEN
Diversified Investors Group
c/o Bill Resner, P. O. Box 32, Route 1
Stephenson, Michigan 49887
Tel. 906-753-4981

Dubuque County Historical Society

P. O. Box 305
Dubuque, Iowa 52001
Tel. 319-557-9445
WILLIAM M. BLACK

Duluth Entertainment Convention Center
350 Harbor Drive
Duluth, Minnesota 55802
Tel. 218-722-5573
WILLIAM A. IRVIN

Echo Hill Outdoor School
Still Pond Neck Road
Worton, Maryland 21678
Tel. 301-348-5880
ELSWORTH

Essex Shipbuilding Museum
28 Main Street
Essex, Massachusetts 01929
Tel. 508-768-7541
EVELINA M. GOULART

Fairbanks Historical Preservation
Foundation
755 8th Avenue
Fairbanks, Alaska 99701
Tel. 907-456-8848
NENANA

John Foss
P. O. Box 482
Rockland, Maine 04841
Tel. 207-594-8007
AMERICAN EAGLE

Freedom Park
2497 Freedom Park Road
Omaha, Nebraska 68110
Tel. 402-345-1959
HAZARD
LSM-45
MARLIN

Friends of the Nobska
P. O. Box J-4097
New Bedford, Massachusetts 02741
Tel. 401-434-6274
NOBSKA

Galveston Historical Foundation
P. O. Box 302
Galveston, Texas 77550
Tel. 409-765-7834
ELISSA

Edward Glaser
P. O. Box 482
Rockland, Maine 04841
Tel. 207-594-8007
ISAAC H. EVANS

Gloucester Adventure, Inc.
P. O. Box 1306
Gloucester, Massachusetts 01930
Tel. 508-281-8079
ADVENTURE

Grand Banks Schooner Museum
P. O. Box 123
Boothbay Harbor, Maine 04538

Tel. 207-633-4215
SHERMAN ZWICKER

Great Lakes Historical Society
480 Main Street
Vermilion, Ohio 44089
Tel. 216-967-3467
WILLIAM G. MATHER

H. Lee White Marine Museum
P.O. Box 101
Oswego, New York 13126
Tel. 315-342-0480
DERRICK BOAT NO. 8
MAJOR ELISHA K. HENSON

Hart Nautical Collections
The M.I.T. Museum
265 Massachusetts Avenue,
Cambridge, Massachusetts 02139
Tel. 617-253-5942

Havre de Grace Maritime Museum
P. O. Box 533
Havre de Grace, Maryland 21078
Tel. 301-939-5189
MARY W. SOMERS

Hawaii Maritime Center
Pier 7, Honolulu Harbor
Honolulu, Hawaii 96813
Tel. 808-523-6151
FALLS OF CLYDE

Head of the Lakes Maritime Society
P. O. Box 775
Superior, Wisconsin 54880
Tel. 715-392-5742
COL. D. D. GAILLARD
METEOR

Hells Gate State Park
3620A Snake River Avenue
Lewiston, Idaho 83501
Tel. 208-743-2363
JEAN

Hudson Highlands Cruise & Tours
P. O. Box 265
Highland Falls, New York 10928
Tel. 914-446-7171
COMMANDER

Hudson Landing, Inc.
725 River Road
Edgewater, New Jersey 07020
Tel. 201-941-2300
BINGHAMTON

Hudson River Maritime Center
One Rondout Landing
Kingston, New York 12401
Tel. 914-338-0071
MATHILDA

Hudson Waterfront Museum
6019 Boulevard East
West New York, New Jersey 07093
Tel. 201-662-1229
L.V.R.R. NO. 79

Humboldt Bay Maritime Museum
1410 Second Street
Eureka, California 95501
Tel. 707-444-9440
MADAKET

Independence Seaport Museum
211 South Columbus Boulevard & Walnut St
Philadelphia, Pennsylvania 19106
Tel. 215-925-5439
www.libertynet.org/~seaport
BECUNA
OLYMPIA

International Shipping Company
4401 West Jefferson
Detroit, Michigan 48209
Tel. 313-843-8800
COLUMBIA
STE. CLAIRE

Intrepid Sea-Air-Space Museum
West 46th Street & 12th Avenue
New York, New York 10036
Tel. 212-245-0072
www.intrepid-museum.com
EDSON
GROWLER
INTREPID

Jackson County Parks & Recreation
Independence Square, Room 205
Independence, Missouri 64050
Tel. 816-881-4431
WILLIAM S. MITCHELL

The Kendall Whaling Museum
27 Everett Street, P.O. Box 297
Sharon, Massachusetts 02067
Tel. 617-784-5642

Keokuk River Museum
P. O. Box 268
Keokuk, Iowa 52632
Tel. 319-524-3286
GEO. M. VERITY

Lake Champlain Maritime Museum
Basin Harbor, Vermont 05491
Tel. 802-475-2317
CG-52302

Lake Michigan Maritime Museum
P. O. Box 534
South Haven, Michigan 49090
Tel. 616-637-8078
EVELYN S.

Le Sault de Ste. Marie Historical Sites
P. O. Box 1668
Sault Ste. Marie, Michigan 49783
Tel. 906-632-3658
VALLEY CAMP

Lewes Historical Society
119 West 3rd Street
Lewes, Delaware 19958
Tel. 302-645-8740
OVERFALLS

The Lobster House

Fisherman's Wharf
Cape May, New Jersey 08204
Tel. 609-884-8296
AMERICAN

Los Angeles Maritime Museum
Berth 84, Foot of 6th Street
San Pedro, California 90731
Tel. 213-548-7618
OCEAN WAIF

Louisiana Naval War Memorial
305 South River Road
Baton Rouge, Louisiana 70802
Tel. 504-342-1942
www.premier.net/~uss_kidd/home.html
KIDD

Maine Maritime Academy
Castine, Maine 04421
Tel. 207-326-4311
BOWDOIN

Maine Maritime Museum
963 Washington Street,
Bath, Maine 04530
Tel. 207-443-1316

Marine Learning Institute
P. O. Box 6
Portage des Sioux, Missouri 63373
Tel. 314-724-1558
STE. GENEVIEVE

The Mariners Museum
1 Museum Drive
Newport News, Virginia 23606-3798
Tel. 804-595-0368

Maritime Center at Norwalk
10 North Water Street
South Norwalk, Connecticut 06854
Tel. 203-838-1488
HOPE

Meriwether Lewis Foundation
c/o Peru State College
Peru, Nebraska 68421
Tel. 402-825-3341

Millersburg Ferry Boat Association
P.O. Box 93
Millersburg, Pennsylvania 17061
Tel. 717-692-2442
FALCON
ROARING BULL

Miracle of America Story Museum
c/o Gil Mangels, 58176 Highway 93
Polson, Montana 59860
PAUL BUNYAN

Moosehead Marine Museum
P. O. Box 1151
Greenville, Maine 04441
KAHTADIN

Museum of Science and Industry
57th Street & Lakeshore Drive
Chicago, Illinois 60637
Tel. 773-684-1414

www.msichicago.org
U-505

Mystic Seaport Museum
Mystic, Connecticut 06355
Tel. 203-572-0711
CHARLES W. MORGAN
EMMA C. BERRY
FLORENCE
JOSEPH CONRAD
L. A. DUNTON
SABINO

National Liberty Ship Memorial
Fort Mason Center, Landmark Building A
San Francisco, California 94123
Tel. 415-441-3101
www.crl.com/~wefald/obrien.html
JEREMIAH O'BRIEN

National Maritime Center
1 Waterside Drive,
Norfolk, Virginia 23510
HUNTINGTON

National Maritime Museum Association
Box 470310
San Francisco, California 94147
Tel. 415-775-1943
www.maritime.org
PAMPANITO

National Museum of American History
Smithsonian Institution
12th Street and Constitution Avenue NW
Washington, District of Columbia 20560
Tel. 202-357-1300
PHILADELPHIA

Naval Undersea Museum
610 Dowell Street,
Keyport, Washington 98345
Tel. 360-396-4148
TRIESTE II

Navy Memorial Museum
Washington Navy Yard, 901 M Street SE
Washington, District of Columbia 20374
Tel. 202-433-3377
BARRY
PCF-1
TRIESTE

New Bedford Harbor Development
Commission
Pier 3
New Bedford, Massachusetts 02745
Tel. 508-993-1770
NEW BEDFORD

Newport News Shipbuilding & Drydock
Company
4101 Washington Avenue
Newport News, Virginia 23607
Tel. 804-380-2000
DOROTHY

Northwest Seaport
1002 Valley Street,
Seattle, Washington 98109
Tel. 206-447-9800

ARTHUR FOSS
RELIEF
WAWONA

Ohio Showboat Drama, Inc.
237 Front Street, Box 572
Marietta, Ohio 45750
Tel. 614-373-6033

Oregon Museum of Science and Industry
1945 SE Water Avenue,
Portland, Oregon 97214
Tel. 503-797-4000
www.omsi.edu/explore/sub/sub.html
BLUEBACK

Oscar Tybring Society
2733 Shelter Island Drive, #369
San Diego 92106
OSCAR TYBRING

Pate Museum of Transportation
P. O. Box 711
Fort Worth, Texas 76101
Tel. 817-332-1161
MSB-5

Patriot's Point Development Authority
40 Patriot's Point Road
Mt. Pleasant, South Carolina 29464
Tel. 803-884-2727
www.state.sc.us/patpt
CLAMAGORE
INGHAM
LAFFEY
YORKTOWN

Norman Paulsen
c/o General Marine Services, 2562 Yardarm
Port Hueneme, California 93035
Tel. 805-984-6179
PILOT

Peabody-Essex Museum
161 Essex Street
Salem, Massachusetts 01970
Tel. 508-745-1876

Daniel Pease
P. O. Box 482
Rockland, Maine 04841
Tel. 207-594-8007
LEWIS R. FRENCH

Penobscot Marine Museum
Church Street
Searsport, Maine 04974
Tel. 207-548-2529

R. J. & Diane Peterson
P. O. Box 511
Douglas, Michigan 49406
Tel. 616-857-2107
KEEWATIN
REISS

Philadelphia Ship Preservation Guild
Columbus Boulevard at Chestnut Street
Philadelphia, Pennsylvania 19106
Tel. 215-923-9030
www.gazela.org
BARNEGAT

GAZELA OF PHILADELPHIA
JUPITER

Ponce de Leon Inlet Lighthouse
4931 South Peninsula Drive
Ponce Inlet, Florida 32127
Tel. 904-761-1821
F. D. RUSSELL

Port of Oakland
P. O. Box 2064
Oakland, California 94604
Tel. 510-839-7533
POTOMAC

Port of Portsmouth Maritime Museum &
Albacore Park
600 Market Street,
Portsmouth, New Hampshire 03801
Tel. 603-436-3680
ALBACORE

Portsmouth Lightship Museum
P. O. Box 248
Portsmouth, Virginia 23705
Tel. 804-393-8741
PORTSMOUTH

Presidential Yacht Trust
1899 L Street N.W. #1200
Washington, District of Columbia 20036
Tel. 703-838-9270
SEQUOIA

Project Liberty Ship
P. O. Box 25846, Highlandtown Station
Baltimore, Maryland 21224
Tel. 410-558-0646
www.liberty-ship.com
JOHN W. BROWN

Radcliffe Maritime Museum
201 West Monument Street
Baltimore, Maryland 21201
Tel. 301-685-3750
MINNIE V.

Richard Reedy
Folly Point
Gloucester, Massachusetts 01930
Tel. 617-283-1232
CANGARDA

River Enterprises
225 South Water Street
Wilmington, North Carolina 28401
Tel. 919-343-8007
JOHN TAXIS

Rogers Street Fishing Village Museum
P. O. Box 33
Two Rivers, Wisconsin 54241
Tel. 414-794-8367
BUDDY O

S.S. Red Oak Victory
Box 70453
Richmond, California
Tel. 510-237-1445
RED OAK VICTORY

Sail-Inn Tours
P.O. Box 358
Tilghman, Maryland 21671
Tel. 410-886-2703
MAMIE A. MISTER

San Diego Maritime Museum
1306 N. Harbor Drive
San Diego, California 92101
Tel. 619-234-9153
www.sdmaritime.com
BERKELEY
MEDEA
PILOT
STAR OF INDIA

San Francisco Maritime National Historical
Park
Building 204, Fort Mason
San Francisco, California 94123
Tel. 415-332-8409
BALCLUTHA
C. A. THAYER
EPPLETON HALL
EUREKA
HERCULES
LEWIS ARK
WAPAMA

San Jacinto Battleground State Park
3527 Battleground Road,
LaPorte, Texas 77571
Tel. 281-479-4414
TEXAS

San Mateo County Council Boy Scouts
P. O. Box 5005
San Mateo, California 94402
Tel. 415-341-5633
WARDEN JOHNSTON

Schooner Ernestina Commission
30 Union Street
New Bedford, Massachusetts 02740
Tel. 508-992-4900
ERNESTINA

Schooner Nathaniel Bowditch
Box 459
Warren, Maine 04864
Tel. 207-273-4062
NATHANIEL BOWDITCH

Seawolf Park
Pelican Island
P.O. Box 3306
Galveston, Texas 77550
Tel. 409-744-5738
CAVALLA
STEWART

Shelburne Museum
U. S. Route 7
Shelburne, Vermont 05482
Tel. 802-985-3344
TICONDEROGA

Sleeping Bear Dunes National Lakeshore
P. O. Box 277
Empire, Michigan 49630
Tel. 616-326-5134

ALOHA

Society for the Preservation of S. S. City of
Milwaukee
P. O. Box 389
Frankfort, Michigan 49635
Tel. 616-352-7251
CITY OF MILWAUKEE

South Street Seaport Museum
207 Front Street
New York, New York 10038
Tel. 212-669-9400
AMBROSE LIGHTSHIP
LETTIE G. HOWARD
PEKING
PIONEER
W. O. DECKER
WAVERTREE

St. Louis Concessions
2241 Edwards
St. Louis, Missouri 63110
Tel. 314-771-9911

Steamship William G. Mather Museum
1001 East 9th Street,
Cleveland, Ohio 44114
Tel. 216-574-6262
little.nhlink.net/wgm/wgmhome.html
WILLIAM G. MATHER

Submarine Force Library & Museum
United States Navy Submarine Base, P. O.
Box 571
Groton, Connecticut 06349
Tel. 203-449-3174
www.ussnautilus.org
HA-8
NAUTILUS
SEEHUND-TYPE MIDGET SUBMARINE

Submarine Memorial Association
P. O. Box 395
Hackensack, New Jersey 07601
Tel. 201-342-3268
LING

Suffolk Marine Museum
P. O. Box 144
West Sayville, New York 11796
Tel. 516-567-1733
MODESTY
PRISCILLA

Sylvina W. Beal
P.O. Box 8,
Cherryfield, Maine 04622
Tel. 207-633-1109
Winter 207-546-2927
SYLVINA W. BEAL

Tabor Academy
Front Street
Marion, Massachusetts 02738
Tel. 508-748-2000
TABOR BOY

Toledo-A-Float
P. O. Box 397
Maumee, Ohio 43537

Tel. 419-698-8252
WILLIS B. BOYER

Tradewinds Education Network
P. O. Box 642
Essex, Connecticut 06426
Tel. 203-434-3890

U.S. Naval Academy Museum
118 Maryland Avenue,
Annapolis, Maryland 21402
Tel. 410-293-2108
X-1

U.S.S. Alabama Battleship Commission
2703 Battleship Parkway, Box 65
Mobile, Alabama 36601
Tel. 205-433-2703
www.ussalabama.com
ALABAMA
DRUM

U.S.S. Batfish
Muskogee War Memorial Park
P.O. Box 735
Muskogee, Oklahoma 74402
Tel. 918-682-6294
BATFISH

U.S.S. Bowfin Submarine Museum and Park
11 Arizona Memorial Drive
Honolulu, Hawaii 96818
Tel. 808-423-1341
www.aloha.net/~bowfin
BOWFIN

U.S.S. Constellation
Pier 1, 301 E. Pratt Street
Baltimore, Maryland 21202
Tel. 410-539-1797
www.constellation.org
CONSTELLATION

U.S.S. Constitution
Charlestown Navy Yard
Boston, Massachusetts 02129
Tel. 617-242-5670
www.ncts.navy.mil/homepages/constitution
USS CONSTITUTION

U.S.S. Lexington Museum on the Bay
2914 N. Shoreline Boulevard
Corpus Christi, Texas 78402
Tel. 512-888-4873
www.usslexington.com
LEXINGTON

U.S.S. Massachusetts Memorial Committee
Battleship Cove
Fall River, Massachusetts 02721
Tel. 508-678-1100
www.battleshipcove.com
HIDDENSEE
JOSEPH P. KENNEDY, JR.
LIONFISH
MASSACHUSETTS
PT-617
PT-796

U.S.S. Missouri Memorial Association
965-A4 North Nimitz Highway

Honolulu, Hawaii 96817
MISSOURI

U.S.S. North Carolina Battleship Memorial
P. O. Box 480
Wilmington, North Carolina 28402
Tel. 910-251-5797
www.city-info.com/ncbb55.html
NORTH CAROLINA

U.S.S. Requin
Carnegie Science Center
1 Allegheny Avenue,
Pittsburgh, Pennsylvania 15212
Tel. 412-237-1550
REQUIN

U.S.S. Silversides & Maritime Museum
P. O. Box 1692
Muskegon, Michigan 49443
Tel. 616-755-1230
McLANE
SILVERSIDES

U.S.S. Slater
330 Broadway
Albany, New York 12207
Tel. 518-463-1568
SLATER

United States Army Corps of Engineers
Bevill Visitor Center, Route 2, Box 252-X
Aliceville, Alabama 35447
Tel. 205-373-8705
MONTGOMERY

United States Army Transportation
Museum
Fort Eustis, Virginia
Tel. 804-878-3603
J-3792
ST-2031

United States Coast Guard Academy
New London, Connecticut 06320
Tel. 203-444-8444
USCGC EAGLE

United States Merchant Marine Veterans of
World War II
P. O. Box 629
San Pedro, California 90733
Tel. 213-519-9545
www.sanpedrochamber.com/champint/lane
vict.htm
LANE VICTORY

United States Naval Shipbuilding Museum
739 Washington Street,
Quincy, Massachusetts 02169
Tel. 617-479-8792
www.uss-salem.org
SALEM
University of Minnesota
110 Rarig Center, 330 21st. Avenue South
Minneapolis, Minnesota 55455
Tel. 612-625-5380

Vessel Zodiac Corporation
P. O. Box 322
Snohomish, Washington 28290

Tel. 206-483-4088
ZODIAC

Virginia V Foundation
911 Western
Seattle, Washington 98107
Tel. 206-624-9119
VIRGINIA V

Vision Quest
P. O. Box 447
Exton, Pennsylvania 19341
Tel. 215-524-0330
NEW WAY

WCO Port Properties, Ltd.
P. O. Box 8
Long Beach, California 90801
Tel. 213-435-3511
QUEEN MARY

Ray Williamson
P. O. Box 617
Camden, Maine 04843
Tel. 207-236-8871
GRACE BAILEY
MERCANTILE

Wisconsin Maritime Museum
75 Maritime Drive,
Manitowoc, Wisconsin 54220
Tel. 920-684-0218
www.dataplusnet.com/maritime/maritime.
html
COBIA

Yankee Schooner Cruises
P. O. Box 696
Camden, Maine 04843
Tel. 207-236-4449
ROSEWAY

Youth Adventure
P. O. Box 23
Mercer Island, Washington 98040
Tel. 206-232-4024
ADVENTURESS

Zanzibar

Revolutionary Government of Zanzibar
Department of Antiquities, Archives and
Museum
P. O. Box 116
Zanzibar
Tel. 30342
SULTAN'S BARGE

Appendix 5 Bibliography of books and articles on maritime preservation

CONTENTS

A DIRECTORIES OF HISTORIC VESSELS – International

A1 Bobrow, Jill and Jinkins, Dana. *In the Spirit of Tradition,* *Old and New Classic Yachts,* New York: W. W. Norton & Co, 1997.

A2 Braynard, Frank O. *The Tall Ships of Today in Photographs* Mineola, New York: Dover Publications Inc., 1993.

A3 Brouwer, Norman J. *International Register of Historic Ships* Oswestry, England: Anthony Nelson Ltd, 1985. (Second Edition 1993)

A4 Deayton, Alistair. 'The Veterans, 1850-1905' (steam vessels), *Sea Breezes,* July 1990-April 1991.

A5 Deayton, Alistair. 'The Veterans: Corrections, Additions and Updates', *Sea Breezes,* November 1992-January 1993.

A6 Ellerstrom, Hans. *All Varldens Museiubatar* (Museum Submarines of the World), Karlskrona, Sweden: Foreningen Marinmusei Vanner, 1985.

A7 Fuller, Benjamin A. G. ed. *Historic Ship Register,* 2 vols. Mystic, Connecticut: International Congress of Maritime Museums, 1981 & 1984.

A8 Heine, William C. *Historic Ships of the World,* New York: G. P. Putnam's Sons, 1977.

A9 Jones, J. Michael. *Historic Warships: A Directory of 140 Museums and Memorials Worldwide,* Jefferson, North Carolina:

McFarland & Co, 1993.

A10 Lund, Kaj. *Vinden er vor 4* (traditional sailing vessels around the world), Copenhagen: Borgen, 1981.

A11 Lund, Kaj. *Vinden er vor 5* (traditional sailing vessels built in Denmark now under other flags), Copenhagen: Borgen, 1981.

A12 Millot, Gilles. 'Les Derniers grandes voiliers', *Chasse-Maree,* No.81, June 1994 and No. 99, July 1996.

A13 Pemsel, Helmut & Stockinger, Heinz. 'Kriegschiffe und Hilfskriegsschiffe als historische Denkmaler' (naval vessels preserved around the world), *MARINE; Gestern, Heute,* 1987.

A14 Schauffelen, Otmar. *Great Sailing Ships,* New York: Frederick A.Praeger, 1969.

A15 Schauffelen, Otmar. *Die letzen grossen Segelschiffe* (revised edition of the previous entry), Bielefeld, Germany: Delius Klasing Verlag, 1984.

A16 Schmidt, Ingrid. *Maritime Oldtimer, Museumsschiffe aus 4 Jahrhunderten,* Leipzig: Edition Leipzig, 1986.

A17 Spies, M. H. *Veteran Steamers,* Denmark: 1965.

A18 Worden, William M. 'The World of Steam', *Steamboat Bill,* Winter 1995.

B DIRECTORIES OF HISTORIC VESSELS – regional

B1 Aatos, Erkko, et. al. *Laivamuseotoimikunnan mietinto* (Historic ships in Finland), Helsinki, Finland: Valtion Painatuskeskus, 1990.

B2 Andrews, Graeme. *Australia's Maritime Heritage,* Sydney, Australia: Cromarty Press, 1984.

B3 Andrews, Graeme. *Veteran Ships of Australia and New Zealand,* Sydney, Australia: A. H. & A. W. Reed, 1976.

B4 *The Boat Museum,* Ellesmere Port, England: The Boat Museum Trust.

B5 Brann, Christian. *The Little Ships of Dunkirk,* Cirencester, England: Collectors' Books Ltd, 1989.

B6 Bray, Maynard. *Mystic Seaport Museum Watercraft,* Mystic, Connecticut: Mystic Seaport Museum, 1979.

B7 Brookes, Douglas S. 'The Turkish Imperial State Barges', *The Mariners Mirror,*

February 1990.

B8 Brown, Leslie & McKendrick, Joe. *Paddle Steamers of the Alps,* Great Britain: Ferry Publications, c.1992.

B9 Burton, Anthony. *The Past Afloat* (Vessels preserved in Great Britain), London: British Broadcasting Corp, 1982.

B10 Butowsky, Harry A. *Warships Associated with World War II in the Pacific; National Historic Landmark Theme Study,* Washington, D.C.: National Park Service, 1985.

B11 Carr, Tim and Pauline. 'Antarctic Legacy' (Wrecks in South Georgia), *Classic Boat,* January 1994.

B12 Clifford, Candace & Delgado, James, eds. *Inventory of Large Preserved Historic Vessels* (Historic Ships in the United States), Washington: National Park Service, 1990.

B13 de Lepinay, Francois. 'Sauvetage du Patrimoine Naval', France: *Monuments Historiques,* No. 130.

B14 Dean, Norman. 'The Norwegian Veteran Ship Club', *Ships Monthly,* October 1982.

B15 Deayton, Alistair. 'European Ship Preservation', *Ships Monthly,* October 1994.

B16 Deayton, Alistair. *Steam Ships of Europe,* London: Conway Maritime Press, Ltd, 1988.

B17 Delgado, James & Clifford, Candace. *Great American Ships,* Washington: The Preservation Press, National Trust for Historic Preservation, 1991.

B18 Detlefsen, Gert Uwe & Lipsky, Stefan. *Veteranen-und Museumsschiffe* (Historic Ships in Germany), Bad Segeberg: Verlag Gert Uwe Detlefsen, 1991. (Second Edition 1997)

B19 Downs, H. 'Sail and Power on Lake Titicaca', *Sea Breezes,* April 1968.

B20 Ewing, Steve. *Memories & Memorials, the World War II U. S. Navy 40 Years After Victory,* Missoula, Montana: Pictorial Histories Publishing Co, 1986.

B21 Garry, Martine et. al. 'Tentative pour une meilleure connaissance du patrimonie peche et cabotage' (French traditional fishing and coastal vessels), *Le Petit Perroquet,* No. 26.

B22 Gaubert, Yves. 'Les dragues a vapeur de La Rochelle',(D-6 and SAINT-MARC) *Chasse-Maree,* No. 44, October 1989.

B23 Gloux, Herve. *Le Musee de la peche a Concarneau,* La Guerche-de-Bretagne, France: Ouest-France, 1988.

B24 Goss, J. 'Guide to Preserved Warships' (Great Britain), *Ships Monthly,* October, 1979.

B25 Headland, R. K. 'Wrecks, Hulks and Other Vessels Remains at South Georgia', *British Antarctic Survey Bulletin,* No. 65.

B26 Hervey, Harcourt & Ellen, eds. *North American Steamboat Register,* South Pasadena, California: North American Steamboat Register, 1980.

B27 Hillsdon, Brian E. and Smith, Brian W. *Steamboats and Steamships of the British Isles,* Ashford, England: Steam Boat Association of Great Britain, 1988; Fifth edition 1994.

B28 Horlacher, Robert & Raber, Anton. *Paddle-Steamers Switzerland,* Lucerne: Verlag Dampferzeitung, 1982.

B29 Langley, Martin & Small, Edwina. *Lost Ships of the West Country,* (old vessels surviving in southwest England) London: Stanford Maritime, 1988.

B30 'Le Tage retrouve la memoire' (restoring Tagus River sailing craft in Portugal), *Le Chasse-Maree,* No. 41.

B31 Leniaud, Jean-Michel. 'The Protection of France's Maritime heritage: achievements and prospects', *Future for our Past* (Council of Europe, Strasbourg, France), 1988.

B32 Lipsky, Stefan. *Classic Ships, Register No. 1* (Denmark), Bad Segeberg: Verlag Gert Uwe Detlefsen, 1996.

B33 Lund, Kaj. *Vinden er vor 1, 2, 6* (active traditional sailing craft under the Danish flag), Copenhagen: Borgen, 1978-1983

B34 Marzari, Mario. 'Le Musee a flot de Cesenatico, Sept siecles d'histoire sur l'Adriatique', (sailing vessels preserved in Cesenatico, Italy), *Le Chasse-Maree,* No. 12.

B35 McKee, Alexander. *A Heritage of Ships* (Great Britain), London: Souvenir Press, 1988.

B36 Millot, Gilles. 'Les vapeurs a passagers des lacs Suisses', *Chasse-Maree* No. 100, August 1996.

B37 Morgan, Richard. 'Sydney Maritime Museum, the First 25 Years', *Australian Sea Heritage,* Summer 1990.

B38 Mortenson, Ole, ed. *Fartojsbevaring i*

Danmark (Ship preservation in Denmark), Copenhagen: Stougaard Jensen.

B39 Muller, Frank & Quinger, Wolfgang. *Die Dresdner Raddampfer Flotte* (sidewheel steamers of Dresden, Germany), Dresden, 1995.

B40 Owen-Jones, Stuart. *Welsh Industrial & Maritime Museum*, Cardiff: National Museum of Wales, 1984.

B41 Pakkanen, Esko and Roitto, Pentti. *The Steamers in Finland* Lahti, Finland: The Finnish Steamer Yachting Association, 1985.

B42 Perks, Hugh & Susan. 'Les Barques du Leman', *Topsail*, No. 21, Winter 1984.

B43 Plummer, Russell. *Paddle Steamers in the 1990s* (Europe), Peterborough, England: GMS Enterprises, 1994.

B44 Rhodes, Tom and Scott, Harley. *Steamboats Today* (United States and Canada), Lancaster, New York: Cayuga Creek Historical Press, 1986.

B45 Roberts, Bruce and Jones, Ray. *Steel Ships and Iron Men* (Surviving United States Naval and Coast Guard vessels that took part in World War II), Chester, Conn.: Globe Pequot Press, 1991.

B46 *Schwimmende Oldtimer der Seefahrt*, Bremerhaven, Germany: Deutsches Schiffahrtsmuseum, 1977.

B47 *Signals* No. 15, Sydney: Australian National Maritime Museum, 1991.

B48 Smith, John. *Condemned at Stanley* (wrecks and hulks in the Falkland Islands), New York: National Maritime Historical Society, 1975.

B49 Smith, Peter C. *Heritage of the Sea* (historic ships in the British Isles), Huntingdon, England: Balfour, 1974.

B50 Soderberg, Bertil. *Goteborgs Maritima Centrum Guide* (Ships preserved at Gothenburg, Sweden), Gothenburg: Goteborgs Maritima Centrum, 1990.

B51 *Spiegel der Zeilvaart*. 'Schepenlijst '87' (List of veteran ships in the Netherlands), Vol. 11, No. 7, September 1987.

B52 Stammers, M. K. *Historic Ships* (Great Britain), Aylesbury, England: Shire Publications, Ltd, 1987.

B53 Stuckey, Peter J. 'Bristol Channel Pilot Cutters - The Survivors', *Maritime South West, No. 6*, 1993.

B54 Suitters, Roger. 'Visit your local Submarine?' *Marine Modelling*, March 1997.

B55 Svensk Sjofarts Tidning. *Svensk*

B56 Tanner, Matthew. *The Ship and Boat Collection of Merseyside Maritime Museum: An Illustrated Catalogue*, Liverpool, England: Merseyside Maritime Museum, 1995.

B57 Tree, Christina. 'Windjammer Days' (Maine schooners), *Historic Preservation*, July/Aug. 1990.

B57a Tsanov, Miroslav I. *Uchebni Vetrohodni Korabi* (Sail Training Ships), Sofia, Bulgaria: Technica, 1990.

B58 Turner, Graham. 'Dining Afloat, A review of Britain's floating Restaurants', *Ships Monthly*, December 1990.

B59 'Un musee de la voile latine a Canet', (sailing vessels preserved at Canet, France), *La Chasse-Maree*, No. 55.

B60 United States Naval Institute. *Historic Naval Ships Association of North America*, Annapolis, Maryland: U. S. Naval Institute, 1982 and subsequent editions.

B61 Vapalahti, Hannu. *Finnish Illustrated List of Ships*, Karjula, Finland: Hannu Vapalahti, 1990, 1996.

B62 Verlag Gert Uwe Detlefsen. *Classic Ships Register No. 2; Niederlande & Belgien: Museumsschiffe & Schiffahrts-Museen*, Bad Segeberg, Germany: 1997.

B63 Verlag Gert Uwe Detlefsen. *Classic Ships Register No. 3; Norwegen: Museumsschiffe & Schiffahrtsmuseen*, Bad Segeberg, Germany: scheduled for 1999.

B64 Vermilya, Peter T. ed. *Union List of Museum Watercraft* (United States), Mystic, Conn.: Museum Small Craft Association, 1995.

B65 Wambold, Donald A. Jr. 'Baltimore's Historic Fleet', *Naval History*, Summer 1993.

B66 Wardle, David. *Murray River Paddle Steamers* (Australia), Canberra: Traction Publications, 1970.

B67 Westphalen, Andreas and Worden, William M. 'Paddle-Steamers in the Land of the Pharoahs', *Steamboat Bill*, Winter 1995.

B68 Wilson, Ian. 'Steam on Lake Saimaa' (Finland), *Sea Breezes*, April 1982.

B68a Wise, Jon & Visser, Henk. 'The Netherlands' Naval Museum's Notable Ships', *Ships Monthly*, August 1999.

B69 Wollentz, Claes. *Skutor ett Seglande Kulturarv* (Sailing vessels of historic significance in Sweden), Stockholm: Statens sjohistoriska museum, 1989.

C HISTORICAL STUDIES OF GROUPS OF VESSELS

C1 Andrews, Graeme. *Ferries of Sydney*, Sydney, Australia: Sydney University Press, 1994.

C2 Andrews, Graeme. *A Log of Great Australian Ships*, Sydney, Australia: A. H. & A. W. Reed, 1980.

C3 Appleton, Thomas E. *'Usque ad Mare', A History of the Canadian Coast Guard and Marine Services*, Ottawa: Department of Transport, 1968.

C4 Baldwin, David. *The Harbour Ferries of Auckland*, New Zealand: Grantham House, 1991.

C5 Bastock, John. *Australia's Ships of War*, Sydney: Angus and Robertson, 1975.

C6 Bennett, J. 'Saints of the Fal' (English steam tugboats), *Ships Monthly*, August 1976.

C6aa Bent, Mike. *Steamers of the Fjords; Bergen Shipping Since 1839*, London; Conway Maritime Press Ltd, 1989.

C6a Boot, W. J. J. *De Nederlandse Raderstoomvaart* (Dutch sidewheel steamers), Alkmaar, Netherlands: De Alk bv, 1990.

C7 Brogger, A. W. & Shetelig, H. *The Viking Ships*, Oslo: Dreyer, 1951.

C8 Campbell, Robert D. *Rapids and Riverboats on the Wanganui River*, Wanganui, New Zealand: Wanganui Newspapers Ltd, 1990.

C9 Churchouse, Jack. *Sailing Ships of the Tasman Sea*, Wellington, New Zealand: Milwood Press, 1984.

C10 Clark, Roy. *Black-sailed Traders, The Keels and Wherries of Norfolk and Suffolk*, London: Putnam, 1961.

C11 Clegg, Paul. 'Tug tenders in the U. K.', *Ships Monthly*, September, 1986.

C12 Cohen, Stan. *Yukon River Steamboats*, Missoula, Montana: 1982.

C13 Compton-Hall, Richard. *Submarine Boats, The Beginnings of Submarine Warfare*, London: Conway Maritime Press, 1983.

C14 Cox, G. W. *Ships in Tasmanian Waters*, Hobart, Tasmania: Fullers Bookshop, 1971.

C15 Crabtree, Reginald. *Royal Yachts of Europe*, Newton Abbott, England: David & Charles, 1975.

C16 Cram, W. Bartlett. *Picture History of New England Passenger Vessels*, 1980.

C17 Cressy, R. 'The Story of the VICs', *Ships Monthly*, July & August 1981.

C18 Crockett, Fred E. *Special Fleet, The History of the Presidential Yachts*, Camden, Maine: Down East Books, 1985.

C19 Cunliffe, Tom. 'Les pilotes de Bristol', *Chasse-Maree*, No. 34, March 1988.

C20 Davies, Ken. *English Lakeland Steamers*, Chorley, England: Countryside Publications, 1984.

C20aa Desgagnes, Michel. *Les Goelettes de Charlevoix*, Ottawa, Canada: Les Editions Lemeac, 1977.

C20a Dennis, L. G. *The Lake Steamers of East Africa*, Egham, England: Runnymede Malthouse Publishing, 1996.

C21 Destefani, Laurio Hedelvio. *Famosos Veleros Argentinos*, Buenos Aires, Argentina: Instituto De Publicaciones Navales, 1967.

C22 D'Orley, Alun. *The Humber Ferries*, Knaresborough, England: 1968.

C23 Dowling, Rev. Edward. 'Lightships of the Lakes', *Telescope* (Dossin Great Lakes Museum), October 1961 & February 1962.

C24 Downs, Art. *Paddlewheels on the Frontier* (sternwheel steamboats of western Canada), Seattle, Washington: Superior Publishing Co, 1972.

C25 Drummond, Maldwin. *Tall Ships; The World of Sail Training*, New York: G. P. Putnam's Sons, 1976.

C26 Eckardt, Gerhard. *Die Segelschiffe des Deutschen Schulschiff-Vereins* (sailing ships of the German Schoolship Assoc.), Bremen: Verlag H. M. Hauschild, 1981.

C27 Flint, Willard. *Lightships of the United States Government*, Washington: United States Coast Guard, 1989.

C27a Friedman, Norman. *U.S. Small Combatants, an Illustrated Design History*, Annapolis, Maryland: Naval Institute Press, 1987.

C28 Gardiner, Robert, et. al., eds. *Conway's All the World's Fighting Ships, 1860-1982*, 5 vols., Greenwich: Conway Maritime Press, 1979-1985.

C29 Gillett, Ross. *Australian and New Zealand Warships 1914-1945*, Sydney: Doubleday, 1983.

C30 Gillett, Ross. *Australian Ships*, French's Forest, Australia: Child and Assoc., 1989.

C31 Gillett, Ross, and Graham, Colin. *Warships of Australia*, Adelaide, S.A.: Rigby Ltd, 1977.

C32 Graham, Philip. *Showboats, the History of an American Institution*, Austin, Texas: University of Texas Press, 1951.

C33 Grant, Alison and Hughes, Barry. *North Devon Barges*, Bideford, England: North Devon Museum Trust, 1975.

C34 Guillou, Jean-Pierre. 'Un voilier irlandais qui refuse de mourir le hooker', *Le Chasse-Maree*, No. 5.

C35 Haigh, K. R. *Cableships and Submarine Cables*, London: Trinity Press, 1968.

C36 Harlan, George H. *San Francisco Bay Ferryboats*, Berkeley, California: Howell-North Books, 1967.

C37 Hawkins, Clifford W. *A Maritime Heritage, The Lore of Sail in New Zealand*, Auckland, New Zealand: William Collins, 1978.

C38 Hilton, George, et. al. *The Illustrated History of Paddle Steamers*, Lausanne, Switzerland: Edita Lausanne, 1976.

C39 Hilton, George. *The Staten Island Ferry*, Berkeley, California: Howell-North Books, 1964.

C40 Hofman, Erik. *The Steam Yachts, An Era of Elegance*, Tuckahoe, New York: John De Graff, 1970.

C41 Hubert, Miroslav & Bor, Michael. *Osobni Lode na Vltave 1865-1985* (river steamers of Prague, Czech Republic), Prague: Nakladatelstvi Dopravy a Spoju, 1985.

C42 Hughes, Emrys & Eames, Aled. *Porthmadog Ships*, Caernarfon, Wales: 1975.

C43 Jones, Colin. *Australian Colonial Navies*, Canberra, Australia: Australian War Memorial, 1986.

C44 Kerr, Garry J. *Australian and New Zealand Sail Traders* Blackwood, South Australia: Lynton Publications, 1974.

C45 Kerr, Garry J. *Craft and Craftsmen of Australian Fishing 1870-1970*, Portland, Victoria: Mainsail Books, 1985.

C46 Kerr, Garry J. *The Tasmanian Trading Ketch*, Portland, Victoria: Mainsail Books, 1987.

C47 King, Johnathan. *Australia's First Fleet*, Sydney, Australia: Fairfax-Robertsbridge, 1987.

C48 Kolesnik, Eugene. 'Thunder and Lightning, The Polish Destroyers BLYSKAWICA and GROM', *Warship*, Vol. 1, No. 4.

C49 Leach, Nicholas. *Lifeboats* (British Isles), Princes Risborough, England: Shire Publications Ltd, 1998.

C50 Leather, John. *The Big Class Racing Yachts*, London: Stanford Maritime, 1982.

C51 Leather, John. *Colin Archer and the Seaworthy Double-Ender* (Norwegian rescue craft), London: Stanford Maritime, 1982.

C52 Lille, Sten & Gronstrand, Lars. *The Finnish Deep-Water Sailers*, Pori, Finland: Satakunnan Kirjateollisuus Oy, 1981.

C53 Loomeijer, Frits R. *Zeilende Kustvaarders* (Dutch coastal sailing vessels), Alkmaar: Uitgverij De Alk, 1985.

C54 Lund, Kaj. *Vinden er vor 3* (Danish sailing training vessels), Copenhagen: Borgen, 1980.

C55 Lydecker, Ryck. *Pigboat, the Story of the Whalebacks*, Duluth, Minnesota: Sweetwater Press, 1973.

C56 *Maine Lakes Steamboat Album*, Maine: Down East Enterprise, 1976.

C57 Malster, R. *Wherries and Waterways*, England: Terrance Dalton, 1971.

C58 Marshall, Brian. *Paddle Boats of the Murray-Darling System*, Burwood, Victoria: Mercury Publishing, 1988.

C59 Martin, Colin & Brouwer, Norman. *The Story of Sail*, Sydney, Australia: Weldon Publishing, 1992.

C60 Marvil, James E. *Sailing Rams*, Lewes, Delaware: The Sussex Press, 1974.

C60a Mayer, Horst F. & Winkler, Dieter. *Als die Alpen Schiffbar Wurden* (steamers on the Austrian lakes), Vienna, Austria: Edition S, 1992.

C60b Mayer, Horst F. & Winkler, Dieter. *Auf Donauwellen durch Osterreich-Ungarn* (steamers and warships on the Danube River), Vienna, Austria: Edition S, 1996.

C61 McDougall, R. J. *New Zealand Naval Vessels*, New Zealand: G. P. Books, 1989.

C62 Mead, Tom. *Manly Ferries of Sydney Harbour*, Sydney, Australia: Child and Assoc., 1988.

C63 Morris, Paul C. & Morin, Joseph F. *The Island Steamers*, Nantucket, Massachusetts: Nantucket Nautical Publishers: 1977.

C64 Navy History Division, *Dictionary of American Naval Fighting Ships*, 8 vols., Washington: 1959-1981.

C65 Niemz, Gunter & Wachs, Reiner. *Personenschiffahrt auf der Oberelbe* (passenger steamers of the upper Elbe River), Rostock: Hinstorff Verlag, 1981.

C66 Norman, L. *Pioneer Shipping of Tasmania*, Hobart, Tasmania: J. Walch and Sons, 1938.

C67 Norton, Peter. *State Barges*, Greenwich, England: National Maritime Museum, 1972.

C68 Olmsted, Roger. *Scow Schooners of San Francisco Bay*, Cupertino, California: California History Center, 1985.

C69 O'May, D. G. *Ferries of the Derwent*, Tasmania: Government Printer, 1988.

C69a Parsons, Ronald. *Ketches of South Australia*, Magill, South Australia: Ronald Parsons, 1978.

C70 Parsons, Ronald. *Paddlesteamers of Australasia*, Lobenthal, S.A.: R. H. Parsons, 1973.

C71 Parsons, Ronald. *Ships of the Inland Rivers*, Ridgehaven, South Australia: Gould Books, 1990.

C72 Parsons, Ronald. *Steam Tugs in South Australia*, Lobenthal, S.A.: R. H. Parsons, 1983.

C73 Pattinson, George H. *The Great Age of Steam on Windermere*, Windermere, England: Windermere Nautical Trust, 1981.

C74 Perks, Richard-Hugh. *Sprits'l, A portrait of sailing barges and sailormen*, Greenwich, England: Conway Maritime Press, 1975.

C75 Petersen, Holger M. *Frem ad Sovejen* (Danish sailing training vessels), Esbjerg, Denmark: Fiskeri- og Sofartsmuseet, 1988.

C76 Peyronnel, Alain. 'Les Moulins-bateaux, Des bateliers immobiles sur les fleuves d'Europe', *Le Chasse-Maree*, No. 11.

C77 Plowman, Peter. *The Wheels Still Turn, A History of Australian Paddleboats*, Kenthurst, Australia: Kangaroo Press, 1992.

C77a Polmar, Norman. *The American Submarine*, Annapolis, Maryland: Nautical & Aviation Publishing Co, 1981.

C78 Porhel, Jean-Luc. 'Les bateaux-feux des bancs de Flandre', *Le Chasse-Maree*, No. 41.

C79 Prescott, A. M. *Sydney Ferry Fleets*, Lobenthal, Australia: R. H. Parsons, 1984.

C80 Reynolds, David. *A Century of South African Steam Tugs*, Pretoria, South Africa: Bygone ships, Trains and Planes, 1998.

C81 Roberts, Franklin & Gillespie, John. *The Boats We Rode* (New York passenger steamers and ferries), New York: Quadrant Press, 1974.

C82 *Royal Barges, Poetry in Motion*, Thai Government Public Relations Department.

C83 Salter, Harold. *Bass Strait Ketches*, Hobart, Tasmania: St. David's Park Publishing, 1991.

C84 Sawyer, L. A. & Mitchell, W. H. *The Liberty Ships*, London: Lloyd's of London Press, 1985.

C85 Sawyer, L. A. & Mitchell, W. H. *Victory Ships and Tankers*, 1974.

C86 Scheina, Robert L. *U. S. Coast Guard Cutters & Craft of World War II*, Annapolis, Maryland: Naval Institute Press, 1982.

C87 Scott, Richard J. *The Galway Hookers*, Dublin, 1983.

C87a Sheret, Robin E. *Smoke, Ash and Steam; Steam Engines Used on the West Coast*, Victoria, British Columbia: Western Isles, 1997.

C88 Stevenson, Gene. 'Submarines of the Finnish Navy', *Warship International*, No. 1, 1986.

C89 Stuckey, Peter J. *The Sailing Pilots of the Bristol Channel*, Newton Abbot, England: David & Charles, 1977.

C90 Thiele, Ron. *Ketch Hand, The Twilight of Sail in South Australian Waters*, Portland, Australia: Mains'l Books, 1987.

C91 Thomas, P. N. *British Steam Tugs*, England: Waine Research, 1983.

C92 Thomson, P. A. B. 'Seychelles Schooners: a Retrospect', *Mariners Mirror*, August 1998.

C93 Tod, Giles M. S. *The Last Sail Down East*, Barre, Massachusetts: Barre Publishers, 1965.

C94 Turner, Robert D. *Sternwheelers & Steam Tugs*, Victoria, British Columbia: Sono Nis Press, 1984.

C95 Ulyatt, Michael E. *Flying Sail* (Humber sloops), Goole, England: Mr. Pye, 1995.

C96 Underhill, Harold. *Sail Training and Cadet Ships*, Glasgow: Brown Sons & Ferguson, 1956.

C97 Van der Linden, Peter ed. *Great Lakes Ships We Remember* (2 vols.), Cleveland, Ohio: Freshwater Press, 1979.

C98 Winkler, Herbert. *Die Schiffahrt auf dem Traunsee, Hallstatter See, Grundlsee* (Austrian lake steamboats).

C99 Wood, David & Elizabeth. *The Last Berth of the Sailorman* (British Sailing Barges), Twickenham, England: The Society for Sailing Barge Research, 1996.

D HISTORIES OF INDIVIDUAL VESSELS

D1 Abelsen, Frank. 'The Torpedoboat RAP', *Warship*, No. 38.

D2 Adams, Keith. 'A Paddle Steamer Voyage on the River Nile' (KARIM), *Paddle Wheels*, Summer 1998.

D3 Aho, Jody. *The Steamer WILLIAM A. IRVIN, 'Queen of the Silver Stackers*, Marquette, Michigan; Avery Studios, 1995.

D4 Albright, Charles L. *The East Coast Cruise of the U. S. Frigate CONSTITUTION: A Philatelic Narrative...*, Richmond, Virginia: Dietz, 1934.

D5 Allington, Pete. 'Old Ways on the last of the Tamar Barges' (SHAMROCK), *Classic Boat*, June 1989.

D6 Allison, R. S. *H.M.S. CAROLINE*, Belfast, Northern Ireland: The Blackstaff Press, c.1974.

D7 Almen, Dag. *Angaren BOHUSLAN: En historik om fartyget och Sallskapet Angbatenk* Uddevalla, Sweden: Zindermans, 1969.

D8 Amundsen, Roald. *The Northwest Passage: Being the Record of a Voyage of Exploration of the Ship GJOA 1903-1907*, New York: E. P. Dutton, 1908. (2 vols.)

D9 Andel, Dick van. *OOSTERSCHELDE de Geschiedenis*, Rotterdam, Netherlands: Herziene editie, 1991.

D10 Anderson, CMDR William R. *NAUTILUS 90 North*, New York: World Publishing Co, 1959.

D11 Andersson, P. G. 'BREMON som museifartyg', *Aktuellt 1997*.

D12 Andras, Dr. Margitay-Becht. 'The Monitor LEITHA (1871), *Sea Breezes*, May 1997.

D13 Andrews, Graeme. 'Sydney Battles for the Last Windjammer' (JAMES CRAIG), *Seacraft*, December 1972.

D14 Ansel, Walter. 'The Dragger FLORENCE', *The Log of Mystic Seaport*, Winter 1985.

D15 Ansel, Willits. *Restoration of the Smack EMMA C. BERRY*, Mystic, Connecticut: Marine Historical Association, 1973.

D16 Arnold, Craig ed. *Euterpe; Diaries, Letters & Logs of the STAR OF INDIA as a British Emigrant Ship*, San Diego, California: The Maritime Museum Association, 1988.

D17 Arnold, Craig. 'MEDEA: A Classic Steam Yacht', *Seaways*, November/December 1991.

D18 Arnold, Craig. *MEDEA: The Classic Steam Yacht*, San Diego, California: The Maritime Museum Association, 1994.

D19 *AUSTRALIA II, The Official Record*, Sydney, Australia: Joyce Childress Management, 1984.

D20 'Auxiliary Schooner ADVENTURESS', *Rudder*, March 1913.

D21 Bailey, S. F. *The CUTTY SARK Figurehead*, London: Ian Allen, 1993.

D22 Baker, William A. 'The GJOA', *American Neptune*, January 1952.

D23 Bakka, Dag Jr. 'Salveson Whale-catcher Preserved in Norway' (SOUTHERN ACTOR), *Marine News*, January 1992.

D24 'Bald wieder Dampfschiff auf dem Thunersee' (BLUMLISALP), *Alte Schiff*, October/November 1990.

D25 Ball, Adrian & Wright, Diana. *S.S. GREAT BRITAIN*, London: David & Charles, 1981.

D26 Bartlett, Capt. Bob. *Sails Over Ice* (ERNESTINA), New York: Charles Scribners Sons, 1934.

D27 Bates, Alan L. *Belle of Louisville*, Berkeley, California: Howell-North, 1965.

D28 Beard, Geoffrey. 'A barge for a Prince' (PRINCE FREDERICK'S BARGE), *Antiques*, June 1997.

D29 Becton, RADM F. Julian. *The Ship that Would Not Die* (U.S.S. LAFFEY), New Jersey: Prentice-Hall, 1980.

D30 Belknap, Harry. 'CONSTITUTION Takes the Sea Again', *The Rudder*, December 1930.

D31 Belknap, Harry. 'Saving 'Old Ironsides'' (U.S.S. CONSTITUTION), *Yachting*, April 1926.

D32 Bencik, Charles A. 'EUTERPE's 1883 Voyage to Sydney', (STAR OF INDIA), *Mains'l Haul*, Fall 1997.

D33 Bencik, Charles A. 'Ferry Steamer BERKELEY, A West Coast Revolution and An American Treasure', *Mains'l Haul*, Fall 1998.

D34 Bennett, Jon. 'Still in Steam, S.S. ADVANCE', *Ships Monthly*, February 1993.

D35 Benscheidt, Anja and Kube, Alfred. *Der letzte deutsche Seitentrawler, Hochseefischereigeschichte auf dem Museumsschiff GERA*, Bremerhaven,

Germany: Morgenstern Museum, 1995.

D36 Benson, Richard & Hopkinson, Francis. 'Wooden Tallship: GAZELA PRIMEIRO' (GAZELA OF PHILADELPHIA), *Wooden Boat*, July-August 1976.

D37 'The Birth of the Welded Ship', (ESAB IV) *100A1*, March 1976.

D37aa Bixel, Patricia Bellis. *Sailing Ship ELISSA*, College Station, Texas: Texas A. & M. Press, 1998.

D37a Blackler, Tony. 'The Survivors - The URI', *Sea Breezes*, January 1999.

D37b Blair, Clay Jr. *The Atomic Submarine and Admiral Rickover* (NAUTILUS), New York: Henry Holt and Company, 1954.

D38 Blake, Joe. *Queen of the Murray, The Life and Times of the Paddlesteamer GEM*, Swan Hill, Australia: Swan Hill Pioneer Settlement, 1998.

D39 Blake, Joe. *Restoring the GREAT BRITAIN*, Bristol: Redcliffe, 1989.

D40 Boell, Denis-Michel. 'Du pilotage a la plaisance; JOLIE BRISE', *Chasse-Maree*, No. 44, October 1989.

D41 Boer, Friedrich. *Everything About a Ship and its Cargo* (CAP SAN DIEGO), Hamburg, 1969.

D42 Bock, Bruno & Paschburg, Hartmut. *SEA CLOUD, Die Story eines eleganten Luxusseglers*, Herford, Germany: Koehlers, 1979.

D43 Bogart, Charles H. et al. 'Naval Actions of the 1941 Ecuador-Peruvian War' (CALDERON), *Warship International*, No. 3, 1994.

D44 Bonner, Kit. 'Can the Pearl Harbor Tug HOGA Be Saved?' *Sea Classics*, May 1996.

D45 Booth, Russell. 'U.S.S. PAMPANITO (SS 383)', *Sea Letter*, Winter 1984/1985, Spring 1987.

D45a Bottum, Lynn H. 'ADIRONDACK, Lady of Lake Champlain 1913-1993', *Steamboat Bill*, Winter 1993.

D46 Boult, Trevor. 'The Lady of the Loch' (SIR WALTER SCOTT), *Sea Breezes*, April 1997.

D47 Bound, Mensun. 'Iron Beam-end Fastenings: Fell's Patent No. 8186. A Puzzle Resolved' (JHELUM), *Mariners Mirror*, August 1993.

D48 Bouquet, Michael. 'A Survivor of the Wooden Schooners' (KATHLEEN & MAY), *Country Life*, September 7, 1961.

D49 Boutelier, E. L. 'A Schooner Reborn' (AMERICAN EAGLE), *National Fisherman*, July 1986.

D50 Boyce, Mike. *Medusa; HDML 1387*, Weymouth, England: Mike Boyce, 1996.

D51 Brady, Alan. *The EARNSLAW, Lady of the Lake*, Christchurch, New Zealand: Bascands Ltd, 1985.

D52 Brady, Cyrus T. *Under Topsails and Tents* (U.S.S. CONSTELLATION), New York: Charles Scribner's Sons, 1917.

D53 Bray, Maynard. 'PRINCIPIA Recycled', *Wooden Boat*, March/April 1995

D54 Broelmann, J. and Weski T. *MARIA HF 31, Seefischerei unter Segeln*, Munich: Deutsches Museum, 1992.

D55 Brotherton, Bruce. 'BATFISH Beats the Boneyard', *Warship International*, No. 4, 1973.

D56 Brouwer, Norman J. 'CATAWISSA: Last Deepwater Steam Tug on the East Coast', *Sea History*, Spring 1996.

D57 Brouwer, Norman J. 'The four-masted barque PASSAT', *Seaport*, Spring 1978.

D58 Brouwer, Norman J. 'The four-masted Iron Ship COUNTY OF PEEBLES' (MUNOZ GAMERO), *Seaport*, Winter 1979-1980.

D59 Brouwer, Norman J. 'The Many Lives of LETTIE' (LETTIE G. HOWARD), *Seaport*, Winter/Spring 1990.

D60 Brouwer, Norman J. 'The Tea Clipper AMBASSADOR', *Seaport*, Fall 1978.

D61 Brouwer, Norman J. 'The 1856 Packet Ship CHARLES COOPER', *Seaport*, Fall 1981.

D62 Brown, Chip. 'The WAVERTREE at One Hundred', *Seaport*, Spring 1986.

D63 Brown, Leslie. 'Return of the GISELA', *Paddle Wheels*, Winter 1986.

D64 Brownlee, Walter. *WARRIOR, The First Modern Battleship*, Cambridge, England: Cambridge University Press, 1985.

D65 Broxam, Graeme. *A Steamship for Hobart, S.S. REEMERE 1909*, Hobart, Tasmania: Navarine Publishing, 1992.

D66 Bugler, Arthur. *H.M.S. VICTORY: Building, Restoration and Repair*, London: H. M. Stationary Office, 1966.

D67 Burmeister, Heinz. *Grossegler RICKMER RICKMERS: Seine wechselvolle Geschichte*, Hamburg, Germany: Ernst

Kabel Verlag, 1986.

D68 Bussel, Troon van. 'Een droom werd werkelijkheid' (JOHANNES), *Lekko*, November 20, 1978.

D69 Canright, Stephen and Miles, Ted. 'The C. A. THAYER 1895-1995', *Sea Letter*, Summer 1995.

D70 Carlberg, Gunnar. 'Fullriggaren JARRAMAS', *Aktuellt 1997*.

D71 Carr, Frank G. G. *The CUTTY SARK and the Days of Sail*, London: Cutty Sark Preservation Society, c.1957.

D72 Carr, Frank G. G. 'CUTTY SARK, Last of the Clippers', *Yachting World*, December 1954.

D73 Castle, Colin. 'Restoring Glasgow's Windjammer' (GLENLEE), *Ships Monthly*, July 1997.

D74 Causey, Cheryl. 'Still Steamed' (BALTIMORE), *Workboat Magazine*, May/June 1993.

D75 Cederlund, Carl Olof. *Folket som Byggde WASA*, Uddevalla, Sweden: Bohuslaningens AB, 1978.

D76 'CERVIA now belonging to East Kent Maritime Trust - Ramsgate', *Lekko*, September/October 1986.

D77 Chapelle, Howard I. & Polland, Leon. *The CONSTELLATION Question*, Washington: Smithsonian Institution Press, 1970.

D78 Chichester, Sir Francis. *GIPSY MOTH Circles the World*, New York: Coward-McCann, 1968.

D79 Christie, Tom. 'NEPTUNE: La Barque en Oreilles', *Classic Boat*, September 1995.

D80 Churchouse, Jack. *Sailing Ships of the Tasman Sea* (chapter on the JAMES CRAIG), Wellington: Millwood press, 1984.

D81 Clammer, R. 'FRESHSPRING, Last of the Water Carriers, ' *Ships Monthly*, November 1987.

D82 Clammer, R. 'SEIONT II', *Ships Monthly*, May 1980.

D83 Clammer, R. 'Still in Steam - SHIELDHALL', *Ships Monthly*, December 1982.

D84 Clare, Capt. Roy, ed. *H.M.S. BRONINGTON; a Tribute to one of Britain's Last Wooden Walls*, Guildford, England: The Bronington Trust, c.1995.

D85 Clark, Malcolm & Iggulden, David. *Sailing Home* (OUR SVANEN), Sydney,

Australia: Angus and Robertson, 1988.

D86 Clark, Roy. 'Crimean Veteran in New Zealand' (EDWIN FOX), *Sea Breezes*, February 1965.

D87 Clarke, M. 'Tug DANIEL ADAMSON', *Ships Monthly*, April 1977.

D88 Clergeau, J.-R. 'Naviguer autrement, Le sauvetage du dernier courpet de la Dordogne' (MERLANDOU), *Le Chasse-Maree*, No. 15.

D89 Collier, William. 'Un cotre Nicholson lance en 1896' (AVEL), *Chasse-Maree*, No. 90, July 1995.

D90 Colton, J. Ferrell. 'Britons, Bring the MOSHULU Home!' *Sea Breezes*, April 1994.

D91 Colton, J. Ferrell. *Windjammers Significant* (MOSHULU), Flagstaff, Arizona: J. Ferrell Colton, 1954.

D92 Compton-Hall, Richard. 'Recovering the Hollands' (HOLLAND 1), *Naval History*, October 1994.

D93 Cooper, John. 'Saving the Heroine of Dunkirk' (MEDWAY QUEEN), *Ships Monthly*, July 1996.

D93a Cooper, Struan. 'LEADER Homeward Bound', *Classic Boat*, May 1998.

D94 Coote, John. 'A Stunning Comeback' (ENDEAVOR), *The Yacht*, August 1989.

D95 Copes, Jan M. & Runyan, Timothy J. 'The Steamer WILLIAM G. MATHER: A Study in Maritime Preservation', *Bermuda Journal of Archaeology and Maritime History*, Vol. 5, 1993.

D96 Corcelli, Richard J. 'WANDA III Now with Muskoka Steamship & Historical Society', *Steamboating*, No. 53-54, Spring-Summer 1994.

D97 Corin, John. 'PORTWEY', *Ships Monthly*, July 1979.

D98 Corin, John. *PROVIDENT and the History of the Brixham Smacks*, Reading, England: Tops'l Books, 1980.

D99 Corlett, Ewan. *The Iron Ship* (steamship GREAT BRITAIN), Bradford-on-Avon, England: Moonraker Press, 1975.

D100 *Coronet Memories: Log of the schooner-yacht CORONET on her off-shore cruises from 1893-1899*, New York: F. Tennyson Neely, c1899.

D100a Coton, Richard H. 'The Remarkable GOETHE', *Paddle Wheels*, Winter 1996.

D101 Coulson, Helen. *Paddle Steamer ADELAIDE*, Wangaratta, Australia: McCabe

Prints, 1985.

D102 Coulton, Richard. 'ROBERTSON II, the Careers of a Saltbanker', *The Mariners Mirror*, May 1986.

D103 'CPR lake steamer takes on new role' (SICAMOUS), *Shipping -Today and Yesterday*, February 1998.

D104 Crawford, Derek, et al. *WAVERLEY, The Golden Jubilee*, Glasgow: Waverley Excursions, 1997.

D105 'Credit Where its Due' (MINERVA), *Sea Breezes*, April 1991.

D106 Crocker, Templeton. *The Cruise of the ZACA*, New York: Harper & Brothers, 1933.

D107 Crockett, David. 'A Short History of the Steamer SABINO', *Steamboat Bill*, Spring 1968.

D108 Cronican, Frank and Mueller, Edward A. *The Stateliest Ship; QUEEN MARY*, Staten Island, New York: The Steamship Historical Society of America, c.1965.

D109 Cross, Hugh. 'JAMES CRAIG Restoration Progresses', *Australian Sea Heritage*, Autumn 1994.

D109a Crossette, George. 'The TUSCARORA; Queen of the Adirondacks', *Adirondack Life*, Summer 1975.

D110 Crumlin-Pedersen, Ole. *Skonnerten FULTON af Marstal*, Roskilde, Denmark: Vikingeskibshallen, 1970.

D111 Cullivan, Lynn. 'EUREKA, A Centenniel Retrospective', *Sea Letter*, Spring/Summer 1990.

D112 'The Cunard-White Star quadruple-screw liner QUEEN MARY', *Engineering*, May 15-June 12, 1936.

D113 Cunliffe, Tom. 'A bord de PROVIDENT, Brixham trawler de 1924', *Chasse-Maree*, No. 93, November 1995.

D114 Cunliffe, Tom. 'La Resurrection de MARIGOLD', *Chasse-Maree*, No. 98, May 1996.

D115 Curdy, John. 'The KYLES Story', *Ships Monthly*, April 1990.

D116 Czok, Thomas. 'Story of a TIGER', *Lekko*, 24 April 1979.

D117 Dale, F. Slade. 'Old 'Emma' Comes to Barnegat' (EMMA C. BERRY), *Yachting*, June & July 1933.

D118 Dalton, Anthony. 'Boats of the Norse; Paddle Post' (SKIBLADNER), *Classic Boat*, February 1993.

D119 Darroch, Vin. *Barque POLLY WOODSIDE (RONA)*, Kilmore, Australia: Lowden Publishing Co, 1978.

D120 Davidsson, Jan. *AF CHAPMAN, ex-Dunboyne, ex-G. D. Kennedy*, Stockholm: Svensk Turistforeningen, 1983.

D121 Davidsson, Jan. *VIKING, Goteborg*, Gothenburg: Forlag Triangeln, 1981.

D122 Day, Jane. 'Old Sardine Carrier is Restored to Sail as a Maine Windjammer' (SYLVINA W. BEAL), *National Fisherman*, August 1981.

D123 de Groot, Edward P. *SAN ANTONIO, Kroniek van een Nederlandse driemastschoener* (GROSSHERZOGIN ELIZABETH), Amsterdam: De Boer Maritiem, 1978.

D124 De Long, Harriet Tracy. *Pacific Schooner WAWONA*, Bellevue, Washington: Documentary Book Publishers Corp, 1985.

D125 De Vos, Alex. *MERCATOR, Histoire des navires-ecoles Belges*, Antwerp, Belgium: Edition Publitras, c.1967.

D126 'DE WADDEN for Mersey Museum', *Sea Breezes*, September 1983.

D127 Dean, Leon W. 'War Sloop of 1776 Raised' (PHILADELPHIA), *Marine Engineering & Shipping Review*, March 1937.

D128 Delalande, Patricia. *L'ARGONAUTE*, Rennes, France: Editions Ouest-France, 1991.

D129 Delgado, James P. *Dauntless ST. ROCH, The Mounties' Arctic Schooner*, Vancouver: Hordal & Schubart, 1993.

D130 Delgado, James P. 'BERKELEY; Hard Worked in a Rough Service', *Sea Letter*, Spring-Summer 1990.

D130a Delgado, James P. *Made for the Ice; A Report on the Wreck of the Hudson's Bay Company ship BAYMAUD*, Vancouver, British Columbia: Vancouver Maritime Museum, 1997.

D131 Dessens, Henk and Hin, Floris. *Geschiedenis en restauratie van de Haringlogger VL 92 BALDER*, Amsterdam, Netherlands: Nederlandsch Historisch Scheepvaart Museum, 1993.

D132 Dessens, Hentk, et al. *Scheepsrestauratie; Met alle restauratie-tekeningen van de Hasseterraak ANNIGJE*, Den Haaf, Netherlands: De Boer Maritiem, 1988.

D133 d'Estaing, Nancy. 'Reconsidering the EMMA C. BERRY', *The Log of Mystic Seaport*, Summer 1990.

D134 Desy, Margherita. 'CONSTITUTION: Where Was She at 100?' *Nautical Research Journal*, September 1997.

D135 Detlefsen, Gert Uwe. 'Seit zwanzig Jahren dampft der Raddampfer KAISER WILHELM auf der Elbe', *Alte Schiff*, October/November 1990.

D136 'DIADEM; Le reveil d'une lady', *Chasse-Maree*, No. 83, September 1994.

D137 Dietz, Theodore A. 'New Life for a Liberty' (JOHN W. BROWN), *Naval History*, Winter 1990.

D138 Dirksen, Louise. 'JEREMIAH O'BRIEN; A Ship That Wouldn't Quit', *Naval History*, Winter 1990.

D139 Dobrin, Michael. 'OUR LADY OF LOURDES: A San Francisco Bay Survivor Rests on Arctic Shores', *Seaways/Ships in Scale*, January/February 1993.

D140 Dodge, David et al. *Steamboat SABINO*, Mystic, Conn.: Mystic Seaport Inc., 1974.

D141 Domizlaff, Hans. *Das Grosse Buch der PASSAT,* Hamburg, Germany: Edition Maritim, 1980.

D142 Drake, Waldo. 'Glorious Stuff' (MOSHULU), *Yachting*, Jan. 1927.

D142a Dudley, David. 'Don't Give Up the Ship' (CONSTELLATION), *Baltimore*, July 1998.

D143 *Due Navi in Museo* (EBE), Milan, Italy: Museoscienza, 1964.

D144 Duffy, Francis J. 'The SABINO Steams On', *Sea Breezes*, June 1990.

D145 Duffy, Francis J. 'A 95-year-old American Schooner Sails On' (VICTORY CHIMES), *Marine News*, October 1995.

D146 Duffy, Francis J. "VICTORY CHIMES', *Ships Monthly*, January 1983.

D147 Dulake, Robin and Robinson, Ian. *H.M.S. WARRIOR, Britain's First Ironclad*, Portsmouth, England: Warrior Preservation Trust, 1987.

D148 Duncan, William J. *RMS QUEEN MARY, Queen of the Queens*, Anderson, South Carolina: Droke House, 1969.

D149 Earle, Capt. James A. M. 'On the Far Reaches of the Pacific' (CHARLES W. MORGAN), *Yachting*, December 1927.

D150 'Eastward through the Northwest Passage' (ST. ROCH), *Ships and the Sea*, Summer 1957.

D151 Edwin Fox Restoration Society. The

Story of the EDWIN FOX*, Picton, New Zealand: Toneden Promotions, 1986.

D152 Egan, Robert et. al. *U.S.S. TEXAS (BB 35)*, Annapolis, Maryland: 1976.

D153 Eifert, Virginia S. *DELTA QUEEN, The Story of a Steamboat*, New York: Dodd, Mead & Co, 1960.

D154 Eijk, Job van. 'Wreck of Dutch steam tug raised' (EBRO), *Lekko*, November/December 1986.

D155 Elgvin, Dag T. 'FRAM-Ferden 1893-96 - en skole i talmodighet', (The FRAM Voyage 1893-96: a Patience Test), *Norsk Sjofartsmuseum Arsberetning 1996*, Oslo, Norway 1997.

D156 Ellery, David. *RMS QUEEN MARY, The World's Favourite Liner*, Blandford Forum, England: Waterfront Publications, 1994.

D157 Emerson, William. 'U.S.S. OLYMPIA', in *Warship 1989*, London: Conway Maritime Press, 1989.

D158 Engvig, Olaf T. 'GJOA, The Ship in the Park', in *Shipping and Culture*, San Francisco: The Norwegian Fish Club, 1996.

D159 Engvig, Olaf T. 'Ongoing restoration of Norwegian steamer', (HESTMANDEN) *Marine Propulsion International*, October 1985.

D160 Engvig, Olaf T. 'Restoring an 'Isles' Escort Ship' (BORGENES), *Marine Propulsion International*, July/August 1990.

D161 Engvig, Olaf T. 'Sole Surviving Steam/Sail ship being restored', (HANSTEEN) *Marine Propulsion International*, February 1984.

D162 Engvig, Olaf T. 'VAERDALEN, A Living Legend of the Fjords', *Marine Propulsion International*, March/April 1992.

D163 Engvig, Olaf T. & Gillham, Skip. 'BORGENES, A Survivor', *Telescope*, January/February 1991.

D164 'ENTERPRISE Restoration Completed', *Australian Sea Heritage*, Summer 1988.

D165 'ETOILE & BELLE POULE, les goelettes de l'Ecole navale', *Chasse-Maree*, No. 92, September 1995.

D166 Evangelista, Joe. 'Last of the Bodensee Steamers' (HOHENTWEIL), *Surveyor*, September 1994.

D167 Fanta, J. Julius. 'The DANMARK in the Coast Guard', *The Rudder*, November 1944.

D168 Fenton, M. E. *ETONA and the River Murray Mission 1891-1912*, Lockleys, Australia: M. E. Fenton, 1977.

D169 Ferguson, Peter. 'Sb. MAY, 100 Years Young', *Topsail*, No. 26.

D170 Fetesoff, Barbara. 'San Francisco's ALMA' *Wooden Boat*, No. 3, 1975.

D171 'The First Modern Ship' (GREAT BRITAIN) *Surveyor*, September 1993.

D172 Flapan, Mori. *Restoration of the Steam Tug WARATAH*, (Bachelor of Engineering Thesis, University of New South Wales) 1980.

D173 Flapan, Mori. 'S. S. KANANGRA', *Australian Sea Heritage*, Spring 1987.

D174 Flapan, Mori & Munns, Andy. 'Restoration of the Steam Tug WARATAH', *Australian Sea Heritage*, May 1984.

D175 Flechsenhar, Kurt. *CAP SAN DIEGO, Ein Schiff und seine Mannshaft*

D176 Fletcher, Daina. *AKARANA*, Sydney, Australia: Australian National Maritime Museum, 1991.

D177 Fletcher, Daina & Payne, David. 'AKARANA Reincarnated', *Signals*, June-August 1998.

D178 Fox, William A. 'JOSEPH HENRY at 75' (THALIS O. MILISSIOS),*Steamboat Bill*, Spring 1984.

D179 Franzen, Anders. *The Warship VASA*, Stockholm, Sweden: P. A. Norstedt & Soners Forlag, 1974.

D180 Fredholm, Christer. 'Motortorpedbaten T 38', *Aktuellt 1997*.

D181 Friedman, Norman, et al. *U.S.S. JOSEPH P. KENNEDY, JR. (DD 850)*, Fall River, Massachusetts: U.S.S. Massachusetts Memorial Committee, 1985.

D182 Friedman, Norman, et al. *U.S.S. MASSACHUSETTS (BB 59)*, Fall River, Massachusetts: U.S.S. Massachusetts Memorial Committee, 1985.

D183 Friendly, Alfred. 'An Ocean Relic is Given New Life' (GREAT BRITAIN), *Smithsonian*, March 1975.

D184 Gallery, Daniel V. *U-505*, New York: Warner Books, 1956.

D185 'HMS GANNET, Ship Restoration in Action', *ICMM News*, Fall 1995.

D186 Garland, Joseph E. *ADVENTURE, Queen of the Windjammers*, Camden, Maine: Down East Books, 1985.

D187 Garland, Vera. *Lady of the Lake: Ninety Years with the M.V. CHAUNCEY MAPLES on Lake Malawi*, Blantyre: Central Africana, 1991.

D188 Garvey, Stan. *King and Queen of the River, The Legendary Paddle-Wheel Steamboats DELTA KING and DELTA QUEEN*, Menlo Park, California: River Heritage Press, 1995.

D188a Gerard, Philip. *Brilliant Passage*, Mystic, Connecticut: Mystic Seaport Museum, 1989.

D189 Gerdau, Kurt. *CAP SAN DIEGO, Vom Schnellfrachter zum Museumsschiff*, Herford, Germany: Koehlers, 1987.

D190 Gerdau, Kurt. *PASSAT - Legende eines Windjammers*, Herford, Germany: Koehlers, 1991.

D191 Gerdau, Kurt. *RICKMER RICKMERS, Ein Windjammer fur Hamburg*, Herford, Germany: Koehler, 1983.

D192 Geuns, W. van. *Om Reis om de Wereld Met de Viermastbarque PASSAT*, Hoorn, Netherlands: Nederlandse Kaap-Hoornvaarders, 1995.

D193 Ghys, Roger and Danckaers, Joris. *MERCATOR en verdwenen kielzog*, Belgium: Uitgeverij Adfrytising, 1993.

D194 Gilkerson, William. 'WANDER BIRD 1977', *Sea Letter*, Fall 1977.

D194a Gill, Ashley. 'PIRNA - Centenary Steamer', *Paddle Wheels*, Winter 1997.

D195 Gillen, Michael. 'The S.S. JOHN W. BROWN: The Ship's People Speak', *Sea History*, Autumn 1986.

D196 Gillmer, Thomas C. *Old Ironsides, The Rise, Decline, and Resurrection of the USS CONSTITUTION*, Camden, Maine: International Marine/McGraw-Hill, 1993.

D197 Godson, Harry. *The MARION Story*, Leabrook, Australia: Investigator Press, 1973.

D198 Goold-Adams, Richard. *The Return of the GREAT BRITAIN*, London: Weidenfeld and Nicolson, 1976.

D199 Goold-Adams, Richard. 'The SS GREAT BRITAIN and its Salvage', *Journal of the Royal Society of Arts*, March 1971.

D200 Gosse, Luc Olivier. *Le BELEM ou le destin d'un Navire*, Grenoble, France: Editions Terre et mer, 1984.

D201 Graham, Tom. 'S.A.S. SOMERSET', *Ships Monthly*, February 1996

D202 Grant, Gordon. *Sail Ho! Windjammer Sketches Alow and Aloft* (BALCLUTHA),

New York: William Farquhar-Payson, 1926.

D203 Grazioli, Luciano. 'The Armored Cruiser AVEROF', *Warship International*, No. 4, 1988.

D204 Greenhill, Basil. *GARLANDSTONE*, Cardiff: National Museum of Wales, 1982.

D205 Greenhill, Basil. 'The Schooner PEGGY: An Eighteenth-Century Survival', *The American Neptune*, January 1969.

D206 Greenhill, Basil. 'World's Oldest Schooner Provides Vital Information on Craft of 1790s' (PEGGY), *National Fisherman*, January 1968.

D207 Gregor, Hugh. *The SS GREAT BRITAIN*, London: The Macmillan Press Ltd, 1971.

D208 Grieve, G. R. & Osler, A. G. eds. *The TURBINIA Report*, 1984.

D209 Grondahl, Karl E. 'Restaureringen av GJOA's kahytt', *Norsk Sjofartsmuseum Arsberetning*, 1993.

D210 Gronstrand, Lars. *SIGYN*, Abo, Finland: Maritime Museum of Abo Akademi, 1980.

D211 Groom, Barry. 'The Mission of the KRAIT', *Australian Sea Heritage*, Spring 1985.

D212 Grossenbacher, Rolf. *LOTSCHBERG, Memoiren eines Dampfers aus der Belle Epoque*, Interlaken, Switzerland: Verlag Schlaefli, 1992.

D213 Hagberg, Jan. 'SPICA', *Aktuellt 1997*.

D214 Hagglund, L. F. *A Page From the Past; The Story of the Continental Gundelo PHILADELPHIA*, Lake George, New York: Adirondack Resorts Press, 1949.

D215 Hainsworth, J. 'Rerigging the COMRADE', *Ships Monthly*, August 1976.

D215a Haley, Nelson Cole. *Whale Hunt, The Narrative of a Voyage in the CHARLES W. MORGAN 1849-1853*, New York; Ives Washburn Inc., 1948.

D216 Hall, Christopher. 'The Restoration of the STANLEY NORMAN', *Wooden Boat*, July/August 1980.

D217 Hall, R. 'Steam tug BRENT', *Ships Monthly*, January 1977.

D218 Haller, Stephen A. 'HERCULES, She was the best we had', *Sea Letter*, Fall/Winter 1989.

D219 Halvorsen, Helge. *Fullriggeren SORLANDET, en skole under seil*, Kristiansand, Norway: Stiftelsen

Fullriggeren Sorlandet, 1987.

D220 Hansen, Knud L. *The Training Ship DANMARK Under the Dannebrog and the Stars and Stripes*, Copenhagen, Denmark: Samlerens Forlag, 1985.

D221 Harmon, J. Scott. *U.S.S. CASSIN YOUNG (DD-793)*, Missoula, Montana: Pictorial Histories Publishing Co, 1984.

D222 Harper, Capt. W. D. 'Cable Ship JOHN W. MACKAY', *Ships Monthly*, May 1985.

D223 Harris, Elizabeth. 'The Early History of the Auxiliary Schooner BONA/BOOMERANG', *Australian Sea Heritage*, Autumn 1990.

D224 Harrod, Mick. 'LYDIA EVA, the Last Steam Drifter', *Ships Monthly*, July 1997.

D225 Hartnett, Rob. 'WAITANGI, Logan's Kauri Racer', *Classic Boat*, November 1995.

D226 Hawkins, Van. *DOROTHY and the Shipbuilders of Newport News*, Norfolk, Virginia: The Donning Company, 1976.

D227 Hayter, Norman T. *The Steam Tug WILLIAM C. DALDY, a short illustrated history to celebrate her 50 years*, Auckland, New Zealand: Amba Graphics, c.1985.

D228 Helmerson, Klas. *Isbrytaren SANKT ERIK*, Stockholm: Foreningen Sveriges Sjofartsmuseum, 1983.

D228a Henry, Tom. *Westcoasters; Boats that built British Columbia* (BCP 45), Madeira Park, British Columbia: Harbour Publishing, 1998.

D229 Herd, R. J. *H.M.V.S. CERBERUS, Battleship to Breakwater*, Sandringham, Australia: City of Sandringham, 1986.

D230 Hill, Alfred T. *Voyages* (CHARLES COOPER), New York: David McKay Company, 1977.

D231 Hill, Ralph Nading. *The Story of the TICONDEROGA*, Shelburne, Vermont: The Shelburne Museum, 1957.

D232 Hillion, Daniel. 'Le BELEM, Histoire d'un grand voilier nantais', *Chasse-Maree* No. 100, August 1996.

D233 Hillyer, Lionel. 'The Story of U-995', *After the Battle*, Number 36.

D234 *History Under Sail*, New Bedford, Massachusetts: Schooner ERNESTINA, 1984.

D235 Hollins, Holly. 'Fragata from the fire' (DOM FERNANDO II E GLORIA), *Classic Boat*, July 1998.

D236 Hollister, Buell. 'Boston Pilots Reluctantly Give Up One of Their Beloved Schooners' (ROSEWAY), *National Fisherman*, July 1971.

D237 Holm, Yngvar. *Den Huite Svane: Boken om SKIBLADNER, 1856-1976*, Hamar, Norway: Oplandske dampskibsselskap, 1976.

D238 Holyoak, Jon. *BALMORAL, and the Story of the Bristol Channel Steamers*, Glasgow, Scotland: Waverley Excursions Ltd, 1992.

D239 Holyoak, Jon & Jones, Nigel. 'BALMORAL's Happy Return', *Ships Monthly*, February 1986.

D240 Horr, A. R. *The Log of the Schooner BOWDOIN*, Cleveland, Ohio: The World Publishing Co, 1947.

D241 Horton, Brian. *H.M.S. TRINCOMALEE*, Windsor, 1979.

D242 Hossack, Gordon. 'Steam Tug WILLIAM C. DALDY', *Ships Monthly*, September 1985.

D242aa Houston, Dan. 'Looking After VIGILANCE', *Classic Boat*, September 1999.

D242a Houston, Dan. ''Restoring ASGARD to sail would not preserve her. It would destroy her', *Classic Boat*, February 1999.

D243 Hoyt, Edwin. *BOWFIN: the Story of One of America's Fabled Fleet Submarines of World War II*, New York: Van Nostrand Reinhold Co, 1983.

D244 Hudson, Jed. *The History of the U.S.S. CABOT (CVL-28)*, Pub. by Author, 1986.

D245 Hume, Cyril L. *CUTTY SARK, Last of the Racing Clippers*, Sydney, Australia: Historian Publishers, 1971.

D246 Husdon, Geoffrey. 'MTB-102, First of the Many', in *Warship 1989*, London: Conway Maritime Press, 1989.

D247 Hutton, W. M. *Cape Horn Passage* (VIKING), London: Blackie & Son Ltd, 1934.

D248 Huycke, Harold. 'Colonial Trader to Museum Ship, The Bark STAR OF INDIA', *American Neptune*, April 1950.

D249 Huycke, Harold. 'The Ship PACIFIC QUEEN' (BALCLUTHA), *American Neptune*, July 1944.

D249a Irrawaddy Flotilla Co 'The RV PANDAW On Her 50th Anniversary', *Flotilla News*, June 1999.

D250 Jackson, Tom. 'Back on Course; A

Puget Sound icon has her most extensive refit yet' (VIRGINIA V), *Wooden Boat*, September/October 1998.

D251 Jaffee, Walter W. *The Last Victory* (LANE VICTORY), San Pedro, California: U. S. Merchant Marine Veterans of World War II, 1991.

D252 Jaffee, Walter W. *The Presidential Yacht POTOMAC*, Benicia, California: The Glencannon Press, 1998.

D253 Jaffee, Walter W. 'The Steam Tug HERCULES', *Sea Classics*, April 1994.

D254 Jansen, Henrik M. *VIKING af Svendborg*, Svendborg, Denmark: Svendborg og Omegns Museum, 1997.

D255 Jea, Tom. *MTB 102; Vosper's Masterpiece - Their First Motor Torpedo Boat*, Norfolk, England: Friends of MTB 102, 1998.

D256 Jeffrey, Bill. *Bulletin* Vol. 13, No. 2 (CITY OF ADELAIDE), Australian Institute for Maritime Archeology, 1989.

D257 Jeffrey, Bill. *Newsletter* No. 48 (CITY OF ADELAIDE), Australian Association for Maritime History, 1991.

D258 Jenkins, Nancy. *The Boat Beneath the Pyramid, King Cheops' Royal Ship*, New York: Holt, Rinehart and Winston, 1980.

D259 Joby, Aho. *The Steamer WILLIAM A. IRVIN 'Queen of the Silver Stackers'*, Marquette, Michigan: Avery Studios, 1995.

D259a Johnson, D. F. 'The York Boats of the Hudson's Bay Company', *Wooden Boat*, September/October 1998.

D260 Johnson, Irving. *The PEKING Battles Cape Horn*, New York: Sea History Press, 1977.

D261 Johnson, Irving. *SHAMROCK V's Wild Voyage Home*, Springfield, Massachusetts: Milton Bradley, 1933.

D261a Johnson, Kenneth C. 'Iraqi Relics' (RIVER GUNBOAT), *Marine News*, October 1998.

D262 Jones, Gordon. 'Coastwise in a Museum Ship' (C. A. THAYER), *Yachting*, March 1965.

D263 Jones, Gordon P. 'The Last of the Bering Sea codfishermen', (WAWONA), *Ships and the Sea*, October 1953.

D264 Jonsson, S. & Olsson, T. *Angfartyget THOMEE, 1875-1981*

D265 Kabat, Henryk. *DAR POMORZA*, Warsaw: Wydawnictwo, 1985.

D266 Kaiser, Joachim. 'UNDINE; Renaissance d'une goelette de Cabotage', *Chasse-maree* No. 103, December 1996.

D267 Karting, Herbert. *HERMANN aus Wewelsfleth, Deutschlands letzter holzerner Frachtewer*, Itzehoe, Germany: Rundschau KG, 1979.

D268 'KBV 238 (TV238)', *Aktuellt 1997*.

D269 Kepner, Charles H. *The EDNA E. LOCKWOOD*, St. Michael's, Maryland: Chesapeake Bay Maritime Museum, 1979.

D270 Kiedel, Klaus-Peter, et al. *The Hanse Cog of 1380*, Bremerhaven, Germany: Forderverein Deutsches Schiffahrtsmuseum, 1985.

D271 Kimberly, Capt. Arthur. *The Wreck of the COUNTY OF ROXBURGH*, (mimeographed report), St. Thomas, Virgin Islands: 1976.

D272 King, Andy. 'Steam Tug MAYFLOWER', *Ships Monthly*, November 1986.

D273 King, Jim. 'Snagboat in Puget Sound' (W. T. PRESTON), *Ships Monthly*, April 1976.

D274 Kinzey, Bert. *U.S.S. LEXINGTON*, Blue Ridge Summit, Pennsylvania: TAB Books, 1988.

D275 Kirby, Martin. *ALBION - The Story of the Norfolk Trading Wherry*, England: Wherry Trust & Jarrold Publishing Corp., 1998.

D276 Kirkbride, P. 'Tug KERNE', *Ships Monthly*, May 1977.

D277 Klebingat, Fred. 'FALLS OF CLYDE', *Oceans*, September-October 1972.

D278 Kline, M. S. *Steamboat VIRGINIA V*, Bellevue, Washington: Documentary Book Publishers Corp., 1985.

D278a Kloser, Reinhard and Fritz, Karl. *Das Dampfschiff HOHENTWIEL; wieder in Fahrt auf dem Bodensee*, Konstanz, Germany: Verlag Stadler, 1995.

D279 Kludas, Monika. 'Finkenwerder Hochseekutter LANDRATH KUSTER', *Das Logbuch*, No. 2, 1998.

D280 Knego, Peter. 'Nuclear Ship Safari' (SAVANNAH), *Ships Monthly*, September 1998.

D281 Kortum, Karl. 'STAR OF INDIA - An Appreciation', *Sea Letter*, Summer 1979.

D282 Kortum, Karl. 'A Working Vessel' (BALCLUTHA), *Sea Letter*, Winter 1997.

D283 Koza, Thad. 'MARITE, Sailing With a Guardian Angel', *Classic Boat*, August 1993.

D284 Krei, Melvin A. *MADAKET Tells Her Story*, Eureka, California: Humboldt Bay Maritime Museum, 1988.

D285 Kruse, Ewald. *AMPHITRITE*, Herford, Germany: Koehlers, 1990.

D286 Kuczera, Andrzej. *Krazownik AURORA*, Warsaw, Poland: Wydawnictwo Ministerstwa Obrony Narodowej, 1981.

D287 Kuebler, Brian. 'Minnesota Transportation Museum restores 1906 lake steamer', (MINNEHAHA) *Society for Industrial Archeology Newsletter*, Fall 1990.

D288 Kuligiewicz, M. *Kuter Poscigowy BATORY*, Warsaw, Poland, 1974.

D289 Kure, Bernte. *Historien om fregatten JYLLAND*, Copenhagen, Denmark, 1995.

D289a Kvarning, Lars-Ake & Ohrelius, Bengt. *The VASA, The Royal Ship*, Stockholm, Sweden: Atlantis, 1998.

D290 Kvarning, Lars-Ake. 'Raising the VASA', *Scientific American*, October 1993.

D291 Lahn, Werner. *Die Kogge von Bremen*, Bremerhaven: Deutsches Schiffahrtsmuseum, 1993.

D292 Lambert, Andrew. *WARRIOR, The World's First Ironclad, Then and Now*, London, Conway Maritime Press: 1987.

D293 Lambert, John & Hill, David. *Anatomy of the Ship, the submarine ALLIANCE*, Greenwich, Conway Maritime Press, 1986.

D294 Lapp, Ralph. *Voyage of the Lucky Dragon* (5 FUKURYU MARU), New York: Harper, 1958.

D295 Larken, Meriel. 'The Ship on the Roof of the World: The YAVARI PROJECT', *Sea History*, Autumn 1986.

D296 'The Last of the China Clippers' (CUTTY SARK), *100A1, The Magazine of Lloyd's Register*, Issue 2, 1993.

D297 'Le chalutier 'classique' HEMERICA conserve a flot a Concarneau', *Le Chasse-Maree*, No. 11.

D298 Le Corre, Daniel and Molle, Jean-Louis. 'La premiere vie de la grande duchesse' (DUCHESSE ANNE), *Le Chasse-Maree*, No. 93, November 1995.

D299 Le Corre, Daniel. 'Le DUCHESSE-ANNE', *Le Chasse-Maree*, No. 107, June 1997.

D300 Le Corre, Daniel. 'Le LAENNEC, Trois-mats carre de Nantes' (SUOMEN JOUTSEN), *Le Chasse-Maree*, No. 106, April 1997.

D301 'Le fregate FRANCE I a la Rochelle', *Chasse-Maree*, No. 39.

D302 Leaper, Genevieve. 'Tall Ship Comrades' (TOVARITSCH), *Classic Boat*, November 1994.

D303 Leavitt, John F. *The CHARLES W. MORGAN*, Mystic, Connecticut: Marine Historical Association, 1973.

D304 Lebech, Mogens. *HJEJLEN*, Copenhagen, Denmark: Burmeister & Wain, 1961.

D305 Lee, Capt. Martin. 'Sailing in the MAGDALENE VINNEN in 1998' (SEDOV), *Sea Breezes*, November 1998.

D306 'Les bateaux-lavoirs de Laval', *Chasse-Maree*, No. 71, March 1993.

D307 'Les derniers chalands metalliques nantais' (LA LEONE), *Chasse- Maree*, No. 94, December 1995.

D308 Levy, *Log: Five Days aboard the Schooner STEPHEN TABER*, Oyster Bay, New York: The Binnacle Press, 1962.

D309 Linard, Andre. 'NOTRE-DAME-DE-RUMENGOL, Histoire et restauration du dernier dundee de la rade de Brest', *Chasse-Maree*, No. 99, July 1996.

D310 Lindholm, Paul. 'Tall-Water Ship PASSAT', *National Fisherman*, February 1972.

D311 Lipke, Paul. *The Royal Ship of Cheops*, Oxford, England: British Archeological Reports, 1984.

D312 Liston, Robert. *The PUEBLO Surrender, a Covert Action by the National Security Agency*, New York: M. Evans & Co, 1988.

D313 Loney, Jack. *Wreck and Rescue; The QUEENSCLIFFE Lifeboat at Port Philip Heads*, Queenscliffe, Australia: The Queenscliffe Lifeboat Preservation Society, 1989.

D314 Longridge, C. Nepean. *The Anatomy of Nelson's Ships* (H.M.S. VICTORY), Annapolis, Maryland: Naval Institute Press, 1981. (earlier editions back to 1961).

D315 Longridge, C. Nepean. *The CUTTY SARK*, 2 vols., London: PercivalMarshall, 1953.

D316 Loomeijer, Frits R. *De Dreimastschoener OOSTERSCHELDE*, Alkmaar, Netherlands: De Alk bv, 1995.

D317 Lott, Arnold S. & Sumrall, Robert F. *U.S.S. ALABAMA (BB 60)*, Pompton Lakes, New Jersey: Leeward Publications, 1974.

D318 Lott, Arnold S. & Sumrall, Robert F. *U.S.S. BOWFIN (SS 287)* Annapolis, Maryland: Leeward Publications, 1975.

D319 Lott, Arnold S. & Sumrall, Robert. *U.S.S. NORTH CAROLINA (BB 55)*, Pompton Lakes, New Jersey: Leeward Publications, 1973.

D320 Lott, Arnold S. & Sumrall, Robert. *U.S.S. TEXAS (BB 35)*, Annapolis, Maryland: Leeward Publications, 1976.

D321 Lowder, Hughston & Scott, Jack. *BATFISH! The Champion 'Submarine Killer' Submarine of World War II*, Englewood Cliffs, New Jersey: Prentice-Hall, 1980.

D322 Lubbock, Basil. *The Log of the CUTTY SARK*, Glasgow: James Brown & Son, 1924.

D323 Lucas, Roger S. *Boldt's Boats* (LA DUCHESSE), Cheektowaga, New York: Research Review Publications, 1998.

D323a Ludwig, Leslie G. 'ROANN', *The Log of Mystic Seaport*, Autumn 1997.

D324 Lundeberg, Philip K. *The Continental Gunboat PHILADELPHIA and the Northern Campaign of 1776*, Washington, D. C.: Smithsonian Institution, 1966.

D325 'The Luxury Yacht HUSSAR' (SEA CLOUD), *The Shipbuilder and Marine Engine-Builder*, June 1932.

D326 Lynch, Thomas G. 'HMCS BRAS D'OR, Ten Years in Retrospect', *Warship International*, No. 2, 1982.

D327 'M.S. STELLA POLARIS - The Largest Cruising Yacht', *Marine Engineering*, April 1927.

D328 MacAlindin, Bob. 'The Lightships of Scotland' (NORTH CARR), *The Keeper's Log*, Summer 1997.

D329 MacHaffie, Frazer et. al. *WAVERLEY - The Story of the World's Last Sea Going Paddle Steamer*, Glasgow: Waverley Excursions Ltd, 1994.

D330 MacIlwain, John. *H.M.S. TRINCOMALEE*, Andover, England: Pitkin Pictorials, 1994.

D331 Mackenzie, Graham K. 'Active Ship Preservation' (SHIELDHALL), *Sea Breezes*,

March 1997.

D332 'MacMillan's New Schooner BOWDOIN a Fisherman Type', *Atlantic Fisherman*, June 1921.

D333 MacMullen, Gerald F. 'Preserving an Old Windjammer for Posterity' (STAR OF INDIA), *Yachting*,

D334 MacMullen, Jerry. *Star of India, the Log of an Iron Ship*, Berkeley, California: Howell-North, 1961.

D335 Mandelblatt, James L. *Rebirth of a Submarine: A History of the U.S.S. REQUIN (SS-481)*, pub. by author, 1995.

D336 Manen, Eymert van. *Museumship BUFFEL*, Amsterdam, Netherlands: Kosmos, 1981.

D337 Marczak, Jan. *Niszczyciel BLYSKAWICA*, Warsaw, Poland: Wydawnictwo Ministerstwa Obrony Narodowej, 1970.

D338 Marin, Pierre-Henri. 'Le retour de la gabare' (DEUX-FRERES), *Chasse-Maree*, No. 88, May 1995.

D339 Marin, Pierre-Henri. 'Les cent ans de MARIE-FERNAND', *Chasse-Maree*, No. 81, June 1994.

D340 Marin, Pierre-Henri. 'Sauver le remorqueur ST 8', *Chasse-Maree*, No. 81, June 1994.

D341 The Maritime Trust. *The Story of the CAMBRIA*, London: Endlebury Publishing Co Ltd, 1973.

D342 The Maritime Trust. *The Story of the LYDIA EVA*, London: Endlebury Publishing Co Ltd, 1975.

D343 Marsh, A. J. *The Story of a Frigate; H.M.S. TRINCOMALEE becomes T. S. FOUDROYANT*, Portsmouth, England: Portsmouth Museums Society, 1973.

D344 Martin, Brian and McLeod, Rod. *The FORCEFUL Story*, Brisbane, Brisbane, Australia: Queensland Maritime Museum Assoc., c.1980.

D345 Martin, E. G. *Deep Water Cruising* (JOLIE BRISE), New York: Yachting Inc., 1928.

D346 Martin, Marian. 'TECLA's Tale', *Classic Boat*, December 1995.

D347 Martin, Robert. 'SEA CLOUD and Her Captain', *Jacksonville Seafarer*, Aug. & Oct. 1984.

D348 Martin, Tyrone G. *A Most Fortunate Ship* (U.S.S. CONSTITUTION), Chester, Connecticut: Globe Pequot Press,

1980.

D349 Martyr, Weston. 'A Western Ocean Passage in the JOLIE BRISE', *Yachting*, July 1926.

D350 Matteson, George. 'A Centennial History of the PIONEER', *Seaport*, Summer 1985.

D351 Matz, Erling. *VASA*, Stockholm, Sweden: The Vasa Museum, c.1990.

D352 'MAYFLOWER Steams!' *Lekko*, November/December 1987.

D352a Maynard, Gary. 'Resurrecting ALABAMA; New life for an aging Pilot Schooner', *Wooden Boat*, July/August 1999.

D353 McCaughan, M. 'RESULT Goes Home', *Ships Monthly*, March 1980.

D354 McDonell, Capt. Ralph. *ALMA DOEPAL, The History of An Australian Schooner 1903-1975*, Burwood, Australia: Brown Anderson, 1988.

D355 McGowan, Gordon. *The Skipper and the EAGLE*, Princeton, New Jersey: D. Van Nostrand Company, 1960.

D356 McGrath, H. Thomas et al. 'Historic Structure Report: WAPAMA', *APT Bulletin*, Vol. IX, No. 1, 1987.

D357 McMullen, Alex. 'Silent centenary' (NUNEHAM), *Classic Boat*, July 1998.

D358 Mead, Tom. *NORTH HEAD Goes South*, Manly, Australia: Newspaper and Media Services, 1987.

D359 Mellefont, Jeffrey. 'A lete-lete from Raas' (SEKAR AMAN), *Signals*, No. 41, Dec. 1997-Feb. 1998.

D360 Meyer, Robert J. 'The Lady of the Lake' (EARNSLAW), *Ships Monthly*, February 1987.

D361 Miles, Ted. 'Restoration is only the Beginning' (BALCLUTHA), *Maritime Heritage*, September-October 1998.

D362 Millatt, Tony. 'A refit for the PRESIDENT', *Classic Boat*, April 1992.

D363 Millinger, Jum. 'The Steamer SABINO on Casco Bay, 1927-1961', *The Log of Mystic Seaport*, Autumn 1995.

D364 Millot, Gilles. 'A bord de l'ONDEE, le dernier vapeur francais', *Le Chasse-Maree*, No. 39.

D365 Millot, Gilles. 'Le BELEM aujourd'hui', *Chasse-Maree* No. 100, August 1996.

D366 Millot, Gilles. 'L'epopee du GREAT BRITAIN', *Chasse-Maree* No. 104, January 1997.

D367 Millot, Gilles. 'A toute vapeur d'Erdre en Loire' (LECHALAS), *Chasse-Maree*, No. 84, November 1994.

D367a Morris, Robb. *Coasters* (LADY ROSE), Victoria, British Columbia: Horsdal & Schubart, 1993.

D368 Morrish, Leslie. *Good Night IRENE*, Windsor, England: The February Press, 1986.

D369 Morrison, Jum. 'Time, Tide and the CARRICK', (CITY OF ADELAIDE), *Sea Breezes*, December 1990.

D370 Moss, Michael. 'L. A. DUNTON, A Brief Encounter', *Wooden Boat*, Vol. 1, No. 6, 1975.

D371 Mulholland, C. B. 'Two Sisters' (TAIOMA), *Lekko*, 29 December 1979.

D372 Murphy, David. 'The Restoration of the Trading Ketch DEFENDER', *Wooden Boat*, January/February 1990.

D373 Murphy, Fernando. 'SEA CLOUD', *Nautical Quarterly* No. 14, Summer 1981.

D374 Murray, Timothy. 'CORONET: Whither Away?' *Wooden Boat*, January/February 1980.

D375 Murray, Timothy. 'Nothing is too good for CORONET', *Sea History*, Autumn 1980.

D376 Myhre, Ivar Otto. 'The Restoration of the Whale Catcher SOUTHERN ACTOR', *Sea Breezes*, July 1997.

D377 National Trust of Australia (Victoria). *POLLY WOODSIDE*, Melbourne, Australia: National Trust, 1978.

D378 Nerbus, Hans. *GJOA var Verdskjende Minneskute*, Oslo: 1980.

D379 Neufeld, David & Habiluk, Patrick. *Make it Pay! GOLD DREDGE No. 4*, Missoula, Montana: Pictorial Histories Publishing Co, 1994.

D380 Neville, Bert. 'Last Steamboat to Montgomery, Alabama' (MONTGOMERY), *Waterways Journal*, 22 April 1961.

D381 'New Swiss Lake Steamers' (BLUMLISALP), *International Marine Engineering*, November 1907.

D382 Newell, Gordon & Smith, RADM Allan. *Mighty Mo; the U.S.S. MISSOURI, a Biography of the Last Battleship*, Seattle: Superior Publishing Co, 1969.

D383 Newhall, Scott. *The EPPLETON HALL*, Berklely, California: Howell-North Books, 1971.

D384 Newby, Eric. *The Last Grain Race* (MOSHULU), Boston: Houghton Mifflin Company, 1956.

D385 Newby, Eric. *Windjammer; Pictures of Life Before the Mast in the Last Grain Race* (MOSHULU), New York: E. P. Dutton & Co, 1968.

D386 Nicolaysen, N. *The Viking Ship Discovered at Gokstad in Norway*, Christiania: Cammermeyer, 1882.

D387 Nixon, W. M. 'Les fantomes de la mer d'Irlande; Histoire et redecouverte des deux plus vieux yachts du monde' (PEGGY), *Chasse-Maree*, No. 27, January 1987.

D388 Norton, William I. *EAGLE Ventures*, New York: M. Evans & Co, 1970.

D389 Nurnberg, Alexander. 'WAL, Dampfeisbrecher wird Museumsschiff', *Alte Schiff*, October/November 1990.

D389a Nutland, Martin. 'SUNDOWNER, The Survivor's Survivor', *Classic Boat*, January 1999.

D390 Olmsted, Roger. *C. A. THAYER & the Pacific Lumber Schooners*, Los Angeles, California: Ward Ritchie Press, 1972.

D391 Olmsted, Roger. 'Wreck of the ship BALCLUTHA', *Ships and the Sea*, Fall 1957.

D392 Orsini, Stephen D. 'The PORTLAND, Last of a Breed', *National Fisherman*, May 1977.

D393 'P.S. ADELAIDE, Back From the Dead', *Australian Sea Heritage*, Summer 1987.

D394 Paget-Tomlinson, E. 'Gas Boat GIFFORD', *Waterways World*, April 1975.

D395 Palmer, H. V. R. 'NOBSKA to the Rescue', *National Fisherman*, July 1975.

D396 'PASTEUR chez les Soviets', *Chasse-Maree*, No. 87, March 1995.

D397 Paul, Wm. Pratt. 'The Versatile CARRICK', (CITY OF ADELAIDE), *Sea Breezes*, April 1952.

D398 Paulun, Hans-Jurgen. *SEEFALKE, Schwimmendes Exponat des Deutschen Schiffahrtsmuseums*, Cologne, Germany: Arbeitskreis historischer Schiffbau e.V. c.1995.

D398a Payne, Stephen M. 'HMY BRITANNIA 1954-1998', *Steamboat Bill*, Fall 1998.

D399 Payne, Stephen M. 'The National Flagship 1954-1997' (BRITANNIA), *Maritime Heritage*, April 1998.

D400 Perez, August et al. *The DELTA QUEEN*, Gretna, Louisiana: Pelican Publishing Co, 1973.

D401 Perkins, John. *The Frigate UNICORN, A Guided Tour*, Dundee, Scotland: Dundee District Council, 1977.

D402 Peron, Andre. 'Les bateaux-lavoirs; A Nantes l'Erdre lave plus blanc', *Chasse-Maree*, No. 46, January 1990.

D403 Peters, Rebecca. 'Iron Square-rigger to Sail Again' (JAMES CRAIG), *Journal of the Institution of Engineers Australia*, February 21, 1986.

D404 Piechulek, R. 'LANGER HEINRICH in Noten', *Das Logbuch*, No. 2, 1997.

D405 Pipping, Knut. *The Museum Ship SIGYN of Wardo*, Greenwich, England: National Maritime Museum, 1980.

D406 Plummer, Norman H. 'The Life, Times, and Restoration of the Skipjack E. C. COLLIER', *The Weather Gauge*, Spring 1993.

D407 Plummer, Norman H. and Lesher, Pete. 'The Skipjack KATHRYN', *The Weather Gauge*, Fall 1995.

D408 Plummer, R. 'MAID OF THE LOCH', *Ships Monthly*, August 1978.

D409 Pollack, Jack H. 'SEQUOIA, A Most Political Yacht', *Nautical Quarterly*, No. 19, Autumn 1982.

D410 Polo, Renato & Collier, William. 'MARIETTE, Back in the High Life', *Classic Boat*, March 1996.

D411 Power, Hugh. *Battleship TEXAS*, College Station, Texas: Texas A.& M. University Press, 1993.

D412 Power, Hugh. *Carrier LEXINGTON*, College Station, Texas: Texas A. & M. University Press, 1996.

D413 Powlesland, Greg. 'MARIGOLD, A Boyhood Dream', *Classic Boat*, April 1995.

D413a Prados, Edward & Warburton, David. 'Al-Hami: A Desert Village Preserves its Seafaring Past' (SAIYYA TYPE DHOW), *Sea History*, Summer 1999.

D414 Prager, H. G. & Ostersehlte. *Dampfeisbrecher STETTIN & die Eisbrecher der Welt vom Holzschlitten zu den Polar-Giganten*

D415 Prescott, A. M. & Willson, R. K.

'SOUTH STEYNE', *Australian Sea Heritage*, Winter 1990-Autumn 1991.

D416 Preston, Anthony. *H.M.S. CAVALIER and the 'CA' class destroyers*

D417 Pritchard, Keith. 'HOSHI Shines On', *Classic Boat*, October 1995.

D418 'Propeller Ferryboat BERKELEY in Service on San Francisco Bay', *Marine Engineering*, August 1899.

D419 Pryce, Michael. 'POLAR 4 - Old Whalechaser At Husvik Harbour, South Georgia', *Marine News*, January 1996.

D420 Putz, George. *EAGLE, America's Sailing Square-Rigger*, Chester, Connecticut: Globe-Pequot Press, 1986.

D421 Pyles, George H. *Modelling the Lightship PORTSMOUTH*, Cedarburg, Wisconsin: Phoenix Publications, 1995.

D422 'Queen of the Willamette' (PORTLAND), *Surveyor*, August 1972.

D423 Raber, Anton. 'Kinderschiff THALWIL in Verkehrshaus', *Dampferzeitung*, No. 3, 1994.

D424 Ransom, P. J. G. 'SIR WALTER SCOTT', *Ships Monthly*, August 1979.

D425 Ransom, P. J. G. 'Thames Tug CHALLENGE', *Ships Monthly*, March 1978.

D426 Rappaport, Amy. 'Reincarnation' (SAVARONA), *Power and Motoryacht*, October 1992.

D427 Rappaport, Capt. Elliot. '70 Degrees North, Maine Maritime in the Arctic' (BOWDOIN), *Mariner, The Alumni Magazine of Maine Maritime Academy*, Winter 1995-1996. and: *Wooden Boat*, March/April 1996.

D428 Reilly, Charles V. 'East for the Horn' (VIKING), *Ships & Sailing*, June 1951.

D429 'Renaissance du trois-mats DUCHESSE-ANNE', *La Chasse-Maree*, No. 33.

D429a Renault, Florence. 'DEHEL, Barque chalutiere de Dives', *La Chasse-Maree*, No. 123, March 1999.

D430 Reynolds, Clark G. *The Fighting Lady: The New YORKTOWN in the Pacific War*, Missoula, Montana: Pictorial Histories Publishing Co, 1986.

D431 Rice, Skip. 'A Star if Re-born' (STAR OF INDIA), *Yachting*, May 1969.

D432 Rigg, W. E. 'Storm Upon the Lakes' (LIEMBA), *Ships and Ship Models*, July 1955.

D433 Riimala, Erkki. *Saimaa ja SALAMA*, Savonlinna, Finland: Savonlinnan Kirjapaino Osakeyhtio, 1978.

D434 Roberts, John. *The Anatomy of the Ship: The Aircraft Carrier INTREPID*, Annapolis, Maryland: U. S. Naval Institute Press, 1982.

D435 Robertson, Dr. E. Graeme. 'The POLLY WOODSIDE Restoration Project', *The Dog Watch*, No. 25, 1968.

D436 Robertson, R. G. 'QUEEN MARY' (QUEEN MARY II), *Ships Monthly*, September 1977.

D437 Robinson, Donald P. 'The Restoration of the JOSEPH CONRAD', *The Log of Mystic Seaport*, July 1978.

D438 Rolt, L. T. C. 'Saving the GREAT BRITAIN', *Country Life*, April 23, 1970.

D439 Ronnberg, Erik A. R. 'Landmark Nautical Archeology Reviewed - The Fourteenth-century Bremen Cog', *Nautical Research Journal*, December 1994.

D440 Roos, Doeke. *Ramschip SCHORPIOEN, een maritiem monument behouden*, Middelburg, Netherlands: De Koperen Tuin te Goes, c.1989.

D441 Ross, Al. *The Anatomy of the Ship: The Destroyer THE SULLIVANS*, Annapolis, Maryland: U. S. Naval Institute Press, 1988.

D442 'Rostocker Fischdampfer wurde neues Bremerhavener Museumsschiff', (GERA) *Alte Schiff*, October/November 1990.

D443 Rowland, E. C. *The Paddle Steamer GEM, Queen of the Murray*, Canterbury, Australia: Mullaya Publications, 1976.

D444 Rowland, E. C. *The Story of P. S. RUBY*, Mildura, Australia: Sunraysia Daily, 1974.

D445 Roylance, Frank D. 'Home City to Help the CONSTELLATION', *Naval History*, April 1996.

D446 Rubino, Thomas C. 'DOM FERNANDO II, A fragata reborn', *Wooden Boat*, January/February 1996.

D447 Rule, Margaret. *The MARY ROSE, the Excavation and Raising of Henry VIII's Flagship*, London: Conway Maritime Press, 1982.

D448 Russell, E. C. *H.M.C.S. HAIDA, A Brief History*, Toronto: Haida Inc., c.1990.

D449 Rybka, Walter. 'The Restoration' (ELISSA), *Sea History*, Fall 1979.

D450 Rydberg, L. *MARIEFRED och Malarbatarna: 150 Ars Trafik med 30 Angfartyg pa Malaren*, Stockholm, Sweden: Tryckt hos Stellan Stal AB, 1978.

D451 S. S. Great Britain Project. *The SS GREAT BRITAIN Official Guide*, London: The Macmillan Press Ltd, 1971.

D452 Sanders, Walter. 'Two Weeks Before the Mast (Yo Ho!)' (GRACE BAILEY), *The New York Times Magazine*, July 13, 1941.

D453 Sannes, Tor Borch. *FRAM*, Oslo, Norway: Norsk Martimt Forlag, 1989.

D454 Saville, Allison. *Ship's Date: The GAZELA PRIMEIRO*, Annapolis, Maryland: Leeward Publications, 1978.

D455 Savours, Ann. *The Voyages of DISCOVERY - The Illustrated History of Scott's Ship*, Dundee, Scotland: Dundee Industrial Heritage, 1993.

D456 'SCHARHORN kehrte an die Elbe zuruck', *Alte Schiffe*, October/November 1990.

D456a Schlegel, Berthold. *Autofahre; Konstanz-Meersburg* (MEERSBURG), Konstanz, Germany: Stadler Verlag, 1989.

D457 Schleihauf, William. 'The Last of Her Tribe: HMCS HAIDA', *Warship International*, No. 4, 1996.

D458 'Schleppdampfer NORDSTERN fahrt Passagiere auf dem Wannsee', *Alte Schiffe*, October/November 1990.

D459 Sclater, William. *HAIDA*, Toronto, Ontario: Oxford University Press, 1947.

D460 Scott, Richard J. *The Story of the KATHLEEN & MAY*

D461 Sexton, Robert & Pickhaver, Gordon. *FALIE, Portrait of a Coastal Trader*, Port Adelaide, Australia: Falie Project, 1985.

D462 'SHAMROCK V, Lean and Mean Again', *The Yacht*, August 1989.

D463 Shaw, James L. 'A Survivor of the Cold War' (SUUR TOLL), *Sea Breezes*, August 1997.

D464 'Ships Preserved; The ROBIN', *Ships Monthly*, December 1974.

D465 Sieche, Erwin F. 'Ex-Austro-Hungarian River Monitor LEITHA May Become the First Warship Museum in Central Europe', *Warship International*, No. 4, 1996.

D466 Sifferlinger, Nikolaus. 'Museum Ship; Boom Defense Vessel S.A.S. SOMERSET', *Warship International*, No. 1, 1996.

D467 Silver, Lynette Ramsay. *KRAIT: The*

Fishing Boat That Went to War, Birchgrove, Australia: Sally Milner Publishing, 1993.

D468 Simper, Robert. 'A Real Lady From Sweden' (L'ATALANTA), *Classic Boat Monthly*, October 1973.

D469 Simpson, Lloyd. 'The Last of a Type' (torpedo boat DERZKI), *Warship International*, No. 3, 1973.

D470 Skec, Paul A. 'S.S. VICTORIA', *Australian Sea Heritage*, Autumn 1998.

D471 Slimin, D. J. 'The Classic Steam Yacht NAHLIN' (LIBERTATEA), *Sea Breezes*, November 1996.

D472 Smith, C. Fox. *The Return of the CUTTY SARK*, Boston: Charles E. Lauriat, 1925.

D473 Smith, Ken. *TURBINIA: The Story of Charles Parsons and His Ocean Greyhound*, Newcastle, England: Newcastle City Libraries, 1996.

D474 Snyder, Dick. *The TRIESTE, the Story of the U.S. Navy's First Inner Space Ship*, San Carlos: Golden Gate Junior Books, 1964.

D475 Sparrow, Alan. 'CLEARWAY', *Ships Monthly*, April 1991.

D476 Spectre, Peter H. 'The ALVIN CLARK: The Challenge of the Challenge' *Wooden Boat*, No. 52.

D477 Spectre, Peter H. 'The BOWDOIN Project', *Wooden Boat*, July-August 1982.

D478 Spectre, Peter H. 'WARRIOR's Figurehead', *Wooden Boat*, January-February 1984.

D479 Spencer, Josh ed. *Gordon Belton, A Sailor's Scrapbook* (PASSAT), Cape Town: Square Sail Publishing, c.1997.

D480 Spies, M. H. 'LIEMBA', *Steamboat Bill*, Autumn 1968.

D481 Spiers, George. *The WAVERTREE, an Ocean Wanderer*, New York: South Street Seaport Museum, 1969.

D482 Stackpole, Renny. 'The Saga of the Arctic Schooner BOWDOIN', *Sea History*, Summer 1986.

D483 Stammers, Michael. 'The KERNE - another tug still steaming', *The Maritime Trust Review*, May 1997.

D484 Stammers, Michael & Kearon, John. 'The Motor Schooner DE WADDEN', *Ships Monthly*, May 1986.

D485 Stammers, Michael & Kearon, John. *The JHELUM*, England: Alan Sutton, 1992.

D486 Stanford, Peter et. al. 'The Last Dreadnought' (TEXAS), *Sea History*, Spring 1984.

D487 Stanford, Peter. 'The Long Sea Career' (ELISSA), *Sea History*, Fall 1979.

D488 Stanford, Peter & Rybka, Walter. 'ELISSA Sails', *Sea History*, Winter 1982-1983.

D489 Stannard, Bruce. *Jack Earl, The Life and Art of a Sailor* (KATHLEEN GILLETT), Willoughby, Australia: Weldon Publishing, 1991.

D490 Stannard, Bruce. *The Triumph of AUSTRALIA II*, Dee Why West, Australia: Lansdowne, 1983.

D491 'Steam Lifeboat to be Exhibition Centre-piece' (CITY OF ADELAIDE), *Australian Sea Heritage*, Winter 1986.

D492 'Steam Yachting in Australia' (ENA), *The Rudder*, March 1906.

D493 Steele, James. *QUEEN MARY*, London: Phaidon Press, 1995.

D494 Steensen, R. Steen. *Fregatten JYLLAND*, Copenhagen: Nationalmuseet, 1965.

D495 Stewart, C. M. *The Blind Fight* (U.S.S. COBIA)

D496 Stewart, W. Roderick. *Welcome Aboard the Frigate UNICORN*, Dundee, Scotland: Unicorn Preservation Society, 1982.

D497 Stillwell, Paul. *Battleship MISSOURI, An Illustrated History*, Annapolis, Maryland: U. S. Naval Institute Press 1996.

D498 Stockman, Christopher. 'Steaming into the Eighties', (WHYALLA), *Ships Monthly*, November 1983.

D499 Stoker, Donald J. 'The Estonian Submarines LEMBIT and KALEV', *Warship International*, No. 4, 1996.

D500 Stonham, Denis and Bellamy, Karen. 'Mud, Sweat and Tears' (MEDWAY QUEEN), *Maritime Heritage*, April 1998.

D501 'Stoomsleepboot LAUWERZEE', *Lekko*, 29 December 1979.

D502 *The Story of the MEDWAY QUEEN*, England: Paddle Steamer Preservation Society, 1974.

D503 Strand, Odd. *HITRA; Med Ingvald Eidsheim og hans menn pa krigstokt over Nordsjoen*, Bergen, Norway: J. W. Eide, 1987.

D504 Streeton, Derrick. 'Japanese Battleship MIKASA', *Ships Monthly*, February 1994.

D505 Stubbs, Laurie. 'Australian Opulence, Restoration of the Steam Yacht ENA', *Classic Boat Magazine*, June 1989.

D506 Stuckey, P. J. 'The Lovely Ketch IRENE', *Ships Monthly*, November 1982. (rep. *Gaffers Log*, Winter-Spring 1994)

D507 Sturges, Michael D. 'She Was No Ordinary Ship' (JOSEPH CONRAD), *The Log of Mystic Seaport*, July 1978.

D508 Sumrall, Robert F. and Walkowiak, Thomas F. *U.S.S. KIDD (DD 661)*, Missoula, Montana: Pictorial Histories Publishing Co, 1985.

D509 Sumrall, Robert F. *U.S.S. MISSOURI (BB 63)*, Missoula, Montana: Pictorial Histories Publishing Co, 1986.

D510 Sutter, Annie. 'The Rebirth of WANDERBIRD', *Wooden Boat*, November/December 1983.

D511 Svensson, Bjorn. *POMMERN, Mariehamn; From Ocean Carrier to Museum Ship*, Mariehamn, Finland: Aland Nautical Club, 1988.

D512 Swahn, Bo. 'U-Baten HAJEN', *Aktuellt 1994 Marinmuseum*, Karlskrona, Sweden: Marinmuseum, 1994.

D512a Taji, Y. 'The NIPPON MARU and KAIWO MARU', *The Shipbuilder*, Nov. 1930.

D513 Tannenbaum, Fred M. 'Museum Report; The U.S.S. SILVERSIDES', *Naval Institute Naval History*, Spring 1993.

D514 Tatley, Richard. *The Story of the SEGWUN*, Bracebridge, Ontario: Richard Tatley, 1981.

D515 'Thames Steam Tug Converted to Diesel Power', (BRITANNIA) *Engineering*, December 30, 1955.

D516 *The Story of the U-505*, Chicago: Museum of Science and Industry.

D517 Thewlis, Alan. 'The Story of the BERKELEY', *Mains'l Haul*, Summer 1994.

D518 Thiele, Ron. 'FALIE Restoration', *Australian Sea Heritage*, Spring 1986.

D519 Thiele, Ron. 'The JOHN OXLEY', *The Dog Watch*, 1993.

D520 Todd, Mabel Loomis. *Corona and CORONET*, New York: Houghton, Mifflin and Co, 1898.

D521 Toghill, Jeff. *The JAMES CRAIG, Her History, recovery and restoration*, Terry Hills, Australia: A. H. & A. W. Reed, 1978.

D522 Tompkins, Warwick M. *Fifty South to Fifty South* (WANDER BIRD), New York: W. W. Norton & Co, 1938.

D523 Tompkins, Warwick M. 'WANDER BIRD and the Blue Waters', *Yachting*, April-June 1930.

D524 Townes, Brooks. 'Century Old Maine Schooner Starts New Career' (LEWIS R. FRENCH), *National Fisherman*, July 1976.

D525 Townes, Brooks. 'The Indomitable WANDER BIRD', *Nautical Quarterly*, No. 17, Spring 1982.

D526 Treadwell, Theodore R. 'K.N.M. HITRA: The Shetlands Bus', *Sea History*, Spring 1988.

D527 Trepa, Helen. 'TU DO: A Boat Called Freedom', *Signals*, Dec. 1995-Feb. 1996.

D528 Tri-Coastal Marine Inc. *Schooner C. A. THAYER, Historic Structure Report*, San Francisco: National Park Service, 1991.

D529 Tri-Coastal Marine Inc. *Steam Schooner WAPAMA, Historic Structure Report*, San Francisco: National Park Service, 1986.

D530 Tri-Coastal Marine Inc. *Tugboat HERCULES, Historic Structure Report*, San Francisco: National Park Service, 1990.

D531 Trost, Heinz. 'Die Irrfahrt der ELBE', *Dampferzeitung*, January 1998.

D532 Trost, Heinz. 'KAISER FRIEDRICH, Berlins letzter Passagierdampfer kommt wieder in Fahrt', *Dampferzeitung*, No. 5, 1993.

D533 Trott, Harlan. *The Schooner that came Home: The Final Voyage the C. A. THAYER*, Cambridge, Maryland: Cornell Maritime Press, 1958.

D534 Trumbull, Robert. *SILVERSIDES*, New York: Henry Holt & Co 1945.

D535 Tuckwell, Frank. *OSCAR W Story*, Goolwa, Australia: Signal Point River Murray Interpretive Centre, 1988.

D536 'Tugboat DOROTHY, Flagship of New York and Northern Railway Company's Fleet', *Seaboard*, May 28, 1891.

D537 Turnbull, Harry. 'Restoration of the ELISSA', *Ships Monthly*, July 1983.

D538 Turner, Gordon. 'A Captain and his Ship' (SEGWUN), *Ships Monthly*, August 1997.

D539 Turner, Robert D. *PRINCESS MARGUERITE, Last of the Coastal Liners*, Victoria, British Columbia: Sono Nis Press, 1981.

D540 Turner, Robert D. *The S.S. MOYIE*,

Memories of the Oldest Sternwheeler, Victoria, British Columbia: Sono Nis Press, 1991.

D541 Turner, Robert D. *The SICAMOUS & The NARAMATA, Steamboat Days in the Okanagan*, Victoria, British Columbia: Sono Nis Press, 1995.

D541a 'The Twin-screw steam yacht NAHLIN' (LIBERTATEA), *The Shipbuilder*, Sept. 1930.

D542 'Un paillebot a greement latin' (RAFAEL VERDERA), *Chasse-Maree* No 77, December 1993.

D543 'Un remorquer dans un musee' (SAINT-GILLES), *Chasse-Maree*, No. 43.

D544 'Un sous-marin de poche au musee de Brest' (S 622), *Chasse-Maree* No. 43.

D545 'Un vaixell historic com a perllongacio del Museu Maritim al Port de Barcelona' (SAYREMAR I), *Drassana*, No. 7, Any 1997.

D546 'Une peniche a Rouen' (POMPON-ROUGE), *Chasse-Maree*, No. 72, May 1993.

D547 Ureel, Urbain. 'DELPHINE Rediscovered', *Ships Monthly*, January 1998.

D547a van Mesdag, Martin. 'BRILLIANT, Olin's shining example', *Classic Boat*, July 1998.

D548 Vaughan, Roger. 'ENDEAVOR, The Woman and the Dream', *The Yacht*, August 1989.

D549 Villiers, Alan. 'By square-rigger to the Cape Verdes' (RICKMER RICKMERS), *Ships and the Sea*, June 1953.

D550 Villiers, Alan. *The CUTTY SARK, Last of a Glorious Era*, London: Hodder and Stoughton, 1953.

D551 Villiers, Alan. 'The Full-rigged Ship BALCLUTHA', *Ships and Ship Models*, July 1955.

D552 Villiers, Alan. *The Making of a Sailor* (JOSEPH CONRAD), London: George Routledge & Sons, 1938.

D553 Villiers, Alan. *Sailing EAGLE*, New York: Charles Scribner's Sons, 1955.

D554 Villiers, Alan. 'Why I Sailed the JOSEPH CONRAD', *Ships and the Sea*, December 1952.

D555 Vine, M. R. 'H.M.S. MEDWAY QUEEN, Heroine of Dunkirk', *Warship World*, Summer 1990.

D556 Viner, Alan. *The Restoration of the*

Ketch-Rigged Tamar Sailing Barge SHAMROCK 1974-1979, Greenwich: National Maritime Museum.

D557 Vralstad, Hans. 'Pa jakt etter Roald Amundsen i Nordvestpassa-jen' (MAUD), *Norsk Sjofartsmuseum Arsberetning*, 1995.

D557a Walters, Tony. 'The Story of S.S. REEMERE', *Paddle Wheels*, Autumn 1993.

D558 Ward, Robin. 'Still in Steam; Paddle Steamer WAVERLEY', *Ships Monthly*, April 1980.

D559 Waters, Colin. 'The GLENLEE Comes Home to Scotland', *Sea Breezes*, April 1994.

D560 Waters, Capt. John M. Jr. *Bloody Winter* (USCGC INGHAM), Annapolis, Maryland: Naval Institute Press, 1984.

D561 Watson, Milton. 'Still in Steam - on Lake Titicaca' (OLLANTA), *Ships Monthly*, April 1981.

D562 Watton, Ross. *The Cruiser BELFAST*, England: Anatomy of the Ship, 1985.

D563 Way, Frederick Jr. 'Luxury Liner of the Mississippi' (DELTA QUEEN), *Ships and the Sea*, February 1953.

D564 Way, Frederick Jr. *The Saga of the DELTA QUEEN* (privately printed c. 1950)

D565 Wegg-Prosser, Victoria. *SS GREAT BRITAIN*, London: The Illustrated London News, c.1970.

D566 Wegner, Dana M. *Fouled Anchors: The CONSTELLATION Question Answered*, Bethesda, Maryland: David Taylor Research Center, 1991.

D567 Wegner, Dana M. 'The Frigate Strikes Her Colors' (CONSTELLATION), *The American Neptune*, Summer 1995.

D568 Wells, CAPT. John. *The Immortal WARRIOR; Britain's First and Last Battleship*, Emsworth, England: Mason, 1987.

D568a Wilkinson, William D. '44-Foot Motor Lifeboat' (CG-44300), *The Quarterdeck*, Winter 1998.

D569 Williams, Steve. 'Tacoma's Fireboat Saved for the Future', (FIREBOAT NO. 1), *Marine Digest*, 10 May 1986.

D570 Wingate, John. 'H.M.S. BELFAST', *Warships in Profile*, Vol. 3, 1973.

D571 Wingate, John. *In Trust for the Nation, H.M.S. BELFAST 1939-1971*, Windsor, England: Profile Publications, 1972.

D572 Winter, C. W. R. *The QUEEN MARY,*

Her early years recalled, New York: W. W. Norton & Company, 1986.

D573 Wischmeyer, Lothar and Nottelmann, Dirk. *D.S. SCHAARHORN*, Cologne, Germany: Arbeitskreis historischer Schiffbau e.V., 1997.

D574 Wood, Gerald L. 'The Ironclad Turret Ship HUASCAR', *Warship* Nos. 37, 38.

D575 Woodman, Richard. 'Restoration or Replication' (TRINCOMALEE), *Maritime Heritage*, June-July 1997.

D576 Wort, Jean. 'Historic Ship Profile; COMMANDER', *Sea History*, Autumn 1995.

D577 Wright, Christopher, ed. 'U.S.S. KIDD', *Warship International* No. 4, 1988.

D578 Zimmer, Frederik F. 'Minner fra M/Y STELLA POLARIS', *Norsk Sjofartsmuseum Arsberetning*, 1993.

E PERIODICALS

E1 *Aktuellt* - Maritime Museum, Karlskrona, Sweden (annual).

E2 *Alte Schiff* - RKE Verlag, Kiel, Germany (1990-reportedly no longer being published).

E3 *The American Neptune* - Peabody Essex Museum, East India Square, Salem, Massachusetts 01970 U.S.A. (1941-present). Tel:508-745-1876 Fax:508-744-6776 E-mail: dori-phillips@pem.org Website: http://www.pem.org/Neptune

E4 *Angbaten* - Sallskapet Angbaten, Box 2072, 403 12 Goteborg, Sweden (owners of steamer *Bohuslan*).

E5 *Australian Sea Heritage* - Sydney Maritime Museum, P.O. Box 431, Rozelle, New South Wales 2039, Australia. Tel:02-810-2299 Fax:02-810-1756

E6 *Bearings* - Auckland Maritime Museum, Auckland, New Zealand (1989-present).

E7 *Chasse-Marèe* - Le Chasse-Marèe, Abri du Marin, 29177 Douarnenez, France (1981-present).

E8 *Classic Boat* - Bradley Pavilions, Bradley Stoke North, Bristol BS12 0BQ, England Tel:01454-620070 Fax:01454-620080

E9 *Dampferzeitung* - Verein Dampferzeitung, Postfach 7222, CH6000 Luzern 7, Switzerland Tel/Fax:041-240-28-86

E10 *Das Logbuch* - Arbeitskreis historischer Schiffbau e.V., Honnefer Platz 5, D-50939 Koln Tel:0221-44-34-62

E11 *The Dog Watch* - Shiplovers' Society of Victoria Australia (1943-present)

E12 *Drassana* - Museu Maritim de Barcelona, Consorci de les Drassanes, avinguda de les Drassanes, s/n, 08001 Barcelona, Spain Tel:301-18-71

E13 *Flagship* - The World Ship Trust, London (1992)

E14 *Gaffers Log* - Old Gaffers Association, 17 Kestrel Road, Newburgh, Aberdeenshire AB41 0FF, Scotland

E15 *ICMM News* - International Congress of Maritime Museums (c.1980-present).

E16 *International Sail; Communications* - An Association of Restored Sailing Ships, Laurel, Maryland. (c.1968-1976).

E17 *The Log of Mystic Seaport* - Mystic Seaport Museum, Mystic, Connecticut.

E18 *Loggen* - (Swedish Society for Tugs and Passenger Ships) Einar Madsen, Box 9007, 250 09 Helsingborg, Sweden.

E19 *Mains'l Haul* - Maritime Museum Association of San Diego, 1306 N. Harbor Drive, San Diego, California 92101. Tel:619-234-9153 Fax:619-234-8345 E-mail library@sdmaritime.com

E20 *The Mariners Mirror* - Society for Nautical Research, Mrs. Annette Gould, Membership Secretary, 5 Goodwood Close, Midhurst, Sussex GU29 9JG, England (1911-present)

E21 *Maritime America* - National Maritime Alliance (1993-present)

E22 *Maritime Life and Traditions* - Le Chasse-MarÈe Publications, PO Box 22, Penryn, Cornwall TR10 8YH (1998-present). E-mail: jbenn@dircon.co.uk

E23 *Maritime Trust Review* - The Maritime Trust of Great Britain, 2 Greenwich Church Street, Greenwich, London SE10 9BG Tel:0181-858-2698 Fax:0181-858-6976

E24 *Nautical Research Journal* - Nautical Research Guild, William J. Fleming, Jr., 19 Pleasant Street, Everett, Massachusetts 02149 USA (1948-present). Tel:617-389-5461 Website: http://www.Naut-Res-Guild.org

E25 *Newsletter* - Common European Maritime Heritage Congress, Bureau Scheepszaken, Scheepmakersdijk 2A, 2011 AT Haarlem, Netherlands Tel/Fax:31-23-540-1704

E26 *Paddle Wheels* - Paddle Steamer Preservation Society
Mrs. G. Anderson, P.O. Box 385, Hazlemere, High Wycombe,
Bucks, HP11 1AG England (1960-present)

E26a *The Quarterdeck* - Columbia River Maritime Museum
1792 Marine Drive, Astoria, Oregon 97103, USA.
Tel:503-325-2323

E26b *Scantlings* - National Historic Ships Committee, 66 Hartford
House, Blount Road, Pembroke Park, Portsmouth PO1 2TW, England
Tel/Fax:023 92 838040
E-mail: colin.allen@btinternet.com
and:
National Register of Historic Vessels, Scottish Institute of Maritime Studies, University of St. Andrews, Fife KY16 9AJ, Scotland
Tel: 01334 462916 Fax: 01334 462927
Website: http://www.st-andrews.ac.uk/institutes/sims/Nhsp.htm

E27 *Sea Breezes Magazine* - Units 28-30, Spring Valley Industrial Estate, Braddan, Isle of Man IM2 2QS, England (1919-present).
Tel:01624-626018 Fax:01624-661655

E28 *Sea History* - National Maritime Historical Society, 5 John Walsh Boulevard, P.O. Box 68, Peekskill, New York 10566 USA(1972-present).
Tel:914-737-7878

E29 *Sea History Gazette* - National Maritime Historical Society, 5 John Walsh Boulevard, P.O. Box 68, Peekskill, New York,USA (1987-present).
Tel:914-737-7878

E30 *Sea Letter* - San Francisco Maritime Museum, San Francisco, California.

E31 *Seaport* formerly *South Street Reporter* - South Street Seaport
Museum, 207 Front Street, New York, N.Y. 10038 USA (1966-present).

E32 *Seaways* - Seaways Publishing, San Jose, California (1990-present).

E33 *Ships Monthly* - 222 Branston Road, Burton-on-Trent DE14 3BT, England (1966-present). Tel:01283-542721 Fax:01283-546436

E34 *Signals* - Australian National Maritime Museum, GPO Box 5131,
Sydney, New South Wales, Australia 1042
Tel:02 9552 7777 Fax:02 9552 2318
Website: http://www.anmm.gov.au

E35 *Skargardsbaten* - Stiftelsen Skargardsbaten, Nybrogatan 76, 114 41 Stockholm, Sweden.
Tel:46-8-662-89-02

E36 *Spiegel der Zeilvaart* - Stichting Spiegel der Zeilvaart, Postbus 653, 2003 RR Haarlem, Netherlands (c.1976-present).
Tel:023-5341801 Fax:023-5345803

E37 *Steamboat Bill* formerly *Steamboat Bill of Facts* - Steamship
Historical Society of America, 300 Ray Drive, Suite #4,
Providence, Rhode Island 02906, USA(1940-present).

E38 *Steamboating* - International Steamboat Society, Route 1, Box 262, Middlebourne, West Virginia 26149-9748, USA (1985-present).
Tel:304-386-4434 Fax:304-386-4868
E-mail: woodenpo@interloc.com

E39 *Tagrijn* - Vereniging Botterbehoud, Netherlands

E40 *Tall Ship International* - Resort Marketing and Publishing,
Suites 1-6, Maritime House, Southwell Business Park, Portland, Dorset DT5 2JS, England (1996-present).
Tel:44-1305-822000 Fax:44-1305-820444
E-mail: tallship@resort-guide.co.uk

E41 *Telescope* - Great Lakes Maritime Institute, Detroit, Michigan, USA.

E42 *Topsail* - Society for Spritsail Barge Research, Northfleet, England.

E43 *Traditional Sail Review* - Anglian Yacht Services, Maldon, England (1981-?).

E44 *Warship International* - International Naval Research Organization, Toledo, Ohio (1964-present).

E45 *The Weather Gauge* - Chesapeake Bay Maritime Museum (1964-present).

E46 *Wooden Boat* - P.O. Box 78, Naskeag Road, Brooklin, Maine 04616 (1974-present).
Tel:207-359-4651 Fax:207-359-8920

E47 *World Ship Review* - World Ship Trust, Peter Elphick, Dorney House, Dorney, near Windsor, SL4 6QW, England (1993-present).
Tel:01628-663836

F TECHNICAL – maritime historic preservation

F1 Anderson, Richard K. *Guidelines for Recording Historic Ships*,
Washington, D.C.: Historic American Engineering Record, National Park Service, 1988.

F2 Ansel, Willits. 'The CONRAD yards: A Close Look at the Restoration Process', *The Log of Mystic Seaport*, July 1978

F3 Ansel, Willits. 'A Ship's Boat for the JOSEPH CONRAD', *Wooden*

Boat, November-December 1981.

F4 The Association for Preservation Technology. *APT Bulletin*;
Maritime Preservation Edition, Vol. IX, No. 1, 1987.

F5 Barkman, Lars. *The Preservation of the VASA*, Stockholm, Sweden: Statens Sjohistoriska Museum, 1965.

F6 Bond, Hallie. 'What is Museum Quality; A curator looks at boat Restoration', *Wooden Boat*, September/October 1998.

F6a Boudreau, Guy Peter. 'Saving CONSTELLATION; A Laminated Shell for an Historic Ship', *Wooden Boat*, March/April 1999.

F7 Bray, Maynard and Ueber, Edward. 'The MORGAN's Knees', *The Log of Mystic Seaport*, Spring 1971.

F8 Bray, Maynard ed. *Taking Care of Wooden Ships*, Walpole, Maine: Maine Sea Grant Publications, 1978.

F9 Cooper, Diane. 'Restoring and Preserving the Victorian Ferryboat BERKELEY', *Mains'l Haul*, Fall 1998.

F10 Craig, Donald. *A New Mast for the THERESA CONNOR*, Lunenburg, Nova Scotia: Lunenburg Marine Society, c.1976.

F11 Delgado, James P. et. al. 'Difficult Choices and Hard-Won Successes in Maritime Preservation', *CRM Bulletin*, Vol. 12, No. 4, 1989 (Cultural Resources Management, National Park Service).

F12 d'Estaing, Nancy and Adair, Gary. 'Documenting the JOSEPH CONRAD', *The Log of Mystic Seaport*, Spring 1989.

F13 Fuller, Gail ed. *A Curatorial Handbook for Historic Naval Vessels*, Historic Naval Ships Association of North America, 1993.

F14 Historic American Engineering Record. *Field Instructions*;
Documenting Technological Sites and Structures, Washington, D. C.: Heritage Conservation and Recreation Service, 1981.

F15 Lewis, John. *Restoring Vintage Boats*, Camden, Maine: International Marine Publishing Co, 1975.

F16 Mystic Seaport Museum; Manuscript Restoration Reports, partial list:
'Restoration of the L. A. DUNTON', M. Bray & C. Haines
'Outfitting Gloucester Fishing Schooners', V. Jones
'Wood Used in Ship and Boat Preservation at Mystic Seaport', W. Ansel
'Interim Report on the Restoration of the L. A. DUNTON', W. Ansel.

F17 National Park Service. *Standards for Historic Vessel Preservation Projects*, Washington, D.C.: U. S. Department of Interior, 1990.

F18 National Trust for Historic Preservation. *Proceedings: First National Maritime Preservation Conference*, Washington, D.C.: The Preservation Press, 1977.

F19 *Proceedings; Common European Maritime Heritage Congress* (Amsterdam, Aug. 31-Sept. 4, 1992) Amsterdam: Nederlands Scheepvaart Museum, c.1992.

F20 *Proceedings; Conference on Technical Aspects of Maintaining, Repairing & Preserving Historically Significant Ships* (Boston, Massachusetts, Sept. 12-14, 1994)

F21 *Proceedings; Third International Conference on the Technical Aspects of the Preservation of Historic Vessels* (San Francisco, California, April 20-23, 1997)

F22 Reynard, Capt. Kenneth D. 'Restoration of an Iron Star' (STAR OF INDIA), *Mains'l Haul*, Fall 1997.

F23 Robertson, Hamish and Palfreyman, Dr. John W. 'A Modern Approach to an Ancient Problem - Frigate UNICORN & Dundee Institute of Technology', *World Ship Review*, March 1994.

F24 Walker, David A. *A Guide to the Maintenance of THERESA E. CONNOR and CAPE SABLE*, Lunenburg, Nova Scotia: Fisheries Museum of the Atlantic, 1984.

G TECHNICAL – useful books and articles

G1 Bates, William H. 'Ship Timber in the United States', *Nautical Gazette*, December 7, 1872 to March 8, 1873.

G2 Bingham, Fred. *Boat Joinery and Cabinetmaking Simplified*, Camden, Maine: International Marine, 1993.

G3 Blocksidge, Ernest W. *Ships Boats; Their Qualities, Construction, Equipment, and Launching Appliances*, London: Longmans, Green & Co, 1920.

G4 Brewington, Marion V. 'The Sailmaker's Gear', *American Neptune*, October 1949.

G5 Bryon, Rita and Terence. *Maritime Information: a guide to Libraries and Sources of Information in the United Kingdom*, London: Witherby and Company, 1993.

G6 Duckworth, S. G. *Ship Joinery, the*

Woodwork Fittings of a Modern Steel Vessel, London: G. Routledge & Sons, 1923.

G7 Estep, Harvey Cole. *How Wooden Ships are Built*, Cleveland, Ohio: The Penton Publishing Co, 1918.

G8 Haines, Charles. 'Ship Preservation in the Old Navy', *American Neptune*, October 1982.

G9 Hall, Elton W. 'Sailcloth for American Vessels', *American Neptune*, April 1971.

G10 Hanna, Jay S. *Marine Carving Handbook*, Camden, Maine: International Marine Publishing, 1975.

G11 Horsley, John E. *Tools of the Maritime Trades*, Camden, Maine: International Marine Publishing, 1978.

G12 Kipping, Robert. *Rudimentary Treatise on Masting, Mast-Making, and Rigging of Ships*, London: Lockwood, 1873. (and later editions)

G13 Kipping, Robert. *Sails and Sailmaking*, London, Lockwood, 1875 (and later editions).

G14 Marino, Emiliano. *Sailmaker's Apprentice*, Camden, Maine: International Marine, 1994.

G15 Middendorf, F. L. *Bemastung und Takelung der Schiffe*, Berlin: Verlag von Julius Springer, 1903.

G16 Payson, Harold H. *Keeping the Cutting Edge; Setting and Sharpening Hand and Power Saws*, Brooklin, Maine: Wooden Boat Books, 1985.

G17 Peck, Edward Cort. *Woodbending in Shipbuilding*, Madison, Wisconsin: U. S. Forest Products Laboratory, 1943.

G18 Reynolds, Hezekiah. *Directions for House and Ship Painting* (facsimile reprint of 1812 edition), Worcester, Massachusetts: American Antiquarian Society, 1978.

G19 Ritchie, L. A. *The Shipbuilding Industry: A Guide to Historical Records*, Manchester, England: Manchester University Press, 1992.

G20 Ronnberg, Erik A. R. 'The Coppering of 19th Century American Merchant Sailing Ships', *Nautical Research Journal*, September 1980.

G21 Ronnberg, Erik A. R. 'Paint and Colors for American Merchant Vessels, 1800-1920', *Nautical Research Journal*, December 1991.

G22 Ross, Robert J. and Pellerin, Roy F. *Nondestructive Testing for Assessing Wood Members in Structures, A Review*, Madison, Wisconsin: U. S. Forest Products Laboratory, 1994.

G23 Story, Dana. *The Building of a Wooden Ship: Sawn Frames and Trunnel Fastened*, Barre, Massachusetts: Barre Publishers, 1971.

G24 Toss, Brian. *The Complete Rigger's Apprentice; Tools and Techniques for Modern and Traditional Rigging*, Camden, Maine: International Marine, 1998.

G25 U.S. Bureau of Ships, Department of the Navy. *Wood: A Manual for Its Use as a Shipbuilding Material*, Washington, D. C.: U. S. Government Printing Office, 1957-1962. (4 vols.) Reprinted as single volume in 1983 by Teaparty Books; Kingston, Massachusetts.

G26 Underhill, Harold A. *Masting and Rigging, the Clipper Ship and Ocean Carrier*, Glasgow: Brown, Son & Ferguson, 1946.

G27 Wall, William E. *Graining, Ancient and Modern*, Dobbs Ferry, New York: Sheridan House, 1988 (originally published in 1905).

G28 Welch, George S. *The Ship Painter's Handbook*, Glasgow, 1927. (and other editions).

G29 Winters, J. C. *Surveying & Restoring Classic Boats*, England: Adlard Coles, 1972 (R1993 Sheridan House; Dobbs ferry,New York).

INDEX

Aside from 'USS, HMS' etc., these are current names of vessels)

Late information

Additional vessels:

CHINA

No 229
submarine

Built About 1958 in China
Original owners Chinese Navy
Propulsion Diesel and electric motors,
4000hp
Tonnage 1712 displacement
Length 251.3ft/76.6m
Breadth 21.9ft/6.7m
Draught 21.9ft/6.7m
Materials Steel throughout
Original use Submarine
Condition Intact, apparently unaltered
Present owners Qingdao Naval Museum
Location Qingdao, China
History One of a series of submarines of the
Russian 'ROMEO' class built in Chinese
shipyards. Now maintained as a floating
exhibit at Qingdao.

Qingdao
destroyer

Built about 1936-1941 by Dalzavod Shipyard,
Vladivostok, Russia
Original owners Russian Navy
Propulsion Steam turbines, 48,000hp
Tonnage 2150 displacement
Length 370.7ft/113m

Quingdao in August 1995

Breadth 33.4ft/10.2m
Draught 13.1ft/4.0m
Materials Steel throughout
Original use Destroyer
Condition Intact, open to public
Present owners Qingdao Naval Museum
Location Qingdao, China
History Destroyer of the 'GORDY' class built
for the Russian Navy prior to the Second
World War. Transferred to the Chinese Navy
in 1954. Torpedo tubes were replaced with
missile launchers around 1971. Vessel is
otherwise unaltered. Now maintained as a
floating exhibit.

GREAT BRITAIN

Research
'zulu' type fishing lugger

Former name HEATHER BELL
Built 1903 at Banff, Scotland
Propulsion Sail, lugger, 'zulu' type; auxiliary
engine added
Length 78.0ft/25.59m
Materials Wood throughout
Original use Fishing
Condition Intact, being refitted as exhibit
Present owners Scottish Fisheries Museum

Location Anstruther, Scotland, Great Britain
History Sailing fishing boat of the 'zulu' type
developed in Scotland in the late 1870s.
Fished out of the port of Fraserburgh, and
later Whalsay in the Shetland Islands.
Converted to an auxiliary sailing vessel, and
later a motor vessel. After an effort of a
number of years to restore her as a floating
exhibit, the museum finally moved her into
a special addition to their building in May
1999.

ROMANIA

Locotenent Comandor Vasile Paun
river gunboat

Former names REPUBLICA, CSOBANC
Built Pre-1918
Original owners Austro-Hungarian Navy
Propulsion Steam, sidewheel
Length c134.5ft/41m
Breadth c19.6ft/6m
Materials Steel throughout
Present location Romania; Braila
Original use River gunboat
Condition In operating condition
Present owners Romanian Navy
History The world's last steam sidewheel
warship. Acquired by Romania after the
defeat of Austria-Hungary in the First
World War. Saw action during the Second
World War. During the communist period
was used by the president of Romania for
tours of inspection on the lower Danube
River. Continues to be maintained in
operating condition by the Romanian Navy
as a protocol vessel

In addition to this vessel, and the two active
passenger steamers listed in the Romanian
section, that country has three more intact
sidewheel steamers: Currently laid up in
need of restoration; the river buoy tenders
GIURGIU, ex-LOCOTENENT COMANDOR
DEMETRIADE, a similar vessel to the PAUN,
and S. H. CETATEA, built as a buoy tender in
1903; and, lately serving as a floating
maritime school, the former river towboat
DECEBEL built in 1917.

Bibliography: Craciunoiu, Cristian. '*Low
Danube Paddle Wheels Steamers*',
(Modelism International, Bucharest,
Romania, 1995)

Chinese 'Romeo' type submarine in August 1995

UNITED STATES

American Victory
cargo vessel

Built 1945 by California Shipbuilding Corp, Los Angeles
Original owners United States Maritime Commission
Propulsion Steam turbine
Tonnage 7612 displacement
Length 455.25ft/138.7m
Breadth 62ft/18.8m
Draught 28ft/8.5m

Tovaritisch

Materials Steel throughout
Original use Cargo vessel
Condition Intact
Location Tampa, Florida, USA
History Second World War American standard cargo vessel. Brought out of reserve for the war in Vietnam. Recently transferred to a group in Tampa for use as a museum and possible operating vessel.

Red Oak Victory
naval supply ship

Built 1944 by California Permanente Metals Corp, Richmond, California

Original owners United States Navy
Propulsion Steam turbine
Tonnage 7612 displacement
Length 455.25ft/138.7m
Breadth 62ft/18.8m
Draught 28ft/8.5m
Materials Steel throughout
Original use Naval supply ship, numbered AK-235
Condition Intact, on exhibition
Location Richmond, California, USA
History Second World War American standard cargo vessel, completed as a Navy supply ship. Placed in reserve fleet after the war. Now serves as a floating museum in the port in which she was built.

Slater
destroyer escort

Built 1944 by Tampa Shipbuilding, Tampa, Florida
Original owners United States Navy
Propulsion Diesel-electric, 6000hp
Tonnage 1750 displacement
Length 306.0ft/93.0m
Breadth 36.6ft/11.17m
Draught 10.4ft/3.25m
Materials Steel throughout
Original use Destroyer escort, numbered DE-766
Condition Intact, restored to original appearance
Location Albany, New york, USA
History Destroyer escort of the DET or CANNON class, built for the US Navy and transferred to the Greek Navy as the HIERAX in 1951. Returned to the US in the 1990s for use as a floating exhibit.

Corrections or additions to entries:

AUSTRALIA

Reemere

Built 1909
Location Melbourne Australia;
History Efforts to restore her in Hobart, Tasmania were abandoned, and a new owner has now moved her to Melbourne.

GREAT BRITAIN

Tovaritsch

Built 1933
History Following an arrangement between the Ukrainian Government and a charitable trust called the Tall Ship Friends, the ship was towed from Middlesborough on 1 September 1999 to Wilhelmshaven in

Germany for a refit. She will return to active sail training.

Vigilance

Built 1926 by Upham in Brixham, England
Length 78.0ft/23.7m
Breadth 20.0ft/6.0m
Draught 9.0ft/2.7m
Original owners George Foster
History Built for fishing out of Brixham. Rebuilt between 1955 and 1971 as a yacht.

MYANMAR

Pandaw

Built 1947 by Yarrow at Scotstoun, Scotland (not pre-fabricated); engines by Denny
History Built as one of a series of paddlewheel steamers that replaced a fleet destroyed at the beginning of the Second World War. Designed for shallow-draught navigation on the upper Irrawaddy and Chindwin Rivers in what was then Burma. Rebuilt with diesel propulsion and some additional staterooms for river cruises of up to sixteen days on the same waterways.

NETHERLANDS

Schorpioen

Built 1868
Present owners Marinemuseum
Location Den Helder, Netherlands

UNITED STATES

Fri

Built 1912
History Owner has now established permanent residence in Denmark and is basing vessel in the Danish port of Svendborg

Jean

Built 1938
Condition Intact, exhibited in County park
Present owner Elmer Earl
Location Near Asotin, Washington. United States
History Sternwheel steamer built for towing on the Columbia and Willamette Rivers based at Portland, Oregon. Now exhibited in a park beside the Snake River, a tributary of the Columbia that forms the boundary between the States of Washington and Idaho.

Picture credits

Marilyn Alexander: 192
G K Andrews: 18 (both), 23 (both), 25, 26, 27 (both), 29, 34, 35, 222
Association 'Nantes-Marine-Tradition': 92
Australian National Maritime Museum: 20B
Ron van den Bos: 214B
City of Bristol Museum and Art Gallery: 165B
Vladimir Chepelev: 4-5, 10, 243B, 245A and B
Dampfeimerkettenbagger 'Ed 9': 104
DCAN, Toulon (by courtesy of J H Chaveau): Colour Plate 11A
Eastern Daily Press, Norwich: (135B)
Gert Uwe Detlefsen: 97, 98, 99 (both), 100, 101B, 102, 103A, 106, 107, 108, 110, 111, 113 (both), 115, 116B, 118A, 120A, 121 (both), 124, 129, 130 (both), 131 (both), 132 (both), 133B
Dundee Industrial Heritage Trust: 148
Ecole Navale, Brest, France: 88A
Ian Edwards, Sydney: 36
Olaf Engvig: 230, 234
Fleet Photographic Unit, Portsmouth: 183B
Friends of MTB-102: 168A
Thomas von Glinski, Berlin: 112, 116A, 126B
D R Goddard: 137B
SS Great Britain Project, Bristol: Colour Plates 8, 9, 155A
Hans Hammarskiold, Vasa Museet, Stockholm: Colour Plate 1, 264A
Hartlepool Historic Ship Centre: 187
Rick Hogben: 146A
Imperial War Museum, London: 138B

Italian Defence and Naval Attaché, London: 195
Stephane Izard: 91A
Japanese Embassy, London: 197 (both), 198 (both), 199 (both)
A de Leeuw: 210B
Boris Lemachko: 227
I Mandrysz: 238B
Marinemuseum Den Helder: 220
Marine Nationale SAVR Atlantique: **94**
Maritime Museum of San Diego: Colour Plate 16
Maritime Trust, Greenwich: Colour Plates 15A, 15B
John Marsh, South Africa: 248
Mary Rose Trust (copyright): Colour Plate 2, 165A
G L Mason, Hartlepool: 181
Melbourne Maritime Museum: Colour Plates 4B, 5
Daan Mujis: 217A
Musée de la Mer pour L'Atlantique, Paris: 86B, 88B, 90
Conrad Milster, Brooklyn, New York: 38B, 61, 164, 185, 266B, 268A, 271A, 277B
Jan Marinus: 213
Tony Morrison: 235A
J Th Mos: 219A
National Maritime Museum, Greenwich: 141A
Nico Nooy: 64
North East Fife District council: 168B
Österreichische Bundesbahnen: 38A
T Pelz, Haifa: 266A, 268B
Nigel Pert: 57A
Philip & Son Ltd, Dartmouth: 149B
Franck Pizzato: 89B
Portugese Navy: Colour Plate 12

Project Liberty Ship: Colour Plate 14B
Jack Putnam: 45B
Paul Quinn Collection (pictures by Admiral Gerald Wood, Chilean Navy): 2-3, Colour Plates 10A, 10B
Lindsay Rex, Victoria, Australia: 6, 9, 19, 20A, 30
Royal Geographical Society: 229
Royal Norwegian Embassy Information Service, New York: 232B
Schiffahrts-Museum Regensburg EV: 123
Dick Schouten: 203, 204 (both), 205A, 206A, 207B, 208A, 209 (both), 210A, 211 (both), 215 (both), 216 (both), 217B, 218, 219B, 221 (both)
Scottish Fisheries Museum: 174C
Rick Shenton: 183A
Erwin Sieche: 373 (both)
Miroslav Tsanov: 42B, 252 (both), 256, 260A, 263A, 265 (both)
Vancouver Maritime Museum: 48, 49, 51B, 52A
Claude Verdier: Colour Plate 11B
R A Verhoeven: 207A
S Visser: 212B
Wiebe Visser: 202B
Peter Voss, Bremerhaven: 105, 109A, 114B
Warship Preservation Trust: 170B, 172
Roy J Westlake, Plymouth: 173A
Councillor P Wilson: 182A
Claus Wolf, Dresden: 103B
Wright & Logan: 188B, 238A

All uncredited photographs: Author

Index <small>(Names in parentheses are former names of vessels)</small>